Edward Weston

THE DAYBOOKS OF
Edward Weston

Two volumes in one
I. MEXICO II. CALIFORNIA

Foreword by Beaumont Newhall
Edited by Nancy Newhall

APERTURE

Library of Congress Control Number: 90-80726
Paperback ISBN: 0-89381-445-8

Printed and bound by Tien Wah Press, Singapore

The staff at Aperture for *The Daybooks of Edward Weston* is Michael E. Hoffman, Executive Director; Jane D. Marsching, Assistant Editor; Thomas Seelig, Editorial Work-Scholar; Stevan A. Baron, Production Director; Linda Tarack, Production Associate

Aperture Foundation, Inc. publishes a magazine, books, portfolios, and presents exhibitions of fine photography to communicate with photographers and creative people everywhere. A complete catalog is available upon request.

Visit Aperture's website: www.aperture.org

Second Edition
10 9 8 7 6 5 4

Contents

I. MEXICO

II. CALIFORNIA

List of Plates

I. MEXICO

II. CALIFORNIA

Preface

As every publisher recognizes, there is a certain kind of book that grants a special, if somewhat implacable, privilege. It is a book that *must* be kept alive, meaning that it must be kept available—in print—and not confined as a near-extinct survivor in libraries public or private. In some ways, that is not a meager definition of a "classic," a work that despite the costs and effort must be kept a part of our lives and our heritage.

The Daybooks of Edward Weston belongs to this category, as one of the classics of autobiography in the history of art.

In his foreword, Beaumont Newhall observes that there is nothing like the *Daybooks* in the literature of photography, evoking a comparison to the *Journal* of the nineteenth-century French painter Eugène Delacroix. Another artist also comes to mind as I read over these insightful, probing, and often rollicking passages. For me, Weston's literary precedent traces back more than four centuries to the immortal autobiography of the Renaissance sculptor and goldsmith, Benvenuto Cellini. Both set out to explore, explain, and understand his artist's destiny; and both men convey to us an almost unbelievable zest for life in all of its lighter and darker shadings.

There are two critical differences. Cellini dictated his memoirs in old age, to a young apprentice, as an elaborate self-justification. Weston penned his own account, of a man in his prime struggling with the day-by-day challenges of life, love, and above all, art. The corollary is that Cellini's story is a collection of fabrications as deftly crafted as his salt cellars and seals. Weston's autobiographical writings, unsparing in his follies as well as exultant in his triumphs, reveal a great artist obsessed with truth.

One other presence fills these pages, whose life was one of devotion and of inestimable importance to the history of photography. If Weston's *Daybooks* is a classic, it is a lasting tribute to the editor, Nancy Newhall. It was she who, with enormous skill and sensitivity, helped translate the huge scrawling handwriting of a man of genius into a work of genius.

This book, and for that matter all of the books which Aperture has published on the life and photographs of Edward Weston could not have been accomplished without the guidance and the beautiful prints made and provided by Cole Weston.

A generation of readers has found inspiration, wisdom, delight, and comfort in the *Daybooks*. We offer this new edition with the hope that this book will equally stimulate and encourage generations to come.

MICHAEL E. HOFFMAN,
Executive Director
Aperture Foundation

Foreword

Seldom has an artist kept a journal as vivid, as intimate, and as sincere as Edward Weston. Day after day, for more than fifteen years, this great photographer wrote down his thoughts about life, outlined his hopes, cataloged his despairs, mercilessly criticized his own photographs, and recorded every experience that was meaningful to him.

The result is an extraordinary document of a struggle of an artist to forge a style, to adjust himself to the world, to determine his position in society, and to appraise his contributions to it.

We know nothing comparable in the literature of photography. In many ways, the *Daybooks* bring to mind the *Journal* kept by another great artist, the French painter Eugène Delacroix, as "a record of what is happening in my life and above all, in my mind." Like Delacroix, Weston wrote with no thought of publication. A few excerpts, however, appeared in the periodical *Creative Art*, August 1928. Years after he had stopped writing the daybook, he reviewed what he had written and edited it. Portions were published in the *Alfred Stieglitz Memorial Portfolio* and in his book *My Camera on Point Lobos*. Shortly after his death in 1958, Nancy Newhall published excerpts in the special edition of *Aperture* dedicated to his memory. Excerpts also appeared in the 1958 Summer issue of *Art in America*.

The two volumes of the *Daybooks* were first published by George Eastman House in 1961 and 1966 and subsequently by Aperture. They are now presented in their entirety in one volume, with the original introductions by Nancy Newhall.

We are indebted to Brett Weston and Cole Weston for their generous help. Professor D. Lincoln Canfield of the University of Rochester, a specialist in Latin-American linguistics, most generously supplied a glossary of colloquial Spanish terms frequently used by Weston.

BEAUMONT NEWHALL

Introduction

For Edward Weston, his *Daybook* was "my way of exploding . . . the safety valve I need in this day when pistols and poisons are taboo." To be alone, to focus on what was happening to him, he rose around 4 A.M.: "Peace again! — the exquisite hour before dawn, here at my old desk — seldom have I realized so keenly, appreciated so fully, these still, dark hours."

It is an utterly frank and intimate journal, so much so that when he re-read it, he was revolted by all the "heartaches, headaches, bellyaches." Once, in 1925, he threw three years of it into the fire. When publication threatened, he went through the surviving eleven years of it with a razor and a very thick black pencil, crossing out names, cutting out "petty reactions, momentary moods" until much of the manuscript is full of holes or sliced to tatters. Even so, as he wrote me in 1948: ". . . it is too personal . . . I usually wrote to let off steam so the diary gives a one-sided picture which I do not like."

Yet because he poured into the *Daybook* his resentment, bitterness, disgust, mercilessly exposing his own weaknesses, egotisms, evasions, he could turn to others with a gentleness, an insight, and a sense of humor that made him deeply and staunchly loved. He seemed at first a quiet little man, rather professorial in appearance. His eyes, a hot brown, were slow and absorbent, as if he were always — as he doubtless was — searching to see and hold the deep inner image of every person, place, or thing. Then you became aware of something inside him that was like a light; it warmed you, and suddenly you felt released. He never laughed out loud — his sister, Mary, recalled that as a boy, he would sit on the stoop of the Chicago house while the glittering Sunday parade of carriages went by, completely deadpan, while a large pet rat, heaving and twisting under his cap, caused astonished gasps from elegant ladies. He was a dancer, a wrestler, and a comic when the spirit moved. He achieved in his later years a simplicity in living that people kept comparing to Thoreau; he was not flattered. Thoreau, with only himself to look after, lived by a lake for two years; Edward, with four sons, two wives, and a legion of loves, had managed, in cities or out of them, to live and work with bare simplicity and a few basic tools for some thirty years. He knew what he had accomplished thereby: "My work has vitality because I have helped, done my part in revealing to others the living world about them. . . ." The *Daybook* is his

Pilgrim's Progress. You can hear him grow, both as a man and as an artist. He began it, as he remembered, in 1917; from this period only the few pages that begin this volume remain.

The Mexican period exists now only in a typescript badly done sometime in the late 1930s or early '40s: "Yes, the MS [manuscript] was 'monkeyed with' by a German girl. It was supposedly just copied. . . . In my original copy, which was longhand, the punctuation was dashes—('modern')— Since the first typewritten copy, each person has punctuated, paragraphed and spelled according to heart's desire." Edward burned the original MS; he had already cut from what the various typists received nearly all references to the agony he suffered over Tina Modotti's other lovers; nothing at all remains of his agony over his eldest son, Chandler, a thirteen-year caught first in the cross-fire between his mother and father, then in the crossfire between Tina and Edward. What remains of the *Daybook* in this period, battered and twisted as it is by the German girl's attempts to give it a romantic Goethean style, is still valid. I have cut only redundancies— the parties, the bullfights, the Mexican toys that in the original become monotonous—and a few vulgarities and sentimentalities of the kind Edward could no longer stand: "Reading, for example, such lines as 'I drew close to her and kissed her' shivers me, makes me out a pretentious prig. I can't take it! Seeing it in a book would turn me into a hermit. Is there much of that stuff?" Otherwise he thought it "not too bad—except when I try to write."

The years in Mexico were only the beginning. "Did I tell you that I have eight years of Day Book, post-Mexico? Memory tells me it makes the Mexican period seem pallid." He was right, and here, though it has suffered heavily from his razor, we have the original manuscript in his massive scrawl. It is briefer, more incisive; his passion like fire eats at what in him was unessential to his purpose: "to present clearly my feeling for life with photographic beauty . . . without subterfuge or evasion in spirit or technique."

When the *Daybook* came to an end, on April 22, 1934, he had solved his crucial problems; his work had achieved the monumental simplicity of true greatness, and he was no longer alone. The last entry is concerned with the coming of his last intense love: "I must have peace, to enjoy, fulfill, this beauty."

Ten years later, he added a brief postscript, recounting main events; this ends like a premonition of what was to happen to himself: "Something almost worse than death came to my only sister Mary—a stroke which crippled her right side. She has come through in heroic fashion, learning to write with left hand, learning to walk, to talk." Edward, stricken with Parkinson's disease, a progressive disintegration of the nervous system, could not achieve such a comeback. Yet even in those last tragic years, when he could no longer see to photograph, when his hand shook too much to hold a pencil, he could remain, as Ansel Adams wrote, "a moving spirit, as always."

Without some sketch of the background, the Daybook is not always easy to comprehend. Briefly, then: Edward Henry Weston was born on March 24, 1886, in Highland Park, Illinois, of a long line of preachers, teachers, and doctors. He and his sister, Mary—"May"—nine years older, were the first children born outside of New England for more than two hundred years. His grandfather, a poet and a Black Republican, was the first to break the tradition: he left Bowdoin College, Maine, to found a female seminary in Illinois. His father, Dr. Edward Burbank Weston, found time during his general practice to teach obstetrics at a local college, introduce the ancient art of archery to the Midwest, and breed fine poultry. Edward, born late in his life, remembered him only as small, grey haired, stalwart, somewhat remote but very kind. The family moved to Chicago when Edward was a few months old. When he was five, his mother, Alice Jeanette Brett Weston, died; he remembered nothing of her except "a pair of burning eyes—perhaps they were burning with fever . . . " and her dying wish that he should break the family tradition and become a businessman.

He was frail as a child; during the usual mumps, measles, and so on, he instinctively fasted, and all his life, though he was never dogmatic about it, he preferred fruits and vegetables to meats, sunlight and cold water to any medicine. He was bored at school, except in painting class and at athletic events; make himself into a track star, took boxing lessons, and became, as his sons later admiringly observed, "a little strong man."

When his father married again, a widow with a teenage son, both of whom Edward disliked, he and his sister were given the top floor of the Chicago house; May brought him up. Always they were very close; after she married John Seaman, an electrical engineer, and moved away, they wrote each other at least a postcard nearly every day.

In 1902 his father sent him a Bull's-Eye camera to play with during his summer vacation on a Michigan farm. Edward was excited; then he found he could not get skies or action, and began reading photographic magazines to find out why. Then he saw a view camera, with what seemed like a usable panoply of holders, tripod, and an "Ideal Ray" filter, in a pawnshop window; he saved carfare and every other penny he could until at last he could buy it. From then on, he played hooky from school until it was obvious his academic career was at an end; he was always out with his camera photographing the southern parks, the prairies, the lakes. When, in 1903, a photographic magazine reproduced a little spring landscape, Edward was lost forever to photography.

His father, obeying his mother's last wish, sent him to Marshall Field and Co., Wholesale, where, under the eye of an uncle, he was to work his way up. He began as a "rabbit"—errand boy—and in three years worked up to general salesman at $10 a week. He hated it; he watched the clock for the moment he could go photographing again.

By 1906 he had saved enough from his salary to go on vacation to visit May, who was now living in Tropico, California. Tropico was then a few shacks in wonderful wild hills; Edward, fresh from the hot Chicago plain, found himself climbing up two thousand feet. He decided to stay, and got a job surveying for a railroad at $15 a week. Then he discovered the survey was a hoax, designed to sell real estate in the orange groves, and got a job with a real railroad, the old Salt Lake. But mathematics in the desert sun, the fifth day of a fast—"I didn't know how to break my fasts in those days"—caused him to faint. He quit, and went back to Tropico determined to be a professional photographer—"At least I would own the tools I needed." He bought an old postcard camera, and went from door to door, photographing brides, pets, everything from the newborn in its cradle to the corpse in its coffin.

Suddenly he found himself the owner of half a house; the idea was to build the other half later. He realized how deeply he wanted a home. He met Flora May Chandler, daughter of a well-to-do local family who owned considerable property here and there throughout booming Los Angeles County. He saw her at first only as "pretty and sentimental"; it was all he needed to fall in love. Obviously, itinerant photography could not support a family, so he went to learn the trade of portrait photography at the Illinois College of Photography. He accomplished the whole course in six months, was bilked of a diploma by a technicality, and went back to Los Angeles to work as a printer for local portraitists.

On January 30, 1909, he married Flora, who, as he gradually realized, was much more of a person than he had perceived: she was vivid, vital, generous—in his direst moments with her Edward recognized her stature—but she gave you her heart when all you wanted was a cup of coffee. Illness sent her into a paroxysm, jealousy into hysteria. A friend of both in those days, the photographer Imogen Cunningham, then married to the etcher Roi Partridge, observed she was "like an electric fan you couldn't turn off." She bore Edward the four sons who were his deepest human relations: Edward Chandler, 1910; Theodore Brett, 1911; Laurence Neil,

1914; Cole, 1919. For Edward, his other loves might come and go like flowers in their seasons; Flora was the mother of his sons, and her generosity was total, even to selling land to help him after they had separated. He did not ask for a divorce until 1937.

In 1911, with the help of his in-laws, he built a rustic little studio in Tropico and set out a garden around it. The first week after he opened it, the total take was $1 for a dozen postcards. Soon he began making a success: he hid ungainly shapes in chiffon scarves, he vignetted down to the head alone, he became an expert retoucher. Customers were pleased, and enough wealthy clients, some of them stars from the burgeoning movie colony in nearby Hollywood, came up his daisy-bordered path to make his little business "'boil my pot,' and support my other work, even then."

Trying to photograph his baby sons, he found himself tearing down the curtains from his skylight and other windows; he threw out a terrifying flashbag device, he got a 3¼ × 4¼ Graflex so he could follow motion, he worked more and more outdoors, and became absorbed by the problems and the beauty, subtle and forever changing, of natural light. His "spontaneous" portraits, especially of children and dancers, became famous.

When change came to Weston, it nearly always took the shape of a woman. In 1912 or 1913, he met Margrethe Mather, also a photographer. He did not see her at first; to the first casual glance she looked mousy. Then he happened to look at her direct, and was stricken—she was exquisite. It was his first experience of the power of understatement; he fell in love with art and with Margrethe Mather at the same time, and for some eight years could not separate them. It was a strange and troubling love. She was elusive, disappeared for days where he could not find her, then suddenly on his doorstep would appear a drift of daffodils, with, on paper the delicate gray-green of acacia leaves, a note of some fifteen words—her attempt at the ancient Japanese poem form called *haiku*. He made her his partner; she was so unpunctual he called her "the late Miss Mather." He complained that she was often slovenly and dirty, slopping about in men's shoes. Yet he still loved her, trying to overcome his natural distaste and achieve a height where "morals" didn't matter. Yet Margrethe with her burning curiosity about what was happening in art, music, poetry, thought, and life brought him what he had never known before; "art," to him, had been something enclosed in a gold frame on a museum wall or in magazines on the family's parlor table. He hadn't realized it was happening to him. Even at the end of his life, he still felt much as he did in the Mexico years—that Margrethe was "the first important person in my life."

By 1914, Weston was becoming nationally and internationally known for his "high-key" portraits, striking tonal arrangements, imaginative use of natural light seen in soft focus. He demonstrated his techniques before national conventions of professional photographers; received numerous medals and prizes; articles were written about him, and many small one-man shows demanded of him. In 1917, he was elected—along with the earl of Carnarvon—a member of the London Salon, then considered the highest honor Pictorialism could give. In the same year, he found himself involved in the reaction against Pictorialism. Stieglitz and Steichen, leading the attack against the decadence that was corrupting the movement they, more than all others, had been responsible for launching, threw out all but 55 of the 1,100 entries submitted to the Wanamaker Salon in Philadelphia. Weston received minor honors; Sheeler and Strand the main prizes.

Weston was becoming sick of shimmer and simper and the human ego, including his own. He sought bolder structure, deep space, sharper seeing, a more humble and objective approach to life. "One does not suddenly change. I never lost my excitement over a sharp, exquisite photograph. What to do with it was a problem from which I was sidetracked. . . . I think success in the 'salons' got the best of me. Then articles by Rosenfeld, Tennant, Seligmann, about Stieglitz began to appear. Later by or about Strand. These shoved me in the right direction. . . . That whole soft-focus period in retrospect seems like a staged act; I even dressed to suit the part: windsor tie, green velvet jacket—see, I was an artist!"

His memory was usually accurate, and he remembered that he began the *Daybook* in 1917. Yet in the first bonfire he records, in 1925, ". . . one brave moment in San Francisco, three years of writing went into the flames." Much later, in 1931, he came across a page he saved from this holocaust, and he was proud he had saved it. It is a savage indictment of his pretenses as he saw them in 1920: "Well I know you, Edward Weston, and I say you have spent a year of writing in trying to build up a fine defence around yourself and your work,—excusing your weakness! and yet, knowing all this, you are not strong enough to destroy most of your work, nor these notebooks." Did he then actually begin his *Daybook* in 1919? Or did he burn the first three years in 1920, when he scraped the emulsion off old prizewinning negatives and used the glass to make a window?

He ceased to send to salons and magazines; little or nothing appears, except in Mexico, for the next ten years.

Tropico was becoming Glendale, Glendale was being absorbed by the huge sprawl of Los Angeles. Weston was horrified by what was happening, and in his naïveté, easily accepted the post–World War I cynicism about America and democracy that led many of the most gifted writers and painters to consider themselves "the Lost Generation," and go abroad to live. Weston tried it himself: around 1921, he met Tina Modotti, Italian-born beauty whose family had moved from Venice to Los Angeles when she was a child. She had acted bit parts in the movies, served as a model to friends such as Diego Rivera and other painters in the Mexican Renaissance. She hit Edward like a tempest, and she had about her a magnificence and a nobility no one who knew her could ever afterwards forget. In March 1922, Tina went to Mexico City to attend her dying husband. She took with her Weston's personal work; exhibited at the Academia de Bellas Artes, it not only roused enthusiasm—for the first time, it actually sold. Edward dreamed neither for the first time nor the last time, of making a living, not out of the human ego, but, like any good painter, sculptor, writer, out of the great images he knew were in him. He decided to go with Tina to live in Mexico.

"The life force within the form"—whatever might be the form when he was "granted the flash of revealment"—this Edward Weston was beginning to see before he went to Mexico. Already the intensity of his vision had much to give his friends among the painters of the Mexican Renaissance—more, he found to his surprise, than they had to give him. But the warmth of their praise and of their friendship gave him the faith and courage he needed to see and to live in his own way. And Mexico itself, dramatic, violent, with its clash of extremes, opened new perspectives— the simple, the stark, the commonplace, even the macabre and the grotesque. "These several years in Mexico have influenced my thought and life," he wrote in his Daybook (vol. 1, September 4, 1926), "not so much the contact with my artist friends as the less direct proximity of a primitive race. . . . Of simple peasant people I knew nothing. And I have been refreshed by their elemental expression,—I have felt the soil."

The return to Glendale, to "a civilization severed from its roots," to "canned people," to an ugly monotonous suburbia devouring the hills, was all the more painful. Absence had not eased the incompatibilities of temperament between him and his wife, Flora, mother of his four sons. "The boys brought me back," he wrote. "I need them—they need me."

Nor had absence cooled the ardor of several feminine friends. "Why this tide of women?" he asked. "Why do they all come at once?" It was a situation that frequently threatened to get out of hand; to his boys who now and then served as traffic cops, it was funnier than anything Hollywood produced, but it bothered Edward. Why he so attracted women also puzzled him. "I am not a stalwart male exuding sex. . . . I am a poor lover. . . . The idea means more to me than the actuality." Sometimes he wondered: "But what is love?. . . Is love like art—something always ahead, never quite attained? Will I ever have a permanent love? Do I want one? Unanswerable questions for me!" Again and again he spoke of love as "bringing beauty." For him it was as important to give in love as in art. Perhaps that is why so many of his loves, later, all passion spent, still came to him as a dear and close friend, and remembered him with pride and tenderness.

To protect them from the perils of publication he slashed at his Daybooks with a razor, cutting out whole pages and many names, leaving behind a frequent confusion of initials. Vivid characterization often renders these attempts at anonymity transparent. Nevertheless his son Brett, who roared with laughter over certain events recalled by this volume, agrees with me that the manuscript should be published much as Edward left it. A few unnecessary intimacies, an occasional hot-headed comment of the kind he usually regretted, obscurities due to the hasty razor, some family quarrels better forgotten—Edward himself would undoubtedly have removed these were he here to supervise the final preparation. Nothing essential has been lost; everything basic to an understanding of this quiet-looking little volcano and the relation of his life to his work remains intact.

His plethora of loves, for instance, is evidence that he had no need to seek erotic forms in his work—an implication by the Freudian-minded that he vigorously rejected. The painter Henrietta Shore was working in a similar direction; her response to his work and then his response to hers— "beyond emotion or intellect, a transcendental force"—ignited anew a way of seeing he had begun in Mexico. In her studio he first saw and photo- graphed a chambered nautilus. Its nacreous spiraling beauty blended in his thought with the nudes he was making of a dancer; he felt "a freshened tide swelling within myself." He began to see "finely moving rhythms" everywhere. "Green peppers in the market stopped me; they were amazing in every sense of the word,—the three purchased. But a *tragedy* took place—Brett ate two of them!" Curving clusters of bananas, subtle ovoids of cantaloupes, melons, gourds, sculptural chard, cabbages— his multitudinous vegetable loves proved anything but inert. They grew or wilted during the long exposures necessary in studio light with the slow films of the time; they showed the strain while they waited day after day, during a rush of business, for him to return.

As in Mexico, the eternal struggle for enough cash to pay the rent, feed his family, and now, launch his eldest sons into their own careers, kept

Edward confined to his studio, fearing to miss a phone call or a visitor. How he welcomed his rare holidays and his still more rare expeditions of a few days! What mighty forms and rhythms awaited him in, say, the desert!

Cities became unendurable to him—even San Francisco. In Carmel he was close to wild beauty again. The Big Sur country—far beyond his power to photograph at the time. "The way will come . . . to see this marriage of ocean and rock." Then Point Lobos—the forces of wind, wave, erosion, life and death, perpetually challenging him into new ways of seeing. "My work is always a few jumps ahead of what I say about it."

His work was leaping ahead of him into the most difficult challenge of all, landscape, wherein all forces and rhythms, human and primeval alike, must be combined, and "the heavens and earth become one."

The accolades and perceptions of friends and visitors—Robinson Jeffers, José Clemente Orozco, Jean Charlot, Walt Kuhn, Walter Arensberg, Merle Armitage, Mark Tobey, for example—the comments by Eastern critics that his work was "theatrical"—its rejection by Stieglitz as lacking "fire, life today," which hurt and puzzled him, until he ceased to care—the assumption by left-wing radicals that he was one of them and should be out photographing the proletariat, which caused him both wrath and amusement—the attempts by academic painters to deny photography as an art—his response to the dance and to music, especially Bach—all these contribute to his meditations in "the still, dark hours." He could always see both sides of a question or a person, and these fluctuations contribute to the final clarifications of his own dynamic and independent approach.

When the Daybook ends, "a most beautiful love" has come to him.

And: "I am the adventurer on a voyage of discovery, ready to receive fresh impressions, eager for fresh horizons . . . to identify myself in, and unify with whatever I am able to recognize as significantly part of me— the 'me' of universal rhythms."

NANCY NEWHALL

*"By the way I have already written my introduction.
Here it is: How young I was. That covers everything."*

E. W.

I. MEXICO

PART I

Fragments from early Daybooks

1. *Boy and Camera*

(One page from a pre-1923 Daybook, undated)

... denying myself every luxury—indeed many comforts too—until with eleven dollars in my pocket I rushed to town—purchasing a second-hand 5 × 7 camera— with a ground-glass and tripod! And then what joy! I needed no friends now— I was always alone with my love. School was neglected—I played "hookey" whenever possible. Zero weather found me wandering through snow-drifts— seeking the elusive patterns in black and white—which covered the ground—or sunsets over the prairie wastes. Sundays my camera and I would take long car- rides into the country around Chicago—always alone—and nights we spent feverishly developing my plates in some makeshift dark-room, and then the first print I made from my first 5 × 7 negative—a snow scene—the tightening— choking sensation in my throat—the blinding tears in my eyes when I realized that a "picture" had really been conceived—and how I danced for joy into my father's office with this initial effort: I can see every line of the composition yet— and it was not half-bad—I can only wish I had kept the print at least for memory's sake—and not destroyed it with many others in some moment of dissatisfaction. Months of happiness followed—interest was sustained—yes—without many lapses —is with me yet—

Last year I talked before the University of California on photography and part of my paper it seems may well be added right here—"I come to you as a photo- grapher—a craftsman I hope. My education was not from the public schools where I dreamed my hours away—but from my camera. Before it came into my life—I had drifted along mechanically—passing from grade to grade—by fair or unfair means—watching the clock for recess or noonhours or vacation time— taking home books for study and returning them still unstrapped the next morning. But suddenly my whole life changed—because I because interested in something definite—concrete. Immediately my senses of sight and touch were developed—my imagination keyed up to a high pitch—because—at last after years wasted—accidentally enough—it is sad to relate—I became interested—

2. Notes from N.Y. Nov. 1922

(copied before destroying daybook 1942)

Near the "penny bridge", a few steps from my room (Columbia Heights). Morning coffee with Jo from the purple cup sister gave me.

The Hurdy Gurdy man who played to our window.

The lone man who wandered by playing a softly quavering flute; 30 years ago I must have heard the same man in Chicago. "God bless you Sir for the money. I surely need it."

Almost daily I haunted the bridges, Brooklyn or Manhattan. One Sunday I walked over Williamsburg Br. at sunset—then down among the tenements on Rivington Street—memorable night.

Two "specials" from Tina, each with 20.00 enclosed: "knowing that (I) would need money, that (I) must see Balieff's *Chauve Souris*."

Other evenings riding the busses, once alone in a drizzling rain.

Stieglitz: we finally met. I phoned him and he promised to see me as soon as his mother died. She was sinking rapidly.

My report of our contact: "A maximum of detail with a maximum of simplification"; with these words as a basis for his attitude toward photography Alfred Stieglitz talked with Jo and me four hours, or rather he talked *to* us, for we had no chance, nor desire, to say much. He spoke brilliantly, convincingly with the idealism of a visionary, enforcing his statements by an ever repeated "You see, you see."

I took my work to show Stieglitz. He laid it open to attack, and then discarded print after print, prints I loved. Yet I am happy, for I gained in strength, in fact strengthened my own opinion. I was ripe to change, was changing, yes changed, when I went to New York. I had shown my portfolio of photographs all over New York, had been showered with praise which meant very little to me, for all the time I knew that I was showing my past. I seemed to sense just what Stieglitz would say about each print, albeit I did not always agree. So I was not disillusioned. Quick as a flash he pounced upon the hands in "Mother & Daughter" (Tina & Mamacita), on irrelevant detail in the pillows of "Ramiel in his Attic" (frankly, I did not always know what he was talking about), bad texture in Sibyl's neck. "Nothing must be unconsidered, there must be a complete release" was an often used thought.

But I feel that I was well received by Stieglitz; I could sense his interest and he did give some praise. "You *feel*, I can see that, you have the beginning; will you go on? I do not know. You are going in your own direction, it is good, go ahead." Stieglitz has not changed my direction, only intensified it, stimulated me—and I am grateful.

Stieglitz said that he used an anastigmat lens of 13 in. focus on 8 × 10 plates, stopped down to f 45 or more, that he used a head rest to enable him to give exposures of 3 or 4 minutes.

In my enthusiasm I do not accept Stieglitz as an infallible master, nor would he want me to. He said: "Friends made me out a god, when all I asked was to be treated as a human being, then turned on me when I couldn't be all they asked— and 291 closed. But I have been thankful to every person who has hurt me. There has been one who has stood by me through it all—a girl from Texas. You see her paintings here stacked all around this room, this room that my brother allows me—and one for O'Keeffe downstairs. I have nothing left, deserted by friends and wife and child—yet in no period of my life have I been so enthusiastic and interested in photography and anxious to work. Yes, O'Keeffe has painted and I have photographed, I will show you." Then he showed us a few of his photographs, perhaps ten; most were in storage. The hands sewing, the breasts, a rather abstract nude. "Ah, you do feel deeply," Stieglitz said, "and that little girl over there trembles with emotion" (as much from the barrage of words as from the photographs!—E. W.) "You will go away and tell of this meeting and some will say 'Stieglitz has hypnotized you,' but I have only bared to the world a woman's life. Every woman has her virginal moments, even a prostitute. I have tried to grasp such moments too. The struggle is to live and express life untouched by the ideas of neighbors and friends. After all we only know what we feel, and I have been unafraid to say what I feel. You see that in my work. I have broken every photographic law, optics included. I have put my lens a foot from the sitter's face because I thought when talking intimately one doesn't stand ten feet away; and knowing that it takes time to get deep into the very innermost nature of matter, I have given exposures of several minutes stopped way down. You see my prints, the eye is able to wander all over them, finding satisfaction in every portion, the ear is given as much consideration as the nose, but it is a task, this desire to obtain detail and simplification at the same time. To make your subject forget a headrest during such long exposures is heartbreaking. If you had come to me four years ago I should not have been ripe to give you what I do now." Nor I ripe to receive it.

Returning to remarks on my work I quote Stieglitz: "I like the way you attack each picture as a fresh problem, you are not formulated. This is very interesting, and this the first complete failure you have shown. There must be an absolute release, nothing left unconsidered. But I will show you! I see you are not satisfied.

You do not think that you are great do you?" Then with a laugh, "I don't think that I am. This print has fine dignity. Treat anything you undertake with dignity, a portrait or a box of matches. If I were publishing *Camera Work* I would ask you for this breast, these torsoes and these smoke-stacks. My last message to you is work, seek, experiment." So ended our day with Stieglitz.

Several days later, and I am still reflecting over the very important day with Stieglitz. His work: solid, nothing neglected, nothing indefinite or wavering, "a complete release." But without minimizing the praise I have bestowed on his work, I think that Stieglitz exaggerates the importance of several portraits he showed. I feel that some of mine are just as important in their way. I have a problem to work out; to retain my own quality and values, but achieve greater depth of field.

My days in New York were nearing an end. My greatest desire was to see Stieglitz again. Then: "Rhinelander 8893 — Mr. Stieglitz? — yes, this is Weston. I would like to see you again but hesitate to ask for more time." — "I am glad you called, in fact expected you to. I told O'Keeffe about your work, please bring it with you."

A Mr. Seligmann was there when I arrived. O'Keeffe responded in much the same way that Stieglitz had, in fact made almost the same criticisms. "This is a fine head." "He is one of my closest friends: Johan Hagemeyer." "Yes, I remember him. This breast, is perhaps the most complete thing you have." (25 years later, I know that this photo was full of striving for effect, sensational, one of least important prints I showed). These stacks too are very fine, they remind me of the paintings of... (can't remember name) do you know them?" I did not.

My audience of three was pretty merciless, yet withal giving me due credit and sufficient praise. Seligmann, silent during the showing, turned and said "I want you to know that these pictures have meant something to me." And Stieglitz' final message, "Weston, I knew from your letters you were sincere. I have tried to give you freely. Your work and attitude reassures me. You have shown at least several prints which have given me a great deal of joy. And this I can seldom say of photographs. Goodbye and let me hear from you."

"Times Square at noon Jo. I have made a date with Sheeler." Stieglitz looking at my steel works photos had said "You should see Sheeler's work," and then in same breath "No, it is not necessary." But I concluded to go — and am very happy that I did. His photographs are a remarkable "portrait" of New York, the finest architectural photographs I have seen.

While with Sheeler, Paul Strand dropped in. We accepted an invitation to see his work. It was splendid, very much under the influence of Stieglitz, but a

1. SHADOW ON A BARN AND MARGARETHE, 1920

2. BREAST, 1920

3. Johan Hagermeyer, 1922

4. KARL STRUSS, CINEMATOGRAPHER, 1922

5. ARMCO, OHIO, 1922

6. Hands & Kimono, 1924

7. TINA, RECITING, 1924

8. Guadalupe Marín de Rivera, 1924

worthy carrying on of the master's tradition. I shall have more to say in retrospect.

But it grew late and train time—we took our last bus ride from Washington Square to Grand Central. Good-bye New York, good-bye Jo. I shall not forget.

In 1942 Weston wrote: Evidently much writing of this period has already been destroyed. I can't find the account of the visit with Strand nor with Sheeler. I do recall that I found too much of Stieglitz in Strand at that time—quite understandable. And I remember that I was deeply impressed with Sheeler's photographs of New York, by far the best I had seen of that city.   E. W.

Excerpt from Daybook, which Weston marked for omission:

Stieglitz said: "Weston, I asked Paul Strand if he knew of you. He said 'Yes, your work was no good.' Now Strand is very close to me, in fact no one is closer, but I took him severely to task for an unconsidered sweeping statement, and let him know how I felt having just seen it. He then admitted having seen only a few reproductions. Strand theorizes, does not work enough."

Chicago: Aunt Emma, Uncle Theodore, and the old home—mine too for a while—at 2213 Washington Blvd; it had gone to seed, a forlorn shadow of the past. I was still "Eddie" to the old folks, I must wear this or that, be in by 12, eat, drink, read as they do, vote Republican straight. But they had not lost their sharp tongues nor dry humor and they did everything in their own way to make me comfortable.

Aunt Em took me to the Chicago Opera Co. *Aida* was playing. I was bored; over all was a veneer of money; it was artificial, but not with the frank, gay artificiality of the *Chauve Souris*. A few voices being exploited, with the same old tunes. How can these people listen year after year! Once I got a slight thrill from a duet between Raisa and Marshall; but most of the time my thoughts went back to a haystack by Monet, sailboats by Manet, a landscape by Cézanne, and a drawing by Charles Sheeler of New York skyscrapers. These in the Chicago Art Institute. I regret to say—but only because of Aunt Em—that once I went to sleep.

Chicago was an anti-climax to New York except for a few fine contacts. Carl Sandburg took me to a tiresome party for which he apologized profusely; and I had a happy afternoon with Eugene Hutchinson and another with Mrs. Bertha Jacques via an introduction from Roi Partridge.

I went to Chicago Camera Club—and left without opening my portfolio. And here I had better wind up by telling the story of getting to New York, the why and how.

7

I had gone to visit sister May and John and family in Middletown, Ohio, prior to sailing for Mexico — a farewell visit for which John sent money. Well John and May got their heads together, decided to help me on to New York since I was already almost there, and might not have such a chance again.

The Middletown visit was something to remember with auto drives through the hills and dales of Miami Valley, all resplendent in autumn colors, and over the river into Kentucky, to Dayton and Cincinnati too. But most of all in importance was my photographing of "Armco", the great plant and giant stacks of the American Rolling Mill Co. That day I made great photographs, even Stieglitz thought they were important! And I only showed him unmounted proofs.

(Editorial comment: 20 years later they still look good — Edward Weston) The reunion with Sis and family was all and more than I had hoped for. John's interest in my work was outstanding and deeply appreciated by me. It was his desire to help me on to New York.

Once more destruction enters in to cut short the visit with May in Ohio. Why, I can't remember.

3. Discussion on Definition

April 20, 1923—Glendale, California. Johan is here—has been here for over a week—Days and nights of intensity—burning discourses on many topics—of course mostly photography!

Johan brought new work—fine industrial things—nicely seen—but lacking in definition—an inexcusable fault when it comes to photographing modern architecture and machinery—even the "mood" could be better interpreted with sharp—clean lines—"-But if I see things this way—Edward—I must render them as I see them" — "Nevertheless—Johan — photography has certain inherent qualities which are only possible with photography—one being the delineation of detail—So why not take advantage of this attribute? Why limit yourself to what your eyes see when you have such an opportunity to extend your vision?—now this fine head of your sister—if it was focussed sharper you would have expressed your idea even more profoundly—Here is a proof (Bertha Wardell) which may explain what I mean"—"By God! I do see now—in this case at least—that a more clearly defined—searching definition would have unveiled and exposed the very suffering and strife I have tried to portray — but in some other prints I show you—it seems almost necessary that there should not be so much revealed—however in the portrait under consideration I realize that I skimmed over the surface and did not penetrate as I might have—I do not accept—swallow—what you say as a whole—but I have gotten something from the talk which makes me see more clearly and will make me surer of what I wish to do—Let me question again—if in a certain mood why should I not interpret that state through my picture and not merely photograph what is before me?—in such instances the use of diffusion would aid me —"

"Yes, it would aid you—to cloud and befog the real issue—and prevent you from telling the truth about the life towards which your lens is pointing—if you wish to 'interpret' why not use a medium better suited to interpretation or subjective expression—or—let some one else do it—Photography is an objective means to an end — and as such is unequaled—It comes finally to the question: For what purpose should the camera be used?—and I believe you have misused it—along with many others—including myself!" And so—on we went pro and con ---

April 25 Quiet again—Johan beat his way north on Monday—I am glad to be alone—we love one another—but wear each other out — I really believe we would finally quarrel if thrown together too many succeeding days—I gave him a print of my "Stacks"—"I have never before demanded a print from you Edward—but I must have a copy of that"—He would return again and again to it—"It is a thing I wish I had made—but I'm glad you did it for me to enjoy—for I feel I *could* have done it."

Together or with Tina or Margrethe — sometimes all four of us — we spent many vivid hours—at Stojana's—the Philharmonic—once an evening with Buhlig listening to his reading of that amazing poem *Waste Land* by T. S. Eliot—and looking over Billy Justema's drawings—listening too—to his reading—That night it rained—and returning to the studio still keyed to adventure—we donned old hats and walked into the rain—I took him to the river—winding our way among the dripping willows—around us the silence of hours past midnight — Bedraggled and drenched we reached home—but thrilled with the beauty we had had—

After the Philharmonic we desired a corner to sit and smoke and sip coffee—but to the shame of Los Angeles could think of barely a place but deadly respectable ice-cream parlors with smug people —sickening sweets—noisy clatter—commercial haste—and most likely bad music—

Margrethe ever curious had heard of a Greek coffee house near Los Angeles Street where sailors gathered—there had been a murder committed there and fights were a nightly occurrence—So we went—and though not favored with a murder or fight had a sufficiently exciting night—yes a fascinating night—

A room full of sailors with here and there a collarless nondescript—but mostly those not in uniform were that type of effiminate male who seek the husky sailor to complement their lacking vigour — One such fastidiously-dressed — unmistakable person—presented to us a most lascivious picture of impatient desire—his foot twitched continually—his whole body quivered—his lips fairly drooled—until finally with several others of his kind—a bunch of sailors were "dated up" and off they went in a limousine — Sailors danced together with biting of ears and open caresses—some sprawled over their tables down and out—every one had a bottle on the hip—while an officer of the law amiably overlooked his opportunity to enforce the 18th amendment—

A negro droned on the saxaphone—or "sexaphone" as Margrethe calls it—another picked the banjo—the four or five waitresses watched their chance to pocket tips or pick the pockets of drunken "gobs"—one sailor prize fighter reeled to our table loudly confiding his troubles—the quarrel he had "with that 'gold digger' over there"—had us feel his muscles and related his life history—

Margrethe was the only girl in the place besides the waitresses—But we were too differently dressed—too conspicuous and I wonder we did not land in the street —I should like to go again under different circumstances.

10

PART II

Mexico, August, 1923—December, 1924

1. "*Romantic Mexico*"

August 2, 1923. Tina, Chandler and Edward on board the S. S. Colima, *four days out from Los Angeles.* At last we are Mexico bound, after months of preparation, after such endless delays that the proposed adventure seemed but a conceit of the imagination never actually to materialize. Each postponment became a joke to our friends and a source of mortification to us. But money had to be raised, and with rumors of my departure many last moment sittings came in, each one helping to secure our future.

Nor was it easy to uproot oneself and part with friends and family—there were farewells which hurt like knife thrusts.

But I adapt myself to change—already Los Angeles seems part of a distant past. The uneventful days—the balmy air has relaxed me—my overstrained nerves are eased. I begin to feel the actuality of this voyage.

The *Colima* flies a Mexican flag, she is small, not too clean and slow—yet I would not change to a more pretentious ship, noisy with passengers from whom there might be no escape. The crew, all Mexican, is colorful and inefficient according to our standards—but it is a relief to escape from that efficiency which makes for mechanized movements, unrelieved drabness.

On board is an Australian sea-captain, a coarse, loud fellow, who continually bellyaches over the dirt, food, service—he goes purple when a waiter's coat is unbuttoned, discounts the whole crew as ignorant, beneath contempt—yet he is the one who suffers by comparison. The Mexicans, at least, have an innate fineness, and they are good to look upon.

Yesterday the sea was rough, the *Colima* pitched and rolled—Tina sick, pobrecita! In contrast, the night before, our ship cut through silent, glassy waters domed by stars—toward what unknown horizons? A night of suspended action—of delayed but imminent climaxes—anything might happen—nothing did.

August 4. A half-moon half hidden by heavy clouds—sculptured rocks, black, rising from silvered waters—shriek of whistle and rasp of chain; 1:00 A. M. and we anchored in the harbor of Mazatlán, my first foreign port.

Morning—and we excitedly prepared for shore. Thanks to Tina—her beauty— though I might have wished it otherwise!—el Capitán has favored us in many ways: the use of his deck, refreshing drinks in his cabin, his launch to carry us ashore.

Did I visualize what I was to see in my first Mexican port? This is hard to say today—seeing, with stranger's eyes, a stageset: blocks of low houses—a continuous wall of alternate pastel blues, pinks, greens. Down narrow streets Indian boys drove heavy-laden burros; around corners appeared vendors of water or chickens —a half-dozen hanging head down, their legs crossed over a pole, all peeping dolorously.

Street stands sold tropical fruits—some new to me and delicious—for instance, the mango is truly nectar. Aguacates—avocados—sold for 5 centavos! There were vehicles for hire, two-wheeled carts and low-swung coaches. In one of these, drawn by a span of horses— decrepit ones I must admit—we drove along the coast at sunset.

Later, exploring the city streets at night, we found life both gay and sad—sharp clashes of contrasting extremes, but always life—vital, intense, black and white, never grey. Glendale, on the contrary, is drab, spiritless, a uniform grey—peopled by exploiters who have raped a fair land.

Often the barred windows framed lovely black-gowned señoritas—and some not so lovely.

Leisurely drinking ice-cold beer in the patio of Hotel Belmar was a fitting prologue to our first day in Mexico. Later we were introduced to Mexican hospitality when we met the captain at noon "for a cocktail". The party grew from four to a dozen— the drinks progressed from cocktails to tequila straight— Strange how one can understand a foreign tongue with tequila in one's belly.

August 6. Sailing again after two days in Mazatlán.
We did not go ashore again—too hot! Water has poured from my body in rivulets—never before have I perspired so profusely—nor so dishonestly loafed dreamy hours away (this thought reveals my New England background!)

I was tempted in Mazatlán to "go tourist" with my camera, making "snaps" of street scenes—even doing Tina in her grand coach backed by a ruin.

But yesterday I made the first negatives other than matter-of-fact records—negatives with intention. A quite marvellous cloud form tempted me—a sunlit cloud which rose from the bay to become a towering white column.

Mazatlán becomes more vivid in retrospect: I recall cool patios glimpsed from sun-baked streets which sheltered coconut palms, strange lilies, banana trees. I see the cathedral, with its crude Christ, horribly real—and the dramatic devotion of those who come to pray, some sprawled in abject penitence at the entrance before raising their eyes to the glories within.

In the cool twilight hour children danced in the streets—as our carriage approached, they stopped to see the extranjeros—foreigners.

August 8. Three days since leaving the boat. Before dawn we had anchored in the harbor of Manzanillo—by eleven, we had passed the customhouse officials,

14

though not without much palavering, suspicious glances at my battery of lenses, chemicals and personal effects, which Ramiel [McGhee, a close friend] had packed so well that I despaired of ever getting the trunks repacked before train departure.

But there was time to spare, so we wandered the streets escorted by el Capitán, ever attentive. As we sat with our beer looking out to the bluest of seas, a sailor from the *Colima* passed, hesitated, returned; saluting his captain he requested permission to order us drinks. A wandering trio of musicians passed—were hailed by "our" captain—played *Borrachita*—slightly tipsy. My Anglo-Saxon reserve was put to test—and lost. But it was more than the music—the hospitality—the blue sea—which broke my resistance: I knew that this day marked an end — and a beginning.

August 20. Avenida del Hipódromo 3, Colonia Nápoles, Tacubaya, México, D. F.—about 40 minutes by trolley from the city. We have leased an old and beautiful hacienda for six months; ten rooms, each opening onto a spacious patio, 85 × 100 ft., filled with vines, shrubs, trees. The house is of brick with high ceilings and tall arched windows, barred, heavily shuttered, seeming to suggest possible attack. The first night there further stimulated the imagination; I was awakened by gun fire under my very windows — then silence, not even audible foot-steps. Well, I did not come here for the ordered calm of a Glendale.

The brick walls of our casa are fifteen inches thick, and plastered in and out. The last occupant had papered the rooms with hideous results, and I, curses be, have been laboriously removing it, while the landlord stands by aghast.

Evidently the middle-class Mexican has no better taste than the middle-class American; the store-windows bear me out with a conglomeration of the most tawdry rubbish imaginable. When the Mexican apes the American he acquires his worst side; and, of course the reverse is true, recalling Mexican or "Spanish" type homes in California. Here, the new architecture is "Hollywood" burlesqued, incongruous beside the beauty of passing culture.

But the past still dominates; old churches stand like impregnable fortresses — quite apart from the new and superficial life which surrounds them. La Catedral is majestic, impressive when its great bells are tolled. "El Zócalo," the square in front, is out of keeping with its bad contemporary sculpture. Nearby two urchins played around a fountain graced by a vapid Venus; impulsively one turned, embraced her, kissed her stony lips, and laughed mischievously.

Beautiful women seem rare—maybe they do not walk the streets—and those of the upper-class dress in execrable taste. Maybe I expected shawls and mantillas! Of course, I except the Indian in native costume, both men and women. Often, they are very beautiful, have poise and dignity. Dregs of humanity are on all sides; maimed, diseased beggars pleading insistently.

The pulquerías — bars — in which the Indian finds solace for his lost glory are the most colorful notes of contemporary life in the city, and the following titles evidence the Indian's romance and imagination.

"Sin Estudio"	Without Thought
"La Primavera"	The Springtime
"Un Viejo Amor"	An Old Love
"El Gato Negro"	The Black Cat
"Las Flores"	The Flowers
"La Camelia"	The Camelia
"La Dama Blanca"	The White Lady
"La Esperanza en el Desierto"	Hope In The Wilderness
"Sobre las Olas"	On The Waves
"La Perla de la Piedad"	The Pearl Of Piety
"El Asalto"	The Assault
"La Muerte y la Resurrección"	Death and Resurection
"Las Primorosas"	The Beautiful Girls
"La Gloria de Juan Silveti"	(Juan Silveti being one of the popular toreros)

Imagine American saloons with such names! Perhaps, if they had had them, we should never have voted the 18th Amendment. That the Indian also has a sense of humor, I concluded from the following inscription noted on a mulepower truck — "Viva el Rápido" — Hail to the Swift One!

Getting established, starting life over from the ground up is not easy, especially lacking money, and with desires none too easy to please. Furniture has been a problem, that found in the average store expensive and hideous, fine examples of the best "Grand Rapids" style, highly varnished, crude and pretentious. Dishes and other details were equally hard to find until "El Volador," the thieves' market, was suggested. There we found every imaginable article to suit any extreme of taste; returning with Puebla ware for both food and flowers, imperfect pieces and modern, of course, but fine in form and color. We also purchased a couple of brass candle sticks at two pesos each, and an old inlaid chest which Gould's in Los Angeles might have sold to some three chinned dowager for a hundred dollars — this, after much bargaining on Tina's part, was ours for fifteen pesos. And, oh yes, the string of eighteen amber beads — lovely uncut ones, half-hidden in the clutter of an old Italian's stall — was purchased for two pesos!

August 23. Will we ever get established! Such confusion! Painters and plumbers at work trying to please the new arrivals. Such dolts!—Labor, too is the same everywhere—-the workmen take their own time; one becomes impatient to no avail. "Bolshevism," remarked our landlord, "has spoiled labor in Mexico. We are a conservative people. We do not want it."

The painters, I am sure, think us "loco" preferring, as we do, the crude beam ceilings to the fake painted canvas which hid them. Our friends, too, think us slightly off for moving so far from the city and expecting our clientele to come

16

out. They are dubious as to the outcome of the venture. Well, surely now I have not come way to Mexico to open a commercial studio on "Main Street" — better have remained where I was! I hardly dare look ahead. Yet—I shall not worry; we may surprise our questioning friends.

A few days ago, Tina took me to see the work of Diego Rivera, murals for a public building. Later we met him. It was the work of a great artist which we viewed; and he was great in another way, tall and of generous girth — a striking figure! I regret not being able to converse with him for he has lived among the foremost contemporary artists in Paris, Picasso, Matisse, and others and he must know anecdotes.

After the inspiration of Rivera and his painting, I received a severe let-down. We went to Sanborn's. What was once a marvellous palace of blue tile has been redecorated, turned into a typical American restaurant.

The murals of Diego Rivera have raised a storm of protest from the conservatives, but the work continues on. I cannot imagine his having the opportunity to start such paintings in any American municipal building. Government "of the people, by the people, and for the people" does not foster great art. However, there are flagrant examples of municipal bad taste all over Mexico City. Statues to every sort of hero abound, line the Paseo de la Reforma, and dot the Alameda; gilded statues, some as vulgar as our own Goddess of Liberty. So, after all, middle class minds and apirations are the same everywhere.

Llewellyn [a pupil] is here, at last, with his police dog, Panurge.

Recounting his trip—brings back my own: The unforgettable train ride from Manzanillo to Mexico City, and those beautiful cities, Colima and Guadalajara. I should like to have lived a while in Colima, but we spent only one day in each place, just enough to excite our fancies. These cities were less spoiled than Mexico City, the natives more genuine.

From Manzanillo to Colima was a touch of the tropics, luxuriant vegetation with stretches of tangled vines, dense growth amounting to a jungle. The Indians sold strange and delicious fruits at every stop — the mango, fresh coconuts and bananas, aguacates, sugar cane. In these foods I indulged — they seemed safe enough — but, tempting as they looked, I hesitated over the tamales and other steaming dishes and sweets. Later I learned that the tamales were not chicken as advertised but iguana, the giant lizard — well, why not? A tender iguana might be more palatable than a tough old hen!

We wandered through the streets of Colima after a well-cooked savory repast. It was there we met little Carmen; she sat on the cement walk, leaning against a pillar under long corridors of arches, in front of her a tray of pumpkin seeds. She dozed, awakening now and then to dish out automatically a dozen seeds or so for un centavo. Again, her heavy lids would droop, once more her pale profile would assume its tenderly poignant outline in the flickering torch light. Tina wanted her. "Will you come with me, Carmen, to Mexico? You shall be my little sister." Carmen's eyes dropped, this time with a shy, almost frightened hesitancy; we must ask her mamma who would soon return.

The mother had evidently been discussing the strange visit and request of the foreigners; she was belligerent, but softened when we gave presents to Carmen, a fan, a jar of jam, and other dainties. "She is all I have — and then she is sick — chills and fever — we cannot cure her — no — her father would never let her go." So we waved farewell to Carmen.

The plaza with its formal trees and arrangement might have been European; it was there the vendor of spikenard passed, an old Indian, barefooted, grey-bearded, carrying spikenard with yard-long stems. Tina should have one; it would complete her own loveliness, but we must bargain — everything is bargained for — even the romantic and beautiful. Finally, after prolonged arguing, the price was reduced from fifteen centavos to ten, but to pay him we found only an American dime! He looked at it suspiciously and another long palaver only half assured him that the dime was worth twenty centavos Mexican. He parted with the "nardo" and we with twenty centavos instead of ten! So ended fifteen minutes of bargaining with the laugh on us; but Tina had her spikenard.

Approaching Guadalajara, there was unfolded a breathtaking panorama — acres of water lilies along the tracks and stretching into the distance — pale lavender hyacinthine stalks — I called them "water hyacinths" for want of a better name.

August 27. We have been out but one evening since our arrival, that with [Roberto] Turnbull, a Mexican cinematographer, but very much Americanized. He took us to La Tapatía, a place famous for its cooking where "down and outs" rub elbows with Senators — Again a delicious meal.

I have yet to eat a poorly cooked dish in Mexico, and, too, they are reasonably priced, unless one wishes the privilege of gazing on the atrocious murals at Sanborn's. Then one pays, and doubly! The other day, for instance, a six course meal: soup, eggs, fish, two meats, pineapple and coffee, cost us $1.25 — less than 65¢ American.

So far, I have concluded that averaging up, living is less here than in Los Angeles, counting two pesos to the dollar; all will be well then if I can earn twice as many pesos as I did dollars.

The panchromatic films show deterioration; several negatives I discarded as hopeless, all show some fog and grain. However, most of them will be printable, and my one great hope, the towering white cloud at Matzatlán, though also deteriorated, will, I believe, admit of enlarging.

August 29. A month since we left California — and not once since the evening at La Tapatía have we had energy or opportunity to see the city after nightfall.

18

In fact, except for the train trip and what I can gather from this secluded retreat I do not know Mexico much better than when living in Los Angeles!

The tile roof to what once was a cowshed is a fine vantage point from which to view the country. Stone steps from the patio give easy access to the roof. Field after field of maize bounded by adobe walls stretch away towards distant mountains always banked by magnificent cloud forms. On clear days, I have seen snowclad Ixtaccíhuatl and Popocatépetl and usually the spires of la Catedral are visible. The castle of Chapultepec is near at hand, and, incongruously out of place, an occasional factory chimney blots the landscape.

Tina and I had a date with Rivera for Monday evening. He was unable to keep the appointment, so Guerrero and his lovely sister, Elisa, substituted for him. We dined at another typically Mexican place known for its good cooking and low prices—Monotes. The artist evidently haunts Monotes, the walls being decorated with humorous, grotesque, and Rabelaisian drawings.

Elisa is a fine Indian type; dressed in the costume of her native state she made a charming picture. Elisa spoke some English, more than I did Spanish. "Next time," I said to her, "I'll bring my dictionary." "When," she asked me, "will you bring the dictionary?" So now I have "una cita" for Thursday — my first "date" in Mexico!

Llewellyn's piano just came, he plays, trying it out. I have wanted music; I find it hurts. I feel singularly like an exile at times, as though I were here not altogether voluntarily...

After Monotes, we walked to *La Catedral*. Every inch of the facade of el Sagrario is elaborately carved, but held together—wrought into a perfect whole.

It pours! A deluge! Every day at 4:00, or so, the rain comes, and often in the night. I like the climate, it is cool, bracing. I sleep under three blankets but never shiver upon rising, nor wish to hover over a fire for a while as I did in Los Angeles. Neither do I back away from my morning cold bath, it is actually enjoyed.

If this, or equally agreeable weather, persists the year around, I cannot imagine a finer climate—and, because of the kaleidoscopic heavens, the play of light and shade over the landscape, monotony is precluded. I found the unvarying sky of Southern California more trying than the lack of decisive seasonal changes.

One attribute of the climate I have not enjoyed — *las pulgas*! The fleas have literally attacked me from all sides — and Chandler too — nothing seems to stop them. I believe they eat and fatten on the powder with which I sprinkle my bed. Guerrero laughs — tells Tina and I that we will become acclimated!

I am to have one of my dreams fulfilled — a whitewashed room; the furniture shall be black, the doors have been left as they were, a greenish blue, and then in a blue Puebla vase I'll keep red geraniums!

Hard work this reconstruction—we are all weary, and inclined to pessimism.

19

My hands are blistered, my back aches, my lungs are tortured with calcimine dust. The reaction comes when I contemplate that all this effort may come to naught.

August 31. Last evening, armed with my dictionary, I kept the appointment with Elisa. We dined at La Tapatía. I glanced at the menu, then shuttinmg y eyes, let fate decide the order. My finger pointed out pozole which with pollo — and tender chicken it was — provided a most delectable repast.

Elisa wishes to learn English, and I, Spanish, so discounting other desires, our mutual aim should provide many a pleasant evening. Just how the subject arose is difficult to recall, but Elisa taught me to say "Yo te amo" — and since she already knew the English "I love you," I taught her "Ich liebe Dich"! We parted early — "You have far to go and los ladrones – footpads – are bad" — "But I have a pistol!" — "No — no — for they are three — adiós — I give you un clavel blanco — a white carnation — have I satisfied you?"

September 1. The studio room finished at last. Walls light grey, doors and windows in their original green-blue, floor darker grey, on the walls a few prints — Picasso, Hokusai — and one of my own photographs — the "Smoke-Stacks" of course — in one corner a blue vase holding red flowers, for furniture two black colonial chairs, the new "old chest," and an inoffensive book case. Temporarily, my cot fills one corner — the room is so large, the furnishings so few — over it thrown an old piece of wool cloth, brilliant in color, flower patterned – probably it is Spanish. Tina acquired it for a song from Cesare, the old Italian in El Volador.

A deluge of rain swept over the building as I prepared for the first night in my completed room. The lighning dazzled, water gushed from the spouts, fell from the roof in sheets. Bare-foot, kimono-clad, Tina ran to me through the rain — but something has gone from between us. Curiosity, the excitement of conquest and adventure is missing. "Must desire forever defeat its end?"

September 13. We must move! — leave our beloved "El Buen Retiro". After two weeks of suspense and anxiety, we received the final verdict — "no telephone." Somehow, I had a presentiment that our efforts here were to be in vain, and so it has proved. A telephone is necessary. I am a "business man" and cannot stick thumb to nose in the direction of my public. How fortunate seems the writer with pencil and pad and any old corner for shelter — or the painter with a few brushes and tubes of paint!

Well, much money has been spent and time lost, the proposed date for my exhibit at "Aztec Land" is drawing near with work to be done and no place to work. Tina and I spent all day house-hunting, finding two possibilities but nothing so lovely as this hacienda which already seems like home — the most charming spot I have ever lived in.

Too, it has proven a wonderful place for work, indoors or out, with innumerable windows and doors and walls. I have photographed Tina — Chandler — Llewellyn and Elisa — two of Tina's I shall include in the exhibit — one of Chandler — three of Elisa. The pictures of Tina, excepting one sophisticated figure in black tailored suit, ebony cane, seen through a doorway against my high white walls, all but this one belong to a "romantic" school not altogether in keeping with my present frame of mind nor attitude towards my work.

I should be photographing more steel mills or paper factories, but here I am in romantic Mexico, and, willy-nilly, one is influenced by surroundings. I can, at least, be genuine. Life here is intense and dramatic, I do not need to photograph premeditated postures, and there are sunlit walls of fascinating surface textures, and there are clouds! They alone are sufficient to work with for many months and never tire.

September 15. Today, we found our future home — in a fashionable neighborhood this time, within walking distance from the heart of Mexico City, Lucerna 12, Colonia Juárez.

I dread the change, no place seems possible after "El Buen Retiro." The new house is a mansion by comparison: It has recently been re-decorated and re-papered with appalling results. It hardly seems possible that these people are not actually trying for ugliness. The only inoffensive rooms are the servants' quarters. How we all fight for them! If he knew, our landlord would be amazed, or amused.

The rent is an item which worries me — 260 pesos a month — a sum to make any craftsman ponder. To one who has never paid rent, this amount sounds impossible, but no such house could be obtained in Los Angeles for 130 dollars — nor anywhere near. Aside from business, I realize several advantages: we four shall not be isolated here night after night, thrown together continually to the point of irritation. We shall be able to see more of Mexico — the city — its life and activities, and meet our friends without such an effort.

This house-hunting has indicated a certain unconcern on the part of the Mexican people as to the personal relations of our unusual party. Not once have we been questioned as to why Tina Modotti and Edward Weston were living together, nor in the hotels has there been once an impertinent query. Viva México!

September 20. . . . Sunday afternoon de la Peña came to renew his acquaintance with Tina. Last year he had purchased one of my prints of her at the exhibit in La Academia de Bellas Artas. Negatives of Tina have proved a profitable investment! He talked of his experience during the revolution; condemned to death by both sides, each thinking he spied on the other. He dyed his hair yellow and otherwise disguised himself, pretending to be a Belgian who spoke only French, and went abroad in the city for a year undiscovered, before escaping to America.

"Do you think there will be more outbreaks, or are troubles settled?" I asked — "Next year at the presidential election there will be renewed fighting," he said. "I hope so anyway — we miss the excitement — it was great fun." Then, with another chuckle, "You know, only two Mexican presidents have lived through their terms!"

We talked of Mexican music, which led to Spanish influence. "The Spaniards," said de la Peña, "were an uncultured race before the advent of the Moors; all their civilization, arts, music, architecture, they owe to the Moors. Come, let us walk to my home, I will play for you typical Moorish music, also a waltz which might have been from Chopin, composed by a Mexican before Chopin was born."

10:30, and the streets were already deserted. "There seems to be no night life in Mexico. Where are all the people?" I asked. "They are busy inside," was the laughing reply. We passed a little cafe. "I have not dined. Will you join me?" queried de la Peña. "Frijoles refritos con queso and cerveza para cuatro – fried beans with cheese and beer for four," he ordered. Into the bright night of a Mexican moon we strolled once more. Only the inevitable dogs were abroad, some skulking, some yapping, some friendly, a sorry lot — crippled and diseased and starving like the beggars.

"What a night!" I invariably exclaim — for Mexican nights are bewitching.

De la Peña served us anise from Spain and black cinnamon coated cigarros. With music and anecdotes the hours passed — a happy night indeed — except for the fleas! — and, shall I confess? de la Pena's obvious infatuation for Tina! — Yet should I be a "dog in the manger"? Next time I'll pick a mistress homely as hell!

September 23. Fairly well established on Calle Lucerna. Best of all, the printing room is ready for use thanks to Llewellyn. I have tried out the roll of W. & C. Palladio [Willis and Clement Palladiotype — printing paper imported from England. See appendix on technique] which I brought along and find it has not deteriorated. Printed a negative of Chandler — little figure seated on the wall to our "cow-shed" — against the sky of an approaching thunder storm — my first print to be signed "Mexico, D. F." Also tried one of the Elisa negatives — Tehuana costume. A fine, strong face is recorded, an Indian face. Will she like it, or will she wish to be pretty?

Elisa is romantic — but I think unsophisticated. "Me gusta la música y las flores, nada más." Are you sure, "nada más," Elisa? — for I recall one evening not long ago, a perfumed evening, the wind fragrant from mosqueta bloom, the moon with its halo of orange, when Elisa displayed desires other than those for music and flowers.

We climbed to the roof that night, up the stone steps from our patio. Over the distant city, blazing parachutes festooned the sky, bombs burst incessantly, flaring rockets died with a shower of stars. From a nearby pulquería — music, laughter, festive noises, a nation celebrating its independence day, El diez y seis de Septiembre —

"I am going away soon," said Elisa. "Indeed! — why, Elisa — I shall weep." "Yes, Weston, I go to be married. I do not love him but I want experience — the experience of marriage. He is American and loves me very much. If I do not like, I go home to my mamma."

I ponder; if Elisa wants experience only, marriage seems a roundabout way. But should I become involved at this critical period? No — it must not be.

The next moment a soft hand, a sigh, an averted face — all is lost — our lips meet. Approaching footsteps, and the breathless instant is over.

Last week I wrote Margrethe to ship my old studio camera. I am dubious as to whether I can depend on her for even this important task. With no word from her since leaving Los Angeles despite urgent requests for certain negatives, I seem to have lost all contact with her, and am now in a mood of complete indifference.

From sister came a message of faith in my success — from Flora words of regret over the past — from the little boys dear tender scrawls — and from Ramiel the most beautiful letters of my life. He alone from out of the potpourri of friends and acquaintances has emerged a definite clear-cut figure from whom I cannot part — Ramiel! keenest of my critics, tenderest and most understanding of my confidants!

October 4–5. Have enlarged the great white cloud of Mazatlán. What a picture it might have been but for the film's deterioration! I have spent hours and many plates trying to improve its technical quality in the negative. Despite this loss in quality, it will be one of my finest and most significant photographs.

October 5. Night noises fascinate: in the still dark hours of wakefulness, a resulting intensification and magnification of one's hearing keys the imagination to an acceptance, an understanding or, at least, a conjuring with the impossible, the abnormal. So, with more prosaic daylight, with logic and common sense in authority, I question quite philosophically that which in the night brings free play to my most excessive fancies. Like an accompaniment to the half heard music of some eerie dream, faint, but clear and persistent above the raucous rooster and barking dog, quavers and trills a tiny whistle, from the distance another answers, and yet another, three notes, reed-like, flute-like, night after night. I listen and wonder. In the morning, I do not ask, afraid to destroy my mood.

Later in the week, I could not resist questioning. De la Peña told me that I heard the whistle of the Mexican police, a whistle retained from centuries back, when, as in the days of Pepy's England, the night watchman, lantern in hand, made his round from street to street, calling out the hour, the weather, and "all's well."

October 6. Sunday, Xochimilco. The beginning to our day's adventure had its humourous side; Tina, Llewellyn, Chandler and I, loaded with cameras and lenses and tripods standing on Bucareli and Lucerna, awaiting the first Ford marked "Listo"—free for hire. It came, and in quick succession half a dozen others, the drivers of which having noted our apparent desire, drew up in long procession to take their turn at bargaining. One by one they left until the sixth capitulated, accepting Tina's offer of three pesos and no more.

The ride to Xochilmico was one to remember. The Mexican sky, always dramatic, presented a surpassing spectacle. Gathering rain clouds, gold rimmed, massed against intense blue; straight ahead rose Ixtaccihuatl, "The White Woman," higher than the highest cloud, dazzling and splendid in the sunlight. Impossible to believe this October! — the springlike green of grass and cottonwoods, the freshness of air.

We raced! The Mexican drivers are the most reckless and most brilliant I have seen. They have to be or perish, for apparently there are no traffic laws. We passed and were passed on either side, turned around or crossed to the left at will, and as for speed, I clenched my fists and held my breath!

We approached the outskirts of Xochimilco. "It reminds me of Italy," said Tina. "Only more beautiful," added Llewellyn. Walls, walls brick or stone or adobe; Mexicans do not parade front lawns. Instead, potted geraniums sprawl over wrought iron gratings, brilliant on the faded pinks and blues of the sun-baked casitas. Now the architecture changed definitely; thatched huts appeared, a bunch of pansies from nowhere dropped into Tina's lap, followed by a breathless Indian boy who jumped into the car to claim his five centavos — then Xochimilco! These once floating islands which comprise Xochimilco were long ago rafts. Upon them the Indians raised vegetables, planted flowers; gradually, the vegetation took root in the bed of the lake and the rafts became islands, flower-covered islands, divided by canals not unlike Venice. Sunday is a gala day in Xochimilco. The water was dotted with canoes or larger canvas-covered boats all bedecked with flowers and filled with festive people, gay people who sang and thrummed guitars and were "borrachito" with pulque or wine.

Soon, we too were gliding down the water ways, past quaint thatched huts, past sad willows, and gardens of pansies, lilies, forget-me-nots, violets. We too laughed and sang and became "borrachito," for across the canal darted a swift canoe to serve us pulque curado. Later, another canoe drew up to our side, this time with elote asado — roast corn — hot from a charcoal stove in the centre of the canoe. The same Indian cooked us delicious enchiladas, so savory that an un-mentionable number were consumed.

24

Then came the flower girl, her boat piled high with pansies, forget-me-nots, carnations — "Señorita, Señorita! Cinco centavos!" waving toward us a bouquet of pansies, almost an armful—We did not resist!

I called the willows of Xochimilco sad. They are poignantly so. They are tall, straight, and slender as an Italian cypress, but more lissome and yielding. With each passing breeze, they sway unresistingly, bending their tops in mournful submission; a bed of river rushes is not more graceful.

Our canoe was "manned" by one Indian who stood in the prow with his one long oar, but some canoes, (or "barge" would be a better name for these larger square-nosed, awning-covered boats) held twenty people, with an Indian at the stern and prow. These were the gay parties with singing and drinking and señoritas, "Wine, Women, and Song." They brought their cocineras—cooks—too, who served hot food from charcoal fires, while other criadas—servant girls— watched that no glass remained empty, or kept the long table from stern to prow laden with viands.

By now, it was raining but it mattered not, the boat was covered. "Parada!"— Stop!—I cried to the Indian and we stopped by a canal on which floated those same lovely lilies of pale lavender I had seen in Guadalajara. From somewhere, far away, came the strains of *Mi Viejo Amor*—My Old Love—, nearer a girl sang *Chaparrita*—Little One—; our gay canoe glided to its landing.

October 30. First Exhibit at "Aztec Land." The exhibit has been open for over a week; it is a success. I have done what I expected to do, created a sensation in Mexico City. Roubicek, the owner of "Aztec Land," told me he has never had such an attendance to any previous exhibition.

I have never before had such an intense and understanding appreciation. Among the visitors have been many of the most important men in Mexico, and it is the men who come, men, men, men, ten of them to each woman; the reverse was always the case in the U.S. The men form the cultural background here, and it is a relief after the average "clubwoman" of America who keeps our culture alive. The intensity of this appreciation and the emotional way in which the Latins express it has keyed me to a high pitch, yet, viewing my work day after day on the walls has depressed me greatly, for I know how few of them are in any degree satisfying to me, how little of what is within me has been released.

Of the future, I hardly dare think, for all I can see ahead is day after day of professional portraiture, trying to please someone other than myself. Eight prints have been sold to date, the first one to Lic. Ramón Mena, archaeologist, who bought *Tehuana Costume* of Elisa. Best came [Alberto Best-Maugard] and has been of much help.

The second day, Robelo [Ricardo Gómez Robelo] came, so unexpectedly after this long silence, it was a shock. We embraced long and with emotion, it was so good to see him. Robelo has been very sick, that was apparent. How sick, he would not admit,—confined to his home, nevertheless writing, in spite of his illness, a book on the Pyramids of Mexico.

An interesting and also interested visitor was Dr. Atl, who came with Nahui Olin, apparently his mistress, a quite fascinating Mexican girl who has spent most of her life in Paris. Tina and I dined with them, then went to Nahui's home — more later concerning the work of Dr. Atl and Nahui Olín — their books and paintings. As I walked down Avenida Madera with Atl, it seemed that he was greeted by every other person. On foot or in machines, they bowed or called to him.

Last evening, Diego Rivera visited the exhibit. Nothing has pleased me more than Rivera's enthusiasm. Not voluble emotion, but a quiet, keen enjoyment, pausing long before several of my prints, the ones which I know are my best. Looking at the sand in one of my beach nudes, a torso of Margrethe, he said, "This is what some of us 'moderns' were trying to do when we sprinkled real sand on our paintings or stuck on pieces of lace or paper or other bits of realism."

With Rivera came his wife, Guadalupe, tall, proud of bearing, almost haughty; her walk was like a panther's, her complexion almost green, with eyes to match — grey-green, dark circled, eyes and skin such as I have never seen but on some Mexican señoritas.

Just now an American girl came in for an appointment. "Do you know," she said, "that you are the talk of Mexico City? No matter where I go — to afternoon tea, to card parties — your exhibit seems to be the principal topic for discussion. You have started out with a bang! — already famous in Mexico!"

Incidentally we are popular — Tina and I have been dined and wined and feted to repletion, yet we have refused more invitations than we have accepted.

Sunday night — depressed and lonesome, I stole silently away from our casa and walked for hours alone; sat in the Alameda and watched the little dramas staged on every bench; strolled along where the "puestos"—booths were preparing for Christmas trade — much utter rubbish made for the tourist, but some lovely things. To assuage my "blues," I did my first bargaining alone, purchasing two lovely dishes of Jalisco ware. I should not have spent a cent, but I needed to, and did!

Then I found a merry-go-round I watched and listened for an hour. In one seat a sophisticated senorita, legs crossed to better show their beauty, nonchalantly lit a cigarette. In front of her, on a rose-bedecked horse, rode an Indian, a flaming flower in his mouth, a green feather in his wide sombrero. There were bare-footed Indian girls with hair to their knees and dandified men with canes, and, of course, children, all swirling around and around and around on this merry-go-round — which being gayer than ours, was sadder.

November 1. To the puestos again last evening, strolling by booths filled with both atrocities and work of the finest craftsmanship; it is evident that the Indian's work is becoming corrupt, and with another generation of overproduction and commercialization will be quite valueless. It was all very gay, festive, colorful — with food as important a display as art. Opposite the puestos, a continuous line of charcoal fires over which, in sizzling pans, cooked enchiladas and other tempting foods. Quite as frequent were the vendors of candies and cakes — the Mexicans consume quantities of sweetmeats prepared with imagination.

Sittings ahead, many dates pending, but oh how tired I am of professional portraiture!

Sunday, November 4. Plaza de Toros. Tina, Llewellyn, Chandler, and Edward. The exhibit is over — the lights turned out last night. Roughly, I estimate that between 800 and 1,000 people visited the "Aztec Land" balcony during the fourteen days — about 250 registered in the guest book, which will be a treasured souvenir. I have made quite a definite break into the consciousness of the Mexican public — especially among the painters and poets and lovers of the arts — many of whom returned again and again, and many of whom would have bought but for their purses.

Of the eight prints sold, six were nudes of Margarethe made that last terrific week with her, before leaving for Mexico. Rivera liked one of the beach fragments of her the best of anything in my collection.

A day of blazing sun tempered by shifting clouds. We had been warned that the Sección del Sol—the bleachers—was no place for a lady, that one could expect a rough, tough crowd, but Tina was game, and besides the condition of my purse precluded the comfort and refinements offered by the shade.

We arrived at the plaza an hour early to choose the best vantage point for comfort and "respectability." Already crowds were streaming in. Outside were vendors of food, frozen dainties or frying meats—the charcoal stove turns any street corner into a kitchen. Banderillas were for sale, supposed to have once waved from the back of some luckless bull. Gaona, el Matador, and the people's idol, was to fight. His picture was being sold in buttonhole bouquets, a leaflet published for bullfight "fans" was named after him.

We entered the the gate to "el Sol." A soldier ste pped suddenly forward, threw his arms around me grabbing at my hip pockets — fire-arms and knives are barred from the bullring! At our baseball games, a pop bottle is occasionally tossed by way of protest, but the Mexican thinks a gun more efficacious.

It was soon evident the sunny side *was* tough: to relieve monotony, apples and other handy articles began whizzing, until the fun waxed furious and a man was lifted bodily from his seat and handed kicking and struggling over the audience. A protest would have been futile—even the victim pretended mirth.

At the stroke of 3:00, a door of the Arena swung open. The announcer of cere-
monies in flowing cape and plumed hat, astride a horse in gorgeous trappings,
crossed to La Autoridad. Saluting, he reared the horse to a stand and with a dig
of spurs dashed back to lead in the toreros. They paraded across the arena, proud,
nonchalant, vain as peacocks and as beautiful in brilliant silks and satins. The
band crashed, the audience wildly cheered and the fight was on.

A tense, breathless, expectant moment—another door swung open to admit the
onrushing bull — in the centre of the arena he paused, tail arched, head aloft,
pawing the sand and snorting defiance. But in this game of life and death in el
Toreo, the bull alone is foredoomed; he is to die, there is no hope. He paused but
an instant and then charged the first flirting cape; how easily, how carelessly,
how gracefully, did the toreros avoid those mad rushes! Until the bull, bewildered
and panting, spied a new enemy — a picador had edged the blinded side of his
decrepit old nag close to the bull. Pica in hand, he was braced for the attack — a
sudden impact of horse and lance and bull — a momentary swaying from the
shock — the long lance in the bull's side — the bull's horns in the horse's bowels
— then, as the picador jumped for his life, the horse streamed pink guts onto the
sand and dropped to his death. This was the ugliest and saddest part of the fight,
though upon reflection one must admit that the horse died a glorious and honored
death! — less sordid than that which otherwise would have awaited him, pulling
his creaking cab at the bite of a lash.

The most spectacular, dramatic and beautiful moment of the afternoon was the
placing of banderillos by Gaona. Green-ribboned banderillas high in his up-
stretched arms, he waited; such brains and daring to match the charge of a
fighting mad brute. Squarely he met the bull, perfectly he placed the banderillas
back of the lowered horns, miraculously he stepped aside, while the bull careened
away, tossing, bellowing and the audience exploded with a roar of applause.

All moments were not so exciting; at times, the action dragged, especially at the
final killing when the bull, already tired, faced Gaona's red-cloaked sword.
Playing for the death-stroke allowed for much technique — beautiful posturing —
and daring too. It made one creep to see Gaona deliberately turn his back and
with never a backward glance walk away from the still dangerous bull. But the
bull was tough and would not die. And the audience was fickle, alternately hissing
and cheering their idol, until finally the sword sank to the hilt and the animal
into the dust. Three mules dragged him out.

Another expectant pause, the bugle and the next contestant. This bull was
afraid, refused to fight and was soundly hissed for his cowardice. I suppose
peacefully grazing on a daisy-covered meadow would have better suited his
desires! The naïveté of the audience in hissing or acclaiming the bulls, as they
did the toreros, was amusing. It was thumbs up or thumbs down as in the days
of the ancient gladiators. Finally, the banderillas were placed and this time we,

as the uninitiate, had a surprise, for they exploded with a bang and poured forth smoke and more bangs which sent the bull bucking all over the arena. But even then the bull turned tail, ran away, and the killing was slow and tiresome. By now, the audience was getting peeved. And when the next bull appeared, a small unworthy beast, they arose en masse and loudly denounced the management for poor bulls, verbally fining the promotors 1,000 pesos and remaining unappeased till the fine had been confirmed —? The bull was chased from the ring and his substitute provided a gallant fight.

And my reactions? Was it a cruel spectacle? Yes, undoubtedly, though perhaps not so bad a way for a nation to release its sadistic emotions... can it be denied that we go to an auto race secretly hoping for some thrilling accident? Of course, not death, but —! Our prize fights? It is only the few who care for a fine display of scientific boxing, it is always the bloodiest slugging match between longshore brawlers which gains applause. While in the Mexican bull ring, it is grace and daring which the audience cheers. Unnecessary cruelty is frowned upon — for example, a picador was recently fined for remounting a wounded horse.

The Mexicans are not hypocrites in their pastime. They grandly stage a mighty pageant with death proclaimed upon their banners. The blood and suffering are but means to an end — like the music — the color — the hot sun — the bellowing bull — that of aesthetic gratification. Yes, I shall go again.

2. "Heroic Heads"

November 9. Have been very sick, fainted away at the opening of Sala's exhibition, and spent the next day in bed — fasted and am better now. I have not mentioned Rafael and Mona Sala, both fine individuals, Spanish, he a painter. We have seen quite a bit of them.

I have been working some with my camera, made nudes of Tina, work not unworthy — what shall I say? — of my lens? — also the best portraits I have done in Mexico — of Nahui Olín.

Last night it rained. In Los Angeles, the real-estate mongers would call the weather "unusual," for the rains are supposed to have been over for a month or more. Llewellyn had a bright idea and we all "fell for it." The four of us, Tina, Llewellyn, Chandler, and myself stripped naked and played tag on the roof in the rain!

Afterwards, a brisk rub-down and we were in a fine glow and ready to read *Moby Dick.* This book has been one of the literary adventures of my life, a great book, full of profound philosophy, prose poetry, thrilling adventure, but I can't stomach his attempts at humour. His jokes are bum; his puns forced!

Just caught a flea — what grim satisfaction — fiendish delight — in contemplating its execrable, nauseous, accursed remains squashed and bloody between one's finger nails! — But they are not nearly so bad as when we first came; in fact, they had almost quit operations until this rain once more drove them in.

Saturday to Sr. Tomas Braniff with Tina. It was one of those futile attempts to bring the artist, musician, poet, intellectual together for the serious discussion of "philosophical and artistic" problems, doomed to failure — for the artist wishes to play, to live, not talk shop on every occasion. Braniff, a Mexican millionare, has opened his palatial home and gardens for this serious purpose, probably with desire to shine in the reflected light of the artist. Robelo was there, and Best-Maugard, and Guadalupe Rivera, also Dr. Atl and Nahui Olin.

Lupe was easily the most striking figure in the crowd, her dark hair like a tousled mane, her strong voice, almost coarse, dominating.

There was brilliant repartee at the dinner table set under the garden trees, the conversation veering, as usual among intellectuals, to sex. Lupe, discussing the homosexuals in Guadalajara, "A group of men there," she said, "actually wore high-heel shoes and lace frills." "Every other man in Mexico is homosexual," added Nahui Olín.

30

When the "regular program" started, the fun was over, everyone tried to be interested or was frankly bored. But we had been well served and Braniff was generous with Cognac and Chartreuse — so, listening to dull theories was the price to pay — and we paid. I shall not forget Lupe's singing of Mexican popular airs.

Last eve was Diego Rivera's birthday. We were invited to six o'clock chocolate. Rivera arrived late from his work of painting frescoes. He was beaming and of ample proportions. I took him one of my prints for a birthday gift, and he gave me a drawing made for one of his murals in return. I had my choice from his portfolio of sketches, but found it almost impossible to choose. Seldom, if ever, have I so thoroughly enjoyed a portfolio. Diego is a master.

Lupe was stunning as usual. She has much of the Indian, so much a child, never a hypocrite: everything she feels is immediately acted out and we were witness to a burst of emotion unpremeditated and unlooked for. Diego had invited Tina and me to see his drawings, so we escaped from the party, dull, as most parties are, to a side room. Soon Lupe appeared, choking, sneering, raging, head tossing, eyes streaming. "Ha! I invited her to see how you two would act together. I did not want her here—you don't think I wanted her!" — and so on, and on about some woman supposed to have been Diego's love. "Estás loca—completamente loca, — You are crazy—completely crazy," was Diego's placid, unruffled defence. Lupe left, still storming, only to return, and this time denounce us for having deserted the party, broken it up, cornering Diego. She was right, but Diego's drawings were more important than the party! We felt uncomfortable — worse, guilty, so prepared to leave. Penitent, Lupe came to Tina with a present — two gourds, fantastically painted, a peace offering. I am to photograph her soon.

Today the first order from a sitting in Mexico, 3 prints — 110 pesos. No platinum paper yet—ordered a month ago from England.

November 19, Evening. Diego and Lupe Rivera were just in, this time cooing like turtle-doves. It was "niño" this and "niña" that, and she wore a new coral necklace. "In Guadalajara, they thought Diego was my father," laughed Lupe, "and when I told them he was my husband, they said, 'How could you marry such an elephant?'"

Diego looked at my Picasso etching — "I saw Picasso etch that, it was done in December 1908 — I don't know why he dated it 1905 — at a time when he was in his cubist period. Many said he had forgotten how to draw, so he did that, among others, to disprove them. Picasso had a failing, he was always falling in love with the sweethearts of his friends, — hence, continually in trouble."

I showed Rivera some of Chandler's stencil designs and he seemed greatly interested. Chandler has done some very fine things, and out of a clear sky, — at least, I can't figure where the influence, if any. Chandler's photographs have been interesting too — one I would have been happy to have made myself. I can see my influence in these, yet they were made entirely unaided. Chandler has had to shift for himself, and having no playmates for baseball or marbles has amused himself by creating.

El Convento de Churubusco is a gem. I think it is the loveliest of the churches I have yet seen, though they should hardly be compared — each having its own special charm. Churubusco is intimate, I wanted to linger and rest in its tiny patio, to caress its mellow tiles, to worship before its lovely golden virgin.

The rest of the party made photographs, one man being a wealthy amateur. I did not, for the churches in Mexico are an end in themselves, needing no further interpretation. I stand before them mute — nothing that I might record could add to their beauty.

Previous to visiting Churubusco, we went to el Convento de la Merced. We met Dr. Atl, who lives there. "I should like to photograph you here, Doctor." "All right." Dr. Atl's "all right" is part of him. His real name is Gerardo Murillo, "Atl" being Indian for water; and "Nahui Olin" is also Indian, standing for the "four movements of the sun." Nahui's real name is Carmen Mondragón. Nahui's books may be interesting, but written in French and Spanish I can make no comment. But neither her paintings nor Atl's have great value, indeed some of his murals I thought very bad, full of half-baked metaphysical striving. But Diego Rivera is so outstanding a figure in Mexican art that much of the rest seem trifling by comparison.

A tiny chapel stands in the centre of a busy market place on Callejón de Manzanares, near the convent. It is quite unpretentious, no carved facade, nor blue and yellow tiles, only bare walls of pastel pink and swirling streams of Indians flowing around it.

November 21. The second order in, this time from Americans here from Tampico, it amounted to 280 pesos, 8 prints from six negatives, a task ahead — six enlarged negatives! So far I have made all my sittings with the Graflex out-of-doors. We eat for another month!

At Churubusco, I picked a daisy to send to Margarethe.

November 24. A few more names noted on the pulquerías:

Charros no Fifis	Cowboys not Dandies
Los Hombres Sabios sin Estudio	Men Wise Without Study
La Hermosa Ester	The Beautiful Esther
Mis Illusiones	My Illusions
Las Fieras	The Fierce Ones
El Gallo de Oro	The Cock of Gold
Alegria del Amor	The Ecstacy of Love

Llewellyn left this morning. I watched the train pull out with much sadness. He has been a delightful and lovable friend. Though his piano, at times, was sorely distracting and his dog a damned nuisance.

Llewellyn has been of much help to us, but, for his own sake, he should have just been coming instead of leaving. I am afraid he has not learned much photography with all the confusion of getting established and the exhibit.

Lupe de Rivera sat to me yesterday — fascinating girl, quite the most interesting I have met here. Results — at least one or two good heads and one figure, but I wish to work with her again.

Thursday last to San Juan Teotihuacán and the Pyramids of the Sun and Moon with Rafael and Monna, Felipe, Llewellyn, Tina, Chandler and Edward, also three cameras, good food, and plenty of wine. I made a few negatives, the best one not of the ruins, but the surrounding country — a typical Mexican landscape made from the summit of the Pyramid of the Sun. We shall go again, for night came on too soon. Next time the stay must be for several days; it is far too much to absorb in a few hours.

Coming home on the train, Rafael bought for Monna and Tina gardenias cradled in a hollowed banana stalk — how tenderly the Indians do things, with what imagination — a stalk eighteen inches long overflowing with gardenias!

November 27. Today a new servant. Aurora could no longer leave her children, and we did not want them. Now Elisa has come, whom we are to room and board and pay fifteen pesos a month, $7.50 American for a month's work! And this is much compared to what they used to get. No wonder then, the revolutions. Elisa can neither read nor write. Aurora could, but Elisa is quick and intelligent, while Aurora was slow and stupid — so much for education.

November 28. To six o'clock chocolate with Diego and Lupe Rivera. Mexican chocolate is generally famous, Lupe's the best I have had. She has it shipped freshly ground from Guadalajara and prepares it with much art.

I took the proofs of Lupe to show — the best heads I have made in Mexico. Everyone was enthusiastic. Diego turned to Tina remarking, "It bothers the painter to see such photographs."

I like him immensely—Lupe too. They are both so genuine and outspoken — too much so for some people. The other evening, Lupe told us, she had broken up a party by appearing, quite accidentally, when it was expressly understood that she would *not* be invited. The party was in honor of the Chilean poetess, Gabriela Mistral, who started to leave upon Lupe's arrival... Now I have no desire to meet the famous poetess. I find myself withdrawing from people who are too nice.

Rivera told us that a group of the Mexican artists had formed a syndicate, that they considered and called themselves "workingmen" and nothing more. I like this attitude and proclamation. A real artist is nothing if not a workingman, and a damn hard working one.

Rafael and Monna told Diego of New York. "If I went there," he said, "I believe I should turn to painting bill-boards and posters." He spoke of the machine, "There is so much beauty in the steel door to a safe vault. Perhaps future generations will recognize the machine as the art of our day." I think so too.

There was much talk of Tehuantepec, the most southerly state on the Isthumus, of the beautiful women and their costumes. The women handle the commerce of the state; the men do the physical labor. Free love is common practice in spite of Catholicism, which is taken seriously only as a festival. The natives speak a language of their own supposed by some scholars to be the tongue of the ancient Atlantians.

The evening furnished much repartee too swift for me to understand. Especially did Lupe and Rivera banter, keeping the whole group convulsed. He is tall and fat, she, tall and slender. "He has breasts like a women," said Lupe, "and I have none — so we make a perfect union." "Diego tries to bind his down," — from Lupe. "Lupe stuffs her front with cotton," — from Diego, and so on, and so on —.

Today again to the Braniff mansion of gold leaf and alabaster; the whole "Painters' Union" was there, some of them, most likely, to get a square meal and a drink. Rivera an animated cartoon, with his two chins, two bellies, and inevitable smile. Lupe with her "Por Dios" and "Caramba." Jean Charlot, a French boy, whom I like immensely, and who gave me one of his excellent wood cuts. Robelo very frail.

We talked on the pyramids. I learned that they are now thought to antedate the Egyptian pyramids. That now, some archaeologists consider that from here went the Chinese to populate Asia, from here went the Egyptians, and also the Semitic tribes. Not the reverse, as heretofore believed, that this country was part of the lost continent of Atlantis. A book recently published in France, after twenty years of research — deciphering of documents in the Vatican, stolen from here by Cortez,—shows actual maps of Atlantis with ports and named cities. Finally, in San Angel, a half hour ride from here, has been uncovered from beneath lava rock a city dating at least ten thousand years B.C. All quite fascinating, nay, thrilling conversation.

Amusing talk from Robelo too. It seems there is a man here so bewildered by Rivera's work that he has decided to give a talk "on the pathological case of Diego Rivera"! Robelo wants to be there and answer him.

In the United States, without art traditions except borrowed ones, we are apt to accept anything new and labeled "modern" without discrimination. Here, in Mexico, they are so hidebound with convention that the work of their greatest painters is ridiculed. Yet they do appreciate and are proud of their pyramids and ruins of the past...

The Mexicans still refuse to accept me as an American. I have secret delight in assuring them that I am a type of the real American now already extinct — that our aristocracy is dead. How uncomfortable my neighbors and relatives of the charming and chemically pure city of Glendale would be to think that one of my "loose morals" and disrepute should be posing in Mexico as a true American type!

The Mexicans have such contempt for Americans as they know them that I have begun to think that God Almighty sent me here to bring about more amicable relations between the two nations!

December 2. The article on Diego Rivera in "The Freeman," is re his work in the Preparatory School. His later painting in the Ministry of Public Education is much finer, and now he tells us he is more pleased with his murals at Chapingo than any he has done. The article goes on about the "Union of Technical Workers, Painters and Sculptors" which adheres to the Moscow International, with Rivera as the leader. It speaks of painting on canvas as painting degenerated, and further — "While feeling that he belongs to the future one is glad that he lives today. Rivera is humble with the humility that comes to those who, having confidence in their own worth, recognize the worth in others, who out of disillusion create beauty, out of human suffering the future —"

Rivera is a vegetarian. He appeared at the Braniff banquet carrying his own dinner of grapes and apples tied up in a red bandana handkerchief... I rather envied him his meal and remembered my own days of intestinal purity. I may return to them again. I have a feeling that eventually I shall. This country with its abundance of tropical fruits should be paradise for the vegetarian.

December 7. To Monna's and Rafael's for chocolate. In Mexico it is 6:00 o'clock chocolate, instead of 5:00 o'clock tea. A Mexican Senator was there, he and his guitar, a tall handsome charro. He had fought in the revolution, two years with Villa; everyone here seems to have been in the fight. "Villa was the best loved man in Mexico," said the Senator. "He was an outstanding personality and made a gallant fight for the oppressed." And we in the United States, thanks to our controlled press, think only of "the bandit Villa." Lupe and the Senator sang Mexican popular songs all evening — some were in memory and love of Pancho Villa.

Diego was there. I watched him closely. His six shooter and cartridge belt, ready for service, contrasted strangely to his amiable smile. He is called the Lenin of Mexico. The artists here are closely allied with the Communist Movement; it is no parlor politics with them. Rivera has small sensitive hands, those of a craftsman, his hair recedes from his forehead leaving an expanse which occupies half his face, an immense dome, broad and high. Chandler gets quite a "kick" from Diego — his ponderous proportion — his infectious laugh — his mighty gun. "Does he use that to defend his paintings with?" he asked.

My days pass monotonously enough, trying to make an ancient American woman, dressed in a black mantilla, look like a Spanish señorita, retouching hours at a time — bah! for professional portraiture! This jotting down of impressions helps to relax and prevents mental stagnation. I write a few words, then retouch a few wrinkles. My writing does not help me physically, however, my eyes suffer and my body is cramped. My only salvation has been fifteen minutes, hard exercise and my morning cold bath.

Aguacates are out of season. I miss the noon meal of hot tortillas and aguacates, but now we have the chirimoya. And for me to dine on chirimoya is to become intoxicated — it is like eating perfume. Also, we have chico zapote, sugar cane, granada de China, and soon the mango will be in again. Northern fruits pale beside these sun-drenched, nectar-filled fruit of the tropics.

December 8. At last the revolution is upon us. Long hinted as a possibility, it is now a reality. Wires are cut between here and Vera Cruz, Tampico and Western points; trains are halted, except those to El Paso which are filled with fleeing Americans. De la Huerta has 15,000 men against the government, several states have gone over to him, artillery is being rushed to defend Chapultepec Castle. Obregón arrived on a special train last night. Soldiers are marching with beating of drums and blowing of bugles. Food prices are soaring — and this is our only concern — for if we tend to our business, danger is unlikely. Opinions vary as to the duration of this outbreak; from three to six months is the average answer.

We have spent a little ready cash on staples, beans, rice, and charcoal. This early morning, before dawn, distant cannons boomed incessant, probably only practise before actuality. —

For the first time in Mexico, that old melody of my aunt's music box has returned — my childhood again —

Jalisco has gone over to the de la Huertistas. Federal troops are preparing to attack Guadalajara. Most of those with whom I have talked opine that the revolutionaries will win, and quickly. Something must happen soon or we shall be stranded.

December 9. My second bull fight. After El Toreo — Matadores "Nacional Segundo" y "Valencia" — altogether the most stupendous, electrifying pageant of my life — I feel for new adjectives to interpret my emotions — my synonyms fail me... They grasp the cape together. The bull charges. Up goes the cape; under and between them the bull, not once, but time after time. And then, with a climax of applause, they kneel together before the bull, each grasping a horn, and salute. But the killing of the last bull was the daring feat of the day — a fitting finale. He was a powerful brute. The six banderillas had been placed – three times had he charged the picadores and as many horses were strewn upon the arena. Blood streamed over his black hide — yet he was fighting and dangerous. With his red-cloaked

36

sword, Nacional played him for a while, then baring the sword, awaited the bull's attack. To attempt the death stroke on a charging bull is almost suicide, a miscalculation possible death. It is seldom done. Three times Nacional met the charge. The audience on tip-toe, the band hushed. The third clash was successful. The sword sank to the hilt. Nacional walked away without looking back.

December 10. De la Pena and Turnbull, old "fight fans," tell me they have never seen a more thrilling fight.

And a "letter" from Margarethe — "To write you tonight — am sending a telegram" — that was all!

And this from Margarethe to Ramiel: "She (Flora) wept around here one A. M. after Edward's first Stieglitz letter (from N. Y.) — blaming herself for holding Edward back — I told her — in front of Tina — that she was responsible for Edward's success — without the balance of her and the children — the forced responsibility — Edward would have been like the rest of us — dreaming — living in attics — living a free life (O God!) etc. etc. not growing and producing *as he had.* Opinions to the contrary Edward as gregarious as anyone I know — Flora seemed grateful for my words but soon forgot them..."

December 14. Definite news of the revolution is difficult to obtain. The newspapers are censored. One paper daring to print the truth was put out of business, its press utterly demolished by "burglars." Mexicans practise "direct action." Politics are as rotten here as in the United States or anywhere. 30,000 men have been fighting around Guadalajara, and there have been skirmishes at Tacubaya, where we once lived.

The Eleventh — to La Festivadid de Nuestra Señora de Guadalupe with Monna, Rafael, Felipe, Lupe, Chandler and Tina. It was not the day of important dancing, but we did see one dance — and in church! Pagan dancing in a Catholic Church: the Indians accepted Catholicism but introduced their own rituals. We met the parade of Indians coming down a narrow walled street, all gaily attired, carrying large half-wreaths of streaming tissue paper, and followed them into the church. There they dropped on their knees and, still chanting, crawled toward the altar. Arising, they danced, simple, rhythmical, monotonous steps, using the wreaths overhead, passing through and under them. An impressive sight, the church with its vaulted roof, its towering columns, with Indians kneeling on the floor, or seated in row after row of wooden benches, many holding lighted candles, hundreds of flickering candles lighting passionately devout faces — such faith! And the priests above intoning their formulae.

Some of the tribes had come great distances, many had made the pilgrimage on their knees. Miraculous cures were reported; evidently the Virgen de la Guadalupe is as potent as Mary Baker Eddy and certainly more picturesque.

All around the church the pilgrims had camped. They were cooking their tortillas and frijoles over the charcoal fires. Some were beautifully costumed; Lupe tried to buy their sashes—she did not succeed. Either they were too proud — one was quite angry — or else they did not understand Spanish. Magnificent specimens in one group—a girl I remember with breasts like cannons and legs like tree trunks, of regal bearing she was. One felt ashamed in scrutinizing her. She could have annihilated me with one arm!

These were the simple, saint-like worshippers, but there were others, for Tina had her pocket picked twice! Across the street from the church, a merry-go-round wheezed out "Yes, we have no bananas" — "Si no tenemos plátanos" — a touch of today clashing with ceremonials from antiquity.

We purchased "modern art" for 65 centavos, brilliant designs on glass which might be object lessons to some "modern painters." The "modernist" cannot merely go back to the primitive, for he cannot compete at all!

As a side-show to the main event of the fiesta, the celebration of the Virgen's appearance, posters announced a special bull fight.!

Elisa, our new servant, is a continual source of merriment. She is quite concerned with my welfare — intensely curious too. I am sure she thinks we are all un poco loco! Especially do our cold baths amaze her. I have had a bad cold in the head; tonight she watched me wash my face, she shook her head disapprovingly, "Señor, cold water is very bad for your 'catarro.'" She has requested a picture of me. So I still have an admirer.

Sunday morning — Beethoven this morning or the bull-fight this afternoon? That is the question. Bulls and bravos versus Beethoven. I can hear Beethoven in New York or Kalamazoo. I can see El Toreo only in Mexico. Why question? Viva los toros!

Next day. His name is Juan Silveti. He is called Juan sin miedo—Juan without fear—and not without reason! I saw him tossed in the air by the bull, I saw the bull mauling his sprawled figure, yet he rose to attack with a daring and brilliance which electrified the audience. One moment to escape death by a miracle, the next to arise, walk straight to the bull, knell before it, kiss its nose, and walk away, back turned, as unconcerned as if he were coming out of church. Facing the bull again with bared sword, he delivered the estocada with the first attempt. The bull dropped and the audience roared in a wild furore for ten minutes.

Silveti wore a scarlet cosume, black trimmed, and salmon colored stockings; Gaona was dressed in gold and blue with salmon stockings, both beautiful. Indeed, it is impossible to over-exaggerate the beauty of the whole pageant, even the mules which drag the dead bull out, with their blue and red trappings. There is a saying in Spanish, "When there are bulls there are no bullfighters.

9. Nahui Olín, 1924

10. Pirámide del Sol, 1923

11. Tina Modotti with Tear, 1924

12. Cross, Tepotzotlan, 1924

13. Manuel Hernández Galván, shooting, 1924

14. Desde la Azotea, 1924

15. TINA ON THE AZOTEA, 1924, 5, or 6

16. DIEGO RIVERA, 1924

When there are bull-fighters, there are no bulls." There must be both elements for a good fight.

The bulls were very poor yesterday. Gaona, especially, had no luck. He is said to be the best banderillero, indeed more, he is acclaimed the greatest matador in the world. My naturally superficial observation would be that Gaona is a cold, scientific fighter, one who takes no chances, but is absolutely sure of himself — an artist, nevertheless, whom I have seen in postures which would make an Isadora Duncan envious, and done with the bull's horns grazing his belly. To return, Gaona's placing of the banderillas was superb — each set with such precision that the completed group was arranged on the bull's back as a perfect star — a star of red, blue and yellow, clear brilliant primary colors too — nothing dilute for the Mexican taste.

December 21. I can't go on this way. I must acquire a formula for my portraits. I compromise anyway — and give far too much of myself to an unappreciative audience.

Yesterday, I quit — put down my prints on which I had spotted all morning. Poor technique? Yes, but not my fault — finger-prints and scratches and bad retouching done by others — retouching necessary to make an American of questionable age look like a vivacious señorita. I quit, I say, and paced the floor the afternoon — the worst reaction to professional portraiture I ever had. It made no difference to me that rent was due and the work had to go on.

As I walked back and forth in my two by four room with its ugly wall paper, its cold cheerless aspect, I pondered much, and a new philosophy of life was presented to me — probably by the devil — that of the Indians who lie in the sun all day and pawn their blankets for the price of a bull fight. They, at least, must be happy, no thought beyond the day, no desires, no ambitions. I became obsessed — overwhelmed by the desire to quit, realizing the futility of effort.

Yet here I am this morning at my desk, working harder than ever, attacking this negative almost with ferocity, as though it were one of the tasks of Hercules. The outward and superficial reason that if it is not done by tomorrow I cannot go to El Toreo Sunday! — and five foot letters announce Silveti y Nacional!

Strange humor, living from week to week in anticipation of the Sunday bull-fight, acknowledging its cruelty, shuddering when a mortally gored horse careens across the arena with its guts wrapped around its legs, but watching the pageant or orgy, nevertheless, in fascinated horror. The Latins have evolved a sport which symbolizes life, its glorious moments and its sordid ones, its dreams and deliriums — and futility, and they can return from such an afternoon to tenderly pet their birds and water their geraniums —

December 28. 5:30 A. M., early as in my old Glendale days. In Mexico I rise late—between 7:30 and 9:00—the latter hour almost never! Christmas passed rather uneventfully. La Noche Buena was the occasion for quite a display of fireworks and much shooting. The Mexicans never miss a chance to use fireworks and La Natividad is no exception.

The moon was full. I walked our white roof alone. My thoughts were with the little boys in California, — hoping they had some joy, a tree with lighted candles and candies. Christmas is children's day.

Christmas day we went to El Toreo, Tina and I, but not for los toros this time; we heard the Mexican National Orchestra render Debussy and Beethoven, indifferently, and Bertha Singermann recite. I felt like cuffing her hands, they were so calculated. Her whole performance got on my nerves. She received an ovation.

After, we walked to the Salas taking them a couple of my prints of La Pirámide del Sol. Rafael had been painting, two large canvases, color and design from the masks purchased at the puestos. He gave me the one I liked. He is blue, discouraged, does not like Mexico City, wishes to return to New York...

December 31, 1923. I reiterate: for a change I enjoy my morning coffee alone. Today, however, "Pancho Villa" is by my side. At him I can curse, to him relate my woes, yet his only response is to show his teeth in a fierce grin. He has an enormous revolver, and an ample sombrero in which I have placed a flaming geranium, also one in his horse's bridle. From his saddle hangs a note, "Para Eduardo — el Niño." He and his horse are made of reed by the Indians. I liked those sent to Cole and Neil so much that Tina gave me Pancho for Christmas. Flora writes: "Neil said, 'Mama, I thought we would get just a little iron horse and man.' They were certainly responsive to that toy, more so than I have ever seen them."

The puestos are thinning out. Chandler and I walked there Friday... I should like to have had a Piñata, one of the life-size figurines which the Mexicans fill with toys and candies for their Christmas festivals, — then break in a blindfold attack. They hung in rows from beams of the booths, fantastic, beautiful, or screamingly funny: marvellous sail boats, brides in flowing veils, charros, a suicide—gun in mouth, streaming realistic blood, and many Charlie Chaplins, clever, clever cartoons.

After my last bullfight, I left with a bad taste in my mouth, a decided reaction against El Toreo. It was not a reaction to the fight itself, which I insist is a glorious affray, but to the audience — the fickle, contemptible audience. I went, hoping to see Gaona for once at his best. He fought brilliantly for a while, but with a gored hand could hardly finish the first bull and did not appear again.

This left Nacional to fight the remaining five, which he did superbly as usual, keeping the crowd in a continual uproar of applause. The sixth bull was a poor one and difficult to fight. It found the body of one of its victims and mounting the dead horse danced a dance of victory — though a rather hollow one since he was dying too. From this vantage point the bull refused to go and it was almost impossible for Nacional to deliver the estocada attempted several times.

Then they started, the audience, whistling, hooting, hissing, a disgusting exhibition of unsportsman-like conduct towards a brave matador exhausted from his fight against five bulls. The bull was backed up to the barricade which separated the arena from the audience, they were yelling almost in Nacional's face. He raised his hand in vain protest, attempting once more to drive the sword home, but they continued the uproar. Nacional was furious, his pride was hurt. He almost climbed the bull's back, driving the sword to its hilt. He threw science to the winds in a suicidal attempt to please the audience and the next moment was tossed in the air — only the animal's death saved Nacional. He arose a hero who had just been hissed! But he stood unheeding the cheers. Torn, disheveled, bloody, he made straight for those whose jeers nearly brought his death and with anger-distorted face screamed at them. Once around the arena he went, acknowledging the plaudits, tossing back the canes and hats,—then fainted.

January 1, 1924. New Year's Party. The party was a success! Lupe Rivera and friends planned it. They came early in the morning to cook and prepare typical Mexican dishes all day — "ponche" too, made with rum and served hot. About thirty came, among those I knew, the Salas, Lupe and Diego, Jean Charlot, Galván, several quite beautiful señoritas with one of whom I had a slight flirtation — armed and aided with my dictionary!

Several Germans came; they had been in Mexico only two days. One of them, an author, I liked, responded to, and he enjoyed my photographs, or rather the only one I showed him, "Pipes and Stacks," made in Ohio a year ago but just printed in platinum. The Salas like it the best of all my work and so does Charlot, — it is a fine print.

The Germans eyed Lupe as though she were some wild animal, and looked hesitatingly at the strange food. They must have been a bit scorched with chile, for after the first dish they refused even olives! Well they might have gazed on Lupe, she was barbarically splendid in red and gold with heavy festoons of gold chain and earrings,—she dominated the evening.

At the stroke of 12 there was much embracing — greetings of "Feliz Anno Nuevo" — and 1924 was here.

January 6. Hace mucho frio — quite the coldest yet, at 7:00 A. M. the thermometer in my window registered 39° F. Last night coming home from la ciudad—the city—I shivered as the wind swirled down calle de Balderas. We had sat in a saloon drinking hot Tom and Jerry, discussing the revolution. "Don't be too sure the government is going to win," said an American here twenty years. "The United States has always picked the losing side and they are helping

Obregón. And don't think that times are abnormal. Four hundred years' history shows that fighting of some kind is a normal condition here."

A contrary opinion came from Salomon de la Selva, poet and politician, who dropped in the other night, "There is only one possible answer re the revolution —Obregón will win, Calles will be elected." Salomon talked long and interestingly on early Mexican history.

No sittings ahead, food prices double, matters appear very bad.

January 7. Our New Year's party was such a success that a weekly gathering at Lucerna 12 has been decided on. The Braniff reunions have been discontinued "because of grave conditions resulting from the revolution." Ours will be inaugurated for the same reason. Unlike the Braniff parties, any discussion of art or philosophy shall be incidental to singing, dancing, food and drink.

Last night was the second party. Galván and Lupe sang again. The same crowd met. Before dancing the men removed their pistols which brought some realization that times are grave.

The sages predict the end of Mexico City January 11th by the eruption of Popocatépetl. Too bad it cannot be postponed till the 12th, the day of our next party. We might dance to our doom.

It remains cold, "unusual" weather say the Mexicans. I believe them—they are not all real estate dealers as in Los Angeles. I smoke my pipe to warm my hands while retouching.

I am finishing the portrait of Lupe. It is a heroic head, the best I have done in Mexico; with the Graflex, in direct sunlight I caught her, mouth open, talking, and what could be more characteristic of Lupe! Singing or talking I must always remember her.

January 12. Popo did not erupt. We are still alive and the party was held as usual ... a young artist danced la rumba Cubana, a very "wicked" dance indeed, the origin of the quite dilute American "shimmy."

I witnessed a new side of Diego. Declining the proffered glass, he drained a part bottle of Cognac. Consequently becoming joyously belligerent, further dancing became impossible, he desired singing and more singing from Lupe and Galván almost wrecked the phonograph when a foxtrot was started. He treated Lupe roughly and I can well believe the reports that sometimes he beats her. What a magnificent melee it must be when those two clash! Lupe calls Diego "Chaparrito" — the little one!

January 18. And no money for rent. The dueña—landlady—is not at all sympathetic with the condition of our pocket books. One sitting ahead but the situation is bad. I started to town with one of my lenses to sell or raise money on, but no luck. Met García Cabral on the way and we had café con leche together.

I am saving his Monday morning sketches from *El Toreo*, they are very fine. "You are not American," said Cabral, "a Russian or Czecho-Slovakian type, but not American." "Soy Americano," I answered.

Last night to visit Señor y Señora Cueto, – chocolate as usual. On the walls were many paintings — her older work. They were — well, not very good, but her present work — how much more vital and important! Brilliantly executed rugs, painted gourds, experiments in other crafts, all very Mexican, very personal. One carpet of an intense green and red vibrated so violently as to actually dizzy me. I could hardly look at it.

Their collection of Aztec antiquities, small but fine, increased my ever growing respect for the civilization destroyed by the Spaniards.

Charlot too had several fine things, notably one piece, a conventionalized sculptured head of a duck, as simple as a Brancusi. "They were greater than the Egyptians," was Charlot's comment.

A horrible night of dreams. I saw my father put a gun to his head and shoot himself — he was holding Cole in his lap at the time.

Just now a letter from Bertha Wardell — "We are finding life interesting in the midst of a Righteous Crusade against the Wicked Dance. It has so far deprived us of the use of our studio but not of our legs so we have nothing really to complain of." Christ! Is this possible! O how sickening! My disgust for that impossible village, Los Angeles, grows daily. To think that Mexico had to abandon the fair country of California to such a fate. I ask every Mexican, "Do you wish like conditions here? If not, then fight American influence in Mexico!" But being an American I like to believe that only in Los Angeles could such a situation exist. Give me Mexico, revolutions, small-pox, poverty, anything but the plague spot of America — Los Angeles. All sensitive, self-respecting persons should leave there. Abandon the city of the uplifters.

Sunday morning — the third of our informal evenings last night. New faces, García Cabral, Revueltas, members of the Cabinet, generals, etc. — absent faces, Agueda and Lila — my tears. — Internal dissensions already — the Mexicans are quick to love and quick to hate. The Germans are amongst the gayest who come. Cabral sang well songs from Argentine.

"When we first came here," said Charlot, "we attempted to have open house as you are doing, but we gave it up. Some of the guests were sure to end the party by shooting out our light bulbs."

Already I sense an end to these gatherings under the present plan. It is too much of a mixture; it may be an amusing contrast, the refined Madame Charlot along with Mexican generals comparing bullet holes in their respective anatomies, but it is sure to end disastrously. As Diego put it — rearranged in my own phraseology — "I want either one thing or the other, a party where I go with the avowed intention of getting drunk, or one with a more subtle prospectus."

January 22. Manuel Martínez Pintao, — we found him, Charlot, Rafael, Tina and I, at Iturbide 27, in an ugly little room, in which his wood carvings mingled strangely with modern chromo calendars and a cheap brass bed. In fact, the carvings, work of many months of love and craftsmanship, were hung directly above his bed, this product of a factory from which one hundred identical beds might have been turned out in a day.

What a personality too! I did not need to understand each word he uttered to feel the import of his prophetic gestures. One knew the man must be as great as his work — or greater. Pintao is Spanish, but he has lived most of his life in Mexico. His motives are usually religious, but never sentimental. Too bad he has not the opportunity to apply his art, for instance in the carving of some impressive door. Diego made a vain attempt to get him a commission with the government. One application of his work is in the carving of bastones—canes—a row of them hung on the wall, beautiful things. How I wanted one! Much of his work was in ebony. "Ebony is so common in Mexico that it is used even as fire wood," said Pintao.

Tonight a full moon, brilliant, almost dazzling — around it a delicate green light and, still further encircling, a halo of orange.

Sunday. Tina, Chandler, and Edward: Galván invited us to join him for an outing. In a high powered car, sixty miles an hour, we climbed the road to Toluca. Up, we roared past plodding Indians and their burros, through old towns, then into pineclad mountains. Once we were stopped by soldiers, ready for action, and significantly reminded of the revolution. But a flourish of Galván's pass, and recognition of a general amongst us, changed the surly attitude to a salute.

Lunch under the pines — tortillas, hot from the ashes of a bonfire, frijoles y carne—beans and meat—and plenty to drink—tequila y cerveza—beer. The Mexicans had with them, naturally, their guns. "Let us shoot, but save a few rounds, we may need them on our return!" said Galván. He placed a ping-pong ball forty feet away and pierced it the first shot from his pistola. The Mexicans broke beer bottles with much cracking of guns and threw knives with accuracy, but I bested them in jumping.

We climbed higher into the mountains. Tina wore tight skirts, not expecting to walk; they were revealing. "You have pretty legs, Tina," I suggested, being slightly borracho. Pablo, our driver, walking with us, roared with laughter. Por Dios! One never knows when to speak in English with safety, least of all, did I think Pablo would understand!

We viewed the simple and solitary monuments to Mexican Independence; would that all monuments were as fine. Dusk was on us before we left for El Desierto de

Los Leones. "Desierto" is not to be translated "desert" as we know the word, but "wilderness," for we were still among pine-covered mountains. Night in the wilderness, the straight black pines, the stately cloister on the hill, — and then the moon rose, la luna sobre el convento. O Mexico, you touch one deeply, poignantly. We loitered along, spellbound, even the ride home was slow, hesitant, reluctant. It grew cold. "I should enjoy a half hour battle to warm me up." said General G.

Chandler plays "El Gato Montés"—The Wildcat—and I remember los toros once more, the opening yell, that wild call for blood from 30,000 frenzied barbarians, — I include myself, — but barbarians who appreciate beauty as well as blood. Black bulls once more charge flirting capes, horses crumble into still heaps of blood and guts, picadores land on their necks, and Nacional saves a life.

January 26. After four cloudy days, gentle rain is falling, much like a January day in California. A sitting was postponed because the young lady could not wash her hair. I wore a smiling mask and changed the date; a cloudy day and a pretty girl's unwashed hair might change another's life, — tomorrow's tortillas depended on that sitting.

The gods always save me at some crucial moment, this time through Flora, who wired me $200. I hope she sold no land at a loss.

Strange not to hear from Ramiel—over a month since he wrote me of his accident, and six weeks since Margarethe wrote "God help me to write you tonight." From both I should have heard, and for not merely sentimental reasons. May's appendix in the slop pail! Dearest sis, when shall I see you again! Johan may be alive or dead, for aught I know; not a line since I have been in Mexico.

Senator Galván in last night to say hasta luego—see you soon. He leaves for the front this morning. His talk of the Indians was refreshing, especially after the depressing opinions from other Mexicans related the last few days, — one felt not only hope, but desire to help. For today, at least, I am a "Callista."

We sat in Monotes talking. "We are going to make Diego Rivera a deputy," said Galván (deputy is similar to congressman in the U.S.). "But you will spoil a great artist," said Tina. "No, he can still go on painting," replied Galván. "Anyhow, Diego is even greater as a statesman."

Interesting faces at Monotes, the derelicts, the dreamers, the useless riff-raff of the world, artists, poets, etc. Always good food there, tamales de pollo y atole, tostadas sabrosas.

Then we went to El Teatro Lírico — Lupe Rivas Cacho y Compañía. I had heard much of her and was not disappointed. The last scene was spectacular, backgrounds, costumes entirely made from sarapes, a dazzling prismatic effect. Everything, it seems, is right in the proper place or at the proper time. Before,

I had not cared for the crude colors of the *modern* sarape, but here the ensemble was stunning.

January 30. The night before we had been alone — so seldom it happens now. She called me to her room and our lips met for the first time since New Year's Eve. Then the door bell rang, Chandler and a friend, — our mood was gone.

Morning came clear and brilliant. "I will do some heads of you today, Zinnia." The Mexican sun, I thought, will reveal everything. Some of the tragedy of our present life may be captured, nothing can be hidden under this cloudless cruel sky. She leaned against a whitewashed wall. I drew close... and kissed her. A tear rolled down her cheek — and then I captured forever the moment...

Let me see, f. 8 — $1/10$ sec. K I filter, panchromatic film — how mechanical and calculated it sounds, yet really how spontaneous and genuine, for I have so overcome the mechanics of my camera that it functions responsive to my desires. My shutter coordinating with my brain is released in a way as natural as I might move my arm. I am beginning to approach an actual attainment in photography that in my ego of two or three years ago I had thought to have already reached.

January 31. To San Angel, the guests of Sra. Oscar Braniff – Beatriz. A grey, still morning, occasional rain drops. We walked through the crooked cobbled streets, winding up and down and around – it recalled Mazatlán, the houses in pastel shades, the barred windows on street level, the walls — such walls! — three feet thick, with blossoming pear trees just rising above them. Pear trees everywhere in San Angel, planted by the Carmelite monks over 300 years ago, gnarled old trees but still hardy. The monastery of Nuestra Señora del Carmen — what a thrill its massive walls of weathered pink crowned by domes of yellow and blue tile.

We went inside the Church. At the door a Christ so life-like in bloodstreaming agony as to shiver even me. What then must be the anguish of those devout Indians who kneel before this tortured figure!

The walls of the chapel were richly and intricately carved and covered with gold-leaf from top to bottom. The ensemble was unusually complete and harmonious, though two or three modern paintings in perhaps unfinished or destroyed portions caused discord.

On the floor, directly under a glass-cased Christ in black satin robes, was a metal spittoon.

Homeward bound at dusk, still raining a gentle drizzle. El Paseo de la Reforma glistened, wet and fresh. Even the gilded Angel of Peace loomed lovely in the transforming mist.

February 3. Galván — Tina — Edward — Chandler — Pepe to El Desierto de los Leones again. We went prepared for emergencies, three automatics and a rifle, much ammunition. Precautions proved not mere unnecessary readiness against fanciful possibilities. For, arriving at the Convent, we found it barricaded and awaiting an expected raid. Two days before the de la Huertistas had attacked and taken away some thirty horses. Now, on the roof, behind sandbags, soldiers leaned on their rifles.

The wilderness around held a grim portentousness. The sky was leaden. The wind whistled through a sea of pines. "Wear this," said Galván significantly, handing me a Colt automatic. I laughed to myself as I strapped it on. I might shoot straight with my camera, but this!

If the sky was heavy and gloom-laden, the earth was not. Scarlet snapdragons flamed. We climbed through purple lupin taller than our heads. And all the time the gale swept through the pines. We climbed up and up, stumbling forward, slipping back. I was the rear guard. My camera slowed me down. It is always so. I pay the price of my love, — perhaps my only love.

At last, the summit, the gale fiercer than ever. Our eyes lied, for the racing clouds seemed to bring down upon us the mountain side, and our ears lied, for the roar of the wind seemed the booming sea.

A sheltered spot for lunch down by the convent. Indian women served us hot tortillas and mole, hot with pimienta; arroz, frijoles y cerveza completed our happiness. The afternoon sheltered by the cloister walls. No storm could disturb the calm of the cloister, the old monks built impregnable fortresses. They were protected not only from the elements and beasts of the wilds, but from prying people, meddlesome outsiders who might probe too deeply into their well-ordered lives, who might discover rust on their instruments for self-torture. They must have been artists in life as well as master builders. We left early – it might be that danger lurked in the dark.

I wanted to catch Galván's expression while shooting. We stopped by an old wall, the trigger to his Colt fell, and I released my shutter. Thirty paces away a peso dropped to the ground — "Un recuerdo — a keepsake," said Galván, handing it to Tina.

February 6. No money for days — we live on Elisa's savings left in our care. The draft from Flora has not arrived, no mail comes through. Persistent thoughts that I must try to leave here, return to Los Angeles, — not to stay there, of course, — merely to use that place as a start towards new fields.

At last, I have heard from Ramiel, such interesting news too — that concerning the children: "I arrived at your house towards evening — Brett was in the yard chopping wood — Neil was playing. I called. They both ran to me screaming at the very top of their voices. Brett threw his arms around me embracing me with great real affection and Neil clung to me for dear life. We all went in together. Flora was joyous over my coming. Cole came in for his share of affection. It was all very beautiful, Edward, and touched me deeply. What a dear child Brett is.

He has grown so fast and is going to be a fine looking fellow. His freckles are disappearing—a milk white skin, heavy, brilliantly gold hair and the bluest eyes, and the most naive manner. There's a lot of the bucaneer in him, a real swashbuckler. Later on, he should go in for exploration, archaeology. Neil is growing tall and weedy, the same pensive, wistful face and manner. Flora will never understand him. I wish you had him with you. Cole so much like you, Edward, the image of you in face. I love his voice — something very original in his accent and speech — and what a fine shaped head and your eyes — so like yours."

And then this about Flora: "How strange it all is — her great respect for me now. She fairly clings to my sleeve, but really, Edward, she is the same — a touch of madness in her, but generous, after all".

Yes, Flora, you *are* generous, and you mean so well, and you have written me so beautifully. But when I think of living in the same house with you or near you, my reactions are definite. It cannot be. Yet— I wish to be near my children, — the desire is strong.

And this about Neil: "The car drove up. We got in. Neil was in the yard, your wistful dreamchild, Neil. I shall never forget the sad pathetic look on his little face as I kissed him goodbye. I shall never forget how he looked up into my face, the tears in his eyes, and asked so wistfully when I was coming back. As we drove away, he stood there a figure of utter loneliness."

And then this to me, always to be treasured: "But you, Edward, stand alone on your pinnacle, the one person really close to me, you are one of the few men I have known, as I have journeyed through life, who understands the privileges and obligations of friendship, and expresses them with a great generosity. You have comprehended and practised it, in the deepest meaning of the word. You have been reliable, sympathetic. Your tenderness and sympathy which began so long ago have continued unabated.

"I have tried to repay them with just as enduring and affectionate gratitude. Your love has been altogether a free gift. How much it has enriched my life, I shall hardly attempt to say. I miss you more and more as the days pass — no one can take your place in my heart."

February 7. A sitting this morning, another tomorrow morning, and this afternoon an order for 315 pesos from an American here, a Mrs. Moats, portraits of her daughter. On top of all this good fortune, a registered letter just came from Flora with the 200 dollars, so we are safe financially for a while. What a mental relief!

Names of pulquerías noted at San Angel: "El Vacilón de la Morena" — The Jag of the Brunette, "El Gran Mareo" — The Great Seasickness, "Las Buenas Amistades" — The Good Friendships, "La Atrevida" — The Daring One, "Al Vuelo" — In Flight.

Pintao visited us the other morning. I took advantage of his presence and photographed him as he conversed with Tina. Some of the heads are rather intense characterizations.

He waxed enthusiastic over my photographs, which pleased me. The approach to his own work is entirely intuitive — hence its great vitality, profundity. He is impatient with geometrically calculated work. With his knife and a block of wood he starts, his mind free from formulae. As he cuts away, the vision — if you will — comes naturally, the form grows unstudied.

I told him that my photographs were entirely free from premeditation, that what I was to do was never presented to me until seen on the groundglass, and that the final print was usually an unchanged, untrimmed reproduction of what I had felt at the time of exposure. "You work in the grand manner," he said...

February 14. The new head of Tina is printed. Along with Lupe's head it is the best I have done in Mexico, perhaps the best I have done at all. But while Lupe's is heroic, this head of Tina is noble, majestic, exalted; the face of a woman who has suffered, known death and disillusion, who has sold herself to rich men and given herself to poor, whose childhood knew privation and hard work, whose maturity will bring together the bitter-sweet experience of one who has lived life fully, deeply, and unafraid.

February 20. The order from Mrs. Moats delivered and received in return 315 silver pesos. I will need a cargaodr — porter — to carry it to the bank. Four more sittings recently, — considering these revolutionary days with everyone "broke" and my work so comparatively expensive I am rather gratified at the response.

Now for the first gossip, scandal re Tina and I living together in Mexico. It naturally came from an American who "thought it was disgraceful and wouldn't send her daughter to me — to such a house to be photographed."...

I accept the loss of a sitting. I can draw in my belt, use one sheet less of toilet-paper per day, eat one less tortilla, and buy one spike of nardos instead of two. Poor woman, I would not hurt your daughter. I am far less dangerous than the sexually unemployed. Do you ask of your butcher his moral attitude before buying a slice of ham? Do you question how many women Caruso has slept with before purchasing tickets to the opera? Do you come to me for a portrait by a craftsman, or to see a marriage certificate garnished with angels?

I am doubting more and more the sincerity of these daily or semi-weekly notes as they concern me personally — my real viewpoint and feelings uncolored by petty reactions, momentary moods. With the passing of time, perhaps the greater part of what I write would not be thought worth writing, either forgotten entirely, or realized as untrue.

I am sure, nevertheless, that my diary is a safety valve for releasing corked-up passions which might otherwise explode — though I sometimes think storm clouds would sooner break with a thunder of words, — but a perspective of months must bring a saner, less hysterical, more genuine outlook.

Certain it is I blush with shame, growing unutterarbly miserable when I remember or reread opinions I have indulged in regarding Tina; especially does this happen after such a night as came to us last Saturday. The pendulum must swing back and forth, the mercury rise and fall when two people live in too close contact, — but the retrospect of years will return to me overwhelmingly only the fineness of our association. I am sure of this.

Six letters all told within the past week from Ramiel, and one to Tina too. How excited we have been, how truly thrilled and stimulated. I have both laughed and wept — the keenest mind you have, Ramiel — of anyone who has been very close to me...

Chandler is in school now, a technical school offering a course in shorthand, typewriting, grammar: Spanish is spoken...

February 21. A hell of a day yesterday. Bitter disappointment awaits the worker in photography.

After risking my neck to get the 8 × 10 camera on la azotea—flat roof—over Tina's room, the highest vantage point of Lucerna 12, and after straining my back and stripping my nerves to capture a sweep of scurrying cloud forms, developement revealed fog — ruinous fog — unmistakably from extraneous light, — and a beautiful negative it was, or might have been!

The demon fog can play such uncanny tricks—always I am confounded, disconcerted, mystified until the trouble has been located. All morning I squinted and poked and probed, finally patching with felt the supposed leak due to a warped back, but I lost my negative, as fine a one as any of clouds I have done.

In a blue funk, I was ready to quit, and when Galván called, accepted his suggestion that we ride into the country and then walk for a while.

North, and out of el distrito federal, he took us, to a barranca—gorge—close by — in fact, hardly twenty minutes drive away, yet, from the desolation of this cactus covered gulch we seemed a hundred miles from any city street. Cactus and rock and the tortuous curves of el arroyo seco—the dry gulch—a bleakness to the spot intensified by a lowering sky, black wrathful clouds, angrily unable to spill their burden of rain. We climbed, we shot, we lay on the dead grass and watched the sunset edge the clouds with rose, and all around stiff cacti in spreading silhouette. Tea with Galván, his three old aunts and Don Pepe, — cajeta de Celaya, te, pasas, — jelly from Celaya, tea, raisins, and sweet bread.

I feel better, to hell with photography, art, women and all.

Yet—I wished for my camera today. Those serrated stalks of the maguey their bold uncompromising leaves cutting the horizon, they would make a fine jagged base to a typical Mexican sky.

February 24. Another outing — Galván's idea. He is certainly a good sport. At his own expense — it cost him at least 70 pesos — he hired a camión for the day and took some twenty-five of us to Toluca. The occasion was the staging of un Jaripeo, lassooing of wild horses and cattle, riding them, — all of which brought back early memories of "round-ups" in California. Never, though, have I seen such beautiful and expert use of the rope. The uncalculated postures of the charros, their foot-work, the use of their hands are as graceful as any dance could be and more genuine than most.

The phrase I love — "form follows function" — is as applicable to these charros as it is to the smoke stacks and grain elevators of industrialism. I could watch with more enthusiasm such exploits than the staged entertainments of our best interpretive or "classic" dancers. Perhaps a thousand years hence our successors will "revive" the lost "art" of the charros or cowboys, with like results, anaemic and colorless.

An exciting moment was that when a charro astride a swiftly running horse placed banderillas in a bull's back. Another charro jumped through his lasso and the next instant his rope coiled over and captured a pony racing by at full speed. Much enthusiasm was shown by the audience, dianas—fanfares—from the band, and amongst other symbols of excitement and appreciation Tina's hat sailed into the ring.

The drive to Toluca was through a fair and fertile country, especially el valle de Toluca. At noon we stopped at an old Indian roadhouse. A meal was served fit for hungry bellies, mole de guajolote, tortillas, y pulque, plenty of pulque, so we were all very jolly after. Galván sang as we jounced along over the rough road, and we interspersed with many a "¡Viva México! ¡Viva Zapata! ¡Viva Pancho Villa!" Burros packed high with produce, crated chickens, pulque in bursting pigskins, charcoal, pottery, scurried out of our way, and to help the excited Indian drivers, we shouted "¡Arre! ¡arre!" — giddap — as we passed.

I had Galván's head printed in time to show at the Saturday night party. It was the cause of much interest and applause all around, but especially from Galván himself who was almost boyishly pleased. I place it along with the recent heads of Lupe and Tina, as one of my very best.

February 26. The revolution? Except for high prices on food, charcoal, and other staples, deserted stores, vacant houses, the war might as well be in Europe for all that we feel. Some shock, death among our friends may bring a realization that thousands are being killed all around us. This is a possibility, for Galván is to head an expedition to the front, some of our closest friends will go with him, familiar faces will be missed from our Saturday nights. Lupe and Diego are leaving too, for Chapingo — political reasons. It is all very sad, this losing of new-found friends, — and some perhaps forever.

Tina and I have been writing joint letters tonight. Smoking our respective pipes, we penned lines to Johan and Ito.

Best-Maugard in today with a stunning Mexican girl, Dolores del Rio, a real beauty. Suggested I photograph her, think I shall.

Best carried bad news of Robelo; he has been very sick. I should not be surprised to hear of his death.

February 28. First to hear Gabriela Mistral, Chilean poetess, give a paper on books for children. We left soon, unable to hear. She had an interesting head. From there to el Anfiteatro de la Escuela Nacional Preparatoria where we heard a very fine rendering of César Franck by el Cuarteto Clásico Nacional, the first good music in Mexico — of course, I mean of its kind, for after all I enjoy and respond deeply to the folk songs of a people.

Then to Monotes for supper, finding there the musicians we had just heard. It has atmosphere, Monotes, a real Bohemian "joint."

At the preparatory school we had opportunity to view Diego's murals at leisure. I like his later work much better. I now recognized many familiar faces he had used as models, Lupe, of course, Nahui Olín, Lupe Rivas Cacho, Sra. Crespo, Palma Guillén.

March 2. "Club" night last night. Some thirty of us went en masse to a circus on Bucareli — Gran Circo Ruso it was announced. Russian refugees, some of them, from the Bolshevist government, and a most unpleasant picture they naturally painted of the Bolshevists. Others from the earthquake in Japan with stories of hair-raising adventure. The circus as always was poignantly sad with little children swirling through space, with sorry clowns, and contorting gymnasts, with all its oppressing glitter. Home to dance and tea, but I left the party and went to bed, slightly weary, and rather sad.

March 3. It so happened, Neil, that last night I dreamed of you. I held you on my lap, kissed your broad forehead, and you cuddled close, and asked for stories. We talked long together, of fierce fanged Aztec Gods, of white rabbits in clover fields, — and we recalled days of long ago. How it used to be at bed time you would climb upon my back for a good night ride out under the tall black trees, waving farewell to Lady Moon, listening to the little pines whisper, or maybe, picking loquat blossoms fragrant in the night fog. Now you are there, and I am here, and perhaps you are so big a boy I could no longer ride you so. Well, came to pass that in my dream you dreamed too... All quiet now, only a distant mocking. I watched your sleeping face, as I looked down upon you, you became not only Neil, but the symbol for all in life of tender hopefulness. They will flout you, insult you, lynch you, but I will protect you, for I have masks that you shall wear, a horned and grinning devil, a sharp beaked bird, a ram in solemn mummery. I have them, I shall keep them for that hour when it must be you shall

52

need them to hide behind and keep inviolate, untouched, the spark within which is yourself. They shall be my only legacy to you, cardboard, painted masks, thicker than your thin skin...

Brett Boy! Hot Dogs! Hot Soup! When are you coming to Mexico? You'll have to learn new slang here, ¡Caramba! or ¡Sangre Santo! or ¡Por Dios! You golden haired, blue eyed son of a sea pirate! — for to see you, who would guess your parentage!... Come through with a letter will you? How's the cheesehound? And do the butterflies still flit before your stumblings? I'll bet you're a handsome devil by now, a real heartbreaker with the ladies, but watch out for them... You'll be the butterfly, and maybe break your wings. Then you can't fly to foreign lands after gold and lost Gods. But if you don't get trapped, you may in your search for gold and conquest, land on some cannibal island to become the Fair White God of a swarthy race. Wear a plumed hat and a jewelled sword, ride an elephant and have a hundred coal black wives to wash your socks and tickle your toes! Quien sabe? Hot Soup! Sizzling Hot Dogs! Dad —

Baby Cole —

Six months since I have seen you! Do you even remember how I look? I wonder, because my mother died when I was five and all that returns to me of her, are a pair of black and piercing eyes—burning eyes—perhaps they were burning with fever. But Mr. Gehee says you are the image of me, so all you have to do is look in the mirror and see Daddy and yourself all in one! Say, my greatest desire is for a ten minute romp at hide-and-seek with you, to hear your shrieks of joy, to see your eyes snap and sparkle, or to have you jump from the terrific heights of some table — jump with a shiver across the yawning chasm below into the sure safety of my arms. So let's plan this prodigious exploit, you and I, — anticipation is good tonic for the blues. We'll pretend hard, shall we? — Daddy.

A recent morning I took my Graflex to the circus, made negatives which please me of the graceful folds, the poles and ropes of the tent. One, "shooting" straight up, recalls a giant butterfly. At least two of them are interesting as experiments in abstract design. Tina too made several good things of the circus...

3. The Thing Itself

March 6. Incredible that I should have been in Mexico six months without visiting the Nacional Museum! But the right day nor time did not come until yesterday, when Tina and I decided to go there. No use in my attempting descriptive matter, I shall only put down my personal feelings.

I had expected much, but what I saw was far beyond my expectations. Besides the gigantic sculptured pieces hewn from rock, more or less familiar through reproductions—things overwhelming in their grandeur, their imaginative attributes, their fineness of conception and execution —there were exposed exquisite jewellery of the most delicate craftsmanship, gold, silver, jade; sculptured heads in obsidian, alabaster, of a simplicity and economy of approach quite a revelation. Even pieces in that perishable medium, wood, remained, a few examples only, to exemplify the supreme art and civilization of the early races who once glorified Mexico!

We were fortunate in having Jorge Enciso, supervisor of public buildings, as our guide, and through him were admitted to the phallic room. This was intensely interesting... There was no note of frivolity in them, they had a religious austerity.

From the fact that no remains of prehistoric man have yet been found in Mexico, Enciso disagrees with Robelo, inclining to the theory that the orientals, Egyptians, and other races came here, but he told us that four distinct epochs lie buried and are now being excavated under Mexico City!

Dr. M. came just before we left for the theatre to take "us" to a merry-go-round he had discovered on Orizaba. I told Tina I well knew he only asked me through politeness, for the Dr. M. is most attentive to her. "Three's a crowd, dear. I would feel quite uncomfortable." "But Edward, I have no desire to become involved with Dr. M." So much for my doubts and jealousy.

The theatre party wound up with tostadas at Monotes. Too much for one day, I am wan and worn this morning and must rest, for tomorrow is our belated Mardi Gras party, everyone to mask, everyone to become borrachito, or plain borracho.

March 9. The Mardi Gras party went off with a bang! Many funny and some quite beautiful costumes. Masking, costuming, and drink loosens up the most sedate. Tina and I exchanged clothes, to the veriest detail. I even squeezed into a pair of mannish shoes which she had just bought. She smoked my pipe and bound down her breasts, while I wore a pair of cotton ones with pink pointed buttons for nipples. We waited for the crowd to gather and then appeared from the street, she carrying my Graflex and I hanging on her arm. The Ku Klux Klan surrounded us and I very properly fainted away. We imitated each other's gestures. She led me in dancing, and for the first few moments everyone was baffled. After awhile I indulged in exaggerations, flaunted my breasts and exposed my pink gartered legs most indecently. Lupe was enraged by my breasts, punched at them, tried to tear them loose, told me I was sin vergüenza—without shame. I treated Tina shamefully in my "take-off"—even beauty can be made ridiculous. I hope I have not "cramped her style!"

Lupe Marin came dressed as Diego, padded, ponderous, lumbering. Chandler in his Indian suit was a real success, he is liked by everyone.

I drank freely of tequila but became only slightly borracho, enough to be a little vulgar, and I think shocked the good Frau Goldschmidt when Nahui Olín, Dr. Matthias and I danced together.

Best-Maugard came in late to bid farewell. He and Ciro Mendez left on the 3:00 a. m. train for New York.

March 10. Visiting the museum last week focussed my thoughts once more on the issue of photography. For what end is the camera best used aside from its purely scientific and commercial uses?

The answer comes always more clearly after seeing great work of the sculptor or painter, past or present, work based on conventionalized nature, superb forms, decorative motives. That the approach to photography must be through another avenue, that the camera should be used for a recording of *life*, for rendering the very substance and quintessence of the *thing itself*, whether it be polished steel or palpitating flesh.

I see in my recent negatives of the circus tent and of the glass roof and stairway at San Pablo—pleasant and beautiful abstractions, intellectual juggleries which presented no profound problem. But in the several new heads of Lupe, Galván, and Tina, I have caught fractions of seconds of emotional intensity which a worker in no other medium could have done as well.

I shall let no chance pass to record interesting abstractions, but I feel definite in my belief that the approach to photography is through realism—and its most difficult approach.

March 12. From the negatives made of Tina lying nude on the azotea, one very excellent result which I have printed: it is among the best nudes I have done. I also printed the arrangement of glass roof and stairway made at San Pablo—a fine print, I like it. Reprinted nudes of Margarethe sold at exhibit and a portrait of Montenegro done last week. Charlot, as planned, sat to me yesterday: I photographed him while he sketched Tina.

I have always had the desire to frequent the pulquerías, to sit down with the Indians, drink with them, make common cause with them. Two things have held me back. First, most of them are dirty! I don't mind a *little* dirt! But even stronger is my second reason for hesitating; I feel my presence would be resented, even to the point of my landing in the street. Imagine sauntering into the pulquería named Charros No Fifis, wearing my knickers and carrying my cane!

However, Tina and I came across a pulquería on Insurgentes: it was quite clean and almost empty. We went in and enjoyed not only the idea of drinking together in a pulquería but the delicious pulque as well, which this time was cured with pineapple.

Another place we went together lately was to a "cine." Nothing unusual to record "going to a movie," except this time we saw Tina herself on the screen, a small part she did some years ago in Los Angeles. We had a good laugh over the villainous character she portrayed. The brains and imaginations of our movie directors cannot picture an Italian girl except with a knife in her teeth and blood in her eye.

This morning I was awakened by running water, just water from the faucet, but never was the sound of water so sweet before. For two days we have had no water, or rather only that which was conserved in advance, and it was running low.

A city of a million people without water, cut off for repairs! A water famine must be fearful—the very thought is terrifying. I splashed extra long in my cold bath though I only missed it twice.

Oh! but those morning baths at Tacubaya—standing naked in the sunlit patio, with the musk-rose, the twittering birds, pouring buckets of ice-cold well water over me, then basking in the early morning sun. I miss the beautiful old house at Tacubaya too, and my whitewashed room. I still dream of having a high-walled whitewashed room opening onto a patio.

But for the wallpaper, my present room has much charm, and could, with a pot of paint and a day's work be greatly improved. But I begrudge the money and time on a place uncertain as a permanent abode. My present effort to make the room livable consists in the placing and use of various native crafts: a sarape over my bed, a petate for my floor, a lovely old flower-decorated chest to hold treasures, the caja de orinar for more treasures—old love letters. The bastones de Apizaco brighten one corner, and my chair is an "episcopal."

March 16. 5:30 this morning and despite the late hour we retired after the party. A bad head: it was considerably jarred last night, boxing with Charlot. He was once an amateur champion in France and certainly knocked me around rather roughly!

56

Some criticized my latest nude of Tina reclining on the azotea because of "incorrect drawing," but Charlot did not mind it: he tells me that Picasso got his "inspiration" to use false perspective from amateur photographs.

Diego had another interesting note on Picasso, that he was never influenced or went to nature for inspiration, always to other "schools" of art.

Another nude of Tina's hands and breasts was well liked: it has a fine flow of line, and despite a loss of texture through movement,—the exposure was forty-five seconds,—it retains solidity and pleasing quality.

I danced many times and furiously,—it was distraction I needed. I am most assuredly not mentally calm. The ghosts of my children haunt, their voices, their very accents ring in my ears. Cole's merry laugh, Neil's wistful smile, and blue-eyed Brett's generous gestures. Some solution must come; I need them, they need me.

The best dance of the evening was with Elisa, yes, our servant Elisa. I dragged her to the floor, despite her protesting cry, "No, no, Sr. Don Eduardo," and we whirled around at a great rate while the crowd applauded.

The mail brought me Paul Jordan's new book of essays, *On Strange Altars*. Glancing through it I note passages which recall and reveal the charm and lovable qualities of P. J. himself, and his delicious humour too. The dedication that is the personal one to me reads, "Whom we call friend we treat with discourtesy." Just once have I had a letter from P. J., that one from London after his meeting with Havelock Ellis, only a short note. I should enjoy one of the all night sessions at "Erewhon," the blazing grate fire, the library lined with books and thick with smoke, and P. J.'s tales of his adventures in England, with Arthur Machen, Thomas Hardy, Havelock Ellis, for there are few who tell tales so delightfully as P. J., nor relate naughty stories with such gusto and with less offense. I still see his twinkling eyes, hear his chuckle, and "Cousin Sarah" stretched on a nearby lounge, listening with smiling tolerance.

March 21. Not yet 5:00 a. m. I awaken early as in my California days, my mind refuses the sleep my body craves. Last night I wrote a love note to Margrethe and received one from Flora: poor Flora, she has had a dirty deal from life. I must try to be tender to her, it is not easy to thrust aside such a great love as she offers me,—that is, when it comes from a distance!

Brett sent me a screamingly funny letter: part of it read—"I have a sweet new girl, she sure is a peach—Old Orville tried to kiss her but I knocked him in the jaw ha, ha."

March 23, Sunday. Three servants this morning! Elisa's sister and aunt descended upon us from Guadalajara and immediately went to work as though they had always been here. I am wondering if they have adopted us! They awakened me too early this morning with their industry and I feel quite spleeny from so short a sleep after the party—quite a crowd last night. I did not enjoy it, excepting the food which Lupe prepared. Her turn always brings something good; count on Lupe to use imagination and not hand out sherbet and stale cookies as did Margarita, the fresh and blooming German girl. We had pozole and pulque curado, and plenty of it.

We went last Friday to the weekly gathering of another group, mostly Americans, the first time in Mexico to a party where "American" was spoken! It sounded almost weird. I didn't particularly enjoy it. When Spanish is spoken one can't understand all the vacuity of the conversation. Carlton Beals, author of a new book on Mexico, was the most interesting person there.

Tomorrow is my birthday. A year ago today—and sometimes it seems but a few weeks past and again distant ages—Margarethe planned a surprise on me, and I sat down to a festive table at Richard Buhlig's,—Ramiel, Henry Cowell, Buhlig, Margarethe and I. Now Henry and Richard are in Germany and I am here.

This being Sunday morning Elisa brought me flowers fresh from the market, clavel sencillo, "simple pink," and pinned one to my buttonhole.

Sunday evening,—After a day of loafing and napping, it is well to let the world slip by occasionally in indolent indifference. The twilight was spent in Tina's room and in her arms, for she had sent me a note by Elisa. "Eduardo: ¿Por qué no viene aquí arriba? Es tan bella la luz a esta hora y yo estoy un poco triste." — Why not come up here? The light is beautiful at this hour and I am a little sad.

There is a certain inevitable sadness in the life of a much-sought-for, beautiful woman, one like Tina especially, who, not caring sufficiently for associates among her own sex, craves camaraderie and friendship from men as well as sex love. How well she indicates this desire and the difficulty of attaining it, when, during a discussion last night over a certain woman, homely, repressed, and probably not able to get a lover, but withal popular with both sexes, she exclaimed, I thought pathetically, "At least she has good friends." So we were just friends for that twilight hour and later Chandler brought us naranjas y chirimoyas y pulque still fresh from the party. When I returned to my room for bed, there on my pillow was a new design by Chandler done for my birthday, a beautiful thing, one of the best he has made.

March 24, 1924. "Thirty-eight" today! My Birthday morning. Elisa is playing music so I shall not be "triste." Chandler came in before I was dressed and beat me up quite roundly. Then Tina appeared with the coffee pot. "Hurry up. Wash your face. We'll have coffee." Returning, my table was present laden. Elisa had bought me one of the naive, realistic figurines in clay, a group, a brave charro in grey and gold, his novia in Mexican pink, holding, we decided, a bottle of tequila. From dear sister a letter enclosing a U. S. "greenback" which will be promptly transposed into ten pesos plus. From Tina a pair of silk pajamas with geraniums in the buttonhole, a little pito—whistle—too,—a crowing cock in clay to replace the one mourned as lost, and, most loved of all by me, a letter, a note of two words and three purple hyacinth buds which conveyed more in simple emotion than pages could have done. The words were only "Edward, Edward!"

March 25. The 24th was also Turnbull's natal day, so Tina supervised a delicious dinner for us with emphasis on Italian spaghetti and red wine. After dinner Roberto and I went to view the private archaeological collection of William Niven. The exhibit represents the five successive civilizations of Mexico covering a period of over 10,000 years! It also represents the unaided labor of Niven who has made important discoveries and has many pieces not duplicated in the National Museum. Niven is Scotch, entertaining, witty and very much in love with his work.

I came away with three examples from the Tlachichique civilization, "the makers of all things," dating 2000 years before Christ, two fine heads and an exquisite hand in terra cotta—they cost me fifty centavos each. If I had only fifty pesos to spend, what a collection I might have! These pieces he excavated at Atzcapotzal- co, buried some two and a half meters below the surface. This civilization was pre-Aztec. The Aztec period lies buried at a depth of one and a half meters and dates much later,—1200 A. D.

March 26. And I have been to see Niven again. A crowd of us had dined with the Wolfs in a vegetarian restaurant they frequent only a few blocks from his museum. So we went there together, spending a full and stimulating hour. Niven is so willing, anxious to talk, to explain. He is 74 years old but vigorous and enthusiastic. He invited me out to dig with him on some Sunday. This appealed to me indeed. I accepted.

March 28, Early morning. The tent of El Gran Circo Ruso is now enlarged and printed. I could wish for a more searching, critical definition in parts: the use of camera without tripod is not conducive to accurate focussing in a dim light which precludes the use of a small stop. Nevertheless, if it is not microscopically sharp, it is visually satisfactory, and I pulled a good print from the negative.

March 29. Without water again. None since yesterday noon, when, without warning, it was turned off during my platinum printing. Surely there is some- thing fearful about a water famine.

March 30. French, Spanish, German, Italian, Mexican, Hindu, American, these nationalities were represented at last night's party. At times there have been more; most always Chandler and I have been the only Americans present. Spanish, of course, is the common tongue though French and German are also heard.

It was Tina's turn to serve, and she gave us, like a true Italian, spaghetti and red wine.

The evenings are taking on a different aspect as new faces come and old ones go. Galván and the fair Margarita are still missing and Lupe is sick in bed, enceinte it is hinted, but that word is too sophisticated for use with Lupe — plain pregnant is better. I genuinely regret the absence of Galván, his guitar, his singing and spontaneity.

Then the advent of the few Americans brings a new note, fortunately acceptable. The Wolfs are both teaching in the public schools; which fact I note that I may mention the waggish humour Mr. Wolf has introduced into his teaching. Wolf once served his day as an I. W. W. soapbox orator and is now helping to perpetuate the delightful songs of that political party by imparting them to the Mexican school children!

For the evening I had enlarged and printed a head of Neil, and hung it over the black table. "What a beautiful boy," was the general comment. I easily agreed. At eleven o'clock Sr. Oscar Braniff will sit to me, the first real sitting in several weeks. I shall pray to the Virgin for cash results!

April 2. Is it possible this is April! The rains must be about over in California, and here they will soon start. This is the most disagreeable time of the year in Mexico City, so very dry, with much dust in the air and frequent high winds. It has been warm too, but not unbearably so. I am told it never becomes warmer than the weather just experienced. Then it is nothing to what Los Angeles can occasionally offer in the way of heat. And when I think of Eastern U. S. with its prostrating summer days and unrelieved nights, this country must be quite a paradise in comparison. This weather has been perfect for printing Palladiotype, so dry and cloudless.

We called on Lupe last evening. She is not pregnant as rumored. I was shocked at her appearance, so pale and haggard. Two months in bed was the physicians' instructions; it seems to be a general collapse. Jacoby, brother to Frau Goldschmidt, bought two of my prints for her birthday. They were "Hands against Kimono," which, by the way, I like as well as anything I have done in Mexico, and "Profile" one of the old nudes of R. W. But everyone working for the government is broke so I got only promise of pay, and this is not well for us, being almost penniless too!

A letter from B. from "her desert": "Now spring is on the desert once more and I spend days gazing at the smoke tree in bloom, a grey exquisite little tree with indigo purple blossoms and they remind me of you as everything lovely which I ever see or touch will do." And more: "Do you think you shall be in Mexico City this summer? I may come up for a few weeks. Let me know. Be well and be sure of my love ever."

It is late, after midnight, but I am wakeful, and the fleas bite. It seems I shall never become acclimated to las pulgas.

We have just walked home from the Salas, a warm balmy night. The evening was spent discussing our proposed trip to Tepotzotlán during Holy Week. We are all quite enthusiastic over the venture, just we six, the Salas, Felipe, Chandler, Tina and I, and, oh yes, Elisa to keep house for us.

A good supper tonight, the Salas have a most excellent cook, spaghetti rivaling Tina's and codfish Spanish style which I could not but compare to the simple creamed codfish or codfish "balls" (what a name) of my New England ancestors: the codfish a la española, a racy, piquant dish, and colourful to the eye: that of New England a staunch, wholesome, unimaginative food, cooked to be consumed.

Upon our return we found that "I" had had a visitor. Elisa told us that Dr. M. had waited a long time for "me." It seems likely Elisa is mistaken in the intent of the call, for a fresh pineapple had been left with greetings for Tina!

I wish I could assume the attitude of Charlot and Féderico, who had great fun at the Goldschmidts, showering Tina with mock attention in the style of the Doctor whose infatuation is so profound he cannot disguise it, or else does not care to.

Sunday morning. The party was a frost, due mostly to the poor food the Frau Goldschmidt served — and not half enough at that. I hinted to several hungry-looking friends where to locate the pot of cold frijoles and they disappeared one by one into the cocina.

Aside from the food, the parties are no longer what they were. The ones who added so much life have gone: Lupe, Galván, and some of the señoritas, who if nothing else were pretty and gay. A German captain came, a striking figure with his military bearing, shaved head, sword cuts, and spats; an exact drawing of him might have been a cartoon, but he was agreeable, entertaining, brainy, and warmed to my work. He is supposed to be, we were told, the best dancer in Germany, but there was no dancing last night. The insatiable Dr. M. was absent and Tina spent her evening enthroned like a queen in an equipal, unable even to walk on her sprained foot.

The roses are blossoming now in California. The "ragged robins" must cover my old studio and the orange trees are fragrant, the loquats too; the fresh spring rains have transformed the landscape. These months are the loveliest in California.

April 9. On top of other troubles, I have had more fog, negatives absolutely ruined. I have found my trouble, or troubles, for my camera leaks light in half a dozen places. Evidently the protracted dry weather of this season has caused shrinkage of the wood. No sooner have I found one leak than another would appear, keeping me in a state of continued consternation.

Experimenting yesterday with Tina as a target, we were interrupted by Charlot and Federico, and, shortly after, Rafael wandered in and then Monna. So we sent Elisa after pulque and idled an hour. The Mexicans have a habit of calling unannounced. Fortunately, we have not, as yet, been greatly bothered. Though, sometimes, it has been necessary to refuse an audience, especially to the frequent calls of Dr. M. whose visits, however, can not be blamed on Mexican habits! Charlot adorned a wall on our azotea with a cartoon of Dr. M. kissing Tina's hand while her head is turned over her shoulder to kiss someone else. It brought much laughter from all including Tina. One way to kill a person is to ridicule.

Much work and experimenting with my leaky camera, mostly using "Panchito" for a model. I believe every hole is now found and stopped and I am ready for the trip to Tepotzotlán. We may go alone, since Monna Sala cannot leave her work.

Tomorrow I am sending with Federico Marín, Lupe's brother, forty prints for a "one man" exhibit in Guadalajara during Holy Week. With what backwardness do I part with forty of my best photographs! Weeks of work and much money they represent. Federico and Charlot have begged us to come along, promising a royal time at very little expense, but it does not seem possible. We can go to no expense, nor spend the time in being entertained.

Lupe called today. After all, she is pregnant, and, though very sick in appearance, much better mentally.

Almost two months since hearing from Ramiel.

April 12. The clouds hang heavy, forecasting rain, also interfering with the progress of photography, particularly in the printing of Palladio. It sprinkled a drop or two at Santa Anita yesterday, not enough to be noticed by the festive throng, gay in their celebration of La Fiesta de Dolores.

On the Viga canal, from bank to bank, floated flower-covered barges filled with the merry-makers, all poppy-garlanded and singing, or strumming guitars, or making love, or drinking pulque. Not only the women and children wore wreaths of flowers upon their heads, the men, too, were crowned with flaming poppies or snowy daisies.

We sauntered down the Paseo de la Viga, Tina and I ...

Everyone was either eating, selling, buying, or carrying celery. Of course, we conjectured, celery must have some religious significance, maybe blood purification. But no, we were told, it was only a custom comparable to our "raisin day" in California, or "apple day," or "eat-a-pie day," celery being the especial crop of this community.

Once we ventured into a crowded cross-street and found it difficult to get out.

A swirling, shoving, confetti covered crowd, borrachito with pulque, surrounded us. I held my breath for fear of harm to the girl's sprained ankle, or a worse calamity. We fought our way out ... Again, we essayed into a tempting patio lured by the sound of music. It was jazz, but very languid jazz and there pulque flowed freely. White geraniums lined the walk; we plucked a spray and left.

The church at Santa Anita was simple, but exquisite; the color pink, weather-worn to expose the coat of blue underneath. A church, large or small, simple or elaborate, I exclaim, "This surely is the most beautiful of all!" Then, remember·ing, or seeing again an old one, I must again exclaim, "Ah, no! How could I have forgotten, this is the loveliest."

Today, in El Café de Nadie, Avenida Jalisco, I am showing six photographs under the auspices of Movimiento Estridentista. It is the same cafe where months ago de la Peña took Llewellyn, Tina, and myself to dine and I watched the pale prostitute with the scarlet mouth. That night I am sure Llewellyn and I were excess baggage! The exhibit is in charge of Maples Arce, editor of *Irradiador*. Others showing are Jean Charlot, Rafael Sala, and masks by Cueto.

The Salas are, after all, able to join us Semana Santa for the vacation in Te-potzotlán, so we are in the throes of preparation, planning to leave Tuesday. A letter from Jorge Enciso gives us the "key" to Tepotzotlán and permission to sleep and live in the convent. Chandler does not care to go and I am not en-couraging him, for after a day he would be restless, want to return, and drive us all quite mad.

Ciro Méndez and Best have been seeing Ruth Wilton in New York. I intro-duced them and today a letter from her tells of their times together. I sent Ruth a little jícara and an Aztec head. She writes, "How I appreciate the fact that you chose these things and sent them to me. It makes me happy! Somehow it typifies what your friendship has been to me."

April, Semana Santa, 1924, Tepotzotlán, Estado de Mexico. Tina, Monna, Rafael, Felipe, Dominga, Elisa, and E. W ... To begin first with the last day:

"If you awaken before I do, call me at 4:00," Tina had said. It was after five when the swallows began circling in and out through the mirador where she and I slept. At my right, a full moon was setting back of the tower of Tepotzot-lán; to the left, over a green fertile valley, the sun was rising through morning mist. The air was delicious after the season's first rain. Birds everywhere over-flowed with song and I thought to myself this is one of the never-to-be-forgotten moments of my life! "Tina! Tina! Awaken! It is time for coffee. We must start early this last day."

There was no lingering over coffee. We, with our cameras, were soon on our way. For a peso an Indian boy would carry the cameras all morning; fortunate, for an 8 × 10 outfit with an f. 3.8 lens is no small item in weight. Looking back toward the church, Rafael and Monna appeared on the horizon and soon joined us for "buenos días." But we separated, Tina and the Salas in the direction of a little white chapel, I into the region of cacti, maguey, and crumbling walls.

Fascinating material to work with, the maguey, the organ cactus in their stark severity; not easy to isolate however, and so, after two hours wrestling with my problem, the boy suggested fresh pulque which idea appealed. Five centavos worth each and we were refreshed with this agreeable mild intoxicant. So I once more attacked the maguey to honor the plant from which is fermented pulque, the plant and beverage so typical of this plateau.

Sharper and sharper I stopped down my lens, the limit of my diaphragm, f. 32, was not enough so I cut a smaller hole from black paper. How ridiculous a "soft focus" lens in this country of brilliant light, of clean cut lines and outlines, —of course, I should add, how ridiculous the "diffused" lens in any country!

This morning's examination of my negatives—for though I returned quite worn last night I could not sleep before developing—revealed a number of satisfying results, things which express well my reactions to Mexico. Technically speaking, I had several disappointments, bitter ones, fog again utterly ruining three negatives despite all my preliminary precautions; but those which were clean were brilliant and chemically fine.

I exposed no film on the church, except a few records with the Graflex for "recuerdos." Many times I pointed my camera towards it—almost longingly— towards this building of such great beauty, but always the lens was finally pivoted away and off into the region of cacti and maguey, or of walled streets and open sky. Of the walls and cacti I had much to say—they, at least, have not been exploited, but the most casual, superficial of tourists would exclaim in rapture over the church, "snap" it with their Kodaks, and then rush back to the hotel lobby.

A group of such tourists we observed awaiting the return train for Mexico. They furnished us much amusement, this family of Americans! How they edged away, nay, shrank away from every sarape-wrapped figure who brushed too close. One imagined a bottle of "Lysol" in each of their pockets and smelling salts ready for use. We soon parted company for they rode "first class" while we piled into "second."

It is evening; already I have printed and mounted one of my Tepotzotlán photographs. Two reasons prompted such celerity: first, intense desire to see finished prints, to gloat over the results; second, to forget, by plunging hard into work, our present precarious condition, for I have just eight centavos left, with rent past due.

The print I made is a lovely thing of the plaza. It has luminous shadows and delightful detail. A huge cross cuts almost the centre of the print. A stickler on "composition" might complain, but rules, like laws, were made to be broken by those who can. This negative was made from aloft, in the tower.

However, it is not my very best one, which is an excellent thing of organ cactus against a crumbling old wall, but with a technical defect, a new and sickening trouble, a round spot of fog, apparently lens flare, appears in the center of half of my negatives. Why I should be thus afflicted I cannot guess, for I have used the "Variable" stopped way down before without trouble and none of these negatives were made against the light for, generally, I avoid back-light as the plague. Well, being a good printer, I can print down those spots, but I don't like the idea, nor fancy the extra work, and it takes some of the joy away that I get from making a straight print from a perfect negative. But for the flare spot, some of the negatives needed not even the work of spotting one dust speck.

La Iglesia de Tepotzotlán, in the churrigueresque style, or at least the facade is (but I must avoid the use of terms and periods, not knowing them), is a church dating back to the 17th Century. Over-elaborate, for me, are the tower, facade, and interiors, yet one marvels at the cohesion of such elaboration. Inside is gold, gold, gold over intricate and beautiful woodcarving; the ensemble fairly made one dizzy. Only a virgin land of untold wealth plus the fanaticism and faith of the Indians, could have made this possible. And these Indians were not merely influenced by the Spanish conquerors in their work. "We have nothing comparable to this in Spain," exclaimed Rafael.

One small room in the dome of which floated a beautiful golden "bird" was anything but Spanish; strange figures holding up fruited baskets, swarthy tropical figures and fruits which had nothing to do with Catholicism. Here the color scheme was a departure from the monotony of so much gold; vermilion and blue combined with the gold to give an aspect of almost oriental splendor. My "bird" which flew in the dome has become a standing joke. "Don't you know that's the Holy Ghost?" said Monna.

Another negative with the pissing Indian: he came out so opportunely just as I was to expose, and stood there serenely, as one is wont to do; I uncapped the lens and have him, stream and all, a touch of life quite unexpected. It might be called, remembering Rosenfeld, an "affirmation of the majesty of the moment."

Living was none too comfortable in the convent, for water was scarce and a daily bath is my one confirmed iniquity. But we ate well on pollo and tender little pigeons. They, at 35 centavos each, were cheaper than meat. So much fun at meal-time gatherings with Felipe's attempts at English, with jokes over our improvised candlestick, a candle inserted in a roll of toilet paper and adorning the tripod top to light the supper table. And so it went—a vivid week to remember.

April 23. I am still in a daze over the result of my exhibit in Guadalajara. Charlot and Federico returned bringing us 280 pesos for eight prints! The ones that sold were as big a surprise as the number—among them several of my very best things. The complete list follows: "Steel," 40. pesos, "Pipes and stacks," 40., "Pirámide del Sol," 30., "Grey Attic," 35., "Breast," 35., "Refracted sunlight and Torso," 30., "Pirámide del Sol," (another view) 30., and "Karl Struss, Cinematographer," 40. Yes, I am amazed!

And then to actually spend money for them! To not only admire them, but to desire to possess them! Los Angelenos would have said, perhaps some few of them, "Yes, they are nice, but so expensive and I need a new tire for the auto; otherwise, we cannot go to the beach Sunday," or, "I must have a new hat for Easter." The Mexicans, impoverished from the revolution, complained of the prices, yet they bought.

I wonder if a trip to Guadalajara would not pay well? I should much prefer living in one of the smaller, less spoiled cities, but never considered the idea as practical. Federico says that living there is half what it is here.

This city has never appealed to me as a whole, not forgetting the charm of certain spots unspoiled as yet, and its delightful climate. But there is Chandler to consider, he is interested and working hard in his school and insists we must go without him!

April 24. Printed more negatives from Tepotzotlán: a subtle, delicate print of a weather worn wall, quite different from the vigorous work I have been doing, pleases me; a couple of the organ cactus and walls also please, but I had a hell of a time printing down the flare spots and find some almost impossible.

Today I received fifty dollars from Flora and an order for 120 pesos. Money seems to be flowing in by way of contrast to the past few weeks.

Evening. Just waiting here by my window for the Salas, who are coming to chocolate at 6:00. It is raining gently, the sky is so soft and grey, the air so clean.

With the brief morning sun, I printed my order and then one more negative from Tepotzotlán, an arch with organ cactus underneath; it might be a stage setting and is dangerously near being just picturesque. I might call my work in Mexico a fight to avoid its natural picturesqueness. I had this premonition about working in Mexico before leaving Los Angeles and used to be almost angry with those who would remark, "O, you will have such a wonderful opportunity to make pictures in Mexico."

From the twenty or so negatives I exposed in Tepotzotlán, I have at least ten worthy of printing in Platinum.

A friend, Dr. Mayorga, an optometrist, also an amateur photographer who has himself made several lenses, came this morning to look for my lens trouble. He opines that I cannot avoid trouble using an anastigmat lens of f. 3. 8 with such a surface of glass exposed to the dazzling [light] of Mexico. A lens shade does no apparent good. Of course, wider open, the flare disappears, but that does not help me. I want depth of focus. This leaves me no lens for outside work. I shall try to pick up a cheap rectilinear of about 15 inch focus, one that will stop down to U. S. 256!

April 26. Chandler's Birthday. I peeked into his room, next mine, and I am sure he lay there pretending sleep to postpone the proposed beating: he is fourteen today.

Our roomer, the engineer, owes now over 200 pesos and tells us he can pay nothing for two months more, wishes to give us a note. He may be honest but we cannot assume this rent burden any longer. We must move and are now in the midst of house hunting and fighting with our dueña.

Ella Wolf served us Borscht, a Russian soup, black bread, and Russian candy this party night: altogether it was a successful gathering. I am no longer under illusions that the *people* of Guadalajara have better taste than those of other communities, for Charlot told me that the Governor of Jalisco purchased five of my prints for the State museum; however, this was satisfying news.

Charlot in looking over my prints laughed outright, then flushed confusedly. "I laugh so at times when I am emotionally stirred," he said.

Federico brought bad news, that another and probably worse revolution was fomenting under General Flores: if I were sure this were so, I should return at once.

Charlot's burst of emotional laughter recalls how in the old days, I, for the same reason, used to laugh at Tina and she would look at me surprised and wondering.

April 28. Sold six prints last eve to an American here from Cincinnati. Needing money so badly, I let them go for much less than I should have, the six for 150 pesos. Mr. Hawley bought: "Head of an Italian girl," "Romantic Mexico," "Portrait of Robelo," "Valle de San Juan Teotihuacán," "White Iris," and one of the new prints from Tepotzotlán.

If only I could make a decent living selling prints instead of doing portraits I should be happy. With the Guadalajara sale and that of last night I have received 430 pesos for fourteen prints within the ten days past.

April 27, Sunday. "El Toro," "La Corrida de la Primavera," the "last" fight of the season, so advertised, yet almost two months ago they said the same thing. However, that insatiable "fan," Turnbull, assured me it would be the last big one. We went together. The day was obscure, the wind high, making fine cape work difficult, and also exceedingly dangerous, for a gust of wind swirling tne cape might cause the bull to charge in the wrong direction with even death as a result. Despite the day, Gaona was superb and I can now well understand why he is crowned king of them all.

I find myself watching the fight with less emotional excitement and more intellectual curiosity than heretofore, and caught myself humming a popular air with the crowd, even as the bull drove his horns into a horse's belly. One becomes hardened to anything, used to all sensations; blood and death grow eventually commonplace, love and romance too. It is only my work that I return to with never diminishing enthusiasm, with untiring energy.

Music, jesting, laughter, "rough-house," color, blood, death! What a wildly tense two hours. And walking home alone down Oaxaca, what hideous humans begged alms, what loathsome dogs yapped, what beautiful señoritas leaned from flower-covered balconies. What a land of extremes! And what can be its destiny?

April 29. Reprinted several of the prints recently sold, also one new one, that of the pissing Indian. It is a fine print technically from a fine technical negative. The photograph reproduces and conveys all the solidity of the house and walls I felt as I viewed my ground glass. Also it has humour!

Tina just called up, "I have gained a real triumph, Elisa is brushing her teeth! I don't know whether she is using your brush, or my brush, or a new one of her own, but she is actually brushing them!" When we first got Elisa, Tina encouraged her to brush her teeth, but she would always say, "O, that is only for rich people!"

Elisa's sister, Dominga, is still here; apparently she has adopted us. We say nothing for she helps Elisa and she has all too much work in this enormous house.

Visiting Roubisec today; he has a copy of *Ulysses* we should like to buy, or borrow. Tina remarked, "A friend told us that soon there would be another revolution." "He lies," answered Roubisec, "there will be not one, but forty!"

April 30. "Elisa! Elisa! — Oiga! Tráigame cafe, pronto, pronto!" Listen, hurry! — Bring coffee, fast, fast! for today I must move. I am the only one who must change The engineer wants my room at 30 pesos per, and we have rented the garage for fifteen, so we have decided to stay here and try to re-rent the front rooms for around one hundred pesos. If we can do this, we might much better stay where we are than try to re-establish, fit up new workrooms, and pay the landlord an extra month or two for breaking our contract.

Despite the ugly wallpaper, I have become attached to this little ladder-reached room in which I have been able to isolate myself to my benefit as well as others. . .

May Day, 1924. Awakened by loud, furious, and prolonged explosions, "The new revolution is upon us," I thought, "or the forty of them" — but then, after collecting my sleep-dazed senses, I remembered this was May Day and being celebrated Mexican way.

I awakened this morning in my new room. My first words were profane and directed toward the wallpaper. It is covered with persistently irritating spots, little spots, big spots, spiteful spots, quite maddening to the eye. My next words, also profane, were for the leaded glass windows and doors which cover one whole end of the room, more spots, red circles of glass, green triangles of glass, blue oblongs of glass; for relief, my eye wandered to the ceiling. My swearing found a complete release, a moulded tin border enclosing lines, and more lines, and then scroll work flourishing around flowers so real one could smell them. A pretty penny the landlady spent to create this luxurious atmosphere, I contemplated, small wonder she refused to come down on the rent arguing the house had "just been redecorated at much expense." Either I shall become used to this room, hardened, or it will "get" me.

But there is always the azotea for retreat, and last twilight found us there full length on a petate, faces skyward, watching the grey, gold-tipped storm-clouds shift; Tina recalling memories of Venice which Dreiser's *A Traveler at Forty*, had brought back, or discussing that subtle and fascinating book by Wasserman, *The World's Illusion*, which we are reading aloud, or just gazing skyward and silently dreaming.

May 2. May Day in Mexico, unlike the United States, is Labor Day, and the proletariat made the most of their occasion. Not a camión nor a streetcar in service, no newspaper published, bread and even tortillas were unobtainable, and in this city of over a million people telephone service was cut off. We passed the day uneventfully, or rather we did not celebrate.

I printed again, to complete my collection, all work of the past. Pulled a fine print of Robelo, which still remains one of my best portraits.

Tina printed her most interesting abstraction done in the tower of Tepotzotlán. She is very happy over it and well she may be. I, myself, would be pleased to have done it. She printed from the enlarged positive, so she has a negative print and shows it upside down. All of which sounds "fakey," and, in truth, may not be the best usage of photography, but it really is very genuine and one feels no striving, no sweat as in the Man Ray experiments.

Still printing! I wish to have everything saleable ready for possibilities. One new thing, Panchito Villa, he halts, saluting, before a mountainous basket; it is humourous, has good technique.

In the afternoon, house-hunting: one place we would take in a minute but for the price of 150 pesos. The house is built on a triangular lot and every room has outside exposure, also a fine azotea from which one looks down on two streets with parkways. It is a cheerful house and many of the Mexican homes are dark and gloomy as tombs, besides being impossibly arranged. One could have no privacy, no isolation in them, each room opening into the next in the most sociable way. Actually, I found one house in which the toilet and bath could only be reached by walking through some half dozen other rooms! I laughed to Tina, "Our temperamental family would separate after one week, or less, of such intimacy."

These are the older homes which from their architectural beauty we are drawn to; the new houses, built American style, may be more comfortable, "up to date," but are so ugly as to be blots on the beautiful landscape. I am not complaining over the arrangement of all the old Mexican homes; in fact, my ideal is such a place as we had in Tacubaya, with every room having its private door like so many little houses opening onto a patio.

May 5, "El Cinco de Mayo," Monday. Sunday, we went with the Salas to San Agustín Acolman, off in the direction of San Juan Teotihuacán. From the roof of the church, we viewed the pyramids at no great distance. The church, built by the Franciscans, in the 16th Century, is a simple massive structure with none of the pompous show and glitter of Tepotzotlán. The murals which covered the patio walls were tremendously interesting, in fact, the whole church important. We decided, then and there, to ask permission of Jorge Enciso to live in there for a week as we did at Tepotzotlán.

Being Sunday, services were held, and though simpler than those of Semana Santa in Tepotzotlán, perhaps even more impressive. The small group of kneeling Indians, the gorgeous trappings of the priest, the Indian at the organ who played and sang Tosti with a voice which moved one to deep emotion. "I felt like applauding in appreciation, Tina." "You took the words out of my mouth, Edward." And as he sang, birds joined him from the vaulted ceiling above. The surrounding country was as fertile and beautiful a valley as we have seen. Red wine, bread, cheese, and crisp lettuce in the shadow of the church...

Gupta cooked for our Saturday night "salon;" curry and sweet rice he gave us; along with Lupe's pozole and Tina's spaghetti, the best supper we have had.

For the first time in weeks, Diego came, wandered smilingly in, paintcovered from head to foot. Regular faces are now Jorge Enciso and Julio Torri,—the latter, Lupe insists, is the best writer in Mexico. Gupta brought a Hindu friend especially to see my work; he was impressed.

"Why don't you dance," I said to Dr. M., who sat forlornly alone. "Tina does not want to dance tonight." "But there are other girls!" "I am a monogamist," he smiled. "For me there is only Tina!" I admired his frankness. Of Chandler's photograph done in the zaguán—entry—at Tacubaya, he said, "I like it as well as the best of yours." So Chandler made him a print.

May 14, Wednesday, at sun up. Some time before the 17th, we are to move, the house on the triangular lot our destination. Tina bargained the man down to

125 a month. We have to pay our present landlord 250 cash before we leave here and 100 a month after till we pay two months in advance for breaking our contract! Wealthy people are usually the closest, stingiest, most unsympathetic. "We, too, have suffered from the revolution," he said, "we must share our losses."

May 16, 1924. Avenida Vera Cruz 42, Esquina Durango. Five-thirty yesterday morning found us through coffee, packing with feverish haste, and in great agitation to move before our dueño discovered us; for we decided to leave Lucerna 12 without paying the 250 pesos demanded. Extortion it seemed, and worth a gamble to avoid payment. Before 9:00 our belongings were waiting at the door of Vera Cruz 42 and soon Tina appeared with the discomforting news that our landlord would bring suit if the money were not paid within two days.

First impression of our new "home." It is much noisier than the other two places we have lived in. A continuous stream of those stinking, irritating, rattling, "busy" assemblages of tin called "Fords" in the form of "camiones" or "listos" tear by. We are close to fashionable apartments frequented by Americans...

[Under my] window is a palatial and pretentious home. It is not quite human, I would prefer a pulquería. The streets which radiate in all directions are parked with trees, fresh, green, well kept. My room is small, but sunny and agreeable. Thank the Gods, it lacks wallpaper and the neutral paint will admit the use of decorations.

On account of its shape we have called this place, "El Barco," the boat: the studio room, a triangle coming to a sharp point, is the prow of our ship; indeed, with two round windows in this room like portholes, we think the place well named. One reason for being attracted to this house was its airy and sunlit rooms, each with outside exposure; but, in gaining light and air, we have acquired noise, and lost some privacy, for though one floor up, we are, nevertheless, "on the street."

May 19. Flies and "Fords" prevent morning dozing, no matter how much desired or needed. The flies enjoy a sunny cheerful room and swarm in each morning as they never did at Lucerna. Like a naughty boy wishing to register protest, if handy in some newspaper headline, I would literally spit on the name of Henry Ford for having created such evil, noisome contraptions. One might write an essay on their "symbolism;" a conventionalized Ford should be printed on the paper banners of democracy. "Time" and "labor" savers? Yes, depending on what one means. But if Henry Ford had lived contemporary with the Pyramids, and had served that age with his efficiency, there would have been no time nor labor for the building of them. Emancipated labor would have spent its time under "Fords," correcting poor craftsmanship, or in them, rattling and jolting along, excitedly and importantly, on errands to nowhere.

May 24. If dreams have any symbolic significance, the one I had last night must be of great import. I only have a thread to go on, I cannot recall nor reconstruct the whole dream. It was this, someone, and it is impossible to remember who, said to me, or rather I understood them to say, "Alfred Stieglitz is dead." "Alfred Stieglitz dead!" I exclaimed. "No," said the person, referring to a newspaper, "not dead but dying."

The obvious way to interpret the dream, if dreams are to be interpreted, would be in the forecast of a radical change in my photographic viewpoint, a gradual "dying" of my present attitude, for Stieglitz has most assuredly been a symbol for an ideal in photography towards which I have worked in recent years. I do remember the pain and shock of this news.

Tina and I were reading *The World's Illusion* last evening and with continued interest. The door bell rang; it was Dr. M., or perhaps his ghost, for Charlot and Federico had assured us they had killed him! I am sure Charlot's sarcastic wit, his subtle ridicule, did kill something, for he did not seem quite the same hand-kissing enraptured admirer as before, or it may be he has changed his method of attack, or it may be that I have changed and am indifferent as to the turn of the tide.

Dr. M. did not speak well of Wasserman's writing in German, said that he was facile and influenced by the greater German authors. I told him how much we were enjoying the translation.

The doctor was overflowing with enthusiasm following his visit to San Juan Teotihuacán. Las Pirámides are the greatest structures in the world he thinks.

We discussed too the proposed exhibit of my work in Berlin which he is anxious to undertake and drank "rompope" to its success. I should want it to be a complete and comprehensive showing and I hesitate over the time and expense in producing the work. If I could feel assured of financial reward, I then might go ahead, but I cannot use the energy nor money to further my glory.

Dr. M. suggested a plan to revolutionize Mexico politically, socially, economically, within twenty-four hours; he would prohibit absolutely the owning or carrying of guns. I am sure the plan enforced would bring immediate and definite results, for the carrying of pistolas is a universal and terribly abused privilege, resulting in a continued performance of tragedy and death, turning each individual, as it were, into an arbiter of law according of his own personal viewpoint and desire. Senators and governors carry guns to their assemblages; Indians to their pulquerías; and little boys flourish them on the streets: the last remark is, to be sure, some exaggeration, but actually I have seen, and more than once, boys of twelve or fifteen with automatics and cartridge belts. This condition would be bad enough in a northern country among people of better poise and self control, but here, in a land where life is cheap and death unfeared, where individuals are quick and hot tempered, the result is appalling.

The same disregard of life is shown in the use, or rather abuse, of the automobile in Mexico. The pedestrian has little enough right to exist in the U. S. at present, here, seemingly, none at all. Fast, furious driving, unmuffled and uncontrolled, is universal, and the wreckage of cars and camiones strewn along the streets and highways becomes a casually noted part of the landscape. One steps into a camión as into the hands of fate, perhaps to arrive at one's destination, but quite as likely to awaken in a hospital, or maybe, according to God's will, in heaven or hell.

The Fords marked "listo" are just as bad. Tina and I had a wild ride in one some days ago. One need not hunt a "Coney Island" in Mexico for thrills; hail a Ford, announce that you must reach a certain point at a certain time, then rest assured that if you get there you will have had your money's worth of excitement, that any thrills overlooked by the driver of your own car will be afforded by numberless others.

We were to meet Charlot at the train for Chapingo; we waited too long on the wrong corner for a camión, there were five minutes left to reach the station through busy crowded streets. "Can you meet the train at two, or no pay?" we asked the Ford driver. He could, and started off with no intention of losing his pay! Pedestrians dodged our car in laughable haste but I well know how they were cursing us! One's psychology is quite different depending on whether one is in a machine or in front of it! Pedestrians were missed by inches, dogs scampared yelping out of our way, we escaped crashing into other Fords miraculously, and, having been jolted and bounced into a state of limp jellification, arrived on time — but no Charlot! Some misunderstanding: disappointed, we made the best of matters and decided to walk for awhile.

It was an old and beautiful part of the city, as yet unspoiled. We came upon "La Santísima." Once before I had seen this church at night. It is a marvel with its fine towers and exceedingly rich churrigueresque facade, my favourite of all the churches I know in this style. We paused long in mute contemplation, then, wandering on, found ourselves in front of that lovely Virgin to whom the prostitutes offer prayer, Nuestra Señora de la Soledad—more exclamations and enraptured meditation.

Then we came upon several examples of contemporary decoration which excited our aesthetic senses quite as profoundly, if differently; they were pulquerías. Assuredly there must be a "school" of pulquería painting, for though diverse, they have the same general trend in color, effect, and design.

If Picasso had been in Mexico, I should feel that he must have studied the pulquería paintings, for some are covered with geometrical shapes in brilliant primary colors to excite the envy of an European modernist. These paintings which include every possible subject, beautiful women, charros, toreadors, "Popo" and Ixtaccíhuatl, engines and boats, are the last word in direct naive realism. With the titles emblazoned over the doors, imaginative, tender, or humorous, one has in the pulquería the most fascinating, interesting, popular art in modern Mexico City.

"After all," I said to Tina, "We have had an enjoyable afternoon and the exciting ride was well worth a peso!"

May 28. It is 4:30 but I cannot sleep.

Yesterday, Sta. Bichette Amor sat to me, a re-sitting, the first in Mexico: small satisfaction in knowing her first sitting was good from my viewpoint. The two sisters, Paulette and Lidia, were pleased and their order of three prints each is already delivered. For once, we were glad to have an excuse for rushing out work; they were anxious to get them for a birthday and we to deliver them for reasons too obvious to state.

With no workroom as yet, finishing has been a problem: hanging blankets over doors and windows, we have developed in my "ropero"—closet—a hot, sweaty, suffocating job; reminding me of boyhood days in photography, the improvised workrooms, toilets, closets, kitchen sinks, bath tubs pressed into service.

How well I recall one brilliant idea for a darkroom, a hoop around which was sewn a long black bag; this bag, open at the bottom, closed at the top, could be lowered by pulley and cord from the ceiling to cover a table below. In this "darkroom" many a now forgotten masterpiece was developed. But that was fun, pure joy, while developing "business" sittings in my ropero, and in my "declining years," is not!

A gentle knock at my door, "¿Quién es?" "Sr. Don Eduardo, ya me voy." I opened, and Dominga stood there weeping, such a forlorn little figure in black. She was leaving for Guadalajara, her home. No work here in the big city of her dreams. Her grief was touching. I took her in my arms and petted her; she sobbed and turned away. "Adiós, Dominga, hasta pronto," but, of course, I shall never see her again. They are so tender, these Indians. We are fortunate in having Elisa and Pedro; she works hard, is appreciative, and ever remembers us with flowers or little gifts. Ella Wolf asked of her if she liked to work for us. "We thank God every day for having such a fine home with Sta. Tina and Sr. Don Eduardo," she answered. Yet all we have done is to treat them as human beings and pay her fifteen pesos a month!

June 3. By moving we have cut our rent in half; but groceries, staples, fruit are so expensive in this neighborhood that if Elisa did not hie herself to the now distant market places, our living expenses would be double. We did not anticipate this condition, neither did we realize how noisy this corner would be.

I do not let the rest of the family know my inner distress and rebellion over the noise. Sunday is especially bad, and as I sat retouching in C.'s room, every camión that roared by made direct and telling attack on my nerves. The "Ford"

74

has become a fixed symbol in my mind for all that is noisy, vulgar, mediocre, noxious. To the doctor's suggested reformation of Mexico through the abolition of promiscuous gun-carrying, I would add a law forbidding open mufflers.

I should like, for a while, a room overlooking one of the market-places, to be able to sit all day long and watch the never ending, ever changing, kaleidoscope of life below. Saturday we went to shop in El Mercado de la Merced, the largest of the many markets—such an amazing sight! Quite every edible thing known to mankind seems on display, and many which only the imaginative Mexican could have discovered as edible.

The fruit astounds one: here are mountains of oranges, carloads of bananas, rooms piled with watermelons, acres of pineapples, mangoes, aquacates. One could describe in a like way the display of vegetables, fresh from their trip down the Viga canal,—not to forget the poultry: blocks of chickens, turkeys, geese, legs tied to prevent escape before doom, all adding to the general confusion with peeps and squawks of discomfiture. Purchases were made, a pineapple for 35 centavos, aguacates two for 5 cents, mangoes 7 cents each, and bananas—I don't know how many, but a basket full for 35 cents.

So we had much to carry, and from somewhere, just at the right moment, a cab appeared; they always miraculously emerge into view exactly when and where one needs them, as though the driver scented his prey from afar. I do enjoy the cabs, creaking, swaying things though they are; one always feels sure they must fall to pieces before the trip is finished, either that, or the horses will drop and gasp their last.

We have had two breakdowns, both ludicrous rather than dangerous. Once, coming from work at Montenegro's, we piled a cab full of tripods, cameras, and gifts, and ourselves. Wes wayed along—not quite two blocks—then the wheels started to wobble in alarming fashion—finally, coming to a dead stop, our driver announced that the wheels were about to come off! We piled out into the street, cameras and all, hailing the first "Ford."

But the funniest experience, with the laugh on Tina, was that which took place in front of the Hotel Princess our first day in Mexico City. To see the city from a leisurely moving cab was a mutual and instinctive desire of both Tina and my-self, so, coincident with our wishes, as if we were Aladins with a magic lamp, a cab drew up "listo." A moment of preliminary bargaining in which the driver discovered that though we were tourists we knew "the ropes," and Tina stepped up into the cab, happy over the anticipated ride. Now Tina is not thin—neither is she fat—but as she stepped in, she also went down, for the cab floor gave way and there she straddled, one leg on the step, the other passing through a hole in the cab floor! Pedestrians and loungers had a good laugh, covert or open; they also had a good look, for Tina's legs are well worth an extra stretch of the neck to see. As gracefully as possible, we regained our lost dignity and bravely hailed another cab, while the first driver, mumbling oaths and apologies, stood contemplating his wreck.

Somehow, this recalls another episode, not humorous though, even a bit dramatic, this time in a camión. We lived in Tacubaya, we had hunted furniture all day; night had come and rain was threatening. Halfway home it started, it poured, the heavens opened, cloudburst and sheets of water fell; the camión skidded through streets turned into rivers and when our stop was reached, we stepped into water to the knees. Home was still a good half mile away, impossible to reach in such a storm, neither could we stand there undecided in the rain.

We made toward a distant light. It proved to be a saloon; it might have been reasonably respectable, or very tough; behind those translucent glass doors who could guess what scene would be disclosed. Not that Tina is squeamish, she is invariably ready for any adventure, but I, as her "Protector," with slight knowledge of Spanish, momentarily hesitated. We pushed in: a crowd of drinking, singing chaffing men stood at the bar; we joined them, put our feet on the brass rail, and, as they eyed us in curious amazement, this evident "gringo" and this Latin girl who spoke Spanish with an English accent, ordered drinks for the crowd. "¡Salud!" At least, they saw we were friendly and "good sports." Then with the usual gallant attention to women that the Mexican man never fails to show, a machine was placed at our disposal. Another short dash through the still-driving rain and river-like streets, and we landed drenched but laughing at "El Buen Retiro."

June 7. La Ciudad de Mexico is clean these days. She is rain-drenched; she glitters in the early sun. The mornings are quiet, serene; nature awakens calm after her bursts of temperament indulged in the afternoons. The sky is the bluest blue ever conceived; the clouds which gather and drift, the whitest white ever imagined; and the shadows cast by an uncomprising sun are not those loved by the poet of anaemic moods.

All morning, clouds float across the sky, great white-sailed boats, pleasure boats on a joyous sea. Then the afternoon: the changing clouds, now grey, now black, a stirring and swaying of trees, a scurrying of humans below, a mumbling of heavens above, an apprehension of tropical discontent. As prelude to the storm, a few drops fall, patterning the street like big polka dots on calico: no intermission, no delay, a crash, pyrotechnics and artillery; first rain, then hail, the wind slanting it this way and that, throwing it up again to the sky from whence it came. The mad frenzy dies from its own passion. The furor is too great to endure. The climax comes with a last violent deluge and suddenly nature lies still, quiet, exhausted.

The reunion is over. Anita [Anita Brenner, writer and editor] served chango, cinnamon toast, and tea. It was delicious. This will be the last time that food plays a part in our reunions. We have found that several of those we like best stay away, not having a peso for the collection hat. Conditions are no better, in fact worse. The government has cancelled eighty days of back pay. Everyone is gloomy, broke, trying to leave, but unable to get away. The Salas, the Goldschmidts, Gupta, Matthias, and others all anxious to get out.

Garduño has loaned me an old R. R. [Rapid Rectilinear—see appendix.] lens which I can stop down to a pinhole. I was happy with fresh prospects until traces of fog on new negatives brought madness to my brain. The trouble was soon disclosed. My bellows have sprung a dozen tiny leaks. Mexico is rough on cameras, but damn American craftsmanship.

My one happiness today is a new yellow table against my grey walls. On it I have arranged my brilliant gourds and painted fruit and jicaras.

Sunday morning came a note from Tina via Elisa: "What do you say to going somewhere this morning? We might happen to find Diego at the Secretaria." He was not there, but we viewed his work again.

One of my favorite panels is of two figures dancing a jota—superb! There were many fine things to exclaim over, but I might offer criticism too. Diego has become formulated, is repeating certain figures and attitudes; but remembering that he is painting day after day at so much a square foot, I rather wonder at the variety of his imagination.

From the Secretaría to el Convento de la Merced: Dr. Atl was not home. We made Graflex negatives looking down on the market, then wandered through its streets, purchasing gourds, baskets, and flowers for a few trifling centavos.

We saw a bit of incongruity over which I am still chuckling; it was in a public toilet. Now Mexicans are never hesitant about using the side of a wall, or any other convenient spot, when called by nature, but in the market so to relieve oneself would be impossible without spattering fruit, vegetables, poultry, or one's neighbors. So here was this public toilet of wooden stalls marked three and five centavos according to the luxury afforded. Well, I have seen shrines to the Virgin in a butcher shop over piles of porkchops, in bakeries illuminating buns and bread, in pulquerías, among hardware, in fact, everywhere, but I never hoped to find one in a toilet! But, there it was and quite resplendent with flowers and many lighted candles! It was the pinnacle to our morning of sight-seeing. We took a cab for home.

June 10, 1924. From somewhere comes the thought, it may be my own or another's, that it is no test of bravery to face unflinchingly danger or death in public; that cowards may rise to an heroic posture given an audience. But to be fearless and intrepid when quite alone is real proof of courageousness. This thought I carried home with me from El Toreo Sunday evening. For otherwise, would that young novillero—novice bullfighter—have risen three times to face his bull knowing as he must have, that less than an even chance with death was all he held?

He was frightened from the start—that was evident. He lost his head time and again, that was fatal. He could have quit with good excuse the last time they picked him up dazed and hurt and horrified, for the audience rose and screamed "No! No! No!" as he once more staggered toward the bull.

Perhaps it was the thought of his ladylove to whom he had so gallantly bowed and tossed his velvet cap before the fight; or, perhaps, it was an assumption of bravery, a desperate false pride, a mask to the hooting, taunting public, for it must be a brave man who dares admit to terror; or it may have been economic determinism, the knowing that this, his first introduction as a "future ace," could make or finish his whole career, which impelled him to fight on so hopelessly.

Of course, he became worse, and more frantic, with each succeeding failure to deliver the estocada, and when one attempt passed through and out of the bull's shoulder, the groans and whistling from the crowd grew to an uproar.

Then the bugle blew, first warning that his time limit was nearly up, then the second blast which was his finish and disgrace. The arena doors opened and in trotted three tame steers to coax the bull away. The bedraggled brute followed willingly enough; he had fought his fight and was the victor; he was glad to return to green pastures.

But the bull was tired. He had charged the bewildering capes. He had gored his horses and received the return shock of three picas. For just an instant, at the gate to freedom, he paused with lowered head and heaving sides, the brilliant banderillas drooped from his shoulders to the ground, the no less brilliant blood streamed over his flanks. It was a fatal pause. From the center of the arena, the shamed and agonized novillero saw one last chance! Crazily running, he reached the bull, poised for a moment, concentrating, gathering together his scattered wits, he placed all hope, despair, defiance, into this last frantic attempt. He once more gambled with death, but he won. The sword went straight and clean to the hilt; the bull sank with no preliminary stagger; the audience rose en masse at this unexpected climax.

The matador walked with dragging steps and bowed head across the arena, heedless of their ovation. To the encircling fence he went, leaned his head into his arms and wept. But they would not let him stay there. They pulled him resisting into the arena again, and with still bowed head, he received the deserved applause. For though he had fought a poor fight, he had returned unhesitatingly to possible death; he had been an object of ridicule and, worse, of pity; but he had been sublime. I have seen better bull-fights; I have not seen a more dramatic one.

June 12. "¿Cómo, Señorita?" I said, prepared to bargain over a bouquet of mosquetas, seductively fresh and fragrant. "Quince centavos, Señor, muy frescas, muy barata — cheap." Yes, they were cheap, I was ashamed to bargain, and took them with no further palaver. It was the market of San Juan, I had gone there hoping to find some little things for the children, but I found mostly food and flowers. The flower market lined both sides of the street for a block, to walk there is to be transplanted into fairyland. Flowers might be had for any mood, all the old fashioned flowers of one's childhood, stock, pinks, forget-me-nots, daisies, gladioli in profusion, and more strange tropical bloom, gorgeous, aloof, at least to an Anglo-Saxon. The display of fruit almost equaled that in la Merced. A mango de Manila for cinco centavos completed my expenditures and I made haste for the bank and more sordid aspects.

Two months rent in advance is our contract with the new dueño; not easy to pay, for my recent sittings have not been profitable. Prospects become less possible to reckon with; I only hope to stay in Mexico long enough to work and create more comprehensively. Then? Well, I ponder much over New York these days. It seems the logical place for my return. Rafael and Monna are to write the Dudensing Gallery about my work, send a few prints, and try to arrange an exhibit for the coming autumn season.

It is a shame to leave Mexico so soon, with much yet to do and see, and with C. interested in his school work as he never was in the States, — at the head of his class he told me last night. But I cannot go on in this uncertainty, this pacing of floors and wondering what will happen next. If I cannot work in peace here, I might better try elsewhere.

It is the instability of Mexico which is maddening: a land so rich, so beautiful; a race, the Indians, so tender, lovable; but all smeared over with a slime of political intrigue and treachery in which my own country has played its shameful part.

I walked to the Salas' last evening. Through a stretch of open landscape on the way, the snowy summits of Ixtaccíhuatl and Popocatépetl floated like white clouds above a grey mist; detached from any earthly base, they rose into the heavens, and in supernal majesty remained there, for they are inhuman mountains. Ajusco was in the distance too, crowned with black storm clouds. He is a dark, gruff, and mighty pile of rock, a friend of the wind, recipient of lightning, resounder of thunder, but he is of the earth—and human.

Sunday morning. As time passes and one gradually eliminates and unconsciously classifies people, the number is reduced to a small group of acquaintances and a still smaller handful of friends. Among these, Jean Charlot remains as the one whom I am most strongly drawn towards, and this despite a slight separation through difference in tongue, albeit his English is usually sufficient. Because of

79

his devout Catholicism, a superficial barrier is presented; though this barrier is not impassible as it might be if he were devoted to Christian Science or Methodism, for at least I can admire the beauty of his religion. Charlot is a refined, sensitive boy, and an artist.

Of course, in mentioning close friends I do not overlook the Salas. I have seen more of them than any other "person," but it is collectively that I always think and speak of Monna, Rafael, Felipe, and their unavoidable dogs.

June 18. A letter from Imogen and Roi Partridge [Imogen Cunningham, photographer, married at that time to Roi Partridge, etcher, both long time friends]: "We want very much to possess a print of your Mexican stuff, whatever you think would interest us most. We can only have one at present. Roi is enclosing your old time price for that."

Besides being happy to hear from them, I was pleased indeed to know that two struggling artists like my work well enough to pay out real money for it, and, at that, without even having a choice.

June 21. For 25 pesos I purchased a Rapid-Rectilinear lens in a cheaply made shutter. Now I start a new phase of my photographic career with practically the same objective that I began with some twenty years ago. My expensive anastigmat and my several diffused lenses seem destined to contemptuous neglect, though it may be I shall dust them off for an occasional portrait head. The shutter stops down to 256; this should satisfy my craving for more depth of focus. Now if I can patch the leaky bellows and straighten my warped holders, I shall be ready to face life afresh, free from fog and flare.

Sunday morning. As usual, last evening, the "reunión." At midnight, Frances said to the few lingering ones, "Let us go dance at the Salón Azteca. It's a tough joint; we'll have fun." There were Anita, Frances, Tina, and there were Charlot, Federico, a couple of Americans, and myself who went to the "Gran Salón Azteca."

It was as tough as promised. Logically then it was colorful. Since no restraints of style and method were placed upon the dancers, one saw an unrestricted exhibition of individual expression, desires, passions, lusts, mostly crude unvarnished lusts—though that French cocotte was subtle indeed and beautiful too. One could not but wonder why she was in such a place among cheap and obvious whores. On her arm was tatooed "Pas de chance." Jazz took a popular place in the music, but the danzón best revealed the temperament of the Spanish-Indian mixture. It is a dance from tierra caliente—tropic earth,—a slow, langorous, sensuous dance of hip movements, the feet scarcely leaving one spot.

As unmistakable foreigners we were eyed, but with more curiosity than hostility. Frances however committed an indiscretion when she asked the orchestra for a waltz. It was received with hoots and whistles, until the leader arose and called out, "'Familia,' remember where you are, this is not the bull-ring." The protesting hoots were silenced and the waltz went on.

Sunday, I took Olga to her first bull fight. Though I knew she would be shocked, I could not forsee the utter horror with which she viewed the spectacle. It was a bad beginning. The first bull charged a picador at once and it was a gory affray. Olga sat with her head sunk into her hands, moaning and trembling convulsively. I pitied her more than the dying horse. I seemed to see momentarily the fight with her eyes and then became introspective. She said, looking at me in amazement, "O, how can you call this beautiful. How can you return week after week to see this awful sight. I don't understand you!" And I wondered about myself; is my reaction to the beautiful and dramatic so intense as to paralyze any other emotion? Or, in my present condition of disillusionment, am I drawn to this debauch of death for its symbolism? Or—is it indulgence in heretofore unreleased sadistic attributes? Or—do I watch with the eyes of a detached spectator of life who sees in El Toreo only another phase of that cruelty and indifference which surrounds and permeates and tinges nature crimson?

The fourth bull brought death to a novillero: he had killed the first bull in fine style, received acclaim and the band's diana. But they try so hard, these novilleros, to please, to show their skill and daring, to win their spurs. He met the bull's charge on his knees. He was caught and gored. He lay so quiet in the sand as the bull rushed over him towards the frantic capes which could not save him now. They carried him from the arena—his head stretched back.

June 27. Tina returned from the city with a pie, the first we have had in Mexico. "Guastaroba bought it for me," she said. "I wanted some pastries from a street vendor, but he said, 'No, they are dirty. Instead we'll go into this bakery and I'll buy you one of those round things the Americans make.'"

I have been assured from many sources that a new revolution coincident with election time is inevitable. I have decided to get out, if for no other reason than that I cannot afford to stay through another such outbreak. But there is another reason, the war between my heart and brain.

For example, yesterday, Rafael, Tina, Felipe, and I went to Churubusco. I did a lot of setting up and focussing, but not an exposure. From there we went to San Angel and el Carmen with the same result.

Both places were quite too beautiful, the element of possible discovery was lacking, that thrill which comes from finding beauty in the commonplace.

All the splendour of Mexico, aside, of course, from nature, lies in its past; the present here is an imposed artificiality, lacking the crude and chaotic but vital and naturally functioning growth of the big American cities.

To be sure, within a few hours ride from Mexico City one may find towns which are as they were two hundred years or more ago. In them I am sure life would be simple, unconstrained and colorful. But questioning myself the answer comes

"No," I could not for any length of time live such a life. It is inevitable that I shall once more be drawn into the maelstrom and complexity of today.

Sunday morning. At Prof. Goldschmidt's last eve, a new Communist group was formed. I shook my head when he asked for my name; I can afford no more complications in my life just now.

The Goldschmidts' house is rather well appointed for that of a "red" leader, and they serve elaborately, buy lovely Mexican things which make me envious – all the time complaining over hard times, and owing me money for a sitting. But the professor is not to blame, rather his dowdy little wife who is a climber and a bore.

After the meeting a crowd decided for "Salón Azteca" again, but I was too weak and dizzy to attempt dancing. For several days a bad head and an uncomfortable stomach have sickened me. Perhaps Elisa's delicious enchiladas started my troubles, or it may be eye-strain, or it may be nerves from varying complications; at all events I have been wretched.

Nevertheless I have tried to work and yesterday attempted to register cloud forms from the top of our azotea work-room. The sky was magnificent but shifted so fast that working with a stand camera proved difficult. My "arrangement" would not wait even the short time required to slip in a holder and squeeze the bulb. Upon developing, I found my subject had moved too fast for a two second exposure: I had stopped down to 256 with a Kl filter. The best negative was one looking down on our boat-like azotea, its "prow" pointing out into the intersecting streets.

July 2. My plans are taking now a definite shape and, unless something quite unforseen happens, I leave before the end of this month, for I have passes to the border which expire then. Tina got them for me. And now, "Elisa is crying over the dishpan. Chandler told her you were going away. She wants to go with you," said Tina.

Just because it seems that I am really going, many sittings are dated ahead; "business" is good! I shall need every penny, for I must raise at least 350 pesos to carry us from the border to Los Angeles. Chandler wants to stay and keep on with his school and Spanish. Tina has offered to care for him—but Flora?

Sunday July 6. Election Day! "Better stay at home today" has been the oft repeated warning. Revolution? Or no revolution? That is the question!

The bull fight needs sunshine, brilliant and hot. I have felt the lack on cloudy days. Without sun the action appears slowed, undoubtedly is. The crowd, too, is less gay and responsive. Even the band seems hoarse and wheezy, while color— the sparkle and glitter of bespangled costumes, all the dazzle of gorgeous trappings—is dulled to drabness. Yesterday's fight was a weary, dreary affair. The fifth bull was killed in a drizzling rain, and there was no protest when a sign was hung from the "Autoridad" which gave notice: "Se suspende la corrida." I watched the wet dejected crowd file out—felt their grey gloom, and was one with it for I knew that probably I had seen my last fight in El Toreo.

July 9. Clouds have been tempting me again. Next to the recording of a fugitive expression, or revealing the pathology of some human being, is there anything more elusive to capture than cloud forms! And the Mexican clouds are so swift and ephemeral, one can hardly allow the thought, "Is this worth doing?" or, "Is this placed well?"—for an instant of delay and what was, is not! The Graflex seems the only possible way of working. Yesterday's results gave me one negative worth considering: to be sure I made but three, but time and patience were spent in waiting and studying.

My eyes and thoughts were heavenward indeed—until, glancing down, I saw Tina lying naked on the azotea taking a sun-bath. My cloud "sitting" was ended, my camera turned down toward a more earthly theme, and a series of interesting negatives was obtained. Having just examined them again I am enthusiastic and feel that this is the best series of nudes I have done of Tina.

Such a day at San Cristóbal with the Salas! Really a wonderful day. We met at the station "Buena Vista" early and had reached our destination before 9:00. The air was fresh and cool, the sky dotted with round little clouds so peculiar to Mexico, the landscape—green stretches of meadow pointed with cottonwoods and maguey—backed on the horizon with hills. I carried my Graflex and before noon had made two dozen exposures, indicating well my response to the surrounding country.

Then came lunch hour: always the noontime lunch and siesta has been an unforgettable part of our excursions. Yesterday was no exception, with Tina's salad carrying off the honors. Before we had finished, the little round clouds had massed into a threatening overcast sky, and when a few rain drops spattered down we made for the nearby historical house in which Morelos was prisoner before being shot. From the upper windows we watched the rain sweep over the landscape, a soft tender rain, soon spent.

Sauntering back the two miles or so to the station, we crossed plowed ground on which was strewn broken bits of pottery. A search was indicated. I made the first find of value, a small idol,—a head— probably Aztec. It was a thrill to find one of those fascinating fragments. And then I found another, and another—four in all. My day, indeed! Monna discovered a head of the Mongoloid period in much better condition than mine which were weather worn and almost effaced. The day ended with a dash for the station to escape another shower. Evening came, and we, homeward bound in a wet train passing through the fields...

July 14. How "fast" the light here in Mexico! Most of my open landscapes of Sunday were on the verge of overtiming, yet they were stopped down to $f/32$ and had $^1/_{10}$ sec. exposure on panchromatic film using a K 1 filter. The Graflex is a spontaneous camera but lacks the precision of a view box planted firmly on a sturdy tripod. Careful as I am in focusing and releasing, many of my negatives — speaking critically — were slightly off in definition, were not as accurately seen as they might have been with my view box. But it is indeed difficult to be accurate on a $3^1/_4 \times 4^1/_4$ plate with the lens down to $f/32$ and a filter over it; and when the result is to be enlarged to 8×10, slight defects are also enlarged. Then, too, the chemical quality is never so smooth — be the care ever so great, and the loss ever so little — in an enlarged negative, as in one made direct. But I say this at the same time defying most anyone to say which are my prints from direct 8×10 negatives and which are those from enlarged negatives.

Of the exposures made at San Cristóbal I have enlarged one, a typical Mexican landscape with a fine and characteristic sky. At the same time I enlarged one of the recent nudes of Tina.

July 18. Sittings and hard work these days; trying to leave the 31st. It recalls the final days in my California studio — tense, hectic, hours. But then, at least, I had some assurance that I was leaving, eventually. Here everything is vague. Even today, less than two weeks from the date set, I am uncertain about two important items: will I acquire enough money for the trip? and — do I really want to go?

July 19. It was 7:00 o'clock of the evening. The storm had passed over but lingered on the horizon — mountainous white clouds illuminated from within by lightning. Sky rockets showered stars and bombs burst to honor Juárez' death. The Mexicans have plenty of national heroes to give them reason for celebration. If they had none, they would invent them! Holidays there must be, and often! I viewed the spectacle from our azotea. Below, from the street, the organ man ground out *Chaparrita* in competition with yelps and snarls from a dog fight. As the clouds sank from sight, a great moon rose — round — cold — metallic — a piece of polished brass. In its brilliant light the white azotea seemed snow-covered, and the chill night air completed the illusion. It might have been a frosty winter evening, instead of July. So many nights I have walked the azotea waiting for my films to wash...

The Salas gave me a farewell supper with Gupta as chef—Hindu cooking of course, and delicious indeed. Only a few were there: Charlot and his mother, Carleton Beals, Khan Khoje (how very much I like him), Olga Wolf, and Federico.

July 24. On a day when a lull or intermission came during the hurry of finishing, we dropped all work, and, cameras in hand, took the train for Amecameca y los Volcanes. It was a late afternoon train. The sun cast long shadows over a very

Mexican landscape—typical of this mesa at least: great stretches of level green, interspersed with pools of water, or sheets of water, on which floated lavendar hyacinths. On the horizon, always hills or mountains, green or grim, and above them, always clouds of infinite form. Then the train would wind through nearby hills and with every few miles, high up on some well-chosen prominence, a little chapel or larger church was patterned against the sky.

Dark! when we pulled into the village of Amecameca. A hotel was sought. There were but two, so we chose the "Hotel Sacro Monte." With tact and respect for my lady's wishes, but with certain desires and anticipations, I let Tina make arrangements for the night. If we would use one bed the price was but un peso cincuenta centavos, the dueña told us, and Tina thought we should save the extra money—to which I agreed!

With stock and white geranium from the patio we covered our pillows, a preliminary preparation to enhance the night. Well—the bed was hard, the pillows harder, and worse, lumpy. Also it was cold! The snowy breath from Ixtaccíhuatl descended upon us, and all the covers from nearby beds did not quite suffice, though snuggling close to each other did help some.

Morning came clear. From the cobbled street we looked up to the "White Woman," so silent, so aloof, above. And Popocatépetl, to the right, belching forth sculptured smoke, a majestic sight. Café con leche, we had been told, would be ready at 5:30. It was nearly 7:00 before we were served a pitcher of steaming milk and extract. But what does an hour or so matter in Mexico—except that for long we wandered chilled and hungry through the cobbled streets of Amecameca. Appeased and warmed by a breakfast simple but satisfying, we hired an Indian boy to carry the cameras, and ascended el Sacro Monte. It was a wonderland we viewed, with green valleys rising up to the snowy volcanos. El Sacro Monte was a dream place too; its church, its chapel, the flower-covered graveyard. Far back to where the graves were few and scattered we sauntered, to where the poor were resting under simple but often beautifully carved slabs.

July 30. A year ago yesterday we sailed from Los Angeles on the *Colima*. Until five o'clock last night I was undecided whether to leave Mexico tomorrow (on which day the passes were to expire), or not. After a terrific inner struggle, both emotional and intellectual, I finally realized, and decided I must stay. From this decision, today, I am having violent reactions, but I still know that I have made the only possible and logical resolve.

I have had many presents—farewell gifts. From Charlot, a watercolor—a serape-wrapped Indian—one of his best; from Pintao, un bastón—his own carving of course—something I had long coveted; from Laura and Negrete, an idol—he himself had unearthed it from his hacienda in Jalisco—a clay figure fifteen inches high, elongated forehead, exaggerated nose, stump-like arms—from which I get a tremendous thrill; and from Olga, a book for Chandler.

85

... thought of seeing the boys: that was a force which almost broke down my better judgment. Mexico seems my only hope, I have nothing else. So I had to say to myself: "Wait. Do not act too hastily. Time—even a month or two—may change everything." And conditions here? No revolution yet. Many sittings, and more in prospect...

Aug. 2. I am feeling the anti-climax of my changed plans: I hate to face my friends though they seem quite happy to find me still on deck. Somehow I remember the boy who was forever threatening suicide, until his friends, weary of talk, waited upon him in a body, requesting him to either "shut up or make good!"

Well, by remaining I can more completely realize Mexico in my work. Time is required for a new land to sink deep into one's consciousness. Also I can go on with my collecting of Indian craft work. An occasional small expenditure, and now and then a gift, has already brought me many lovely objects and recuerdos. I must make the best of my time while in exile!

4. *Landscapes and Still Life*

August 4. For months — until it had become a standing joke — I had been promising an "American breakfast" to Tina and Chandler. Sunday morning, after a long walk to insure hearty appetites, the event took place. We went to a "Lonchería Rapida" — one of those places into which drift unassimilated 100% citizens of the U.S., looking for a little "home atmosphere" and "substantial" American cooking. I don't know whether hot cakes and corn syrup are more substantial than tortillas and frijoles, but they tasted good for a change, and so did the ham & eggs, and coffee American style. The atmosphere was American enough, being that of our great institution for prospective dyspeptics — the "Quick Lunch Counter."

From this nourishing repast Tina and I went on another lark; we had our pictures taken! This too had been talked over and the idea flirted with, for if ever I have seen ludicrously funny "portraiture" it has been in Mexico City in the show cases of the cheap photographers. After much hesitating and speculation over the various displays, we climbed the steep stairs to a comical little studio and were waited on by the "artist" in person — himself a cartoon.

"We have been married just a year today," said Tina coyly. "We wish a photo to commemorate our anniversary. El Señor is very religious, perhaps you can put a church in the background; and I should like to hold these lovely flowers," pointing to a dusty, dirty bunch of roses. "But you will have better ideas than we — your pictures are so artistic!"

The photographer beamed with satisfaction from the compliment and bustled around in excited preparation. I was seated; Tina stood with her hand on my shoulder; to one side a plaster Christ; the background a vaulted church interior. Purposely I sat as stiff as possible: feet together, hands outspread on knees. But alas, I couldn't get away with it. The artist insisted I cross my feet, and, in desperation over my hands, placed a book in them.

It was all over before we knew it. "Your light is very good," said Tina. "Yes," said the photographer, "I study the latest lighting effects from the U.S.," pointing to a pile of *Studio Light* magazines!...

Presto! and the church behind us changed to a spring landscape, the Christ to a beflowered pedestal, and we held hands while the artist snapped his shutter. The last, in which the romantic temperament of the Mexican reached a climax: in front of the same leafy landscape, on a rustic "something," Tina sat reading a book. (As I leaned over her shoulder I noted it was tables of U. S. Railway statistics!) My hands were on her shoulder and at the critical moment she was told to turn and gaze up into my eyes — click-click — and "exhibit A" for a future divorce case was made. "Funny if he should put this in his show case, Tina!"

"You wish a deposit?" "Any amount you wish to leave." "And the proofs?" "They will be ready Tuesday." Out on the street again?: I thought I must explode with laughter," said Tina. "How did we keep a straight face?"

To complete a full day, and to celebrate my remaining in Mexico, I went to El Toreo in the afternoon. Until the fifth bull I cursed my luck and came near to leaving, for the bulls were but heifers which ran away so fast that neither man nor horse could approach them — it was a game of catch-the-bull rather than dodge it, and I was thoroughly disgusted. But the fifth bull brought a sensation. I had seen advertised that "Armillita Chico" would fight, which — since I did not know of him, meant nothing to me.

This is what I saw. A thirteen-year-old boy, dressed in a black conventional suit, wearing a school boy's cap, stepped into the arena, faced his bull — which though small was a spirited animal — and fought not only bravely, but with such finesse that he was awarded that great honor, the bull's tail! Diana after diana was played for him during the fight; the audience was in a bedlam of uproarious joy; a future hero had appeared on the horizon; they stayed on their feet shouting appreciation, and I was one of them!

His cape work was fine; he kneeled to the bull, among other tricks of the trade; he placed the banderillas and executed the estocada like a veteran. It was a perfect fight. The boy was modest too. He looked around almost bashfully, smiling appreciation as he held up his trophy — the tail — to the thundering applause above. Not only hats, canes, overcoats, but money too, showered down upon him, and with the fight's finish, a crowd of excited little boys broke into the arena, hoisted him to their shoulders, and marched triumphantly away.

August 8. Ricardo Robelo is dead... and though this has been expected for long the news is saddening. I have seen nothing of Robelo since my exhibit last autumn; in his sickness he preferred to remain away. Our actual contacts — even in LA — were few, but always intense, and he will ever be recalled as a vivid personality and fine friend.

Have finished one of the San Cristóbal landscapes, and also printed a cloud negative, photographed last month. Both please. The cloud print is a subtle, delicate and emotional thing.

Yesterday, from a Prof. Millard Rosenberg who came to be photographed, I had one of the sincerest appreciations of my work that I have received in Mexico.

Sunday evening. We sprung a surprise, that of our late photographic adventure, on the Saturday night crowd. The one holding hands, and the other group with the plaster Christ, were finished and placed conspicuously in the studio room. They brought shrieks of laughter, and they were worthy! To Jean and the Salas we presented copies.

August 13. After several hours — spread over a couple of days — of nerve-wracking effort, I at last pulled a good print from the negative of the "Valle de San Juan Teotihuacán." I did not waste so much paper as the foregoing may indicate, but made endless tests for time and contrast. I wanted the maximum of brilliancy in the clouds while yet retaining detail. The addition of Bichromate to the developer — to the point where my clouds were satisfactorily brilliant — rendered the sky dark, apparently over-corrected. Yet, I would ponder to myself, those brilliant clouds against the deep blue sky can only be shown as very white against a background contrastingly dark. But the dark sky of the print — correct in monochrome — was to the eye a most resplendent blue.

The final achievement, and I am pleased with the print which is *straight*, shows the trees as the darkest note; then the sky at the top of the print next in tone, which becomes lighter and lighter as it blends to the horizon, quite as though I had used a graduated filter; then the distant hills which are darker than the valley itself, and finally the white and static clouds which hang over the landscape as though permanent, unchangeable. For actual visual correction the use of even a K2 — 3-time filter with panchromatic film, is dangerous here in Mexico, and a K3 filter (for "absolute correction") would often produce a quite incorrect result.

The most pleasing compliment that a Mexican can give me is to say that I have really *felt* Mexico deeply and sincerely. This compliment I have had on numerous occasions.

August 14. Another landscape from San Cristóbal now printed. It rings rather novel for me to be writing of my "landscapes," practically the first I have done since I began photography as a boy some twenty years ago. The reason, lack of time and opportunity — though, after all, mainly lack of desire. But I do respond to nature as she is presented here in Mexico. This view is a beauty, a real joy to me: silhouetted trees against low hills for a narrow base line, and a sky expanse showing cloud forms quite at variance — a long line of cumulous clouds forming another base, and above, a reach of delicate fleecy clouds — a combination of contrasts quite typical.

An evening with Pintao — smoking his cheap but good cigars, eating his medley of sweets, and sharing his wine. It is all but incomprehensible to me how a man who does such really great wood carving can display such poor taste in other things. He showed us a head of Christ which some friends had painted and presented to him, which was not even an interesting abomination — it was simply inane — and he showed it with pride. But one does note such anomalies amongst simple naive peoples who produce unconsciously craft work of great beauty, but are completely lost outside of their own narrow circle of comprehension — are utterly lacking in discrimination.

August 15. Photographed Marguerite Agniel, an American dancer here on vacation. Made nudes: except for two negatives of legs, failed. Was too worn out; must rest. Expect to go to Cuernavaca, Monday, for several days vacation.

Sunday, August 24. Back home after five days in Cuernavaca, where we had the use of Mrs. Moats' lovely house for the week. The place was a surprise to us — a pleasant one, for the country home of a wealthy American was pictured in advance as something quite different from the delightful place we found, with rooms high up overlooking and surrounding a sunken patio. From the patio, steps led to the balcony and rooms above.

Cuernavaca is built among hills, in a country luxuriantly tropical; the houses with sloping roofs of tile, the streets cobbled and well kept — in fact Cuernavaca had an air of well-being that few Mexican towns have. There are many things to remember...

(The Borda Gardens)

Here was a synthesis of Mexico's tragedy and decay, though the Gardens, being of Italian design, took one somewhat out of Mexican or Spanish atmosphere. One evening we swam the great lagoon lined with banana and coffee and mango trees. Impossible to work photographically in the Borda Gardens, quite too picturesque.

But in the garden of Fred Davis I responded to a towering palm which, seen through my short focus lens with the camera tilted almost straight up, seemed to touch the sky. I have already printed from the negative and those who have seen it respond with exclamations of delight. It's a great cylindrical, almost white trunk, brilliant in the sun, topped by a circle of dark but sungleaming leaves; it cuts the plate diagonally from a base of white clouds. Then one day I photographed details of a small but most interesting pyramid near the city, a structure contemporary with those of San Juan Teotihuacán. From four of these negatives I have printed; fine technical negatives, revealing well the massive solidity of the masonry which has stood the weathering of centuries.

The town itself was again too picturesque to photograph. It was so theatrical, so dramatic, that unless one became used and hardened to it, living there would be as mentally exhausting as spending all week in an art gallery or sitting all day in a theater.

Jean Charlot, Federico Marín, Anita and Dorothea Brenner spent two of the days with us.

90

August 26. I have returned, after several years use of Metol Hydroquinone open-tank developer, to a three-solution Pyro developer, and I develop one at a time in a tray instead of a dozen in a tank! I am quite pleased with my new negatives, and with the flexibility of my pyro developer, nor do I bewail the extra hours in the "cuarto obscuro," though now I shall be more than ever careful not to expose on an ill-considered subject. My professional portraits I shall continue to run through a tank in the old way. More and more I realize I must conserve my strength for the work that I love.

Another conserver of strength and saver of time has been the retouching of all my professional sittings by a paid retoucher. The work seldom means anything to me beyond money, the public does not appreciate any difference in results, so why should I ruin my eyes and tax my nerves! My one regret is that I must sign these prints; may they soon fade into obscurity!

The purchase of that cheap Rectilinear lens was of the utmost importance to me: gone are all my flare spots, internal reflections — yet unknowing ones remark on what a fine lens I must have! I have, but it is relegated and forgotten.

The print from the new palm negative is chemically and emotionally beautiful. It is the result of only two attempts, the first one — but for a defect in the paper — would have been as good. Most of the prints from negatives made with direct creative intent are also the result of but little experimenting; usually two or three prints suffice. Or rather I should say that because of the cost I can afford to make but few prints, sometimes but one — and of course I am not always entirely happy. "If I could only use one more sheet of paper," I say to myself, and then stoically, though regretfully, seal the can of palladiotype, promising myself to someday reprint all my favorite negatives. By that time, perhaps far distant, all my present favorites may be in the discard!

August 31. Monna said to me last night, seeing my new photograph of the palm. "Ah, Edward, that is one of the finest things you have ever done. Aesthetically it has the same value as your smoke stacks." Monna's opinion is always of interest to me.

Just the trunk of a palm towering up into the sky; not even a real one — a palm on a piece of paper, a reproduction of nature: I wonder why it should affect one emotionally — and I wonder what prompted me to record it. Many photographs might have been done of this palm, and they would be just a photograph of a palm — Yet this picture *is* but a photograph of a palm, plus something — something — and I cannot quite say what that something is — and who is there to tell me?

Sunday, September 7. ...today I am so weary, so very, very tired; and the bull fight was a poor one...

September 11. Rain and an overcast sky for over a week. Unable to print palladio. Sittings though, four of them; if I don't watch out I may make money. That would be funny. Remembering my inspired manifesto — "To work, Edward Weston" — I'll state that I have been working hard enough, but not in the intended sense of my proclamation, when I had a vision of glorious new achievements. My work has been drudgery. I should be glad of these sittings — as a means to an end; that end, money for more films, more paper, for other work that I want to do.

There is definite talk of Brett coming here, if someone is found to bring him. Flora wants him with me. Better with me, to be sure; no woman is fit to bring up a boy. How can they possibly understand them!...

September 16. I am desperate over this continued cloudy weather, yet I used to love grey days: it must be that now it prevents my working. After having lived in California and more especially Mexico, I feel that never again would it be possible to remain long in a land of rain and mist. I am not even provoked to make negatives these drab days.

One should do something just as significant while the rain falls and clouds hang low, but I at least am not aroused; perhaps because I am not visually excited as by the definite form which the sun invests. Today I am going to expose at least one negative on anything or person that passes my lens, if it be no more than to again open and close my shutter—

September 17. I kept my vow and exposed several negatives on Felipe. Today is Tina's big day: she appears in the initial performance of the Mexican *Chauve Souris* — el *Teatro Mexicano del Murciélago* — Mexican Theater of the Bat.

September 20. That tinkling tune from my Aunt's old music-box returns again to recall my childhood, and her earthenware crock of fresh doughnuts and white sugar cookies.

The *Chauve-Souris*? Well done for an initial attempt though somewhat reminiscent of the original production and lacking its finish. Tina? A difficult part, which might easily have become melodramatic, done with restraint and understanding. The native dancers brought from tierra caliente in the acts "Juego de los Viejitos" and "Danza de los Moros" were excellent — the latter indeed superb. The act "Camiones" was a side-splitting burlesque, but of local interest only. Those who had never seen Mexico City would not appreciate it.

Sun at last! Orders printed and new negatives made, which show a return to life! I worked from the azotea, pointing my camera searchingly in every possible direction. The best negatives, those looking down on nearby roofs and houses: an attempt to amalgamate widely diverse objects, to unify them, to present them as a complex but coherent whole.

Sunday. Today [at Azcopotzalco] we, the Salas and Westons, had agua miel—honey water—for the first time, freshly drawn for us from the maguey. ¡Qué dulce! ¡Qué fresca! ¡Qué sabrosa—delicious!

The patio of the most important church there captivated me. The only vegetation was a superb banana tree in the exact center, offering as interesting an object for the attack of my camera as did the palm at Cuernavaca. I shall return there, for with my Graflex I could not register definitely what I felt might be done with the 8 × 10 view camera.

September 22. Over the roughest road yet encountered in Mexico — and that is damning it sufficiently — Turnbull, Chandler, and I... to the Santuario de Nuestra Señora de los Remedios. The sight there was not the church, but the old aqueduct with its curious towers like those of Babel, built by the Spaniards in 1620. The span of the aqueduct is of simple and elegant lines. It drew me to expose two negatives, looking up from almost directly underneath.

Difficult to work when one is guest, and the rest are waiting, even though good-naturedly. But these free trips to remote points are not to be overlooked, rather considered as scouting expeditions, for one can always return if sufficiently interested.

The evening I spent alone among the ever-fascinating puestos, purchasing for ridiculously small amounts more animals of clay — a bull, a horse, a pig — executed with fine feeling for essential peculiarities of form, or as in the pig, painted with a keen sense of decoration. Then the tiny figures in metal: the charro a-horse with raised banderillas — what grace! what elegance! what understanding of anatomy! These Indians never went to "Art School." And again the sense of humor shown: the long-legged, pink-legged, lamb, with its silliest of faces...

Always when I go to the puestos I think of my little boys, and picture their wide-eyed wonderment and their sure cries of delight — "O buy this, daddy!" Then, arm-laden, we would walk joyfully home together.

September 30. A big day of printing — the first day possible for palladio printing in three weeks: results, fourteen prints from as many negatives. Perhaps I attempted too much. I view the results rather pessimistically tonight, but "the morning is wiser than the evening," recalling a saying from the Russian Folk Tales which I used to read the boys.

Today I feel is the first day of winter, not by the calendar, to be sure but because not all day long did one cloud appear—¡qué milagro—how micraculous! Too, there was a crispness to the air not of the balmy rains.

Several negatives printed are new, made during this last cloudy week when I turned to my camera for diversion and consolation. Still-lifes they are, and pleasing ones: two fishes and a bird on a silver screen; head of a horse against my petate; chayotes in a painted wooden bowl. The animals of course are from the puestos. The bird is a beauty indeed — a blue heron, bill and feet red, neck turned over its back to almost a completed circle — a lovely thing in line, but done by nature (albeit nature improved by man) for the bird is a painted gourd. However the horse and leopard owe nothing to nature but inspiration. The horse is Chinese in feeling — a 7th century porcelain perhaps! Charlot, seeing it, hied himself at once to the puestos to find another; disappointed, he playfully attempts to steal mine on every occasion.

These still-lifes, strange to say, are the first I have ever done; and feeling quite sure they number among my best things, I would comment on how little subject matter counts.

Other new prints which please are the complicated "arrangements" of our neighbor's azotea and nearby houses. My technique and understanding of photography improves. A torso of the dancer Agniel is as fine a nude as I have ever done — a simple and very sensitive rendering of line. Unfortunately, due to careless use of an old developing hanger, the negative has stained edges and I was forced to use lamp-black on the print — very little — and not one person in a hundred would know — but I do — and it spoils my joy!

A block of houses, though rather ugly new ones, crowned by a pyramid of fine clouds gives me a real kick. Again technique and understanding of photography.

One of my favorite new negatives I despair of getting a good platinum print of: it is a sky with delicate white cloud forms. After repeated attempts I must admit that my original print on Azo, made to study, pleases me more than the platinum. The *Gaslight* print is more nebulous, more subtle, and its colder color more suitable. I shall try once more. The portrait of Sala is a good likeness, and a satisfactory print.

October 2. After trying again to improve my printing of the new cloud negative, I have given up until some future day, to try it on white-stock platinum. My print of yesterday is an improvement, but not yet what I visualize! The trouble is this: the slight tone of the stock is just enough to destroy the more subtle gradations in the clouds, their delicate brilliancy, and with the addition of bichromate to gain the brilliancy of the Azo print, I cut the clouds out against the sky in a way that makes them look pasted on. Admitted, indeed, that one peculiarity of the summer clouds here is this very way in which they are "cut out" against the sky — great white everchanging, swiftly shifting forms, against a ground of the deepest blue — still there is an exaggeration in my print that is not satisfactory. I shall bide my time. I cannot afford to keep white stock on hand — I seldom need it, the buff being better for my professional work. But I did pull a print yesterday to compensate for my other failure: a new printing of my palm. It is dazzling in its brilliance, and the improvement shows what might be done by repeated experiments.

I mounted and had ready the new prints to show at a supper Tina and Federico prepared Wednesday night — she cooking spaghetti, he furnishing the wine. An agreeable and congenial crowd: the Salas, Felipe, Federico, Gupta, Khan Koji, Anita, Charlot, Tina, Chandler, and myself; how many nationalities! Catalonian, Spanish, Mexican, Italian, Jewish, French, Hindu, and Gringo! I had sufficient interest and enthusiasm shown in my new work to repay my efforts — such opinions as: (from Felipe) "The best you have done in Mexico..."

Now I have set me a new task — that of making ten enlarged negatives from Graflex films selected from my work of the last eight months. I have in mind a new exhibit, to be entirely Mexican, and every print made since the last show of a year ago. Something must be done to stimulate "business," for alas, finances are very low again.

October 4. Tina sat to me yesterday morning. We had long planned that I should do her as I have often seen her, quoting poetry — to attempt the registration of her remarkably mobile face in action. There was nothing forced in this attempt, she was soon in a mood which discounted me and my camera — or did she subconsciously feel my presence and respond to it? Within twenty minutes I had made three dozen Graflex negatives and caught her sensitive face with its every subtle change.

Monday October 6. We have been like a couple of happy excited children, Tina and I, over the results of our recent sitting — but also sad with disappointment, for though the series of heads are the most significant I have ever made, though my vision on the ground glass and my recognition of the critical moment for release were in absolute accord with her emotional crises, I failed technically through underexposure, just the slight undertiming which destroys chemical continuity in a set of negatives made under a strong over-head light.

But why should I of all persons fail on exposure? I had figured to a nicety, $1/_{10}$ sec., $f/11$, Panchro film, Graflex, knowing though that I was on the borderline of underexposure. I had placed Tina in a light calculated not to destroy expression in her eyes, and then to augment it cast reflected light down from above with an aluminum screen — an unusual procedure for me — to be using light accessories. But the sun moves in its orbit, and I, working in a state of oblivion, did not note that my reflector no longer reflected! I feel the weakness of my excuse, my intellect should not have been overwhelmed by my emotions, at least not in my work!

With a stand camera, my hand on the bulb, watching my subject, there is a coordination between my hand and brain: I *feel* my exposure and almost unconsciously compensate for any change of light. But looking into a Graflex hood with the shutter set at an automatic exposure, a fixed speed, is for me quite different. I dislike to figure out time, and find my exposures more accurate when only *felt*.

Then came another disaster in the darkroom — pure carelessness and quite mortifying. Ready to develop, I turned white light onto a dozen exposed films, ruining half of them. So Tina and I tearfully contemplate what might have been! But there are several that I simply must try to pull a print from; they are too fine to relegate to oblivion.

October 7. 4:30 A. M. and all's not well! Confound all Mexican Saints and Virgins for giving the people excuse to make noise, awakening me from a hard-earned sleep with their firecrackers. Such a night! Preparatory, I had sprinkled my sheets with flea-powder and lit three sticks of incense, which act was neither cabalistic ritual nor aesthetic indulgence, but merely self-defense against hungry hordes of mosquitos. My precautions proved futile; the fleas came and playfully leapt admist the powder, the mosquitos joyfully sang as they sailed through the smoke which nearly smothered me — not them, and it seemed I had only gained sleep when the volley of bangs in praise of the Virgin started me out of bed. "Another revolution," I thought. "Or—our neighbor, the histrionic zapatero— shoemaker—after too much pulque, has decided to exterminate his enemies." But no; once awake, the answer was simple — just a prayerful exuberance was being expressed, that was all!

Mist-like rain is falling. This irregularity forecasts the Season's end — now sun and cloudless days for many months — and next Sunday the first big fight in El Toreo.

My exhibit is to open the 15th; hard work ahead, though if necessary I could open tomorrow. Reporters came last night, and their enthusiasm indicates much acclaim. But business is what I need — not praise!

Yes, my work is far in advance of last year; the striving, the sweat — though expended — is not so obvious in the prints.

October 8. Tentative discussion under way with Flora over the possibility of my returning New Year's for a visit. I favor the plan, for I cannot remain away much longer from the boys.

I am utterly exhausted tonight after a whole day in the darkroom, making eight contact negatives from the enlarged positives.

At dusk, clouds over the moon's face were pink fading into grey against a sky ground of pastel blue.

During lunch hour we were interrupted by an Indian who beseeched and besieged us to buy carbon because his poor burro was too tired to carry it further!

October 11. Have been quite sick — fever and incipient sore throat. Lay all day on my bed in a half stupor, unable to work; fasted and sweat myself and am practically well again. I am ever thankful that doctors play no part in my life — that is, doctors with pills and knives — nor Christian Scientists, nor their like. A day lost.

96

With the opening day of my exhibit near, it is too bad — for we have endless detail ahead.

Too bad also that I should have blamed the Virgin, or some Virgin, for the recent cannonading: it was the celebration of the Eucharist taking place. A great conclave is now here. The city is bedecked in a ridiculous fashion —Independence Day in comparison becomes a minor event. Catholicism has yet a tremendous hold on the people, despite the government and constitution. The priests must have much inward satisfaction and security these days. Everywhere are more or less pretentious signs announcing, "Viva Cristo Rey" — even over a dirty pulquería named "La Gran Turca" — The Great Drunk! My mistake in blaming the Virgin for all this noise — my biblical knowledge is lacking!

Sunday, October 20. Wednesday the exhibit opened. I have had — as last year — applause; real homage — yes, even more than last year — and as before, the men far outnumber the women in attendance and interest. I am pleased, not satisfied, with my prints as they display themselves to me on the wall. No question but that I have gone ahead. And then comes the question, what next? An exhibit is always a climax to a certain period: once shown, a print becomes definitely a part of one's past; if not actually discarded, it is relegated to a portfolio of old loves, to be referred to at times with perhaps no more than tender memories.

Three prints sold the second day — all nudes — and to the same person, for ninety pesos. One was of Tina, one of Marguerite Agniel — "Dancer's Legs," and an old one of Ruth Wilton.

The most talked of photographs in the exhibit are the heads of Galván, Lupe and Nahui Olín, and several of Tina. The clouds excite much interest, praise and comment; also the new work done with my Mexican toys. Nahui is a bit "enojado" – annoyed – that I should display such a revealing portrait of her, though I had her permission before hanging... Now she wishes me to do nudes of her — and I shall. Several sittings seem assured as the result of my show, so for awhile yet we eat and pay rent.

Amazing news: for the first time in Mexico, a letter from Johan, and quite characteristically Johan. "What shall I say — I have so much to say — how can I say it — but why — why shall I say it here — in a medium so inadequate — when I can choose a better one — and have chosen! I shall come to see you in Mexico — visit and talk with you to my own heart's desire: Yes, I shall come — I must — and if fate is not against me — not so very long from now. I shall get things in readiness here for my going — perhaps in a month or so. Edward — I am happy — the joy — the thrill to see you again —. to be together once more and in Mexico at that — until I see you! Au revoir! Johan."

Well, this is astounding! Unbelievable. Yet I am perplexed. If I return for New Year's to see the boys, should I encourage Johan to come now? If he waited we could return here together. But the question is always flitting through my mind, will I ever return to Mexico again? What a joy indeed to have Johan here — for us to see Mexico together!

And another letter came which brought memories, it was signed "your own J." She is in California; perhaps we are to meet again!

And yet another letter, a screamingly funny one from Brett. "I weigh 113 pounds of meat — blood — bones — fat — grease and especially brains and muscle. I am 5 ft. 3¹/₂ inches tall — Have you (still) got a cute little mustache? I sure did like those pictures you sent of Chandler — He still has that big nose and fat chin and dirty mouth and sticking-out ears and yellow cat eyes. I could take on about 13¹/₂ just like him and maybe more, but of course that has nothing to do with my *good looks*. I am just about the craziest writer in the whole school and everybody knows it too. I'm sorry I can't write you a half way decent looking letter. Just before we went to the beach I had my head shaved clear off. Hot soup — Brett." Dear old Brett Boy! I'll appreciate you even more after this long separation.

October 31. Diego and Lupe came to the exhibit yesterday — he large and lumbering as ever, she big with child. Diego showed his usual enthusiasm over photography, and immediately became involved in an argument with some other painter on the subject. "I would 40,000 times rather have a good photograph than a realistic painting," he stated, and dismissed his opponent with a wave of his hand. He liked my "Circus Tent" best of all, also the new still lifes of fishes and horses and birds immensely.

Dr. Atl has visited too, and registered in the guest-book as finding even greater interest than last year. Viewing my "Colonia Condesa," he said, "This means nothing, yet it means everything." Dr. Atl is a unique personality, and far more valuable as such than as a painter. Maria Appendini wrote in my guest book, "Un Nuevo Tormento—a New Torment."

The general attendance has been good — greater than last year: many promised purchases, but so far no money! With the evening hour arrive familiar faces who drift in to talk and smoke: Charlot, the Salas, the Quintanillas, Felipe, Roberto. Felipe, by the way, is to open a puesto in "El Volador"! With books and antiques, it will be called "El Murciélago—the Bat—" and decorated in *Chauve-Souris* style. What a unique adventure!

A few lines from B.: "You are ever a definite part of me — people's lives are like threads — some of them cross our own and remain forever part of the pattern – the Attic days of ridiculous and delicious humour, of daring and romance — I shall ever bless you for that fall — Saw Jack Taylor — he is well and happy in New York — Be well and be near to me always for I love you —."

October 22. Came Herr Goldschmidt, with his hearty embrace — more like a bear-hug — his tickling of the ribs, his infectious laugh. ¡Qué hombre más simpático! He insisted again that I must exhibit in Berlin.

How tiresome it becomes to be polite to all those who come — yet the pleasure from genuine appreciation is compensating; and the Mexicans can be so intense, so excited, so passionate in their felicitations as to buoy one up into a like state of exaltation and belief in one's work!

Of course, I hear that I must have a marvellous lens or extraordinary camera— instead of a lens with shutter and all for 20 pesos, and a camera quite gone to ruin! Not many realize that good photographs — like anything else — are made with one's brains.

Charlot said, "I am going to work out the geometrical plan from some of your photographs which are so exact as to appear calculated." No, Jean, to stop and calculate would be to lose most of them.

Diego, Tina tells me, also expressed delight over my "Fruta de Barro"—Clay Fruit—and "Caballito de Cuarenta Centavos"—Forty-cent Horse. When Galván saw the title to this picture of my little horse, he said, "You're Gringo all right; you paid too much."

But it is not my little horse any more; Charlot's desire for it was so great that I could not be comfortably selfish any longer, and sent the caballito to fresh pastures. Charlot's pleasure was expressed concretely — he wandered in last night with a water-color sketch under his arm. "To Edward, my first Boss — Horsie." It was a humorous thing, and I told Charlot that either he had fed horsie too well on beef-steak or else "he" had become a wee bit pregnant! The painting was signed "Fot. Silva", which starts another tale.

That mad Mexican photographer came yesterday, tells Tina, and after raving and waving and tearing his hair went up to a certain "Torso", exclaiming, "Ah, this is mine — it was made for me — I could —" and with that he clawed the print from top to bottom with his nails, utterly ruining it. Tina was horrified and furious, but it was too late. "I will talk to Sr. Weston," said Silva. "The print is mine, I must have it!" Tina was called away and later found that the mount had been signed — "Propiedad de Silva". I don't know whether Silva is really mad or only staging pretended temperament; if the latter, I could quite graciously murder him. Either way the print is ruined.

October 25. Dr. Peter, who has been my best patron in Mexico, bought from the wall "Pirámide del Sol" for 30.00. Mr. Fred Davis, in whose Cuernavaca garden I photographed the great Palm, purchased a copy for the same amount, and Mr. McGuire was so in love with the head of Neil that I sold him an extra print for half-price, knowing that he could not afford to pay the full. A lawyer who purchased three nudes has failed to return with the money, so this is the rather discouraging way sales stand at present. I have assured sittings ahead, so something has been accomplished besides glory; but the glory has been sweet and I shall ever be grateful to the Mexicans for their fine attitude and appreciation.

Lupe has her baby, a girl. Diego says it looks like a tadpole and that he could put it in his pocket!

Sunday evening, October 26. On returning from "El Toreo" — Matadores Valencia I y Valencia II — and bad bulls. My ideal of a toreador is Valencia el primero ...he fights with such dare-devil audacity, such smilling nonchalance, such dazzling nerve, and he maintains such mastery over the bull, controlling its every move with his elusive flourish of the cape and fearless posture...

With poor matadors, nothing is so tiresome or so disgusting as a prolonged attempt to deliver the estocada; it reeks of the slaughter-house. With certain toreadors, no matter how brave, one feels their imminent danger, awaits in a tense and uncomfortable excitement their inevitable fate; with others — and they are the real artists — one loses all sense of their personal danger, watching the pageant in all its elegance, entirely oblivious to possible death. So does the great artist, by ease and command of execution, dissemble the means to his end.

Roi Partridge writes me, after receiving the forwarded prints: "I am always most agreeably surprised by your technique. Sir, aside from what you may or may not be as an artist, you are a damned good craftsman — none better."

October 28. Rain fell in my dream last night; this morning the streets are dry. I have a desire to work after this long spell of inaction: day after day at the exhibit, seemingly a waste of time, though between visitors I have some moments for writing, also much opportunity for contemplation, a chance to size up my work and more especially myself.

The most important visitor recently has been El Señor José Vasconcelos, ex Ministro de Educacion Publica. He was deeply interested, particularly in the clouds, and requested seven prints for publication in his magazine *La Antorcha* – The Torch.

A much bejewelled and super-haughty French dame came, who, asking my prices, drew up in feigned surprise or misunderstanding. How I despise that trick of pretending not to hear correctly! "What? Three for ninety pesos!" "Yes, Madame, really quite *cheap*, eh?" I overlooked her pretenses and she was properly squelched. She could not resist telling me that Zuloaga had painted her. Then I scored, for she made a date for a sitting!

October 31. Jean Charlot wandered into the exhibit at evening, rather woebegone and discouraged: that is Mexico, it either raises one to ecstacy or dumps one into depths. We took him out to dine, Tina and I, prosaically filling him with hotcakes. Nahui Olín joined us, we met her on the way; then all four of us went to Nahui's house. Jean, who knows her well, defined Nahui as genius opposed to talent. At times brilliant in the extreme both in writing and painting, she is again commonplace, without discrimination, discounting her own best work, insisting on her worst. We spent two hours listening to her poems and prose and satires written in both French and Spanish.

November 1. The exhibit is over. The naked balcony walls presented a sad and stripped void as we glanced back to be assured no print was forgotten; but no time for tears, for already a new exhibit is on! Tina and I for the first time are showing together; indeed, it is her first public showing, and I am proud of my dear "apprentice." We went directly from the "Aztec Land" and under the auspices of the Secretaría de Educación Pública hung ten prints each in the Palacio de Minería. It is a big affair: Rafael, Charlot, Felipe among our friends are also showing.

November 2. El Día de los Muertos. Like mushrooms magically appearing over night, los puestos — in celebration of the Day of the Dead — once more are with us. More numerous, more varied than ever, they line both sides of two blocks and the street centres as well, I wondered and searched untiringly for my occasional concrete reward; this time I found more "Mexican porcelains" — animales de barro – clay animals — a magenta-colored dog mouthing a green basket, excellent in form, and, at the same booth, a wildcat biting into a green snake...

Returning late from the puestos, company awaited. Bert and Ella Wolf had brought to see us Scott Nearing, American Socialist. From one hour's contact I would say that he was a typical labor-leader, a preacher, pedagogic and pedantic — but then, that is his mission! And, after all, he may have another side on closer acquaintance. Few of us give ourselves freely on first contact.

Yesterday, with the band's salute, President Obregón formally opened the exhibit at the Palacio de Minería. Our photographs are simply and well displayed. Tina's lose nothing by comparison with mine — they are her own expression.

Sunday Evening. D. H. Lawrence, English author and poet, in with Louis Quintanilla. My first impression was a most agreeable one. He will sit for me Tuesday.

Monday. After experiencing the ever-recurrent condition of being "broke", I have sold two prints: "Palma Cuernavaca", and a nude; besides, I have four definite dates for sittings. Such prosperity is overwhelming!

Tomorrow I dine at a luncheon in honor of the United States Ambassador to Mexico. God knows his name — I don't — but duty calls. In preparation I trimmed the fringe from my trousers and borrowed a hat from Rafael. Now to buy a collar and I shall be ready for the fray.

Tuesday Evening. The sitting of D. H. Lawrence this morning. A tall, slender, rather reserved individual with a brick-red beard. He was amiable enough and we parted in a friendly way, but the contact was too brief for either of us to penetrate more than superficially the other: no way to make a sitting. Perhaps I should not have attempted it; now I actually lack sufficient interest to develop my plates.

The dinner to "our" ambassador! How "United States," how childlike! "Our country right or wrong," "moral example to the world," "business — business — business —."

Wednesday. The D. H. Lawrence negatives were not technically up to standard — damn the ambassador's banquet for my hurry! Now it amounts to this: unless I pull a technically fine print from a technically fine negative, the emotional or intellectual value of the photograph is for me almost negated, no matter how fine the original feeling and impulse.

Thursday, 6. I dread these two months to come before Christmas, despite the foreseen influx of pesos. Many sittings are in prospect, meaning a period of concentrated hard work. One might as well be in Java or London or anywhere else during this work which closes one in the dark-room or hides one under a focusing cloth.

My "life" in Mexico is already over, for I am returning to Los Angeles after Christmas. There can be from now on but little time for excursions or work that I want to do. I have a quite definite feeling that once I leave Mexico I shall never return, at least not for many years; once with the children again, I know how difficult it will be to part with any of them, and I cannot have them all. Also Tina and I must surely separate forever.

November 10. Saturday night with Charlot to Teatro Hidalgo, where was given the annual performance of an old traditional Spanish play, *Don Juan Tenorio*, the hero being that same gallant knave whose name we use when alluding to one who is a devil among women as a Don Juan. He was surely a hero to the audience, who watched wide-eyed and listened breathlessly while he conquered innumerable women and killed his rivals. All the time we were constrained to silent laughter at the naïveté of the performance, at the quite ingenuous presentation, the obvious hocus-pocus, and stage clap-trap; indeed, we enjoyed the show so much that when the curtain went down upon the last scene — Don Juan and the beautiful nun on their heavenly throne surrounded by a bevy of pink-clad girls, both fat and lean, dancing to Mendelssohn's Spring Song — we too joined in the applause, though from quite a different reason.

Tina and Pepe also came, joining us. Between acts Pepe and I went out to smoke; we wandered up and down, arms about each other's waists, each thinking his own thoughts — but speaking of the weather!

November 11. Madame Charlot served Jean and me one of her delectable suppers — "Mexican," she called the meal, but methinks it had a marked French accent!

17. Pulquería, Mexico, D. F., 1926

18. NEIL, ASLEEP, 1925

19. Johan Hagemeyer, 1925

20. NEIL, NUDE, 1925

21. NUDE, 1925

22. EXCUSADO, 1925

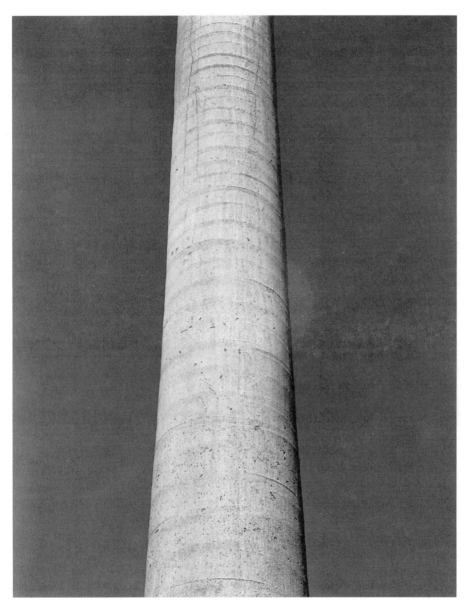

23. PALMA CUERNAVACA, II, 1925

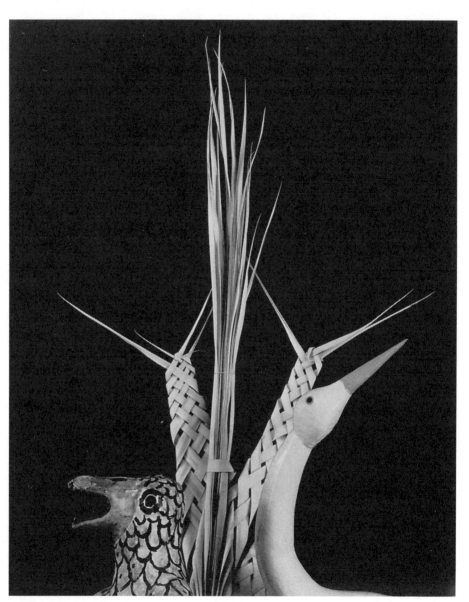

24. Palma Santa, 1926

Jean is a prolific worker. "I am never happy unless I am working," he said; he is a tireless, never satisfied experimentalist. I note a tremendous growth in his work since the year ago I met him. He renders the quintessence of Mexico...

For me he is the most important artist — aside from Diego and Pintao — whose work I have known in Mexico, and I somehow sense that someday he will be the greatest of the three.

We talked last night of a joint exhibit — his paintings, my photographs of Mexico — to be given some day in New York. The idea appeals to me indeed.

Mr. Fred Davis of the "Sonora News Co." is, as Brett might say, a "good scout," for when I boldly suggested, in desperation over my ragged clothes, that I would exchange photographs for clothing from his store, he fell in with the plan at once. "Get what you wish," he said. "The more you take the better I shall like it." I came away with new pyjamas, shoes, hat, suit, neckties, amounting to 200 pesos.

Well, dawn is upon me. I go to prepare, and, despite the foreseen enrichment, rather reluctantly, for the ten o'clock sitting.

Chandler wears his first pair of long trousers — my old suit with but little alterations!

The next morning. Through my window a pink and blue symphony: the background sky-blue, the pattern geranium-pink. I awakened to it from profound slumber, almost startled. Where was I? Why, yes, Mexico, of course! And last night Tina and I had talked and talked for hours, trying once more to reconcile and adjust our lives to each other.

The conversation centered on the future, should I return here or not. "You must not decide now, Edward, wait until you reach California, then you will have more perspective. As for me, my mind is clearly focused, I want to go on with you, to be your 'apprentice' and work in photography —"

Questions and answers back and forth, a quite deep and tender and hopeful final understanding — clearer and closer than ever before. Now some five weeks of hard work; then, California!

November 15. Printed the profile of D. H. Lawrence; he, at least, is very well pleased. Jean and I visited Diego's new murals on the walls of the Secretaría stairway — quite the finest of his work. Luxuriant, tropical, complex, yet in the last analysis a conception simple and powerful: a great piece of work.

Jean and I, plus a bottle of Vermouth, took a camión for my home. We set the table and poured a glass for the unknown guest as well as ourselves; the unknown one came — it was Tina!

November 19. Tinita and I visited Diego and Lupe last eve to pay our respects to the new baby. We drank its health with a bottle of port — old Spanish, which proved to be unduly potent! We found ourselves frankly borracho and unable to conceal the fact as we swayed arm in arm down the street toward the Zócalo. "We must seem to have come straight from a pulquería, Tina!" In a laughing, rollicking mood we leaned, to collect our wits and exchange a kiss or two, against the great door to some Zaguán – entrance hall; it swung open and the astonished porter almost received us in his arms!

"Roma — Mérida — Sonora —" cried the camionero. The camión was empty and remained empty the way home, which was fortunate since our conduct and posture was a bit undignified. "Durango" was near to being passed unnoticed, but we tumbled off, handing the surprised camionero an extra diez centavos in sympathy for his poor business...

November 21. To Frontón — Juego de Pelota — with Pepe, Chandler and Tina. "You may find it more thrilling than 'los toros'," said Pepe. I did not, though it was exciting, to be sure — a game to make, by contrast, our tennis and baseball appear quite tame. The Latins evolve sports that are spectacular, sensational, dangerous, and always elegant. Every second of the play was scintillating; one fairly gasped as the pelota shot through the air like a bullet while the players executed most miraculous passes, involving dramatically tense and beautiful postures.

Preceding our departure for Frontón, a surprise was afforded us by the arrival of Charlot, Nahui Olín, Federico, Anita and several bottles of wine. They had come to celebrate! And this is why — at the recent exhibit in the Palacio de Minería, I was awarded first prize for photographs (one hundred and fifty pesos)! Quite unbelievable. I shall await undue enthusiasm until the money is collected. The honor of winning amounts to nothing: we had no real competition. Diego Rivera was on the jury, who else I know not.

November 24. Sunday in the "Secretaría" patio I made two dozen Graflex negatives of Diego Rivera. As yet they remain undeveloped. Also started an undertaking which I have already given up, that of copying his work for reproduction in a book to be published about him in Germany. It looms as too great a task without ample renumeration, which is uncertain.

There are some who feel that Diego's work is too calculated, too entirely a product of his brain. For me it is emotional as well as intellectual. For a man to paint murals twelve hours a day — sometimes even sixteen hours at a stretch — and day after day working quite as a day-laborer might, not awaiting "mood" or "inspiration", it is amazing to me how much feeling he attains in his work. Only a man of great physical strength, possessed of a brilliant mind and a big heart as well, could have done what Diego has.

Yesterday I felt, as I have before, the preoccupation of his work. Direct questions were often entirely unheard, his eyes would be utterly oblivious to surroundings

— then suddenly he would start out of himself, break into a broad, genial smile, and for a few moments Diego the dreamer was gone.

November 25. I said to Tina, having noted several interesting items in a downtown bookstore, "Let us go on a book-hunting expedition, I am hungry for a new thrill." We were successful in acquiring a number of additions to our library, mostly books reproducing the work of contemporary painters. Ferat, Grosz, Dérain, and a volume on African sculpture — what splendid things! — and how fine is Dérain!

Now my orders are printed and the stage set for more sittings. It will take many orders to pay the expenses of our return trip.

I am so lonesome to hear a word from Ramiel — why is it he does not write!

November 29. Diego, refering to my head of Galván, said, "Es un retrato— portrait—de México."

I cannot work in such feverish haste as I do with my Graflex and register quite the critical definition desired. F/11 is the smallest stop possible to use without undertiming when making portrait heads in the sun, —setting the shutter at $1/_{10}$ second and using panchromatic films, —thus when depth is required my difficulties are increased. Diego's ample belly as he sat on a packing box in the Secretaría patio, swelled forward quite like a woman pregnant, presenting much difficulty.

Jean thinks they are the most interesting set of proofs from a sitting that I have done in Mexico. Well—I do like some of them, yes, a number of them, yet I could wish, especially with Diego, that I had made something to be very enthusiastic over. In each proof I find a fault, granted a minor one, and I had hoped for a quite perfect negative from this sitting, not just because Diego is a big artist, rather because he is especially interested in my work.

Last evening we went to a "studio tea" at Fred Davis's home: a genial host, delicious food and drink, many beautiful things, mixed to be sure with an overwhelming number of bad ones. But I am impatient, I cannot enjoy social gatherings; the meeting with a few friends, one or two at a time, is the only form of contact that appeals to me.

I face the fact that I find myself really happy only when I am lost behind my camera or locked in my dark-room. So today I became happy for a while: I photographed more of my "juguetes Mexicanos", this time the "pajaritos"— little birds — in blue, —exquisite things in line. I combined two of them on my ground glass. Perhaps three negatives will be considered worth printing.

Martial music, – soldiers pass below,—a bedraggled lot but with brave front: not to be denied, dogs of sorry mien march with the procession somewhat lowering its essayed dignity. Tonight Chapultepec Castle is a blaze of light.— All this is preparation, for tomorrow is Calles inauguration.

Surely here in Mexico we live in another world for Thanksgiving Day was passed quite unremembered! — perhaps it should have been —

Sunday. Technically dissatisfied with what should have been my best photograph of "los pajaritos", I spent another several hours attempting to duplicate it: impossible to place even inanimate objects exactly as seen before. I still think my failure the best seen negative though the actual difference is ever so slight.

December 2. In the same way that I ruined part of my last sitting of Tina done two months ago, I fogged today's by turning on the white light during the development. It almost seems that fate has decreed against my doing what I wish to do in the way of portraying Tina. But one of the negatives made this morning pleases me: the glare of light on the azotea destroyed all the delicate modulations in Tina's face. It was flat and uninteresting, — too, the eyes were filled with unpleasant catch lights. I must call the sitting a failure. We shall try again tomorrow —

After ordering prints on our exchange, amounting to 230 pesos, Mr. Fred Davis intimated that he would like at least four or five more prints, so I shall have clothing to the value of some 380 pesos. Good luck indeed!

Tomorrow a big day: in the morning Tina again, in the afternoon Jean Charlot. Diego was pleased with his proofs. They are, I will say, well seen. His choice was one in which his huge bulk was exaggerated, and his face expressed a cynical sadness.

December 4. I have approached Galván for passes. "Not on a basis of friendship, my dear friend, — only if you think the work I have been doing in Mexico has value to the country so well loved by you."

...from these last two sittings of her [Tina] I surely have recorded something worth while. I know how difficult it will be to please myself after our first attempt in which both of us were attuned to the moment, and failure was only through my faulty technique. The faces from that group of negatives will always haunt me: they were without a doubt supreme registrations — that was my moment — and I failed.

Rafael gave me a new name for my list of Pulquerías: "Mírame Bien" — Look At Me Well.

December 5 — night. It is a lonely walk to the Salas, but I take it often, — they are such altogether agreeable and "simpatico" people. I usually arrive in time for cafe con leche and then to their amusement, take an after dinner nap, curled up with "Peggy" and "Xóchitl" [the dogs].

Chilly tonight walking the deserted streets home. Mexican streets are always deserted at night.

December 8. After a beautiful day in the mountains with Galván, Pepe, (Galván's Pepe) and the Salas, we went to the latters' home for cafe con leche. There happened a near tragedy, for Pepe, playing with Chandler, fell onto the pike of an iron gate and seriously tore his leg. We rushed him to the "White Cross" for first aid. What a terrible place!—dirty, inefficient,—and what sights I saw! Two men, victims of auto accidents,—heaps of raw bloody meat.

The brilliant driving of the Mexicans cannot save them from their recklessness. We noted a half dozen wrecks on the road to Ajusco,—and we passed these wrecks going a hundred kilometers an hour over a none too smooth road. A rut,—and Monna, Tina and I struck the auto's top. Tina was hurt, painfully hurt, and lay almost senseless in my arms.

Early breakfast in Las Tres Marías,—then a morning tramping the hills around Mt. Ajusco. Lunch was delicious: Chicharrones, cheese, mescal, and solid food it was for hungry people. Four generous drinks of fiery mescal did not phase me, yet at times a glass of wine will turn my head. I worked some with my Graflex, interesting cloud forms, surprising at this time of year. The landscape fine too. As to results I am in doubt,—the festivity of our party prevented concentration.

December 10. Rain! A rumble of thunder, then a gentle downpour. Preceding the shower, clouds assembled on the horizon. One strange serpent-like form I captured from the azotea with my Graflex: it borders on freakishness, exciting interest through strangeness of shape. But I feel it has enough value to include in my cloud series—in fact my only hesitation is over its bizarre quality.

Night time after the rain — clouds — white like sweeps of drifted snow, moonlit, dazzling. I watched them from the azotea.

To Fred Davis yesterday with a portfolio of photographs for a last exchange. He took 190 pesos worth. I returned with clothing for Chandler to the value of 70 pesos, and there is now a tidy sum left for Tina and myself. Chandler and I will return to California looking quite prosperous. Alas, "business" is quite slack again.

Fred Davis thinks he has a wonderful collection of my work,—he has not. His sellections were from my unimportant prints. He invariably passed by unconsidered my best things. I shall have to reprint but a few from out the entire exchange of 420 pesos worth of photos. I am sad and glad!

Considering my recent photographs:—a landscape done near Ajusco I shall finish; it is simple, quite dependent on a delicate sky of horizontal clouds, almost ruled lines across the nagetives. Then there are the latest cloud forms done from our azotea,—all are well worth finishing, surely one of them I shall do. It is a sensational thing, like some strange monster, but it is also technically good and fills the plate well.

Jean by the way is enthusiastic over my "Pajaritos", and so is Tina.

Sunday. With Felipe to "la Merced." Again that most charming little church in pink, again the overwhelming array of tropical fruit, the scent from heaps of pineapples. But the day's most interesting sight was a meat-market. I must say that the proprietor was a good business man. We were attracted from afar by the strains of a danzón: it was played by an orchestra seated in the street fronting the market. As is customary, great sides of beef hung from the ceiling,—ice in cool dry Mexico being superfluous. But the beef here was in gala attire,—artificial flowers, large, brilliant tropical blooms patterned in profusion the raw and bloody meat.

Felipe and I were enchanted and watched with admiration the rushing trade of this enterprising market... Speaking of carnecerías – meat markets – their names are even more amusing than those of the pulquerías – at least more incongruous, for one rather expects a poetic title or an imaginative one over the door of a house of dreams: but to name a butcher shop "La Lluvia de Oro", The Rain of Gold, or "El Paseo de las Ninas", which one might translate as the Promenade of the Flappers, is quite a delightful absurdity. Another pulquería title recently noted,—"El Misterio del Comercio"—The Mystery of Commerce —I well understand and sympathize with!

December 14 – Sunday in El Toreo. "I want to go with you", said Tina. I was surprised. Tina had not shown my interest and enthusiasm in los toros. I understood her though,—it was a gesture to please me rather than herself.

Three vivid impressions I shall record, though surely I can never forget them. So then – there was Ixtaccihuatl, "The White Woman," suddenly revealed to us through parting clouds: raised high above the topmost seats of the arena, her snow covered figure glittered in the setting sun.

Now, eyes down into the Arena's pit, sunless but for one long ray which streaked in through an open gate. The last bull was being fought, one of its victims lay stretched in the sand,—a horse, once white now crimson: and there it lay, light from the sun ray like a halo resting on its head.

The third impression was Valencia's fight with the first bull, as dramatic as I have yet seen. Valencia appeared in royal purple trimmed with black jet, his bull was a perfect one, a super animal, valorous to the core. The fight was beautiful, the enthusiasm supreme, the arena rocked with applause; but in an attempt to cap the climax Valencia hurled himself into the kill too recklessly. The steel entered to its hilt,—Valencia lost his balance, literally fell onto the bull's horns, was tossed and dropped heavily to the ground. He lay face down an instant, then in a last effort raised to his knees, arms outstretched as though in supplication, and fainted into the sand. He was carried out unconscious, but a moment later ran back to attack once more the mortally wounded but still standing bull. There was no need, the bull was really dead, but Valencia, in half crazed bravado tried to finish him with a short dirk from in front. He did, and then was retired to the hospital for repairs! To my disappointment he was not able to appear again in the afternoon. The last bulls were worthless, and so ended what I feel sure to be my last viewing of a bull fight, unless I return to Mexico.

December 12. Notes on this year's festival at Guadalupe, with Tina and Charlot. We lost Jean in the terrific crowd pressing into the Church, and so spent the morning alone.

The church was quite as impressive as last year: the strange Indians from far away as interesting,—they were gypsy-like in attire with beads and bracelets and brilliant colors. Tina coveted their fajas of unusual fineness. After much persuasion and bargaining and difficulty too—for the Indians, many of them, spoke no Spanish,—we possessed three fajas—quite a triumph, for last year Lupe and Monna had each tried in vain to convince the owners that they should part with the sashes that held up their very skirts! We purchased too a weird flower, like a witch's claw, blood stained: flor de manitas. We ate food typical of the day, bizcochos called gorditas de la Virgen or little fat ones of the Virgin!

A few side lights of the day: A blind man with a flute played "It Ain't Gonna Rain No Moh", and an aeroplane whirred overhead,—modern touches to costumes and customs of centuries past. As we entered the church a leaflet was handed us: on one side a picture of Nuestra Señora de Guadalupe and a prayer to her, on the other a patent medicine advertisement for the cure of sexual debility, urinary disorders and diarrhea!

A dream I had of the night just passed: someone, and to my regret I cannot recall whom, perhaps Tina or Chandler—came running to me and called, "Come quick.—There are the most wonderful cloud forms for you to photograph." I hurried, regulating my Graflex as I went. But once out of doors I was terrified, for black ominous clouds bore down on me, enveloping me: I seemed about to be overwhelmed, I dropped my head into my arms to protect myself from the sweeping forms and slammed the door to keep them from me.

December 22. Charlot has reserved several prints from which to choose two, in exchange for one of his paintings. The selection interests me so I will record it. First of all, and with no further question, he chose "Bomba en Tacubaya"; the others are "Lupe Marín"—"Two Bodies"—"Caballito de Cuarenta Centavos" —"Circus Tent"—"Hands against Kimono".

Last evening I tried to select one of his paintings. It was difficult! Hardly one that I could not have been happy with, yet he had several in reserve which I wanted and probably might have chosen from. Finally I took the hand of an Indian girl holding a bouquet of flowers. He handed me a number of ink sketches of "Luziana", maybe thirty or more for my choice. It narrowed down to four. "Now I shall see how our taste agrees," said Jean. I chose the one he would have indicated!

109

Sunday afternoon. Nudes of Tina, indoors this time. I used my new anastigmat, it has fine quality. My sitting pleases me.

December 23. No word of the passes—greatly distress—edworry over vaccination and income tax—what a difficult world we live in! and it seems as though it should be so simple. Several last moment sittings have added to the confusion. I don't know if I should even attempt to make an appointment with General Calles—(I had a letter of introduction)—better not than fail.

Two of the last series of nudes of Tina ready to print, elegant things in line, fine technically.

The Christmas puestos are like last year, – colorful, indeed the ensemble even more picturesque, but little of real value to purchase. The craft work is becoming greatly corrupted,—crude, formulated, commercialized, and a flood of cheap German and Japanese toys has crowded out the delightful native espression.

December 26. No passes to date! Packing now — in go those damn day-books! Adiós a México—

December 28—On the train. We faced each other speechless at the parting—a hand clasp—tear filled eyes—a last kiss—

Jean came to the station though I had warned him not to. Of course Elisa we brought with us, dear Elisa, pathetic little figure in black, and she cried too, indeed has wept by spells for two weeks past.

I lay in a half stupor all day—emotional exhaustion, the shock of parting, worry and work. Awakening once, I saw a sky as magnificent as any I have seen in Mexico. Twilight came on and a superb sunset, long streaks of scarlet clouds over black hills: they changed and were black against a lemon sky: above all hung the first delicate half circle of the new moon. I think at every station a blind man on his harp has played, the last one at Irapuato.

I seemed to realize that I was leaving not only Tina but dear friends and the land of my adoption too.

Of course I must record a new pulquería —"Después Te Digo"—I'll Tell You Later.

One was besieged at each new town or stop by vendors of every thing imaginable: food stuff, fruit, dulces, sarapes, baskets. One Indian insisted that I should buy a basket for my Señorita. "But you have a novia,—fiancée"—he retorted with mischievious eyes. "Tampoco—neither one," I finished the argument, and we both laughed.

I got no passes,—it was a financial blow, the spending of 200 pesos for tickets. Our train is trailed by an armored car with soldiers ready for action.

Finally, I did not "do" Calles,—the opportunity came too late. But this chance for fame and business awaits my return. I sense my return, but for a while I shall no longer hear "Zócalo por Tacuba!"

PART III

California, January—August, 1925

1. "I Felt Myself a Foreigner"

January 3rd, 1925. Los Angeles. Sitting here at my old desk, my much loved desk where I have worked and written, where I have shared morning coffee with Tina, Margrethe, Betty, Ramiel, Johan and how many others! But the desk is now in the "ranch," the home place where I am living. Flora has moved to the house of her parents, which was empty.

Joyous greetings with the boys!

The little ones, though taller, have not changed—are still babies. But Brett has, a big strapping fellow with amazing energy and a rebel! To leave him in these surroundings would mean his landing in a reform school; he must return to Mexico with me. Yes, I must return; I have already announced my intention.

I walked the streets of Los Angeles and found myself a stranger,—more, I felt myself a foreigner. Who were all these drab grey people!—not my kind! It was not merely that they were Anglo Saxons, for in New York I am sure the reaction would have been different. No, what I saw was a parade of Christian Scientists, Angeles Templeites, Movie Stars, Arty People and Iowa Farmers. To be sure there are in Mexico just as vulgar a class,—but there is also something besides!

Flora?—the same—she tries to be nice, I try to be decent, but underneath a thin skin is irreconcilable antipathy. Margrethe?—the same—almost submerged in mystery and intrigue.

Peter Krasnow saw my work, the first of all my friends—"our" work, I should have said, for his response to Tina's several prints was keen. Now I must see Ramiel at once!

January 7th. It is surely cold here in winter. I literally shake in my shoes after a night walk, and hover over the stove mornings. As for a cold bath, the very thought terrifies. On the other hand the days are hot and uncomfortable. Comparisons to la ciudad de México are unfavorable to Los Angeles.

Yesterday with Margrethe to Redondo beach and Ramiel. Who would have thought that we three outcasts from respectable society would ever be together again by the old sea-side! It was not the meeting I wished with Ramiel, and another must be arranged alone. I hardly need comment on his fine response to my new photographs, his appreciation war a forgone conclusion. We talked all day until my jaws ached and my throat was raw!

January 9th or thereabouts. I lose track of time,—and Christ how cold! Evenings usually with the little boys, reading *Robinson Crusoe* and telling tales of Mexico. Last night with Millard Rosenberg whose kindly face recalled our meeting in Mexico. Betty and Miriam have been out and I see Peter often, but other than these I have seen no one, nor want to.

From Tina letters. The parting has brought us closer together. Last evening a joint letter of New Year greetings from Tina, Monna, Nahui, Felipe, and Rafael, written from the latter's home, and another from Johan. "God! I want to see you!" I echo the thought, Johan!

I have sold two lenses and am bending every effort towards acquiring money for the return. Whether to attempt an exhibit in San Francisco I am undecided. The glory means nothing for I can show my work to the few whose praise and pleasure I would enjoy, but it might result in added income. My cameras are being overhauled, a new bellows for the 8 × 10 and new lenses fitted. Altogether I am a busy person!

EDITORIAL NOTE: Entries in the 1925 Daybook stop here, and do not begin again until August 21, when Weston was once more sailing to Mexico.

Back in Mexico City, on December 17, 1925, he writes: "I have been reliving the past— that period recently spent in California—from reading letters sent to Tina. So—to save a few notes, but in no particular order, for it would take hours to arrange consecutively this fumble of letters—" he begins copying into the Daybook what he considers significant passages. These entries occur intermittently from December 17, 1925 to January 23, 1926.

I have arranged these as far as possible by date or internal evidence into what seems to me a reasonably coherent sequence. N. N.

2. *Letters to Tina*

Undated, from El Paso: "Well it's all over, the border crossed and we are in the U.S.A. I confess no thrill upon reaching my native land, in fact a certain reserve came over me as I noted foreign faces — people with whom I could never have one common thought. A typical middle-west family is across the aisle, a drab worn-out mother, a flapper daughter, a gawky boy. Chandler remarks, "I hope all Americans are not like these." On the American side a detective accosted me, — he had noted my "foreign accent." I convinced him at last that I was 100% American!

"It is quite cold — praise be: the desert exquisite, fantastic, enticing. I have always been fascinated by barren wastes, — even the mid-west prairies, especially in winter. One tries in vain to pierce the distance, the white silent level unrelieved by even a mound. The sky is white, there is no horizon, all is a shroud of white."

Glendale — the old home — January 3, 1925. "Too bad for me to have returned to this! — this worn out spot, surrounded by my dead past, the once-blossoming fruit trees I cared for so tenderly, sapless, brittle, naked, the plow and garden tools rusty, scattered, — the house with shattered window panes and sagging sides doomed to tumble soon unless new life and love comes to save it. But who is to bring that love? Not I! For I am only a camper, using this ruin for temporary shelter. Almost as a stranger, I speculate, philosophize, try to pierce the past of this abandoned place, to revision it peopled, ringing with children's voices, fragrant from roses and honeysuckle, alive with desire, intention, potentialities. This is not sentimentalizing on my part, — my tears are unshed, — I am merely reminiscent.

"The Mexican juguetes with which I have tried to decorate the place seem strangely out of keeping. I rather pity them. — The tropical tiger, the bright blue heron, the scarlet jicara shiver with me, and as for my comrade 'Panchito,' that tough rough-neck, with a faded flower in his horse's bridle, I am afraid any moment that he will turn and shoot up his best friend for bringing him to this land of grey sky, bootleg, and singing evangelists.

"My little studio presents even a sadder, sorrier aspect, surrounded on all sides by brick blocks, business-like and efficient, which scorn the falling shack and seem to say, 'Soon, soon we shall crush you, crowd you out, tear up your garden, cut down your trees, clean out this eye-sore to a wholesome, right-thinking commun-

115

ity.' The sign *Margarethe Mather* is falling too, in a week it will be gone forever. I go on. Is it my will, am I stronger, or do I have better luck? Even the faces and voices of my old friends come to me as in a dream. Yes, I used to know these people, but now who are they, and what have I to do with them? But I knew it would be this way, I had no illusions —"

Los Angeles — January 17. — "This morning I dressed in the dark — it was early. Just as I was tip-toeing out, bound for the ranch and coffee, a little roguish face peeked out from under the covers, greeting me with, 'I want to go with you, Daddy.' So here he is, to interrupt me as I write. He sings and chatters and is altogether delightful." (Cole)

Los Angeles January 27. — "Last night, as I kissed Cole good night he said, 'I wipe off other people's kisses but I don't yours daddy!' Surely it will be a sad and difficult thing to leave them again...

"The reading of *Robinson Crusoe* to Neil and Cole has been a very precious thing, to be looked back upon as more important than a supposedly exciting adventure. Neil's fair hair, his grey eyes, his finely pointed chin: Cole's determined little jaw, mischievous eyes, saucy nose, — they are two delightful boys."

Carmel. — "Johan and I! You know what that means to me? — of course you do! In his attic, — the rain falling through the pines outside, conversation intense and vital inside: my craving to show him my work satisfied, his response, arguments on technique, approach, our quarrel on 'definition'."

January 29 — Carmel. — "We leave tomorrow for San Francisco. I am glad, you know how restless I become. Besides I am being pursued by a 'poetess' and feel quite uncomfortable, even embarrassed, the wooing is so open! I'm sure it's much easier for a woman to say 'no' than for a man, one feels like being polite, or accommodating."

February 6. — "I have treated this exquisite spot rudely, glanced over it hurriedly, exclaimed and turned away my head, almost afraid to be seduced by its charm. The pursuing poetess I treated likewise. I said to her, 'I shall return — and then —' but I knew that I would not. She handed me a poem that 'you have written' — and faded into the sea-fog."

San Francisco. "Neil is beside me, chattering his head off in great excitement. We arrived last night. I arose at 5:30 thinking to be alone and write awhile — but no — he was wide awake in a moment, eager to have his first view of the bay and boats."

February 11. — "At last the end has come for Margarethe, and my old studio passes into alien and vulgar hands. A letter from her, 'Today — my last Sunday in the Studio — raining softly — like tears — for you and for me — and for the willowed river we never walked to — a terrific nostalgia envelops me.'"

116

Exhibit at "Gumps" [store specializing in art goods]. "The opening days have brought many enthusiastic people. There is something vital about photography — *not* art photography — that draws and holds people from all walks of life. A significant note is the interest taken by the store's employees who return again and again. Miss Starr, in charge of the room said: 'They are fed up on 'art' and never come to see the exhibits of paintings.' Though men come too, it is of course the women who form the majority. Some very intelligent ones, but most of them I despise: club-women — just curiosity seekers who come to 'rubber' and bore one with insane comments on art. And do you suppose they ever ask the price of a print? No it's a free show in which they idle away a leisure moment of the shopping hour, a moment stolen from their more important business of buying fripperies."

San Francisco. — "A brisk tattoo of rain on my roof of glass awakened me at four. Always the first impulse is to gaze out over the bay. It is white capped and sullen, — one tiny tug, a black speck trailing smoke and foam, buffets the waves. One pink cloud, a rift in the grey, a rising sun. I am endeared to this studio, to this spot, to San Francisco, and yes to several fine new friends: Jean Roy, Lester, Consuela [Kanaga, photographer], Dan."

"Do you remember the name or work of Sidney Joseph? — Knowing that his pet aversion was photography and photographers, Mrs. Celrion arranged a meeting between us. Innocently unaware of the trap — before my portfolio was opened, there was a long discussion over the evening's subject, with Joseph emphatic, definite, unswerving in his opinion. 'Photography could never be a personal expression, it had spoiled public taste, had hurt the painter by making him see nature wrongly.' I was stimulated, I had a worthy foe with a good mind.

"Finally, deadlocked in our differences, I opened the portfolio to prove a point. The first two prints were enough, he retracted everything, he capitulated absolutely. His admiration was deep, enthusiastic, sincere: he proved one of the keenest critics I have met lately, thanking me for having changed his attitude. Once he said, 'Anyone seeing that line and recording it could have done great things in any art!'

I liked his remarks on art: that it is being taken too seriously, reduced to mathematical problems, lacking in the sheer joy of creating, the thing from the heart, the fun. I don't know Joseph's work — but I like the man."

San Francisco. — "This is the morning after the night before — such a night! of course with your [the Modotti] family! Easy enough to say one had a good time. This was a glorious time! I do not — could not exaggerate. Of course we got beautifully borrachito — no — I should not have added the diminutive — at least in regard to the condition of Johan, Benvenuto [Tina's brother] and myself

— and if Mamacita was not, she didn't need to be, for she was quite the gayest person in the room. I made love to her and then to Mercedes [Tina's sister] with intense fervor and shocking indiscrimination. O she is lovely! Tina mia! I am quite crazy over her. With a few drinks, Johan is always a scream. Last night was no exception. Benvenuto was superb — gave us Grand Opera in the kitchen and acted all over the place. We jazzed — sang — did mock bull-fights. My sides really ache this morning from last night's laughter. I have had little sleep — yet I have no 'head' and am still exhilarated. So much for good wine and a good time. And the dinner! — what a feast — with little pigeons so tender one ate bones and all — fresh mushrooms too — and then for emphasis I repeat — the wine! — the Wine!"

San Francisco. — "Blake said, 'The eye sees more than the heart knows.' And I say, 'The camera sees more than the eye, so why not make use of it!'"

"Neil goes to play every day at Carter's with their little girl, four; when he starts to leave she threatens with tears. Rather young to pull this feminine stuff. I shall have to warn my sons early."

March 4. "The fog sweeps by like smoke. The sirens shriek dismally. I am alone in this great room — no, you are with me, but only your counterpart on the wall, forming a kiss I never got. I read a bit, walk the floor, smoke nervously, try to write but cannot. I question which of my friends who have begged me to call I shall telephone. The answer comes—none, so I shall open a can of Campbell's Soup and try to find solace in eating.

"Later: the soup was not inspiring. I don't stand inaction — that's *my* trouble. I must keep going towards something—if it be but a blind alley or a locked door. Intermissions of relaxation, yes, but not this uncertain waiting and wondering. I shall go out and walk in the fog."

"Consuela got me a sitting for next Wednesday. She has been so anious to help and so upset because she could not swing things faster for me. Imagine another photographer — in business in the same city, so helping a stranger, — and she struggling too. Well—they are the kind who do such things.

"Slept ten hours again last night. Exhausted nerves I realize. Thank God I sleep when overstrained. Johan does not, he lies awake to think and go crazy. I protect myself by giving up at night."

San Francisco. — "May left for Los Angeles an hour ago, taking Neil with her. It was a sad good-bye, marking the end of another period, never to be repeated. He clung to me at the end, sensing perhaps the same in his child-like way: he has been a trial, but he has brought me much beauty."

Weston comments in the Daybook, December 19, Mexico, D.F.: Besides Neil's companionship mentioned in the above note he afforded me a visual beauty which I recorded in a series of Graflex negatives of considerable value. He was anxious to pose for me, but it was never a "pose," he was absolutely natural and unconscious in front of the camera. When I return he may be spoiled, if not bodily changed, in mental attitude. Last spring in San Francisco at eight years, he was in the flower of unawakened days before adolescence: tall for his years, delicately moulded, with reed-like flow of unbroken line: rare grey eyes, ingenuous, dreaming, and a crown of silken blond hair. He is a lovely child!

March, 1925. — San Francisco. "I have been here almost three months, almost four months since leaving Mexico. I had expected to be in San Francisco not longer than a month, had hoped indeed to be in Mexico ere this. Yet the end of my stay is not in view, — even more indefinite.

"Rain has fallen all day. Not for one second has the beating on my skylight ceased. It seems to fall directly on my brain, while I, tied hand and foot, writhe and twist and turn in hopeless effort to escape the seeming symbolism of this incessant downpour.

"I am tired of thinking, my mind is a vortex of negated plans and desires, my thoughts find no rest in coordinate intentness of purpose. Whatever the cost — a fusion of apparently incompatible wishes must come, or else some vagrant hope will be buried forever. But to finally dismiss a hope is as sorrowful an act as to inter a beloved friend — I hesitate — and so returns the unanswerable question.

"One does not necessarily act for the best, nor even nobly, in destroying personal aspiration for the sake of others. The greatest if less apparent gain, even for those others, must come from the fulfilling of one's predilection rather than in sentimental sacrifice. Yet I realize that I face sacrifice, no matter what the decision, thus involving the whole situation and complicating any plan or proposal. So all questions remain unanswered today as they have for days past."

Thursday, April 9 — San Francisco. "It is the hour before dawn, a time I love, so very still. The whole world sleeps—for aught I know I may be the only living person. For the moment this thought pleases me yet if it were true I imagine one would commit suicide, for—craving aloneness—yet some human contact is necessary to rebound from or identify with. Anyhow at this hour I seem Lord over my dominion and preside in mighty isolation.

"My remark at Jean Carter's that, 'The artist needed an audience,' started an argument. I should not have used the word audience, for it pictured perhaps a group of from a hundred to ten thousand applauding people, when I meant not necessarily more than half a dozen, or even one. Neither did I mean the artist creates to *please* his audience—not primarily—but the feeling of having given is as important an item in art as it is in sex. Misanthropic as we may be or become, we are basically a social group and only grow anti—from bitterness, disgust, weariness. Arguments are so futile, the loser in his own eyes is never defeated, he starts with an a priori premise, his attitude remains stolidly incontrovertible, debating becomes absurd."

Undated. "There's too much 'swooning' in Lawrence—too much 'sweat' and 'surging'— overemphasis on 'vibrations' and 'anticipations'—repetitions of 'white fury' — 'voluptuous ecstasy' — 'sardonic look' — 'demonical soul' — 'fine hate' — 'convulsed moment' — 'drugged eyelids' — the writer of *Nick Carter's Weekly* never rose to such melodramatic heights. His characters are over-drawn—for instance, 'Hermione'—he's too anxious to make plain their patho-logy. Better to write a book of facts and statistics on sex psychology. Lawrence is unrelieved by a single laugh, which might, by contrast, strengthen his drama.

"He is keen indeed—has much to say on 'love.' He sees, he feels, he knows: his baring of impulses, his revealment of the cause, the why and wherefor is profound. But in the *telling*, in the *words*, he loses by repetition and obvious statement of fact.

"But *I* do not attempt to criticism of Lawrence! I am indulging in passing thoughts. To me he is [a] head higher than contemporary novelists that I happen to know. But my reading is limited, so after all I don't know much!"

San Francisco. "It is not best, this reading of one book after another in such quick succession, as I, in this insatiable spell, am doing. Moore lessened my pleasure in Lawrence, and now after Rosenfeld's verbosity, his sky rocket of words, I find relief in the mature direct elegance of Havelock Ellis. You remember how Rosen-feld loves to 'toss the glass balls' before a bewildered audience. He must write with a well-worn book of synomyms by his side, cigarette stubs scattered around him and certainly one feels that a typewriter nervously clicked as he wrote. In Ellis one senses the repose and dignity of a goose-quill which I am sure he used."

San Francisco — April 12th. "Morning, with fog so dense that vision penetrates scarce half a block. Sounds of fog-horns are muffled, the wail of a siren on Alcatraz is faint and chokes abruptly. The sailors on the anchored battle fleet must gaze out into nothingness.

"Sailors I like, but do the strutting soldiers that infest San Francisco never realize their humorous pomposity? And why does the sailor offend less? — is it merely a difference in uniform, or has the sailor from long night watch or day-dream over the sea, acquired a deep self-questioning? In answer he *wears* his uniform, he never flaunts it."

San Francisco — April 15th. "After an overcast muggy day — earthquake weather, I heard whispered — this morning came clear. The bay is blue — blue — every detail of the other shore revealed. 8:30 is late for my coffee, but I went last night to a 'movie'. Unusual form of dissipation for me, but I would go more often could such films as last night's be seen. Fine acting — fine photography and real

120

life. No sub-titles were used to insult one's intelligence—nor needed to make shift for poor directing or acting. The added 'happy ending' was unfortunate. It was evidently an after thought to please the American audience who so dislike to face the truth. The film is German — titled *The Last Laugh.*"

May 18th—San Francisco. "I have had another rotten contact with a newspaper man, the general-manager, the big cheese of *The Chronicle.* Really I boil when I think of him and what he represents. Realizing that this man caters to, and knows the taste of, several hundred thousand readers, and that these readers average like millions of others all over the country—one becomes appalled, hopeless.

"His remarks: 'Well — what are these pictures — what do they all *mean*? I can't get any *idea*, they may be very fine technically, but they have no *art* value' — and so on! He finally selected begrudgingly a dozen for one page, saying — 'If you had to buy this it would cost you a thousand dollars.' It took him five minutes to look over fifty prints. I did not return."

June 3rd "Is one after all ever *influenced* by anything? Is it not an abused word? Would not a better word be awakened or stimulated? I feel one is *influenced* only because one already has inherent qualities — maybe dormant or unused or misused or misdirected.

"Your individualistic attitude towards life is not selfish, at least not unnatural, in fact it is most natural, a law of nature touching everyone, everything. Are not your thoughts a reconsideration of 'the survival of the fittest'? — to consider oneself first is in the last analysis the least selfish attitude. My eternal question over my children is between my emotional, personal love for them, my selfish love! — and the impersonal consideration, realization, that to do the best thing for them — unselfishly — I must think of Edward Weston first.'

"George Stojana last night. We met at arm's length, we kissed on parting. I cannot hold a grudge against such a person,—anyhow the parting gesture was was his. There were no explanations. A trifle worn was George, and older, much of his past work destroyed,—he would show me but five wood carvings in relief, fine things...."

June 16th. "Someday I shall tell you of the beauty and drama of my leaving S. F. —how Jean Roy, breathless, reached the train to wave farewell just as it pulled out: it was a perfect gesture."

Exhibit in Los Angeles given before a Japanese Club on East First Street. August, 1925. "The exhibit is over. Though weary, I am happy. In the three days I sold prints to the amount of $140. — American Club Women bought in two weeks $00.00 — Japanese men in three days bought $140.00! One laundry worker purchased prints amounting to $52.00—and he borrowed the money to buy with! It has been outside of Mexico my most interesting exhibit. I was continually reminded of Mexico, for it was a man's show. What a relief to show before a group of intelligent men! If Los Angeles society wishes to see my work after this, they must come to the Japanese quarter and rub elbows with their peers — or no — I should say their superiors! I owe the idea for this show to Ramiel — and his help made it a success."

Venice, California, no date. "So this is 'Venice!' I live on the Grand Canal — isn't that grand! I am a nurse girl, policeman or something quite objectionable. I wasn't made for the job. The boys fight and bicker all day: my last memory of them will be wails, whines, and scoldings.

"It is tawdry as ever here but I am amused and amazed watching humanity enjoy itself. They come for the week end, get burned fiery red and raw, buy salve and return home to suffer. The thrill-producing rides exceed one's wildest imaginings. Is it sex repression? Skirts are worn well above the knee, — the question is are they more provocative or *less*!

"A man just returned with a catch of fresh fish. His red-faced slovenly wife called out, 'Eat a lot of 'em, 'Sam, they're good for your brains!'

"Well the boys are awake and the first fight has started. I don't stand confusion, I want to run — run away — my fingers in my ears."

PART IV

Mexico, August, 1925—November, 1926

1. *"Life through My Camera"*

August 21, 1925. On board S. S. Oaxaca. *Brett and E. W.* Sailing! Once more bound for Mexico, returning to my unfinished period of work and life. There were farewells yesterday. Sad acknowledgments of the pang of separation. Partings with friends and loves, old and new. Leaving the children, the most painful. But it had to be, this going away again.

I have enjoyed my new cape—its ample encircling folds, the swish and flap of it in the stiff breeze—long coveted, I now possess a cape. So, warmly wrapped, my pipe glowing with good tobacco from Miriam and with many a thought of her, I dreamed away the hours before bedtime.

Today the sea is rough. Our little ship rides mountainous waves. I enjoy its careening but Brett "feels rotten." He cannot eat the good cooking and Brett unable to eat is an anomaly.

The boat is clean in contrast to the *Colima* of two years ago. We are the only passengers, it seems quite like our private yacht. Cabins and decks are deserted and silent but for the engines' rhythm and the lament from a love-lorn Mexican youth singing to the waves.

August 22. The morning is cool and calm. The *Oaxaca* steams ahead with scarce a roll. Brett is more himself and in his irresistible way, making friends with all the crew.

Eight months have passed since I left Mexico, unable after eighteen months' separation to be longer parted from my boys. Leaving, I no more than half expected to return, and why I return, questioning myself, is not so simple to answer. Pages of reactions to people and places might be indulged in without conclusive reason. There might be more than one answer from more than one self. I simply packed my trunk and left before becoming once more too deeply involved in a mire of routine or imagined responsibilities.

But I am sure if my studio were not awaiting me intact and ready for work and if Tina were not in Mexico I would have hesitated longer or never have considered the return at all. At least I have some idea of what to expect of conditions and surroundings. I am not blindly venturing unchartered seas. I am not ready for another adventurous change.

To the cackling overheard from busybodies I can say that Tina's presence in Mexico is not the magnet supposed, since she has expressed a willingness to leave for any place of mutual desire.

The moon set early. Only a spectral lantern sways from the masthead. We plow on through the black night noiselessly, except for the plunging piston and plaintive cries from sea fowl overhead. A sudden jarring impact and we have struck a whale,—then on again. The chief engineer, rotund and waggish, kids Brett. "Tomorrow is Sunday. We no work. I stop the engine and fish for sharks." Brett, wide-eyed, ingenuous, half believes him or wants to.

August 23. I am disinclined to exertion, mental as well as physical. Better had I used animal instinct, were that possible, instead of exhausting myself in an attempt to reason out the why of everything. The best thing to do, though it may well be that my instinct has played a part in finding me this August day southward bound.

August 24. I have written thirteen letters today. Really I should call them notes of farewell. What a volume the history of these several persons would make if detailed episodes of their part in my life were to be recorded. I did record much from day to day, even as I now am doing, but one brave moment in San Francisco, three years of writing went into the flames. No doubt this period will meet the same fate, but write I must, no matter to what end. It is the safety valve I need in this day when pistols and poisons are taboo.

August 25. We are anchored in the very beautiful Puerta Vallarta having arrived here from Mazatlán yesterday morning. I did not expect to lose a day here. However I deserve reproof for calling time spent here loss. Green mountains, palm-covered, meet the waters of this small gulf. Only a narrow strip of sand gives room for the pueblito of white tile-roofed houses and thatched huts, set against steep green inclines.

Tobacco is being loaded, canoes the means of transportation. The water is a thousand fathoms deep, even close to shore. So we are near enough to make this primitive way of loading practical if slow.

Our day at ever-remembered Mazatlán was spent with El Capitán Arenas of the *Colima*, and a fine reception he gave us. Many incidents recalled my first visit of two years ago, especially when Brett and I took a coach over the same winding road which follows the coast. We have been ashore twice in this Puerta Vallarta, Brett casi loco over the flitting myriads of tropical butterflies which he ineffectually tried to catch with my newly blocked panama, quite ruining it, but in a good cause. Finally, hot and exhausted, we stopped under cool arches and protecting trees to be served coconut milk; with a two foot machete an Indian hacked off the coco's end, inserting a soda pop straw!

September 14. — Mexico D.F. I have been sitting on the "hypo" barrel in the dim green light of my dark-room, reflecting upon the past, pondering over the future... However, I willed myself in Mexico again—and here I am!

September 22. Musing over events en route from Manzanillo to Mexico, I shudder with aversion remembering the landing,—the confusion, heat, officials,—but after all it could have been so much worse, and certainly the Mexican officials were courteous and lenient. Only my deep rooted antipathy to all "red tape," to all uniforms demanding a dreary consistency of acquiescence, of submission to formulae, brings this always disagreeable revulsion.

At last we were accepted as proper people to land on Mexican shores, my letter to President Calles having had due and immediate effect in the consideration, and weary but relieved we relaxed in the train for Colima.

Towards evening, approaching Colima—a sudden lurch—a grinding of wheels —and we went off the track, destined to a six hour delay before reaching the hotel. To bed at one, up at five,—then Guadalajara in the afternoon. There they were! Tina and Elisa excitedly waving from the station platform.

The ten day stay in Guadalajara excepting for a few bright hours, was a boresome period. The proposed exhibit took place in the State Museum. Every day we went, waiting for sales which never happened, every day we grew more irritable and despondent, the governor's purchase of six prints for the museum bringing quite inadequate reward for the effort expended. But hail to Sr. Zuno for being such an appreciative patron!

The bright hours were Sunday dinner with the Marín family, the venerable parents and seven children, including Lupe, with them for a short visit. Almost without exception the children were individuals in every sense of the word, but Victoria to me was an outstanding figure even amongst this unusual group.

Another happy evening was the mask party at Carlos Orozco's. Tina and I exchanged clothing as once before in Mexico. That our make up and acting was well done may be judged from the effect we had upon the Orozcos, who were frankly disappointed that we had merely masked! — until gradually they perceived that "Tina" was not Tina, nor "Edward," Edward! Brett appeared as a California Bathing Beauty: in his blue bathing suit crowned by a wig of golden curls—a wig such as is worn by the adenoidal "movie queens" of Hollywood— with flapper lips rouged to a cupid's bow, his blonde eyebrows delicately penciled, he startled even us with his girlishness.

After the exhibit, we made two excursions of interest,—one a descent into "La Barranca de los Oblatos,"—Valley of Forgotten Men—a famous gorge near the city. Diego had said, "It is the strongest landscape in Mexico," so, visualizing great mountains of bare and precipitous rock, forbidding black abysms, etc., I prepared enthusiastically to do my first photographic work of the new adventure into Mexico. We hired an Indian to carry the weighty 8 × 10 camera, and Brett of course made ready to capture the butterflies which flit through his dreams even as photographic images are preexposed in mine.

All day long we explored, making but two exposures, one of a sunset cloud, another a detail of the rocky trail beneath my feet. The expected barren landscape was completely covered by luxuriant tropical growth, gorgeous to the eye, impossible photographically. Diego afterwards complained we had been directed down the wrong descent. Nevertheless I do not believe that the tropics can ever show the austere grandeur of a northern landscape, wild, insidious, intense as it [the tropic landscape] is in other ways. But I am expressing disappointment from only one angle, for the day was rich in experience.

The descent of 2000 ft. was leisurely made, except by Brett, who surely covered twice the distance we did in his chase for butterflies: prepared this time with net and box he captured many.

The bottom of the gorge was under cultivation, all tropical fruits flourished in the humidity and heat engendered there. The ascent was even more leisurely made, but not from carefree indifference! An overhead sun dispelling all shade, the heat became intense: water, which was not to be had until near the summit, became our preoccupation, — so when at last a spring gushed from the rocks we literally threw ourselves into the spreading pool beneath.

With twilight and the end of our ascent we rested in the open country above. A storm was gathering, — great clouds afire in the sunset, flashed lightning, rumbled, roared, and massed together to an approaching deluge.

One other remembered day at Tonalá, amongst the potters. On the way, Indian women passed, balancing great water jars upon their heads, though "balancing", which seems to indicate effort, — is that the word? For the jar and figure were a synthesis, moving with exceeding elegance.

We found at last the adobe home of Amado Galván, most famous of potters. He squatted on the earthern floor, — delicately moulding his clay.

That afternoon we left Guadalajara for good. I shall recall it as a city, clean and gay, with sparkling skies and balmy air, with beautiful and, more surprising, smartly dressed women. I noted but little poverty, less begging than elsewhere, yet if there is any over-indulgence in, or worry over, work or business in Guadalajara my observations failed! Incomprehensible to the Anglo-Saxon, life sailed serenely on! In none of the 1001 proudly progressive, despairingly new California Cities, with red, white, and blue Standard Oil Stations, and "Cash is King" grocery stores, have I seen such a blaze of street lights. Night became day even unto dawn, for not until then did the extravagant display end.

The press notices concerning the exhibit brought us screams of laughter. I was announced in head lines as "Weston the Emperor of Photography, who, notwithstanding his birth in North America, has a Latin Soul." This was the usual style, but Alfaro Siqueiros, painter, writer, radical, wrote a most intelligent, brilliant article which though directly concerned with the work exposed, might be read as a exceptionally understanding treatise on photography. I quote one paragraph:

"In Weston's photographs, the texture, the physical quality, of things is rendered with the utmost exactness: the rough is rough, the smooth is smooth, flesh is alive, stone is hard.

"The things have a definite proportion and weight, and are placed at a clearly defined distance one from the other. In one word, the beauty which these photographs of Weston's possess is Photographic Beauty!"

Tina insisted on riding second class the journey to Mexico. Brett and I had our first class tickets straight through from L. A., so I bought a berth for Brett,—too cruel to make such a sleepy head sit up all night, I thought, and I spent the night alternating between a watch over my cameras in first class and Tina in second, in the dim light among the Indians, sprawled over each other on the hard seats, dozing or drunken or garrulous.

September 29, 1925. I have been very sick since arriving, a terrific cold, chills, and fever,—perhaps malaria? Today, my old self has emerged, weak and gaunt but on the mend. The weather has aggravated my condition, a continued dreary drizzle or downpour, till I who love rain have prayed for a moment's sunshine to warm my shivering bones. It is still cloudy,—most un-Mexican weather.

I have met many old friends, — Monna, Rafael, Felipe, and Jean Charlot,—also Diego, Carleton Beals, Frances and Pepe. I have seen the new work of Jean and Diego,—they have not stood still, nor, considering my own new negatives from California, have I.

Prolific I have not been these past months in the States. I have seldom been aroused or had opportunity to work, yet from each brief period with my camera, some sensitive recording has been achieved. The majestic old boats at anchor in an estuary across from San Francisco, [Neil] who, naked, seemed most himself, the full bloom of Miriam's body, responsive and stimulating, the gripping depths of Johan's neurasthenia,—the all-over pattern of huddled houses beneath my studio window on Union Street—in these varied approaches [I] have lately seen life through my camera.

October 2. And the first day I have printed palladiotype since returning. The rocky trail and storm cloud from La Barranca, several of the new industrial scenes from Los Angeles and two heads of Diego.

Diego has painted a self-portrait into one of his murals in the Secretaría, copied quite exactly from one of my photographs of him, one which I could not use because of poor definition, though it was my favorite as well as his.

I am now in a fine mood having printed once more after so many months, despite a very bad night previous. We loaned our house for a "wild" party,— some have the idea that "wild" is to hold hands in a dark corner. Fortified with cognac, I did not become bored for quite awhile, even played at being wild myself, but alas, ready to retire, I found my room occupied by spooning couples, and I an outsider! When the party finally dispersed, F. was left behind, down and out: with difficulty I steered her to my room, got her shoes off, tumbled her into bed and found a corner for myself in the studio,—rather cold and rather uncomfortable.

October 3. Rereading letters before burning. Love like art returns in measure the emotion one carries to it,—one finds what one seeks—

Well, already I have been compensated for my loss, and surely this is the strangest love of my life. A little brown Indian girl came to live with us, to help. At first it was a timid, distant admiration, then she would softly caress my hair, then stroke my hand or cheek, until one day, seeing too well her passion, and feeling deeply, I took her to me and kissed her lips; since then our embraces have been often and impassioned, no less genuine from me than from her. There is indeed something exquisite yet sad in this love between such extremes of age and tradition,—for what can ever come of it!

My little room is once more assuming character, a corner to hide in, enjoying my retreat the while. A new "trastero"—whatnot—which, stained brilliant yellow, stamps the room at once as Mexican: of course by "Mexican" I mean the indigenous race, for no sophisticated Mexican, always excepting the artist, would have a trastero in his room. So—starting with a trastero, a petate, a sarape, the room irresistibly becomes fixed in character: no additional properties could find place near such direct, vigorous, primitive expression. On the trastero I have placed my new juguetes—toys, a crimson spotted dog, a leopard, a couple of viejitos, and pigs with bursting bellies.

I never tire of the juguetes, they are invariably spontaneous and genuine, done without striving, fancied in fun. One imagines the Indians laughing and joking as they model and paint. My old flower-bedecked chest, a new orange and black sarape, a drawing by Diego, and a small canvas by Jean complete my exposed treasures.

Charlot seeing my delight in his new oil, said, "Take it, you have many photographs I want to choose from." It is simple, this painting,—two terra cotta [arches?] over a base of Mexican pink, surmounted by a mountain-top and sky of deep blue-grey,—a subtle thing in color and construction,—aesthetically satisfying.

October 10. After all, life is not so difficult for me,—I slip a new disc into my musicbox of emotions, grind the crank and out squeaks another tune. To be sure it may be a more or less familiar melody, but one can always change the tempo and use imagination!

October 12. Brett and I were guests of new American acquaintances yesterday. First the bull fight in which the bulls were victorious, matadores being carried

130

to the hospital for repairs after their first encounter. Complete demoralization of the lesser lights followed and the fight continued on in confusion—a sorry spectacle. Later we picked up Tina and Jean and were treated to a good supper with wine.

Wednesday, October 14. Brett at thirteen years, wanted a cane! Last night I got him one, incidently a new one for myself, of ebony,—another trade with Mr. Davis. A great event this first stick!—the selection an occasion for prolonged and profound deliberation, though I should confess that my own consideration of shape, size, surface was quite as extended!—then off we went down Madero, swinging our respective "bastones." Brett handled his well, albeit with some self-consciousness. "Dad, you don't carry a cane for show do you?—you just like to swing it?" So—I assured him! Now we are both happy!

October 15. With Brett to a nearby "movie," perhaps a little worse than the usual average of mediocrity. Yet why is it that I can be emotionally moved at the most vapid climax, the while I intellectually deride the whole false and mushy mess? It is of course but the awakening of memories by some act or gesture related to the past,—some unrealized hope is returned, a lost thread is for the moment woven into reality. However, the absurdity of my Jekyll and Hyde situation, with my mouth in a grin and my throat choked, and this from viewing some quite preposterous melodrama, ridiculously conceived, acted by imbeciles, presented for bovine clodhoppers, brings the question am I infantile? senile? maudlin? or also beef-witted? With a superlative stretch of the neck I answer these questions, "No!"—yet feeling uneasy over the sureness of my self-estimation. Better to wink at my weakness than to discover it a truth!

October 17. It was a rare joy, my first view of the paintings of Carlos Mérida. We had been told that Mérida was one of the first three painters of Mexico,—the others, of course, Diego and Jean, but one learns to expect nothing, so the visit was an unlooked-for treat. He may be amongst the first three, though more than that I shall not put down, knowing the hazard of first enthusiasms—my own, I should add—for I am so liable.

Mérida himself is a finely organized type, more that of Jean than Diego.

From Mérida's work and glowing with a fine heat of aroused ecstasy, we went to call on Pintao. Almost too much for one day, the painting of Merida and the carving of Pintao! It was a foregone conclusion that Pintao would again bring us full satisfaction: he did!

We sat on his funny brass bed,—he offered us the same crooked cigars and his night-pot for spittoon: then he talked while we watched his remarkable eyes and prescient gestures.

In New York following the showing of a wood-carving by Pintao, a "critic," quite with usual stupidity, wrote that Pintao is one of the "moderns" who played at being naïve. Pintao! who is naïveté itself!

October 21. "Form follows function." Who said this I don't know, but the writer spoke well!

I have been photographing our toilet, that glossy enameled receptacle of extraordinary beauty. It might be suspicioned that I am in a cynical mood to approach such subject matter when I might be doing beautiful women or "God's out-of-doors," — or even considered that my mind holds lecherous images arising from restraint of appetite.

But no! My excitement was absolute aesthetic response to form. For long I have considered photographing this useful and elegant accessory to modern hygienic life, but not until I actually contemplated its image on my ground glass did I realize the possibilities before me. I was thrilled! – here was every sensuous curve of the "human form divine" but minus imperfections.

Never did the Greeks reach a more significant consummation to their culture, and it somehow reminded me, in the glory of its chaste convolutions and in its swelling, sweeping, forward movement of finely progressing contours, of the Victory of Samothrace.

Yet the blind will turn longingly back to "classic days" for art! Now I eagerly await the development of my exposed film.

October 22. I awakened this morning to the song of a bird. Yes, this is rare enough to comment upon! There seems to be almost no bird life upon the plateau: city, parks, country alike are lacking, and why, I cannot conjecture nor ascertain.

But we have music,—forsaken by birds there are compensating melodies. Early amongst the street songs comes the cry, "Tierra negra para las macetas—black earth for the flower-pots!" and an Indian, sack on back, passes. Or he may sing— and it is a real song—"Tierra de ocha para las macetas—earth of leaves, etc.—!" Follows the woman with "Los tamales! los tamales!"—and soon the scissor-grinder, always from Spain—blowing his plaintive tremulous notes on a Panlike pipe, carrying one away from today, perhaps to ancient Greece,—a whistle traditional, archaic. Later, the organitos serenade beneath one's window, delighting with wheezy melodies, from well loved popular airs to jazz.

These are a few from the many songs of the street,—and with night, safely tucked in bed, one shivers a bit, listening to the eery shrill of the police whistle and the faint far-away answer from another shrouded figure. Or perhaps a sharp clatter of hoofs startles one from half-slumber and peering out, a half-dozen black-cloaked, lantern-lit mounted police spur on their horses into the drizzling night.

October 23. The portrait of our privy could not have been finer but for a piece of carelessness on my part: during exposure I shoved a sheet of cardboard within

132

range of the lens. So today I am working again with my new enthusiasm. It is not an easy thing to do, requiring exquisite care in focusssing — and of course in placing — though the latter I am trying to repeat. Elisa had only this morning polished up the bowl, though hardly in anticipation, so it shines with new glory.

The household in general make saracastic remarks re my efforts, — Brett offering to sit upon it during exposure, Mercedes suggesting red roses in the bowl, while both criadas believe me quite crazy. I showed the first negative to Felipe who unhesitatingly offered congratulations, — and Felipe is one of the first persons among my friends whose opinion is invariably sought for and well considered.

Evening of the 23rd. A good negative—technically at least—of the W. C. is washing, together with several enlarged negatives from my evening's work. My head is sublimely swimming from plenty of excellent Vermouth. Best of all I'm alone! Brett asleep and the rest—even the servants—out. How precious to be alone!

October 24—evening. Already the W. C. negative is printed!—a beautiful print too. Charlot and Paul have seen it and agree that it is one of my most sensitively observed photographs. Now that it is printed the tile floor does not distract, in fact quite takes its place as a satisfactory base—suggestive yet unobstrusive. What absolute joy to be working again.

October 26. Several days full to crowded with work, and more unusual, divertisement. Saturday night, supper with Rafael, the occasion his saint day. There we encountered Dr. Atl already accoutred for the ascent of "his" mountain "El Popo,"—and he was to walk there besides! He gave me a new spelling for that glorious mountain, "Itztatzihutl," and a new meaning which appeals most of all—"The Ice Woman."

Also, there was Dr. Gruening, one time editor of the *Nation*; he knew Stieglitz and his "group," admired his work but thought him a poseur, at least to the public, ridiculed too, the exaggerated worship of his followers, and the bunk mysticism read into his photographs.

Rafael's supper of fish—Catalonian style—and fried mushrooms was delicious, but as usual the wine befuddled my brain and I slept erect in my chair.

Sunday afternoon, the bull-fight, with Brett and Mercedes,—her first. The furor, in which I joined, created by "Chicuelo" and the magic fifth bull: "there is no bad fifth bull," a traditional superstition.

Tea with Diego and Lupe,—the three of us, Tina, Brett and I. Of course I must carry my portfolio of new work to show Diego, saving for the climax the "Excusado." After his first exclamation,—"In all my life I have not seen such a beautiful photograph," Diego sat silently considering the print for many moments. This was more significant to me than any praise. I gave Diego two portraits of himself and left with two drawings chosen from his collection.

October 28. No use to "kid" myself longer, I am not absolutely happy with the toilet photograph. My original conception on the ground glass allowed more space on the left side, hardly a quarter inch more, but enough to now distress me in the lack of it. Not my fault either, excepting I should have allowed for the play of holder in the camera back. I finally trimmed the right side to balance and though I admit a satisfying compromise, yet I am unhappy, for what I saw on the ground glass, I have not,—the bowl had more space around it.

I spent hours yesterday contemplating the print, trying to say it would do, but I am too stubborn and refused to say. This morning I am no wiser which may mean that I should do it over. Yet if I restrain my impulse and put away the print for a week, I may become perfectly satisfied, not acquiesing to something badly done but accepting a different conception quite as good. And I am anxious to work more!

October 29. Mariposas—mariposas! Brett's net swishing through the air, butterflies captive in its meshes or sailing away to his chagrin. This was our day together in Tlalpan, a happy day for both, though my joy was most in seeing his!

The evening, Frances took us,—which meant Carleton Beals and the Weston-Modotti household — to Teatro Lírico. Too much "carne"—though I am not moralizing. I was finally bored by all the wiggling arses and wobbling tits. We wound up the party at Monotes where food is good and the crowd congenial. But to bed at 2:30 has never been my way, less than ever now! Seldom that I do not regret the time lost and energy spent.

October 30. Trying variations of the W. C., different viewpoints, another lens. From certain angles it appeared quite obscene: so does presentation change emotional response.

Only one more negative so far, which I might have liked, not having done the first one. However I am not through, the lines seen from almost floor level are quite elegant, but to work so low I must rig up some sort of camera-stand other than my tripod.

November 1. It was more simple than I had thought: by placing my camera on the floor without tripod I found exactly what I wanted and made four negatives with no change of viewpoint except that which came from substituting my short focus R. R. Unhesitatingly I respond to my new negatives, and shall choose one to print from.

November 4. Questioned—I could hardly answer which of my loves, the old or the new privy I like best: perhaps the first, yet the second, or rather the last which is such a different conception as to be hardly comparable, is quite as elegant in line and as dignified as the other. Taken from floor level the opening circle to the receptacle does not enter into the composition, hence to nice people it may be

134

more acceptable, less suggestive; however, "to the pure"—etc. I like best the negative made with my R. R. lens of much shorter focus, for by getting closer and underneath the bowl I attained finer proportions.

But I have one sorrow, all due to my haste, carelessness, stupidity, and I kick myself with pleasure. The wooden cover shows at the top, only a quarter inch, but distracting enough. Of course I noted this on my ground glass, but thought I must make the best of it; such a simple act as unscrewing the cover did not occur to me. I have only one excuse for myself, that I have done all these negatives under great stress, fearing every moment that someone being called by nature would wish to use the toilet for other purposes than mine.

Now shall I retouch the cover away—difficult to do—being black, or go to the effort and expense of doing my "sitting" over? I dislike to touch a pencil to this beautiful negative—yet it is in the unimportant background—and to do the thing over means a half day's work and confusion plus expensive panchromatic films. I shall start to retouch and see how I react!

Afternoon—Now that I am "nicely" stewed from beer imbibed at Mercedes' birthday dinner, for which we bought a keg, I see with more clarity.

To take off the toilet's cover, either by unscrewing or retouching, would make it less a toilet, and I should want it more a toilet rather than less. Photography is realism!—why make excuses?

November 5. Following the custom of this season, *Don Juan Tenorio* is being played at almost every theatre in town.

We went, a half dozen of us, with great expectations, remembering last year, and were not disappointed.

The same handsome devil played *Don Juan*: he had taken on a few extra curves, especially noted fore and aft of his umbilical region, presenting a most voluptuous silhouette. Unfortunately, the *Doña Inés*, fat and "cursi"—vulgar—of last year, had been replaced by a quite beautiful woman: nevertheless when *Don Juan* grappled to carry her away, she needs must jump up a bit to aid him in the abduction—but why not grant this often true to life!

The last scene—*Don Juan* and *Doña Inés* were in heaven. Heaven was presented like the "Venice Amusement Pier" or "Coney Island." Back of the throne on which sat the lovers, now awakened to life immortal, were great windmills of swiftly revolving colored lights; more lights of every gorgeous hue played from the wings and front, while to the strains of soft music, a chorus of fat angels in pastel pink tights cavorted, wriggled, floundered to regale the deceased. The hero and heroine in heaven, in quite unheavenly embrace, — while the colored wheels went round and round!

November 12. I have sometimes said or written, that "I am in a fine creative mood—period." This is misleading, it seems to indicate some hour, day or week when I happened to be in an especially exalted state of mind, or raised to emotional heights. This of course is the way of all artists as portrayed in novels, "best sellers," and is indeed a pretty picture to palpitate the hearts of kindly spinsters, male or female, in need of someone or thing to mother; a dog or cat would do as well!

But fact is not indicated in such sweet fiction: peace of mind and an hour's time, given these, one creates. Emotional heights are easily attained, peace and time are not. Yesterday I "created" the finest series of nudes I have ever done, and in no exalted state of mind.

I was shaving when A. came, hardly expecting her on such a gloomy, drizzling day. I made excuses, having no desire, no "inspiration" to work. I dragged out my shaving, hinting that the light was poor, that she would shiver in the unheated room: but she took no hints, undressing while I reluctantly prepared my camera.

And then appeared to me the most exquisite lines, forms, volumes—and I accepted,—working easily, rapidly, surely.

Today, reviewing yesterday—with my new negatives at hand—comes the emotion which did not arouse my "creative mood."

Afternoon—The "peace of mind" aforementioned I would indicate as that state of being, in which one is reasonably free from petty worries of a material sort: the heart-ache of tragedy is not so devastating as the belly-ache of poverty. A broken heart is more easily cured than a shrivelled stomach.

November 13. I made fifteen negatives of A. Eight I may finish, six most surely. My first enthusiasm has not abated, I was not unduly excited. Under cool reconsideration, they retain their importance as my finest set of nudes,—that is, in their approach to aesthetically stimulating form. Most of the series are entirely impersonal, lacking in any human interest which might call attention to a living, palpitating body.

Not that I am prepared to say this is a finer use of photography than the rendering of realism, the frank statement of fact, the capturing of fleeting moments from life, as I have done, and never better than with Tina,—in fact I have always held the latter approach more important, since no other medium can possibly picture life so well: but one must satisfy all desires and at present my tendency seems entirely towards the abstract. If this is not so fine a use of my medium, it may indicate a more introspective state of being, a deeper intellectual consideration of subject matter. But I am not prepared to argue these debatable issues: enough, if I work, produce, and let the moment direct my activities.

November 14. It is—well, most fortunate that I took advantage of A.'s presence the other day. She was badly hurt in an automobile accident the night following the sitting and is now in a hospital with various cuts, contusions and a broken

136

ankle. Poor girl! I shall send her a set of proofs to cheer her. The reckless driving of automobiles in Mexico is appalling!

November 14. This afternoon billions of diamonds fell from the sky. The sun shone upon a terrific hail storm backed by leaden thunder clouds. Arched high over all, framing the downpour of brilliants were two complete rainbows. We were printing in the little dark-room on the azotea. Hail stones attacked our paper-roof like fire from machine-guns: work became impossible from actual confusion of senses.

November 17. I am flirting with the idea of giving up cigarettes. There is no morality connected with this proposed restraint of appetite—but wait!—it gave me an immediate reaction to write down "there is no morality"—am I indeed afraid of becoming moral!—for then I am as weak as one who fears to be immoral! No, I have no wish to attain any height of morality nor immorality, but I am impatient with my lack of poise in smoking: it has become a nervous habit which half the time I neither need nor enjoy. Yet there must be a need or else why do I forsake my pipe, in which there is such serene enjoyment? Well, I do know why I desire to limit my cigarettes: they may be lowering my vitality—and I need it all, every ounce, for my work.

Friday the 20th. Day follows day of gloomy weather. Without a watch, noon might be twilight. The sun seems in permanent eclipse, and only with sun, is Mexico—Mexico. O for a crackling, roaring grate fire these days! But it is colder and sadder indoors than out.

Yesterday we drove to Chapingo, Carleton Beals having procured a government auto. The attraction other than viewing new country and the National School of Agriculture was Diego's new murals in the school. The ceiling and top panels were almost complete. Two tremendous nudes dominated the room—to the right a prone figure from a drawing of Tina—to the left a semi-erect figure from Lupe—both majestic, monumental paintings. The ceiling with figures in exaggerated perspective was intellectually provocative, stimulating, but effort and calculation were more evident,—while the first mentioned nudes were presented with such grand manner as to bring no questioning. The are worthy of anyone's pilgrimage and homage.

At Chapingo we met Khan Koji, most lovable friend of last year. Dinner with him,—then a hurried drive home to escape the menacing storm.

The sun is at last unveiled. I feel more like working and happily it shall be work for myself. I have found a retoucher who can prettify all the obese and wrinkled hags who expect full value for keeping me in salt. I have been tortured by such work for weeks.

Ten minutes, no more, the sun shone. Then I donned my bathrobe over a wool shirt. Even the glow after my morning inquisition, the cold bath, does not stop my shivering for long, and the ceremony of morning coffee warms but briefly. Everyone wears a long face offering no compensation. To spend the day in bed with a congenial... [fragment missing].

November 21. ...but I only sneer to hide a hurt, my sarcasm is a defense against my emotional self. I know this even while I ridicule and scoff and grin. The hurt may come from my own false gestures or the guile of another—either way I acknowledge disappointment with contempt. Better if I could start with a premise admitting possible incompatibility and hold a philosophical attitude throughout. But no, my fault or not, the protecting grimace comes.

From Paris yesterday arrived a most beautiful, tender letter from Miriam. Here is a letter I may turn to, not only for its contents, but also for the memories it recalls, when I find myself indulging in that perennial weakness of mine—unwarranted cynicism. Diverse reasons returned me to the States last winter: if nothing else had been attained but the new love and friendship of Miriam I have reason to be ever grateful.

She had always attracted me. For the last several years she had appeared and reappeared to me in person and in thought,—but the right time delayed. Then came the night on her hill-top. The Rabbi's good wine—God bless him!—the first kiss—the assent—the affirmation. But from the vagrant episode which might have died that night, grew rare affection which has never lessened. Each fresh contact brought me finer appreciation, fuller understanding and ever increasing ardour. To be with Miriam was a fulfillment. She is in Paris, I am in Mexico—a few thousand miles away. Three months ago we parted, today I retain impressions as of yesterday of all our times together. I find myself climbing once more to her hill-top, or racing with her over the white sand of Carmel, or listening to Stravinsky, or pointing my camera towards her naked body.

Sunday—November 22. The weather condition unchanged,—cloudy, cold. I cannot print and am most impatient to do so. The nudes of A. have caused more comment than any work I have done. All the group of friends,—Diego, Jean, Rafael, Monna, Felipe showing much enthusiasm. I visited A. in the hospital, finding her happy with the proofs. She has a broken ankle and is quite badly bruised and cut.

For me too, her accident was unfortunate. I should like to have continued on working with her in the same frame of mind and direction, correcting my mistakes,—the worst of them being in the use of a distracting background. I knew it to be bad at the time, but in my fear of losing lines and postures never to be repeated, grabbed the first thing at hand. Now I pay penance: I shall repent for my haste when I attempt to simplify a messy background in the printing.

Tuesday the 24th. I am told that when Clemente Orozco—a Mexican painter—and considered one of the best, went into the States via New York, his drawings of nudes, a life's work, were destroyed by the U. S. custom-house officials: he was not allowed even the alternative of sending them back!

November 25. Cuernavaca—guests of Fred Davis. From the chill, dark gloom of Mexico, to the frosty pine-covered heights of Las Tres Marias, then down, down to tierra caliente, into paradise—the Valley of Morelos.

Today, staring out upon the drab sky and sad city street, yesterday returns as a tantalizing mirage, a favored moment in some Eden.

I was incited to work, the stately palm in Davis' garden... [page missing].

...than that of last year,—though so different in intent, as to be perhaps, not comparable.

Brett echoed my thoughts—"I don't like Mexico City any better than Los Angeles, Glendale or any other city." But I might add, if it is to be a city, let it be a real city, New York or San Francisco.

December 2. Diego Rivera received first prize, 3000 pesos, in the Los Angeles "Pan-American" exhibit. All we "Mexicans" are happy, though for my part I wish Jean might have won, if for no other reason than his actual financial need. I think Jean is quite in distress, his demeanor indicates worry. And Felipe is another whose condition is revealed in his bearing.

Tuesday—In Mercedes' honor, we gave a party. It was so much like the old reunions at Lucerna 12, that I quite expected Chandler to appear. Galván came with guitar and song; Jean, Carleton, Frances, Diego, Lupe, Pepe Quintanilla, the Salas recreated the past, and A. bandaged but gay, was carried to her first fiesta since the accident.

The weather having favored me at last with printing days, I had ready to show a print of the new palm. Why should a few yards of white tree trunk, exactly centered, cutting across an empty sky, cause such real response? And why did I spend my hours doing it? One question is simply answered—I had to!

December 6. "While the cat's away the mice will play"—only I should not indicate Tina as a "cat"—not in the shrewish usage of the word. Nevertheless the "fiesta" of yesterday would not have been possible had she not been away posing for Diego.

Brett and X. and I sat down to the table for dinner together. There was a half keg of beer which we tapped—with unforseen consequences, for not always from a few glasses of beer does one attain such hilarity. But it was a day forecast for inebriety, Bacchus in the ascendancy, and we honoured him well! First X.'s eyes began to roll heavenward, then Brett suddenly turned his beer upon the bread and with a gesture quite as bombastic as a matador tossing his velvet hat, let fly the empty glass over his shoulder.

There was no work that afternoon, but singing, dancing, grandiloquent words and nonsense. Brett was a burlesque worth a price of admission: we wept from laughter.

Yet how I would be criticized, berated for allowing my son to so shame himself —even taking part in his downfall!

But I know Brett! So full to overflowing with life! I did not scold him when an "obscene" drawing from his pen was turned over to me by his teacher; I put it in the waste-basket with a chuckle. He could be ruined by a tight rein or a long face. He needs to explode naturally. He is bound to adventure much, to experience much. He is open-faced, laughter-loving, amenable to suggestion. I hope to help him when he stumbles or give him a gentle kick in the right direction —if I am able to decide which is right, at the time!

I was forced to make a hasty decision when we first arrived. An obvious homosexual made pressing overtures to Brett. And what was I to do, with a personal distaste, but no moral objections? If a woman of the right kind had desired him, I would have aided the affair, but to have Brett at thirteen thrown into a perverse relation, unformed in tendencies as he is, perhaps to be physically drained by this very sophisticated older man, I could not give in to. So the person suddenly disappeared from his life. With my attitude towards so-called perversions, which is certainly understanding and tolerant, I retained some feeling of guilt over what I had done, for the man was infatuated, and wealthy, would have done for him in ways that I cannot. Well, in three years, I shall not stand in the way of any experience which opportunity may afford him.

December 6. A letter from Johan—always an event: and a letter from Alfred Stieglitz, postmarked Lake George, N. Y. He has been very sick—but, "For the past four weeks I have been able to work like one possessed," and, "I want O'Keeffe to stand on her own feet through her work. She is developing greatly. And is taking root if taking root is possible for any real artist in our country."

December 9. Following a telegram with advice of her mother's precarious condition, Tina left for San Francisco this morning! The house is so strangely empty.

December 10. In writing of the street songs of Mexico City, I did not put down that one most often heard, the song of the Indians in conversation. No matter what chance the Indians are given to regain their lost dignity as a race, which seems the present political tendency—though I must guess from reasons not wholly altruistic,—ulterior motives such as brought prohibition in the States— how can they fit into a material world, this present commercial age?

The Indian needs a new shirt,—does he buy it?—not if first he sees a fancied bunch of flowers! When hungry does he consider calories for maximum nourishment?—no—he eats and drinks for pleasure, most likely wandering to the nearest pulquería. Or he may prefer to starve all week, tightening his belt in anticipation of the Sunday bull-fight. So one questions—what hope is there for such uncalculating lovers of life?

December 13. Days of professional printing, tiresome indeed, but the weather not permitting work with platinum, I did not rebel.

Well, I have been rebellious enough in another way and do not know just how to handle the situation. Since Tina's departure, X. and Elisa too, have hovered over me and pestered me till I am half crazy, never knowing a sure half-hour to myself. They imagine that Tina's absence means one long fiesta of play and love-making. If the North American is too much concerned with business, the Mexican is over-steeped in love. Granted it is a more colorful life, one becomes nauseated with "amor" and it becomes quite as boresome as business. The two races might well mix to advantage, attaining an agreeable balance. So I am paying a price for my conquest.

December 15. The catalogue and papers at hand reproducing canvases from "Pan American Exhibit"—L. A., reveal scarcely a stimulating achievement. I am not surprised. This is an age of "scratch my back and I'll scratch yours."

I am guilty too. Afraid to offend with my true opinions for fear of ten centavos loss. I should like to test myself someday with just enough money ahead to allow of snapping my fingers at public opinion.

The Anglo-Saxon is eminently equivocal. He goes beyond hypocrisy in self-deceit, actually believing in his formulated buncombe, so warped in judgment, and blinded by "should" and "should not", that his real self no longer responds to uncoloured "likes" and "dislikes."

The water stops, maybe for an hour or maybe for a day or two. Fortunately, I have had no catastrophe from [safe] light failure during development. I have that to expect.

December 17. I went to Jean's for chocolate at 7:00, taking reproductions of the Pan American exhibit. "Really though," he said, "I am so angry with painters and 97% of paintings, I get to hate them," and turning over the newspaper, "Now look at this, it is something fine"—a news photo of a football player in action!

One can always expect to find a fresh new attitude in Jean's work, or rather he has no "attitude," is continually experimenting, changing. I spent three hours going over his new drawings and paintings with the greatest interest and pleasure. He is growing into an important figure, while Diego, unless he gets out of his rut, has reached his limit; he is going around in circles, repeating successes, but cold and calculated in their formulization. Charlot has no mannerisms, not in colour, brush-work, arrangement, subject nor medium.

I saw at Jean's a drawing by a young Mexican, Pacheco, it was excellent!

December 18. Destroying old negatives, saving others for possible sale, reconsidering some for printing.

Today dawned clear and cold. After a hard rain the hills much lower than Ajusco are topped with snow, and the Ice Woman is resplendent, dazzling in her fresh white shroud. At last! I can print palladio, and God help visitors who bother me.

Besides a number of 8 × 10 negatives I have decided to print contacts in palladiotype from a series of 3 × 4 Graflex. Aesthetically they will be quite as satisfying, and the time used in enlarging two dozen or more small negatives, I might better spend in doing new work.

December 21. I had a curious experience last night which well proved that my habit of going to sleep evenings no matter where, is not disinterest in my surroundings nor lack of mental stimulation. I fell asleep viewing *The Gold Rush* — Charlie Chaplin, — dozed off while those around me were shrieking with laughter and I too had been just a moment before. I felt it coming on, my brain fought desperately but hopelessly for mastery over my physical self, so I missed some choice bits. Charlie is as great a tragedian as comedian, and he makes use of those less obvious, little ironies of life, more poignant than standardized sorrows. An article I recently read by "Sadakichi" [Hartmann] contra Chaplin, sounds like the wail of a misanthrope embittered over failure and envious of success. For though Charlie may be spoiled and overrate himself—he stands alone in Filmdom!

Carlos Mérida back from N. Y., having successfully arranged for an exhibit: the dealers fighting for the privilege. Latin American art will yet be the rage.

December 22. X. can never understand how one would at times rather work than make love. I was actually driven from the house the other night by her persistency and spent some preferable hours alone wandering the streets and sitting in the Alameda.

Brett and I to "El Toreo" yesterday. If I were not blasé over bull-fighting I might write pages of enthusiasm about Sánchez Mejías. His marvellous and daring work with the banderillas, his perfect control, mastery of the bull. I have seen no one fight so close, nor with such seeming risk. He fights not merely with bravura and elegance but with brains. Brett is quite as much interested in "the bulls" as I am and always anxious to go.

I have been offered a government position, to teach photography in a technical school for girls. Two hours daily, five days in the week and pay during vacations, the salary 120 pesos a month. Small but sure income.

December 23. I'm acquiring a fine complex over the weather question. How quick I would take the next train for Cuernavaca, Guadalajara, or any place of genial warmth if I dared spend the money. But no sittings lately and none ahead. I shall yet have to accept the "professorship."

The Principal of the Gabriela Mistral school is short and fat, two watery blue eyes fade into the alcoholic patina of her face streaked with hasty dabs of powder. She sits sideways, braced as though fearing a toboggan slide to the floor, her plump hands discreetly folded amidships over what once was a stomach, now seen as an unbroken swell progressing from the chin. Her eyes roll unctuously, her head nods knowingly, while Rafael explains that I would rather accept 90 pesos a month as professor than prostitute my art by commercialism!

Yesterday I worked with the 8 × 10. A mask against petate: a pig-tailed "Pancha" of woven reeds against an equipal. But it was too cold to develop; I went to bed to keep warm.

One so easily gets into a rut. Why I have not used the white stock palladio before can only be answered by admitting myself addicted to buff from years of professional usage. And to use a tinted stock is a form of affectation near to "artiness." The white stock is clean, direct, unpretentious: it presents unveiled all the negative has to give. It reveals the best of a good negative and exposes the worst of a bad. There is no hiding behind a smudge of chemical color. Now I am troubled, for I would reprint most of my past work that still satisfies, but have neither time nor money. From the new negatives, the print on white stock which most pleases me, is a nude, a torso of Neil. It is a simple, artless conception and one of my best.

December 24. I have rolled with laughter, reading Brett's day-book entry of December 23. He writes delightfully, impulsive and natural as his way of speaking. Also his photography has been well seen,—done with constructive instinct.

December 25. Christmas day. It is raining, the city presents a forlorn aspect, especially the puestos which should be so gay. This year they hold more junk than ever, cheap tin toys, German and Japanese,—hardly a thing worth buying, except the piñatas which are gay in color, fantastic or funny in conception. It is remarkable that such plastic beauty can be achieved from the use of tissue paper.

La Noche Buena was spent with the Salas, Carleton and friends. Gayety forced with habanero and vino rioja, an immense guajalote—turkey, dancing and games until 4:00. Up at 9:00 to keep a date with Anita. Luziana cooked a tasty meal—real Mexican. ¡Qué bravo la chile! I sweat while eating. Conchita in her inevitable pink bonnet was the important guest. She was handed in turn to each, down the table's length, always bright and cooing. Charlot swears she said "¡Ay Mama!" at two months.

December 26. "Two things are necessary for the poet and artist. He must rise above literal reality, yet he must nevertheless remain within the sensuous. When both these exigencies are fulfilled equally there is aesthetic art."   Schiller

"Life proceeds not by burnishing up the existent ideals, but by the discovery of new and more vital ones, thanks to the imagination, which reaches out into the unknown whither the intelligence is able to follow only by a long second."

Van Wyck Brooks

December 27. ¡Qué mala suerte!—what bad luck—to be serenaded in Mexico for the first time and sleep through it all! Xmas night it was, but who honored me I do not yet know. The story came from our roomer with Brett's confirmation. "There were wild songs ended by the persistent cries of ¡Viva Weston!' They tried all the windows in turn and in vain. I came to your door and called, but no answer so thought you out." Well how, how sad. I missed a chance to respond with flowery speech. And think of the poor serenaders singing to deaf ears!

I have forgotten what the sun looks like! The streets are drenched this morning and fine rain is still falling. The fleas have decided summer is here and attacked with after-hibernation appetites. Elisa is cooking pozole de pollo for a dinner to Sr. Darday Abriani, a young Hungarian whom we met on the boat. I liked him at once. Jean and his mamma are also coming and I have provided plenty of vino rioja.

Yesterday, worked with juguetes again: three negatives with possibilities.

That professorship? No! the "salary" is not worth the distraction and effort —

December 28. 4:30 a.m. Rain! I'm a bit "nutty" on the subject. Warmer though, —that's something. But the warmth has brought mosquitos with the rain. They are a nuisance but don't like my flavor as do the fleas. It is rather a pleasure to scratch flea bites, if one did not feel them crawling on the job!

Elisa cooked a marvellous pozole, and received felicitations from all guests, — Jean and mamma, Sr. Darday, and Miss Goldstein my new roomer.

The best of the still-lifes is one of a rag-doll and sombrerito against my black and grey striped sarape from Texcoco. I satisfy my desire to make calculated arrangements by still-life: it used to be an attempt to introduce life into a preconceived placing of Studio properties,—pictures, pots, what not,—always forced, though I was better than my co-workers in creating these artificialities. Now I am content to take life as I find it.

December 29. 4:00 a.m. again.—I made five negatives all told of the juguetes and shall print from five: not all masterpieces to be sure, but each with some interest. I seldom make an exposure now that it is not printed from, for I never make a random shot. I am not speaking of portraits, when I battle to bring out or find an elusive expression, nor do I mean that I am always certain with my Graflex used without tripod, but the 8×10 view-box firmly screwed to a sturdy base usually yields results. As for exposure and development, their correctness is a foregone conclusion, which should be so with my experience.

I was working on one of the nudes of M. when a letter came from her, from Paris. "O Edward, I wish I could give over to you the feeling of complete immersion in love and affection your recent letters have given me. I can truthfully say they have been the one satisfyingly personal thing to me since my arrival here." And she writes further, "I am intensely interested in your writing. Betty and I discussed it."

I only wish I had this confidence in my writing. I seem to read between my lines something quite different from what I wrote, yet I try to be genuine, and imagine myself so at the moment. But when I glance back over myself speaking on such and such a day, I either snicker with amusement, or get a belly-ache, or "see red." If I could write in the "style" of Brett, with all his boyish uncalculated enthusiasm, then I would be content! But write on I shall, I need to, I derive personal pleasure, it is my way of exploding, my way of self-indulgence, self-communing—so quite enough. I even regret destroying my day book prior to Mexico: if badly written, it recorded a vital period, all my life with M. M., the first important person in my life, and perhaps even now, though personal contact has gone, the most important. Can I ever write in retrospect? Or will there be someday a renewed contact? It was a mad but beautiful life and love!

December 30. The only possible way to stay warm these days other than sitting on the oil-stove, and our stove is quite temperamental, refusing to function properly in crises, is to soak in a boiling bath or stay in bed: but these are temporary alleviations, and one soon proceeds to shiver.

A.'s body as the camera sees it, is mottled and blotched. The nudes I did of her, required a skin quality of exceeding smoothness, otherwise,—and this happened, the eye is disconcerted from full pleasure in the enjoyment to their fundamental offering,—form.

In fresh gingham of checkered pink, a contrast to her brown skin,—I admit almost unwillingly, quite agreeable, X. appears on duty after a hot scrub. I say "admit unwillingly" to emphasize a point, for consciously, I am willing at any time to change an opinion or alter a view. But nature protects from too sudden change which might unbalance, by making unlearning more difficult than learning. We cling to old ideals, we are easily shocked, we disagree with opposing conceptions of a foreign port and find fault according to our most cherished presumptions with politics or food, with morals or color combinations. Until suddenly or by degree, it is revealed,—unless we are impervious 100% Japanese or American, that what once was assumed as right in "Centerville" is not right in "Tlaxcala," or perhaps not right at all. And this is rebirth! Then how delicious

145

taste maguey worms, how natural becomes the Indian who buys a flower with his last centavo, and how charming is the pink and brown dissonance of X!

January 1, 1926. ¡Feliz Año! I saw the old year out asleep in bed!—invitations did not tempt me, nothing but oblivion. I start the new year holding no new resolutions and forseeing no financial security. I do believe, granted leisure and frijoles, the coming year will be my best in photography.

Came a Mrs. Swift from San Francisco with introduction from Imogen. I spent all day "showing off" Mexico, she being so thrilled that I received many a second hand emotion. Considering her first day I withheld from acquainting her with mole de guajalote y pulque—too sudden a break from ham and eggs, I thought—and took her to Sanborn's. I have before rebelled against the desecration of this architectural gem by the hideous modern murals, now I have a new reaction. The mural by Orozco on the stairway, granting its intrinsic value, has no more place in the building than the aforementioned paintings. It is to me, simply another desecration! But it is a powerful conception and I must know Orozco better.

January 4. The artist is considered the most impractical of mortals. Quite contrary, I would say, perhaps in personal defence, he is the most practical. Because he will not recognize as important much of the complicated machinery and useless superfluities of average life, the artist is damned as a visionary—which is true enough. He attempts to travel a straight line to his goal, cutting all possible corners, instead of deviating in tortuous spirals. For his contempt of custom as ordained by his peers, the ventured goal may end in gaol, it being incorrect, even naughty, to overlook "Keep Off The Grass," though the grass be withered or dead.

January 6. The sun hot and brilliant after his weeks of seclusion. Printing of course! Printing exhausts me. If I am ever temperamental as story book artists are, it is while printing. The reason is based on economics. The first print must be perfect, which is of course expecting the impossible. If it comes almost right—my purse says—"Good enough." But the craftsman answers—"Good enough is not enough." By nightfall the quarrel between "common sense" and "extravagance" has torn me asunder. If there was someone to pay for the ideals of craftmanship! One nude of Neil is "almost right." Should I reprint? Or is it "good enough?"

January 7. Printing of yesterday yielded five more prints, the most pleasing, another nude of Neil, though I must say that I am not happy with the rendering of deep black in the white stock, which seems to solarize more easily than the buff. The deepest blacks are not clean—they have a chemical quality—yet Neil's whitest of white bodies should be printed on white.

January 10. Diego came Thursday eve. I had fine contact with him. Being alone, I was forced to enter directly into the Spanish conversation and allow no thought to escape. He stimulated me greatly because of his remarks on photography, and on divers topics,—what actually amounted to his feeling for life. He speaks well, and I envy one who can so clearly express in words his thoughts. My own, clamoring for release, too often stick in my throat. If they did not, I might write instead of photograph, and that would be too bad, for there are few good photographers!

Diego is a profound admirer of photography. "I want to write about your work sometime," he said. And—"The exhibit you mention of machinery and modern paintings must reveal the painter's weakness. The best brains of our day, the strength, has gone into the machine. All the modernists are sentimental. Picasso is, except in his cubism. I like the work of Marcel Duchamp, but I like your photographs better."

I showed him Johan's work. "This man has a feeling for composition but not for the aesthetic value of his medium. Seeing his work I think at once of where it was made or of whom. Your work leaves me indifferent to subject matter. There is no attempted interpretation of a mood. Now this print of his would be excellent but for the indecision of presentation."

Then many topics were touched upon. "Europe does not interest me now. I dislike Paris. I am a typical American. What difference if the U. S. makes conquest of Mexico? The sooner the two races mingle to produce a greater race, the better."

Later, in came that sociable "social uplifter," a Russian Jewess rooming with us. She moaned, "I am so musical and there is no Grand Opera here." She always irritates me to exaggeration. I said, "The organitos serenading our windows are preferable to Opera, and an Indian's voice from out a pulquería I choose before all Carusos bellowing." Diego laughed and nodded in approval.

Another admirer of photography lunched with me yesterday—Jean. I repeated Diego's conversation, he often agreeing. "I too like the painting of Duchamp, but your photographs mean more."

January 15. Photography is, or can be, a most intellectual pursuit. In painting or sculpture or what not, the sensitive human hand aids the brain in affirming beauty. The camera has no such assistance, unless of course, the process after exposure has been interfered with, and hence ruined, by manipulation, manual dexterity.

My technique is never quite equal to my vision, but this is preferable to the reverse. The last few days, besides printing new work, I have reprinted several old negatives, especially of clouds. The results are far ahead of my printing of a year ago. Perhaps it is not so much a finer technique as it is a surer feeling for that which I wish to say aesthetically.

Reviewing the new prints, I am seldom so happy as I am with the pear-like nude of A. I turn to it again and again. I could hug the print in sheer joy. It is one

147

of my most perfect photographs. If (the saddest of words) if I had not needed to remove the spots in that patterned background, so carelessly used, I might be almost satisfied.

January 16. The weather, turning cloudy again, halted my printing debauch. But I shall register no complaint. I have worked steadily, intensely, and gotten myself into a state of nerves demanding a change, so I turned to my camera. Long eyed and considered as a desirable victim, I subpoenaed into service the armless, legless torso of a wooden church Cherubin. I found it all and more than I had hoped for, exposing seven negatives during the morning.

January 16. Evening. The letters of most importance come from the little boys – illegible scrawls—mostly the same refrain, "Dear Daddy, when are you coming home?"

January 18. Outside, yesterday was a dull dead day indeed; but inside with a keg of beer, hot pozole and pleasant company, the hours sped swiftly enough. Came the Salas and Eric Fisher, to whom I have taken a great fancy. Eric presented me with a most exquisite cigar-holder of carved amber he got in Vienna. It is to be counted as one of my treasures...

One does more in Mexico because one dreams; more time for dreams. You can't hurry because no one hurries. No one runs for a camión, they back up a half block,—you leisurely swing your bastón, puff your pipe, and they wait.

"Mi querida" "Mi morena"—my darling, my dark-haired beauty—they can love—these brown skinned Inditas. Thank God they don't talk "art." Mexico hasn't a group of "arty" people, mouthing boresome nothings, sitting around at studio teas. Too much talk—not enough work. Life—the passion of love—the passion of work—these count—these and nothing more...

Elisa sat near, planning pozole for our fiesta. I patted her cheek, saying, "Qué simpática Elisa."

She put her arms around my head. "I don't want you to leave for the States—ever, Don Eduardo." (It sounded nicer in Spanish)

"But Elisa, I may have to go."

"What is there to do there—vámonos todos a Guadalajara—let's all go to Guadalajara."

"But I can't earn a living there."

"We don't need money, we shall have a ranchito, raise chickens and pigs, and you can photograph the chickens and pigs all day long!"

January 19. 4:00 a. m. This is my hour—a time when I am most alive—eager— clear headed. This is the hour Johan and I always split over, he, most likely going to bed or at least going to sleep, as I arose! If we did happen to arise to- gether we had another difference, he would have his tea and I would have my coffee. I wonder if I would so write down these thoughts if it were not for my hour with morning coffee,—my early hour alone.

Every morning when X. dusts the studio-room, she puts out of balance two candlesticks placed formally under a framed print. I as regularly replace them and explain, while she shakes her head despairingly. She does not see, she has no sense of proportion. This irritates me more than the gaudy calendars collected from butcher shops and baker shops with which she plasters her room.

January 23. Even knowing Jean is to be vastly benefitted by his change, it was sad to view the breaking up of "Independencia 50," so long his home. He leaves today for Yucatán and I question if I shall ever see him again.

I wish Brett knew how my heart was warmed by a request of his last night. "Dad." "Yes." And then hesitantly as though asking a great deal, "I should like to have a couple of your photographs for my own."

No request from my most sophisticated admirer could have pleased and complimented me more. And his first choice was interesting to note, Johan stretched out on the couch at Union St.,—the long table above strewn with cigars—tea-cups—milk bottles—laundry—canned soup and what not from our bachelor days.

Sights I have seen in Mexico: A barefoot Indian wearing a wrist-watch; a charcoal vendor, face black from unwashed days of grimy toil, twirling his moustache with gestures elegant as a dandy; an Indian seated on a curb of the fashionable shopping district, trimming his great sombrero with a peacock feather; the owner of a street stand for tobacco, creating a doll,—yes—creating! for he smiled at it as he worked, oblivious to surroundings, and held it off for better perspective, head cocked as a painter might to view his canvas.

The "sights seen" to be continued.

I worked well that day in the Los Angeles industrial district. So far six negatives from the series have been printed. Now it has been clouds again. Brett called me to see them. One with fish-like form, quite exciting—and I have it.

Yesterday I felt the time could no longer be postponed to attempt finding beauty in our ugliest room, the "Louis XV" dining salon! It is festooned with wreaths of roses, embellished with fruited cornucopias, bedizened with scrolls and gewgaws, all panelled and stuccoed in most elegant rococo style. I took Monna's straight-laced rag-doll with "feminist" face, placing her against one fragment of floridity. She appears delightfully indignant, forced into surroundings so compromising to her starched reserve...

February 4. At last I have met again and photographed Victoria Marín—here visiting Lupe and Diego. I still hold the opinion that she is an outstanding personality. But she does not belong here in the city with conventional hat and clothing. She does not belong to this day of "flappers" —"pelonas."

Juguetes have continued to hold my interest. I did three fishes on a silver paper sea,—quite fine in form and in technique—and I did an amusing group of the little figures woven from rushes: two buglers announcing the arrival of Panchito Villa—two women gossiping oblivious to that important event: and I placed in front of a flowered petate, a parrot and a pile of painted fruit. All these I like very well indeed.

February 8. I have made the juguetes, by well considered contiguity, come to life, or I have more clearly revealed their livingness. I can now express either reality, or the abstract, with greater facility than heretofore.

But should we use "abstract" in describing a photograph? Better "elemental form" or "simplified form." But again, should one use "abstract" in connection with painting or sculpture? The most abstract line or form, of necessity is based on actuality—derived from nature, even as God is pictured a glorified man. If "abstract form" was used to indicate form abstracted from nature, then I have no quarrel. But no, its usage has come to mean, and I speak in connection with "art," something apart, something metaphysical, something done by the artist whose feet are where his head should be, whose head is muddled in the mire. These nebulous persons believe themselves soaring, but like those who indulge in a clatter of cryptic words they really grope for the very spirituality which they lack. To keep one's feet firmly planted on terra firma is to keep the head poised and receptive. To leap with wildly kicking legs towards the unattainable is but to giddy the brain, to miss the attainable. The higher the leap—the harder the consequent crash.

February 20. The coldest morning I have experienced in Mexico. If not the lowest in temperature—the most penetrating. In my dark-room at 7:00 the thermometer registered 38°, but outside I noted ice on the side-walk. I sit here with a bathrobe over my wool blazer, none too warm, though the oil stove is close to my shins. But a brilliant sun forecasts a quick change, and if the cold will only kill off the spring crop of fleas and mosquitos, already noted, I will gladly shiver on.

These are exciting days in Mexico! The government has closed all catholic schools in the republic—1000 catholic priests have been deported without even personal property or money. In Brett's school, fortunately exempt from this drastic measure, every indication of Catholic tendencies was quickly obliterated, crucifixes hidden beneath mattresses and morning masses discontinued. The result will be worth noting. A lid is not suddenly and peremptorily clamped over a still seething kettle without a resultant explosion—a reaction, as witness prohibition in the States. Calles has played a dangerous card which may undo him. Was he attempting to forestall another revolution? And will he cause one instead?

February 21. "Carnaval" week just passed. I "stepped out" but once. If Eric had not shown desire to go, I would have gone to bed and so missed a funfull evening at the Mendizabels'. Lacking enthusiasm I planned no costume until almost time to leave. But one idea came at that late hour, to look at Tina's left-behind clothing—dress as I have before—become a girl. So "Miss Weston" took the arm of "her" gentleman friend and walked down Avenida Chapultepec!

Gendarmes eyed us suspiciously—or was it my imagination?—but we wavered not! Once there, my mood changed. Helped by countless drinks of habanero, I became a shameless hussy! Monna, you were a beautiful boy! Frau Gold-schmidt, you, balancing on your snub nose a painted, perfumed rose—you were the burgess personified—as always. Herr Blank, you in monkey costume, were a dull monkey. But the antipático elements left early—and we danced and sang till dawn.

I recall chasing a pretty criada—my specialty—around corners, through doors. She escaped! I recall lying beneath the piano, groaning and shaking with ill-suppressed laughter at the Grand Opera bellowing of some ponderous male.

I remember our genial host placing a revolver at Eric's head, a subtle suggestion to cease embracing his wife. Eric murmured "Don't kill me yet," and waved away the menace. Of course there were seductive señoritas, and coloured snow falls of confetti, and tangles of ribbons which wound around and bound us, a laughing, swirling, dizzy whirlwind of "borrachito" fun.

February 22. This contact with Brett in Mexico has given me a clearer under-standing of the boy. The swagger he affects, the loud, bold words of self-esti-mation, his posture of a braggadocio, hide an over-sensitive personality. This I have noted in divers situations. He is physically clumsy, forever hurting himself or breaking something. But this aspect will pass. Mentally for a boy of barely fourteen he is well integrated—indeed beyond his years. His reactions to people and conditions are violently colored. He is able to formulate his opinions with fine perception of salient points. That someday he will write—or can if he so wishes, I am sure. And because he enjoys writing, I am sure that he will write. [fragment missing]

...horse-man, a sombrero and a straw-rain-coat to make an all grass symphony. And I tried, in various combinations, three black clay ollas de Oaxaca. These latter have been especially fascinating to work with.

February 27. Dr. Mayorga does not pose as an "intellectual," yet I always enjoy showing him my work. His response delights me, his enthusiasm warms me. He explodes with rhapsodic speech—not the calculated club-woman style—which is the more charming when he intersperses broken English with flowery Spanish. "Tell me where I can buy anteojos (spectacles) to see as you do," or "I want a pair of scissors such as you use for cutting prints."

When I showed him my series of Mexican toys, he exclaimed, "You are a god—for you make these dead things come to life!"

February 28. They came to cut off our lights for non-payment. Next it will be the telephone—that instrument of torture with which undesirables can invade one's privacy at any hour of the day or night. The telephone is the special joy of all the busy-bodies, live-wires, Rotarians, who lacking brains, want action. "Speed up life," cry these people of pep,—"hustle, bustle, meddle, push, we'll make this world efficient, we stand for Service, we'll bestir the dreamer, and put a red, white and blue oil-station at the very foot of the Pyramid." And phones and Fords will help them.

But I want to simplify life—my life. Christ! what a lot of excess baggage and blah we civilized moderns carry. We pay a pretty price for these extras, sweating to support supposed necessities which are superfluities.

If one could have slaves as did our ancestors—but alas, "all men are born free and equal"—something like that—there are no more slaves—or better—we are now all slaves.

March 4. Weak—from an attack of influenza. I tried to fight it off, but finally took to bed. Nevertheless, here I sit at my desk, dressed and writing, before 4:00 a.m. Tina arrived Sunday night—which was a big event, though not for X. who is bathed in tears. And I am genuinely sorry for the child.

March 7. Tina met many old mutual friends in San Francisco and Los Angeles, and several new ones: Jean Roy and Lester, Consuela, Dan, Cristal.

I have a feeling that I will see much of Cristal in Los Angeles, or even here in Mexico. She writes of the possibility of coming, and I would welcome her! A fine, sensitive girl, Cristal. From that chance meeting—or was it chance?—at my Japanese exhibit, a deep attachment has developed, stronger now than when we parted.

Ramiel tried to keep us apart,—that was not possible. I can understand him. He thought, "God—another female!" But the inevitable happened.

March 12. Today for the first time since my sickness, I feel again my real self. But matters have not been at a stand. A new exhibit is under consideration, as a move to stimulate business. This time prominent persons of the city, politicians, generals, artists and bull-fighters will be exposed to awe the buying public. To give added "class," the show will be presented under the auspices of the "League of Writers of America," Dr. Atl having offered the assistance of this distinguished group of pen-pushers.

What an irresistable combination, "The Emperor of Photography"—the "bellisima Tina Modotti"—"the League," with flowery phrases and flowing ties—generals, bristling with pistols and moustaches—toreadors, brave and bespangled

—a liberal dose of titillating señoritas—and nudes, plenty of them! My poor juguetes will be overlooked in such dazzling company!

But the juguetes have had their day of glory recently. Diego saw them and later Carlos Mérida. They both were so delighted as to augment my own certainty that I had seen them well.

Brett to my great satisfaction has been working in photography and has done several things which I would be pleased to sign as my own.

March 16. After reading Bernard Shaw's *Saint Joan,* I exclaim why have I not read Shaw before! What clear unfrosted thinking, what biting arraignment of the credulities of today which are quite as fantastic as those of Joan's day.

Vaccination!! Are we indeed more civilized, more intelligent, who poison our blood with pus from diseased cows, than they who burned witches? A century or so from now our system of inoculation will be referred to in wonder and horror. But then—the enlightened race to follow will substitute their own imbecilities, quite equally stupid, brutal, insane.

March 17. Having gone to bed early, I awakened early. The stars were just paling in the dawn, when I dreamily peered into the murky morning-light of my shuttered room. Nice to laze awhile in half-sleep, I thought, to evoke the imagery so delicious in the langor of awakening hours.

And then—is this fantasy or reality?—this spectral white bird poised upon my flowered chest?—this most elegant form—from where? Either it is an exquisite sculpture by Brancusi, or a creation granted me by Morpheus. With a rub of my eyes, it became neither—*only* a juguete, fashioned by some unnamed Indian.

Paul sent it for me to work with. I shall today!

Open season for fleas is now on. I have made several small catches. I should perhaps let them live and feast undisturbed, remembering the passionate pleasure from scratching their bites, but to feel them crawling excites me to murder.

I now have a pupil in photography. A well-to-do Mexican who will pay me $4.50 an hour, and I hope to teach him six hours a week. Finances being low I welcome this drudgery ahead.

March 19. Eric entertained last night,—not in the common usage of the word, with tea and marmalade, nor chocolate y bizcochos, but with his ever brilliant conversation. Excepting Paul Jordan, I have known no other whose conversation is so thoroughly diverting. He has achieved a style, not to indicate by style a formula. The most insignificant yarn he turns with wit, mimicry, and riot of racy, piquant words, into a finely woven fabrication which holds one charmed throughout—and leaves a memory.

As an artist recreates from the commonplace, so does Eric, reaching the climax with an ease of execution attesting his command of words. This he has—and besides, a lovable personality.

March 23. The white heron Paul loaned me, has been all that I could ask for to work with. Every turn of the body tempts an exposure, though so far, I have done no more than slight variations of the back.

The best recent negative is of three ollas, of black clay, grouped on the azotea—well seen and technically fine.

March 24. 5:00 a.m.—and my birthday morning. *And* 40! Sounds quite ancient! Estoy triste—but not over my age. I wish for the children around me!

X. and Elisa came, bringing coffee. They sat beside me singing birthday songs. X. told of the beautiful bed-spread she was to buy me. I heard her horrified! I protested, that she should so spend her money—"A little potted plant as greeting if you wish, but nothing more." My protest brought a scene—"One should sacrifice to give pleasure to a loved one"—she almost wept.

The Xmas gift of a ghastly Tlaquepaque water-bottle was bad enough—but imagine me with a lace bed-spread! I must prevent this catastrophe!

March 25. Celebrated my birthday by putting in hellish hours of hard work. First my student—a session of pretended profundity. Then a sitting, members of a wealthy Mexican family,—mother, child and dogs: the mother alone, the daughter alone, the dogs alone, the mother and daughter together, the dogs and daughter together, until my brain was a muddle of mother, daughter and dogs, wriggling and posturing, barking and smirking.

I was given a fiesta in the evening, with Pepe, Carleton, Felipe, the Salas, Eric and Dr. Atl as guests.

More pulquerías: "Acuérdate de Mí"—Remember Me; "Vamos de Nuevo"—Let's Go Again; "El Corazón de Maguey" – The Heart of the Maguey; "Horas de Consuelo y de Olivido"—Hours of Consolation and Forgetfullness; "La Reforma de la Providencia"—The Reform of Providence; "Me Estoy Riendo"—I Am Laughing.

March 26. 3:30 a.m. Black morning—star sprinkled—empty streets. We started for Mixcalco 12, Diego's home, planning to be in Santa Anita by sunrise for the annual fiesta.

"Yes"—they would be ready by 4:00 was the promise. They were not! Gringos are usually on time,—most Mexicans never.

Not a light, nor sign of life,—so we called to the window above, "Diego!—Lupe!" Diego sleepily answered. He had not heard the ring of his alarm. We walked the streets—waiting. It seemed they would never come down. Lupe leaned from the balcony—"Diego can't get his shoes on"—she chuckled. Another long wait. Lupe again, "Diego is sitting on the toilet." Derisive laughter, and a longer wait.

It was break of dawn before we left.

154

Arriving at sunrise, Santa Anita was already alive. A surge of people, mostly Indians, swarmed along the Viga Canal, jostling, singing, calling their wares, which were flower wreaths, fresh vegetables, wax canoes,—moulded facsimiles of the colourful boats crowding the canal: and, besides other symbols of the day, pale reeds were woven into diverse and ingenious designs, of which each of us bought several.

The canal was overhung with fronds of brilliant tissue, and the water below, agitated by gliding, colliding canoes, blended the colours into a vibrating kaleidoscope. Diego remarked, "Good material for the impressionistic painters!"

Finally we too were floating down the water amongst the singing, bantering, vacillating throng, perhaps out of place in our civilized costumes. Yet, one of us, rebozo-wrapped and flower-crowned belonged there. It was Victoria.

March 30. The woven palm-leaves from Santa Anita—which I had called woven reeds until corrected by Rafael—proved tempting material to work with. I have made several negatives, one especially significant in form, exquisite in texture, and symbolic of Mexico. Then I have a queer fish or an animal, or bird, but the likes of which was never seen on land nor sea. It is quite a creature of the imagination—perhaps a penguin with webbed feet and scales. Diego loaned me this amphibian of papier-maché. I have two negatives—jolly records of this humorous beast.

With what aversion I await the arrival of my new student!

Last night I literally ran away from the house—to be alone. After a long walk I found myself in a "movie," more to sit awhile than see the show. I had not even read the program before entering.

The Passion Play, photographed at Oberammergau was showing, which was of interest, since I had not much idea of the production. But of much more interest to me were the inconsistencies in the program as presented by the theatre management.

Before the Passion Play, a Buster Brown Comedy was shown, and after, a Wild West film by Tom Mix. While Christ was healing the blind and raising the dead, an orchestra rendered the Anvil Chorus from *Il Trovatore*. While Nuestro Señor was being nailed to the cross, a sensuous danzón was played, and his descent was enlivened by a blare of jazz!

April 4. Came Dr. Peter, the best patron of my work I have had in Mexico, or anywhere else. He purchased as usual. It was a print from the boat series—San Francisco, price thirty pesos.

Have printed the black ollas, Diego's queer fish-bird, and the Palma Santa—the palm decoration from Santa Anita. The latter I foresee is destined to be well liked by those whose opinion I value.

I have a new and charming friend—this is also a forecast—for I have met Mr. Pat O'Hea but once,—the day he sat to me. Yes, he is Irish, quite Irish!

April 9. Another pupil! I should welcome this good fortune—this opportunity to earn an honest living. But I am instead quite depressed. I have no time for myself now, and my juguetes stare down from the trastero reproachfully.

April 14. Ten new platinum prints,—result of two day's vacation. My student away, the sun favorable,—I worked!

In trying to analyze my present work, as compared to that of several years ago, or even less, I can best summarize by indicating that once my aim was interpretation, now it is presentation. Also I could now, with opportunity, produce one or more significant photographs a day, 365 days a year. Any creative work should function as easily and naturally as breathing or evacuating.

April 16. These days bring no moment of loneness—not even with morning coffee. X. comes early, if I tell her I am busy, tears follow. Then Eric, who stays overnight quite often, may knock, and much as I enjoy him, I resent morning intrusion, one is not always ready for conversation. Then Brett follows; unable to use his badly strained eyes for study or work, he is more sociable than ever. Finally Elisa arrives with her never failing question, "How much milk shall I buy today?" which receives my never failing answer, "The same as usual!"

Tina alone hesitates before knocking.

April 17. Even as I wrote down the above description I was interrupted! However there has been no item of much importance to record lately. Yesterday Galván purchased two prints; in the evening Miss Moore, my new pupil, brought a "gringo" to see my work—another sale, and she too purchased; which, with the print Dr. Peter bought, brings my total this month to over 100 pesos, an unusual amount from an unexpected source of income.

Manuel (Galván) is now president of the Mexican Senate.

There is a possibility that our lives will be full of adventure and new scenes. A proposition from Anita may take us to Michoacán, Jalisco, Oaxaca and other points. I live in this hope, for I hate this city life and would gladly leave for anywhere, even the States.

Frances just returned from Tehauntepec, telling tales to arouse one's desire for like experience. But these are for her to relate. May our itinerary include Tehauntepec!

Just one joke I must remember—a true story. Frances went to a "movie"—they have them even there. A melodramatic Italian film was showing. The heroine, chained, was unable to escape from a mass of descending rock, the hero could not release her, their last moments were spent in agonizing embrace. The situation was too much for an Indian in the audience who frantically screamed "¿Por qué no se chingan, cabrones?" or "Why don't you_____, you fools?"

April 23—4:30 a.m. Rather early even for me! I sleep soundly, while it lasts, but awaken with a start, my brain active in planning the next move. If the contract is signed for my proposed tour, I shall, at the end of four months, leave Mexico. If the tour does not materialize I shall take Brett somewhere, perhaps Tehauntepec, and then leave. In any event, I hope, expect, and plan to leave.

April 24. In Mexico most everyone has suffered, so they don't bother over another's affairs. One need not pose. It follows then, that there is less hypocrisy here, for actions succeed feelings. But the Anglo-Saxon lives on self-deceit or wears his mask and becomes a neurasthenic or a hypocrite. What one can't feel, one can't be. To play a part too long is death to instinct with consequent introspection.

However the Mexican has formulated politeness. It is quite pleasant to be thanked by the conductor for paying a car-fare, or flattering to a lady when she is greeted with "I kiss your feet." But—in a camión a pretty girl is offered a seat while a tottering old hag stands; in public places, banks, ticket offices, post offices, there is more crowding, pushing rudeness, than I have seen in the more brusque "States." And the unreliability of the Mexican in keeping promises and appointments discloses their want of courtesy, their ill-breeding. Naturally one generalizes. Just now I am bitter over our treatment by Dr. Atl, who with fine face made elaborate promises to aid us in presenting an exhibit, and we were naïve enough to actually believe him! ...

These black clay toys and pottery from Oaxaca, I like extremely well. Some toys are in the tradition of the ancient idols,—direct descendants indeed. I also worked with a great bellied cat—or bat—I know not which: the creature's arms or wings, terminate in little bats, yes assuredly bats, for they are winged. Then Paul brought a most laughable startle-eyed bull, whose tail is the mouth-piece of a whistle. In fact all these juguetes are whistles. Interested in my present tendency, friends bring all sorts of toys for me to use. My trastero is strewn with them, awaiting their turn,—an inexhaustible source of pleasure.

April 30. Having sold, in the morning, another print to a visiting gringo, I hied myself to town, and purchased a f/4.5 Zeiss Tessar lens of 21 cm focus, for 80 pesos. Longingly I had viewed this lens from the street, in the window of an antique shop. I wanted it for my Graflex, having worked too long with a lens not suited to my needs. Anyhow I made the reason for purchase easy by many plausible arguments—and then bought.

Afternoon—"C. R. O. M."—the "yellows" as the real bristling "reds" call them, marched the city streets today in their annual labor manifestation. The parade lasted hours: we watched from Paul's roof. Every imaginable group was organized

157

from vaqueros to opera-singers. In the latter group was a bloke in derby hat and loud checked suit. He might easily have been a character drawn from a novel. He raked up the past of some last century melodramatic stage.

I wonder why there was no parade of prostitutes? They should organize for a six hour night and double pay for day work.

80,000 marched—80,000 hoping—

May 3 [?]. From a recent sitting, a six hundred peso order! One print each from seventeen negatives! But O! the memory of that sitting! The maddest jumble of grandmother—grandsons—granddaughters—great grandchildren—sons—and daughters—in every conceivable combination. I made four dozen negatives in one hour, thanks to my Graflex, without which I would not have earned six hundred pesos. This sitting I made on an empty stomach the third day of a fast!

May 4. Sunday, Anita and I went to Coyoacán for a visit with Orozco the painter. I had hardly known his work before, which I found fine and strong. His cartoons —splendid drawings, in which he spared no one, neither capitalist nor revolutionary leader—were scathing satires, quite as helpful in destroying a "cause," heroes and villains alike, as a machine gun. I would place Orozco among the first four or five painters in Mexico, perhaps higher. Monday eve he came to see my work. I have no complaint over his response.

I wish I had known him sooner,—now it is almost too late.

May 5. Frank Tannenbaum called recently—though, I am sure, not to see me. A superficial observation, quite superficial I admit, would be that he has all the petty dogmatisms of the average labor leader. One remark he made which at once gave the clue to his intelligence was in regard to Havelock Ellis' *The Dance of Life.* He "could not read it!"

May 6. I am not going to have the signing of this contract dragged out Mexican style. I have given the officials until Saturday to sign if they wish my services.

I carried X. from her bed into the cheerful studio—into the sunlight; she cried out in agony, "¡ Me voy a morir!—I shall die!" But she will take no advice. She should have water, air, sunshine. The doctor gives her injections and pills.

May 7. Moonlight and morning light combined to awaken me at 4:30, after a night of fitful sleep. I am overstraining my nerves to finish the 600 peso order while a spell of sunshine lasts. I want the money in my pocket, then I can leave here if the contract is not signed. My decision is quite definite, I only lack money.

May 8. Dr. Morley, chief of Carnegie expedition in Yucatán, came with letter of introduction from Charlot. He said that Jean was the "find" of the year for them.

After seeing my work, he asked what amount I would consider for my services next season.

How quickly would I accept any reasonable offer but for my family. Almost a year now, since I have been with my boys.

May 10. Monday—Rafael, lucky fellow, leaves today for the south, into the tropics, with an expedition which will hunt the breeding ground of the "langosta,"—the locust, so devastating to Mexico. My "expedition" is still uncertain, and uncertainly is demoralizing to me. The big order is finished—if not paid for, I will have enough cash to leave, but just enough, — and that is not enough. I want to return via Guadalajara. I want to live there awhile, but how could I earn a living?

May 11. Not only was the order paid, but a re-order received for 400 pesos more—a total of 1000 pesos—the largest amount, from one family, I have had in Mexico. Hardly comparable to the W. A. Clarke order of 2400 dollars which I had some six years ago in Los Angeles. In those days, orders for 500 dollars, while not common, were not unknown.

During a brief breathing spell, I printed my "changos negros de Oaxaca" and my black cat too. Both please me, except perhaps in minor details.

I used to wonder why the ollas from Oaxaca were made with rounded bases. They would not "sit up" in proper fashion, always rolling around on my floor. The Indians place them on the earth, give them a turn or two and there they sit secure. The soil conforms, the olla takes root, the union is complete.

May 13. Just as the light dimmed to prevent further work, I placed the last touch of chinese ink on unacceptable wrinkles, and finished the 1000 peso order. The tension, working against time and weather has been severe. To relax I should like to drink a bottle of Vermouth with someone. But with whom?

May 14. Let no one say to me that Mexico City is fogless. I watched the sky grey over and veil the city in a soft, wet mist. But it is rare.

After an apparent deadlock over terms, the expedition seems assured. With the signing of our contract, we leave for Puebla and Oaxaca next week. This is the opportunity I have awaited three years.

May 15. "The morning after"—a bit "crudo"—though I was more drunk from laughter than from tequila. I laughed at Eric, we all did, indeed we roared, for Eric drunk is a three ring circus. I needed just this hilarious evening. Of late my only laughter has been like D. H. L.'s, sardonic. Now, after the churning around of my liver, I am quite buoyant.

May 20. Martial music brought me to the window—it always does. Much as I despise the military, a drum and bugle thrills. But even more, the fife and drum of our Civil War veterans actually causes my hair to creep.

With dragging out of negotiations by the University, I am mentally prepared to leave this very week for the States. I am starting to pack.

Diego often said he would write an article on photography. He did, and Frances [Toor] published it in the current *Mexican Folkways*. The title is "Edward Weston and Tina Modotti." Though personalities enter in, it is really a lucid commentary on the art of today—and photography. "Few are the modern plastic expressions that have given me purer and more intense joy than the masterpieces that are frequently produced in the work of Edward Weston, and I confess that I prefer the productions of this great artist to the majority of contemporary, significant paintings." I should be pleased—and am—by such words.

Monday the 24th. I have had a definite offer from Morley to join the Chichén-Itzá project next season in Yucatán. The salary small—250 pesos a month—but all expenses paid and R. R. fare. I asked however for fare from the States, for I surely will be there. Jean will join the expedition again, and to be in Yucatán with Jean would be jolly indeed.

Tuesday. Did more work for the family of the 1000 peso order. I photographed the young señora in exactly the position she was painted by Zuloaga,—then copied the painting for her. They are taking the enormous canvas way back to Paris, so that Zuloaga may put a black mantón over her shoulders! What a waste of money and energy! There were half a dozen of Zuloaga's hanging around. Yet they overlook the far greater painters of their own country.

Saturday next I am *supposed* to receive the first 500 pesos on the contract for our expedition. If it is not forthcoming I am through waiting. This I swear!

May 26. Tina told a delightful story which quite demonstrates the Indian's indifference to time. Passing the tower on Bucareli in a camión she could not see the clock so asked an Indian sitting by "¿Qué hora es?—What time is it?" "Las tres en punto, señorita—exactly three, Miss," he answered. But Tina knew it was much later and told him so. "Entonces, señorita, son las cuatro—then, Miss, it is four!"

May 29. Brett with his butterfly net, I with my camera, went a-walking way out on the plain beyond Ixtapalapa. Mountains, which at dusk, might have been man-made pyramids, cut the horizon with geometric precision. The sun burned deliciously, the great plain, once the site of a pre-Spanish city, quivered in the heat, slender dust columns spiraled into the air, while we, so far as eye could see were the only human beings: until Abe came down a hillside, his fire-red pate flaming in the sun. Strange, for we of the genus "pale-face" to meet in such a place.

Today is the day—the question,—money or no money?

May 30. A check for 500 pesos in my pocket—letters for civil and military authorities—a program outlined—the expedition assured!

June 1. I was surrounded immediately by a rabble of gaping, gesticulating men and boys, mostly ragged Indians. Perhaps many had never seen such a big camera, not in action, certainly not pointed at their special haunt the "pulquería." They pressed close, interfering, but not intentionally, though I feared they would not understand the spirit in which I worked and cause me trouble.

We went to some eight or ten carefully chosen pulquerías,—Frances, Diego and I, to make records for an article Diego had written for the *Folkways*.

I have enthused before over the pulquería,—my feeling has been sustained. The aspiring young painters of Mexico should study the unaspiring paintings— popular themes—popular art—which adorn the humble and often—most often — filthy pulquería. This he should do, instead of going to the degraded impotent art of the self-glorified academician.

I photographed brave matadores at the kill—white veiled ladies, pensive beside moonlit waters—an exquistitely tender group of Indians,—Diego himself could not have done better—and all the pictured thoughts, nearest and dearest to the heart of the people.

June 3. We leave today!

2. "Mexico Breaks One's Heart"

July 4. Mexico again after a month in Puebla and Oaxaca. If I had not so much finishing to do, from over a hundred negatives exposed on the trip, I would be depressed indeed to be here. Mexico City is not Mexico at all.

Oaxaca, city raised from rock,—a mellow, yellow-green rock. After the rain which swept the country afternoons, the glistening rock turned to jade,—one walked on flagstones of jade.

The train trip to Oaxaca, a twelve hour ride, was varied in aspect and climate. Miles of waste-land interspersed with little oases brilliantly green,—hills dry, and prickly with organ cacti, followed by ravines where fields of sugar cane galloped in the wind.

Contrasting to the drab railroad stations in the States, each little stop had some interest,—a new food to try, new costumes to note, new types to discuss. We gorged on mangoes at three for five cents and on aguacates even cheaper. We chanced tamales which proved savory, steaming hot, and burning with chile.

A "bad man" impressed us all. He outrivaled a movie make-up in acting and in costume. He lounged wickedly on the station platform, clad in black shirt and scarlet neckerchief,—sizing up the crowd from furtive eyes,—fumbling his six shooter true to all tradition.

Travelling in Mexico has not the comfort we spoiled Americans expect. On a narrow gauge track the antiquated cars swayed and bumped along appallingly. Everyone carried at least ten bundles, and we, three cameras, tripods and suitcases. As usual cargadores mobbed us at the station.

When one arrives in a new city after dark, dawn holds out such eagerly awaited horizons,—to spring from bed and view for the first time a new land! And Oaxaca,—rain bathed, sweet and fresh in the morning sun, musical with bird song,—with water playing over cobbled streets, encircled by green mountains, topped by lingering clouds—fulfilled all expectations.

The architecture, dignified and massive, appealed to me more than the tiled walls of Puebla,—often exquisite but disquieting to live with. In Puebla one wearied of seeing daily the same portraits, allegories, flowers in tile. In Oaxaca the green walls,—plain or carved with simple elegance, achieved a satisfying visual harmony. And the people of Oaxaca are more agreeable, more open than those of Puebla.

The church dominates Puebla. Bleeding Christs beckon,—veiled Virgins implore,—the bells from sixty churches clangor arrogantly, demanding penitence and servility from funereal puppets who scurry by with averted eyes,—who cross themselves or doff their hats when passing a church portal. I noted one man, speeding by in an auto, remove his hat!

Being cheaper and quicker than train, we took a bus to Puebla. The road, newly constructed, was in fine shape,—the trip comfortable. Dusk,—when we stopped in front of the "Gran Hotel,"—every other hotel in Mexico is "Gran." A hurried wash—then out for a stroll. Fine luck—a fiesta was on in the plaza,—this was surely planned in our honor!—but, it so happened that we were passed unnoticed in the surge of people strolling by the puestos, around the band stand,—and around again. Well, here were new juguetes,—something different. Gayly coloured images of papier maché,—cartoons they were—of fat men—but really fat—burstingly fat,—and ladies of haughty contour, dressed in the bustles, the railing gowns, and peaked bonnets of long, long ago. These Indians caricature with exquisite sarcasm,—keen observation. The fat men had faces of surprised, baby innocence, revelant to the obese. The ladies swept by with high held chins, quite on their dignity. Of course we bought.

My note book shows June 3rd as dating the first negatives done. I worked in a private home,—a collection of antiques belonging to Sr. Bello. Rather uninteresting work but many exposures made to count in the necessary total. The four hundred negatives to be done appear at present as a herculean task—for each one must be exceptional in interest, technically fine, and must be finished within a few months, in my own interest as well as Anita's.

While developing the first night, Ray Boynton, here from San Francisco knocked at the door. We thought to have missed him, so were happily surprised.

Developing was a real labor,—funny only in retrospect. My manga de hule—sleeveless rain coat—proved its impermeability used as a hypo tray! And after, to conserve the hypo only the night-pot was large enough. That there should be no mistake as to its content swe placarded the pot—"Don't empty!" And always there was a commandeering of coats, blankets,—anything to keep out stray gleams of light. It seemed like a return to my amateur days of long ago.

Our first excursion was to Cholula. How insolent the Spaniards to crown the great pagan pyramid with their flimsy Christian temple! However, they chose a magnificent site, and from a distance the ensemble was perfect. Climbing the pyramid was worth while only for the view afforded,—the church itself had suffered from abominable restoration.

The Indian women wore elaborately embroidered camisas—blouses—but they were not for sale,—and I would have one. Finally one Indita, wearing an especially fine example, made known through an interpreter,—for she spoke but little Spanish—that in her village we might buy them. She was on the way,—we could follow, it was only a few miles away. We *followed*! I emphasize "followed." She started with that space-covering walk of the Indians, which is almost a run.

It was a hot, hot day,—we sweated and panted after her. An hour passed and Tina questioned—how much farther to go? "No es lejos, Señorita—it is not far, Miss." Another hour passed and we pantingly questioned again,—a like answer! This was now too indefinite—this hag ahead was laughing up her sleeve, we knew. A passing Indian was hailed: "How far to so and so?"—"About two hours away," he assured! We called "Adios," to the Indian woman now far ahead. She did not so much as look around! However, I had my camisa after all, bought it literally from the back of an Indita,—but only after much persuasion, while an amused bantering crowd gathered around us.

On the return to Cholula we stopped to investigate a little church,—no one was around, so we entered the forsaken weed-grown yard. Ray and I climbed a tumbling wall to better view and photograph details of the tower.

Just then appeared several excited Indians, one of whom in peremptory manner ordered us down. "What right had we there?—would we enter another's yard without permission?"—and so on. "Well, the House of God is for all," was Tina's retort, which seemed to rather stagger them,—and before they had time to retaliate we produced letters which might or might not have had any effect,— but fortunately did, more I think because the "jefe"—head man, mayor—took great pride in being able to read off the letter with much hesitating pomposity. A tense moment passed,—we shook hands all around,—and gladly parted!

There was great joy in finding important things in unexpected places,—for instance the stone angel in Hotel Jardín,—a squat heavy-set angel which only an Indian could have done. The bell-hop insisted it was no angel—that it was pagan. Evidence enough that our instinct was right—for it was an angel in every detail,—only the execution proved that the Spanish had but changed the names of the Indian Gods. Another instance was a ponderous stone cross. Christian symbols done with pagan mind,—and stronger for the pagan interpretation!

Everyone goes to San Francisco Ecatepec—the guide books insist. It does astound, this gem in vari-coloured tile,—even to me, blasé from seeing much, it brought emotion. The encargado—agent—would bring the keys,—"Vengo pronto—I return soon." "Here, leave us your sarape,"—otherwise he would never have returned!

Despite the elegance, the complete beauty of San Francisco Ecatepec, it was a nearby church which is outstanding in my memory. It was Catholic in name only,—it was completely Indian, and having been newly painted in crude colour, it held a barbaric splendour. The Indians were excited by the strange invasion but they were friendly and willing to help. I wished to photograph a bloody Christ with weird angular arms. His loin cloth was missing,—maybe in the wash, they chuckled, and grinned over his predicament while Tina scolded them for being sacrilegious. They teased us by speaking "Mexican" and roared at our bewilderment. Altogether a pleasant episode.

164

I am sure there are as many churches in Puebla as in a great city like Chicago, —the least of them more beautiful than Chicago's best. All, except a Methodist Church,—a crude, cold invasion from the north. The Catholic mind demands beauty.

No alarm clock was needed in Puebla,—the din from sixty church bells could awaken the deaf,—and out the window, black veiled women scurried to early mass. Here for contrast I record a pulqueria title—"Me Voy Fuerte—I Go Forth Strong." A little competition for the churches.

Hunting "retablos"—the votive offerings to this or that virgin who has miraculously cured or saved the donor—has been one of our joys. They range in execution from the crudest expression of simple minds to exquisite and sophisticated paintings. Almost our first thought on entering a church was—are there retablos? Not less interesting are the dedications. For instance, a child fell head first into a pot of hot soup, but through the intervention of so and so escaped serious injury. Another,—a woman in the throes of childbirth feared the deliverance of twins. She implored divine help and as a result but one child was born!

Pottery, Mexico's most important craft, had too brief mention in the guide. The splendid loza of Oaxaca receives not a word, though Terry deals at length with the sadly commercialized sarape. He could not overlook the famous Talavera ware of Puebla, but this loza is far removed from the truly indigenous pottery of Oaxaca—the Puebla ware has Chinese influence, and Spanish of course, though I am told and was shown, that it is far superior to the machine-made Spanish article of today.

We watched the making of tile and dishes and vases,—it seemed sheer magic to see the clay blossom into form from the potter's wheel. More magic at the glass blowers—molten glass forming like great soap bubbles. This cheap green glass of Mexico has great vogue now in California,—selling as something quite exclusive to the wealthy gringo for twenty times the price in Mexico.

But my thoughts of Oaxaca blot out those of Puebla,—and my first thought is always of the market,—and the market meant first of all loza—crockery!

I bought and bought—dishes, jars, juguetes,—of the dull black or grey-black ware, and of the deep green glazed ware. It was all so pure, strong,—really Indian. There were great hills of piled up loza,—the black round ollas, flanked by baskets heaped with juguetes,—bulls, horses, monkeys, birds,—every animal the Indians know, and some entirely imagined! And there was Cortés the conqueror, stiff in armour, draped in his cape. Very well do these people reproduce, make use of the essential quality of a material, —splendidly do they observe and utilize to advantage the very essence of a form. A race of born sculptors!

With my meagre collection of Oaxaca juguetes I envy no one's collection of "modern" sculpture. The little bells of clay which tinkle so sweetly, are exquisitely elegant,—a great flare of skirt forms the base, which narrows to a swaying waist and to up-stretched arms for the handle.

From the dull black hills of ollas, one came to pyramids of glazed dishes, gaily splashed with color, sparkling in the sun. And then to puestos of giant baskets, or little bird-cages, or fresh petates, or coils of rope.

Besides this visual feast, the nostrils were gratified by the scent of pungent herbs, of spicy fruits, or the bouquet of flowers,—fresh clean smells,—none of the filth of La Merced in Mexico. Nor was the sense of hearing neglected, a busy hum rose to complete a sensory feast,—the buzz of conversation,—gay repartee,—sing-song of vendors.

Market day—"dia de la plaza"—was a climax of activity. Hordes of visiting Indians came from far away. It was sarape day. We were besieged to buy even at the hotel door. Gringos pay well for sarapes which an Indian would not be seen with. Sarapes made to sell, with a great calender-stone woven in the center. But I found the Germans and French buy just such disgusting sarapes. Well, the poor Inditos had no luck with us. Instead we bought such sarapes as they with good taste wear,—black with a flaring red center, a few stylized flowers or whimsically fierce tigers. One questions how long they will keep their fine colour, for aniline dyes are universally used,—another sad result of commerce.

Bargaining with a group of Indians in the market, we talked on varied subjects. Thinking that like Tina, Brett and I were also Italian, they gave us a rather distressing idea of their attitude toward Americans. "The gringos?—we kill them and eat them!" It is unpleasant to feel this antagonism,—I admit justified on their part.

One is always the pivot for all eyes, and I would rather be the onlooker. Yet in the States I managed to be conspicuous, wearing my "knickers" long years before movie stars adopted the convenience of knee breeches.

But the Indians—the Zapoteca—were friendly,—so agreeable that I find in my note-book—"A misanthrope would change with contact of the Indians near Oaxaca." They are clean, have an air of well-being, and I noted few beggars. The women wear valuable gold jewelry,—earrings and necklaces,—and refuse to sell. They have fine carriage and noble breasts. Skirts are worn to the ankle with ample flare. Their dignity makes modern woman of the knee skirt—all too revealing, disillusioning,—look cheap,—awkward. The men dress in white with wide fajas of red or black tied in front and reaching to the knees. Sometimes a kerchief of like colour in worn,—and usually finely embroidered sombreros. They go barefoot or wear huaraches of excellent weave.

Two notes on huaraches,—Brett saw an Indito sitting in the plaza having his shined!—and in the market we noted many for sale with buttons!—a climax of corruption but very funny!

166

25. Pulquería, Mexico, D. F., 1926

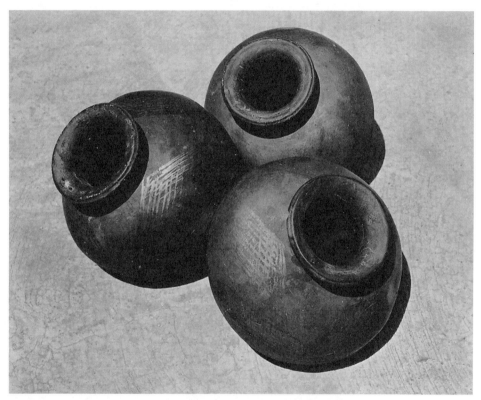

26. Tres Ollas de Oaxaca, 1926

27. ROSE COVARRUBIAS, 1926

28. MAGUEY, MEXICO, 1926

29. JANITZIO, PATZCUARO, 1926

30. Dr. Atl, 1926

31. Casa de Vecindad, 1926

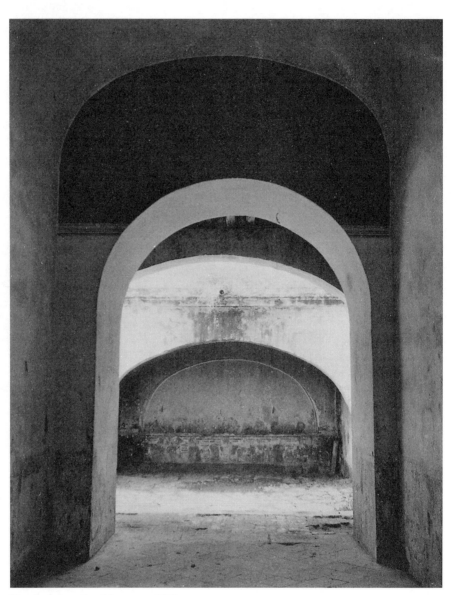

32. ARCHES, LA MERCED, 1926

These Indians continually suggested a remote Chinese ancestry. The slant of the eyes, the drooping moustache, the sound of their language,—they say "Chan!" for greeting!

Besides the pottery purchased in the market, I bought an animal water-bottle from an antique dealer—though the bottle was modern—which is quite as fine an expression as any prehispanic piece I have seen. It is of red clay. Water is poured into the body, which forms the container, and pours out from the open mouth. The neck of this bottle, which is the animal's neck, rears up stiff to meet the handle, curved over the body. Braced legs perfectly conform with the reared up neck and form a solid convincing base. This is major art. The same dealer sold me a fish,—a painted gourd, the like of which I have never seen. Nature attended to the form, but some Indian, noting her incomplete effort, decided to "gild the lily." Nature never created such a funny fish, with great, round, surprised eyes, a tiny, silly nose stuck on to a jolly fat body. A most perfectly logical tail helps him to buffet the waves. He is scaled all over, excepting his red checkered belly. Minor art—excellently conceived.

We lived well in Oaxaca. Hotel Francia I recommend with all augmenting adjectives. First item: it was clean,—then it lacked the usual hotel aspect,—then it was reasonable in rates,—and finally the charming French lady was a perfect hostess. The meals we still speak of with gusto,—a six-course dinner for a peso. But that does not tell the tale, for the food was abundant and well cooked,—more, cooked with artistry. Our room opened,—each side,—on to a patio, and there at night we would sit on the edge of a little stone fountain, the air fragrant from jasmine,—no—not indulging in romance—but washing developed films.

Yet when it rains into a patio,—that patio in Oaxaca,—one becomes perforce romantic.

Ushered in with full ceremony of celestial pyrotechnics, a few great drops spat, spat onto the flag-stone court, then the heavens open, the stone water-spouts piss from bursting bladders, the patio becomes a lake, the tropical foliage droops heavily,—then suddenly all is quiet,—all but a soft drip, drip, and the scarce audible, half-imagined rustle of night.

We haunted the market, hunting for loza, juguetes, sarapes, or merely for the pleasure of being there,—to watch the whirl of activity. We became familiar figures. "Ahí vienen!—they are coming!" we heard an Indita call out one morning as we approached.

I worked there with my camera,—the big 8 × 10 box drawing a crowd of curious spectators. I did a "close up" of the heaped black ollas and of the little glazed dishes arranged in pyramids.

The Mexican always displays his wares,—fruit or pottery or what not—with an instinctive sense of proportion. No matter how meagre the stock, it is arranged,

167

—and I do not exaggerate in writing that a stock may consist of three bananas, two oranges and a handful of peanuts!

Curiously thumbing the hotel register, I noted the signature of D. H. Lawrence. We decided to call on Padre Ricardo,—an English Padre, with whom Lawrence spent some time. We found him gone,—arrested and deported to Mexico the night before by the military. The neighbors spoke in hushed voices but with flashing eyes,—the criada we found in tears. He had been well loved. This was a hint to us of that which followed in the religious war.

The first excursion out of Oaxaca was ahorse to Cuilapam. There was a splendid Dominican church of the 15th century, built on a magnificent site, overlooking such a sweep of valley, hills, mountains, as to bring desire to return the horses and stay there with a fig for the future. I found some work to do,—strong hieroglyphs imbedded in the wall,—and a painting on another wall, standing alone amidst fallen arches, to do which I cut my way through dense tropical growth.

The next trip was to the ruins of Mitla. No camiones were going direct, so we took one to Tlacolula, a several-hour ride. There we waited with no luck for a connecting camión,—they went irregularly on account of the rains. Impatient, we hired horses and started on a long, hot pilgrimage, burdened with cameras, suit cases, tripods, butterfly nets, and rain coats. We furnished, I'm sure, a curious spectacle to the passing stream of Indians bound for Oaxaca,—the usual cavalcade on their way to market that one encounters on any highway in Mexico, —with a very beautiful addition—that of oxcarts, great creaking carts with solid wooden wheels, arched by a sun-shading canopy of petate. And the oxen, majestic, sculptural forms,—their heads held immobile, grappled together, bridged by a massive wooden yoke. The ox manifests power in every heavy move. He cannot be hurried beyond his deliberate measured pace. He submits to the yoke, but in his own way,—he obeys, but holds out a rigid plodding resistance.

Weary, hot, dry adventurers at last reached San Pablo Mitla to find a not half bad hotel. We went immediately, after dining and a brief siesta, to the ruins,— not in tourist style, to quickly satisfy insatiable curiosity, but to plan work for next morning.

Lacking time and money for roaming the country at leisure, we have had to carefully calculate our itinerary,—attempt to plan activities ahead, sometimes too suggestive of a forced march. But if we cannot travel as might a carefree globe-trotter, the very nature of our work has made us keenly observant, open to impression.

Our guide, *Mr. Terry's Guide*, was impressed by the dramatic desolation of the ruins and surroundings. I was not, not after deserts I have known in Western

U. S. But one's impression depends much on the day,—and ours was balmy, with rain clouds forming.

I am not one who can view ruins no matter how magnificent, and these were, with the same thrill of pleasure that comes from discovering a fine contemporary creation, though it be only a five-cent piece of pottery.

But I was fascinated by the stone mosaics of Mitla, for besides a variation on the Greek fret, there was a unique pattern,—oblique lines of dynamic force,—flashes of stone lightning, which remain my strongest memory of Mitla.

Adjacent to the ruins was a church. The Spaniards had robbed the ruins of ready cut stone for their far inferior construction. Here Tina made an important discovery. A stone angel bearing a cross, which made such an impression that every curve and cut I recall without reference to my negative. It was modern, we were told,—done last year by an "albañil"—a brick layer who recently died. The world lost an artist! I count this real discovery,—not the digging up of primordial ruins. Here was something done in the grand manner,—with tenderness and love and power,—done by someone who felt stone and cut it with decisive command.

The excusado in our hotel was like a throne. One ascended several steps and felt quite regal sitting there. And there was no way to shut out others who aspired to like heights,—one could not sit and silently brood without possible invasion. But the excusados in Tlacolula—can I call that terrible place we stayed one horrible night a hotel?—were even more amusing: just a large room with some six openings, where a group of sociable people might sit together and discuss the weather...

What a night in Tlacolula! We had to stop there on the return, for work planned in the church. The bed made one itch to see it. Better to sit in the plaza awhile before going to our room! The Indians wore striped sarapes, wrapped close, full length. One leaned against a lamp-lighted wall,—like a tiger in the night. For twenty minutes he leaned motionless, maybe longer, for so we left him.

We were not without reason for misgivings. They began at once their invasion,—the bed-bugs, and midnight found us sitting bolt upright, wild-eyed,—questioning what next?

Breakfast was offered us in a bed-room just vacated after the night! We took coffee from the store-counter,—flies were preferable to fusty, bed-room air.

Work in the church was delayed,—a fiesta was on,—Mass would not be over till nine. We waited in the church yard. Midway of the Mass came the tatoo of a war-like drum—prodigous cannon crackers burst—burros brayed—startled dogs howled – and the low rumbling bellow of oxen mingled with distant anthems from the church.

All memories of Tlacolula are disagreeable. One *waits* in Mexico for camión or train,—but there we waited—waited—desperate—for three hours. Here I might

169

hint to any young lady in a delicate condition that sure relief would result from a camión ride—Tlacolula to Oaxaca—in the rainy season! We went through roads which were rivers bedded with mud. Oaxaca and our nice hotel seemed like paradise!

Etla followed,—a short trip but not without excitement. We had walked to a tiny settlement adjacent,—not to say Etla is large, and in the church found a Virgin,—black robed,—quite exquisite in taste, so simple and unadorned, so unusual in this respect. Permission to photograph her was easily obtained from a gracious sacristan. She was however in poor light,—so the three of us, with ceremony and reverence, out of deference to a few onlookers, moved the effigy, dusted her, arranged her robe and made her portrait.

We had just packed and were leaving the church yard when a sharp command halted our exit. The jefe of the village and all his cabinet had arrived to demand with what right had we entered and taken such liberties in their church. Our official letters had no effect,—neither [did] the permission from the sacristán. It was evident the "mayor" felt his dignified and illustrious position as chief of the town had been slighted. He scolded the poor sacristan and argued pedantically with us. After twenty minutes of palaver in which he duly impressed us with the seriousness of our offence,—the barred window of the town calaboose was just across from the church!—the jefe ran out of official lingo and bowed us out of town. He had a wonderful opportunity to show his official power while we melted in a broiling sun.

A group of small uncovered pirámides near Etla kept us hunting idols for an hour, with no luck. But Tina bought from an Indian a prehispanic whistle, done quite in the spirit of those sold in Oaxaca today. One other recollection of Etla,— not an unusual one in Mexico, is the hours, long wait for a return train.

I wanted to stay on and on in Oaxaca,—and today, given leisure and money, I would return. But many other states ahead indicated the end of work and play in Oaxaca.

Little incidents often remain with one more vividly than apparently important ones. A drizzly night I took Tina's shoes to the Plaza for a shine. One little barefoot urchin donned them, and assuming lofty airs, lit a cigarette while the other, on his knees, shined.

It was in Oaxaca also that I saw underneath a shrine to the Virgin, all draped with red plush, gold embroidered, a table cover of blue-and-white scalloped oilcloth!

Another note—though I have seen like exhibits elsewhere—a coffin swinging on a bracket over the sidewalk to advertise a trade. Once I saw coffins painted bright blue and decorated, which seems a sensible variation.

Torrents of rain had fallen for days before our departure from Oaxaca,—flooding the country, washing out tracks. There was some doubt as to whether we could make the trip, but we found an antiquated engine waiting to take us to the worst washout where we transferred ourselves and luggage to the regular train, a quarter mile away. The cars lurched along as though at any moment they might leave the track. Finally they did,—with a shocking crash, grinding and plunging over the ties, amidst crashing glass and screaming voices. A moment of panic,—then we faced each other on terra firma with white faces and knocking knees. The engine had not jumped the track and with some manuevering the cars were shunted back in place. Proceeding cautiously,—the cars now creaking and groaning in protest,—a few miles later, around a curve, the engine struck rock. The cow-catcher doubled up, but on we went. Any pretext to feel one's feet on solid ground; so the toilsome pilgrimage over a washout was a relief.

Puebla at midnight—well worn out.

No less memorable was the trip from Puebla to Mexico. The bus left at 7:00,—one half hour later it was stuck up to the hubs in mud near Cholula. Once free and on a fine road, our driver made up lost time. On the straight-away the Cadillac went 100 kilometres an hour; over dangerous mountain roads, around curves even, so fast as 90. Only one who knows the fool-hardiness of Mexican drivers will appreciate this episode. When sign boards indicated danger ahead we speeded up a bit! I vowed to dedicate a retablo (ex voto) to any or all of the Virgins if saved from what seemed inevitable death.

When we stepped within our long vacant house it seemed but a cardboard toy after the stone strength of Oaxaca.

Through Michoacán, Jalisco, Guanajuato, Querétaro — Two weeks of developing and printing,—then off again,—Acámbaro the destination. From the train,—purple hillsides,—lupin purple,—or corn fields far as eye could see. One seemed to hear the pat-pat, pat-pat of tortillas in the making. The city, Acámbaro, lacked interest, but the country side was fair indeed, and continued so the trip to Morelia. Green, rain-drenched hills and valleys,—instead of lupin, purple water-lilies. Lakes, lily covered,—meadows of orange wild flowers,—orange shading to yellow, splashed with purple.

We were ready to leave Morelia after working in the Museum. The Indians lacked the character, as did their crafts, of those in Oaxaca. The church interiors had been stripped of all interest. But the city was clean,—had much fine architecture, and again the surrounding country was alluring.

In this day of the pedestrian's decadence—when even those who would walk, find no place,—we chanced upon a promenade, a flagstone walk, wide and long, lined with stone benches, shaded by elms. Here one might rest and dream, or leisurely stroll, unmolested by the insolence of automobiles.

Of course it was built 200 years ago when legs were still in use!

On July 22nd we waited two hours for the train to Pátzcuaro. Rain—rain—

171

water flowing over tracks,—spectral mountains opening cuts, red and raw, for the train's passage,—then Pátzcuaro—Michoacán.

Whenever we did not have advance information,—providing of course there was more than one hotel in a town, the question was always which to chance. Sometimes one look would suffice to turn us away, convinced of bed-bugs,—or the room would lack privacy—or be poorly ventilated. Hotel Concordia was unhesitatingly adopted. Rooms with floors of red flagstones—waxed,—ceilings of uncovered beams. And who could have resisted Pedro's infectious smile, his open face, his willing service. He tended our rooms and confided to us his woes. He wanted to return to his "tierra," but he never could save enough from his wages. He had hoarded two pesos, only to have his room robbed. He was sad, for he did not like this "metropolitan life" and his sweetheart was far away. I am certain no guest in that hotel had ever asked Pedro to sit down and have a smoke as we did.

Our arrival was well timed,—the next day was to be "dia de la plaza"—market day. The street below swarmed and buzzed with Indians cooking over improvised fires. One wondered where they slept,—so many vendors and buyers from far away,—certainly not in the hotels!

With us in Pátzcuaro was "Count" René d'Harnoncourt. He had [the] right to use "count,"—but did not take his title too seriously, except when with that species of democratic American eager to hobnob with royalty,—then his title proved a financial asset.

When René joined our little party we were a bit distressed. Conspicuous enough as new arrivals are in a small city, we were now destined to be heralded far and wide like a circus come to town. For René was just six foot seven, wore checkered knickers and white spats. The small-statured Indians looked up, stretching their necks as though René might be a New York skyscraper,—first amazed, then convulsed. But René was so charming a companion that we forgave him this undesired publicity. Evenings in the improvised hotel-dark-room, he regaled us with stories of court life in pre-war days, and sang to us the folk songs of Austria. Brett still recalls René's version of the *Marseillaise*, which he thundered forth to what must have been the amazement of all the natives within a city block.

That night we overslept, and René beat us to the market, returning in triumph with a water bottle,—a fat, round little duck,—a gem in red clay. Leaving coffee half finished, I scurried to the plaza and bought one,—the last, for myself. Later I purchased a bird,—a transfigured gourd: now I no longer envy Paul for his.

Again to write down admiration for the Indian in his sense of balance, knowledge of anatomy,—for in painting and amplifying upon the gourd, they actually recreate. The perfect placing of the legs upon the round gourd's body,—slightly straighter or more sharply angled, and the fine continuity of line would not have

172

been achieved. As it stands I cannot imagine a great sculptor creating more sensitively.

Market day in Pátzcuaro was next to Oaxaca in beauty and interest. The arranged produce [was] an incentive to buy: neat little pyramids of green chiles, bouquets of lily-white onions, a half block spread of sombreros. The sombreros served not only as head protection, — they logically enough became a convenient "catchall," a receptacle in lieu of bag or pocket. Glancing down at the sombrero of one squatting figure, it held — chiles, cigarettes, matches and a handful of tiny silvery fishes.

The costumes, even for "picturesque" Mexico, had unusual distinction. The women wore pleated skirts of scarlet or black, — pleated anew each day, for at night they unfolded to become bed covers, — and fajas, sashes of exquisite craftsmanship, and silver earrings. The old sarapes, even when in rags, held brilliant color, — were simple and dignified; the new ones often hideous. Red was a favorite color, and also black. Their wrapped figures became a scarlet flame against the grey sky which hung that week over Pátzcuaro, or loomed black in the drizzle.

One man with a rare old sarape, continually crossed our path, until Tina approached him to buy. Yes, he had worn it about eight years, — he would sell for three pesos. For once Tina did not bargain! Later that day we saw the same Indian proudly strutting through the plaza wearing a brand new sarape, — an ugly modern one. He surely thought, what a stupid gringa to buy that dirty old rag from me!

Good as hotel cooking may be, one tires, — so we were happy through Señor Solchaga to discover Buenos Aires and Panchita. "Buenos Aires" was made up of out-of-doors lunch counters. Panchita was owner, cook, waitress and dishwasher in one. She performed her fourfold obligations quite miraculously over a single charcoal fire. Panchita cooked for us better meals than the hotel served, at one third the cost, and, best of all, whatever we wished, if in the morning she was forewarned what to buy. This might be the dinner "menu": caldo (soup), arroz, (rice) aquacates well seasoned with onion and chile, jokoke (sour cream) served with tortillas, and of course frijoles.

"Buenos Aires" nestled at the foot of the "Santuario de Nuestra Señora de Guadalupe." *Mr. Terry's Guide*, with characteristic lack of appreciation, dismisses this sanctuary with the words, "It is uninteresting." On the contrary it has such great interest that we often walked out of our way just to be "inspired" (apologies to Terry) by the four great sculptured figures which crown the campanario. They were grandly conceived, executed by a master, — attributed to Tresguerras, but now supposed by some who have documents in proof to be the work of one Casas. The controversy seems immaterial, — sufficient these superb sculptures which have the strength and fineness of archaic Greek. Casas, or Tresguerras, (three wars) — the latter name conjures up a more vivid imagery —

173

is called the Michelangelo of Mexico, to indicate his importance rather than any similarity to the maestro.

Impossible to photograph these figures from the ground; I climbed the campanario,—even then only a profile was possible with the 8 × 10. So I crept out onto a narrow ledge, hugging close to the wall, not daring to look down,—and with the Graflex obtained a $^3/_4$ view. The slight jar of the Graflex shutter seemed enough to overbalance and drop me down into the charcoal fires of "Buenos Aires."

Unconnected notes—Offered for sale a lacquered screen from Uruapan of marvellous technique, but of deplorable taste, of picture post-card realism.

Encountered a store in which coffins and bread were sold from the same counter. The staff of life and the symbol of death,—take your choice,—on Monday buy bread, on Tuesday a coffin.

Have I yet mentioned how often one sees, both in painting and sculpture, black Christs? Or how unusual it is to find a Christ, gashed and gory, but wearing in place of a breech cloth, a lace petticoat and pantalettes!

Encountered the coldest weather in Pátzcuaro since leaving sunny Southern California. San Francisco papers will copy.

Delicious candies we overindulged in,—sold in the plaza, but surely not made by the Indians. It was hinted to us they were made by ladies of the old aristocracy, now in poverty, who turned to this covert way of earning pennies,—yet remaining ladies.

I had been wondering if our stay in Pátzcuaro was to be prolonged because of a threatened strike on the Railroad. It did not happen. Calles ordered all engineers who would not start their trains to be shot and replaced at once! Direct action in Mexico.

Analysts get busy—an entry of July 20th in Morelia—dreamed Cole was dead—awakened weeping and crying out "O my baby!"

I was possessed by a great uneasiness while in Pátzcuaro, in view of the government order to officially end Mass in the Catholic Church. One felt the tenseness of the situation affecting the whole community. The severity of the ruling might result in civil war. I recall one morning,—4:30 it was and pitch dark. I was awakened by a delirious clangor of bells,—more than protest, I thought,—an insinuated rebellion. Then came Sunday, August 1st—when no bells rang—a heavy silence, more alarming than the foreboding bells, threatened the city.

No longer did Tina, for favors, have to kiss the greasy hands of lecherous priests —but I insisted more seriously than heretofore that Brett join me in doffing my hat to every church door,—for now the attitude towards strangers,—possible government spies, or at least unsympathetic aliens,—made our situation precarious. We were marked. If we entered a church some fanatical old hag would

174

follow, or a crowd of sullen faces would eye our activities. A source of importance to our work, the sacristy, was closed, locked and sealed by the government. With the going of the padres, permission to work in a church was not easy to obtain, for no one cared to—or would not—assume responsibility,—so often we went around in maddening circles.

As I review our travel and adventure from the vantage ground of my comfortable desk I think this: that if a woman had not been in our party, especially Tina, with her tact and sympathy for the Indians, a woman which made the group seem less aggressive, Brett and I would never have finished the work.

Pátzcuaro, built on the slope of hills which flank an exquisite lake, is "picturesque." In the hands of American business men it would soon be a world-famous all-year resort. But the hillsides and shores are so far free; bill-boards have not yet conquered Pátzcuaro. Instead, green hills with scarlet skirts of women and scarlet sarapes of men scattered here and there like exotic tropical blossoms.

In La Iglesia del Calvario we found work to do,—several important paintings —though Mr. Terry again played the blind man. To reach the church one must climb a rocky road to Calvary, and the camera became my cross which I shirked when an Indian would bear it for a peso a day. The way up was stationed with little shrines painted as a child might see. Near the church, a hilltop commanded a great sweep of the valley, lakes and hills.

Idling an hour, we watched the Indian dugouts gliding from island to island or across to the far away shore.

The daily storm, approaching, alternated sunshine and gloom,—burnished the lake or turned it leaden. There was the islet of Xanicho [or Janitzio], and on the horizon Tzintzuntzan,—both places we were soon to see,—to retain vivid and not altogether pleasant memories.

The name Sr. Salvador Solchaga, to whom I had a letter of introduction from Anita, will always be linked with Pátzcuaro. With him we spent much time, and to him we are indebted for his courtesy as host and guide.

The night before,—to be sure of no delay, a Ford had been engaged to carry us to the launch, which also had been hired for the morning, with Tzintzuntzan the destination. That the Ford would not be punctual was expected from past experience,—that it would be an hour late exceeded our worst fears. ¡Qué gente tan informal!

The gasoline launch was out of place,—a modern trespasser upon this lake which once held the royal canoes of Tarascan emperors,—canoes we may imagine all brilliant in lacquer. Even today the slow-plying dugouts rule by right of affinity, —the motor's "put-put" and the stench of gasoline seemed sheer impudence.

In Tzintzuntzan "the centre of attraction" for guide book tourists is the famous Titian (or Titianesque) painting. It was supposed that we went as most do, for no other reason. Out of courtesy we had to glance at it. Not a single line do I recall! But, under the arches of the patio, well-remembered frescoes. In abandoned corners the stink from bat dung nauseated. Several women swept the church. They would sweep a few moments, then kneel in prayer. Up and down they bobbed, most of the time down. I wearied of the droning mumble from prayerful señoras, whose religious emotion, from over-indulgence, had become a formula.

But I was often awed by the fervor, the agony, of the Indian man as he knelt with outstretched arms before his God.

News of our arrival spread, and vendors came even into the church. Mostly prehispanic fragments were offered,—the usual clay heads, but I made one purchase of exceptional value,—a pipe, probably not less than 400 years old, most likely much older. The bowl was smoke black.

A more notable day was that in Tupátaro,—a long ride ahorse from Pátzcuaro. "Venado"—the deer—carried the cameras, coats, and numerous incidentals to a strenuous trip. Venado, a little grey burro, deserved his name,—not once did he allow the horses to nose him from the lead.

Few had seen this church of Tupátaro, far from tourist tracks. The Indians told us that only a "gringa" whom we knew was Anita, had visited their village before. She had insisted that we include Tupátaro, in our itinerary as being of great importance to her book, which it certainly was. The ceiling was entirely lacquered, even the beams,—a notable achievement in colour, design and craftmanship. Already ruined in portion from the seepage of rain water, another few years of neglect will allow irreparable damage to this fine monument.

Here in Tupátaro the villagers were more than hospitable, and excited as children when I asked permission to photograph their Santiago. Santiago was a childlike expression. They must feel more than mere reverence for a saint, he must be like them,—one of them. So Santiago was. He could have been displayed in any American department store amongst the toys,—a super toy. All details had received careful, tender attention. He was booted and spurred, over his neck hung a little sarape, around the waist a real faja, and his spirited hobby horse had been branded! Because of a recent fiesta the horse was still wreathed with roses. "Should we remove the wreath?" "No, no, please no!"

That was a hard day of work, so much to do that must be done before the afternoon storm. Exposures were prolonged to even [fifteen?] minutes with additional flash light, the while I must remain quite still upon a rickety balcony for fear of jarring the camera, which was real torture with more fleas biting and crawling than I ever knew could jump from a few square feet of space. Fresh gringo meat was evidently a rare and toothsome treat.

The cordial villagers vied to have the honor of serving the "extranjeros" dinner.

176

And who could have thought that in such a tiny, smoky hut, we could eat so well!

"Venado" led the return procession, going sure-footed while the horses slipped and stumbled. The storm behind promised a soaking, but never caught up, though it grumbled and spat rain on our backs, blowing us ahead fullspeed to Sr. Solchaga's ranch,—the night's destination.

Tired,—exhausted I was, yet the sunset over the valley,—two white clouds racing in the dark sky above darker hills—brought me to my feet and my camera out in a hurry.

"Would we care to dig for idols in the morning?" "We would!" and did. I made the first find—a tiny clay torso lying in the furrowed ground. The rest were envious for it was a perfect piece, but nothing more was found except fragments of no value, though Brett dug deep with pick and shovel. The Tarascans threw away all pottery and images every two years, creating anew,—they liked things fresh and bright. Being real artists, no tremendous effort was required to replace their pots and Gods with new ones equally good. So the earth of Michoácan is strewn with broken bits.

The Mexican government has become very strict concerning what "art" is taken from the country. This is an admirable stand, yet there comes a question,—is it not better for a nation to be rid of its past,—even more so if that past were a mighty one?

Better for the present generation not to live in the reflected light of great ancestors, imagining the glory their own.

Xanicho [Janitzio] of disagreeable afterthoughts! We were eager to go,—more eager to leave. It was a small rocky island of fisher-folk, who received us with hostility, which made me bristle in turn. Upon our approach the church was locked and remained so despite our letters and entreaties.

Maybe our visit was an intrusion,—one felt so wandering through the narrow streets,—like private property, like invading someone's back yard, it was that intimate,—personal. Before landing we heard music,—distant orchestra,—song and laughter. What a gay place! A wedding feast was on and we were the uninvited guests. This was the second day of celebration,—half the villagers were drunk. A reeling Indian greeted us, swearing uproariously. My inclination was to knock down the filthy beast, but not wishing to commit suicide I half embraced him instead; surprised, he staggered off still swearing.

Upon a cliff by the church, fishermen mended nets,—yards of mesh stretched on poles to dry, sunlit and sparkling. To gain our end we affected great sympathy, denouncing the government for ending Mass. But they were taciturn, aloof, answering with laconic sarcasm. One offered to take us where there were prehispanic idols. He asked five pesos, which so incensed Tina that she berated them for greediness. "Well, when we go to the capital," he retorted scornfully, "we are cheated and know it, but we pay for our fun without question."

Hopeless now,—sure that the church would not be opened, I turned my camera toward the huts and lake below: the tiled roofs a jagged foreground,—the lake a sheet of silver,—the hills of Pátzcuaro beyond, murky under storm clouds.

And as I focussed the wedding procession approached. Up the rocky lane they wound, stumbling, staggering, led by a drunken hag whirling round and round, wildly gesticulating with a pair of steer horns, lunging at the bridal couple, retreating, crazily screaming,—while the orchestra blared forth barbaric music. The others waved flags or empty bottles, drowning the music with hoots and shrieks.

"We had better leave," I suggested, "before meeting that mob. They might decide on a funeral march for variety. Let us hunt for old lacquer from Uruapan in the village below." We went down, — the wedding up. Then happened a near tragedy, for to my horror the old horn-waving witch charged my camera, left standing on the cliff's edge in charge of our cargador. What he did or said to dissuade her I don't know, but the boy had an extra peso in his pocket that night...

Brett and I acquired new names in Pátzcuaro. Brett—"El León"—the lion, and I—"El Señor de los Milagros"—the miracle man, because they said I worked miracles with my camera!

Uruapan was not included in our itinerary, but the temptation to go down into "tierra caliente" was so strong that August 2nd found us on the train headed for the land of lacquer.

Suddenly Tina gave a horrified "O!"—then she was speechless,—and following the direction of her staring eyes, I in turn became mute,—stricken with grief. A newspaper headline announced the burial of Señor Manuel Hernández Galván! No room for doubt—it was our own fine and beloved friend. But how? Details were not given. He could not have died a natural death,—not Manuel. He was marked,—he knew this, and we had half-jokingly told him that "he would get his" sooner or later. Surely he was killed from ambush, no one dared face him on equal terms. How often have I seen him draw his pistola and dent a peso the first try at thirty paces!

Only a few days before we left for Acámbaro he had dropped in. "Phone me when you are near Guanajuato," he said, "I'll plan a real fiesta with barbecue and song and dance." Now he has gone—dear Manuel! A Don Juan of today, a brave cavalier, handsome, charming, generous, the wit and life of any gathering. Many will mourn his going.

From every important stop, a varied assortment of purchases,—loza, fajas, juguetes, had to be expressed back to Mexico City. A large, strong basket, lined

178

with grasses, sewed over with petate, was invariably chosen for container. Not one piece of pottery was ever broken en route. I doubt if a box would have been easily found had we desired one,—not in the smaller cities,—for shipping in baskets is quite universal, and the idea is beautiful. The sweet-smelling grasses, the sturdy basket, the flexible cover of petate, all from the handicrafts,—an intimate, living ensemble.

Our guide book would probably read, "The landscape between Pátzcuaro and Uruapan is inspiring." It is. But what is the matter with words! Have the poets so abused them that they have become anaemic, dulled,—robbed of all suggestion?

The track formed an unbroken curve over which the train creaked distressfully. My thoughts would revert to the horror of Galván's death. Rain fell to make the day more dreary. I recall a valley, rain-filled from mountain top to mountain top.

"The best hotel in Uruapan" was pointed out. It had running water in each room, but every vacant room opened onto the street, and all had wooden floors. This would never do,—wooden floors in Mexico! We searched and found a hotel with flagstones.

I half imagined the streets of Uruapan would be paved with lacquered bateas, —trays—and it was almost so. The industry, though flourishing, has become corrupted to such a degree that one can only hope for its ultimate death. It is dead in feeling,—only the technique remains. We watched Cruz Hernández, super craftsman, wasting his time and skill over piddling knickknacks to clutter the rooms of the fat-minded burgess. Truly it was sad!

Others had preceded us in the search for old lacquer,—Uruapan was stripped. But an unexpected joy was the discovery of the green loza from Patambán. I would rather have one piece of this pottery than all the Talavera ware of Puebla. Like that of Oaxaca this loza has retained its indigenous character. It is never shipped to the Capital, hence there has been no concession to hybrid taste. The output must be small, barely supplying nearby villages, for even in Uruapan none was to be had on Market day and our few purchases were all from private homes.

Sr. Solchaga had first shown us this pottery,—then, seeing my delight, presented me with an exquisite dish. The pattern is almost always a vivid green on a brown-black ground,—sometimes a touch of ivory is introduced. The better dishes are painted underneath,—green and ivory patterns over the natural red-brown clay. If it came to parting with all my pottery but one piece, this green dish from Sr. Solchaga would be under consideration as my favorite. For in it all the Indians' imagination, their lyrical spirit, their plastic reconstruction of nature is manifest in essence. Chained to the outer edge of the plate, a little animal, maybe a deer, balances on leaf sprays. No deer could stand on such

179

delicate stems, but what cares the Indian for humdrum truth? Another dish presents a gambolling deer, so elongated, that without legs he would be a snake. On another a bird hovers, about to alight, drawn with one sweep of a brush.

A jar I have from Patambán is crisscrossed with a mesh of lines, forming diamond shapes or squares quite like a Scotch plaid. It is round as a ball, a big one, with a small base and a generous mouth. It is a jolly jar,—and has a story. We first spied it on a counter in the market filled with milk,—that was its use, to bring milk to market every morning on the head of a nice Indita. Would she sell it? No, she needed it for her milk. But she could get another and we could not. No, they were only brought to market after the rainy season. Finally she remembered having another. If we would come to her home that afternoon she would sell it.

She lived far in the outskirts,—but what a memorable walk into an extravaganza of surprises! The way led through lanes carpeted with moss, under a canopy of trees,—mulberry, banana, coffee, chirimoya,—and flowers,—scarlets, pinks, whites,—and lush ferns.

Arriving at our destination, a cordial welcome was extended, but not a word about the reason for our visit,—the green jarro of Patambán. After courtesies, I had to question. She had changed her mind! The other jar had a round base, it would not balance alone on her head, she would have to hold it there the several miles to market, and that was too much effort. Besides she really liked the jug and might not find another quite the same. Raising her original price 25 cents each time I reached an offer of two pesos, and since she had paid less than a peso for it and yet allowed us to walk away without capitulating, I'm sure this Indita had real love for her jarro. I am equally sure that she finally sold it, not for gain, but because she was kindly, and saw how we loved it too.

It was misleading to write that "the technique remains", in speaking of the bateas. Some few workers use the old technique in which the pattern is cut out of the ground and the paint inlaid, whereas the modern facile method is to stencil. The old tradition never approached realism. The leaves and flowers were stylized,—presented as flat geometric forms. But now all dimensions are in mode, and being dexterous and imitative the Indians copy nature perfectly, with results which delight the burgess and outrage the artist. Even when adhering to the old tradition the craft lacks interest because of a universal crystalization of idea in design. The bateas are with but slight variation alike,—seeing one is to see them all.

In contrast the little candy boxes from Paracho are gayly imaginative and the furniture, cheap in construction but finely carved, was far from being commercialized. A chair brought to market many miles on burro back could be had for 50 cents. Maybe the candy boxes influenced the painting of coffins, decorated with similar flower designs. Rather a tender idea!

180

In the States, a grocery store in California and one in Illinois are prosaically alike. Each with its shelves of standardized foods. Rows of "Quaker Oats," "Campbell's Soup," "Heinz 57,"—canned conveniences allowing our feminists time to hunt culture and invade man's last retreat—the barber shop. This is digression, the point is that from coast to coast the stores are depressingly monotonous. Not so in Mexico. Each market place has a new note in display, besides peculiarities of costume and variety in food. The Inditos of Uruapan for instance, offered their fruits on long green fronds of the banana tree.

While in Pátzcuaro René loaned us Lawrence's new book on Mexico, *The Plumed Serpent*,—such boresome reading that we could not force a finish there, but, curious to find out Lawrence's reactions to Mexico, we brought the book along. Despite its entire lack of humor, we were at times convulsed with laughter. His chapter on the bull fight in which he belly-aches, weeps and ridicules, is full of absurdities. Lawrence tries, it is evident, to bolster up his symbolism by indicating the customs of one locality. I never found a market where the Indians "never asked you to buy,"—they are usually clamorously insistent. Nor do the women hold their water jars as he points out, to show their lack of poise. More often, they walk free handed, with regal bearing. Throughout the book apparently trivial inaccuracies persist, and form a wrong or one-sided impression of Mexico. Lawrence was bewildered by Mexico, he was frightened, but he over-dramatized his fear. There are fine descriptive passages, intelligent analyses, accurate prophecy, but such a padding of tiresome allegory about Quetzalcóatl that excellent material has been used to create a volume of unconvincing mysticism.

There was no excuse of work to let us dally in Uruapan,—so August 5th found the "expedition" Guadalajara bound, over a branch line which led to Penjamo, the night's destination.

The more I travel through Mexico, the more I am impressed with the tremendous wealth of its natural resources. An Italian newspaper headed an article, "Poor Mexico, she is too rich!"

We passed neglected orchards in which cacti had regained their lost dominions.

After an unexpected dearth of food, unusual on Mexican railroads where every station affords fruit at least, we bought gorditas at a siding—maize cakes filled with a savory medley of meat, potatoes and chile.

Except that awful night in Tlacolula, the hotels had been clean, airy, comfortable and reasonable,—but I had a premonition about the night to come —

We arrived in a driving rain, slipping and stumbling a block to the "Hotel." My premonitions, I swore, were about to be fulfilled. So, preparing for the worst, I wet my face with melisa for mosquitos and powdered the bed for fleas. The room had no windows,—there are few fresh air fiends in Mexico,—to leave the door open would have been financial suicide. I erected a barricade of table and chairs, coyly viewed my bed, crossed myself,—and—awakened next morning remembering a sanguine, night-long battle with fleas,—batallions of them. The dead lay strewn between the spiteful little hillocks of my mattress, between which I had found no vale of rest.

Hot baking powder biscuits and good coffee cheered us at 4:00 a.m.—a Chinese Restaurant in Panjamo station! On the stone floor of the waiting-room, Indians had slept all night. They lay there like so many animals, sprawled or huddled together for warmth. Over them we gingerly stepped to morning coffee. Waiting for the half hour late train, the grey smoke from a standing engine turned golden in the sunrise.

Ugh! The entry into that fetid train,—the bleary faces! Two men having beer with breakfast! I smoked to kill the stench.

Terrific rains had wasted the land. Acres of drowned corn rotted in new made lakes. And still it rained, while the train wavered over shifting tracks. Alongside were water hyacinths,—lavender lagoons under a rose dawn sky.

An Indita offered tortillas with chicken, chile and onions. No sale. Disgusted, she flung a sarcastic, "What *gentlemen* in first class, so delicate they cannot eat my food—" Of course I bought!

For the third time we are in Guadalajara. This had to be a cheaper visit. No one questions morals in Mexico. Not even in the Casa de Asistencia kept by the highly respectable Morales Hermanas,—the only concern is board-and-room bills. So we lived as we often had before, three in a room, to save a few pesos. Morality is a personal issue in Mexico. A large corner room was ours for 2.75 a day, with dinners for .85. Imagine living so well and yet so cheap in a hotel!

It took a straight ten hours sleep to recover from Panjamo,—no, not quite uninterrupted, for the slats clattered out of Tina's bed in the night, and three chinches aroused me in time for breakfast. The weak bed was repaired, the inhabited one removed, and there were no more misadventures.

We were not strangers in, nor to Guadalajara. The Marín family would have us live with them,—no?—then eat with them—no?—then "our" home was open for any time we could spare. Such unbounded hospitality.

They told of Galván's death. Shot by political opponents, as I had guessed. The murder took place in "The Royalty," where three years ago Llewellyn and I used to sit over hot rum punches. He had no chance,—fell dead across his table, shooting as he fell, but shooting with eyes already dead. I suppose one might say he died as should a man of action,—but it was a monstrous tragedy.

The electrical storms of Guadalajara were noteworthy. Our solid stone building would tremble from crash after crash. The streets became impassible rivers. Ragged little urchins made good on such nights, building plank bridges over-which they demanded toll of "un centavo".

182

More negatives were done in Guadalajara than in any other place. Work was concentrated. The museum furnished many. The new home of Governor Zuno also. This "colonial" house represented a fortune. With splendid details, — as a whole it was not convincing. Governor Zuno—he who had bought my work—and later Tina's—for the museum where it now hangs, —almost to my sorrow, being work of my past, —sat to me in charro costumes, of which he had the most extravagant collection. Then in the University were the frescoes of Amado de la Cueva and Siqueiros to be done. I thought them a splendid accomplishment, a synthesis of color and idea, —realism geometrically expressed.

Admitting all the charms of Guadalajara, —perfect climate, cleanliness, beautiful and chic señoritas, progressive spirit, —I would choose to live in Oaxaca in preference. I felt a pretentiousness in Guadalajara, —consequently a superficiality. The new "colonia" of vulgarly ostentatious houses irritates me, — indeed the very commendable progressive spirit was not acceptable. As yet it seemed but a weak graft upon dissenting roots.

Guadalajara was not gay. What city could be during this crisis! Black prevailed, — the Catholics in mourning. A boycott of all luxuries, all pleasures, emptied the streets and stores. Street fighting between soldiers and Catholics, —the majority women, armed with bricks, clubs, machetes, —resulted in bloodshed and death.

To work in such a belligerent atmosphere was embarrasing. Every movement out of the ordinary was noted. Setting up my camera in front of a church was next to training a gun upon it. I wished that instead of puttees and leather breeches, I had the most conventional suit.

Two Mexican engineers—(suspected of being Government spies)—had been lynched in Acámbaro shortly after our visit...

This recalls a story from Aguas Calientes. A General said he would have no black-dressed women mourning for the church in his town. He arrested a number, had them stripped and sent home in their underwear.

In Guadalajara for the first time we did not need to turn our hotel room into a dark-room. A most hospitable photographer allowed me the freedom of his. However it was the fine old colonial building he had turned into a "studio" which I must mention, —or more explicitly the stairway leading up to his rooms. I think it furnished a striking example of a difference between that period and this. There was no economy of space, —the stairs were built for a leisure-loving people. Broad, low steps compelled a slow and dignified ascent, —one could not climb jerkily, —hastily. The rise was so gradual one walked as on a level promenade.

Victoria cooked us wonderful meals, —real banquets. Caldo with aquacate sliced in, chiles rellenos, pipiano de pollo, —a sauce of pumpkin seeds over chicken, fruit salad of guayava, —delicate and refreshing. And then another well remembered meal, —supper at Valentina's in the outskirts of town. Valentina was a famous cook, a magnet for all classes. Food was the thing. Formalities she would not be bothered with. We asked for knives and forks, — she had none — only food! — and we had hands!

Except the farewell to the Maríns, there was no sadness as the train pulled out from Guadalajara. I was glad to leave there, — it would have been the same elsewhere, — just to be leaving, to be through, was the desire.

Mexico breaks one's heart. Mixed with the love I had felt was a growing bitterness, — a hatred I tried to resist. I have seen faces, the most sensitive, tender faces the Gods could possibly create, and I have seen faces to freeze one's blood, so cruel, so savage, so capable of any crime.

The first station-meal at Yurecuaro. Fresh cream in earthenware jars, gorditas fat with goodness, and a sort of pudding, — a work of art, — I guessed it was milk, cheese and burnt sugar. "Chango!" the vendors cried.

A hard day with two changes to reach Guanajuato. We arrived in the night. Our train had no headlight, — but lightning flashed to reveal a mountainous landscape, and the train puffed and wheezed up a heavy grade.

I stepped out on the balcony of our hotel room to view the city, — and — Galván faced me like a ghost. No Manuel to greet us but a great poster across the street, done from my photograph, announcing his candidacy for re-election. It was printed in a ghastly green, — rain-streaked and sodden. On every corner in corner in Guanajuato we met that portrait!

The first day at dinner a disagreeable and tense episode happened. A party of men took an adjacent table, — and casually noting them, I recognized General G. — who had been with us on those first excursions during the revolution, when Galván had driven to El Desierto and Las Tres Marías. We had been gay friends together. Then General G. had turned traitor, had become Manuel's bitter enemy, had plotted against him. He recognized us, I'm certain. I turned away as casually as I had looked, but pent with emotion.

Apart from the mines and the mummies the only great interest in Guanajuato was the situation of the city. "Picturesque" it was, Mr. Terry says so, but saved from this damning label by its ruggedness. The house of the poor grew from solid rock, — out of the hillsides, but the pretentious homes were the most vulgar we had yet encountered, — frivolous, unrelated excrescences imposed upon an austere landscape. The climax of bad taste was the "Teatro Juárez", described in our guide as "the pride of the city." I could no longer tease Tina about Italian Art, for the bronze allegorical figures "crowning" the edifice were by an American! Yet the building had its value, — it was amusing! And so was another, — a pulquería named "A Ver Si Acaso — Let's See If By Chance."

I had looked forward to finding much fine pottery in Guanajuato, — but no — the industry was in decadence. The younger generation had not learned the craft,

184

few workers were available, and those few unreliable from drink. From door to door we went in search of such fine loza as Guanajuato had once been famous for, —a heavy, durable loza, broadly painted in bright yellows, blues, greens on a light ivory ground. And we found it, quite unexpectedly in a grocery store. The little old lady did not wish to sell. The dishes had been in the family for years,— they were for festive occasions,—but—"What would we offer?" It was evident she was poverty-stricken and forced to grasp this opportunity and I felt guilty in tempting her. But if we did not buy, another surely would, so without too much bargaining, excellent examples were ours.

All the activities of Guanajuato, all energy, all life is directed into the subterranean. It impressed me deeply, the idea of this great underworld army of men burrowing, tunneling day after day for silver and gold for someone else. We heard the story of one mine, "El Tiro de Rayas,"—The Gunshot—of 1000 men working 1500 feet down,—then—through the courtesy of the manager, Mr. Harold Mapes, we were taken there.

To the uninitiate the first look down that shaft must be awful. 1500 feet deep, from 40 to 60 feet wide,—a dark, dank bottomless pit,—the depths of which the sun reached but two days a year. My ears popped from pressure as the lift went down, and looking up to daylight, the steel cables were but threads too trifling for a safe trip. "The miners sing hymns as they descend to work," remarked the guide,—"and one slipped off the other day. He made a nasty mess." At the bottomless pit's bottom was a little shrine, tenderly decorated with pretty rock crystals.

Another subterranean visit was quite as awful as that down the mine shaft. In the underground vaults of the Pantéon (cemetery), we paid our respects to the dead. Circling the entire room, they stood there naked—not a sheet, not even a breech cloth to soften the ghastly sight. A gruesome, grinning crew whose tanned, taut hides had warped them into monstrous grotesques. They held an appalling beauty. But not all were naked. Two old men still wore their evening finery. Skulls and skeleton hands thrust out from tattered glad rags. One woman had been buried alive, her mummy writhed in horror and agony. Another had died in childbirth, she clasped the foetus to her breast—and grimaced. I repeat,— they had a fearful, shocking beauty. I wanted to photograph them, do details of contorted hands, of shrivelled breasts and gaping mouths,—it would have been a monumental theme. But the caretaker would not move the bodies, and the vault was too narrow for work, also the fusty air of the locked room almost overcame me,—so I have no records, but I have ineradicable memories.

My camera was not removed from its case while in Guanajuato, though we wandered looking for material through, or rather up and down the narrow streets, which sometimes changed to steps, and again to bridges.

The same story was repeated in Guanajuato. Every time a church was entered a spy would follow us, — usually a woman. She would drop to her knees simulating prayer but watching our every move. I became nauseated by churches...

Rain fell every day of our stay in Guanajuato. I recall mines, mummies and a dismal, reeking landscape. My frame of mind accentuated my view-point. I wearied of insults. I vowed to practise shooting and throwing a knife, — to learn every curse in the Mexican tongue. My love for Mexico turned to something near to hate. It was forced on me though I tried to repress my feeling.

The worst day of all was that spent in the station of Guanajuato and the subsequent journey to Querétaro. My God, *what* a day!

Torrential rains had fallen. The train was chalked up four hours late. We gasped. But that four hours was nothing. Six hours passed, — eight, ten! No one dared leave, more than to pace the platform in turn. Romantic Mexico! Twelve hours after we had *hurried* to the station, at dawn, we left, or rather, — thought we had left! The train carried the extra weight of "La Burra" as the Indians had facetiously named the dead engine, — and "El Burro," straining and snorting, could not make the grade just outside the station. Four times dauntless "El Burro" dashed for the summit, four times it slid back to the station. "La Burra" was cut off, — then the second class was cut, and a steaming, reeking crowd was jammed in with us. The air became poisonous, it was a cattle-car, — no one could move, — hardly stretch. And we had two changes ahead before our destination, Querétaro!

Silao at 10:30 — waiting again. The extra basket of loza from Guanajuato was almost the last straw. Other passengers eyed us disapprovingly as we crowded in upon them. The train barely crept along, while uneasy travelers leaned out over dangerous crossings. A sigh of relief at Irapuato, — the last change. And when it was announced that the connecting train from Guadalajara was two hours late I only shrugged my shoulders. There was no spirit left for temperament, — just a dull acceptance. Even bad station coffee at outrageous prices did not bring a protest. Querétaro might be reached at dawn, — my watch read 3:00 a. m. At Celaya, a barefoot blind man stood ankle deep in mud, shivering, and fiddling a water soaked violin. He played a well-remembered tune of Manuel's, and earned the few centavos that I tossed him.

Twenty-four hours after arising in Guanajuato we went to bed in Querétaro! Two hours sleep had to suffice, or miss the early hours of market day. Besides we did not want to be charged for a night, after arriving at sunrise. Beds were carefully smoothed out, and, braced with coffee, Querétaro, the last city of the grand tour, awaited our conquest.

Here was greater activity, and the sun shone cheerfully! I began to feel almost enthusiatic again.

Tresguerras, or Casas, whichever you will, had worked in Querétaro. The "Palacio Federal" had noteworthy figures, and the flying buttresses of the church

186

"Santa Rosa" were a powerful expression. The base, perhaps, was too weak a support for the great inverted arches,—but I only say "perhaps." How sad to compare the sculpture of today in Mexico to that of the glorious past! But it is not even Mexican. Porfirio Díaz, that tyrant of bad taste, imported Italian "art," —portrait busts, fountains, monuments, the "Teatro Nacional." Enough said! With his vulgar mind he of course had no understanding of the more intelligent, finer Indian. He should have been dethroned for aesthetic reasons, not political. In such a revolution I could joyfully take part!

Seven o'clock that night found us unanimously ready for bed. Not the band playing in the plaza below, not the long, snaky, bumpy pillow kept me awake five minutes. No less than twelve hours dreamless sleep sufficed to revive us from that twenty-four-hour harrowing train trip from Guanajuato.

Thanks to Tresguerras much work was found in Querétaro,—church interiors as well as exteriors,—sumptuously carved doors and confessionals,—altars splendid in gold leaf,—wrought iron. The sacristy of Santa Clara was sealed and locked by the government. We never discovered what treasures were hidden there.

After learning to take the cue from Mr. Terry we found him an excellent guide. When he said a sculpture or painting was strange, queer, bizarre, we hurried to it and were usually rewarded with a find. When he praised unduly we avoided going out of the way. He is a good guide for historical dates, natural history, geology, climate and—bad art.

At last we were through with Querétaro, which meant the end of travelling, except to nearby towns. Over a month had passed since leaving Mexico City and all were travel worn and weather beaten.

Blond, blue-eyed Brett,—ingenuous, 200 percent gringo, was the marked one in the party; he could not escape. Loafers sneered as he passed, and he it was who received the last parting curse from a fat old bitch on the steps of Santa Clara. Tina could pass as Mexican or at least what she is, I could pass as European, but Brett was always definitely damned as Yankee.

The train from Laredo was jammed, our extra basket of loza was again cursed, and hunger made us irritable until, Mexican style, we bought chicken from the window which challenged the cooking of any famous chef. And farther on, cheese, which Brett exclaimed was the best he had ever eaten,—and tostadas as big as a big sombrero, thin as a wafer, crisp and toothsome.

187

3. "The Beginning of a New Art"

August 26. Distrito Federal again, surrounded by the beautiful new loza from Patambán and Guanajuato which came through safely, — the Guadalajara shipment to arrive this morning, — that from Pátzcuaro mysteriously missing, causing me considerable concern.

The first visit was of course to the Salas — dear, dear people. Shocked to see Rafael so very sick — the torrid zone was too much for him. He brought me a coat with collar and cuffs of monkey fur, from Chiapas. It seems anything but Mexican in character, rather as coming from the arctic regions.

Hearing that we were at the Salas, Eric, Frances, Mary came later. Much talk of the tragedy of Galván's murder. Everyone is dazed. The man who killed him walks the streets free! Mexican law allows a "diputado" to go free no matter what the crime, until his term expires. Then, or by then he will be gone. What a convenient law! How fantastic!

Mexican Folkways published, with my photographs of the pulquerías illustrating Diego's article.

Professor John Dewey, here to lecture before the University Summer course, called yesterday to see my work. A quiet, dignified gentleman, but how can I comment after a short hour's contact? He left to pack for his return to the States.

August 29. Came Frances, Mary, and René—René had not yet seen my work— He burst into superlatives, excited gesticulations. " The modern painters are all off. They have chosen the wrong medium to express their ideas — but they would not dare admit so if they saw these photographs. This print (Three Ollas of Oaxaca) is the beginning of a new art."

August 30. I called on Jean. I always go to see him with expectations. I am never disappointed. His new work from Yucatán in contrast to the sombre, heavy painting done here, sparkled with delicate, but brilliant, jewellike color. I loved his old work and I love the new equally, if differently. He showed me also a delicious caricature of Mrs. Nuttal of Coyoacan.

All the loza has arrived — but alas! My favorite dish, an elegant old piece found in Tonalá, was broken. I have cemented it, or rather Rafael did, but it can never be the same to me, though it appears quite well, — for I buy not in the spirit of an antiquarian but to have beautiful things for actual use. I am much happier when I find a modern piece of value than I would be to discover the most precious antiquity. And it is sad to note that the pottery done in Tonalá today is either indifferent, bad or actually ghastly!

I am told that Dr. Atl is responsible for the present corruption and formulization. If so, may he suffer in hell for his sin. He told the Indians, "Your ancestors used the greca [Greek fret], you inherit the greca, make grecas." So they stopped painting their spontaneous rhythms of birds, flowers, animals, and, one and all, do "grecas."

We went from door to door in Tonalá in hope of finding something different; we always turned away disgusted, — except in just one hut — where, on the wall was sketched a delightful landscape. "Why don't you paint your dishes so!" we exclaimed. "I would like to, but we can sell only grecas. I must live," he said. Then I discovered in a corner a little dish, done in the same spirit, a gem! The theme was a tiger hunt. A ferociously funny tiger, two white clad hunters holding guns in impossible [positions], treed in trees whose dainty elegance presaged slight safety from the wild beast. In a corner two deers gambolled oblivious to the pending tragedy, prodigious butterflies fluttered, birds sailed in long lines, and a scared little rabbit jumped over stylized grasses in the foreground. I must have shown my delight and desire too plainly. It was not for sale! Only after waiting and pleading for half an hour did the dish become mine for a peso, which amount, large compared to prevailing prices, I did not begrudge.

The other fine dish, broken in transit, I discovered, dust covered, discarded, and bought without much bargaining for fifty centavos. It is more elegant, less realistic, more sophisticated. On a cream ground the figures are painted in warm browns and black browns. A flowered border surrounds a fern and bird harmony. In the center are three long-legged, long-billed herons circled by twining leaves. Ferns sweep over them and two larger birds, birds which in life would be actually much smaller, complete an outer circle with a flourish of plumed tails. But the black brown herons in the center are nothing less than a poem in line. The three in silhouette, all alike, with just a slightly varying tilt of their elongated necks and extra long bills to save from monotony, are a tour de force in repetitive form.

That day in Tonalá we had stopped first to see Amado Galván — he of more than local fame. I bought a signed vase, and Victoria bought for me a plate. When an artist begins to sign his work it is indicative of a certain self-esteem, self-consciousness. And Galván, finding himself recognized, has felt his importance. It shows in his work, he repeats, — only the very great do not repeat their successes. One must admit its beauty, yet it is a bit cold, — calculated, while amongst the cheap botellones—bottles, demijohns—one finds many a gem. I have one which cost me forty centavos. I would rather own it than the vase or plate of Galván. Whoever painted it did not take himself seriously, he had no formula, he just dashed off the first thing that came to his head, and he must have been in a jolly fine mood that day. The painting pulses with life, — swirls with energy. A full throated black bird bursts into song — two flaring magueys top a pink hill — leaves and grasses, dots and lines cut hither and thither — done with carefree surety.

They are painted alfresco, these botellones, — the colors are dull, but never dead, — the ground is always the natural color of clay as it comes from the oven. There are hundreds of them to choose from and one might choose blind-folded and be happy.

Another ware almost always good is a cheap, friable pottery, brilliantly glazed red brown. The patterns or figures are cream with accentuating lines of green or black. Again one might choose at random and make no mistake. It is very personal, this pottery, indigenous, done with no desire to please an alien public. It is obviously cheap ware, the burgess would never display it, so there is never a concession to burgess taste. It is gay, irresponsible, imaginative; it could not be placed in a room with silk lamp shades, lace curtains and pompous furniture. Tonalá is a city of potters, yet not one potter's wheel did I see. "Hand made" can be applied to their work without reservation.

There were seven of us wandered this day in Tonalá — Chavala, Pancho, Carmen, Victoria, Tina, Brett and Edward.

September 4. A copy of Spring *Little Review* at hand. It is "old fashioned" — *The Saturday Evening Post* is far more exciting. I used to eagerly await it — to devour it. Now I find myself impatient, irritated or indifferent to most of the contents. I feel but an attempt to force attention by bizarrerie, or a fierce, puerile effort at being intellectual. Either I am becoming conservative or else I am more discriminate, more aware, less deceived by affectation of knowledge. Naturally I place myself in the latter class, — yet, to be fair, or to build a defense — I claim no intellectual apirations, — I even confess a lazy mind. So my reactions may be an admission of weakness.

The photographs by Zwaska are trivial mannerisms, the centre one least offensive. I would quite as soon have a dark smudge by Genthe. The "N. Y." done by Charles Sheeler, had a genuine grandeur, — nobility — these photographs by Zwaska are an effort to be smart. Neither do I contact with the photography by Moholy-Nagy — it only brings a question — why?

I would not change one piece of my green loza from Patambán for any thing in the *Little Review* and this may explain my attitude.

These several years in Mexico have influenced my thought and life. Not so much the contact with my artist friends as the less direct proximity of a primitive race. Before Mexico I had been surrounded by the usual mass of American burgess — sprinkled with a few sophisticated friends. Of simple peasant people I knew nothing. And I have been refreshed by their elemental expression, — I have felt the soil.

190

September 6. No, — I should not say I have "a lazy mind" — rather, I do not have a studious mind. That which seems to concern me, I go to eagerly and dive deep, but I cannot memorize, or ponder over problems of irrelevant interest. Though they may appear important, my intuition says no, and that is the end of them.

At Rafael's I glanced over a German magazine — it had an article about the photographs of Man Ray. I suppose it was a laudatory review, but not being able to read the German I was spared. This photographer has been much praised and why, I wonder? The photographs reproduced show nothing beyond the usual, — even the best of them — and the worst are what one might expect from anyone of a hundred commercial photographers in New York, — theatrical postures and soft focus "effects" — Picasso done in a blurr — well, well, how funny!

In another magazine reproductions of buildings constructed for recent Paris exposition — again the sweat of effort to do something striking, different. No dignity — no reason for existence.

September 4. Roberto is grinding his camera for a movie to illustrate the popular song *La Casita*. It is to be done in a style especially suited to the Chautauqua course, and will serve to show these serious students the sweet romance of life in Mexico. An influx of enthusiastic Chautauquans bent on a realization of their dreams will follow. But not if they first read D. H. Lawrence' teeth-chattering, hair-raising nickel-novel, titled *The Plumed Serpent* or a timorous tale of dreadful days in demonic Mexico.

September 7. X. has gone to visit her mother in Guadalajara. I walked to the camión crossing with her, — we kissed good-bye and I slipped her ten pesos I could ill afford to spare. I feel that she has gone forever and though she irritated me sorely at times, with child-like lack of consideration, — yet she was tender and sweet.

September 13. They are artful, these Indians, — good liars — clever to a certain point at least. They can sit on a pin and claim comfort. X. did not go to Guadalajara, she was seen near .... Now I wonder what is up?

Brett has been ill — his condition worries me, and I am not one who becomes excited over sickness — I must get him away from here soon — and myself too.

September 14. Brett still sick. I cannot work with this worry. He must have an intestinal infection. My heart aches to see him so gaunt and sad. I fear my own judgment, the assumption of authority — but I fear the pill and knife doctors more. Have delivered to Anita 450 prints from 150 negatives all done on this last western trip. Adding those from Puebla and Oaxaca I have yet to finish some 140 negatives. And now I am very anxious to be done.

September 15. Brett better. I am still his doctor. Made eight more negatives of things around the house.

September 23. Pintao came. He will not allow his work copied for Anita's book. We — Anita, Tina, and I — have failed to persuade him, he remains obstinate, — not firm, not holding to some principle, but just cussedly obstinate. He is at outs with "Art" — "It does not pay — better to sit in a cool patio and thrum a guitar,', which is only the surface Pintao speaking in a crossgrained mood. He is one who could never do "Art" for money — he creates because he has to.

Later Covarrubias and Rose Roland came to see their proofs. Of Rose, I have one at least for myself. Miguel I should like to do again, but they leave for New York tomorrow. They are both very agreeable, jolly persons — I like them.

Well, X. returned. So much for my premonition. Yet I was not far off perhaps, for after two days of tears and kisses — and the consequences — she left again. Her brother came to take her home. I confess being sad — the house is lonesome. She was a nice little plaything to love. I did not need to waste energy making love, she brought it to me with outstretched arms and upturned face. She was charmingly wanting in brains, — and that was nice.

September 24. "In Union there is strength" — Yes — commercial strength — mob strength — fine motto for labor-unions, — for politicians — but for the individual who would create — no.

In the early morning, when all the rest are snoringly asleep, then one feels strong — untouched — released from the drag of personalities, for one pays a price for beloved friends — granting of course that they pay too!

With the first sounds of life, the bugle to awaken soggy soldiers, the first careening camión, the snarling of dogs, — then my enthusiasm wanes, then I feel the imposition of social service.

September 26. Surely this is a strange turn of life. X. and her mother and brother and sister are now on the way to Los Angeles and in a month I will be there!

September 30. A representative of the Berlin *Tageblatt* wants to reproduce a number of my photographs, but how to spare time for making prints, I question. I am so "fed up" on this work I am doing. I go to bed thinking negatives, prints, failures, successes, how many done, how many to do — and awaken with the same thoughts.

I received the most unique love-letter of my life — an almost illegible scrawl from X. She was full of sadness, going so far away. But she will blossom forth as a real flapper in Los Angeles, and soon forget Mexico in all the excitement of a big American city, where everything is offered to distract one from self-communion. Life is offered predigested. Not that X. could ever be introspective!

October 1. "Diez a Guadalupe — ¡Carrera! — Guadalupe — ¡Carrera!" "Ten cents to Guadalupe — Racing!" I have gone faster, but it was fast enough, —

and five cents cheaper than street-car. I took a day off from this work, — deserved, I swear.

Though market day, the town was empty compared to the two feast days of December 12 I have seen, when the streets were an almost solid suffocating mass of Indians.

Market day, — yet I was disappointed, for I found few things to purchase. Fortunate for my pocket-book, — or no — the price of most things in Mexico, the things I love, is so low that even a scanty purse is scarcely lightened. It is my trunk space I always consider — even now the overflow is appalling and I dread to consign my treasures to freight. But purchase I did — of course loza! A lion of tremendous mane, and I hardly need add of elegant form. I call him a lion though he has five horns. His legs are ridiculously small, yet considered as an integrity there is no disproportion. He is a pulque bottle, glazed brilliant metallic black. A real beauty!

A large gathering in the church conducting their own songs and service indicated a Catholicism revivified by suppression. A large marble figure of some venerable prelate kneeling before the main altar was having his face scrubbed with soapy maguey fibre.

Returning, I noted from the camión a pulquería, named "Risas y Llantos," best translated "Laughter and Tears!"

October 4. Sunday, — Jean, Brett and I went pulquería photographing for Anita's book. I dreaded the day, — even the day before. The pulquerías are always in crowded sections; closed Sundays, yet in their shadow the habitués linger per-haps because some small side door may be ajar, or perhaps from habit.

It seemed difficult to find just the right ones to illustrate the point. One week a fine example is noted, the next week it is gone, — repainted or painted out, or covered with posters. These fine examples of popular art are treated with scant respect. Too, many new paintings are in bad taste! The "art of pulquería paint-ing" is in decadence.

Nothing untoward happened for a time, but just as I heaved a sigh of relief that we were out of the crowded, tough districts, and set up in a quite respectable, quiet street, an unpleasant incident took place. A Mexican of the middle class really quite a fifi, accosted us. He was boiling with hardly suppressed anger. We were to use such pictures to ridicule Mexico, to show her worst side to the North Americans, – and so on. Words with such people are futile, but Jean argued, then became sarcastic. "You think the Teatro Nacional is a finer expression?" — which naturally he did! I thought he would use personal violence, but he hurried half running away, — "to get a gendarme," so I hastened the exposure and we were off. But such people form the mass, the world over — except, in Mexico, they seem a bit more touchy.

Our search took us even to Guadalupe. There I found not a pulquería, but more loza! I am becoming ashamed of my repeated adjectives, fine, elegant, naïve, — but what is one to do? For I bought a siren, to which I might apply these and more. She is of the same ware as my lion, black brilliant glaze, but gorgeously decorated, painted and gilded with flowers and leaves. She too is a pulque bottle, her tail the container, her head and waist the neck. On her shoulders are two great gilt roses and she lures the mariners to destruction with an orange and black guitar.

René came in the evening. He is painting parchment lamp shades adorned with coats-of-arms for democratic American women with a hankering for royalty, — wishing to cut a figure with armorial bearings acquired in the good old days before all men were born free and equal. So Count René is purveyor to their inhibitions. René also gives lessons on "art," — tells these culture-hungry people which is the greatest picture ever painted, which one sold for the most money, when Velásquez died. To one eager lady, René showed a painting in gouache. One day she brought her husband, and all in a flutter to to exploit her attainments, exclaimed, "Look, dear, at this pretty picture painted by Gouache!" So René finds his discounted title soaring above par in the American colony.

October 6. Not 4:00 a.m. yet. Rising at such an unseemly hour accounted for by retiring before 8:30. Yesterday a full, tiring day of printing. I have cut the number of negatives down to 45. They want me to return to Querétaro. I balk. I have worked hard enough for the money. Working here I could finish in two weeks, print a few platinums for myself, — then leave. Sporadic rebellions everywhere, — talk of another real revolution. Better to leave soon. No place this, to work in a peaceful frame of mind.

Monday — I smashed my camera to the tune of thirty pesos. Brett thought I had hold — I thought he had. It fell from tripod height to the cement floor of Museo Nacional. I just stood and looked at it.

A sitting ahead today — must try to find some half-decent clothes to don. Funny people who think a good photographer, or a good anything, must have money!

Sunday 10. Thirty more negatives to make! I work at high tension to be done and go. But these last few negatives seem — or are — more difficult to assemble than the hundred preceeding ones. With so many illustrations already settled, the choice of subject matter has been narrowed with consequent slowing down of my work. Two weeks more?

October 13. Mr. McL. called on me last evening. I had not had the pleasure of meeting him before. He furnished me an evening of intellectual stimulus amounting to inspiration. He came to me on a quest for nude photographs.

"We are furnishing a bachelor apartment, you see. We want a nude study about 2 ft. × 1 ft. to hang above an inverted red light. Of course I'll cover it with black chiffon, — more discreet, you know. I don't want anything esoteric either — a tall, slender model with long hair." Quite a bill for me to fill — I despaired while my pocket book itched. My prints were either the wrong size or perhaps too "esoteric". "Well, we might hang these two to fill the space, but can't you bring your pictures to our apartment? I want my partner to help choose — he's the artist."

So, with some thirty nudes, we mounted his waiting limousine. Money, evidently! "F. and I have been together twenty-five years, — learned ship carpentering. When the war broke out we started two ship yards — built a lot of ships for the government." Ah, I see, from one suspender to spats!

At the door we met a short, stout baldheaded lackey, an ex-bartender turned butler, I thought. "Meet my pal and partner, Mr. F.," said Mr. Mac. Caramba! — how deceiving is appearance!

"María, bring cocktails for three. Shall I play a Caruso record or a blackface dialogue?"

House and Garden had helped them a lot in furnishing and decorating their home. But — "I don't like this round table in this square room, Tom — what do you think, Mr. Weston?" "A fine time to doubt, Jack, after I have just spent five hundred pesos for a blue satin cover — and besides — I saw a picture of Henry Ford's living room with a round table." I felt safe in agreeing with Henry Ford's good taste!

In blue-and-yellow-striped satin panels, gorgeously framed, hung life-size heads, "hand-colored" photographs — fried photographs — by the famous Mexican artist-photographer, Silva. "But we are going to change these for steel engravings, — one of Washington and one of Hidalgo. These two closets are to be turned into niches for statuary, draped with blue velvet, — this lampshade Tom designed and I am having miniatures painted of our friends to hang around the border. — Over these spaces we want two painted pictures — good color, you know — of Xochimilco and Popocatépetl."

They turned my nudes every which way to find the right way, with no success, they were too esoteric!

"Will you come to dinner? Tom is the cook, our girl makes fine native dishes, but we'll give you a real American meal — do you like roast beef? — but we can't find turnips — good American turnips, — big yellow rutabagas." By this time six cocktails had been finished and I felt relieved when the car was ordered to take me home.

"None of these nudes are quite right, Mr. Weston — don't fit the space — but I want my portrait done in platinum. Sorry we did not meet sooner — we go in the same crowd you know — read the same magazines — *The Dial, The Little Review.*" "But," I feebly protested, "I only read *The Saturday Evening Post* and *The Ladies Home Journal.*"

October 17. Since writing the above the Messrs. McL. and F. have become bosom friends to me!

The famous dinner party took place with M., Frances, Tina and Edward, the invited guests, and Ann Gorlick brought along half-protesting, from a chance encounter on the street.

I have every reason to be grateful to our hosts, for in their home I first discovered M.'s lips, and they were sweet indeed, and her Irish blue eyes were bluer than ever in contrast to her flushed cheeks. We danced and danced and loved and loved — but she would not leave the party — "because of Tina!" How ironical!

I protested and explained — but no! Now this is a sad situation, for M. is a girl I could care for deeply. I must have another talk with M.

October 18. M. and Frances came the day after to gossip a bit about the party. I found urgent need to develop some plates and took M. with me. More kisses and embraces in the dark-room. "But this must end, Edward. We have all believed in the legend of Edward and Tina, you are leaving now, and I want to still believe. It was a beautiful picture." "But I insist, M. darling, that I have no one else, not by the farthest stretch of imagination!" M. would not surrender her fabulous picture. "I shall not be a persistent suitor, I never am — it is seldom worth while — but you are unusually worth while." So I wrote M. after we parted. Now if she does not change, then I forget M. and indulge in derisive laughter at the irony of my position, an unwilling participant in an imaginary idyl!

October 15. Packing trunks now — leaving soon. Yesterday a crate came, ordered for my Spanish chest. It was a poor job, roughly thrown together. The lumber cost at the most a peso, I could have done the job in an hour, I was charged seven pesos. This was the price agreed on, but I had expected a strong, neat box. "Labor" is all powerful these days! But I am becoming a reactionary. Too much sentimentality over the proletariat. Too much deification of the Indian. Labor thinks itself underpaid — the fact is, that it is usually paid too damned much. What incentive is there to excell as craftsmen with uniform wage scales and set hours? Injustice is a stronger way. The weaklings are weeded out, the fit survive. But I am only talking and without statistics. Yet statistics can always prove things either way.

October 20. Just five more negatives to do! My herculean task nearing the end. The trip to Acolman and Texcoco netted seven negatives. To make the two towns possible in one day I hired a Ford. Ten hours and a half, — sixteen pesos.

The road to San Agustín Acolman led out towards Guadalupe. In the chill early morning we passed processions of barefoot Indians and women of the wealthier class, also barefoot, flower laden, bound for the shrine of Guadalupe. No men of the better class, barefoot; it is the women who remain religious fanatics.

Then we passed a typical Mexican landscape,—a Ford wrapped around an iron lamppost. Later another head first in a ditch. Acolman — that strong, fine temple — there I copied many frescoes — which seemed however to have but little Indian influence. I recalled the happy day of two years ago when we and the Salas, with ample lunch baskets and good red wine, dined and whiled away the hours in the church yard. But this time it was work — and hurried work — for we had yet to make Texcoco. The road to reach the highway for Texcoco was a mere clearing through a cornfield, — I give credit to a Ford for accomplishing almost what a burro might!

I had always wanted to work with that most magnificient plant, the maguey — here on the highway was my chance. I took it. But I hurried, — each hour was costing pesos. Always the preoccupation of money!

Bulls and cows and calves wreathed with marigold! We passed them near Texcoco.

This chapel in Texcoco is said to be the oldest on the American continent. It is strongly Mexican. Angels, which are delightfully unangelic, flitting over the portal, and on the church facade were sculptured Indians with plumed head dresses. The old padres may have watched the work with dismay and surely contempt — but they were wise to let them have their way. The return ride to the city is surely one of the most beautiful out of Mexico.

October 22. Well, here I am until the 1st of November, at least — and through no fault of mine. Sr. Pallares cannot pay me the balance due of seven hundred fifty pesos before this date. I was furious — having more than fulfilled my end of the bargain — and to stay on here means extra rent—expenses I had not counted on. But it may be the fates are kind to me for M. seems to have changed her attitude, and when she returns from Guerrero, Tuesday, I am to see her.

What probably are the last negatives I shall make for the book I did Wednesday in a "casa de vecindad" — neighborhood house — in Colonia Soreto — la S. Antonio Tomotlan 10.

This was a community home, a sort of tenement house. A fine old convent, converted to this more utilitarian purpose, admirably served to house the obscure.

We met Goitia, a Mexican painter, in the patio of this place the night before. He had promised to show us a typical casa de vecindad. "I will have an organito there to play *La Golondrina* — so the *light* will be perfect," he said! We found him sketching the patio, though he could not possibly have seen it through the wall of washing hung from a cobweb of ropes. The organ grinder did not come but the "light" was made perfect by the collective noise of cats and dogs, children laughing and crying, women gabbling and vendors calling. A great opportunity to do something for myself, — this maze of ropes and festooned washing, the zigzag of the cement community wash tubs — but the life? — how could I render that and retain definition, minute detail of objects near and far, all fascinating and necessary?

The next morning I went early. I must "stop down" — the exposure would be at least a second — it was a gamble. I waited for a moment of arrested motion — I tried at least eight times. I think from out the lot, one or two may join my collection.

Brett too has been working with the camera and I give the boy great credit for fine vision, — accurate observation. A sureness that I did not have six years ago. So much for contact in life. He has lost a year and a half of school stupidities. But he has gained.

October 23. Cold frosty mornings — cloudless days — the rain is over; the season in El Toreo is on — tomorrow Chicuelo fights — I must see one more corrida! Bless Frank and Bob my *House and Garden* friends for that evening with M. Tuesday seems many days away.

Rafael's condition no better — Monna near to collapse with worry and work. I want so much to return by boat — Soon I shall see those little rascals — and the big one — once more — Cole — Neil — Ted [Chandler].

October 25. El Toreo — yesterday for the first time in many weeks, and for the last time in Mexico, I am sure. A perfect day — cloudless — hot. A great crowd, expectant and enthusiastic, for it was the season's first appearance of Chicuelo, last year's idol. The music! The suspense! The great empty arena, like a blank sheet of paper ready for the recording of comedy or tragedy, beauty or ugliness, life or death! The bugle! Chicuelo — Barajas — Rayito! Chicuelo acclaimed with a roar of applause and a rain of hats, canes, flowers. The bugle! The first bull! A magnificent brute. But Chicuelo killed in bad form and was hooted and hissed. The bugle! Another superb bull. Barajas — an unknown quantity. A whirlwind fight — a perfect kill — a new hero. Twenty thousand white handkerchiefs, a swirling snowstorm of acknowledgment — a thunderstorm of voices. Each bull was a fighting bull — tremendous animals.

There are those who see a bull fight — for example, D. H. Lawrence — and all they see with with their unseeing eyes and all they feel in their unfeeling stolidity is a fight between a man and a bull with a few gored horses to groan over. Sentimental? an abused word — flung around too easily by modern "intellectuals." Bourgeoisie? also lovingly mouthed by those who read *The Dial* — what then? Apathy to the aesthetic quality of the fight — granting its undeniable sordidness—bars such persons from feeling and understanding its symbolic pagentry. Perhaps they are more humane, if less human, but they miss in life those fearful forbidden heights from which some see beauty masked and arrayed in alien guise. Refinement of aesthetic response or shocking sensuality; one may seek and find, each in his own fashion, in El Toreo.

October 28. Printing palladio! near to six months since I have indulged in this rare pleasure — also yesterday I made the last two outside negatives to be done — the arches of that fine patio in the ex-convento de la Merced, and a new prehispanic discovery — a large model of a temple, a sculptured stone, found while remodelling the Palacio Nacional. One more negative only, a painting by Goitia to be copied, then I am free! I am quite gay and carefree to be through. Now for a few happy days with M. and I'll sail away forever!

Brett worked with my Graflex from the roof of la Merced, and made negatives technically fine and equally as well seen. The boy has a great future, and I believe he realizes it. For a boy of fourteen he is remarkable well balanced and free from "spooks".

Lupe had phoned to come for tamales and atole at six. A crowd was there — too late to back out — Anyhow I might never see them again. Lupe with her racy tongue convulsed us all as usual. Her topic, which allowed of caustic and flippant garrulity, concerned two girls, friends, who had published a manifesto against men in general. A warning to long suffering women to awaken. They published even to intimate details their relations with men and also the names of their betrayers! Then personally distributed the propaganda to prove their courage.

This morning I awakened with tears from a half dream in which Diego said, "No te vayas, Edward," as we embraced farewell. It was reacting our parting of last night! I suppose in the dream Diego was a symbol for all that I shall be sad to leave in Mexico.

The "tamalada" was a success — couldn't have been otherwise with la Señora Marin supervising.

October 31. Tomorrow I am to receive my last payment — or I should say I am supposed to!

We have decided to return by boat via Manzanillo — stopping over a day or so in Colima, — the few glimpses of that city leaving impressions which tempt me to further exploration, and Brett knows that there must be an unexcelled hunting ground for butterflies.

But best of all must be a week upon the water — enforced idleness — that sort of idleness which allows the brain to function clearly – unharrased by daily duties.

November 1. M. came — and M. went!

She came early. For a birthday present I had asked her to select one of my photographs. She chose my Three Ollas de Oaxaca — of all my work maybe my present favorite.

Then we went out Guadalupe way. Another religious pilgrimage was on. Singing and crying "Viva," hordes of people marched into the church. To have entered would have meant suffocation, so we climbed high above the fanatical mob and watched the sunset over a truly noble landscape. "El Popo," whose white blanket changed to rose then faded to grey — black geometric forms in the foreground hills — lightning over Lake Texcoco.

I had asked M. more than once to go away with me — but always evasion of this culmination to our episode — "To Oaxaca — to Colima — anywhere, darling —" But always evasion — even to my "Why not?" — except a vague "After, come so many pains, so much sadness."

We descended to the plaza and sat for awhile in the dusk — very close together — yet very far apart — little flashes of recognition — a touch of finger tips and exchange of the eyes — her head on my shoulder — and then, when I might become insistent, a barrier of casual remarks — behind which sat M. with who knows what thoughts — yet she cares, I can see in her eyes.

November 2. And no money yet — Pallares promised yesterday. I cannot make boat reservations with no surety of my pay. What a ghastly day it was — too cloudy for printing — all other work finished — M. away — Brett haunting my heels. I don't blame him — he has not enough outlet here — he is sociable but has no friends — I have to be father — friend — teacher. I want to be — am glad to feel I can be — but not every moment of the day.

The puestos are open for "El Dia de los Muertos". For the last time we walked the alameda. Kewpie dolls, tin toys, Japanese screens, horrible abortions from Tlaquepaque, — such rubbish was offered and sold from two thirds of the puestos. Yet it was colorful despite the corruption of taste. Massed gewgaws may be visually delightful — but taken separately become abominations.

The indifferent familiarity of the Mexican to death — the macabre viewpoint is indicated in the puestos on this day of the dead. "Death for sale" is the vendor's cry — Death from every realistic and fantastic angle is sought and sold. Great candy skulls, tin trolley car hearses, tombstones, puppet skeletons who fiddle and dance, gruesome death masks — while a jolly crowd banters and buys.

November 4. At last my money — all but forty pesos. The boat four days late, — I should leave the 13th. A party has been planned at Frances' to bid me farewell. I don't want it. Just sitting around, talking, tea sipping, joking. A dancing party at Frank's and Bob's, yes, for there I could lose myself with M. There a party would mean dances, drinks, embraces, kisses with M. — and the rest go hang! My last gesture in Mexico with M. — that is my wish — She comes in half an hour for her portraits — this early morning — 7:00 a.m.

200

November 5. No M. came — She must go, as guide with a group of labor delegates from Europe. These laborites have played havoc with my love affair. I must in revenge become more conservative than ever.

Before the clouds came — I pulled a brilliant print of my palm, better than the one Diego has. In the afternoon Jean sat to me. He has given me a number of drawings to dispose of in Los Angeles—they are so fine that I almost hope they do not sell!

With the greatest satisfaction I note Brett's interest in photography. He is doing better work at fourteen that I did at thirty. To have some one close to me, working so excellently, with an assured future, is a happiness hardly expected.

Both Jean and Diego, who came late, like a new negative done in Xochimilco of cactus and rock. It yields a hard contrasting print, — in spots where the sun reflected from cactus or sand the value is represented by almost clear paper, but how else could such eye-blinding portions be registered? The same with a lake reflecting the sun, seen above a foreground of Indian huts heavily shadowed, which I recorded from Xanicho [Janitzio]. The lake is a blank, — quite without detail. I know just the people who will criticize these prints. But I know that I saw correctly.

November 7. My boat delayed again — now it does not leave till the 17th. I do not feel so badly — for it will give me more time to print palladio, but Brett is quite cross, and all for leaving by train, which can't be done, for all my papers, passes, idols, chest, photographs are for the officials at Manzanillo.

Brett hasn't a friend of his own age in Mexico, and I feel sorry for him, but I'm afraid when he returns, his old friends will not satisfy him either, for he has gone beyond them; they will no longer speak the same language.

I did not say that the delay will also give me more days with M. For what is the use? I have given up hope that she will "run away" with me. Yesterday she sat to me, and there came moments when we forgot the purpose of her visit, but always her answer to my "Why not?" was "Because." Could ever a word be more exasperating!

November 8. Two Tarahumare Indians ran from Pachuca to the Mexico Stadium yesterday, a distance of 100 Kilometres or 62.5 miles in 9 hours and 37 minutes, close to seven miles an hour for nine hours!

Frances, Peter, Claire, M. and I hired a car and met them about twenty miles out. They were running strong, these huarache-clad interlopers in modern athletic games. I was told that several had once been sent to the Olympic games in Paris, expecting to clean up the world in long distance, but had failed because they tried to run in modern running shoes and bandaged ankles. So they wore huaraches yesterday, an amusing contrast to the usual track uniform, with the colors of Mexico on their breasts. But the huaraches were not the only note which showed them out of place, for each wore a string of bells, which jingled merrily as they ran, and peaked straw sombreros.

The finish took place in the Stadium, where as a reward for their performance, officials tied around their necks silk handkerchiefs of gaudy red.

M. and I ditched the crowd for the bull fight, in which "El Chato" fought gloriously.

I saw her but once again, alone for a moment, but with nothing more to say. We met at Frank's — a farewell party for me. Successes can not be repeated — it was a sad and tiresome affair.

Tuesday—9th. Rather sleepy — not having slept off the wine which Madame Charlot served with a little farewell supper for me. Just the three of us, Madame, Jean and I, were the party. I took Jean a print, the new "Maguey", and he gave me an oil, which I hardly need say delights me. Jean was happy with the proofs, especially one head against a brick wall, a perfectly fine negative and a strong likeness.

Pulled some fine palladio prints yesterday and want to continue printing today with such perfect weather. But I have very bad news. — The boat we were supposed to take does not stop in Los Angeles. A nice time for the stupid agents to discover this! Now all my letters of introduction must be changed from Manzanilló to Juárez. And we must take that miserable train trip, — hot, dusty, and quite uninteresting.

As usual I have last moment sittings. A bride! — and Sra. Llamosa who says I cannot leave Mexico without once more making her portrait. Also I have sold a print. Dr. Boehme, professor in the German School, purchased my petate horseman — the second German who has chosen this print. With Dr. Boehme came the wife of the German Ambassador to Mexico, who made a fine impression on all of us, as a strong, intelligent woman.

On the train. The leaving of Mexico will be remembered for the leaving of Tina. The barrier between us was for the moment broken. Not till we were on the Paseo in a taxi rushing for the train did I allow myself to see her eyes. But when I did and saw what they had to say, I took her to me, — our lips met in an endless kiss, only stopped by a gendarme's whistle. Our driver tactfully hinted that public demonstrations were taboo, — for shame! Mexico is surely becoming United Statesized.

Dear friends came to the train, — Felipe — Pepe — Roberto — Frances — and M., — others sent messages and love.

Vamanos! — last embraces all around — Tina with tear filled eyes. This time, Mexico, it must be adiós forever. And you, Tina? I feel it must be farewell forever too.

II. CALIFORNIA

PART I

Glendale, January, 1927—July, 1928

1. Return to the Past

January 24, 1927. In my old studio, Glendale. Months have passed since I have sat here at my desk with morning coffee recalling the past, reviewing the present. I will revive this stimulating hour, but not until tomorrow, for soon a marcelled flapper aged 70 will sit to me to boil-the-pot.

8:00 a.m. the 25th—a late arising. C. came. She said "Women in love never know when to go." Right, C. Too many have been coming, and now K., tall and fair with gold-brown hair, hazel eyes, lovely and 21. For 3 months I have focussed my camera but once on subject matter for myself. I could blame 3 loves—but no, time could have been found. I am not yet a part of my new surroundings, one foot is still in Mexico. New surroundings! Too many faded flowers. I should never have returned to my past. But the boys brought me back here, and here I will stay until I can make some positive, constructive move.

February 3. Peter's party [Peter Krasnow, painter] was one of the gayest ever. Dressed as a fine lady, evening gown and trimmings, I had a chance to burlesque the ladies, and did. The "bootlegger" failed us, but we did not miss him. Only dawn ended the fun. Peter made great cartoons which covered the walls; they were far more than jokes, he achieved creative expression. One was of E. W. with his camera, another Dr. Frankl, knife in hand, after decapitating a patient. Galka Scheyer had begged my leather breeches, putees, pistola and Texano, so I got in exchange her outfit even down to panties, and a marvellous make-up job to boot. As a ravishing woman I was a success with the women.

February 5. Two days of retouching on that 70 year old flapper. So do I boil my pot. Pretty disgusting, this simulating of Jazz babies by mimicking, mincing old ninnies. But I worked for myself Monday. An event. Two negatives, nudes of C., both well seen. We started so late that exposures were of necessity prolonged to 5 min. with some resulting movement. A start has been made. C. has a body of exaggerated proportions. To overstate her curves became my preoccupation. The ground glass registered sweeping volumes which I shall yet record more surely. C. is a fine girl—unusually fine; generous, considerate; really great hearted. I regret diversions.

February 7. Saturday is the boys' day—the little fellows, Neil and Cole. I close up "shop" and we wander away wherever their fancy lures, to the zoo, rowing, or to the museum. This time I suggested the latter goal; for while they marvelled over stuffed bears and old bones, I could see the show of "Synchromists," Wright

3

and Russell. Their published credo was brave enough but I came away unconvinced. S. Macdonald Wright's work was no more than *Sat. Eve. Post* figures seasoned with splashes of unrelated prismatic color. I hurried away before seeing Morgan's to escape culture hungry throngs who filed in to hear Wright explain. The stuffed animals were beautiful.

February 8. Nudes of C. again. Approach similar to those made of A. in Mexico. Repeating my successes? No, I have always felt that I could go on with variations. I am in fine humor to have done new and good work. C. wants me to go with her to Germany, her home. She "will work hard, earn the expense money!" A generous offer from an uncalculating woman.

February 10. Why this tide of women? Why do they all come at once?

Here I am, isolated, hardly leaving my work rooms, but they come, they seek me out,—and yield, (or do *I* yield?)

Five years ago M. came to this very room for her portrait. Her reason for coming was drowned in kisses,—but—nothing more—she would not. Again she came two years after,—more kisses—that was all. Yesterday she did not deny me,— not after a few weak protests.

M. had been drinking—I saw this at once—her flaming cheeks, and excited talk,—irrelevant words which did not conceal her desire. Maybe she drank to suppress a vigilant, puritan self,—I rather think so. She left me gardenias,— and I drifted retrospectively home to fry pork chops for the boys' supper.

Saturday, February 12. An evening was *given* me at the studio of Ed Langley— Hollywood. Rather—I was used to furnish an evening's amusement for a group of serious people. They were so serious that from the first print shown to the last there was not a sound from one of the melancholic congregation—Maybe they were overwhelmed,—at least they were polite,—deadly polite. Before my performance, Mr. Langley gave his. Upon a velvet-curtained easel he showed his paintings,—prefacing the exhibit by admitting he was not an artist, with which charming modesty he at once won approval. Back of the luxurious curtains he placed in turn the paintings,—Presto!—and Art was revealed. With controlled lights he made sunsets more sunsetty—"so pretty!" gasped the congregation. K. would dig me in the ribs, Brett would lean over with a wickedly mischievous grin, until we gagged from suppressed laughter.

Ruth Shaw swept grandly in! No one had told me we were to appear on the same program. I had not seen my quondam friend since her clacking, wagging tongue caused our estrangement. My bitterness has long ago passed, I am only indifferent, I cannot be bothered with a missionary. I did not avoid her, perhaps she did me,—we did not meet, and that was well. F. in her usual tactless manner saw to it that K. and I went home in different cars. Does she smell a rat? And even so, why should she be a cat!

4

Last night K. held me close and said, "I want to tell you something darling,—that I really love you very, very much,"—a sudden change from her flippancy.

Just don't grow to care too much dear girl. I must remain free — — I also care, —but not too much.

February 13. Brett and I are exhibiting together,—his first public appearance. The University of California invited me, and I included him as quite worthy. I am showing around a hundred prints,—Brett twenty. We hung the exhibit yesterday and were exhausted by night. He should be stimulated and has sense enough not to become conceited.

February 14. Peter came with Marguerite Zorach and Henrietta Shore to see my work. Mrs. Zorach I remembered from published reproductions, but could not definitely connect her name and her work. Henrietta Shore I knew only by name,—from Peter. Now I know her very well, for they took me to her home and there I saw fine painting.
Women as creative artists soar in my half contemptuous estimation when I see such work. . . .

February 16. This is the 16th and the formal opening of our exhibit with a "tea" and invited guests,—reporters, "critics," etc. It is also the fourth day of a rain storm which has become a veritable flood, with no sign of cessation. My little shack leaks in a dozen corners, rainwet branches whip the thin board siding,—while "Sin Verguenzo," my simpatico Tomcat, wild from excitement and four days imprisonment is on a rampage attacking imaginary foes, especially the straw horseman "Panchito Villa," who, biting the dust, stiffens in proud salute
I will blame no one for staying home today from our opening. A letter from Tina, [Modotti—see Vol. I.] who writes that John Dos Passos called to see our photographs,—she has a few of mine. To quote, "He like all keen persons appreciates photography as it should be. We talked of Stieglitz. He spoke of his cloud pictures. Does not like them. Too vague he says and with such absurd titles." Later I want to comment upon Dos Passos' remarks.

February 17. I should feel gratified that so many came to the exhibit in the storm. Among others were Betty and Harriet, with whom I promised to spend the weekend at Lois's home—Palm Springs. I have an excuse for myself of work to do,—Lois's horse to photograph, for actually I have no desire for a holiday, much stronger is the urge to create. I will take my 8 × 10, and maybe find something for myself,—there is the desert! Those who met me yesterday, after these several years, note a great change. Some say I appear younger,—pleasant thought! Marcella said I was more brusque, but I would answer that I am more direct.

To briefly remark on Stieglitz:

He is a prophet who suffers from the exaltation of his disciples. This thought in no way indicates that I do not appreciate him,—fully. Again I feel that he weakens his work by too much explanation, tries to read into each photograph esoteric derivation. Perhaps he does this wisely, knowing his public who expect reasons.

I question whether now, after four years, I would be as deeply moved either by Stieglitz' work or talk as on that memorable afternoon with Jo in New York— Perhaps I might be more *understanding* with less youthful hero worship.

[*Undated*]... This is a turn unexpected, but too beautiful to be disregarded. When an experienced girl, though she be young, writes,—"I love you"—one can no longer remain untouched—Love is too rare and precious for flippancy. Her love has changed the incidental attitude I held. Now I would give her all that I can spare.

February 23. Life seems to afford me a sequence of dramatic episodes. I probably make them so. This act was staged on the desert bound for "Fool's Folly,"— Lois' home. Four of us went,—Betty, Harriet and "Brandy," were the others.

We knew the highway was impassible from landslides and washouts,—but there was a detour across the desert. Leaving late, night came on, the detour was found by moonlight. Far into the wasteland we drove before the storm swept upon us,—sand not rain,—stinging, blinding sand, blasted along by the desert gale, shrouding the landscape, hissing fiendishly, obliterating the road. A silent, snow-crowned mountain towered hardby. Foot by foot we made our way through the drifts and against the gale,—digging—pushing. For miles Harriet and I walked, floundering along, wind buffeted....

[*Undated*] One day the knot-hole in a fig tree tempted an exposure, —and after, another of the same tree trunk. The former is slightly blurred,—wind-shaken I guess, which is too bad for I had hopes.

February 24. A trip to our exhibit showed by the register, not many, but important visitors had called. I was glad to note the name of Henrietta Shore. Liking her painting, I felt sure she would like my photographs. She wrote—"I spent an hour enjoying the sheer beauty of your work—free from mussiness or effect." She could have written nothing better.

February 26. ... Seeing the exhibit, Bertha [Wardell—dancer] wrote "Even to think of them gives me a feeling of reality, of things falling and fallen into their proper relations... The effect seemed to be a sum-total reaction." Then she offered herself as a model.

Sunday morning. The boys and I went out on our Saturday adventure to Ramiel's. [Ramiel McGehee, see Vol. I.] All these months I have only seen him four

6

times: of all my friends the most discriminating,—understanding,—human. We live too far apart,—yet each knows the other is very near in spirit.

The boys swam: Ramiel and I talked,—of the past, the present and the future. It is seldom I exchange thoughts with anyone,—really talk.

Returning, from the train I saw a "Studio of Photography"—named "The Be Saw Studio." Mexican pulquerias have nothing on us in imaginative titles!

From habit I wrote "George" Stojana—I should have written "Gjura," for he has changed, or rather taken his real name, dropped when he came to the States. I like it better, "George" never suited him, but knowing a person six years, a name becomes a label hard to change.

Gjura then—is still the child he always was and will be. A simple, credulous person trying to intellectualize his words and work. He speaks in farfetched metaphors which he may understand but no one else does, and becomes impatient if his equivocal talk and gestures are not immediately comprehended—and agreed to!

The elect may read his mystic symbols; I have not reached that plane. Add to his unintelligible expression, a misuse of English and a great desire to set forth his ideas, for he makes few friends to confide in, and one is confronted with an exhausting contact. Yet I like Gjura, with all his querulous temperament. He is a poseur, without knowing that he poses. He has the ego of one who really doubts himself. He said—"Rivera is my only contemporary, a great painter but I am greater,—I say this without blushing!" But his work did not move me as it once did. I see no progress, only a re-hashing of his Bali themes—now stale. He needs to return there, for Gjura works from outside impression, he has not the spark within. I contrast him with Peter Krasnow who has quietly, steadily, surely progressed until now I feel he is more important than George. I played with Gjura at first, made him try to explain his nebulous jargon, until he went around in circles, contradicting himself. Finally he burst out, "You are playing with words!" And I retorted "So are you!" I took Brett, but I'm sure he got nothing from the day. "I like Peter's work better, Dad."

[*Undated*] A letter from Jean Charlot,—the first since leaving Mexico. He is in Chichen-Itza, Yucatan. "I am pretty sure we shall meet again, Edward; I learned much from you about painting and if you want to send me from time to time some bad prints of your best negatives, I could still learn something."

[*Undated*] I have partially fulfilled a youthful covenant with myself. For—one day before my twenties—I answered my sister who questioned what I would do in life, "I don't know yet, but I will be successful." I have never forgotten this. My words sounded strange to me then, as though someone spoke for me. This inner conviction I have held and shall always hold. I ask nothing more than to be able to grow in strength, and achieve the ultimate from my possibilities.

[*Undated*] ...more critical each time I work, I am not dissatisfied when in an afternoon I make one negative worth printing.

Sometime I want to give an exhibit printed on glossy paper. This shall be my gesture of disapproval for those who try to hide their weakness in "arty" presentation. This long-held plan received fresh impetus after viewing the "International Salon of Photography" at Exposition Park. Unable to definitely use Form these pictorialists resort to artistic printing: unable to feel Life, except with the surface emotions of a pugilist or an old maid teacher, they produce only fogs and "light effects." Pretty stories poorly told!—moods—instead of the Thing itself.

That exhibit, excepting two or three prints, if reprinted on glossy paper, stripped of all subterfuge, would no longer interest even those who now respond: those photographs without varnish, without evasion would mean nothing.

Those "pictorialists" were deadly serious, I grant,—so serious that the result was often comic. I took Brett, hoping to find material for discussion: there was nothing to discuss, he was highly amused for awhile, by this work of the most celebrated "pictorialists" in the world, then wandered off to the butterfly room. After noting the numbers of four photographs that had some value I referred to the catalogue, finding that each one was by a Japanese. Perhaps my exhibit in the Japanese colony has borne some fruit,—I could feel my influence.

Sunday, March 20. I was given a party last night—O Jesus! What a party! Drink reveals what a person is made of: drunk, the burgesses lose the thin veneer which hides their crudeness. I don't mind noise, foolishness, amorous display,—it is the WAY in which one is noisy, foolish, amorous.

Some people have no more right to get drunk than a dog has: or I should say that I had no business with them,—for they had a glorious time. I was ashamed to have Elena's old mother,—the girls too,—the several Mexicans, see the performance.

X. knowing how I dislike the "artistic" evenings she pulls, thought she would give me a good time. This is the pitiful side,—her effort with energy, time, money,—her generosity. I tried hard to fit in, but I feel the party thought me stiff, cold, indifferent, and probably were disappointed, for although I knew but two or three who came, they knew of me, from talk,—and pictured me as a gay Don Juan.

I stole away at 1:30, an unpardonable breach of etiquette! I could not stomach the mess longer.

This morning I am consumed by disgust. At least I am not "crudo,"—I only pretended to drink with the rest.

March 22. C. came for our Monday together, bringing besides the "goodies" she always so thoughtfully contributes for supper, a cup and saucer for my morning coffee,—a gay cup, yellow, with red posies.

She is going to Fresno for several months,—perhaps the Gods are taking her away for awhile! I shall genuinely miss C.,—she is one of the most thoughtful, considerate of mortals.

Despite feeling half sick,—a hangover from the party, I tried to do more nudes. Exposed twice, one nude,—back and buttocks again, and one head.

The cup was a birthday gift,—I shall be forty-two, Thursday.

2. The Chambered Nautilus and the Dancing Nude

Thursday, March 24. Forty-one years I have today,—not forty-two when I came to figure! The boys gave me ten dollars: of course it was from Flora, and indicates her extreme generosity, which I have never denied.

I have given myself a birthday present, it may be for a day, a year or forever, —I have quit smoking. This plan only happened to come on my birthday,—I have long considered to stop.

B. sat to me again: six negatives exposed, all of some value, three outstanding, but two of the latter slightly moved. However, the one technically good is the one best seen. As she sat with legs bent under, I saw the repeated curve of thigh and calf,—the shin bone, knee and thigh lines forming shapes not unlike great sea shells,—the calf curved across the upper leg, the shell's opening. I made this, cutting at waist and above ankle.

After the sitting I fell asleep, sitting bolt upright, supposedly showing Bertha some drawings,—I was that worn out.

These simplified forms I search for in the nude body are not easy to find, nor record when I do find them. There is that element of chance in the body assuming an important movement: then there is the difficulty in focussing close up with a sixteen inch lens: and finally the possibility of movement in an exposure of from 20 sec. to 2 min.,—even the breathing will spoil a line. If I had a workroom such as the one in San Francisco with a great overhead and side light equal to out of doors, I would use my Graflex: for there I made $1/_{10}$ s. exposures with f/11,—in this way I recorded Neil's body. Perhaps the next nudes I will try by using the Graflex on tripod: the 8 inch Zeiss will be easier to focus, exposures will be shorter, films will be cheaper!

My after exhaustion is partly due to eyestrain and nerve strain. I do not weary so when doing still-life and can take my own sweet time.

B. has a sensitive body and responsive mind. I would keep on working with her.

March 25. Well, I have not quit smoking! I felt during the day that to stop so suddenly the accustomed poison was too severe a punishment, so I cut the amount to half, and will try to gradually reduce,—smoking the last within four or five days.

It is this: I feel that I owe my self the strongest body possible to carry out the work I am surely destined to do.

Came a letter from B. which well indicates her response: "You seemed possessed for an instant not only of a physical but of a psychical fatigue... What you do awakes in me so strong a response that I must in all joy tell you. Your photographs are as definite an experience to the spirit as a whip lash to the body. It is as if they said, 'Look—here is something you have been waiting for—something you have not found in painting nor even in sculpture, something which has been before only in the thought of dancing'." This letter also indicates why I would work more with her.

March 26. With K. to see Ruth Draper, an actress of unusual ability, who presented an enjoyable evening's entertainment. She has a great vogue, but I came away with not more than a pleasant feeling: I would rather have seen a Chaplin comedy, or "Frisco" dance.

I am disgusted this morning for not having slept longer,—I needed to. Probably I overworked yesterday, having made 12 enlargements from as many negatives on an order. It will bring me $120, then I'll sleep better!

On my birthday there came,—sent by Tina,—seven drawings by Pacheco, on commission. I decided at once to make myself a birthday present: seldom now do I desire to possess drawings or paintings,—but this one,—a deep sea fantasy I guess,—I want to live with.

It is, of course, more than a fantasy,—a spiritually moving conception. The boy touches the same chord in me that Henrietta Shore does. He has that which is beyond emotion or intellect,—a transcendental force. To buy this I would sell my Picasso dry-point or one of Diego's drawings. Having this work of Maximo Pacheco causes me to meditate over the Mexican painters. Diego Rivera has arrived—he is "*It*" with the public—those who echo the voice of the Art dealers,—but there are others. I have before this placed Jean Charlot ahead of Diego, now I place Pacheco also ahead: and there is Siqueiros to consider, no minor figure—and Orozco of great importance. No, not with less admiration for Diego, I say he is now overrated, or better the others are underrated, that there are several his equal or greater,—Jean and Orozco are surely greater.

I recall a consignment of drawings I sent from Mexico to San Francisco for a Mrs. Swift who was to exhibit them for sale. All of Diego's were taken, all of Jean's came back. The name "Diego Rivera" sold, not the superiority of his work. Jean and Diego both showed at the Pan American Exhibit here. Diego won the grand prize,—but—Jean's canvas was the finer.

March 29. — 5:00 a.m. Only the mocking birds are awake with me. There is a jolly one who lives in my elderberry tree,—he is the busiest, sassiest fellow, and always bursting with song. I have the greatest admiration for the mockingbird, and protest a name as slurring. If they mock, they most certainly recreate the

11

stolen song, give forth in their own way, and I dare say improve upon the original version.

California is lovable these days, with all fruit trees blooming, with lush grass and soft skies. Today it is raining—maybe the last rain of the season.

After cutting down my cigarettes to comparatively nothing I smoked too many yesterday. I don't blame myself! I spotted nine enlargements on an order which had been very poorly retouched,—had to be retouched or I never could have delivered the prints. I worked all day, until my eyes were a blur, and my nerves raw. I hoped someone, anyone indeed, would call that I might talk and forget myself, but nary a soul came, even Brett was away. I would have been happy in my aloneness some days but not yesterday. I worked awhile, smoked between spasms, cursed, paced the floor, played a record, worked again, and all the time kept saying to myself $120 — $120!

I have three more, and the worst ones to do this morning. They must be done— I have just ten cents left — — —

March 20. Consuela Kanaga is here...[on her way to New York; apparently while discussing Stieglitz, she commented—]..."but he will keep you in your place, you will always be known as one of the Stieglitz group, and his power in New York is tremendous."

Henrietta Shore asked me to sit to her. I am sure no one else could tempt me to so spend time, but certainly I respond to this real opportunity.

The shells I photographed were so marvellous one could not do other than something of interest. What I did may be only a beginning—but I like one negative especially. I took a proof of the legs recently done of Bertha, which Miss Shore was enthusiastic over.

April 1. Nudes of ———— again. Made two negatives,—variation on one conception.

I am stimulated to work with the nude body, because of the infinite combinations of lines which are presented with every move. And now after seeing the shells of Henrietta Shore, a new field has been presented.

April 2. Consuela took to New York three platinum prints and several glossy prints of mine to try for an exhibit the next season. She will see Stieglitz,—so I told her that if he expressed desire, to show him my work. And I especially hoped that Charles Sheeler would see the work. This may bring an opening for me to go on to New York, for which I have desire and equal aversion.

Good Lord! Anne Brigman is here! Worse she wants to use my darkroom, which I cannot deny her, nor would I, for Anne is a dear soul. But how she does talk and always of herself,—living on her past glory, still expecting "the one man

12

in the world," with whom she would go to the world's end. Remarkable to have such faith and enthusiasm,—Anne being well over sixty.

The last nude of B.,—good.

Sunday, April 3. Monna and Rafael on their way here from Mexico—they should arrive today or tomorrow — — — I want to see them very much—yet I am unwilling to be interrupted by even my best friends—these days which find me in the swing of work again.

I made an excellently seen negative of my desk lamp, which I have considered doing ever since purchasing it. My placing and timing were near to perfect but the base was fogged. This is depressing: I have had no fogged negatives for months—indeed not a sign of fog in all the weeks of travel in Mexico, working under most trying conditions.

It must be that a holder leaks, for last week I carefully tested my bellows and back. I will try to repeat the negative today, and also do a bunch of bananas which I intended to photograph in Mexico, where they are much cheaper.

April 4. 5:00 a.m., though I was awake at 4:00, with my mind full of banana forms! How exciting they are to work with! I am torn between two new loves, —bananas and shells.

I made one negative, and it is a failure because of inaccurate focussing,—a rare defect in my work. I shall repeat the same arrangement of bananas, an orange and my black Oaxaca olla, and do many more besides.

A new negative of the desk lamp is quite perfect.

April 6. I can foresee that bananas, even as a bouquet of posies, are to be elusive material if I wish to repeat a negative: they too wilt and change, and there is yet another danger, which concerns the afternoon appetites of small boys: the last bunch was consumed before I had thought of hiding or warning. Brett bought another bunch, but the grouping was so different I could not carry out my original idea.

Nevertheless I attacked the problem from another angle and have a new negative worth finishing. I am not through with bananas: and I shall watch the markets for other fruits and vegetables. Strange, loving flowers, that I have never used them. Why, I cannot say. Maybe because I was not ready to do them as they should be done. Someday soon I shall see exactly what I want. I have been printing on bromide paper,—no more Palladio for lack of money.

Yesterday came a Japanese photographer, Kinsaku Asakura, who purchased two prints,—the hand of Galván and the one of Rose Roland. This is the second time I have sold "Galván" to a Japanese. I asked fifteen dollars for each. When I am in New York I shall raise my prices. I was rather sad to see these fine prints go, but I certainly needed the money.

13

How rarely I sell to Americans! How appreciative, understanding and courteous the Japanese!

April 7. — Early! Monna and Rafael here at last. Seeing Rafael again was a shock,—he seemed worse than ever. They are both so lovable!

In the afternoon came Winifred Hooke and Mrs. McLouth, curator of the L. A. Museum. I have been invited to give a one-man show there,—and accepted. It is with no desire for glory that I will exhibit, other than the glory of a few extra dollars in my purse, and that consequence is not worth considering as a possibility: but it is to make my gesture of disapproval towards the Pictorial group,—their tendencies and policies, their control of the annual exhibition. I may reach a small public who will like my work better.

Another visitor was a sculptor, a young fellow, Stanley by name, who brought a wood carving of considerable beauty.

April 9. Could not sleep this morning after 4:00, so wrote Henrietta Shore before dawn. I want to see more of her.

My work rooms are spick and span in readiness for the coming of Monna and Rafael today!

Made negatives of Kathleen singing, but cannot consider them successful: more another time.

Have a student at $3 the hour: only an hour and a half from her the first day.

Must consider *"business."* Money again low,—the check from order nearly gone.

I want to work with bananas today. Fortunate they can be eaten, I could not afford to buy them for Art's sake.

A letter from sister [Mary Weston Seaman—see Vol. I.] —in which she poured out her sorrows. I have been fortunate to have a sister so close to me.

April 10. At 6:00 a.m. the temperature in my dark-room was 43°: outside the roofs are white with frost. San Francisco papers copy!

A 35 cent bunch of bananas made me happy. The children eyed them covetously but I hung out danger signals: they are not eaten yet .... This is an especially fine bunch, though so unlike the first grouping that I cannot yet carry out my original intention, which was a vertical point of view, the concave side to the camera, the columns of bananas filling the entire plate, curved at the top to a common focus.

In yesterday's two negatives the concave side was down, the bananas horizontal, with a splendid sweep of lines. Both attempts successful.

April 11. — The morning after a confusing yesterday: five boys here, most of the time in a turmoil,—the rain precluded sending them out. I did not accept the situation with inward grace.

No sooner had they gone when C. W. arrived. I thought I had shown him long ago my distaste for his company. I was courteous, but I do not think he will call again — — — —

Rafael has been too sick to leave his room. I'm thinking it will be many days before he comes here.

April 12. The date for Japanese exhibit postponed: they are surely an appreciative and understanding group, shown by this extract from a letter from Toyo San: "Our club 'Shakudo Sha' will pay for use of gallery and no commission for sale of photo also."

April 13. Tuesdays are now definitely B. day. She enjoys working with me, and I respond to her. Her beauty in movement is an exquisite sight. Dancing should be always in the nude. I made 12 neg's,—for the first time using the Graflex: arrested motion however, for the exposures were three seconds. But these negatives will be different in feeling, for the ease of manipulation of a Graflex allows more spontaneous results.

Today, fortunately, I have a real sitting: Marie Haggerty, a lovely and wealthy girl.

Friday, Henrietta Shore will start my portrait.

Flora is "snowed in" up in the moutains and maybe all this week I'll have to be house-keeper and policeman for the boys. Though I refuse to take my position too seriously, there is more or less confusion and preoccupation.

April 15. I received by mail from Cristal a box of lilacs, white and lavender, so exquisite that my eyes filled with tears. I had to hide them when K. came last night: she too brought spring blossoms. No use hurting K. or causing doubt to rise.

Printed some of my new negatives which I want to show Henrietta Shore. I go to sit for my portrait today.

Tina writes she is "crazy about the two nudes"—the backs of Cristal. And now I am almost "crazy" over several of the recent negatives of B. I shall work with the Graflex for awhile.

April 16. Not so early as usual: Henrietta Shore and I talked till late. The portrait started. She asked me not to look at it until much more work had been done. "I work slowly,—I am not a brilliant painter,—but I used to be!" she added, her face expanding with that characteristic, full-blown, generous smile. I saw for the first time one of her drawings. "I rarely show them, I never have exhibited them." "Why?" I questioned—"I am selfish,"—her answer.

This one drawing was not a quick sketch, it was done with as much care and thought as her painting: a superb piece of work. My admiration grows.

Of my new work, she liked well the legs of Bertha,—the forms Peter thought were great shells: also the second banana negative, my desk light and the

15

chambered nautilus, front view, agreeing with me that the background was too heavy—

Monday, April 18. Sunday was spent with Paul Jordan and Cousin Sarah,—the first visit since my return: always, time spent with them is well spent.

Paul has been painting! He always had contempt for "modern art," an undiscriminating contempt, but partly justified. So, with his sense of humour, and joy in ridicule, he set about to perpetrate a hoax. He painted,—he sent his work to independent exhibits under an assumed Russian name,—and—he was acclaimed, reviewed, his paintings reproduced!

But the joke is partly on Paul. Painting in a really naive, childlike manner, he actually achieved in at least one canvas that which many contemporary painters consciously try to do. This canvas of a Negro woman at the scrubbing board is really a gay, spontaneous thing, not great of course, but much better than most "efforts" seen at modern exhibits. The literary element which he tries to put in each painting is happily almost lacking in this, though he can explain his allegory with many a chuckle. A hand reaching in from one side weakens by adding symbolism,—and distracts, but as a whole the canvas has much real merit.

If he could paint along in this attitude,—gaining in technique, he might become important.

Anyway the whole episode is delightfully amusing.

April 19. Rafael must die!

I was with Monna when the doctor told her — — — — her face I can never forget. How ironical,—cruel, after these months of heroic sacrifice on her part, and terrible suffering on his. They operated, but could not remove the malignant growth which completely enveloped his kidneys. Too late now for natural methods,—though I shall consult McCoy today.

I have only contempt for these "scientists" who have doped him with serums and drugs and X-ray for months.

What brilliant minds!

April 20. I am having coffee from a new and delightful cup,—from M. It came in yesterday's mail: it was received with mixed emotions. I have been here now over five months, yet I have seen M. but twice...

B. came for her Tuesday session: when she went our association had assumed a new aspect! I had before, vague questionings as to whether her coming was an entirely impersonal interest in my work, knowing definitely how strong that response was, but though she has been with me these many afternoons,—danced before me naked, I have never felt the slightest physical excitement. I admired her mind, I thought her body, especially in movement, superb,—but nothing more.

16

Even yesterday, it was not until she was dressed and we sat together exchanging thoughts, that I became fully aware of her real feeling for me. Our hands clasped,—our lips met,— ... then I had to go before a fulfillment. As an artist, B. is more definite than anyone I have met since Mexico, excepting Henrietta Shore. Our association should be constructive to both.

My life may become complicated with three lady loves to consider, and I don't want that: quite the contrary, I crave simplicity.

Ito brought four Japanese friends to see my photographs. Real homage, deep respect always comes from the Japanese,—and concrete appreciation. I sold two more prints,—a head of Diego and an old nude of Tina, for $10 each.

Then one of the party, as spokesman made a little speech, very timidly, in halting, broken English.

Would I like to come to Japan? Many Japanese would be honored if I did,— that was the thought expressed. Of course I told them what a pleasure that could be,—but I had no money. "Japanese artists want you come our country, if we send passage, you come?" What real honor they bestow upon me! One cannot disregard such tribute. How can I accept, considering family complications, I don't know — — — —

April 23. Sat to Henrietta again. I have not seen the canvas yet. She would exclaim often during the sitting—"I am getting something!" We always have supper together, and after I read from my daybook at her request. Reading that part written during the period of my toilet photographing, she said, "Wait, tell me something frankly,—from what motive did you photograph the toilet?"

"Why, it was a direct response to form," I unhesitatingly answered. "I felt so,—that was my reaction,—but others have thought otherwise. I think them very fine."

So!—well, I could expect misunderstanding from the others;—most others.

"I told Mr. Poland, director of the new San Diego museum, that he was going to have an exhibit of your photographs." Mr. Poland, never having seen my work, nor even heard of me, must have been surprised!

"I showed him the nude I have, and he said that if I vouched for the rest, the exhibit was already arranged. I did, assuring him the work was important,— and—I don't often say work is important."

This exhibit will be in midsummer.

I showed Henrietta the last nude of Bertha: legs and feet in action.

I had a direct, plain-spoken reproof. "I wish you would not do so many nudes, —you are getting *used* to them, the subject no longer amazes you,—most of these are *just* nudes." (I knew she did not mean they were *just naked*, but that I *had* lost my "amazement.")

17

Maybe if I had not shown her the whole series, but one or two selected ones, which is all I would *ever* finish from a series of Graflex negatives, her reaction might have been different. "You see, Henrietta, with the Graflex I cannot possibly conceive my complete, final result in advance,—as you can. I hold to a *definite attitude* of *approach*, but the camera can only record what is before it, so I must await and be able to grasp the right moment when it is presented on my ground glass. To a certain point I can, when doing still-life, feel my conception before I begin work, but in portraiture, figures, clouds,—trying to record ever changing movement and expression, everything depends upon my clear vision, my intuition at the important instant, which if lost can never be repeated. This is a great limitation and at the same time a fascinating problem in photography.

"Imagine if you had to create in, at the most a few seconds of time, without the possibility of pre-visioning, a complete work, supposed to have lasting value. Of course my technique is rapid, and serves me if coordinated at the time with my perception.

"So, not being able to anticipate,—depending on quick decisions,—many negatives are destined to be named failures.

"This should not be when dealing with inanimate matter,—and the fact is, working so, I discard very few attempts.

"However a quick decision is different from a hasty decision, and there is danger in acquiring the latter habit, growing from the necessity of having the former ability.

"I am explaining the limitations of photography rather than apologizing for it: if a medium needs apology it is already dead. I accept the limitations trying to make the most of photography's possibilities. At times I have felt the need of a more fluid, less rigid way to release myself, but always I have put aside other desires, and tried to realize all that I can in my own way.

"I like the manner in which you speak your mind straight out. It is invaluable to me as coming from you. Please, *always do so*. Few persons there are whose judgment has more than a passing interest for me—you are a fine stimulus!"

April 24. What have I, that bring these many women to offer themselves to me? I do not go out of my way seeking them,—I am not a stalwart virile male, exuding sex, nor am I the romantic, mooning poet type some love, nor the dashing Don Juan bent on conquest. Now it is B.

April 28. Every day finds me working, or at least thinking of work for myself,— and with more enthusiasm, surety and success than ever before. Another shell negative,—another beginning of something, from yesterday.

One of these two new shells when stood on end, is like a magnolia blossom unfolding. The difficulty has been to make it balance on end and not cut off

18

that important end, nor show an irrelevant base. I may have solved the problem by using another shell for the chalice, but I had the Devil's own time trying to balance those two shells together. In the first negative, they slipped just a hair's breadth,—and after a three hour exposure! The second attempt is technically good.

And then the dancing nudes of B.

I feel that I have a number of exceedingly well seen negatives,—several which I am sure will live among my best.

B. left me a record of one of Chopin's *Preludes* played by Casals. Starting a tender, plaintive melody, it suddenly breaks, quite without warning into thundering depths, and then in a flash rises to electrifying heights, which makes my scalp tingle.

April 29. I am realizing that law and order of court and church is not such a bad plan after all. When I consider, would I be without police protection from the mob or be irritated by symbolic uniforms?—There can be only one answer! Anything must be preferable to the people uncontrolled.

When I play *Canto Salvaje* it is as though I were challenging all the grey surrounding minds of Glendale. Sitting in the doctor's office with Monna, she remarked: "Good taste has been so standardized in the States it is almost unbearable."

This is well put. I have had the same thought,—unspoken. Everything in that room was harmonious,—painfully correct: furniture, rugs, hangings, walls all prudently considered,—nothing out of keeping, nor out of place,—and of course spotlessly clean. The boisterous, extravagant bad taste of some Mexican interiors was at least amusing, provoking,—these American interiors bring desire to start a riot for diversion!

The last dancing nudes of B. were 24 neg's: 20 have interest,—14 can be considered for finishing,—7 I do not even hesitate over,—they will be added to my collection, and hold there with my very best.

This is seeing well!

The two 8 × 10 shell negatives I do not respond to fully. I was too anxious to start. But I have hours of joy ahead.

Saw Rafael in the hospital last eve: his vitality is amazing! He may fool the "scientists" yet!

It rains this morning. My flowering acacia a yellow glory in the grey.

April 30. Sat to Henrietta yesterday. We do have good times together! She is a jolly companion, keenly alive with word and thought, besides being a really good artist.

I want to write about her work,—yet to find words?—It would be a difficult subject, maybe beyond my ability. Well—this time I got an absolute response to my last nudes,—and of course I must admit the first ones are weak in comparison. Henrietta liked the two shell negatives also,—thought them very fine.

My own doubt I can recognize as a failure to realize fine print quality,—the negatives being slightly undertimed despite three hour exposures! If I cannot pull better prints they must be done again,—perhaps only repeating the arrangement, for my vision was all right.

B. came with undiminished enthusiasm, but I did not work so well: I was tired and confused: it was a hectic day! Peter brought me a carving to copy in a rush: E. arrived with a birthday gift, only six weeks late! Chance found us alone....

B. had not gone when K. arrived. I wonder if K. comes out of curiosity over my attitude towards B.? It seems more than coincidence that she has called several times on Tues. I had to be very diplomatic. K. is a bit of an exhibitionist in love making. Well B. had no sooner gone than E. came again! I call this day a mad one, with three loves to respond to!

Henrietta was here Wednesday eve—or "Henry" I now call her. She wanted to select 8 or 10 prints to show Mr. Poland of the San Diego museum. She selected about forty,—saying now and then "We can't leave out this one." So the pile grew, and had to be reduced. She gave me amazing news, that I am to have one of her paintings! "Not yet—but I am going to give you one." This will be an event in my life!

May 7. The neg's developed and proofed, I find that I worked better with B. than I realized despite my weariness. Three proofs, duplicating movements before recorded, are definitely stronger and finer than the first attempts. I did not intend to duplicate, knowing how futile it is to try,—I was even surprised when I compared the old with the new prints, and noted my unconscious repetition. These three twice-seen movements should be finished, for the sake of my insistent intuition. Besides the aforementioned proofs there are five others to consider: two exquisitely delicate, of legs, three powerful ones, which might be thought masculine.

After, B. came, bringing me a dainty glass fish,—M., a rare visitor, arrived with gardenias, followed by K. with a passion flower. Another day of near complications!

I have not heard from Tina for over a week, which worries me, for last letter she was in bed with severe grippe. She wrote distressing news of Diego: "He has an infection of the ears and nose, and seems resigned to die!"

[*Undated*] ... I think the Chambered Nautilus has one of the most exquisite forms, to say nothing of color and texture, in nature.

I was awakened to shells by the painting of Henry. I never saw a Chambered Nautilus before. If I had, my response would have been immediate! If I merely copy Henry's expression, my work will not live. If I am stimulated and work with real ecstasy it will live.

Henry's influence, or stimulation, I see not just in shell subject matter, it is in all my late work,—in the bananas and the nudes. I feel it not as an extraneous garnish but as a freshened tide swelling from within my self.

An amusing tale came to me, re the association of M. and Edward: that when she came within my horizon I was "still doing babies on bear-skin rugs." Not true! I could never have afforded a bear-skin rug, it must have been imitation. I put myself now on record as owing a great deal to M.,—taking from her all she had to offer—and leaving her, not when I had all I could get, but because she was draining me of all I had: it got to be far from an even exchange.

I will take from anyone all they can give me, and try to return them as much more.

M. tells me she was doing toilets when I was here from Mexico last time. I don't remember, but offer thanks if the idea came through her. I was sure to have done my toilet, suggestion from outside or no!

Monday morning. I worked all Sunday with the shells,—literally all day. Only three negatives made and two of them were done as records of movement to repeat again when I can find suitable backgrounds. I wore myself out trying every conceivable texture and tone for grounds: Glass, tin, cardboard,—wool, velvet, even my rubber rain coat! I did not need to make these records for memory's sake,—no, they were safely recorded there. I did wish to study the tin which was perfect with the lens open; but stopped down I could not see sufficiently to tell, but was positive the surface would come into focus and show a net work of scratches—it did. My first photograph of the Chambered Nautilus done at Henry's was perfect all but the too black ground: yesterday the only available texture was white. Again I recorded to study at leisure the contrast. The feeling of course has been quite changed,—the luminosity of the shell seen against black, gone; but the new negative has a delicate beauty of its own. I had heart failure several times yesterday when the shells, balanced together, slipped. I must buy a Nautilus, for to break Henry's would be tragic.

Thursday, May 12. B. danced for me! This time I was spectator,—not photographer. A definite feeling is not always easy to put down in definite words, but I know I was privileged to have her dance for me,—to me. The work I do today must be finer than that of yesterday because of B. dancing: she has added to my creative strength. B. danced nude. What a pity all dancing cannot be in the nude: or no!—some dances may well be covered for illusion's sake — — —

I have my work room barricaded,—for there, are two shells delicately balanced together awaiting the afternoon light. My first version of the combination was done Sunday: Monday a slight turn of one shell, and I gained strength: Wednesday the second proof decided me to try a lighter ground with the same arrangement,—but desiring to repeat, I again saw more clearly.

Wednesday, after developing. I thought—before putting away the shells I will see what a still lighter ground does, in fact a white ground. Seeing, I knew at once that now I had what I was fighting for! But the hour was late, the light failing, I could not expose another film. So there stands my camera focussed, trained like a gun, commanding the shells not to move a hair's breadth. And death to the person who jars out of place what I know shall be a *very important* negative.

Henry wired me from San Diego that my exhibit date could be either now or in September. I decided now, and expressed my prints yesterday. The opening day will be Sunday the 15th. I sent sixty carefully chosen photographs.

From B. dancing I went to another dance,—a fiesta in honour of Elena's birthday. I would rather have remained home with my clear impression of the afternoon, but no—the familia Ortiz would not have forgiven me.

The food was not all it might have been,—the pianola hurt my ears,—nevertheless one little Mexican girl I found a perfect dancing partner and took her so often that an older brother began to give fierce glances.

Elena was dressed in new green silk, a cheap brilliant silk of vivid green which contrasted exquisitely with her dark skin. As she danced the short skirt worked up higher and higher till her plump brown legs were exposed, which pleased me, but not the old mother and aunt who shook disapproving heads. The poor souls are quite the hens with ducklings they cannot understand.

May 13. After watching my shell arrangement all day,—repeatedly warning Brett to walk lightly,—even keeping the windows shut for fear of a slight breeze, though the day was hot,—a cardboard background slipped, fell onto the shells, and completely disarranged them. I was literally on the verge of tears from disappointment, knowing the impossiblity of repeating anything absolutely.

But now I see the Gods meant well. I took off my shirt, for the room was like an oven, and half indifferently, half rebelliously, retired under the focussing cloth. After twenty minutes' struggle in which I tried to register my previous negative over the ground glass image,—almost but not quite succeeding, I suddenly realized that the slight change was an improvement! I shall remember the making of this negative.

In the morning I enlarged the first five positives of B.—dancing nudes. They appear to advantage blown up. I am pleased with my day's work.

Saturday, May 14. I must do the shells again! That is the last combination. If I did not have the third proof to compare I would be very happy with the last:

in some ways it is better, but one important upright line is not quite as fine. Henry agrees, though she thinks I have done a very important negative. Also she responded fully to six of my last dancing nudes. Says they are among the finest photographs I have ever done.

Four of the six I shall enlarge: two I shall try to improve by doing the impossible—repeating.

Henry showed me the portrait in its present stage. She is pleased,—and I am.

Coincidence that we are exhibiting at the same time in San Diego. A friend of hers, Katherine Wagenhals, noted at once the analogy of our work: yet we knew nothing of each other except by name until a few months ago.

Tuesday, May 17. I could not be at peace until I had made the fifth attempt to improve the shell arrangement by a fifth negative. The result has been that I have printed my fourth negative, and am quite pleased. Also printed two former shell negatives, worthy recording if not so important. The fig tree done at Palm Springs is at last printed and the first of the dancing nudes: the former comes close to being fine,—the latter is fine,—a kneeling figure cut at the shoulder, but kneeling does not mean it is passive,—it is dancing quite as intensely as if she were on her toes! I am in love with this nude — — —

Late in the afternoon I took out the Chambered Nautilus thinking to improve on the first negatives: instead there came to me a new group over which I am absolutely enthusiastic! It was too late for an exposure so I must be patient until this afternoon. I find myself, every so often, looking at my ground glass as though the unrecorded image might escape me! I can see that I am to have days of struggle with the later group also. There are so many slight variations I can make. The last negative is better in most ways,—just one line I'm not so sure of. Also the background might be varied. But I shall enjoy the struggle!

3. Subject Matter and Life Today

May 20. A letter at last came from Conseula, who took six or eight prints of mine to New York. I wanted to have her arrange for an exhibit, and to show the work to several persons, among them Alfred Stieglitz.

She writes: "Stieglitz seemed disappointed. He thought your technique was very fine but felt the prints lacked life, fire, were more or less dead things not a part of today." (!)

If I had sent my toilet, for instance, how then would he have reacted? And must I do nothing but toilets and smokestacks to please a Stieglitz! Is his concern with subject matter? Are not shells, bodies, clouds as much of today as machines? Does it make any difference what *subject matter* is used to express a feeling toward life! And what about Stieglitz' famed clouds? Are they any more today than my subject matter? He contradicts himself!

Great art of any period may portray, use, contemporary subject matter,—but the spirit of art is ageless,—it may have national characteristics but the appeal is universal. If it is not universal it is no better than propaganda, and as such must die. Rivera's frescoes, if they live, will not live because of their revolutionary character,—they may interest a historian from that angle: nor have they aesthetic value because he depicts an Indian woman rolling out tortillas, they may have future value to an ethnologist,—they will not live as art.

But this is old stuff!—too obvious to write down!

I recall the dream I had two years ago in Mexico—that Alfred Stieglitz was dead. If dreams are symbolic—this was an important dream to me — — —

Sunday, May 21. Re-reading my notes of yesterday, more thoughts come: I am full of protest over Stieglitz' opinion, because it is biased, unfair, and Stieglitz I had on a pedestal as many others have—too many others. One admits the fall of a hero unwillingly!

My work could not be "dead"—lack "life, fire:" it was done with so great an enthusiasm, love, "fire,"—all that I felt must show in my work, and does, for I have profound response from so many intelligent and important persons.

I am one who has always been keenly alive to the life of today: never have I mourned for the past of "Greek glory" or any other period. I have protested whenever it was obvious that a contemporary artist had merely gone to the past either in technique or subject matter and assumed a pose,—but, to avoid

24

using a palm, or Mexican pottery or what not because it does not belong to our day is merely silly!

But this is what I feel: if I had lined up as one of the Stieglitz group, if I had remained a second rate Stieglitz, I would have pleased Stieglitz. He told me, "Go on in your own way." He says one thing,—he means another.

Some years ago, Laurvik said to me, "Stieglitz would not like your work, he would fear it." Laurvik may or may not be an important critic, but I think he sensed the truth.—I recall what Diego once said to Jean, "I like Weston's new smoke-stack better than his old;" the new smoke-stack was the trunk of a palm! So much for aesthetic reaction to subject matter.

But now I have spilled enough words: the subject should be a closed issue,— Stieglitz a dead issue!

May 30. We returned from San Diego late Saturday night, or rather early Sunday morn for it was 2:00 a.m. when Chandler, Brett and I drew up in front of the shack—my studio—having deposited Henry on the way—Henry went with us, and we did have a jolly two days.

My photographs had a room to themselves, but were not well hung, being crowded too close and in a double line. Mr. Poland apologized, saying that they had not facilities for hanging prints. However, I am quite pleased in that the committee on selection is going to purchase three prints for the gallery's permanent collection. Henry's exhibit was hung to great advantage: never have I gotten so much from her work before. And Henry said that nowhere has her work been so finely arranged in such a perfect gallery.

I liked Mr. Poland at once and think San Diego fortunate in having a capable and discriminating director.

He is direct, outspoken, either that or noncommital; so Henry purposely questioned him, "Do you think the work of Stieglitz or Weston has the most *Life?*" He answered in my favour: and Poland is a great admirer of Stieglitz.

I record this opinion not to indicate any finality as to the merit of my work compared to Stieglitz, but to show that another person feels the *Life* I have recorded,—which Stieglitz does not.

We saw a collection of shells in the museum which added greatly to my knowledge, and several plants in the hot-house, one especially, called "Antherium," —if the gardner really knows, which were quite amazing. Chandler deserves great credit for his driving and repairing of that old Nash. He has practically rebuilt the car.

May 31. C. came: I admire and care for her so much that I wish I could respond to her love side more fully. My mental and physical regard for a woman rarely accord: an approximation was attained with M. and T. Now, I am most completely satisfied,—physically, by K. or E. To be sure K. has a good mind for a young girl, but E. has nothing for me but an exciting body! A strange twist of life has found one of my loves working for another: E. is now B.'s maid,—and neither know!

C. has opened to me vistas of the metaphysical in which I find myself becoming deeply interested. Years back I would have scoffed; now my mind is at least open,—receptive. Too much that cannot be explained otherwise.

At last I have gotten the shell arrangement which has bothered me for two weeks out of my system, or at least I am through with it for awhile. I suppose any one of the numerous attempts could be considered good,—but always a slight change would start me trying to improve, until yesterday I grew weary and changed to another approach. I found a strong, fine group almost immediately, one after another.

June 1. If I can only control myself, my tendency to match F.'s hysteria with destructive words, until she calms,—we will manage to stand each other somehow. I must realize she can no more accept my viewpoint, than I can hers. But one look at her handwriting is enough to destroy my equilibrium!

The new shell negative I definitely like. In none of the shell photographs am I quite satisfied with the backgrounds,—they are not disturbing—yet seem unrelated. I have considered them, but so far have not solved. . . .

Tuesday, June 7. Rafael died Saturday after another operation. After seeing his fine, sensitive face in death,—all suffering gone,—the old Rafael again, it seemed that he had attained reality, after wearing for months his mask of pain.— Monna had been composed,—brave, but when she saw his face again, a hysteria possessed her which was awesome.
Surely what we call "life" is neither the beginning nor the end.

Wednesday, June 8. Last evening I had printed, and ready to show all shell negatives: two "interested" girls, pupils of B. wanted to see more of my work after B. had shown them a print she has of the first shell.

Of course, they were "interested,"—"thrilled,"—but not to the point of spending money, yet they were wealthy girls. Do they think I show my work to be flattered?—That I am hungry for praise? Well I'm hungry for money and discouraged. The Japanese would have bought,—I never waste time with them! I don't know what move to make next: Enrique Jackson wants to start a business with me, and though I hate the idea of a partner even so agreeable as Jack, I think I must do this,—or something.

I have to show my prints so often that I detest every one of them. I suppose this is all right if I am forced by my reactions to create new.

26

June 9. My one thought is money! I have tried to make a living here, in a quiet unobtrusive way,—because of M. But no such way is possible: the American public want noise, steam-roller methods,—they must be forced to buy. Woman, who is the buyer here, is not genuinely interested in art: with her, it is a pose, along with other ways of culture hunting: all she wants is sex, and all her gestures are directed by sex,—she would not spend one cent on art,—yet pretending to be deeply moved, if a new hat would make her more attractive,—for sex sake! And the poor boobs of American men are but money machines to further her ends.

God help me to some day return to a man's land,—Mexico or Japan or Some-where — — — —

For three days I have not had one penny. I borrowed ten dollars from Rose Krasnow,—that has gone.

Sunday, June 12. My period of working with shells has been broken: not through lack of desire, however. The days have been so grey it may be just as well....
But I worked with B. and I'll swear they are the strongest yet done! Now she goes away for awhile, so we shall be forced to see each other in perspective. Last night I saw another dancer. The Schindlers persuaded me to go with them to the studio of Elise Dufour where a young Polish girl, Eugenia Liczbinska, gave a program. The girl had been lavishly praised: I went half expectantly. Today I recall that she was lovely, that she had moments of strength,—but—would I make an effort to see her again? She was personally beautiful,—and... Madam Dufour wishes me to make a series of torsos of her.

Friday I was so depressed that for diversion I called on Betty,—when Betty was out! E. and I had an hour alone — — — — Maybe I'll attempt my shells today.

June 13. Started to work—interrupted at the critical moment—that is my story of yesterday. C. K. came,.... I had not met her for years, not since the night she spent here, and wanted to be seduced but wouldn't. I'm sure she is no longer virginal! Someone had more persistence or desire than I had.

C. wished she had known I was here two weeks ago,—now she was going to Santa Barbara. Thank God she didn't know! She hoped I would make some negatives of her. That would be better than entertaining her for an hour, I thought.

C. is a dancer, or at least she dances. I would see how I responded to her after working with B.

"Take off your clothes" I said. I felt not a flicker of response to her. Instead of figures I made a few heads. Her body was youthful, strong, brown from the sun, and sea winds,—yet I was repulsed.

She inveigled me out of a faja, and I'm so angry with myself for being easy. I don't know how to meet such open nerve,—brass.

Wednesday, June 15. Twice I have repeated the shell group,—the latest, which is one of the strongest, but blurred from slight movement. Monday I got a perfect negative and an improved arrangement: but Chandler was using my cardboard backgrounds to press flowers between, so finding nothing else, I used a square of black velvet, which I knew was too black,—and proved so. Why I went ahead I don't know! Yesterday, I tried again: result, movement! The exposure was 4½ hours, so to repeat was no joy, with all the preoccupation of keeping quiet children and cats,—but I went ahead and await development.

Cats—yes—two orange kittens Flora brought me: delightful little rascals, but worse than four boys for mischief.

The San Diego museum bought my Palm trunk and one of the cement factory roofs. Miss Wagenhals bought a shell print,—my first. But no money from them, nor any other source. I am becoming disgusted and depressed.

Saturday, June 18. The shells again moved! It must be the heavy trucks that pass jar the building ever so slightly. Anyway I have quit trying: I can afford no more film.

The money question is disturbing me mentally.

Sunday, June 19. It has been the greyest, coolest Spring I can remember here, and continues so into the summer. I enjoy the weather, but "business" complains.

A check for $9 from shell print sold in San Diego, comes to me like a hundred dollars! Money is so important for one's ease of mind: just enough to get by on!

From the last series of dancing nudes (I made 20 negatives) I consider for finishing, 13: 8, I am sure of—2 of these heads.

Shells again yesterday,—trying to better one of the recent negatives. I have not exposed yet but think I have improved.

Monday, June 20. Monna came for the first time yesterday—also Abad, Edith, and the children. Peter brought two friends and Olive Taylor paid a visit, so the afternoon was confusing enough. O yes, K. came just before the crowd.

I am almost despising my work, having to show it so much.

Sunday morn. June 26. I have had very bad luck: Chandler lost a five dollar bill, just given him for groceries. This was part of ten dollars received from a print sale,—one of the first nudes of B. Five dollars!—Enough for *me* to live on a week!

I shall work with new shells to forget this tragedy! Three shells and a piece of coral came as a present: fine material for much thought. Ramiel has promised to pay me a visit for several days: he will arrive this morning.

July 13. I would enjoy writing for hours today,—given leisure which I have not,—for I am stimulated with many thoughts after the long considered Japanese exhibit which took place last week. Financially, it was the most successful showing I have had. Prints sold amounting to $180 mostly of inexpensive work, old prints or imperfect prints. Ramiel was with me every day, and they were long days, from 10 to 12 hours on duty!

July 16. It seems as though I shall practically have to stop writing, except for the briefest notes for memorandum. Too bad indeed, for I have much interesting material to discuss with myself,—thoughts stimulated by the exhibit, and by letters from Tina after receiving my shell photographs: opinions, impressions, and reactions from her, from Felipe, René, Diego, Orozco. The shells have been deeply felt!

But now what a program I have ahead! A new exhibit opens Monday at the University of California: I must prepare for my very important showing in the Los Angeles Museum: Cristal and Ramiel calling for my manuscript [the Mexican Daybook] which they are to go over together: Enrique Jackson preparing to deluge me with sittings in the new business venture: invitations coming from everywhere to dine out,—which I shall refuse. Enough! I am almost confused!

July 19. The heat was terrific yesterday: I stripped to my underwear and worked with shells and gourds. I see with surety not lessened after my "vacation."

I did not want this anger from H. I had to write her so—and now await her answer. Can we resume the former fine exchange? . . .

July 20. The heat continues: I had to bathe my head and neck and wrists while working. And I am working with a perhaps conscious desperation, knowing my days of freedom must soon end when Enrique comes for "business." Yet I do not force myself: the creative spark is still strong. One new shell and two or three gourd negatives will hold their own with my best.

July 21. Last night I dined with Madam Scheyer and Mrs. Greenbaum. Why it should be "Madam S.," I don't know!—except that "Frau Scheyer" wouldn't "go" very far here! Well, between "Frau" and "Mrs." there is not much choice —both disagreeable words.

Madam Scheyer—clever, vivacious,—with a nice line of talk for club women and art students: she has climbed all over the culture hungry! However, I don't dislike her as some of my friends do. She amuses for awhile and can be simple when she knows the futility of pose.

I definitely like Mrs. Greenbaum: really the visit was with her. She wished to show me etchings and lithographs by Feininger, Kandinsky and others. Several Feiningers were truly fine, in fact I might have bought one etching of roofs but for the price,—only $9, yet more than I could spend: but I did buy a Kandinsky lithograph,—how could I resist it at $3?

Kandinsky seems to me one of the few moderns whose work will live: he has something very personal, genuine,—he has both intellectual and emotional ecstasy. This print will bring me much joy.

Today starts out very hot! I don't like the climate of S. California.

Friday, July 22. Last eve—I spent with M. the third time we have met in these many months. She had wired, wanting to see me. What were my plans? Of course that I was going into business here,—which could not have pleased M. Once from Mexico I promised M. that I would never return to start business in L. A. Foolish promise, and quite unjust if she held me to it, which I am sure she wants to do.

However we had a long talk on many things, with no hysteria, which I half expected.

Another shell yesterday,—and—the heat continues.

July 24. I am alone: the family away at Topango Cañon. Blessed by aloneness! A bright idea,—my pipe, months since I have smoked it.

I thought that I felt like writing,—and yes, I do—but other thoughts distract me.

July 25. What bothered me yesterday was that never-finished manuscript,—I could not face Cristal's question! When I tell her I would destroy it, I bare myself to a hearty scolding. She is such a fine girl!

So I worked two hours on the ms., protesting the while. One thing that has turned me against it has been Ramiel's corrections. I have to agree they are well considered, and yet I no longer feel myself in the writing: some of the spontaneity is lost, and not having a writer's technique, there is not much left of me after corrections!

I rebel too, reading my opinions of a few years ago, but these I can at least pass with a shrug and a smile, as I will this writing two years hence—

4. The Shells in Mexico: Letters from Tina Modotti

July 25. — continued. I must take time to write about the reactions to my shell prints, as written by Tina from Mexico after showing them to several old acquaintances. First, to quote briefly the most salient remarks. "My God Edward, your last photography surely took my breath away! I feel speechless in front of them. What purity of vision. When I opened the package I couldn't look at them very long, they stirred up all my innermost feelings so that I felt a physical pain."

Later—same morning—

"Edward—nothing before in art has affected me like these photographs. I cannot look at them long without feeling exceedingly perturbed, they disturbed me not only mentally but physically. There is something so pure and at the same time so perverse about them. They contain both the innocence of natural things and the morbidity of a sophisticated, distorted mind. They make me think of lilies and of embryos. They are mystical and erotic."

Same day—evening—after showing them to Felipe and Pepe—"On the whole their reactions were very similar to mine—Felipe was so carried away he made an impulsive promise to write you.

"We three spent about two hours discussing the photographs and all kinds of problems stimulated by them—

"Since the creation of an artist is the result of his state of mind and soul at the time of creation, these last photographs of yours clearly show that you are at present leaning toward mysticism.

"At the same time they are very sensuous."

Next morning—

"Last eve, René called. Without my saying a word he used 'erotic' also. Like me, he expressed the disturbance these prints caused him. He felt 'weak at the knees.'"

July 4 —

"At last Diego saw your photographs! After the first breath-taking impression was over, and after a long silent scrutiny of each, he abruptly asked: 'Is Weston sick at present?' Then he went on: 'These photographs are biological, beside the aesthetic emotion they disturb me physically,—see my forehead is sweating.' Then—'Is W. very sensual?' Then—'Why doesn't W. go to Paris? Elie Faure would go wild over these things.'"

July 7 —
"Last evening Orozco was here. I got out the shell prints. Well, in a few words, he liked them better than all your collection put together. Of one he said, 'This suggests much more than the 'Hand of God' than the hand Rodin made.' It is the one that has made everybody, including myself, think of the sexual act."

From the above quotations it will be seen that I have created a definite impression, but from an angle which surprised me!

Why were all these persons so profoundly affected on the physical side?

For I can say with absolute honesty that not once while working with the shells did I have any physical reaction to them: nor did I try to record erotic symbolism. I am not sick and I was never so free from sexual suppression,—which if I had, might easily enter into my work, *as it does* in Henry's painting.

I am not blind to the sensuous quality in shells, with which they combine the deepest spiritual significance: indeed it is this very combination of the physical and spiritual in a shell like the Chambered Nautilus, which makes it such an important abstract of life.

No! I had no physical thoughts,—never have. I worked with clearer vision of sheer aesthetic form. I knew that I was recording from within, my feeling for life as I never had before. Or better, when the negatives were actually developed, I realized what I felt,—for when I worked, I was never more unconscious of what I was doing.

No! The Shells are too much a sublimation of all my work and life to be pigeonholed. Others must get from them what they bring to them: evidently they do!

July 27. Gjura Stojana happened in: I can't say that I was happy,—for I dislike unannounced calls, even from friends, except they be in the evenings.—A visit from George, (I revert continually to his old name) is not what it once was. I must always be alert to avoid argument. He started on my Kandinsky print,— God knows if there is anything he really admires,—he didn't like it and was all primed for a windy wrangle. I simply stated that Kandinsky stimulated me, and put a record on the phonograph!

Gjura brought a loaf of his famous bread, but it was too salty: all his arts are failing. But I do feel kindly towards George, so that I gave him one of my pipes, —his being broken. And if I don't respond to his work as I once did, at least I can admit its importance compared to most of the "art" produced in this neighborhood.

July 28. My heart sank when Elena and Elisa arrived early, all primed for a day at the beach. They had misunderstood the date,—and I was not ready. What could one do but capitulate! To reason with children would be easier.

Once on the way, I was not sorry and certainly I have no after regrets: we all had a good time,—especially the girls,—actually my pleasure was in watching their joy.

I took them to Redondo, with an ulterior motive: I could visit with Ramiel at the same time. So "my family" and I descended upon Ramiel in holiday mood. After all, there was no opportunity to visit with Ramiel: not with Elena, who would listen to no reason, until she had donned an old purple bathing suit and plunged into the breakers.

July 29. I went with Peter to see an exhibit of sculpture by a young boy, George Stanley. It did not meet my expectations: exquisite work, but too clever,—imitative of Archipenko,—Mestrovitch. But he has many years ahead to assimilate and grow towards a more personal expression. Today, Elena and her mother and I go to Topango Cañon, for a visit with my boys,—and F. Too bad that I dread so to be near F. and, I must . . .

I shall try to come closer to F., I want to, but the breach seems ever-widening. . . .

Monday, August 1. Back again, and with me a bad enough case of sunburn. I was careful of my body, but my face I could not protect. I have always laughed at those who burn themselves to a lobster red and suffer a week for one day's outing: now the laugh is on me. But I was caught in a trap. Chandler took his mother home early, leaving Brett, Elena and me on the beach until 4:00 while the wind and sun played havoc: even Elena's dark skin grew rosy. How I respond to women of dark skin! Yes—I like them all—but especially the swarthy.

August 2. Jean Roy, Lester and Collier are spending their vacation at Santa Monica: they drove down to our picnic grounds on the beach, and later up to the cabin. I had not seen Jean Roy since she waved good-bye to me as my train pulled out from San Francisco. . . .

Yesterday I did the first work at Balboa Beach,—the home of Dr. Lovell.

I responded fully to Schindler's construction. It was an admirably planned beach home with a purity of form seldom found in contemporary houses unless they be mere reproductions from another age or. . . .

August 4. A sharp earthquake awakened me early. I could not return to sleep: my mind became too active,—it went from thoughts of bills and poverty, to my approaching doom. . . .

Saturday, August 6. Oh, for money!—Not for a single luxury, not even for food,—money enough to leave here,—to get away from — — — —

I am deeply concerned about the return of my old bitterness: it will distort or destroy all that is creatively fine within. I thought I could stand her proximity, —that I was strong enough, but I am being gradually undermined again.

We should be miles apart, for her sake as well, for I know I have the same effect upon her, I would want never to hear of her again,—not even to see her hand-writing on an envelope: that dreaded handwriting!

But the boys!?

The eggplant again: and this time better. I gave over five hours exposure,—more would have been better, but my light was failing. The Graflex bellows cut when extended, so the 8 × 10 was used: and, —the negative might be sharper.

August 9. Henry sat to me: I had not yet gotten what I want to of her, nor did I Saturday. She was very conscious the first days, so I decided to work out of doors: results better,—she was more natural, but my focussing off. I held the Graflex: next time I shall use tripod. I have been having poor "luck" lately: the eggplant not critically sharp, and a cactus branch, done yesterday, moved. But I have a new shell, done late last eve,—definitely good.

Both eggplant and cactus were well seen: I shall someday do them over.

So—I have been working. Henry loaned me a book by Kandinsky. I copied several thoughts: one, "The artist is not born to a life of pleasure. He must not live idle; he has hard work to perform...." I could change this: for instance, what pleasure is so supreme as that which the artist derives from his hard work! —and I would say, he *cannot* live idle,—no question of "must not" enters in!

I have been going over my daybook from Mexico, preparing it for Cristal to type. I have been impressed by the amount of emotion, hysteria, gloom, cyni-cism, written into page after page. I am amazed that I could have created anything worth while. I seemed to be reading about another person: these days are so serene in comparison. I am glad after all that I did not destroy this record, it makes a valuable contrast.

C. and I celebrated "our day," last Sunday. Two years ago she came to take dictation: but the Gods had planned that something else should happen.

Now we are very close: I have not been true to her,—but no one else is closer to me.

August 10. Enrique's early arrival, (our business venture) clearly indicated what my future, at least for awhile must be. I was working with the cactus, but her presence diverted my trend of thought: I put the camera away. Perhaps I have no complaint,—having been granted a long period of freedom.

I have been nurse-girl and policeman to the boys for almost a week: this is not particularly conducive to clear thought.

Bob Sanborn, Peter, and Rose spent last evening here. I don't have visitors often, so I enjoyed them. I like Bob.

August 11. Just as I reach bottom, and wonder where the next meal will come from, something happens to tide me over: this is so regular an occurrence as to seem providential.

My meal-ticket this time came from Germany, a check for $20 from the *Berliner Tageblatt*. Somehow it made me unusually happy, and something sang within, —the check was unexpected. The amount was small for four prints, but the newspapers in the States expect donations,—the privilege of seeing one's name in print is supposed to be enough!

And the *Tageblatt* has asked for more prints.

I had confidence in Herr Klötzel when I gave him these photographs a year ago in Mexico, and I was not mistaken.

Last night Cristal and I saw *Metropolis*. Fine "shots" of machinery,—but as a whole not convincing: it could have been much stronger.

Made a new shell negative,—and a good one.

August 12. 5:00 a.m.—but I went to bed at 9:00! My hours are quite regular,— I will them so. I have such a time making excuses to avoid dinner appointments. I think from now on I shall simply state that on account of my work I go nowhere: this should be sufficient!—and true enough. I can always break this rule when the occasion warrants.

I spotted a swiss chard in the Japanese Market, so fine in color, form, livingness that I bought it at once, and made two negatives: one is good,—but last eve I saw another even finer, which shall serve me today.

Writers, even such a brilliant one as Rémy de Gourmont, are seldom intelligent critics of the plastic arts.

"Beauty is so sexual that the only generally accepted works of art are those which show, quite simply, the human body in its nakedness. By his persistence in remaining purely sexual, the Greek sculptor has placed himself above all discussion for eternity."

Greek sculpture, of that period, which Gourmont evidently means, judging from the thought of this paragraph, most assuredly does admit of discussion: in fact the decline probably came when the Greeks copied the human body in its nakedness with no other thought or reason. And why say "the only generally accepted works of art?" "Generally accepted" art is not likely to be fine art.

The phrase, "beauty is so sexual," admits no argument, but his explanatory remarks are ill chosen.

The book *Decadence*, I have thoroughly enjoyed, especially the chapter on "The Value of Education," and that on "Subconscious Creation."

August 16. The second swiss chard, which was a solid, sculpture-like head, and almost white, I did against a light ground, standing alone with no accessories. It pleases me. Then Sunday I did an eggplant but again failed. I bought three to arrange: they did not arrange, except in too-well-known combinations. My greatest danger is in imitating myself—not others. I tried one alone: again it

35

was reminiscent, for the logical way was to center it, and I have used that way of seeing often and am tired of it. But in forcing another viewpoint I failed to convince.

Today I have the eggplants, though some withered, and an exquisite head of lettuce! Good luck to myself!

August 20. The lettuce moved,—wilted—during the prolonged exposure: the eggplant fruit group is perhaps too obviously arranged: but three long radishes have excited me quite as the shells did. I combined them into a finely-moving rhythm, into something that will live.

Thursday I showed forty prints before the L. A. Camera Club. What a curious group of people! Naturally to them I was curious. I talked to them, and am sure my talk was no more comprehended than my work, though God knows I am not even capable of indulging in esoteric oratory.

One member said: "Are you a philosophic realist?"

I had to admit my ignorance! Where would this classification place me?

August 23. I took Monna to see Henry and her work. She was deeply impress-ed....

Every time I see that cactus, I have renewed emotion: it is a great painting.

Henry gave me one of her semi-abstractions: a fine one, she thinks one of her best. I am happy! Yet I must add, given my choice, I would not have chosen this. Now Henry is going to Mexico with Helena Dunlop. This is an exciting turn! I am happy for her.

A letter from Jean. He is weary, and discouraged by the hard work in Yucatan. He thought the shells were my finest expression of their kind: but prefers the series of dancing legs. To quote—"The shells are symbols or abstract shapes while the legs are legs described in function of their utility. There is perhaps the same evolution from your abstract photographs to these legs, from your ladies smelling orchids to the abstract photographs."

I cannot say that I agree with Jean. I certainly like the legs, but the shells, I believe, are so far my most important work.

F. has bought a new car! A 7-passenger Nash sedan, for over $1300. She mort-gaged the studio property to buy it. She is absolutely mad!

I want to become financially independent and then move out.

Sunday morning at 1:30 a.m. she found E. with Brett in *apparently* a compro-mising situation. But there was no question on her part: she always hangs on circumstantial evidence. She almost forced her way into the studio: her face was one that could have burned witches in the early days of our country. I hunted for a new home all day. When she knew this, she appeared, begging an audience, and asking me to please stay for the children's sake. I am still here: but for how long?

36

5. *"Finely Moving Rhythms"*

August 25. I have been training my camera on a cantalope,—a sculptural thing. I know I shall make some good negatives for I feel its form deeply. Then last eve green peppers in the market stopped me: they were amazing in every sense of the word,—the three purchased. But a *tragedy* took place. Brett ate two of them!

August 27. Henry offered to loan me anything I could use from her studio. "It will be closed for several months, you might as well have what you wish." So I took shells, a number of beauties, a couple of cactus, many books, records, an old chair of fine line, and finally her painting, "Semi-abstraction No. 3." She gave me a parting gift of *Tertium Organum* by Ouspensky, "because I am enjoying it, and want to feel we are reading it at the same time."

Had two sittings, both from Enrique's "press agenting": yet they were old clients of mine.

Well, I am joyful over my green pepper negative. If I can get some quality into the background it will rank with my finest expression. The cantalope is worthy of printing too, but I shall do it again, and of course I am not through with peppers.

August 29. No—I am not through with peppers: now I have another as fine or finer,—the same pepper from another angle. Saturday I made the first exposure: it was moved!—not badly, but enough to destroy that precision in my work which I want. I tried to say to myself, it would do; but no, I can't fool myself.

Yesterday, I did the pepper again,—and what a satisfaction to have a clean-lined, brilliant negative! This, and a shell negative, done yesterday too, were made with a $5 R. R. lens bought a few months ago second hand. I like the quality, and being of shorter focal length it is easier to focus and requires less exposure. I stop down to U. S. 256.

This pepper sits on top of a milk bottle. It has amazing convolutions. The shell was an accidental find: or at least rather so, for I was working with a cantalope, and not feeling fully its form in connection with the olla, I tried the shell which gave me just the swing, the flying quality I wanted.

It may be only enthusiasm for a new negative which causes me to say "one of my best," but I really believe that all these recent photographs are "my best," for I am working too surely to expose with indecision.

Fortunately I overexposed on this shell: the day was half cloudy, and that, with the change of lens, caused misjudgement.

I shall repeat this morning, for the camera is still focussed on the arrangement exactly as was.

August 31. Margrethe has been out for the second time since my return: she came to choose prints for the photographic exhibition in connection with the formal opening of the new Calif. Art Club house, Olive Hill, Hollywood. Three of Brett's photographs will be hung, four of mine, and one of Chandler's. This may please and encourage Chandler. My one-man show at L. A. museum only a month away. I have much printing to do and enlarged negatives,— more than a month's work! Yesterday Miss Upton showed me the rooms at my disposal,—two fine galleries, with space for more than 100 prints.

"All aboard!" Soon it will be "Vamanos!" I waved farewell to Henry and Helena Dunlop leaving for Mexico! I did not envy them. I have had enough of the confusion of travelling for awhile.

September 1. The last day of August was full: nine enlarged negatives, no tests made, all satisfactory. It was a hot day too,—but I do not feel the heat these days of my simplified diet.

Not that it has ever been complicated, but lately I have eliminated all excess, and am eating two meals a day of fruits, vegetables, nuts. Meat I rarely touch,— only when dining out. Cigarettes, which I long ago thought to stop, I still use, though some reduced in number. Is it lack of will? I find myself automatically reaching for the ever-ready package, especially when nervous or excited. But one or two puffs and I'm through, half disgustedly! The day will come when the last one will be finished!

And why all this intestinal purity? To clear my mind for my work! I know, absolutely, it has helped me to a more sensitive reaction and unobstructed thinking.

Tuesday, September 6. For the first time in at least twelve years I have sat down without morning coffee,—and with no cigarettes. This is a heroic gesture on my part!

But I don't feel very heroic just now!

September 10. I do not enjoy my morning writing without morning coffee! An old friend has gone — — — —

Perhaps I am over-scrupulous with myself. Should I take just one cup? Or a substitute? But I have always laughed at substitutes! At least I have proved to myself I can stop,—and it's good discipline. I can understand those who have nothing else in life, pampering themselves, indulging their physical desires with stimulants and gross eating. But why should I?

The other day while working in the back room, I casually glanced out, to rest my eyes upon Roi Partridge, quietly gazing in and munching his inevitable banana. And there sat Imogen in the car.

We had a hectic one day and night together.

Roi bought a nude,—one of the dancing figures of Bertha.

I have been printing: have ten new prints,—three shells, a gourd, the rest vegetables. I like especially the radishes and pepper, the swiss chard, and one of the shells.

Tuesday, September 13. Cole fell from a walnut tree yesterday, when a rotten branch gave way, breaking both wrists,—double fractures. Poor baby! How he suffered. Now he will be helpless for weeks. How we will get through with it all, nursing him every moment, I don't know! And my exhibit only two weeks ahead. I was planning to work every spare moment.

Too, Flora is "broke," and my condition no better,—nay worse. I am disgusted with her extravagance in buying the $2400 car,—mortgaging everything,—running bills everywhere,—taxes due,—not a cent to pay with,—hardly enough to eat — — — —

October 20. A long period has passed without writing: it has been the most difficult period of my life,—and this is no exaggeration. Trying to finish prints for the exhibit, and a large order as well, and nurse Cole,—wait on him, listen to his suffering, his childlike impatience over inaction. Now the exhibit is well under way,—half way through, and Cole is nearly normal, though still with me from 8 to 12 hours a day.

I thought that I should burst with nerves at times,—intensely concentrating, then Cole would interrupt me. He has been a patient child, but nevertheless a great trial.

Brett is showing with me, and a fine showing it is. He has hung 18 prints, I have 102,—all on one line, well-spaced, and in rooms well-suited to photographs. It is the finest exhibit I have ever given, both in general appearance and individual prints.

As usual I have there a guest book in which some comments of interest have been written.

Nothing has been sold as yet. Not much like the Japanese exhibit!

All the shells, coral, plants loaned by Henry remain unused. Lately there have been days I could have worked, given a day alone: but not with Cole around. I have looked longingly at this fine material,—and put it aside.

Now comes Cole—my day of nursing has started.

Saturday, October 29. I am having coffee this morning!—the first time in weeks. It is no breaking down of my morale, rather the morning is so cold that I automatically lit the gas stove and put on the coffee pot.

I have no intention of starting coffee again, but I do miss a hot drink. I dislike gas and hope to afford a little wood heater.

39

If there were only beautiful places to walk nearby, I would enjoy warming up by a brisk hike through the hills: but one must go through blocks of smug bungalows, or by rows of squat business blocks to reach any point of open country: and worse, pass longfaced, bleary-eyed commuters, going to work after a breakfast of warmed-over potatoes or bran breakfast food for constipation.

Well, Brett is getting his morning walk these days. He left for parts unknown two days ago. The only clue is from a boy friend who saw him—and Dick—in San Fernando, headed north.

I admire his guts in getting out, his adventurous spirit. What has a deadly monotonous place like Glendale to offer Brett? He wants life! I can make my life,—here in this little shack,—but he must expand.

I do not blame Brett for going: nor am I worried, but he should have left me some farewell word. We have been too close as comrades for him to leave me this way. Also he should have been more considerate in the time chosen for leaving. Now I am alone with Cole, a large order on hand, and the probability of much Christmas work ahead.

Youth is thoughtless.

November 11. Brett is back, but not from his own volition, and I am sorry he did not have his fill of adventure. A telephone call from Modesto, 300 miles or more away, came from the Chief of Police.

"Have you a son, Brett Weston?"—"We picked him up—with another boy—under age to be on the road—we'll hold him for instructions."

I think I had not more than 35 cents in my pocket: but the next morning I was on my way to San Francisco, via Modesto, with Chandler driving Flora's Nash Sedan, Cristal as company, and $100 for expenses! It seemed like a dream, and still does — — — —

The money came from the sale of my bow: Mr. Bauer had fallen in love with it the same morning of the phone call. "If you ever wish to part with that bow, I have $100 for you." He must have been surprised to hear from me so soon: and he was a good sport to stand by his word.

We left before noon and were in Modesto by midnight. Rain fell, and Chandler's driving over wet roads was breathtaking. Early in the morning we had Brett out and that noon were waiting for Johan and Elsa, Jean Roy and Lester.

November 12. Bertha invited me to the second symphony directed by George Schnéevoigt: Stravinsky's, *The Fire Bird*, was given.

I had only heard it on the phonograph,—which I now realize is entirely inadequate. What amazing music! It held me thrilled: my hair stood on end!

We should have left at the finish of *The Fire Bird*, for the following Mendelssohn violin concerto was like drinking milk after tequila. And even Beethoven's

40

Eroica, the last number,—I heard as in a daze. Indeed I slept through parts,—reacting from the tremendous stimulation of Stravinsky.

Schnéevoigt I thoroughly enjoyed. A bigger, more human figure than Rothwell. Yesterday was the first symphony I had heard in three years, so the effect on me was the more profound. Something to be said for Hellenic moderation.

Bertha returned with me for supper: aguacates, almonds, persimmons, dates, and crisp fresh greens. A steak is sordid beside such food for the Gods.

December 7. I now possess an automobile! Reason for exclamation — — — Edith and Abad went to Mexico last week, following Monna, whose 6 months permit was not extended by the immigration authorities. What stupid dolts,—what asinine laws!

They went to live,—sold everything. Abad let me have the car with no down payment. All I must do, is to keep up the payments of $47.50 a month. All!

Why did I take upon myself such an obligation?

First of all because business cannot be conducted these days without a car: one must fit into the speed of our time. My late work has been mostly on the outside: for the Pacific Electric Ry.,—an iron foundry,— and home portraits.

Flora was willing to loan me her car, but I needed one here on the job, ready for action. Besides the big Nash cost too much to run.

Then by enabling me to do my work more quickly, I can have more leisure. And leisure to think and create is the most important thing in life!

The car will be a stimulus to Brett, and enable us to get away from these drab surroundings, to breathe freely away from cities, to work quietly in far away places, to see distant friends.

I also bought for almost nothing a fine bed spring,—the first real night comfort I've had for years,—a sofa, a red chest which Monna painted, and several shelves for books, and Oh, yes, a magnificent cat,—Pirracas.

Now I am trying to sell many things to pay for my extravagance. My creative work has stopped: I have done nothing since before my exhibit.

That exhibit brought me no results,—financial I mean. Not one print sold: Quite different the Japanese — — — —

However, I did make some interesting contacts.

Peter scolded me about the hanging of my prints: far too many he thought. Well—maybe my desire to show all possible bettered my good judgment: but I think they looked well.

His feeling was that of confusion from overstimulation. So perhaps being used to all my prints and tired from showing and seeing them, I underestimate their value.

Brett did write me before going away, and a beautiful letter. "I care for you more than anyone else, Dad, and you will never know how hard it is for me to leave you like this."

6. "My only reason for existence—"

January 5, 1928. Yesterday, after four months in which I did no work for myself, I looked through my camera at an exquisite squash, which has been lying around here for many weeks. The light failed before I found an important viewpoint, but maybe today — — — —

And maybe this renewal of personal expression will cure me. I have been miserable with swollen glands in my neck. I know that my sickness has been mostly a result from psychic break—when I do not function in my work my only reason for existence is stopped.

Whether this long inaction,—an artificial inaction, for I was not ready to rest,— has deadened my vision, I have yet to find out. Much will depend on whether I can get hold of myself mentally, and whether I can spare time.

If I thought myself in a mess before,—what now!

Flora in bed for six weeks from an auto accident: Cole in bed with measles: my own sickness: and expenses greatly increased. Oh, if I only had a little shack somewhere in the desert or wilderness, with no possessions. But how can I ever achieve this?

January 6. Yesterday was spent dry mounting with my new secondhand press. It seems a solution for my mounting troubles, the cockling and curling of bromide prints, a trouble which never vexes a platinum printer. So far as print quality, I am very much pleased with my bromides, they are fully equal to the Palladiotype,—for some things, I dare say, better. I am using a smooth white matte, single weight because it is better for dry mounting, and is cheaper. I use both Gevaert and Illingworth bromide, for contact and enlarging, and an Amidol developer.

Among those mounted yesterday is one of O. G. Jones, a head done in 1925: it is strong. Peter thinks it better than the head of Galván, "one of the finest portraits" he has seen. Have also mounted my pepper and milk-bottle, which Henry and Ramiel do not care for, but Peter and I like it immensely. I say, as I have often said, no matter how important the person who comments on one's work, listen with interest and respect, then go ahead with one's own opinion. I say this even to a beginner. Mistakes must be self-realized!

I must in some way rise above conditions, or, I am done for — — — —

January 8. I record today with capitals—I Am Working Again! Yesterday a negative—the day before two. And best of all my long enforced rest has not hurt me,—I realized that at once.

42

My subject matter has been squashes. What an ugly word! Pumpkins may be better,—at least sounds humorous. I shall say pumpkins. They are really gorgeous: one exquisite as a Brancusi, another a human embryo,—another wartlike, malignant,—a little round one, quite jolly. I found also a cabbage of unusual shape, the leaves folded to a definite point: it is a beauty.

Well, believe me, I was excited to be working with them. All three negatives are good.

B. came in the late afternoon to dance for me. She made her own music with large cymbals, little finger cymbals, and tambourine. She danced nude. It was a rare privilege to see her in these several dances,—an inspiration.

I have worked on with cabbages: two more negatives,—one of the two little pointed ones against a tall Mexican basket,—the other of a large round cabbage, a much more cabbage-like cabbage, in a round basket. These sound in description like the usual run of still-life, but they have more — — — —

This little shack is now for sale—or rather the property. No one would pay much for the shack! But it has been the most important building in Glendale! The "For Sale" sign marks the end of an epoch—the beginning of another.

No tears can be wasted over a change: all changes are important.

Today I must stop work and start wondering how I can meet the payment on my car within four days.

A letter from Tina: "You don't know how often the thought comes to me of all I owe you for having been the one important being at a certain time of my life when I did not know which way to turn, the one and only vital guidance and influence that initiated me in this work that is not only a means of livelihood, but a work that I have come to love with real passion. My heart goes out to you with such a deep feeling of gratitude — — —"

January 12. A small duplicate order decided me to print: so I made a day of it, printing two new negatives for myself and reprinting several old ones. I must say the new cabbage is quite fine in movement, volume, texture. The pumpkin is rather a morbid thing: maybe I get this reaction from memory of its stench. It was rotten inside and almost made me sick. I can smell it as I write!

A letter from Henry tells me she will soon return. I anticipate evenings of great interest, comparing notes on Mexico and people there.

Jean writes me that I am to be invited to exhibit with Mexican contemporary artists in New York.

January 13. Shades of Mexico—who should appear last night but Nahui Olín and Matias Santoyo! I certainly gasped with surprise on seeing Nahui. Matias did not enter into my notes from Mexico. I had only met him casually there. He cartooned me last night, recording salient points in my anatomy. He works simply with clean-cut lines and geometric forms: almost too clever,—facile at times,—but he is young.

I returned with them to their hotel,—they are living together,—where he showed me several cartoons in sculpture,—Calles, Cabrál,—excellent.

Nahui gave me a recent book of hers. As a frontispiece, one of my photographs of her was used—but not one I am proud of. Too bad, for her portrait I use in my collection still holds its place as one of my best. I enjoyed the evening, but sense they will try to monopolize my time, maybe unthinkingly: Nahui I guess is somewhat of a sponger.

Sunday, January 15. I took the new arrivals out to the Museum. Matias took his work: The result may be an exhibit. Gjura was there. I find him more mellow these days,—tamed down. He has an exhibit on at the museum and I am glad to be able to say that I responded with pleasure to much of it. He seems to be in a period of working out very complicated problems: if digested this may be followed by work of fine simplicity.

Nahui and Matias were staying at the Biltmore: how they landed there I wonder! I helped them move to nearby apartments, so had a chance to enjoy the Biltmore. How funny it all is! I wished I was a cartoonist to record the amusing people, the lackeys in blue, gold-braided,—tricked out to look very English you know. Matias was paying $8 a day for a little hole called a room.

Bertha took me to the Orpheum in the evening, especially to see Bill Robinson, Negro dancer and comedian. He was the real thing—worth sitting through the other numbers to see. His dancing was a perfection of subtle rhythms—his stories delicately told!

But the other numbers *were* worth seeing—for the same reason, "The Biltmore" was enjoyed: one could laugh at their ludicrous and successful attempts to overwhelm the audience with frippery,—or touch them with bombast and bathos. God knows I can be moved by a simple and entirely sentimental love song—but this stuff was just cheap.

Monday, January 16. A gentle whistle at my back door—it was Johan Hagemeyer!—An expected surprise—I knew he would come after the holiday—I fe his approach. An intense day followed,—always so with Johan. Today will be the same, for he will only be here a short time.

How cold it is; clear and frosty after a cloudy day.

January 20. Johan stayed until last night. If I had money, leisure, these days would have been joyful. As it was I kept wishing he would go, despite the desire I had to keep him here, despite my love for him. A difficult state of mind!

Too, our habits are so different, and I tried to please by joining him: drinking, and smoking, and eating, in a way I never do when alone.

I feel internally clogged up, and the glands in my neck sore again.

Well, I had mental and emotional stimulus to counteract the physical strain. This sounds as though I am sorry he came. No!—It was a rare treat worth any reaction. The showing of my work to Johan was a joy. He was so responsive: we have much in common.

From my collection he chose to have "Shell No. 1."

January 21. A bitter cold morning with frosty roofs and grass. I think So. California can be the coldest place on the American continent—and the hottest! "Realtors," and Chambers of Commerce, please copy.

K. came last night: She was full of eternal love declarations. This is not what I wanted K.,—I cannot respond to an idea of undying emotion,—only youth could hold such a beautiful concept.

She is in a state of mind needing tender consideration and devotion. She wants encouragement,—a crutch to lean on, and turns to me for help.

A sitting yesterday: a wealthy, middle-aged, repressed woman, who wanted an exalted portrait—head to heavens. I felt anything but exhalted after my effort.

Sunday. Johan's visit broke my spell of work: now orders come to further interrupt me. I have promised myself tomorrow, to continue with the pumpkins, better, *the* pumpkin, for I have one which is beautiful beyond all others I have seen.

Henry irritates me at times: if she had not such fine qualities and great art to counterbalance, I could not easily overlook a certain prosaic, unreasoning way of pigeon-holing people. She is apt to be critical in a sort of humourless, puritanical way.

Recent letters indicate that Monna and she discussed me, and I am in some way excommunicated until I can prove that I am not taking advantage of some "foolish woman's love" for me. Evidently Monna is under the ban too, for having talked. Well, Monna would never say aught to disparage me, this I know. My impulse is to say, "—I don't care to hear nor explain anything, Henry, take me with my faults or not at all." Henry can be so damnably serious!

Every recent morning there has been heavy frost. I am eager for long summer days, for warmth and light.

January 24. B. came last eve and brought for me to see a new printing of the *Book of Job*, illustrated by Blake. A rare treat! A great artist, Blake! An hour with his engraving means more to me than a month of reading,—more spiritually,—for my eyes receive—and give—more directly, surely, than any other of my senses. Listening to music, I must always close my eyes: a common practice, yes,—but with me a necessity,—otherwise I see the action of the musicians, their expressions, the shapes of instruments.

Ramiel, and Monna too, criticize the portraits of me by Henry and Peter as showing an intellectual type when I am intuitive.

Henry's portrait is that of an ascetic: I am surely not that, though.

Later same day. I am making an exposure: my favorite pumpkin the model. It fell this morning and split, fortunately on the "wrong" side, so I must do it now before decay sets in.

Waiting, I am thinking this: I always work better when I do not reason, when no question of right or wrong enters in,—when my pulse quickens to the form before me, without hesitation nor calculation.—I am using the centre of a sarape for background to the pumpkin, its zigzag lines in opposition yet rising with the upward movement of the pumpkin, achieving a strongly vibrating whole.

I am also thinking of the days when I was concerned with "light effects," etc. Surface ideas never touching the real,—the object unaffected by atmosphere, moods of the changing weather.

Now I want to see the eternal, basic quintessence each object has and its relation to *the* great whole.

Tonight my pumpkin will achieve its final glorification, in a pumpkin pie!

January 25. Yesterday's neg's? The first with sarape ground has interest, yet what I originally felt in the pumpkin has been lost: it appears a bit squatty. I made another, raising it on the neck of my black olla, against a black ground. How it shows in all purity of form, as simply exquisite as Brett's magnolia bud. But I have overworked that olla as a base for shells: and I have done too often a lone form,—centered, isolated.

I was interrupted by Brett, who wants to trade the Essex for a 1924 Packard, and I believe he is right, that it will be a good exchange, outwearing the Essex and certainly more beautiful.

The Packard exchange will mean a fifty dollar first payment of which I have but twenty-five. So far I cannot foresee from where the other half will come. And then how will I eat afterwards?!

But somehow feel that we are destined to own that car,—and for some good reason.

January 26. We own that car — — —

Now I am more in debt than ever. How to deal with finance corporations I don't know. I'm afraid they got the best of me. By the time insurance and interest was added, my total surprised me! The first $50 I must pay in two weeks, plus interest of course!

I have been trying to sell things without much luck: $7 worth of books yesterday. As I said, and feel, there must be a reason for this seemingly reckless plunge.

46

My better judgment was against further financial obligations: my intuition. forced me into buying this car. The future must tell me why.

January 27. No sales, though a prospect of selling my father's old bow and his collection of archery scrap-books. Am I lacking in sentiment? Perhaps — — — But I will do anything to further my work,—and acquiring this car will. I need to get away from here once in awhile, to get closer to the soil. I cannot on foot. Am I merely making excuses for myself?

I went to the University: some of the younger teachers had expressed a desire that the art department should have a series of my shells. Miss Gere, the director, whom I have known for years met me in her private office.

God save me, and the youth of today from teachers!

Miss Gere is a nice, sweet, old lady with exquisite taste, of a sort. I know that I could learn much from her about composition,—according to formulae: but she could never learn from me.

She at once assumed a teacher's prerogative, starting a detailed analysis of each print. Ten years ago or more I used to eagerly listen to her criticism, yesterday I was impatient and bored. I went there to sell, not to have a lesson in composition. She could not realize that our position had changed, that I had gone beyond her, that she no longer understood my language. I realized how pedantic a teacher can become.

She hardly glanced at my shells, liked best the weakest ones. My nudes, the backs, I fear repelled her, though she was apologetically polite. She cannot go beyond loveliness,—to beauty!

January 29. Through Harriet,—Ahna Zaesek sent me tickets to *The Idiot,* in which she and Reginald Pole took the leads. I thought Ahna showed a mature conception, compared to those Ibsen days of, I guess, ten years ago. Both she and Reginald were excellent, though the cast was weak in some parts.

After, Ahna joined us: Harriet, Sam and myself, to supper and an evening of dancing and reminiscencing at the Freeman home. (The house is by Frank Lloyd Wright: a fine conception except for the insistent pattern on cement blocks which weakens by over-ornamentation.) Ahna can cook as well as act. Some of her idolaters should see her in kitchen array! I teased Ahna, remembering the day years ago when she posed in the nude: a modest virgin who insisted on covering herself at certain points with a towel after each negative, and quite hampering my way of seeing the critical moment.

Harriet dances well: if she were smaller—in bulk—she would be ideal for me. We danced many times to exquisite Spanish tangos.

February 1. Brett drove us to Redondo Beach, Sunday, for a day with Ramiel: we included Nahui, Matias, and Cristal.

47

The notable hour of the day was sunset on the Palos Verdes hills: not a gorgeous sunset,—but exquisite in rose and grey of water, clouds and hills. I realized how much one misses living in an ugly, squat, city like Glendale, surrounded by box-like abominations in brick,—or worse, stucco and cardboard pretentions. Ramiel came here Tuesday bringing Lee Jarvis. The evening was spent with Paul and Cousin Sarah. Arthur Millier and wife were also there and a jolly time we had. A good laugh is cleansing! We screamed with laughter,—one always can with Paul, and the combination was especially congenial last night.

Saturday, February 4. Raining!—after a month of drouth,—of hot days and cold nights. I must go to Dr. Lovell for an examination of my mouth. A congestion of the salivary glands again which I realize is only the effect,—the cause I must locate: maybe a tooth.

Henry will arrive Sunday. She asked me to save Wednesday eve for supper with her.

I am very anxious to see her work done in Mexico. I am not so anxious to listen to certain matters she seems primed to tell me.

The "why" of this and that, about so and so,—including myself. What does it all amount to? Why bother? Loosen up, Henry!

I feel towards persons as I do towards art,—constructively. Find all the good first. Judge by what has been done,—not by omissions or mistakes. And look well into oneself! A lifetime can well be spent correcting and improving one's own faults without bothering about others.

February 14. I have suffered greatly the last few weeks,—my mouth much worse,—but with this writing am free from pain and on the road to recovery. A tooth infected from an old crown caused the trouble: the crown removed and a fast of two weeks on water and orange juice cleaned out the poisons. I went through hell,—physically, mentally.

Henry returned, bringing important new canvases, huaraches for me and dulce de leche for the boys. She called on one of my worst days, and I was worse as a result of her visit! She is so intense that she wore me out, in her desire to help! Mr. H. C. Bentley of Boston,—a retired business man who is collecting work of the most important Calif. artists, and who has already bought one of Henry's paintings was to call the next day to see her Mexican canvases. Henry said: "I want to take back a few of your prints, expect nothing but maybe I can interest him."

The following afternoon I stopped by as requested. Mr. B. was still there. He had purchased seven prints and one of Henry's new paintings!

This is an important opening for me I feel sure. And as to the ninety dollars —
————! Prints he selected were: palm trunk—Cuernavaca, radishes, maguey, nude—Miriam, two shells, cloud Mazatlán.

A payment on the car is indicated!

Today I am preparing to ship seventy-five prints to Seattle. Peter Krasnow and I are showing together before the Seattle Fine Arts Society.

— *This is Feb. 16* and a bitter cold morning following a terrific windstorm yesterday. I feel much better physically and mentally after my long fast on orange juice. I could easily have gone another week and enjoyed myself, but such a fast ties one to the source of supply and I must be able to get out and hunt the dollar. Miriam here last eve, and later Paul Jordan came. Miriam has moved back to her hillside home in Edendale. On the opposite hill lives Cristal! Cristal took Brett and me to the *Chauve Souris*. Many numbers I had seen six years ago in N. Y. The glamour of seeing the show for the first time—and in New York— was missing,—but we thoroughly enjoyed every moment.

I have been printing,—new negatives,—new last summer—but only now printed, and a few reprints: one of three gourds is rich in values, deliciously smooth: two pumpkins on a woven tray has fine movement: a lone pumpkin blossoming from an olla might be Brett's magnolia bud,—only I like his better: but two pointed cabbages against a towering basket, pleases me most, it is so exquisitely sparkling with delicate highlights on clear grays. Today I mount, then go to visit Henry.

Friday. A visit with Henry—and after, sheer exhaustion! I slept through part of the concert that Bertha took me to that night,—even through Carpenter's *Skyscrapers* ballet, which I wanted to hear,—went to hear.

Henry has a certain possessive sense re her friends, or at least re me: She will have them act just so, according to her light, or, they are no longer friends! I hardly knew whether to politely refuse answer to her very personal questions or to attempt explanations, whether to be angry or to inwardly smile and "defend" myself. Henry thinks she's a profound psychologist, but does not read me,—while I read her as an open book. She is a child in her betrayal of motivating reasons for word and action. She does not hide them, if indeed she would, because she does not realize or know the very causes deep within her which bring out these words and actions.

Henry has taxed my patience times before this with her entire lack of humour, her positiveness. I have stood that side of her, knowing her preponderance of fine qualities, as one must with any friend, as I would have friends do with me: but yesterday was near to being the limit.

There are moments when I positively dislike Henry, and then the feeling passes, overwhelmed by her definite fineness.

I don't want to lose her as a friend — — — —

February 21. A climax to my sickness came Sunday. I hope it was the climax for never before have I suffered such pain. I started feeling worse again Friday, and Sunday morning an abscess formed on my gum which finally burst bringing relief. Well that's over!

Not caring for a repetition of the irrelevant nonsense which spoiled my last visit with Henry, I wrote her, scolding her as I would a child.

Her answer was typical,—psychologically interesting in the way she turns the tables, pretending to be highly amused at my "anger." It was she who was so deadly serious that her face flushed and her lips trembled when she talked to me, gave me a "third degree."

But I shall not be concerned how we settle our difficulties, just so such nonsense will not be repeated. She can have the feminine last word!

A sitting today of Shibley Boyes, pianist. Having cut prices in half for a "fellow artist" I will not greatly enrich myself.

Wednesday, February 22. Last eve to Arthur Millier's where a small but finely chosen group of prints collected by Merle Armitage was shown. Armitage I had not seen for years. He had seen the two prints Arthur has of mine, and wishes to come out to see more. This may mean more than a social and interested call. I hope so.

Francine Millier is a striking person. I have asked her to sit to me.

Dalzell Hatfield, manager of Newhouse Galleries came yesterday. He wishes a portfolio of my portraits and other work also, to place on view for commission and sale. This should develop into an important opening.

I am stronger. I shall print again today.

February 23. Printed as planned,—all told four negatives,—all reprints: three of best shells, one of chard. From each negative I pulled a finer print than ever before. I was thrilled, though very tired, not having over much reserve.

Peter and Rose, Brett and I had supper with Henry.

Of her new work done in Mexico I especially like a flower study,—oil, a water-color,—nude torso of Indian girl, and a drawing, Indian mother and child,—the latter one, the finest thing she has ever done in any medium.

I suppose I should lie in the sun and build up my strength today,—I crave sun: yet the desire to print again is strong.

February 24. I am quite disgusted with myself,—for a number of reasons, and have decided that unless I can prove otherwise, I am a weakling.

Cigarettes for one thing; I still use them though not so many. I always say "to-morrow," then find some pretext to have one in the morning, which starts the day. I might much better give up the idea of quitting, then I would not weaken my morale by giving in, and losing self respect! Yesterday I was especially disgusted.

February 25. Uncle Theodore writes that Aunt Emma is dying — — — — —
With her passing, goes one of the important figures of my life. She has mothered me since my own mother died, when I was five years old. Even in recent years a letter almost always held a check or a dollar bill, admonishing me to buy a good steak, that I did not eat enough! The dear woman always worried over my vegetarian propensity.

Printed yesterday,—four negatives. Again I improved over old printings, and am quite pleased with the day's work.

March 2. I took Armitage, at his request, and my desire, to Henry's. He had thought there was no art on the West Coast. Since seeing my work and then Henry's he has changed his mind. He said,—"Why, she is one of America's greatest painters!"

On the subject of art again, I repeat a thought which I wrote down several years ago in Mexico: that modern artists who go back to the primitive,—try to recall the past, the feeling and technique of simple, artless people,—fail absolutely. The way is ahead, not back, no matter how great the past may be.

Peter and Rose invited Henry and me to supper, and a good supper it was, in the popular idea of a meal. But give me a head of crisp lettuce, and aguacate, a handful of California dates.

Two nights out in succession is too much: and besides I have been seeing too many people, I need aloneness and work.

March 3. An exquisite morning after rain,—tardy rain needed for weeks. I printed all afternoon,—again some negatives from last August: a shell which holds its own,—a gourd—my fish from Oaxaca—also good, except the painted scales are a bit insistent.

Then I printed the pumpkin and cabbages,—Henry thinks it appears arranged, or in other words I didn't "get away" with the arrangement. Maybe — — — but why not admit it to be an unusually sensitive arrangement.

Carleton Beal's name is plastered all over the *Nation*,—the first American to interview Sandino. Carleton added a thriller to his adventuresome life. This government's war on Nicaragua is a disgrace,—a crime.

March 6. When first I met Henry over a year ago and saw her work, I acclaimed her greatness as an artist at once. I indulged in superlatives, until my own words and enthusiasm nearly brought a reaction. Then she would paint such a canvas as the cactus to bring forth from me a renewed tribute.

Yesterday she showed me a drawing in pastel,—the greatest work she has done, and that means it is really great. A nude female torso,—an astounding thing so sure, so powerful. It "knocked me cold." Slang seems stronger to express my feelings.

Hail Henry! This last work places you among the immortals.

Merle A. purchased 2 prints: the all-over pattern of ollas, and a nude of Tina, 1924 period. Also wrote a letter to Rockwell Kent.

"There are a few artists on the Pacific Coast (not many) who are doing work of a character that I think warrants national attention. Two of them H. Shore, painter, and E. Weston photographer, I am certain of. Would you be interested in having some photographs of their work sent on with a view to your using articles on them in *Creative Art*?"

This and a letter I wrote the Weyhe Gallery in view of an exhibit for next winter should start things in New York.

March 23. Bertha took Brett and me to the Persinger String Quartet. I went to sleep. I insist I was enjoying myself, had been looking forward to this event for days,—and it was no disappointment, but a combination of tired eyes, Adagio lamentoso, and overheated room, proved too much. Part of the heat was generated by a jam of hog-fat women,—the same idlers, parasites, curiosity seekers who patronize exhibits but only with their presence,—they never buy! Brett and I sent exhibits to a new "Salon" of photography formed in San Diego,—the incentive being a purchase price of $25.

Brett has been doing some splendid work in the industrial district. I think if I have any real competition for the prize, providing the jury is competent, it will be from Brett.

I need so much to work again. All I do is to scrape money together for the monthly car payments.

March 29. White and purple iris, pale lavender poppies, delight my room, a birthday greeting from Cristal. She also brought me sweets of her own making, orange-peel candied in honey, and best of all an exquisite cactus, a tiny thing in a glazed mauve jar. A grey day, rain softly falling, was my birthday. This pleased me.

I worked yesterday with leek,—a fine subject matter. My negatives do not thrill me. Then I enlarged a negative from the Bertha series. A strong thing, well liked. Today I hope to work again. Henry, Brett and I are going on an outing! A rare treat.

Sold another print, again the nude of Tina. A lady met at Millier's wanted it for her husband's studio!

April 6. The outing was a fizzle: no use for a painter to pick out a spot for the photographer to work in,—the weather eye of one is far different from the others. Henry's suppers are too rich, even when she thinks they are simple. I come away uncomfortable.

A loaf of unmistakable bread, coarse and heavy, and a jar of jam indicated Gjura had called. So I returned the visit.

The same old story: an evening trying to avoid certain topics of conversation, and when unavoidable, holding my tongue.

Now Gjura is all for the "abstract." "Nothing which in the least represents nature."

"But Gjura, each line or form you draw is after all taken from nature. And absolute verity can be abstract — — — —"

Why discuss with Gjura, he is all wise!

Miguel Covarrubias sent me $50 owed by Rose since Mexico days.

And I sold a copy of the "Maguey" to Poland of the San Diego Museum, and two prints, one of the "Knees," another of Bertha's legs, from my Seattle exhibit,— also Brett sold one! So we are comfortable today. Sunday to a Bach Oratorio, Saint Matthew's "The Passion," at the Philharmonic. A chorus of 350, in which Kathleen sang. It was most impressive, but. . . .

April 8. "Haw Haw!" laughed Chandler awakening me from a sound sleep. He had slept the night on my sofa to be near his girl's house. They were going to a cross-crowned hill for Easter service at sunrise,—and the sun was veiled by heavy fog.

I have Easter flowers,—royal red tulips with blue centers from Cristal, and a single rose from B. A new coffee cup from C. too: but now I do not use coffee!

Last night Nahui and Matias cooked Mexican style. I took Bertha. Mushrooms fried in olive oil with garlic and chili,—green peppers, cheese and sausage, chocolate and bizcochos,—a meal well prepared but not in my present way of thinking. I have a bellyache this morning, and worse, I must eat another Mexican meal today,— a long delayed birthday spread for me from the Ortiz family. How can I refuse those simple, generous people!

Matias dances beautifully, with gestures of a torero. I could watch him all evening with more pleasure than the best of stage performers. I know Bertha was fascinated too. He is naturally a dancer,—none of the tricks of a professional, no mechanical perfection.

April 11. Spring is here with the blossoming fruit trees, the wisteria, and acacia: my little tree—no, it is no longer little, —is a fragrant yellow glory. Will it bloom next year or be uprooted to make room for business!

I feel springtime in my marrow, but I am trapped,—I cannot become a part of the blossoming. This auto is possessing me, I slave to support it,—to what end I begin to wonder. Perhaps it is a lesson I must learn, to show me more clearly the possessive quality of possessions.

April 17. One fine day last week Henry, Brett, and I packed cameras, paints, lunch, and went to Santa Monica for work and outing. I had grown tired of "still-life," of confinement,—I wanted air and soil. Santa Monica was chosen because of a fine group of sycamore trees.

One negative I have already printed,—there was no hesitation. It is a detail of trunk at the base where roots go into the soil. Sunlight outlines the main form: it has the feeling of a strangely beautiful torso.

The technique is about perfect. The exposure was 90 sec. at noontime using my $5 lens at f/256 without filter....

B. is to dance on Olive Hill next Sunday. The program is rather well done. On the cover is reproduced my photograph of her knees which holds its own as one of my best.

Mrs. Agnes Strauss invited me to show recent work to Mr. Strauss who is confined to his home through sickness. He bought the "Knees," and she bought my first shell negative. I have sold three copies from each of these neg's. Best sellers!

Merle Armitage is showing his collection of prints at the L. A. Public Library. My "Ollas de Oaxaca" is the only photograph in the exhibit which includes such names as Bellows, Rockwell Kent, Whistler, William Blake, Mestrovic, Matisse, Picasso, John Marin. I think the photograph well holds its own.

Peter Krasnow needed a portrait for publication—in a hurry. The results indicate what I can do with him, for I shall work again. One of Peter and Rose together is exceptionally fine in feeling, though technically weak.

I have worked with two gourds recently: a truly marvellous one, black lacquer, belonging to Henry—which inverted, is like a strange balloon—and a slender fish-shaped gourd. I used these as flower and stem; it is an exotic print. Is it tricky,—getting away from life? Brett said "I don't know whether to like it very much or not at all,—I'm puzzled?" The forms fascinated me, and the print does too. After all it suggests life and quite profoundly. I have printed another of the sycamore tree which I like without question. It is life first hand.

A letter from Jean Charlot, still in Chichen Itza: a long interesting letter. He writes: "I saw some Stieglitz photographs lately and I lacked entirely the emotions the first ones I had seen produced in me. I prefer your best last prints in Mexico to his." This comment does not necessarily mean a thing, despite Jean's good judgment,—for who knows what prints he may have seen. Maybe even Stieglitz has prints out not up to standard.

A letter from Lee Simonson who wants an article (by me) and five photographs for *Creative Art*. He writes, "I saw some of your photographs in Mexico, and think they are among the most remarkable I have ever seen." This should be an important showing of my work. For the first time in America it will be in a magazine of the Arts.

I asked J. N. Laurvik, Nahui, Matias and Cristal out to dine and dance. We had a rather gay evening. I am taking the same crowd to see Bertha dance.

54

Perhaps the most fun I have had lately has been in a swimming hole discovered by Cole and Neil. It was reminiscent of Huckleberry Finn, with bonfires, rafts and naked boys. Fed by fresh river water this hole gouged out by steam shovel is deep enough for diving, and much larger than the local swimming tanks. It is hidden from public gaze so no spinster can be horrified by naked boys and men.

May 2. After Bertha's dance program on Olive Hill we went to Laurvik's to a party, a perfect evening which was prolonged into the morning. "We," included Cristal, Brett, a couple of Laurvik's friends and Bertha, whom we begged to join the gaiety. There was wine aplenty,—good wine. My glass seemed ever full,—with consequences. I have not been joyfully borrachito in many moons. However there was no shadow to mar the fun. Hours of dancing and laughter, and a fine supper prepared by Laurvik.

The setting for Bertha's dance was perfect: The green lawn, the wall of straight young pines: and the rays from a setting sun, converged upon her figure, glorified her auburn hair.

A party the following night was too much,—an anti-climax. It might have been another joyful evening,—the group was a happy one with Peter and Rose Krasnow, Ericka Webber, Agnes Strauss. I took them with the direction of Toyo San to a Japanese restaurant unfrequented by Americans. Supper was cooked on the table, saki wine was served, and it might have been an outstanding evening except that I was too weary.

On the way home Ericka Webber presented me with a flowering stalk from her banana tree. What an amazing growth, what a marvellous creation in color and form.

May 4. Bertha, Brett and I to Pasadena to see *Lazarus Laughed*—Eugene O'Neill. The stage version was almost something,—surely worth seeing. I think it could have been cut with no loss,—but I have not read the play. Caligula was the outstanding figure,—fine portrayal. I wearied of Lazarus' ever-impending laughter, I felt like tickling him to bring a giggle.

I had more real enjoyment from the Russian film, *Czar Ivan the Terrible*. More such productions would remove the stigma from motion pictures.

May 6. Eleven hours sleep indicates unusual exhaustion on my part. I had a heat stroke last night after eight hours in the darkroom: heat, bad air, nervous hurry, and the empty chatter of my "student" brought on collapse. In the first place the day was burning hot outside. But I had to get off several prints for *Creative Art.* I stripped naked and worked in comparative comfort, finishing within five hours. Then came the student family, mother and two children, which meant three hours more confinement. After, I went down and out! Too bad for I missed a party at Roy Rosen's which Peter said was great, with a barrel of wine and everyone joyous.

May 8. Shipped air mail the ms. for *Creative Art* and 14 of my photographs. I have a bad taste, rereading the article today. I copied it from my daybook which was actually as much effort as writing an original, connected article.

May 10. No one should say to another of vivid imagination,—"It was the greatest this or that I've ever seen," for then the one of imagination conceives the impossible, creates such an illusion that no actuality ever equals.

I had heard too much about *Potemkin*,—God knows what I expected to see! And I will say it was a great production, so far ahead of the usual that I shall go again, and maybe again. If I had chanced upon this film, never having heard of it, surely I would have come away so full of eulogies as to likewise spoil it for others.

Potemkin was the most dramatic film...dangerously near at times to the melodramatic,—in details of the Cossacks' advance: indeed the emotional content was overwhelming, one's sympathy overstrained. Propaganda played a part, granting a true picture, and honestly expressed. At the same time mob psychology was illuminatingly portrayed. The ghastly results, shown in every bloody detail, and a logical sequence which showed fine directing.
A great picture!

May 11. I sent six prints each from Brett's work and my own to the first exhibit of the "Camera Enthusiasts" of San Diego. The name of this new group should have been sufficient warning that our kind of photographs would not be well received, but a first prize of $25 and a second of $10—how ridiculous the amounts! $100 or $1000 would sound more dignified—tempted my wasted purse. No jury was announced, but I gambled, sending six of the finest things I ever made. I had the prize money all spent, 1st for me, second for Brett!

Yesterday the prints returned. I did not win! nor Brett!—worse—three of mine were rejected and five of Brett's — — — — Well, what an amazingly stupid jury, turning down several of the greatest photographs ever made! But what could I expect? History repeats itself. Calender Art wins. The language of form cannot be read except by those with the key; to others it is no more than meaningless hieroglyphs.

I understand the first award went to a bromoil. Naturally it would, with most photographers no more than disappointed painters.

I have a mind to make several negatives especially for next year's contest, sending them under an assumed name. They would be hung, even win, for I know what these people really want! I could turn out their kind of work by the ream: then I would expose the hoax. But I have had my effort in submitting work rewarded. Mr. Poland sent me $20 for a shell print.

7. The Desert

May 23. B., Brett and I have been guests of Theodore and Olga Stack,—Big Bear Lake, San Bernardino Co. We left last Thursday morning at 3:00 a.m. arriving at 9:00 p.m. The trip could have been made in five hours,—but we "loitered" on the way.

I had planned to work with Joshua trees on the desert, and did, but if I had known what was coming farther on, no stop would have been made for Joshua trees,—or anything else. B. said, "Would you be interested in great piles of rock? We will pass them beyond Victorville." I immediately sensed something ahead, but was hardly prepared for the dramatic scene to come. Without exaggeration I say, it was one of the impressive moments of my life. No mighty mountain, snow capped, touching the heavens ever stirred me as did these amazing rocks. Stark-naked they rose from the desert, barren except for wisps of dry brush: belched from the earth's bowels by some mighty explosion, they massed together in violent confusion, in magnificent contiguity. Pyramids, cubes, rectangles, cylinders, spheres,—verticals, obliques, curves,—simple elemental forms, complex convolutions, opposed zigzags, at once chaotic and ordered, an astounding sight!

The sun was near to setting when we arrived, but Brett and I set up our cameras. Days or weeks of study before working would have shown more respect for the magnitude of our theme, but to live there, or even near enough to make the trip daily could not be planned nor financed on short notice: it was a good two hours from water and provisions.

However, long years of work with a camera have trained me to see and grasp essentials quickly, so several negatives were made before sunset. We planned then and there to leave Big Bear early enough on the return, to allow some hours before the noon time desert heat became intolerable.

Monday at 6:00 a.m. we were there again. I had fourteen 8 × 10 films unexposed. At 1:00 my last one was used and Brett had finished too. He said "My brains are fried!"

It was so easy to work, that it was difficult! One could expose a thousand negatives and be there weeks without exhausting possibilities. To go there with one negative and have to decide *the one* most important viewpoint would be maddening. I worked with fine surety, without mental sweat, though the physical sweat near drowned me!

The day after returning I developed, spent seven hours in the darkroom while important "business" waited. I would have developed the night we arrived but for exhaustion. I fell into bed at 5:00 and opened my eyes eleven hours after!

I believe I am not merely enthused in writing that these negatives are the most important I have ever done. They have all the forms I felt and revealed in shells and vegetables plus greater strength and vitality. So writing I do not mean to belittle my former period,—it led to this.

My technique matched my vision,—two or three slightly overtimed, but printable without alteration. The light was blinding. Brett with less experience did not cut down enough and overtimed most of his.

The Joshua trees were a problem,—too fantastic. I have two or three to finish. But two details of Junipers rank along with my best rocks. Cristal wept when she saw one negative of bark, roots, needles, and rock. The pines of Big Bear had true grandeur. I studied them for hours and some day shall do them. But I knew that every film should be saved for the rocks. It may be that the heat will be too great this summer, if we make the trip again, hence further work impossible.

Theodore and Olga Stack,—Frantie, Rosemarie and Kit, their children,—friends of B. with whom we stayed, extended every hospitality, and showed discretion by leaving me alone to work unmolested. A cabin with roaring fire, comfortable bed and cupboard well provisioned was ready for Brett and me.

When we left, a cordial, sincere invitation was extended to return and occupy the cabin at any time we wished. They loved the country and would have me the interpreter.

May 26. I made 27 negatives on the Big Bear trip. Two of Joshua trees were discarded,—one rather too pretty and usual, the other a repeated idea. Three of rocks were discarded, all duplicates which I made thinking the wind had shaken my camera. Actually I only destroyed one negative as unimportant, and will print 22 without hesitation. I worked intensely and well! At last my purchase of the auto has been justified! If I should lose it now I will nevertheless feel repaid for the effort.

Today I must meet the payment of $55 and I have but $25 all told.

Last eve I talked on Mexico before the Arts and Crafts Society. I believe from all response I stirred them.

May 28. My pupil paid $38 due, and I paid the car installment. But no other bills have been paid this month.

Peter and Rose Krasnow, Henry Shore and I joined Ericka Webber in meeting Kern, returning from N. Y. where he furnished and decorated a three room apartment at Macy's "International Exposition of Art in Industry."

Peter, Henry and I were each represented in his rooms.

1. Chambered Nautilus, 1927

2. KNEES, 1929

3. SHELLS, 1927

4. PEPPERS, 1927

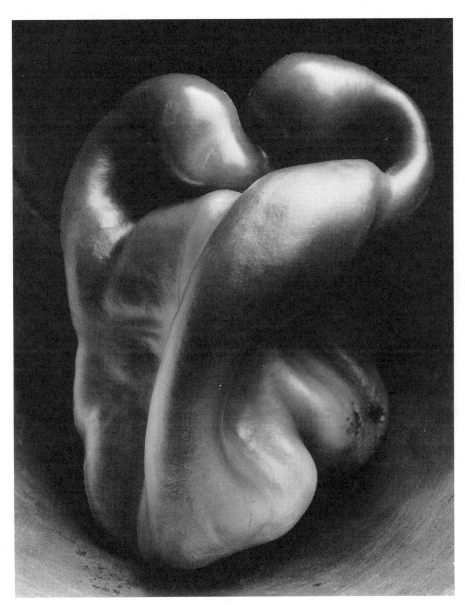

5. Pepper No. 30, 1930

6. CABBAGE LEAF, 1931

7. ARTICHOKE HALVED, 1930

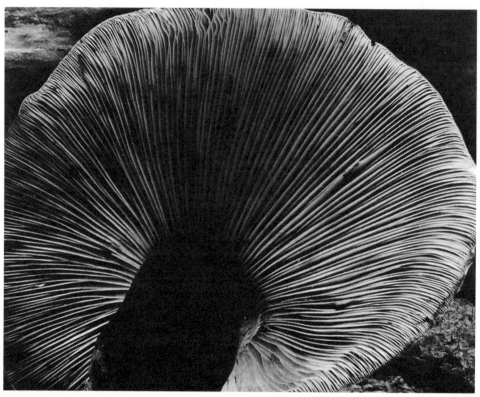

8. Toadstool, 1931

We went home with the Webbers where numerous bottles of good homemade wine, peach cordial, and cocktails, served to enliven several hours.

Dr. and Mrs. Witte, recent arrivals from Germany, and friends of the Webbers, returned with me. I found them intelligent, fine people. I liked them at once. They intend to buy.

May 30. The excerpts from my daybook and photographs will be published in August issue of *Creative Art.* This should be an important means of establishing me. Best of all, Mr. Boni, the publisher, "seems distinctly interested in a book on Mexico, a holiday volume, of which your photographs and daybook would be the basis and asks that you communicate with him on his return in July." So writes Lee Simonson.

It seems my fortunes are to change for something better. Now I must spend all spare time in cutting and correcting my manuscript.

June 1. Tonchi's four kittens are a continuous vaudeville,—comedy, acrobatics and dancing! They furnish free entertainment, more comical, more amazing than any "Orpheum" act. Tonchi seems burdened and bored with maternity: but Pirracas who is papa to at least one of them watches their antics, fascinated. Suddenly, as though the kittens had suggested mice, he pounces upon one,—then what a squealing and skedaddling follows to escape the monster's jaws.

Prince Pirracas I call him, or Your Satanic Majesty, for in the feline world he must be titled. His aloof elegance, his diabolic moods, his cryptic movements denote Black Magic, suggest allegiance with hobgoblins.

Keith Corelli, a young pianist sat to me recently and yesterday bought a print,—a portrait of Cristal. Not often I sell a portrait unless it be of a prominent person. Merle Armitage brought three friends last eve. All seemed quite moved by my work. One of them will buy after seeing my rocks finished. I am anxious to finish them. They are nice, clean negatives. I spotted the entire 22 in a couple of hours.

One of the party was a girl, a dancer,—Fay Fuquay. She became enthused over my dancing nudes of B. and offered herself as a model. I accepted. She interests me.

— — — To friend grocer and buy a can of beans without paying! Gjura mailed a m/o for the amount about a week after I needed it most. With it a silly little note in broken English,—Maybe a pose—

"This used not occured...." No it "used not," George, but by the Gods I am tired of working for nothing.

Peter and Rose are the other extreme. They pay before delivery. I appreciate them!

June 3. Dr. Witte purchased a head of Tina, one of the series done as she recited Venetian poems. It was a beautiful print and I was sorry to part with it. I sold

it for only $10. He also bought 10 glossy prints from the expedition collection at
$1 each. The Weyhe Gallery, N. Y. through Carl Zigosser, has asked for a
consignment of prints.

This should be a good move for me. I believe sales will follow. Now into the
darkroom for a few hours printing of my new rock negatives. A friend of Armitage wishes to see them before leaving for N. Y. He has promised to purchase.
I believe the sales from my personal work during last year would add up to a
tidy sum. This is most satisfying to me.

June 4. I picked up Brett's daybook and spent an hour of the keenest enjoyment.
I roared and shook with laughter, especially over the Mexican period. What
refreshing, spontaneous writing!

June 6. A mess of a party—and my fault. Nahui Olín and Santayo were coming
out—it seems I could no longer avoid them! So to prevent boredom I asked
Kathleen, which meant inviting her sister for "chaperon"—since K. is in bad
with her family—which in turn meant inviting Flora. After all I thought, Flora
has not been here to a party since my return,—it may please her.

Then I phoned Schindler to come: he has asked me many times to meet Nahui.
Neutra answered the phone, that meant inviting him and his wife,—but I was
not sorry for I like them both.

Well when Neutra arrived who should be with him but Sadakichi Hartmann
whom I had not seen for a good eight years,—not since I had told him to stay
away following an unpleasant episode with Margrethe, which served as a good
excuse for I was disgusted enough with his grafting. . . .

Neil and Cole and the six cats squeezed in to add spice. I began to move in
circles. Sadakichi was a sad old ruin, I was shocked. He is paying for a dissipated,
malicious life.

Flora thanked me on parting. I really think she enjoyed the evening.

June 7. I have printed and mounted 18 photographs from the Mojave desert
trip. Two I decided to intensify before printing, and two I discarded: the
form,—construction was good but the evening light in which I worked was too
soft and flat for the strong subjects.

Cooling down after my first enthusiasm, I doubt, forced to decide, if I would
discard the shells before these rocks. But this does not mean I have lost interest,
nor consider them less important. And I shall return there when finances permit.
One of the finest is the close up of a juniper tree. A Joshua tree of exquisite
delicacy and perfect technique grows in importance. It does not smash one in
the face as do the rocks, but it lives well.

Karl Howenstein gave a farewell party to Anita Delano, going to Europe.
Shibley Boyes showed a side of herself I did not know and quite approved of:

60

she was the life of the party,—a dynamo of energy. We popped olive pits at other tables to liven several who seemed a bit too dully reserved. A great bonfire followed supper, in which was burned a papier-maché figurine of ghastly form and mien, pillaged, as the story goes, from the Pot Boiler's theatre at that hour when life ebbs low, etc.

Later Shibley played. If my opinion has value she is destined to a great future. I have heard no one, neither man nor woman play with such power. Of course it was in a small room — — —

But these young folks, growing up here in America, they amaze one!

June 8. Of all days in the week I dread Thursday,—the four hours with my pupils, a mother and two children. It is not the children but their mother who exhausts me: an overworked, hysterical woman, who talks from the moment she arrives till she finishes with an extra fifteen minutes on the front porch to say good night, while I stand there,—hand on latch, ready to close and collapse. Most of the work is in the darkroom: four of us closeted together four hours! I earn my ten dollars.

June 9. Weary after a day of spotting, and restless from three days confinement here, in which I did not once step outside, I hied myself to Peter's. They were going to a party and took me along. Sitting in a back room, with Peter and George Fisher, I heard amongst late arrivals a familiar derisive guffaw: it was Sadakichi again,—the second meeting after all these years.

I had never seen Sadakichi dance, though from time to time I had heard enthusiastic comments.

I add my eulogies. He is a much finer dancer than a writer. His gestures and facial expression were often superb. He knows the dance. No woman dancer could have approached his feeling and understanding. Again the male in art transcends the female,—and in a field almost monopolized by females.

June 10. It seemed as though I were wasting yesterday: still restless, but with no definite desire to go to any particular place. If Ramiel had been a mile away,— yes, but I could not consider a long train ride and Brett was not here to drive me. I could have been happy alone on beach sands, but again too far. Reading was impossible, correcting my ms. also, and certainly I could not have gone into the darkroom. So when Laurvik loomed tall in the doorway I welcomed him. He is a fine person, and I always enjoy him.

After awhile I thought to show him the new Mojave desert rocks. He viewed them with real enthusiasm,—thought I had made a definite advance,—that I had found myself most decisively. Later Reginald Pole arrived. He knows the desert well, and told me of rocks at Twenty-nine Palms, and at an altitude high enough to be cool even in summer.

61

I know the danger of accepting another's word about subject matter for photography, but this seems worth a chance.

June 12. Sunday started out to be another bad day. I could have worked joyously out of doors, with rocks or trees, but not here, not indoors. I moped around, rather wishing for a new amorous adventure, it being about time. Finally I walked over to Peter's. He was taking a sun bath in his garden. I joined him and we lay there talking for several hours. Then Chinatown was suggested for supper. I was ready for anything!

The night presaged merrymaking. We stopped at Kern Webber's. A quiet party was gathered around the fire place, but with our arrival six bottles of wine were brought from the cellar.

We left at three a.m., after such a swirl of dancing and tomfoolery as I have not known in months.

The last act found me in the rumble seat of Peter's car, with Ruth in my arms, our lips fused,—going somewhere. Ruth's last name I don't know, and I will probably never meet her again.

I was sick Monday. But the good from that night overbalanced the bad. I was not so sick that I had to postpone the Monday afternoon sitting with F. I even made several negatives that developing must reveal as well seen.

June 13. I just embraced and kissed Brett good bye! He has left for San Pedro to get work on board a ship bound for—who knows where—Maybe around the world! I shall miss him. I love that boy! We needed money. It was necessary that he work this summer. But Brett's imagination could not be satisfied with a local job,—clerking in a grocery store or chauffering for a laundry! This is a delayed adventure, the last one interrupted by the police of Modesto. He had to have this experience, to get it out of his system. May the Gods watch over him and treat him kindly!

June 16. A dejected and weary Brett returned last night: he had walked the streets of San Pedro hunting work in vain, until his money gave out. Dick who went with him got a ship for England, but Dick had discharge papers from former work. I was sorry for Brett, but relieved.

Have had a wire from the East West Gallery, S. F., for fifty prints to show July 1st to 15th. I accepted, providing terms are mutually agreeable. I sense sales up there.

Showed my work last night at Neutra's to a small group. Dr. Epstein, exchange professor from Russia at Cal. Tech.; Edstrom, sculptor, and Katherine Edson, dancer, whom I had not seen for years were there. Much interest in my work. Neutra is always enthusiastic.

Sunday, July 17. To the Olympic tryouts yesterday, on a free ticket. There had been so much ballyhoo about "the race of the century" that I was on tiptoe to go. Nor am I sorry. I had not been to a track meet since the days when I wore spikes. My distance was the century and I was better than average: built for distance with the necessary nervous energy, I might have, under a wise coach, developed into championship timber. I held for some time the Junior record for two laps (I believe about 185 yds.) at Central Y.M.C.A., Chicago. I dreamed and lived on the cinder track!

But photography entered in and my track days were over.

So, with the crack of the gun, starting the 100 metre dash yesterday, I tingled with excitement.

I had never seen Paddock run: nor can I say that I have seen him now, for out in front of his field, never to be headed, flew a slender boy with a big "G" on his breast,—Wyckoff of Glendale! All eyes focussed on that flying youth, surely Paddock would head him at the tape. But no!—and 50,000 wildly excited persons acclaimed a new hero. The 200 metre race was a repetition,—and Wyckoff equaled Paddock's world record time. I lived over my past in those breathless moments.

My back, repaired by Dr. Lovell, held out remarkably well and my mood was gay, having been revived by a check for $24. I must have been a dancer in some past incarnation.

June 30. "I am inclined to see in this orgy of painting not primarily a spiritual need but a purely economic symptom"—Adolph Basler.

I copied this from an article in *Creative Art*. It caused me to consider my own work. So far no economic need has tainted my personal work, for I have never depended upon it for a living, indeed not until the last year have I even thought of placing my work with dealers; not until I exhibited in Mexico had I sold more than an occasional print. Even now I am sure that no thought of selling enters in when I photograph something for myself. A personal joy and need is the motivating force. This accounts for what I know my photographs possess,— honesty.

Some years past when exhibiting in various open "salons" I may have considered, at least in selecting prints for submission, those which I thought the average jury would pass, but soon realizing the stupidity of juries I quit exhibiting except in one-man shows, and since then my work has been only for myself. Of course I am not including portraits done for others.

July 1. I start the new month with a new love! I am not surprised. F. and I were forecast to have this experience—at least once.

She came to be photographed again. From the last time I have one extraordinary negative. She bent over forward until her body was flat against her legs. I made a back view of her swelling buttocks which tapered to the ankles like an inverted vase, her arms forming handles at the base. Of course it is a thing I can never show to a mixed crowd. I would be considered indecent. How sad when my only thought was the exquisite form. But most persons will only see an ass!—and guffaw as they do over my toilet.

Yesterday was not meant for work though I loaded my magazines in preparation. "I have a pint of liquor over home," said F.

We drove to Pasadena. We drank. We kissed. She was an artist with those lips — — — —

July 5. . . . We should have a few pleasant weeks together, and a very good time it is for me, with K. working—I almost never see her—and B. away. C. comes occasionally but the physical side is on the wane. Women are presented to me in abundance so that I may suffer from no inhibitions! I never think of them, nor search them out, for they always appear at the right moment.

This is well for my work. How different from those years in Mexico!

I am trying to scrape together enough money for a trip to San Francisco. I believe it would pay me to be there while my exhibit is on. I have had much publicity. A whole column in the *S. F. Examiner* with reproductions, written by Jehanne Salinger, begins: "If a book on the art of the western coast is ever to be written one name will stand out as of unusual significance—Edward Weston of L. A. is the man."

Arthur Millier wrote in the *L. A. Times* an article headed "Three print makers and a master artist." It was rather hard on my co-exhibitors, Franz Geritz, Aries Fayer, and Will Connell.

"Each of the last-named three has something to say but it was not made to be said in the presence of a master." I was criticized for showing with them, but I well knew my work would not suffer by comparison.

Henry wants to accompany us north where she goes to live for two months, and will pay for gas and oil. It would be a trial for me, she wears me out and bores me to death with attention. But to have the gas paid is no small item and she means so well and has been so kind that I should like to please her. Henry is a bit mad. I see that same wild look in her eye even as in Flora's and in Mrs. Jones my pupil. . . .

July 8. Days and hours of "watchful waiting." A telegram is due which may indicate enough work to warrant a trip north. Otherwise I do not go. This way I have decided. Too much expense is involved for a holiday. I would rather spend the same amount on a trip to some place where I might work. Besides so many friends are away from San Francisco—Imogen and Roi are here, Johan in Carmel, Jean Roy and Lester maybe in Ojai. It is difficult to decide.

Imogen spent the afternoon here. I like her,—and I like some of her new work. I always felt she would do something given leisure from house and children. She is a bigger artist with her camera than Roi is with his etching needle.

Either someone razzed Arthur Millier for his article comparing my work to the other three exhibitors at the library as gold to lead, or else his conscience hurt, for in today's paper he "realized that an injustice had been done the three last named artists, whose work, while I do not believe it as masterly as that of Weston, cannot fairly be classed as bad."

I think you are getting in deeper than ever, Arthur!

PART II

San Francisco, August, 1928—Desember, 1928

1. *The Skylight*

San Francisco, August 24, 1928. 2682 Union St. Three years ago or more I sat under this same skylight, with morning coffee,—gazing out over the bay,—writing, dreaming. In those days my writing was mostly in letters to Tina! Romantic days!

How very strange to be here once again: the same sirens warning the same ferry boats, the same fog drifting over to shroud the bay and obliterate the horizon. I loved this place. I sought it again,—and it was empty awaiting me.

Months have been crowded into weeks since leaving Glendale. I hesitated for long before deciding that I should be here during my exhibit: until the day before leaving I had not definitely made up my mind. Yet is that literally true? For all the while I knew I should and would make the trip.

Briefly, I found the stage all set for me to stay in San Francisco. Enough prints sold to give me ready cash, sittings dated, and Johan's studio empty until he returns from Carmel in October. He urged me to stay and make use of it.

We left our few belongings, drove to Los Angeles, again returning within four days with all necessities for a long stay,—and Cole!

I wanted to give the boy a long-promised trip,—his turn. But my imagination got the best of me. I did not foresee that work would keep me in that office all day, day after day. Cole got well tired out waiting around, and after two weeks, for the good of all, I shipped him home on the train.

Somehow I felt a change from Glendale was in order, that something was about to happen. If I had trusted my instinct, I would have come prepared, saving a hard trip there and back again.

The grind of work has been hard on me, especially my eyes. I have made more sittings in these few weeks than I made down south all this year. But I have accepted confinement gracefully, almost lightheartedly, whistling at my work as of old. Only a temporary physical and spiritual confinement I would say.

I am not broke! No worry about car payment this month. I would not go on this way,—no—death would be preferable.

But a pocketful of money means another temporary release: maybe to camp on the desert near those beloved rocks!

Sunday morning, August 26. Late last night, came Johan and Elsa from Carmel, both fairly well "lit."

"To celebrate getting away from the small town stuff of Carmel," said Johan.

I took a few drinks of gin to help meet their mood,—or rather his, for Elsa was wanting home and bed. And I was sleepy having been roused by the late arrivals. Johan was gay, but only Brett responded to his 2 a.m. desire to have ham and eggs at Tait's. If there had been a party on somewhere, with dancing, wine and women, I could have risen to some heights, but to sit in a public restaurant— where I am always out of place—did not appeal. But we went. Johan in such a state can be sweetly stubborn.

As usual he was a comedy,—stopped traffic with outstretched arms at a busy corner on Geary St. and blockaded a movie set in front of Hotel St. Francis.

I wanted to respond, but was frankly bored,—one must be in a like condition. Elsa was angry. Only Brett got a kick. It was a new story for him.

Friday, August 31. Besides about fifteen sittings from San Francisco, twenty prints sold,—five of them Brett's, totaling $211. Thirteen sold from East West exhibit on budget plan from which they took 50°/₀ commission accounting for the low total. But the most interesting and significant note in the sales is that all but the tree prints Bender [Albert Bender, San Francisco art patron] took, were purchased by children of eighteen or younger.

My faith in the new generation of Americans is maintained.

Mrs. Charles Liebman of New York purchased seven of my best prints, choosing with excellent judgment. I also sold her two of Henry's lithographs. Henry is devoting all her time to lithography and doing some fine things. She gave me two.

Mrs. Liebman is a friend of Stieglitz, and will show her prints to him. I wonder will he like them, and will he say so if he does?

After knowing Henry better, I am not so sure but that her estimation of Stieglitz is very much colored by her personal peeve, which would be natural, even as my own reaction followed Consuela's letter quoting Stieglitz' opinion of my work. I might have more simply said,—instead of exploding as I did—if Stieglitz likes my work I am happy, for I admire him,—if he does not, I'm sorry—for Stieglitz. The very fact that I bothered to notice his opinion shows that I did care.

But evidently the rumours of Stieglitz' favoritism, autocratic rule,—the ex-aggerated reverence demanded before the shrine of O'Keeffe and others are not unfounded,—they come from too many different sources: or else the gossip comes from envious inferiors.

Maybe Stieglitz is a Napoleon of art. Napoleon was a great man—to the masses— a spectacular figure to anyone. The popular tendency has always been to idolize spectacular leaders,—ruthless, selfish climbers, while the really great, the noble, but less dramatic are passed unnoticed. Even a Christ is forgotten unless his end is theatrical,—nailed to a cross, or somehow headlined.

70

No—Stieglitz, who has, or had, idealism could not in justice be so labelled. But it has come to me of late that comparing one man's work to another's, naming one greater or lesser, is a wrong approach.

The important and only vital question is, how much greater, finer, am I than I was yesterday? Have I fulfilled my possibilities, made the most of my potentialities?

What a marvellous world if all would,—could hold this attitude toward life.

September 4. What can be the matter with me?—This awful headache,—the nerves at the base of my skull: almost steady for over a week.

I have overworked, strained my eyes and nerves, in my desire to get ahead. I knew I was abusing myself, but thought to counteract by regular hours and much sleep. But every morning I awaken with this maddening tightness. I have not retouched for a week, yet I am no better. If I had the price, a chiropractor might slip something in place. I am usually able to cure myself.

And there is work ahead—retouching alas—which finished will bring me $100. I have a check for $110 due. With this in hand, I would close up until Monday—go to the warm hills, lie in hot sunshine. But rent is due, all first of the month bills, and we have nothing to live on. Brett and I walked home last night. Not a cent for car-fare nor supper.

September 6. Afternoon in the Post St. "Studio." My headache disappeared just now as if by magic. I am well enough to feel rebellious. I am afraid to start retouching again, afraid to work in darkroom, afraid to read, afraid to leave this office for fear of losing business. Why all this fear? Am I merely one of the millions of slaves who submit to the daily grind?! Shall I go on this way? Must I? No—I will not!—it is not my destiny. I am willing to work,—love work, but not this!

I must find a way out. I have spoken so before. But this is a climax. I cannot be a puppet to please the public's vanity—it is destroying me.

All this bowing and scraping to land an order, showing my work until I despise it. Straining eyes and nerves, destroying my health, degrading my spirit, all for the dollar.

To what purpose all this? For the boys? Yes, but am I better dead or alive? Johan returns soon. What then?

I must and will have peace and quiet, away from this dirt and noise, and contact with people. I want my mind in order, —not this chaos: a shack far away—no phone, water, gas, light bills,—no landlord.

I expect too much,—know this as I write. I am better off than most. Acclaim on every side, pilgrimage to see my work, praise, real devotion, women in love with me,—that I cannot care for—don't want—But what does it all mean? I want a chance to work, to contemplate that work, search myself, improve myself, fulfill the very reason for my existence.

The phone rang in my ears: The shock renewed my headache.

I must get hold of myself and go through this present hell. No one can do it for me!

Next day. I seem practically normal. Perhaps a $50 check helped cure me — — —

September 9. A new portrait of Johan, the finest I have made of him, is attracting much attention in the Post St. show case. I have also done a good portrait of Alan Seabrook,—and of Brett. Albert Bender got in range of my lens, while I was doing Mrs. Liebman. I made one negative, which he will not like,—it is too revealing, the skin texture quite marvellous.

So after all I have been working for myself, and rather pleased in doing new and strong portraits.

I would stay home and rest today but expect a check from Dan who bought three prints, then I can pay room rent.

Sunday. No check from Dan—he surely is away—for I know how he would come to my help: but Lula paid me $10 due on a shell photograph, so we eat over the holidays.

Johan will return soon now,—a change for me in order. I shall try my luck out here on Union St. Even if I leave S. F. it should not be until after the Xmas holidays.

I need money to start with: must have some furniture,—screens, mirror, stove. I can get away with a certain "Bohemian" atmosphere, but not quite with an empty room. Also I should have a show case on some important downtown street, quite an expense to make, and rent space. Then a phone is necessary. If I had even two hundred dollars to start with, I could have been successful without half killing myself.

Monday, September 10. Margrethe Mather here to buy antiques for a holiday shop. She spent Sunday with us. We drove to Golden Gate Park and spent hours in that marvellous place. The unbelievably exquisite butterfly fish, enormous turtles that swim like a bird flying, jolly bull frogs, sinister eels in their ritual dance, the seals! For exhilaration from sheer amazement—the aquarium! We returned here. I warmed Margrethe's soul with a bottle of gin. Five years ago, madly in love with her, what an exciting experience this would have been,— together in S. F.—far away from local discords. Now, light gossip, bantering, but not a thrill. What is love! Can it not last a lifetime? Will it never for me? Do I only fool myself, thinking I am in love, and really never have been?

And these girls, all friendly after,—corresponding, meeting. Does it indicate the affair was not so deep: otherwise might not the end come with an explosion, and a parting forever?

Supper here: that was the unanimous decision. The best restaurant pales before our banquets. Avocados,—Brett found at 5 cents each!—an enormous Persian melon, crisp lettuce and peppers, swiss cheese, rye-crisp, comb honey, kippered cod: all for less than $2. Who would eat out? Not since Mexico have I had aught alcohol on tap for my friends,—I never drink alone. My bootlegger calls every Monday to inquire for my health and suggest that I may have run out of gin over the week end. The order is delivered promptly to the front door, as casually as the grocer might bring a bottle of vinegar. This town is wet!

My bootlegger, who also supplies thirsty U. S. Senators, who vote dry, is a tall venerable Dutchman: always immaculately groomed, with high stiff collar, grey spats, gloves and stick. Before the important question, am I dry?—we chat for awhile,—current events, even art. His call is a social event, though he is a bit too sociable.

September 12. Last night rain fell to give San Francisco its first bath of the season. The heavens especially needed a washing. Fog had settled into every nook and crevice, houses, hills and heavens lowered in dismal grey. This morning all is sparkling and gay.

I delivered three prints yesterday as my entry in an international invitation salon at the Legion of Honor. I had thought that they were not inviting me because of prejudice toward my late work,—certainly it is not the same work once lauded by these same "pictorialists." But Imogen assured me that on the contrary I was now supposed to be quite aloof, rather contemptuous of others. I don't want that feeling about me. I would only remain aloof as a defense. I understood these photographers perfectly, but most of them could never understand me. So I have the more enviable position. I am willing to show in a "no jury" exhibit. I can stand comparisons.

"Ollas de Oaxaca," "Galván," and a shell,—these should hold the attention of even those who do not know why.

I started retouching again yesterday, and must continue today. So far my head remains clear.

Sunday morning. 6 a.m.—after 11 hours sleep! I needed it — — For the first time in my life I went down and out at a party—plain drunk I might as well say. And I got sick too,—perish the memory. I have phoned my apologies around, but that does not give me absolution nor erase my chagrin.

I don't remember passing out, but I vaguely see a compassionate girl hold a flowered bowl for my disgorgement, and wondering why she chose a thing so lovely for such a purpose.

It was a jolly party at Margaret Nicol's,—only nine of us. I took Elsa and Ida, or we did, for Brett drove. Walt Kuhn, painter, here from New York, Long-feather an Indian—I suppose a chief, they all are chiefs or princesses when they leave the reservation to exploit the poor whites—and—well I cannot recall the other names, were guests.

73

The episode of the evening for me was a dance with Margaret Nicol,—she a professional dancer. I can easily call it one of *the* dances of my life. We were both well "lit." I put on "La Pintura Blanca." It was perfect for both of us. Reservations were cast aside: I had heretofore made no gesture because of her lover. The dance became wilder, a mad whirl, kissing, biting, mauling,—ending by a crash to the floor with the last note, where we lay unable to move.

I needed just such an evening—a release from my sordid grind. I went hoping to become gayly borrachito,—not drunk.

No matter, I shall have pleasant memories.

Brett and the girls got me home. Never have I been so helpless before. Elsa swears I mixed drinks. I think not. I was depleted when I went there, and the bartender was too attentive.

Walt Kuhn is a person I hope to know better. A strong, vital, clear thinking type that will lay a foundation American art must grow from.

Sunday evening. Brett and I to the opening of the photographic exhibit at the Legion of Honor. I recall scarcely an outstanding print. The finest things there—as in Los Angeles—were Imogen's. The usual crowd of tired business men, lawyers and butchers who take up photography as a Saturday afternoon hobby, gathered to discuss composition.

But I'm glad I went for we met Walt Kuhn again, and wanted to. I like him,— like his talk. I asked him to sit to me,—he has a splendid head.

Monday—and fog again. I can't say I will be content here without more sunshine. Kuhn said, "America is the only place. I went to Europe recently and came away satisfied they had nothing more to give us. We can't go on painting imitation Rousseaus. . . .

"Stieglitz' work is too sentimental. He is colored by his racial background. People are no longer accepting without question his exaggerated publicity. He whines too much,—always complaining that people do not appreciate all he has done for art."

September 18. I lay in bed an hour listening to the moaning, groaning, wailing, shrieking from the fog-hidden harbour.

An order for $130 yesterday. I have $370 ahead from work finished or ordered. This is quite satisfying. Yet how am I to pay for the car and eat for the next week if nothing comes in? I suppose I should hold no doubtful thoughts. But I cannot help wondering!

Walt Kuhn came to visit and see my work. He said what Carl Zigrosser wrote me, that my photographs were the outstanding art expression he had seen in the West. It was my group of portraits he especially liked.

"The finest I have seen. No one has done anything like them," he said. "You should show these in N. Y. Just an exhibit of these portrait heads. There

74

will be no other work to compare them to. If you show your nudes, still-life, or industrial things, they will knife you, or even worse be so silent you will be utterly quashed. No matter if your things are better than another's, if there is any chance for comparison in subject matter or approach, they will get you. And it is perfectly natural. Their bread and butter are in danger. If you fail the first time in New York, you couldn't come back for ten years. Create your sensation with the heads,—*then* you can show anything."

Margrethe came in later. We had supper at Il Trovatore. Brett and I both agree to liking best our fruits and nuts and fresh greens. One does not feel all stuffed and bloated.

September 19. Another order in for $50—a total of $400 ahead—and checks received for $40. Though I have not enough for the car payment, the way ahead is clearer. Next month should be easy.

Last night to the Salingers',—a party of a dozen or so. Just the kind of a gathering I don't like,—circled in a little room, passing casualities with strangers, who might be delightful alone. Then heavy refreshments at midnight. Now I am up late, still sleepy and a big day ahead to get off the Liebman order to N. Y. I made some contacts of value and an invitation to talk before the art section of some refined Rotary Club!

It has been a long time since I have had the delights of love! Letters full of tender thoughts have come from K., B., and C. But one cannot live on such vicarious love. Twice I have noted indications of desire in rather interesting girls, but I have "manfully" resisted. Too busy, preoccupied, or indifferent,—the indifference maybe a result of the former condition.

September 20. How I sleep!—ten hours again last night, going to bed at 8:00. Eye-strain no doubt accounts for some of my drowsiness, but a less obvious reason is at the base,—sheer boredom, lack of any mental stimulation, the desire for oblivion.

I must retouch and print two orders today,—spot, mount, and deliver them to-morrow, hoping that I collect. I have put a larger previous order aside—these amount to only $60, because the latter have hardly any retouching—a child and a very sensitive man, Mr. Shevky. He is also a fine type,—a Turk, and discriminating. He purchased the head of Galván. I am later to visit his home in Mill Valley and make some outdoor heads in my favorite way.

Recently a strange episode took place, which suggests the old platitude, "The world's a small place after all," etc. A man came in to look at work whom I recognized in a flash as a boyhood playmate I had not seen for thirty years, or since I was twelve!

I was really startled, as though a ghost appeared.

75

"I know you," I said. "What is your name?" I did not need to ask, only to be formal, for he did not know me,—had been attracted by my work.

"Louis Edbrooke," he answered.

"I am Eddie Weston."

"Not Eddie Weston I played with in Chicago!"

Then followed reminiscencing, looking backwards to youthful days,—3975 Drexel Boulevard—once a fashionable street,——Gertrude, his sister, my first calf love,—Lake Michigan, playing in ice caves, jumping the ice floe,— fishing for perch in the sunrise,—the haunted barn. What child does not know some haunted place?

"I have not been in an artist's studio for years," said Louis.

"I am a realtor."

I suppose we only have the past in common now, and that cannot last long.

September 21. A hot day past. I guess it rose to the 80's,—really not so hot except by contrast. A check from Jake Zeitlen for $10. He sold a Roi Partridge etching from the consignment I left him. With what care did I buy that print ten years ago for the same ten dollars!

Now if I can deliver even the child portraits with a balance due of $10, I pay the car installment today. This continual dwelling upon money matters is devastating. My daily entries indicate a sordid state of mind. Only four more months and the car is mine,—only!

Mr. Dyer of *The San Franciscan* wishes a back stage photograph of a chorus rehearsing. With this in view we went to see *Good News*, a clever musical comedy,— funny, snappy, delightful, with a number of excellent ensembles. I can't remember having seen a musical comedy since I was a boy in Chicago, and a first nighter at the old La Salle theatre. I came away refreshed. Not a bad idea for a tired business man. Back stage life is fascinating. Plenty of good material. But I don't see how I can work with a slow lens and a hand flash gun.

4:30 a.m.—And I just got Johan off to an early start for Carmel. He has been here since Saturday. I am always happy to welcome him and relieved to say farewell!

He is packing now to return for good. Queer anomaly if Johan's return would eventually cause my departure! Our habits are so contrariwise — — —

He drinks—not heavily but continuously—which I cannot do,—and one does not easily say no to Johan. He loves restaurant life, which I cannot afford, nor like except on rare occasions. He is very European, and I am—?—not that, nor 100°/₀ American either.

I love the man, but we should not be together too much.

Walt Kuhn sat to me yesterday. He leaves Friday. I wish I had known him sooner: a type of American I like. German-Spanish parents, but American, a pioneer type of this continent, a forerunner of this new race. I think we could become good friends. He said again, with added significance, "Yours is the *only* real art I have seen on this coast. All the others are doing applied art."

He chose from my work, a head of Tina. He gave me a lithograph and promised an original drawing.

That backstage job was nerve wracking. I suppose one could get used to such work, or I could. The confusion,—shifting scenes, yelling orders, impatient chorus,—and the flash failed twice! But I have a rather spectacular, jazzy, negative to please the editor. Tomorrow I must talk before the Commonwealth Club. This week I must retouch and print five negatives in order to enrich myself to the amount of $150!

Wednesday. Por dios, what a damp morning. My leather coat is clammy, the sleeves stick to the table. Leather is not suitable for wear in S. F.

Went to see Emil Jannings in *The Street of Sin.* But I have seen enough of him. A clever actor, but too much sob stuff. Perhaps he is poorly cast by American directors. And yet when I remember the German film *The Last Laugh,*—that was just as sentimental. I can't see that Americans are more to be condemned for optimistic endings than Germans for their playing on one's tear ducts. Either becomes monotonous.

To mention Kuhn again, his remarks re my photographs, "I marvel that your work shows no Mexican influence, the superficial, romantic, picturesque side. Few can stand the life there and not be spoiled."

2. "Now that I stand almost alone—"

Thursday, September 27. Many mornings I wonder why I even start to write, with nothing worth recording in my humdrum existence. If it were not for my pot of coffee I am sure there would be no inspiration. The talk at the Commonwealth Club was announced as "Photography,"—it turned out to be "Mexico." I got in bad with Albert Bender by my attitude toward Diego, roasting all the worshipful disciples, "Little Diegos" springing up here and in Mexico, stating there were other painters of equal or greater import in Mexico, notably Orozco, that his [Rivera's] work had too much propaganda, sentimentalizing over the Indian. It seems Diego is sure to come here in November for a fresco commission, and the opposition is hungrily on the watch for any adverse remarks.

Kuhn phoned that he had been considering my situation and felt I must come to New York, that he would pave the way with talk. Fine fellow. Also said, he had bequeathed his harem to me,—given letters to a couple of girls. Fine fellow?! Yesterday a day of steady retouching. Today the same.

Friday. And the same today! Walt Kuhn came to say goodbye and so interrupted my routine. Two hours lost and two hours gained. His has been the most stimulating contact I have had for many months. Just because he rated my work so high? No. Praise can be boresome or of less interest than criticism. But I never meet valuable opposition, only the kind one wastes time with. Ten years ago, considering my attitude and technique, the right opposition might have been invaluable, but then I had only flattery from a lot of imitators,—now that I stand almost alone, the barking of these same people only wearies me. What I need now is someone to criticize my technique, urge me on to greater perfection. But since I know my own failings, even the latter is hardly necessary.

Yet I had a sort of opposition from Kuhn, for in considering my portraits my finest achievement, he gave me fresh interest in portraiture which I have been neglecting for still-life.

"Still-life is usually applied art, your portraits are fine art."

This thought, his enthusiasm comes at an opportune time, for I had already done several fine portraits recently,—Johan, Seabrooke, Bender. Albert does not want me to show his! A real document! I will have to put it away for secret enjoyment.

There will be some who no longer will hold a friendly and praiseful attitude toward me and my work. Heretofore I have been almost alone amongst photo-

78

graphers. Now the painters will ostracize me. Kuhn said, "I told a group of artists that there was one man out here, who had it all over them, saw ahead,— Weston."

"Artists" will never stand this. Kuhn and I are both finished with them! But I cannot be alarmed, for who is there I care for?

October 1. Saturday night Brett and I sailed away on the yacht *Flirt,*—guests of Dr. Eloesser. We had never met the doctor,— he knew us only through the East West exhibit, where he purchased two prints. He took a chance, inviting strangers, and we likewise as guests of a stranger. However, the night and day passed amicably enough.

I said we "sailed." The sails were raised but only flapped in a gentle breeze, and gasoline took us to the night's anchorage, far up the bay. A full moon shone,—when not befogged,—through floodlight into gloom we hugged the shoreline,—changeful, restful hours. To bed at 2:00, up at 7:00. Breakfast on the beach. Pork sausage and fried applies, cake, jam, and coffee. Washing greasy dishes in the ocean, hunting firewood,—a disagreeable waste of time! How differently Brett and I alone would have done it. Fresh and dried fruits, Brazil nuts, pecans, maybe an aguacate apiece,—we have found them quite inexpensive up here—then the waste overboard!

A roaring bonfire at night on the beach to gather around for good cheer— yes!—for frying apples and pork sausage—no! Destroying the flavour and goodness of a delicious apple, eating a dead pig! Well, we are the abnormal ones, cranks I suppose. The doctor enjoyed it and went out of his way to give us a good time.

The memorable hour of the day was after a dip in the bay,—loafing on deck naked in the sun and wind. What a tonic for weary minds and bodies! I hope to plan my life so that one hour every day can be spent naked in sunlight.

October 2. I have finished the order for Mrs. Walter Haas,— eight prints, $110. If she pays at once, my first of the month debts and a few old ones will be cleaned up. Also printed one negative of Kuhn—the one he liked best. It is good, all but the back sleeve line.

I recall another comment of his. I said, "Once my aim was to interpret, now, to present." He chuckled. "You only think you 'present'. This work could not be done, unless you had been through the other. Let a commercial photographer present, and see the result." Well, words can make a mess of thoughts. Of course I meant presentation through *my* eyes. I might have elaborated on my thought, made it clearer.

Once my aim was to interpret a mood, now to present the thing itself.

I will have imitators who will "present" atrocities. Better if they stay with their moods.

October 4.—And the beginning of our new venture at 2682 Union St.—the end of Room 404, 117 Post.

Johan phoned yesterday noon from Carmel that he was moving his laboratory up, would arrive that night.

I finished retouching, directed Brett in some printing, packed nearly everything, changed P. O. address, showcase, took a last hot sponge-off in the dressing room, God knows where or when I'll have hot baths again, and was ready to help Johan move up and myself down when he arrived at 9:00.

Rain this morning. I awakened with a tight head from yesterday's strain.

Johan sleeps. He will stay here until an apartment is found. He is a sick man, coughed all night. He cannot last many years,—or less than years, this way.

Such confusion! No place to put things, no furniture,—the floor a dumping ground. I don't like it. I have an appointment for a sitting with Margaret Nicol at 10:00, at my request and expense. Why I invited her is yet to be seen. A poor day to work: rain and the room a chaos.

October 5. As I worked with Nicol, the tightness in my head vanished. Music and dancing!—The excitement of capturing evanescent gestures!—I became one with the transient moment and worked en rapport. After came a let-down when I viewed the room, strewn with everything from clothes to chemicals, and no closet nor drawers to store in,—and no money to buy the cheapest secondhand furniture. Money, always money!—After all, I have nearly $300 to collect. But it must come soon — — —

What a relief not to look forward to a day in the office. Johan, Elsa, Brett and I went to Pantages, after a good dinner at Coppa's, —went to see Mae Murray dance. She was worthwhile, lovely, joyful, and a fine dancer. The rest of the bill was amazingly stupid, with not even the interest from crude presentation,—one recalls *Don Juan Tenorio* at the Teatro Hidalgo.—Last night was just pretentious blah. — — — What do the skulls of those applauding people hold?

October 6. Our first day here,—warm, sunny, joyous. A great deal was accomplished: the darkroom ready for work. Brett developed three dozen negatives of Margaret Nicol,—he does most of my developing now, and does it well.

A staged dance may be artificial, and this dance before my camera could be called staged. But she well forgot the camera, and the negatives show spontaneity. There are a number that I may use for myself,—better things than one usually sees of the kind,—rhythmical, feelingful. Technically, they are extraordinarily uniform in excellence, sharp and well timed: 1/5 second exposures at f/4.5 with new Dupont panchros, which are faster than E. K. Co. They are more likely to have imperfections though.

A letter from Jean Charlot, enclosing a new print, and a beauty. He will soon be in New York,—and hopes to see me there! Might as well hope to see me in Mexico!

80

Johan groans from a troubled sleep: always he is tortured at night. He came home last night well lit, and orated for an hour while I tried to keep awake. He can be cruelly analytical with a few drinks, and his ego rises to extraordinary heights. But stray remarks reveal him, possessed with a devastating inferiority complex. He delivers a tirade against those who are trying to "work" him, especially on the subject of women.

I may see as clearly, but am more likely to shrug my shoulders. I seldom antagonize people by a frank opinion as he does, so I am more generally liked. Maybe I show myself the weaker in this respect. I keep my thoughts to myself.

How could I tell Johan himself, that his work does not thrill me, not often. What good would it do? It would hurt him, and he could not change if he would. I could tell Brett frankly my opinion, or Tina, both my apprentices, I could tell Henry, would have, about the seals, if I had seen it in preparation,—but with Johan I find myself silent. His work must be always colored by his weakness.

October 9. Mrs. Kytka, our good landlady, considered renting "my" room to a dressmaker for $100 a month with a ten year lease. We were all rather distressed, awaiting her decision, which finally was no. "I like artists around, I have the soul of an artist."

I must live up to my label!

And I fear we can have no gay parties here, for she also likes "quiet, respectable people."

I will go to great lengths to keep this place, so ideal for work, and a continuous joy to live in.

Yesterday I made 1/10 second exposures, holding the camera, and got very good negatives. A business man, Walter Haas, sat to me. He came, figuratively speaking, with watch in hand, and left on the run. A fine way to respect my work, expecting me to make a living, lasting portrait. I fired away, and surprised myself with results.

Later came Otis Oldfield, an artist Kuhn is interested in. He wants to "put him over in New York."

Oldfield wanted a portrait in a hurry too, for an article about his work. I liked the way he approached me, asking an exchange, and though I did not know his work, wanted to help him out.

Kuhn said to me, "He is the only other artist on the coast doing anything creative. It is not great work, but honestly his own."

A funny little shrimp,—Oldfield. Imagine me being able to call anyone a "shrimp!" Wisps of long hair straggle over his baldish pate, an enormous Adam's apple wobbles around as he sucks a pipe, he speaks in a rather selfless, appealing way, wanting so much to be friendly. One feels like mothering him! I can see that he will do his part on an exchange, for seeing my prints tied in wrapping paper, he offered at once to make three portfolios. "You and Brett will come to our home for supper this week? No spread, just what we would have, but you might like a little home atmosphere."

Brett and I are forever being pitied for the way we live! And we prefer our way and are quite happy!

An order in yesterday for $70. Today we have 50 cents. Yet counting this order I have over $400 coming in.

Johan groans and coughs, sleeping. A sick man, and depressing to be near.

October 10. Our last 50 cents gave us a good supper,—1/4 [pound] of butter to eat with some rye-crisp we had, a package of raisins—15 cents, the balance in bananas: the most filling meal for the money we could plan. But what about today! I could fast till tonight when we dine with Oldfield, but I want Brett satisfied.

I made a couple of heads of Oldfield, either of which I can add to my personal collection, augmenting it. Now to print one today in a hurry, and to print the $70 order, which I retouched yesterday. I have never gotten work off in such a rush,—so promptly. I have only one objective, to get hold of some money. —

October 11. A gale whipped up a sea of whitecaps last night, and cleared the distance of all "atmosphere." Mountains barely seen before appear quite neighborly. Otis Oldfield has a finer vista than we, from his shack on Telegraph Hill. All the great ships dock under his window, ferry boats spread out fanwise, packed with weary commuters, bound for the city's bedrooms,—Oakland, Berkeley, Sausalito. Shunting freight cars crash,—a confusion of lights, moving, flashing,—horns, shrill or deep, toot and moan,—a modern symphony. And the sour odor of wine press is on the air. Ours is a comparatively respectable and "burgess" community,—quiet, orderly. Yet the confusion of sounds from Telegraph Hill cannot be so startling as the Union St. car, clattering, groaning up the grade in the dead of night.

A rather jolly place Oldfield has, stimulating to visit, though our place is more conducive to serenity of thought.

His wife, heavy with child, served supper, and went to great lengths in the preparation. And there was good wine.

I agree with Kuhn that Oldfield is the best man here,—that I have seen. An experimenter, and a hard worker. His drawings, notes on the life seen from his window, especially the boats, were exceptional. He became a different person with his work,—more positive. He actually seemed to grow in stature!

October 12. The $70 order ready to mount for delivery this noon, and $80 order in from Walter Haas.

A sitting yesterday from a Spaniard, a painter who knows many of my friends from his Paris and New York days,—Diego, Jean, Miguel,—Sr. Moya del Pino.

82

My total ahead when delivered passes the $500 mark! And yet we are broke. Mr. Haas wants his prints in a hurry. Another concentrated effort ahead. I am weary of rushing. Another dance, and a bottle of wine, and a girl to love is what I need. The latter has not yet appeared on the horizon.

October 15. Always—and at the right time—my wishes are fulfilled: last night I took A. into my arms, and found her lips were waiting mine. . . .
We met two days ago at Margaret Nicol's.
Hardly a word was exchanged that night, but I noted her beauty of face and form, her fresh loveliness and refinement. We drove her home, and parting, I read her eyes. Next day, all day, she haunted me, until I called up Margaret to get her telephone. We planned a day together—lucky that Sunday followed—a day far away in the hills, lying in the sun, dreaming, each knowing well the others thoughts and desires,—and yet I did not touch her,—could not. I am always so, I cannot be aggressive. But I knew the evening was ahead!—and I would have surprises for her: music, a bottle of wine, the beauty of my room. And how we danced!—with the ecstacy of knowing, yet waiting the moment. What an incorrigible romanticist I am. Who would not be with A.! Rich chestnut eyes,— frank, open eyes, golden hair to match, a slender, almost fragile body, yet well rounded,—seldom does one see more exquisite legs—and sensitive hands. All this is A. plus the freshness of youth. She may be virginal,—I almost think so. She is only twenty,—which means nothing, but seems untouched,—mentally wise but bodily inexperienced.

So I have what I wished for in my last entry,—dancing, wine, and a lovely girl. And to make my happiness complete, a check for $120, and new orders to $100.

Friday. A. came to supper Wednesday eve. We served one of our typical meals: a dish of avocados,—five of them, which may have appeared extravagant for a poor artist but cost only 10 cents each, a big bowl of cottage cheese, rye-crisp, gorgonzola, plenty of greens, muscats turned almost to raisins, and coffee with honey.

Later who should appear but Margaret and Irving, surprised I'm sure to find who was with me. Dancing followed,—the tango, the danzón, and A. and I renewed our episode of Sunday. She is, I am sure, quite as excited as I am,—and that is enough! We are to have a dance, Saturday night, for which I have a gallon of Burgundy, and Sunday A. will come here. I await what should be our day!

The *Evening News* has made arrangements with me to photograph prominent San Franciscans for a series of articles to be published daily for a month or so. They are to make all arrangements,—bring them here, and give me important publicity. I of course take a chance on orders. Whether I get cash returns or not,

I will be quite well-advertised. The idea was hatched between Irving and Millie Bennet, who presented it to Reed Hayes. I dread the confusion of a sitting a day, the rush and added expense, perhaps without immediate returns. But I must do something to give me a more definite place here.

October 24. What a dawn! I thought of Whistler,—then knew I was wrong. It had not the elusive, befogged quality of a Whistler: rather, a rich, black, clean-cut solidity,—heavily clouded but brilliantly clear. Ferries slipped quietly through glassy water, lights of the night still sparked on far away shores. Peace!—no moaning horns, alarming shrieks of danger.

I have been busy enough God knows: two more sittings, one a resitting of Mrs. Stern,—another failure, bad luck!—the other a direct result of my article in *Creative Art.* Also sold a print to a New York man through the same source, and answered another inquiry.

Saturday night our first party here. Just Margaret, Irving, A., Brett, and Edward with a gallon of Burgundy. We danced—A. and I—and loved till I was sick of love—in a flame! Then Margaret suggested a drive to the beach, a run on the sands.

"Stay with me," I said to A.

"No, not tonight, I have complications. I'll tell you why later," she answered. O hell, I thought, another virgin with inhibitions. I will not try much longer. But I wanted her. I was full of passion. . . .

We drove far and fast, seventy the hour at times, until kisses became more like clashing of teeth. And then she left me.

She came next day with evident desire, and I said to her, "I want you, do you want me?" "Yes—I did not stay last night, because we had been drinking, and because the others would guess. I am not an exhibitionist." I liked her delicacy of attitude though it certainly was hard on me and took the edge off our first coming together. I was fooled. She was not a virgin, no indications at least. Maybe I am lucky, there will be no tears and regrets. But she gives me much beauty, and I have desire to reach a closer understanding and finer rhythm with A.

October 26. A new experience is mine! I am wiser than I was.

And sadder?—not so very much—a little though. I will miss her dancing most of all. We danced well together, A. and I. An impassioned courting—the surrender—then the rocks! Sunday night after she had left I was just dozing off, feeling rather balmy over my success, when the phone buzzed—I have it well muffled.

"Is Miss ——— there?"

"No."

"Do you know where I can reach her?"

"No."

84

I hung up and dove into bed. Again the phone—this time I was asleep—and rather peeved to shiver in my nakedness.

"Is Miss ——— there?"

"No!"

"A friend of hers is dying—are you sure she is not there?" Now I was angry,— being called a liar—indirectly, though I would have said "no" if she had been here! I hung up abruptly. But now I was wide awake and smelled a rat.

A jealous lover, of course! Well I want no triangles,—no one is worth such a mess.

Two days later, a note from A., certain things had happened, and she thought best not to come out again, regrets, etc.

The name given me over the phone was someone Lula Boyd knew. I will go to her, perhaps she will enlighten me. She did!

A. had been using me to incite jealousy, or perhaps using both of us. So thought Lula. She told the whole long story, in confidence.

Who would have thought it of you, A.?

Well, I shall be fortified if you should change your mind or heart and come again — — — —

October 27. The broken rhythm has let me down. I am not so depressed as I am wistful. I play *Horas Tristes* that we danced so often together, wondering what next. I was gay and happy these last weeks, I needed just what A. gave me, to relieve the daily drudgery. It surely was not real love I felt for her, I was in love with the idea. But what is love? What has happened to the many girls I have thought I loved? Is love like art—something always ahead, never quite attained? Will I ever have a permanent love? Do I want one? Unanswerable questions for me!

I have been working very hard. Another fifty dollar sitting paid this time in advance! !Qué milagro! I sent forty-five to Edith and Abad—the balance due on Essex. What a relief—though it leaves us almost broke. I could not delay longer—they needed it. Now we have only three more payments, $165, to make. Never again things on time: the strain has been killing. I felt the car possessed me! Now will I be glad to have it? For Brett—yes.

October 29. Sunday found Johan, Brett & me—with no females—by the seaside: a quite perfect day, a restful day. Men alone are more honest,—women I grant the same. No reason for smart persiflage,—effort to strut at one's best. Just a relaxed indifference,—each fellow for himself, yet part of an understanding whole.

We drove to Moss Beach,—walked far down the shore line: low tide bared rocks and sea growth,—the colors and forms were amazing. A pool left by the receding water tempted: we stripped and plunged into the chill water, then danced and ran over the sands.

Homeward bound, an unexpected thrill,—too much thrill. Fog—such fog as I had never experienced. The powerful spotlight barely found the roadside to keep us from going over. Once I thought we were gone, but Johan shouted and the brakes held.

Today I have more desire to go on with the grind.

October 31. A tragic day passed.

Mrs. Stern phoned for another sitting. I was pleased that she still had confidence after two failures.

She was two hours late in her appointment,—which meant that I paced the floors two hours. I can start no other work when awaiting a sitting. Profuse apologies, and I suppose legitimate excuses on her part: but she did not feel she should sit, having another appointment at 12:00.

"I could give you fifteen minutes if you think it worth while."

"Let us try, Mrs. Stern, we might get something."

I knew she might not come again, for she was leaving for Paris in a week. I was prepared: background placed, camera focussed on Brett in advance, film loaded, even the slide drawn. I knew she would be hurried, though hardly prepared mentally for such a rush. I did not intend to fail this time. I would gamble wildly to catch a certain expression—that was my problem—before she froze. I made three dozen negatives in that 15 minutes. I worked well, and she responded. I was rather pleased when she left. I knew I had done well. I visioned any order from $100 up.

I developed,—and my tragedy was revealed. I had grabbed one of the exposed magazines again, and double-exposed, ruining twenty-four possibilities!

Strange with what indifference I viewed the debacle — — —

But last night I walked far and went to a cheap movie for diversion.

I have had a definite feeling that my contact with A. was not over: that she would return, and that she was not merely using me. I know when a woman really cares. There came a beautiful letter while I was developing. Maybe my indifference to the tragedy was due to the renewed joy this letter brought. She did not ask to return. She did express her love and sorrow, and hope of forgiveness for the hurt. I would not have liked an open request for return. But A. is too fine for that.

I admit I want her. She complements me well.

We walked by Lula's last night. I stopped to ask her to join us for supper. A. had talked with her! And Lula had changed her mind. "She sincerely cares for you. I misjudged her." It seems Lula is destined to be the mediator.

86

I wrote A. I did not ask her to return. But I told her I had no bitterness, and would make no embarrassing gesture if perchance we met. She, if wise, can read between the lines. She will. We are fated to be together again. And maybe the stronger for this test.

But A. must make the first move, and show me clearly her desire.

November 2. Merle Armitage, Fay Fuguaey, Jake Zeitlin and Edith, surprised me Wednesday, on their way south after a three thousand mile auto trip.

All work stopped, a gallon of wine ordered, a party sprung, after a dinner at Coppa's.

I have laughed a lot: Merle has a Rabelaisian tongue.

Merle took us to some friends of Jake's in Berkeley, radicals. I felt far removed from the group that gathered, as far as I would from the bourgeoisie! Much poetry was recited, all seemed to be doing it, I might have belonged twenty years back. The host gave an oration which in content and delivery could have been from a Baptist preacher. I see no difference. I left early!

Today starts the first of my sittings for the *San Francisco Daily News*: George Noville—one of the transatlantic fliers. I hope I can enter into the spirit of this adventure, make each sitting a personal experience, try to do something for myself. Otherwise my spirit, already low from too much drudgery, may flop lower.

November 3. Two sittings yesterday: an elderly lady,—kindly but homely, so conscious of her age and looks that I had to make 1/5 sec. exposures before she froze, and Lt. Noville whom I tried to do in front of a great amphibian plane. The light was flat,—deadened with rain clouds. I made three negatives, and then returned to work here. It grew so dark I could not see to focus,—exposures with lens open were 10 sec.—and they may be underexposed.

A bad beginning for my *News* series!

If the elderly lady is pleased, she is the kind who will replenish my pocketbook. After all my hard work I am precariously low in cash. Money seems hard to get hold of, people reluctant to part with it. One bill of $60 due since August, another for $100 due since September.

Johan has moved. We have less confusion,—more room!

Sunday, November 4. Very low yesterday: possessed by a mood, rare for me. I may grumble and worry about money or lack of opportunity to work, but I seldom give up, quit the job,—certainly not when quitting means actual money loss. I was calm about it,— gave up a chance to do Mrs. Stern over,—a last chance, put aside proofs that must be out today if I am to get an order in at all, said to Brett, "I am going—where—I don't know—come if you wish." We locked up and walked for miles in silence. Finally I said, "Shall we stop at Lula's, take her out to supper?" The logical sequence to an unfinished episode happened. A. was there, —is living with Lula!

They insisted we stay for supper. I felt the strain of changed conditions—last time we parted from the bedside! but considering all, the evening was a jolly one, A. is a lovely child, attentive and tender. We parted late. Next!

November 5. A seeping, sopping, sodden day. The whining, yapping, roaring from the Bay sounds like a wild animal zoo at the feeding hour.

I am pretty well fed up on fog and gloom. A little southern sunshine—even with heat—would be welcome. . . .

I have returned to my old habit of early awakening: 4:00 found me wide-eyed. I tried in vain to lose myself. I did not want to face the day's issues so early.

Printed yesterday, and was sick at heart,—or stomach, after. Yet why blame myself for those poor negatives: one of the three dozen in 15 minutes group of Mrs. Stern,—another made before I realized that these yellowish walls would not give enough contrast as background. The only print that half way pleases is of Lt. Noville. Yes—another, A. prone in the grass, sunlit. Just a sentimental record. M. said, "Looks as though she had been knocked cold." Meow!

A. told Lula, M. is sore at her "because she wanted an affair with me." I had not sensed this, because it had not occurred to me, not seriously.

I have no illusions about the women who fall in love with me. I am in the same boat with the man of wealth. He attracts with gold, I with the glamor which surrounds me, much as the torero or champion pugilist or matinee idol fascinates. Women are hero worshippers. I suppose it has a biological reason, and unconscious selection of the finest type—according to their light—as a father.

I would like to be loved for myself: which means I would like to be a highly sexual animal. But would I? We can't have everything!

I am a poor lover, in that I have no time nor desire for sustained interest. I make a grand beginning, then lose out through indifference. The idea means more to me than the actuality. . . .

My ego is gratified by all these easy conquests over the cream of the crop,—many of them I know to be girls not easily persuaded.

I "kid" myself, and yet I don't. If anything should give me honest satisfaction, it is the friendship, and regard these women feel for me after all passion is over.

Wednesday. Election day Nov. 6, will be a long remembered date: not because of the election. I believe it was said last night that Hoover swept the country. A sad commentary upon the American people, indicating a smug conservatism, fear of change, lack of the spirit of adventure. Probably the Democrats would have thieved as readily as the Republicans have, but conditions could not be much worse. Al Smith represented danger,—radicalism to the mass mind, and fear was in the hearts and bellies! So they will go on, thankful to own a tin Ford, (the new ones are quite as tinny) have 10 cents for a "talkie," and drink synthetic gin. Smith could not have changed anything, but a vote for him symbolized desire!

Well, the election was only a casual note in the background of my busy yesterday. Gertrude Atherton sat to me in the morning, another casual note, except for the amazement, chagrin, and inner laughter when I met her. I knew nothing about the lady nor her looks,—but she was California's famous female novelist. I looked forward with interest to meeting and sitting, ready to welcome some forceful Amazon. I could not believe my eyes, when Squires from the *News* introduced a watery, washed out, squat scrubwoman, bursting out of her bespangled evening gown. She sat, or slumped down, pulled the gown off her shoulders, exposing a lump of fat at the base of her straw colored, unkempt crown, removed her glasses and said, "Do me from this side, my hair is better, (it shot out in all directions) and I am always taken in profile."

I could have done a beautiful caricature for myself. I did something better calculated to fill my pocketbook.

Then came the next casual note: Oldfield painted my portrait. It was very bad in every way. Why painted portraits in this day of the camera? I say this in the face of even the greatest contemporary painters.

Finally the last incidental garnish to a memorable day. A Japanese evening at The Womens' City Club. I took Lula and A. The artist of the evening demonstrated his way of working. But, shades of Hokusai, why copy the manner of those great men of another day?

The Japanese music was fairly interesting. I have heard much better. But I was not bored, for all the time A. sat next to me, and I felt a definite response.

The plan had been to have coffee after the show, somewhere in town, and listen to returns. But the Hoover landslide had killed all interest, the streets deserted early.

"Come out to the studio," I said, "We'll dance and open a bottle." Everyone was delighted,—especially myself!

I started a danzón. Once in my arms I knew she was mine again,—and Oh, what a dance — — — "Are you glad you came A.?" "Yes."

November 7. A check for $80, still due, counting orders unfinished, $420. But no new sittings ahead, excepting those on *News* schedule. Today, a Mrs. Kahn just re-elected to Congress. I hope she is an improvement on "Gertie" —

No love affair in years has so deeply moved me as this with A. and the renewal was more profound than the beginning. I had felt at the start that she, though excited and responsive, was withholding something of herself. But the coming together of the other night was perfect. She completely surrendered. A sweeping, surging, unrestrained rhythm coursed between us: we two became as one. That ride home in the back seat, Lula and Brett to the fore: what exquisite intoxication.

—this moment she phoned—and will come here tonight — — —

November 9. Mrs. Florence F. Kahn I liked immediately: an unaffected, human person, with broad vision and keen wit. If I were a voter I likely would cast my vote for her! Unless I am greatly mistaken she will not want to appear twenty years younger than she is, not in life nor in her photographs.

Squires told me Gertrude Atherton was seventy-one: which certainly amazed me. I would have guessed under sixty. Of course she has had her face lifted, and I'm sure wants to simulate fifty. This lying about one's age nauseates. Even when it cuts off ten years—apparently—one senses a sham and instinctively recoils.

I would never retouch proofs for Mrs. Kahn, removing the last vestige of age the way I did before sending Gertrude Atherton's.

Brett went away for the evening so A. and I were alone to talk.

She will be my mistress, wants to be, cares for me,—but Lula does not approve. This is not going to be pleasant,—she is living with Lula. Probably Lula is being ethical, A. must have talked with her as with me: that she cares for this boy who has gone away for a year or two, but sees no reason why she should be true for so long a time.

I, of all persons, have no right to complain, not when I have had three affairs at once, three or a half dozen! Yet my ardour is somewhat cooled. I want to be the whole thing, or at least not second fiddle, which I very likely am.

I am basically constructive, much of the home builder in me. Many would laugh to hear this, but I feel it is so—I pretend to myself—not always—that this affair—the latest—is a lasting one. I start to construct the future—I believe in my plans. I would take A. out of her office work, teach her photography, make her independent of a job. But how can I build enthusiastically, knowing some one else is in the background.

Yet my whole reasoning becomes ridiculous in the face of my past record. And how can I promise anyone anything—with four boys to consider!

Saturday, November 10. An adventure ahead: A., Brett, and Edward leave for Carmel this noon, to stay until Monday night. A vacation, Armistice Day, gives A. three days in succession. Johan has given me the key to his studio and home. A phonograph is there, all necessary bedding—and two beds! surely I will not sleep with Brett—a cozy fireplace will cheer us, books—but who will read! Even the kitchen stove is ready — — —

Too bad that it rains today. The weather has been perfect. Rain may be romantic, but it also means Brett will be shut in with us. Not so good for love, even when the third person is sympathetic.

90

I am told that Gertrude Atherton, besides having her face lifted, tried gland rejuvenation. Considering again my reaction to her, it was this: that here was a woman, prematurely old. Instead I was meeting a woman unnaturally young. The effect was horrible. Such people only fool themselves.

November 14. The weekend of A. and Edward is now a memory,—a rare and perfect one. Hours of exquisite delight for me,—and I am sure for A. too,—seeing, feeling, her response.

I have had women, burning with passion, women stirred with romance, sensual women: but no one who has quivered in my arms so sensuously responsive to my caresses as this slip of a girl.

So—my own approach being sensuous rather than passionate, the union was well-nigh perfect.

We danced!—tangos & danzóns: A. is always ready to dance. Jean Roy furnished a bottle of wine, "to help along a good cause." The second night a few glasses at Ray Boynton's fanned the flame—though fanning was superfluous—and the last night a bottle of gin found in Johan's cupboard cheered our departure. A roaring grate fire fed by driftwood was the focus for lazy, dreamy hours: we kept it crackling day and night—

Acordate—Mocosita—Sonsa—Horas Tristes!—music that will always recall you, niña de la primavera!

Going—on the San Juan grade we had a rather terrifying experience: our lights burned out. Fog, nighttime, and a tortuous road with no lights. Two women driving alone were just ahead.

"Christ! Do not let them get away, Brett!"

For harrowing miles we followed them to a service station at the grade's end.

Sunday, November 17. A busy week last,—rushing again—and I had promised myself not to rush, but what was I to do with two orders which must reach N. Y. before the 23rd or miss the parties who then sail for Paris: and miss my pay! Next week will be heavy too. Monday Alfred Hertz, symphony leader, and two sittings for myself,—Hertz coming from the *News.* I have had no sittings for myself the last two weeks, bad business. Albert recommended me to the proximate sittings. Bless him!

The two last sittings from the *News* were Thomas W. Hickey, politician, who seconded Al Smith's nomination, whom I photographed standing, head raised—perhaps in oratory—to hide a heavy jowl: and Wm. P. Stanton, labor leader. Of Stanton, I made some corking things,—fine characterizations, and good negatives. A tall, loosely-knit, jovial person, with a contagious smile, which I captured,—a typical labor leader.

A. came to supper last eve. We became gay with wine and wound up at Margaret's, dancing until 2:00. These diversions are most salutory for me. She is coming this afternoon, and will sit to me. Question—will the sitting be incidental?

November 18. All else was incidental to the sitting. She had to leave early, and we were both wan and weary from the night before. But I worked well, despite, and have her, —captured that childlike loveliness,—golden hair circling her face like a halo, frank, tender eyes, wistful smile: eyes and mouth that fooled me, so virginal they are. Yet they will never grow sophisticated, never hard, calculating: too sensitive, too delicate her gestures and attitude toward life.

November 20.—from the *News*, came Alfred Hertz. I told him he was worse than a business man, for after ten minutes he had to go. I was disappointed, having looked forward to this sitting as offering possibilities for myself. That great bald dome of his and grotesque body could have given me some hours of exciting work. Considering the negatives, I have not failed.

In the afternoon two sittings for myself. Jews they were,—most of my sittings have been Jews, certainly the best ones.

So I had a busy, wearing day, for orders had to be finished as well.

November 21. General Ligget was my last *News* sitting, and one of the most enjoyable. I have an ingrained antipathy for the military, so was happily surprised. I know nothing about him, but can well imagine him to have been a very human sort as an officer: yet those piercing eyes and firm jaw indicate command.

I am quite interested in this series: so many walks of life represented, and each person a leader in their way,—if not a great one. If only one order would come in to pay my expenses! The old refrain is due to be sung—"Car payment in arrears and how can I meet it?"

November 22. Hail! Emil Jannings!

I saw him in *The Patriot* last night. My recent reaction was swept aside by his great portrayal of the mad Tsar,—acting so vivid it became actuality. I became so absorbed as to forget stage artifice, all means to the end. I could not analyze. Jannings must have lived the part, and I lived the moment with him.

I came near to missing *The Patriot*, for I confused the title with *The Last Command* which I had seen and was not greatly enthused over. But Brett wanted to go, and A. said it was her favorite picture,—which surprised me. Well—I thought—I will not be bored, I want a chat with my lady anyhow. Imagine my surprise and delight when a new and exciting film unreeled before me.

Monday, November 26. Rabbi Newman sat to me: the *News* again. A vain, sleek, self-satisfied person,—a poseur, probably so flattered, that he now believes in his pose.

92

Yesterday might have been worse than many another day, but for my mental state, my fierce rebellion.

Today, with no material change—still waiting—I have calmed down: but it is a hard, cold calm. I have drafted an "appointment card," to be sent in advance to all prospective sittings, stating clearly my terms. There will be no loophole to escape payment when prints are ready, and a check will be due at time of sitting as well.

And I have thought out a plan to go into effect if I am ever independent enough to carry it out. All those rich enough to be rated over, say $10,000, will pay five times what the poor pay. In other words I openly make the rich pay for my losses on the poor,—the latter being usually the ones who really want my work, understand it, and sacrifice to have it.

I am having another reaction, from my statement that I could go through life with one woman! Ridiculous thought! Imagine never again having the thrill of courting,—the conquest,—new lips to find,—new bodies to caress. It would be analogous to making my last print, nailing it to the wall forever, seeing it there, until I would despise it or no longer notice it was there. No!—let me stay free!

I have been re-reading *South Wind*, Norman Douglas, started in Mexico, but unfinished when I left there: a delightful book! I chuckle continually. The discourses of Count Caloveglia fit in with my present state of mind: chapter 10, on the strenuous northerner,—a pretty picture of what I am now, but will not remain!

These *News* sittings have been an education to me. Yesterday I had an appointment with Judge Waste, Chief Justice of the Supreme Court—California. Having the same antipathy for courts as I hold toward the military, I had built up a stone wall around me, expecting some pompous, arrogant person, whose first word would antagonize me. Instead, I found the Judge a most agreeable, human individual, with whom I had a fine contact, whose first greeting immediately broke down my barrier. I am being broadened by these contacts, and the expense I am under I will not charge to advertising, but to education.

November 29.—Thanksgiving Day. Shall I count my blessings? Easy to find I suppose: health fairly good in spite of minor dissipations—food in pantry—near owner of a Packard car!!! Brett as a pal and co-worker—A. as a novia—my work considered by some few as the most important on this coast.

But when I think of my work, I slump mentally, spiritually. Not a pretty picture, this year compared to last. 1927—when I jumped eagerly out of bed to study last night's negatives, or a new shell, vegetable, fruit: 1928—when I lie in bed wondering if a check will arrive "in time." 1929 must bring a change — —
I finished and took to "mi niña" one of her new portraits. It could be sentimental,

will be thought so by most of my friends. I say "could be": if I had told her, "Now put your hands so, under your chin, and register dreaminess," then it *would* have been. But the actuality was quite different. She sat there in the sunlight, waiting, dreaming: perhaps her thoughts were of me, maybe—more likely—far away with another love,—it makes no difference, I saw a moment, lovely but not banal, and caught it.

More difficult this, more subtle, than to record an heroic head of a strong man. There is danger in always searching for obviously powerful subject matter, or using obviously perfect forms.

November 30. My holiday spent at hard labor: retouching an order for one print to be done by Saturday, and making a sitting from which a glossy print must be ready today! Where are all my resolutions not to rush?

Well, the last rush order delivered yesterday afforded me a pleasant surprise. Mrs. Schwartz had not been overly pleased with her proofs but ordered ten prints nevertheless. Ten minutes after the chauffeur called for them she phoned. My heart sank—a complaint probably—my own reaction to the work—though they were flattering portraits—colored my imagination—as it often does.

Instead—"I want to thank you for the perfectly beautiful prints, they are so much better than I hoped for. And please send me a bill!!"

This made me happy, especially after a mean experience with a cheap woman who runs an expensive tea room. She caught me when I had to have money, claimed I overcharged and forced me to reduce my bill for a copy. I wish I had been in an independent mood! But I shall have my revenge by writing her my opinion. A waste of time, for on her thick hide my sarcasm will make no impression.

3. *Weary of Cities*

December 5. In less than three weeks we will be in Los Angeles to spend Xmas with the family unless some large order delays us, and if we have the price of gas and a new battery.

A new sitting dated for tomorrow, and a duplicate order for $50, yet not a check in lately. If Cristal with her usual thoughtfulness had not sent $5, we would be broke! A ridiculously ironical situation,—$600 standing out, after weeks of steady grind,—to be penniless.

We went with Johan to Carmel Sunday, —he drove as well, gathering together as much of his household effects as we could crowd into and tie onto the two cars. A hurried and wearing trip, quite a contrast to the last episode with A. But I was glad to help Johan. Returning we found Peter and Rose here, with the ceremonial chest for Rabbi Newman. We were together last eve, first here, then at Henry's. She is becoming more impossible than ever to be around, or else I have less patience, the fresh interest of a new conquest having worn away. Peter brought photographs of late work, especially a group in brass, an important piece with a new strength. He seems, is, half sick, and Rose has aged, appears all dragged out.

I had hoped to have a rather gay party to celebrate, but they seem quite low for fun making.

I had Haig Patigian, sculptor, on the *News* series,—went to his studio in fact at their request. He is supposed to be famous, and probably is amongst the most "burgess" element. His reception room was a nightmare, his work room, cluttered with atrocities, worse, and the man himself impossible. I made eight negatives and left as soon as possible.

The lamplighter is just turning off the gas, though it is still dark. I awaken very early, a form of insomnia—awaken to think of past due accounts. But at night, or even afternoons, I sleep if my head touches the pillow.

Brett and I have discussed taking over Johan's Carmel place. Both of us enthused with the idea. Foolish after the start here? Perhaps,—yet health and contentment count, and we are weary of city life, the noise, dirt, confinement. Johan did well there. I should and could.

I will talk with Johan. We could move down on our way to the Southland. Then bring back my own furnishings from there, and maybe a stepmother for Brett! I will give A. a chance if she wants to. K. would be ideal—in many capacities— but I doubt if she would dare leave home.

Mr. McNab, who nominated Hoover sat to me: another *News* sitting and a most enjoyable one. He has a warm, strong personality, and infectious smile, magnetism.

December 7. A real sitting, for pay! I boldly requested a deposit, and got $14, evidently all he had. Enough for a few days at least. The rest of my hours were spent retouching.

Johan and I went to a costume ball at the Beaux Arts Gallery. He did not understand it was a costume affair, so we were among the few not in fanciful array. The party dragged at the start, but after midnight the few remaining, led by Lucien Laboudt, had a gay climax. I danced with M. a beautiful woman, —an artist of no mean ability. I have asked her to sit to me! Alas she is married, and I have scruples — — —

A.? Am I so fickle? Something is wrong with our affair. My fault or hers, I don't know.

December 8. Back from a long walk through the early morning streets,—hunting cigarettes: lamps blear in cold fog, walks slimy. I skidded along to find at last a little lunch counter fetid from rancid grease: a row of labourers, a lone policeman hunched over ham and eggs, gulping dishwater coffee. I should have slept this morning, needed to, wanted to, but could not.

I awakened with thoughts of A. She is coming this afternoon—and I know beforehand what for: to tell me that we should part. She has been avoiding me with various excuses, too obvious excuses. Real desire overcomes all obstacles. She claims deep melancholy, megalomania, and I know she is subject to depression. But if I had even temporarily "inspired" her, she would be buoyed up and happy. Somehow I have failed,—why, I shall try to find out for my own education!

Am I sad with the thought of parting? No, though I wish the affair could have lasted longer. Now unless the aspect of our association changes, I want it definitely over.

I need someone to be gay with, not one who needs continual cheering. I "kid" myself better than most of my friends. I have my work to fall back on.

At the ball was a popular table, where one's character was read from handwriting. For one thing I was said to be given to enthusiasms. This is true enough, and I am thankful that I have this quality. Like the thought of suicide it "helps one through many a bad night."

Thinking over A. again, maybe I am all wrong as to why she wants to come today. Maybe my thoughts are prompted by *my* desire.... Maybe I am the one who wants to end it all and she receives my wish.

96

My heart has been lightened by a check for $100! Most of it already spent on first of the month bills,—but what a relief! Now I will start rushing again with renewed fervor.

December 9. A raw, dank day. I shiver in front of my miserable, stinking gas stove. The thermometer read 46° in my darkroom. Well, I slept until 8:30, that's something to my credit.

A gathering at the Salingers' in honor of Peter: we sat in a circle trying to make conversation,—Henry gurgling out remarks of an eight year old child. I could hardly look her way—such a reaction I have. Too bad!

A. came, and went, with no change in our status. She was distant, though her eyes held tenderness, blaming herself, explaining her mood which bordered on suicide, apologizing for bothering me, —with her self-consideration. She did not so much as remove her hat. I took her home. She said, "I am not a nice person to be around. When I come out of this state, I'll let you know." She hesitated as though to kiss me, but I bent quickly and kissed her hand.

Was I wrong in my yesterday's conjecture? Not altogether.

I should go into the darkroom today: orders ready to print. But I'll be dammed if I will! I am not willing to punish myself to that extent. I still have $20 in the bank. But news from Flora that she is in a mess financially. Any more troubles!

December 10. Rain beating on my skylight awakened me,—a driving, sweeping rain. I will not look out longingly at the sunlight before entering my darkroom, and the thermometer has risen 10 degrees. I really must print: $150 tied up in two orders.

Yesterday was given over to Peter. First driving around with Albert Bender to see his various public donations, then back here for a glass of wine before picking up A. We dined together at the Trocadero, stopping off at Greta Hilbert's, where a distressing hour was spent listening to the babble and cackle of old man Cowell, that impossible senility, father of Henry.

We stayed too long, five minutes would have been enough, but Peter is more polite than I am. Once home, a rather jolly night we had, dancing, chatting. A "rather jolly night,"—no more than "rather." I always expect too much from my rare free hours.

December 11. If my gas bill for this one room last month was $6.80, this month will be double. The only way to keep warm is to sit on the damn stove. Go for a walk?—and miss possible calls!

I feel most virtuous today, having printed thirty enlargements in three hours: two orders and another negative of A. Now for hours of spotting and mounting, then for hours of waiting to collect. To the *Patriot* again last eve—a nearby theatre showing.

Jannings held me as much or more than the first time. People around us would laugh at the most pathetic and subtle bits of acting. To them it was a comedy. Confronted with such manifest misunderstanding, the hopelessness of any contact with people at large is all too sadly evident. No wonder they can be stampeded like cattle into war, or to lynch a Negro, or to destroy the frescoes of a Rivera.

December 12. After a clear day, rain again,—which means a sitting postponed. I was to do Dr. Eloesser in the City Hospital, going the rounds of his ward,—or perhaps performing an operation. A commission which intrigues me, yet questioning whether I could go through with it. Fate has been kind to me, in bringing this rain storm: I needed another day on finishing more than a new sitting.

An interruption to routine came when Peter took me to see his ceremonial chest, carved for Temple Emmanuel. I take off my hat to you Peter, for a superb piece of work both in conception and technical execution. Tears came to my eyes, which would not come hearing Al Jolson. No doubt some of the emotion was from a very personal angle: knowing Peter, his life struggle, and details of the story woven around this chest. After the months of heartbreaking work, mental strain and physical effort, he will receive exactly what he spent out in cash expenditures,—$1000. Nothing for his ability as an artist, not a red cent for his time as a day labourer. But he knew what he was going into, as I knew when accepting the commission to illustrate Anita's book on Mexico. Neither he nor I can complain, yet we were exploited. This church spends $20,000 on a banquet, I have this first hand. Peter should have $10,000 in his purse,—even that would not be relatively fair.

Later we went to hear Ernst Bloch tell now he created his "America." Some were disappointed in his talk, Rose for instance, expecting a grave, profound sermon on art. Instead he kept us all chuckling or roaring with laughter, revealing homely, intimate details of his life during the period of creating. I heard the opinion that he was a good ballyhooer, used mob psychology to hold his audience. I felt he was just a naive, simple person, having the best sort of time laughing at himself and with his audience: one who could not talk profoundly,—that went into his work. Yet his jokes had depth, his gestures had pathos, and he already wore, anticipating fame, a rakish laurel wreath.

We wound up a full day at Alfred Honigbaum's, a friend of Peter's who has purchased before and did last night, a number of his lithographs. I am to dine with him tonight, then we will come here to see my work. He is a beginner as collector, hence enthusiastic, he must have money from all appearances so I have fond hopes! He served us excellent whiskey—not bootleg—and Benedictine!

December 13. No sale—I wasted an evening. Honigbaum is a nice enough fellow, but I could have used my time to better advantage. He certainly tried to entertain me, took me to Solari's for a supper of wild duck. They brought the damnable bird on whole. And what did I know, who cracks nuts and peels bananas, about carving a duck! I did not know where to start. I might better have tackled a football, it was that round, taut and slippery. It slid all over the plate, potatoes went overboard onto the table. I began to sweat!

I have seen cartoons of poor boobs in just such a situation that were no funnier. But I felt anything but funny at the time — — —

December 15.—5:30 a.m. I am needing, or taking much less sleep than I am used to. Staying out late, arising early. I feel no ill effects. My mind is full of plans. Carmel is assured. We pack everything next week, and down goes the curtain on the stage at 2682 Union St.

I am quite happy over the prospect—and Brett is overjoyed. At last I am to live within five minutes of the open country and hills, only a short walk from the beach. Yet four hours of steady driving would land us in San Francisco and a day's driving in Los Angeles.

This room, I could never forget,—the magnificent panorama from out the great window, the honest construction, the fine light, a working room but not a living room: no bath, no closet,—the darkroom serving for both, and as a kitchen, besides its intended purpose.

It is just too much to expect, Brett and I living in one room even under normal, convenient conditions. The future looms bright. I am stimulated,—already visualize working again for myself.

I have another reason to be happy. $150 in the bank and $50 more in my pocket, besides outstanding accounts to the amount of $515, and several prospects. This should enable us to make the trip south, give Flora a Xmas check, pay up the car, and have a little left to live on while starting in Carmel.

There will be those who will criticize me for changing again but I know what I am doing.

We took supper with Henry, Thursday—then all went to see Anya Kubert dance. It's Anya now, yesterday it was Vadah, five years ago she was Chloe,— really her best name.

I didn't go to see Chloe dance, knowing well enough she would be a mess: she was! I hoped to make certain contacts, and did: landed a sitting of a dog! How people, supposed to be above average intelligence, could be enthusiastic over her dancing amazes me. It makes one more hopeless than over the crowd who laughed at Jannings.

After the dance, I had to greet Chloe, not knowing what to say, but there was no escape. She saw me approach, stretched out her arms, enfolded me and kissed my cheek before the assembled multitude! Chloe is a little climber, an opportunist.

Monday, December 16. It remains cold, 44° in my room—frost on the house tops. The sun, though bright, does not warm the day. In the southland the days at least are comfortable. This gas stove has no apparent effect upon the room. One might as well try to heat the out-of-doors. I shall be glad to go—have already gone—mentally I am no longer here.

I have left A. too. Yesterday I said good-bye, and she it was who wept—though maybe not all the tears were for me—since M. also left for Germany. I was emotionally torn, she seemed so sad and worn—physically—psychically.

But I knew the time had come,—after the farewell party at M. Saturday. I hardly seemed to touch her that night—and she flirting desperately with some tall blonde. Perhaps I should have tried to win out. But it's not my way. I shrug my shoulders, freeze and indulge in mocking laughter.

The party too was a mess. Indifferent people, drinking bootleg—poisonous stuff. Girls sick. I was out of it—couldn't get into it—and I was sober, beastly sober—I watched my chance—sneaked my cape and hat—and vanished.

She called me next morning, her voice had remorse, "I am miserable—for many reasons, will you come and sit by the fire?" I went to her.

"Have I hurt you, Edward? Tell me."

I told her she had not, but circumstances, life had hurt. Hurt may come from chagrin, disappointment over wasted affection. The feeling of having given to another is so very important, more so than the smug satisfaction from receiving only.

So I said farewell, that this would be our last meeting, that I was busy packing. She choked, and said, "Go quickly, Edward."

What did I do, or not do, to quench the flame which seemed to flare at Carmel?

December 18. Nearing the last day now. Just when we can get away I cannot plan, depending on work. Another $50 order brought my cash on hand up to $270, with $500 standing out. We feel quite respectably prosperous.

I went personally to collect one old account of last August—something I cannot recall having done before—and I got it! The person owns a bookstore on Post St. She had ignored bills, letters, and phone calls. I must have been desperate and angry to have turned collector, yes, and hurt too, for I liked the girl and worked hard for her.

I planned carefully. The store would be open these holiday shopping nights. I sauntered by. She had but one person buying. I waited, watching the door. Soon she was alone. I faced her, twitching with nervousness. I so disliked the job. Before I had time to say a word, she handed out $60 in cash! Which so surprised and overwhelmed me that I bought two books for the boys' Christmas.

I would not let myself go at Margaret's party,—though I drank enough, my mind refused to give in. Last night with Johan, Dan and Frank Gregory, three drinks of gin, and I was nicely lit. We had a jolly time, laughed our heads off and all voted for the same picture at the Beaux Arts contest, because the nicest girl had painted it. One might have chosen a worse way to vote! The paintings were mostly bad enough, and I must say our judgment was not so dulled by gin that we were far off aesthetically. Ina Perham paints well.

Today my last day of enlarging, tomorrow finishing—and then?

December 20. All work finished. Just packing several prints to ship today,—then unless last hour work comes in we pack our belongings and go forth toward the new horizon.

Who would have guessed that Weston would be identified with the "Art Colony"—Carmel!

I have spent much of my new wealth: tire, battery, monthly payment, only one more to make! And I sent Flora $50 for Xmas. But I still have $340 due, and $200 in my pocket. It seems like a lot to us who have counted pennies, but by the time we get settled in Carmel, and wait for sittings— — —!

I would like some girl to come with me, to share the interest and growth of this adventure. But who? I shall not go in search of one, I am not that desperate. I am glad now that A. and I parted. She would not have been the right one. Too weak to pioneer, physically, mentally. She has a good mind, but it lacks the directness of purpose to carry through. My momentary enthusiasm got the better of my judgment. C. would come in a moment, but alas dear girl, I could not have you around me long. Yet no finer, truer person ever breathed.

K., I would be willing to take a chance. Whether she is strong enough to face the disapproval of her family—and it certainly would cause an eruption—I am not sure. An opportunity for someone willing to gamble with me on a sure thing!

December 27, at my old desk in Glendale—Last Friday noon I was developing negatives made of Dr. Eloesser as he went the rounds of his ward in the City Hospital: not one thing had been packed. At 5:30 we left S. F., the place stripped and clean-swept. Midnight found us in bed,—Carmel. The next morning after repacking, sorting out necessary articles for the trip south, calling on several newspapers to announce our arrival we were on our way again. Starting at 1:00, with steady driving—the car performing beautifully—we landed in Glendale at 11:30.

I am not all here: on edge to get away, to start again a new adventure. There have been too many changes of recent years, too many for the good of my purse, too many for peace of mind. I pray this will bring me a reasonable period of constructive building toward some future. I am weary of this moving,—from Glendale to San Francisco to Carmel!

Christmas eve and day with the boys: Neil grown so tall, Cole too frail,—I don't like it and wish I could have him for awhile. I could build him up.

I have seen K.,C.,E.,—all demonstrating their love, and wanting to return with me. From indications it will be K., who will come in February, after her school is finished.

January 1, 1929. One should, I suppose, write down the new year date with much enthusiasm, full of noble thoughts and burning desire: but I feel quite flat after a New Year's eve of hunting gayety—and missing it just around some corner. If we had been successful, achieved that elusive condition, I would not mind today's weariness after a brief nap, nor even feel it. Peter and Rose, Brett and I, started out gayly enough, but found our way blocked at every turn, with every move. I should not say "we." Maybe the rest had some fulfillment, though I take the floor with some surety. The party at Hansen's had potentialities, others had a grand time I know: the food, one could ask for no more in quality and quantity, the presentation and achievement, and wine flowed freely. But the dance room was two by four, the music foxtrots, which I couldn't get into after the danzón and tango, and there were but three or four girls for the same in dozens in men. Finally Flora arrived just before we could escape. We were bound for a party at Ben Berlin's, and I could not see taking her along. Chandler, who had another date, also wished to lose her. So Flora, feeling her position, rather out of it with her family, expressed herself in her own particular fashion which can be damnably disagreeable. I always feel it, because Flora, being so generous, trying always to please, I want to see her happy, though I usually manage to hurt her.

Another party was given, for my benefit at Peter's: Ramiel, C., B., Flora, the Hansens, Brett and myself—rather a difficult combination! Flora had to be asked,—living so near, and I thought B. and C. would combine agreeably as they did at Laurvik's. I made up my mind to be myself, and was,—showing my interest in both ladies, and dancing once or twice with Flora. All was jolly enough, even Ramiel dancing, with superb use of his hands, which I had almost forgotten in the past years. But Brett knocked over a boiling coffee pot on Helga, which ended the party. He took her to an emergency hospital and we drifted over here. We talked till near five in the morning, and I began to realize the situation: which of the two, B. or C., was to stay, which to go! I tried to joke about it, suggesting we all camp here for the few remaining hours, until dawn. Finally B. asked to be taken home, and C. left, flew into a rage, interpreting a parting remark of B. as "catty." C. was all for walking home at that lone hour, and stormed around until we got her into bed, almost by force. Methinks C.'s rage was partly self-incrimination for allowing B. to be more generous, stronger, and partly because she felt, as she said, "in the way." She knew instinctively I was more excited over B. though I tried to be fair. Well, we have had a wonderful renewal, B. and I.

January 3. To Richard Neutra's for supper: other guests were Mr. and Mrs. J. R. Davidson, and Dr. Alexander Kaun and wife. Dr. Kaun I met years ago at

Margrethe's, but only casually. I like Richard Neutra so much, and found Kaun and the others stimulating, so the evening was a rare gathering I do not regret. Even the showing of my work was not the usual boresome task. I felt such a genuine attitude. Neutra is always keenly responsive, and knows whereof he speaks. Representing in America an important exhibit of photography to be held in Germany this summer, he has given me complete charge of collecting the exhibit, choosing the ones whose work I consider worthy of showing, and of writing the catalogue foreword to the American group.

And Mrs. Salinger, writing a book on the most important Western artists—I am one of the seven—wishes more notes from my daybook to include in the foreword to my work. I don't feel particularly complimented, when I note F. among those chosen! I have busy days ahead — — —

PART III

Carmel, January, 1929—December, 1934

1. *"This new life—"*

Carmel, January 17,|1929. We arrived a week ago today: we leave for Los Angeles tomorrow morning! I intended returning in a month or so to collect the rest of my furniture and incidentals to good housekeeping, but a couple of prospective sittings and the need of more furnishings for comfort and appearance brought an immediate decision: better to go now, have it over with before settling down too comfortably, I thought. I am not enthused over the thought of that 400 mile drive again,—and back again within a week! And the ancient trailer wobbles along as though to fall into pieces any moment.

But this effort being constructive, I go ahead with desire to be done. An amazing amount of work has been already accomplished: cleaning the three houses, placing our effects to advantage, even printing and developing. Besides work we have had recreation, a dip in the ocean, long walks through the hills and along the beach. This is what I wanted, knew we would have in Carmel. In Glendale there was no incentive to walk, or even stick one's head out-of-doors,— nothing but cheap ugliness to face: San Francisco had interest of course, but I wearied of cement walks to clatter and pound along on. But there was another reason I discovered, questioning myself, for leaving the city, any city,—a psychic rather than a physical reason. And when I think of the unbroken rows of houses, people canned as it were, the massed emanation from these huddled thousands, I catch my breath and draw away, and am glad to be here with pine trees instead of people for neighbors. Every time we drove away into the country from S. F.,—returning, nearing again the city streets, my heart would sink, my stomach turn in revulsion. This new life should bring fresh stimulus to my work. Already I have sorted out ten negatives laid aside these many months to finish. And I shall be doing new work too. I feel it in my bones!

Carmel, January 26—early morning in the studio. I cannot write in this big room again, not before sunrise, it is too cold: the little oil stove is inadequate, and the big fireplace burns too much wood. I will try the board desk in the work room upstairs.

I am glad we made the second trip south, it resulted profitably in many ways: Dr. Lovell gave me $50 advance payment on sittings of his family, and I sold two prints, one to Merle, one to Jake Zeitlin. Besides we are now more comfort- able, with almost everything I own moved up here,—a heavy load it was, which nearly brought us grief. Neither Brett nor I know much about packing, or rather roping. After the first hundred miles or so, we stopped to stretch, piss, and warm our hands, for it was still moonlight,—a chill, clear morning, so clear that driving into the path of the moon, Brett turned off all lights,—an amazingly beautiful ride. Our load had shifted, and ropes loosened, and an hour was lost, in which we learned a lesson. The next misfortune happened, fortunately near our destination; the trailer threw a tire,—and after a few more miles the other! But here we are, quite well organized, ready to work and I hope play.

When I see all of my possessions around me, and recall the little shack in Glendale, quite stripped, I feel that at last the end has come to that place so far as I am concerned.

I have one hundred dollars and over, even after these weeks without work, and the car is paid for! But there are other debts unpaid, and Flora needs help, so I must pull every string that might start things moving.

Startling news has come from Mexico. Tina is featured in the headlines of every paper, even in California papers, as the only witness to the assassination of a young Cuban communist, Mellá. Indeed, she was more than witness, the boy's beloved it seems, and walking with him when he was shot. The murder may cause a break between the Cuban and Mexican governments. My name was brought in, but only as having gone to Mexico with Tina. Poor girl, her life is a stormy one.

Yesterday,—Sunday, Alfred Honigbaum visited us from San Francisco. I talked art all day and was repaid by a good dinner at the Highlands Inn, and the purchase of two prints. I have an exhibit on at the Inn,—invitation of Janis Johnston: while hanging it, met Dolores del Rio whom I had not seen since Best brought her to me in Mexico, as a beautiful type of Mexican girl I might like to photograph.

Well she is still lovely and apparently unspoiled. I had a short visit, recalling Mexico and the vicissitudes leading up to our meeting here. I wanted her to sit to me, but she was to leave that night. I have a promise of a sitting in Hollywood.

February 4. Days of rain have drenched Carmel, and to my discomfort, both living room and studio: the roof leaks like a sieve, —literally! The air is so moisture-heavy that salt which, "when it rains it pours," does not; and sow-bugs seek out my bed for warmth to dry their feathers.

We have stepped out to one gathering already, which the paper mentioned as "young Bohemia!" Will Johan get a kick from this, E. W. with young Bohemia! There I met M., I liked her and wasted no time telling her so. There seemed to me a response, but I dropped any thought of a definite conquest after sensing a third party. No triangles for me—no one is worthwhile.

February 16. I have been reading mornings, and evenings too,—for we have not yet become involved in Carmel society. Fielding's *Tom Jones*, I enjoyed immensely, could hardly put it down! Jack London's *Martin Eden* suffered by comparison, but it held me nevertheless. I am sure it was a sentimental sympathy I felt for Martin. Yet I did not admire his giving up to suicide, his disillusionment. Some years ago I would have agreed.

Tristram Shandy, which I note that I started to read in 1917,—probably I laid it aside, not having time, for it needs a certain mental freedom to be patient with Mr. Shandy's digressions, even when they are really enjoyable. I always sit me down to write when I have something disagreeable to groan over: to spare my friends the groans I guess. Today I must explode over a $25 fine some — — — of a judge in Uplands—a village I will avoid by going forty miles round-about—levied on Brett for coming down Mt. Baldy out of line. Considering all circumstances, the fine was quite out of proportion: certainly it is a hard blow! We could have lived two weeks on that money — — —

Sunday last we drove to S. F., remaining until Wednesday. Only one sitting resulted, and that a dog! Johan is so miserable—physically—mentally—that it is distressing to be near him. We lived there to save hotel bills—and I was glad to leave. If one could help him—but no — — —

The happiest part of the trip was spent in buying food with which to stock our larder: a gallon of olive oil, twelve lbs. of walnuts, a gallon of honey, a box of apples, and vegetables fresh from the soil. The saving was enormous, buying direct from the producer.

K. is having an emotional storm, trying to decide whether to come here to live with me or stay at home and pay back the debt she owes for her education. The professed love and desire never to be parted from me almost makes me cold! Indeed her burning words have quite the opposite effect she must desire! Yes—I would like her here for a while — — —

I have tried to answer so that I can never be accused of false encouragement—for there will surely come a time of regrets if she leaves. But I could not resist expounding one belief of mine which I wrote down for my own benefit before returning to Mexico: that one's first duty is to oneself, that one must be discreetly selfish, that actually and most certainly one does more harm to others by sacrifice of personality, that only by making every move to advance and improve oneself can others, individually and collectively, be benefited. But how few will understand such an apparently un-Christian doctrine! Writing of Mexico,—I just had an offer from Alfred Honigsbaum to go with him, all expenses paid, to Mexico. What a temptation! I did not hesitate in answering "no"— — To go would have been—at this time—a selfish act for pleasure only. Theories have to be applied with discretion.

Sunday. Returning to yesterday's thought on self-consideration: it might appear that I am merely defending with a guilty conscience certain selfish acts,—but

I say it is much the easier way to give in, sacrifice, say "yes," instead of "no." A long period of personal conflict was required before I finally decided to break away and leave my family for Mexico. To the outer world I was a deserter, but I was not. If I had remained under conditions which could not have been, and never will be changed, I would have mentally poisoned all around me; destroyed them, my work, myself.

I had the desire to write this morning—and the hour is early— but find I have nothing to say! If I could only have the enthusiasm from new work accomplished, then I might write down pages — — but I cannot start new work until I have a clean slate—all orders finished, and certain portraits printed for publicity.

February 21. About this time last month I was making my car payment, and now that period is over. Whatever material benefit may come from the car, the act of buying it had significance: paying the installments with money saved penny by penny was a discipline not to be underestimated. Brett profited even more than I. Owning a car was something I would not have dreamed of two years ago. A letter from Tina disclosing her strength through a terrible ordeal: she has maintained and proved her innocence. And letters have come from ... nine old loves who reach a higher significance through continued interest. All these women—what do they mean in my life—and I in theirs? More than physical relief—one woman would be sufficient for that .... Actually it means an exchange, giving and taking, growth from contact with an opposite, more to be learned than could be possible from a close friend of my own sex, chosen maybe because of similar tastes and ideas. Such a friendship is stimulating only through a bolstering up of our own egos, a sympathetic assurance that we are not alone in thought and desire. But the opposite sex provokes, excites growth, and most important, affords an opportunity to give. We cannot give to a man of our own pattern—only accentuate what they already have or clarify their thoughts—and to give freely, to withhold nothing from one or many who come with desire, seeking the answer to their riddles—this is the very meaning of life and the way of personal growth.

The spoken word need not enter in to an exchange: only to be near another, to read their eyes may be sufficient. Of course this is all idealistic. How can one *give*, when continually worried about the actualities of life—I mean eating and a corner to sleep in. Coming generations must work out a better plan.

My one way to give is through my work, for which I find so little time apart from earning my salt. Somehow, somehow there must come a solution. I have not had a period of real concentrated work for nearly a year. I believe I am ready, ripe to begin once more, and the way will be clear.

March 2. The 1st of March I should write in color and capitals—I started my work again!—and in the most exciting environs,—the Big Sur. We, Brett and I,

110

with Mina and Eddie ... as guests, left Carmel at dawn,—and returned at dusk. The excursion was exciting: over a steep tortuous road high upon the cliffs overlooking the Pacific, then down into valleys, hardly more than cañons, where great Redwoods, majestically silent, doused the light. The coast was on a grand scale: mountainous cliffs thrust buttresses far out into the ocean, anchored safely for an eternity: against the rising sun, their black solidity accentuated by rising mists and sunlit water, the ensemble was tremendous. But I lack words, I am inarticulate, anything I might write down would sound as trivial as "ain't nature grand." I hope the one negative made from this point will, in a small way, record my feeling. My desert rocks were much easier to work with, and quite as amazing, or more so. They were physically approachable, I could walk to their very base, touch them. At Big Sur, one dealt with matter from hundreds of feet to many miles distant. The way will come in time to see this marriage of ocean and rock. Yet I did respond—it is rather that I must find the right spot to see clearly with my camera.

March 6. Finishing my first Carmel order—the minimum of $40—I made a full day of printing. The print of the Big Sur is not important: a thing of emotional mood, rather than a revelation of essentials. A painter could have done it better. Made against the light, all detail, surface texture is absent—that important asset of photography. In comparison there is my negative of the juniper tree detail: it has exciting rhythms plus exquisite detail which no painter could record,—or if attempted must appear niggling, while in the photograph—an exact transcript of Nature and therefore exactly true—it is honest, convincing.

I also printed a nude, which in contrast makes the cliffs pale: the latter visually tremendous as seen in reality,—the former transformed by my way of seeing and understanding into something greater. This nude is months old,—and of F. She leaned over in her acrobatic way—which might be called artificial, but is not artificial to her—until her breasts touched her thighs,—her arms followed the movement toward the base, completing a form of architectural solidity and significance. My best work is more analogous to architecture and sculpture than to painting. I made a posterior view, in flat, but very brilliant light, which outlines the figure with such a definite black line, that even photographers swear I have pencilled the negative,—I have used this light before on the dancing nudes. The figure is presented quite symmetrically, great buttocks swell from the black centre, the vulva, which is so clearly defined that I can never exhibit the print publicly—the lay mind would misunderstand.

Another negative printed was made a year ago. The fact that I am now printing it, indicates its importance. B., weary after an hour's dancing nude before my camera, leaned, slipped down exhaustedly against the wall. It is poignantly, searchingly, a revealing of the inner self usually masked. Then I printed fine portraits of Cole,—all befreckled, and Brett, refreshingly strong in sunlight.

111

And yes, many more too,—several reprints of the rocks which sold—improved in the second printing: a number of prominent citizens from the *News* series,—quite fine characterizations, but too much cut out and pasted on the background—what amounts to improper relation to the background, and finally a negative of Mina—the first done in Carmel (this time). It is very much Mina, the first negative I made of her—done the moment she sat down to wait my preparation. But I was prepared,—saw her and have her.

I am feeling myself, with all this release of force, this action. I cannot be passive long.

Money low—not enough for this month's bills!

Tuesday, March 12. Rain has fallen to cheer the ranchers, but to my discomfort: fallen on my shake roof, thence through it!

I wrote for the first time at my desk in the studio...

Why write at all? I often ask myself. Do I not waste time?—my cry being for time to spend on my personal work. I am getting a clearer idea of the necessity which causes me to write. It is more than the recording of anecdotes, more than emotional release,— it is a way of learning, clarifying my thoughts. I know, now that it is too late, that I should not have destroyed my daybook from 1920 to 1923, it contained a most important period of growth, besides one of the most intense emotional periods, days of dramatic interest, of exciting personal adventure. My desire to destroy was natural,—to look back over immature thoughts and excess emotion was not pleasant,—but I should have locked the books away—to reread them was too much. The same will happen to this period. I pray for strength not to destroy.

K. will not come to me for two years, having decided she must pay off her educational debt to her parents. Does this mean she will never come? What will she mean to me in two years? Where will I be? But I do know this—despite all my protests—and actions— to the contrary: I need some one woman to go through life with, to build up something not based on an erection of the moment. I have been going over my past as represented in old negatives, selecting a number to finish: several of them dating back to 1923. This indicates—not as might be considered—a weakness, and inability to go on, but rather to clean my slate so I can go on. Besides, my selection must have importance if they still hold me after these years. Quite a few however, belong with work I might be doing now: nudes of B. done in 1927. One of them already enlarged—and I have been printing direct from small negatives instead of projecting 8 × 10 positives—is as strong and fine as any in the series: a prone figure, but not relaxed, rather one of the most tense, alive moments of all.

March 16. To the Kedroff Quartet: the most exquisite vocal music I have heard. The folk-songs were especially thrilling, and a Strauss waltz! I always respond to a Strauss waltz! But in music as in all the arts, there is something tremendous coming just ahead, and from this country. I may be enjoying music, or painting or architecture, but with this joy is mixed a drop of impatience for that greater expression to be.

"Just ahead" may mean one hundred, two hundred years,—I will not know it, but it will come. After, I went with Pauline to a reception for the Quartet, and there met Carmel "society," everyone that I should meet, I suppose! I have certainly been flatteringly presented to Carmel with many newspaper columns of flowery praise. One could easily become "a big toad in a little puddle" here. Not my intention!

March 17.—At Caroline Blackman's the other day—an afternoon tea it was—I noted on the mantelpiece several bones. A close inspection revealed their great beauty: the jaw bone, of an ass or horse, vertebrae, maybe of a cow, these amazingly like flower forms,—white iris. I have borrowed the bones to photograph. I felt that I was through with still-life for the time, but could not resist these.

Amongst old negatives, I printed yesterday,—one nude of Tina prone on the Azotea. After five years,—is it possible!—I have decided this one to be better than the ones finished from same series. Another cloud form is at least as fine as the one chosen from that exciting hour's work in 1926. Then, a print of "O. G." which Brett seeing it in the wash exclaimed over—"one of the best heads you have ever done,"—is from a series in 1925. A nude of B., 1927, very brilliant in technique and action, completes yesterday's work, excepting six prints of Ray and Peggy Boynton,—an exchange for signs Ray painted for me. There seems reason enough for my resurrecting the past.

But I have discovered material exactly to my present way of seeing—rocks! They are on the coast beyond the home of Robinson Jeffers. One group is just in front of his home, I think his property. We can drive the car almost to the rocks which will mean time and effort saved.

A sitting Thursday and another Monday. I am encouraged—

2. "Point Lobos! I saw it with different eyes—"

Thursday, March 21. Point Lobos! I saw it with different eyes yesterday than those of nearly fifteen years ago. And I worked, how I worked! And I have results! And I shall go again,—and again! I did not attempt the rocks, nor any general vista: I did do the cypress! Poor abused cypress,—photographed in all their picturesqueness by tourists, "pictorialists," etched, painted and generally vilified by every self-labelled "artist." But no one has done them—to my knowledge—as I have, and will. Details, fragments of the trunk, the roots,—dazzling records, technically superb, intensely visioned. Brett and Merle Armitage exclaimed over the negatives: one "like a flame," Merle said.

I worked first with rocks near Jeffers, but though they are good, [they] do not equal the desert rocks, and certainly take second place to the cypress. But I shall do them again, the hour was a bit misty: the material is there. But again the cypress!—amazing trees—those stark, bone-white, aged ones, storm swept and twisted into the most amazing forms. This sounds all too picturesque,—but wait—I have seen them with *my* eyes, at my best.

Merle here for a few day's rest. His stories—very naughty — — I have laughed—and Brett has laughed—better say we roared!

March 22. Yesterday Brett and Merle went riding,—horseback — — the horse slipped, fell on Brett, breaking his leg — — — he is now in the Monterey hospital. The X-ray shows the bone so twisted that only an operation can put it in place with any surety. The suffering of that boy — — — the bond of deep love between us—has come to the surface — — not to say it was ever deeply hidden — — — but living so alone together—seeing each other constantly—many realities become matter of fact—are taken for granted.

I cannot forget the way in which Merle has stood by us in every possible way.

March 23. How cold-blooded hospitals and doctors can be, or seem to be: that is re financial details,—I would not want an emotional nurse, or physician. Well, they are in business, have to live. I ask a deposit on my work, why shouldn't they? But when I was told they wouldn't operate without cash on hand,—$75, which, though I know it is a small amount, I have not. I asked, "If I cannot get the amount by Tuesday, what will you do,—send the boy away?"—They evaded the question! $35 is all my purse holds. Merle, bless him, has assured me he will send $50 immediately. And how fine the neighbors and friends have been!—offering every kind of help.

114

This is a hard blow,—the worst, Brett's suffering and confinement,—but the money question is staggering, and the time I must and want to give him is a problem: all the work he so faithfully performed, now up to me, with less time to do our combined duties.

Now I wish that I could drive. Brett is miles away in New Monterey.

March 24, 1929. My birthday—and what a day! Cold—raining—hailing—Brett writhing in the hospital, and I broke after paying $75 advance for his room. Enough of this self-pity, actually I am thinking of Brett,—nothing else matters. He must come out of this perfectly well,—normal. One of his first questions was, "Will I be able to dance and run the same as before, Dad?"

We had planned to drive south, be in Los Angeles for my birthday,—rather using the birthday as an excuse for going. I wanted to see the boys, my friends, — and we both had desire to be with our several amantes — — —

C., bless her, phoned from L. A. last night to send birthday greetings. I am afraid the conversation was not the joy she had expected: mostly about Brett.

Friday. Chandler drove all night Tues. last, to be with me, to help Brett: a fine gesture on his part. He is a great comfort and help, now I can get to Brett whenever I wish without depending on friends and the infrequent bus. Many new acquaintances have been very kind in driving me over, and offering their aid. Marcella, and Amelia,—a new friend, have been especially lovely. From letters, I know how much Brett is loved.

The operation called "successful." But how the boy suffered after! I could hardly retain an outward calm — — —

Dr. Dormody says he may be on crutches in a week! I pray so, that I can get him away from the stupidity of hospital care!

April 2. I saw the X-ray made five days after the operation: the bone which had been broken in five places appeared to me as perfect as ever. Dr. Dormody is so jubilant over his work, quite as though I had made a new negative of importance. But Brett must stay in the hospital another two weeks, in bed another month, and then be on crutches three or four months! I mentioned the stupidity of hospital care: I will say they have acted to the best of their knowledge. But an example,—a full meal, including pie and ice cream served the day before operation, which Brett refused, and then a dose of castor oil to clean him out, which Brett promptly vomited up!

After the operation they served him, (next morning) a good breakfast, to build up the bone! As if he could digest and assimilate anything in his condition! Of course he again refused. The whole force have been very much alarmed over Brett's fasting. Yet they marvel that he was not more nauseated after the ether. Now that he is again eating, I take him fresh fruits and vegetables and dried fruits, avocadoes, and so on. When the nurse brings his supper, I eat it myself, and they are happy that he is again being nourished! I don't want them to hold antagonistic thoughts, hence my white lies,—which if discovered would be thought—from the doctor down—very black ones.

April 4. Beginning Tuesday night, ending last night—a round of visiting: Marcella the cause. Tuesday she took Vasia [Anikeef], Sybil, [his wife] C. and me to the Flavins'—he a playwright—living at the Highlands. I guess we "the artists" were supposed to perform, but I have not much to offer without my portfolio, and Vasia wouldn't sing,—so—a quiet evening of no import, except the bourbon and White Rock warmed my soul. But unless this artificial warmth can be released, objectified,—why drink! Then the next noon lunch with Lincoln Steffens and wife: a much more stimulating event. Persons worth knowing. And they served well, a delicious meal plus pre-war wine.

I said to Marcella as we drove away, "why this way?"

"I want to leave some things for Robin and Una Jeffers."

I did not want to go in: Jeffers must be pestered to death with sight-seeing tourists, curious meddlers. Marcella insisted. Jeffers opened the door. He was cordial, simply so: also his wife, but more voluble. We stayed on and on, sipping excellent homemade wine,—the recipe promised me. A Jeffers' sort of day, with rain sweeping over the ocean.

I have only read *Cawdor*: a gripping poem. I feel that we will become friends. And I am to photograph him, when I know him better.

Chandler left last night. He has been of so much help: staying hours with Brett, driving me back and forth. I shall miss him!

A letter from Jean Charlot, with sad news of his mother's death. A blow to him,—they were inseparable. Such a triste note!

April 10. Albert Bender phoned me from S. F.—hearing of Brett's accident. Full of sympathy of a very concrete kind he said, "You must need money, Edward, would $200 help?" I could hardly answer. I stammered and choked, with surprise and emotion — — — Next day the check came! This really noble gesture made me self-satisfied. To explain—many have sneered at Albert—behind his back—in a half contemptuous way, over certain crudities,—buffoonery, garrulity: I have always stood up for him, recognizing the fine, warm, tender person within, hidden by his almost grotesque shell, and braggadocio.

Then Peter Krasnow wired $30 and John Seaman $40,—even more in proportion to their means. And I'm sure they had no idea how soon I could pay it back! Merle of course sent the promised $50,—Uncle Theodore $20, and Flora offered $50. Combined with several checks on old accounts and a couple of

116

sittings and sales of prints, I find myself richer than in many months. I'll need it. —Sunday a Mr. Vaughn Flannery, N. Y., friend of Sheeler and Steichen, touring through, chanced to see my sign. I showed work for an hour and was rewarded by the purchase of two prints.—$25.

Yesterday Lincoln Steffens and wife called to see work, again two prints sold. He had already purchased a head of Diego,—a best seller: then as he was leaving I brought out an unmounted print of my new cypress root. He said without hesitation, "Print me one of those." A painter by name Nash, of Santa Fe, spent a recent evening here. Name is familiar, work I cannot connect with name. If it matches his viewpoint, it is good. He said, "I thought Paul Strand was at the top amongst photographers, until I saw your work." Then aside, "How much are these prints?" "Is that all! I'll have a couple when I return to Sante Fe."

I am behind in all work these days. Take the 9:30 bus to Monterey, stay with Brett until 1:30. By the time I have tended to odds and ends the day is spent! Brett laughs at my "odds and ends," but they are only too real! One item, about fifty letters of "sympathy" to answer. I'll have to get a secretary (a pretty one) to help out. She might answer a double purpose! A. is here with Ray and Peggy—maybe she'll do!

Last night supper with Vasia and Sybil Anikeef. A good Russian pudding, and fireside conversation. Fine persons, both.

Saturday, April 13. Last Thursday was a full day. Back from seeing Brett, I found a note from Una Jeffers—would I come over?—Friends of Stieglitz—wanted to see my work. They came after me. She proved to be Mrs. Blanche Matthias, whom Walt Kuhn had sent to me.

The Jeffers' had not seen my work, so I had a very interesting audience,—and they responded. A man may be a fine poet, and yet not respond to other art forms. But Jeffers is a great poet plus—

Mrs. Matthias said, "You have no idea how much you are being spoken of in the east. Walt has spread the news all over N. Y. that you are the greatest photographer in the world." Then—after seeing the portfolio through—"I guess all that Walt Kuhn says is true." The same afternoon I found a note from Ella Winter,—Mrs. Steffens, "...want to be gay tonight and dance—Do come. Just the Boyntons, Woods, a few people like that." She had left three books for Brett and a check for $20. I went, wanting to be gay. Brett's suffering these last days has depressed me. A. was there, as I expected—and hoped. We danced for the first time since certain well-remembered days,—and her cheek against mine, as of old! What does it mean? She has been very sweet. Is it only friendship? I would not mind something else! She excited me and of course she knew it.

Undated. Time: 3:30 a.m. Place: the white sands of Carmel shore—the moon setting over the ocean. Characters: Sonya [Noskowiak] and Edward.

Edward: "Sonya!"

Sonya: "Edward!"

—and then the first embrace—the first kiss.

Literally they were not the first. I have to thank wine and dancing at a party I gave for A. last Saturday for the prelude.

I danced many times with Sonya, there was an immediate, mutual response. I kissed her cheek and neck and ears as we danced—she did not resist. Then she invited me to supper Tuesday night. We talked, played many records, and she sang until way past midnight: but I made no attempt to renew familiarities. I was sober—she was sober,—and I am always backward, afraid to make a false gesture. Perhaps, I thought, the other night her yielding was only due to wine.

"Me voy, Sonya, es tarde!"

"Pero no es tarde, esperate."

How stupid I was! But I put on my coat. She did too!

How wise these women! How subtle was Sonya.

I took the cue—and walked with her toward the moonlit water and what I knew was inevitable.

We returned to her "Playhouse,"—"for hot coffee."

She resisted just long enough. Wise little Sonya — — —

No sleep that night,—no desire to. Tender, lovely, passionate Sonya!

Brett comes home today! I have prepared his room, and am ready to be nurse for some months to come. It will be wonderful to have him home again and near me, away from that really awful hospital.

Saturday, April 20. After over four weeks without sitting up, indeed scarcely moving, Brett had a new cast put on, and I have him home!

The people of Carmel have been very kind in many ways, even comparative strangers.

Wednesday, April 24. Ramiel will be here Friday week!—driving with Winifred Hooke, who comes for Buhlig's concert. I will only have him for two days, but we'll make those two days sing! Brett and I are thrilled—

Another possible guest will be—my little sister! Not until this summer, but what an event—four years since we have been together.

These are busy days—difficult ones. Brett needs much attention: daily baths and meals. But if I start rebelling against my lot, I think of his—and calm down at once. And Brett is wonderfully patient, considering his type, his usual active and gay life. He is appreciative too, and considerate in his demands.

April 26. Just had a catalogue of Paul Strand's recent exhibit. His subject matter, trees and rocks! He on the Atlantic coast, I on the Pacific, using same material. I wonder how they differ in viewpoint and technique?

Which makes me ponder.

I made a statement months ago, that it was immaterial whether one man was greater than another: the important thing being a matter of personal growth. Yet a few days ago I wrote down the opinion of Nash, that my work was more important than Strand's. Do I really mean what I say! Have I really gotten rid of the personal angle? Am I big enough to? I would not have put down that opinion if I had been really honest in my former statement. I need to grow,—beyond personalities.

Sunday. Brett had a bad night: the first time he has called for aspirin to ease his pain and bring sleep.

Dr. Dormody called for an examination: said he would have been pleased, or at least satified with 50% the result he has with Brett, and wants to show the X-rays to Dr. Eloesser when he returns. A good sign, for Dr. Eloesser is held in high esteem.

"Get Brett up now, as fast as his strength will allow." His parting word. I have managed to get in a couple of days printing: orders a month old, and several reprints of personal work—among them my "Flaming Cypress Root." This new print is an improvement, with greater contrast: actually more contrast than the original had in nature. It is a dazzling print, technically superb, with rhythms like flames. I have never made a negative that pleased me more.

May 1. I have been the recipient of a package of photographs from M. Alvarez Bravo of Mexico, D. F. When I was assessed $2.50 duty, I felt rebellious, but upon opening the package that feeling vanished—I was enthusiastic! Photographs of better than usual technique, and of excellent viewpoint. One of a child urinating, just the little round belly, his "trimmings" in action, and an enameled dish to catch the stream: very fine! So many were of subject matter I might have chosen,—rocks, juguetes, a skull, construction. I wonder if this person, Sr. Sra. o Srita, quien sabe?—does not know my work, or Tina's? In fact I had a suspicion—and still wonder—if these prints are not from Tina—under assumed name,—perhaps to get my unbiased opinion. The inclusion of a delightful petate recuerdo also excites suspicion. And the prints are mounted on the same cover board we used in Mexico. It is all a very nice mystery!

The month starts well: a sitting today of Mrs. O'Shea, and two Saturday from Pebble Beach. I have a feeling I am to do well here.

Saturday, May 4. Well, Ramiel did not come: his sister died Saturday—or the funeral was Saturday. Both of us deeply disappointed. But I couldn't have given him much of a welcome: I went down and out yesterday. It was a climax to

119

six weeks of worry, and working on my nerves. Not feeling well in the morning, I thought it would pass, so went ahead with my daily routine: Business letters with morning coffee — — bath, change sheets for Brett — — sweep house and studio — — marketing — — breakfast,—mine swallowed standing the while (I might better have gone without) mix chemicals—develop five dozen films — — greet visitors — — cut wood—Brett's supper—and my collapse. I was to take Sonya to Buhlig's concert,—instead she took tickets, protesting she would stay with me. But I want to be alone when sick! The dear girl came back after concert to see if I needed her.

I suppose a contributing factor to my break was a doctor bill for $300. I don't consider it too much, but the awful actuality of what those figures meant, overwhelmed me. Too much sob stuff in this day's writing. I must face all this, and pull through. No other way out.

Sunday, May 5. Yesterday afternoon I had three sittings within three hours, and all from Pebble Beach: came in a Rolls Royce! I had one foot in bed in the morning, but by afternoon I was feeling fairly well. I'm a tough viejito—have much reserve. This is the biggest week, business considered, I have had in Carmel, and a forecast of what I may do in the season. All told, five sittings so far—and another this morning—Winifred Hooke. By the way I felt last night I should have slept twelve hours, but instead I was sleepless at 5:30, and provoked with myself.

With a sitting coming at 9:00, magazines to load, bath to give, and six dozen films to develop for rush proofing, it is well I arose!

Friday, 5:30 and sunrise already —I had forgotten how long Northern days are in summertime.

Have been reading *You Can't Win* by Jack Black, ex-criminal—convict: so exciting an autobiography that despite my unusual exhaustion I can hardly lay it aside for honest work! My sympathy always with Black, hoping for his escape, may indicate certain tendencies in me! After being lashed in the Canadian prison he quotes Nietzsche, "What does not kill me strengthens me." A good fireplace "motto."

Another one "for the day"—by Blake—"Great things are done when men and mountains meet. They are not done by jostling in the street."

Brett now sits out in the sun all day in his wheel chair: at night by the roaring fireplace—

Saturday, and 5:00 again —I hoped that I would sleep—or expected to—having retired rather late. Why I should want to sleep I don't know—so much more time for my work if I can do with five or six hours instead of eight—but being used to eight—I imagine that I must have eight.

I feel rather piggish, having consumed a large portion of baked ham, several yams, succotash and wine at the Bechdolts'—he is a writer I believe. Rather jolly evening, most of the party being old timers in Carmel who entertained with stories, mostly woven around George Sterling. I spent some time discussing music and musicians, local events, with David Alberto. He said Buhlig played like a crazy person, which agrees with Winifred's remark that Buhlig was in an hysterical condition. We spoke of imre weisshaus—I write his name as he does—but I cannot see any advantage in doing away with caps—periods —in fact all division —spacing—as in the mode with some "moderns." I feel an affectation—or a straining to be different—legitimate enough for advertising— but resulting in a page more difficult to read.

weisshaus is being "rushed" by Carmel art patrons—the ladies of course. Like most musicians, his taste outside of music might be questioned,—but he talks glibly on all the arts, and "modern" life, his remarks published at length, and quoted at intellectual gatherings. For example—"Beauty is not a word which the modern artist allows himself to use." I admit it is an abused word—so is "art"—but because they are misused is no fault of the words. Further he writes, "Besides there is beauty in everything. It takes only seeing to know that." Well, any real artist "knows that,"—they always have! The word beauty used by an artist simply indicates that the essence of the object has been seen, understood, or put down in his medium. I suppose it is youthful enthusiasm which gives to many young moderns the idea that they or their group have at last discovered "art." But many of them are actually academic. weisshaus is—I pick him as a firsthand example—at least so I label him from a few chance remarks. He saw my work one night—then Brett's,—whose prints impressed him more than mine. Why? Because mine were mostly of rocks and trees—I'm tired of showing my smoke stacks and toilets—while Brett's were of machinery, industrial things.

"Rocks!" he after said to Alberto, "Who is interested in rocks today?" And a similar line of talk to Brett. I see in this attitude a viewpoint as narrow as any academician, bound by subject matter.

I say,—subject matter is immaterial—the approach to the subject, the way it is seen and recorded is the critical test of a worker.

I feel beforehand that my work will not be greatly admired in Stuttgart—indeed it may be severely criticized—for, from what I can gather—a group very similar to weisshaus have the exhibit in charge.

I await with interest.

I will laugh at—no, pity, anyone not liking, not feeling my cypress root — —

Tuesday, May 14. Had to supper an Irishman, O'Malley by name, whose tales of his part in the rebellion—1916–23, made me realize what a comparatively unexciting life I have had. But excitement can come in different ways,—mine, through my work. Can I ever forget certain days, periods, places? One of the earliest,—the scene in a Chicago apartment, printing from my first negative made with a stand camera purchased with money saved penny by penny, walking ten miles to save ten cents, denying sweets, selling rags and bottles: a second hand camera I had seen in a downtown window, with tripod and filter it cost $11. I can even recall my ecstatic cry as the print developed out—"It's a peach!"—and how I ran, trembling with excitement, to my father's library to show this snow-scene made in Washington Park,—a tree, a winding stream, snow-covered banks. I slipped into the stream and rode home on the Cottage Grove cable car with my trouser legs frozen stiff as a board.

My enthusiasm over this print did not last long: I soon realized that the tree was too black, the snow too white, and my struggle began, caused by dissatis-faction, to improve my technique,—a long, tough struggle without help, for I was a bashful boy, dreading to hear my own voice when making purchases,—to ask questions would have been impossible.

I often compare Brett's start in photography with mine. Has his been too easy, having me to question? Or will he be strong enough to make the most of an easy beginning and then fight on, going much further than I have?

Yesterday I printed two more negatives from Point Lobos: branches of a cypress, sweeping horizontally across the negative, and another of roots, both quite satisfactory. From the sittings made that day I was so miserable, two orders amounting to $290! And another yet to come. Business is good! This afternoon I am to photograph Jeffers — —

9. CYPRESS ROOT, 1929

10. KELP, 1930

11. PELICAN'S WING, 1931

12. OAK, MONTEREY, 1929

13. ERODED ROCK, 1930

14. KELP & PEBBLES, 1934

15. ROCK EROSION, 1934

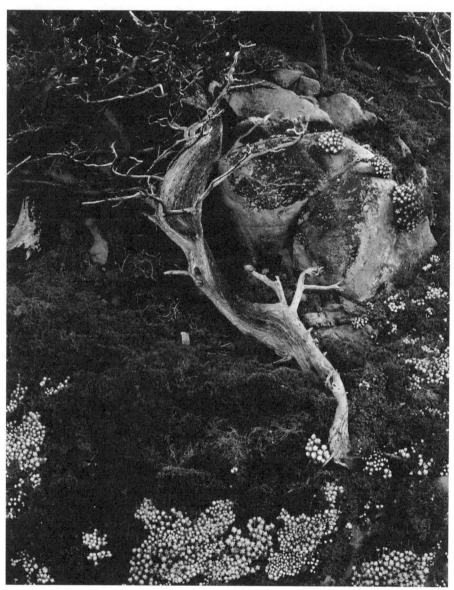

16. Cypress & Stone Crop, 1930

3. Robinson Jeffers

Wednesday, May 15. Fog drifted in, dulling the sky, obliterating the horizon, before I had even started for Jeffer's home. I planned to do him out-of-doors, in surroundings that belong to him,—the rocks and the ocean. The heavy sky was suitable in mood but sunlight would have carved his rugged face into more revealing planes. I made but twelve negatives, mostly profiles against the sky, and then quit, until the next time.

I couldn't get into the sitting: the light so flat—Brett sitting alone for the first time except for my hurried dash to P.O.—and then finding him unexpectedly conscious, not nervous as some are in front of a camera,—that tendency can be usually overcome, but Jeffers really posed, tried to appear as he thought he should be seen. I caught him looking out of the corner of his eye at me, and then would come a definite attempt to assume a pose,—throwing back the head, feeling the part he was to play. This was disconcerting.

I am inclined to think there is much "bunk" talk about Jeffers,—about his way of working, unconscious of what he is doing. Any great man, artist, is quite aware,—conscious of his unconscious, if that means anything, if my words make clear my thought. And so Jeffers.

Another order for $80 brings my total for three hours work on a sick afternoon up to $370. Actually the work has just begun with eleven negatives to retouch and thirty prints to make, but the important effort to please and bring consequent orders was made with one foot in bed and the other wishing to be there.

May 18. Thursday last, Brett stood alone on his crutches just eight weeks after the accident. The doctor told him he would remove his cast as soon as he learned to walk with ease and confidence alone: so Brett practices to the limit of his strength.

Chandler and a friend arrived last evening: "bummed" rides from L.A. Ted [Chandler] wants to drive Brett and me back to L. A.—but I cannot leave work, and Brett does not want to go,—he says that he would soon tire of "home life," but I know that he fears Ted will abuse the pride and joy of his life,— "his" Packard.

Several negatives of Sonya are quite Sonya. And of Jeffers I made a good start, —better than I hoped. I wrote of Jeffers, he "tried to appear as he thought he should be seen." Maybe I should have written "as he *knew* he should be seen." For a man to know himself is legitimate, indeed quite right.

123

I showed the Jeffers portrait at a gathering here last Saturday. Both Lincoln Steffens and Ella Winter thought I had seen him too heroically. They hoped I had caught a shy, retiring side which he has. I see that quality and perhaps will catch it today when I go again,—but gestures, attitudes, moods are not made to order—they happen—and when they do I am usually ready to catch them. I photographed Jeffers out on the rocks, his face oceanward. Almost anyone would become heroic in such surroundings—certainly Jeffers.

Monday. Friends and acquaintances,—neighbors, have brought to Brett, soups, salads, sweets, books, flowers, and—wine! Most of the delicacies Brett has wisely put aside,—people have strange ideas about pampering an invalid's appetite. But their spirit has been unforgettable. So I have been living on the donations: maybe soup and pudding for breakfast! Or I have served Sonya suppers, the menu made up from Ann Dare's soup, Mrs. Clark's salad, Sybil's pudding, the O'Shea's wine.

May 25. Printed Jeffers—a head in profile—very much Jeffers—the dull day gave no modelling to face—it is a silhouette against the sky. I hurried the printing—did not get from negative its full quality, and must reprint.

Photographed Sean O'Malley—and did well. Have grown quite fond of him. He shares our vegetable stew and often sleeps here.

Chandler just left for the south—without Brett. The doctor would not let him go. Had a very bad night,—up every hour to help Brett stand, and relieve his pain. I can't go on this way much longer.

May 28. I was showing to Sonya and Brett a portfolio of photographs I had made of some twelve old loves,—one fell out and was found on the floor later, one of M. I walked home with Sonya—the first night she has slept at home for a week—on the way stopping at P. O. I had one letter,—from M., the first in months. She has been in a mood similar to mine. "I am sick of temporary relations, of making beginnings that are endings. I want a relationship that has some stability, some mutual foundation of companionship, and as you say, building."

M. would be a fine person to consider as permanent. But what of Sonya? Yes —she has already become very close to me, and I can easily imagine a lasting association. And K. whom I asked to come here, with whom I have a sort of agreement? She attracts me physically, she apparently loves me—but I wonder would it last — — —

Sonya is young—maybe not ready to settle down — — —

May 29. I made three dozen negatives of Jeffers,—used all my magazines: and developed the moment I got home. It was another grey day, but I now realize, knowing him better, that Jeffers is more himself on grey days. He belongs to

124

stormy skies and heavy seas. Without knowing his work one would feel in his presence, greatness. His build is heroic—nor do I mean huge in bulk—more the way he is put together. His profile is like the eagle he writes of. His bearing is aloof—yet not disdainfully so—rather with a constrained, almost awkward friendliness. I did not find him silent—rather a man of few words. Jeffers' eyes are notable: blue, shifting—but in no sense furtive—as though they would keep their secrets,—penetrating, all seeing eyes. Despite his writing I cannot feel him misanthropic: his is the bitterness of despair over humanity he really loves.

My negatives show better technique, though I may have nothing finer in feeling than several from first sitting.

Jeffers gave me a copy of *The Women at Point Sur*—autographed. I would never have asked him to autograph a book, but coming this way it has meaning.

May 30. After proofing the last Jeffers' negatives: I have done well,—very well! —at least twelve, from which I could choose any one, and show with my finest portraits. Three or four are great, using my own work for comparison. So I am happy! This is Jeffers' week: last night I read to Sonya and Brett from that gripping poem *The Women at Point Sur.*

June 6. Sean O'Malley just left for the South—and I suppose out of my life forever: but no, not out of my life, even if we never meet again, for our few weeks together made us real friends. We embraced and kissed at the parting.

And today the Jeffers' leave for Ireland. Sonya and I walked out to say goodbye, and take them several of his portraits. They were so pleased with them. Una Jeffers said: "Robin will never again have such fine portraits, unless you make them." Indeed, everyone seeing them has been impressed, and I too know that I have seen and worked well.

The last visit to the doctor's marked another milestone in Brett's progress: the cast was left behind him for good.

And yesterday he surprised me by dressing alone!

imre weisshaus has been in several times of late, bringing photographs for my criticism, of a young Hungarian,—and various drawings which had value. He had said that he would like to play for Brett and me some evening, so yesterday I phoned and arranged for last night.

Well he can write his name without caps or upside down, and I'll not protest: he can be pedantic—for he is young—or misunderstand the plastic arts and I'll forgive him, for he gave me something last night. I had expected only an intellectual stimulation, but my emotions were also moved: first by Bartok—a group of Xmas songs, then by a dance of adolescence—Stravinsky—which was superb—and to my untrained ears, superbly played. Also one of his own compositions—which seemed to hammer directly onto the nerve centers—brought me—what can I call it —— pleasure?—immaterial—labels superfluous if one can be stirred. Who can label the sexual climax!

Rain—a drenching downpour—fell Saturday and continued a gentle shower Sunday—when Brett drove us—Sonya and me—far into the valley. Brett drove! Astounding! One recent morning a horn honked and I could not believe my own eyes when Brett waved from our car. He manages well without his $1000 leg!

June 12. Another drive into the valley—with "Paul," so I have renamed Pauline to her great delight,—but not to indicate masculinity—she remains pure female. We dined with Dene Denny and Hazel Watrous. The evening's conversation mostly on how to run the *Carmelite*, and its aspirations. I, being on the editorial staff, had to listen in until after midnight though bed called me, having retouched all day.

Village gossip mostly about the divorce of the Lincoln Steffens.

A letter from Una Jeffers, written on the train, again expressing their pleasure in the portraits.

And a catalogue from *Film und Foto*—Stuttgart: they reproduced my head of Galván, and published my article, hung 18 of Brett's photographs and 20 of mine. I sent 20 from each of us.

I must have an exhibit here to make propaganda. No sittings for a long period—

Saturday, June 15. Ramiel will be here tonight!
About two weeks ago, when I thought to have reached my limit, I wrote him to come if possible—that I would send fare. Now my nursing troubles are over, Brett requiring comparatively little care, but we will have all the better visit—and I still need help around the place, everything so much run-down,—my orders far behind. Aside from his assistance, just to see Ramiel will be a great joy. The jolliest party took place last night at Sonya's sister's, in the Presidio at Monterey,—Stanton, her husband, being a lieutenant. Just a few close friends,—I, the new element,—but soon felt quite at home. The evening was one long continued laugh —until my sides ached. Drinks were not necessary! Each one of the half dozen had been in amateur or professional theatricals: and each had a sense of humor. When Kelly and Sonya appeared as man and wife, laughter became uncontrollable. Kelly is a six footer—and he was the wife: Sonya is not much over five feet,—she was the husband!

Sunday, June 16. Ramiel is here!! He has been very sick—but did not tell me—knowing well that his troubles would become mine—and that mine were already heavy. Now we must and will grow well and strong and happy together. It is a great privilege to have such a friend.

Chandler is here too—came to take Brett south. I shall miss Brett, but a separation is indicated, really necessary for a short while. We have been constantly together—day and night—for nearly a year,—or since coming north. Too much for two who love each other: though there has never been friction. Brett is an ideal companion for me: very few that I could stand day after day and not weary of, or worse. We seldom clash.

July 6. Is it possible,—Ramiel has been here three weeks! He always brings peace and order, has these past weeks, enabling me to nurse an enormous boil, or carbuncle—I think a doctor would have called it—which appeared on my side, and grew and grew. It came just below the belt on my hip—either I had to go naked or to bed. I'll carry a scar. Whether I became infected from Brett, whose leg "boiled" over after the cast was removed or whether I was depleted and needed purification,—who knows. To me there seemed almost a mystic symbolism indicated—of my close relation to Brett.

Recovering without a doctor—in their methods I have no faith—cleaning out— then suppressing the balance—I let it drain, grow until it stopped naturally — — recovering—I put in a week of hard work—cleaning up orders a month old.

The three of us, Ramiel, Sonya, and I have led perforce a quiet life. No company—except Richard Buhlig over one night — — evenings by the fire—reading —talking.

I tried to photograph Richard, but failed. It was a cold, damp day,—not his kind of weather. I made but one negative and destroyed that. But I made a successful sitting of Lincoln Steffens,—and an eggplant—which later became part of our respective blood and body.

4. *"Peppers, my wonder and vision increasing—"*

July 8. A recent evening I thought to read Ramiel passages from my daybook,—those concerning my work. I was appalled and disgusted how often I had indulged in self pity. Most of the writing seemed to be a wail over my financial condition, and the rest about my love affairs.

But now I am working again. I must thank Ramiel and Sonya,—each in their own way for having given me mental and physical freedom. To them I owe much: clearing the way, bringing peace, understanding love, stimulation.

I am working now with two green peppers of marvellous convolutions. Yesterday's negative will be finished: which indicates its value.

Recent sittings include Hans Ankersmith and Perry Newberry. Perry proved an especially fine person to work with, and I made a number of excellent portraits.

July 9. The aforementioned pepper negative will not be finished despite my yesterday morn's enthusiasm: the reason—I have far surpassed it with almost any one of eight negatives made yesterday. July 8th, 1929 I will remember as an important day—and I feel the beginning of an important period—in my work. I worked out-of-doors in the sunlight—a trying but exciting way, for the sun playing through pine branches changed so rapidly the direction of light, that it became a matter of chance as to whether or no the peppers were well illumined: but no chance entered in to my decision as to the right moment for exposure.

July 13. I have been working so enthusiastically with the two peppers,—stimulated as I have not been for months, and with my conscience clear, having all orders printed and shipped. Money a bit low, but a check from the East due on my order for $290,—so I was not worried. A letter would come in time to save us. It came,—but no check! She liked her husband's portraits, but was "very much disappointed" in hers, there were too many "shadows," by which she meant to indicate lines and hollows. And I spent half a day on each negative, retouching until her face was near to putty. She, a woman of maybe 45, I made into a woman of under thirty, and that was not enough!

This is a moment which brings a tremendous reaction to portraiture, a moment when I swear I'll get out of it as soon as possible. But I am even more disgusted, outraged at her action in withholding the check. A person lousy with money, introduced by a friend, and who well enough saw my condition. Her gesture should have been to include the check with her complaint, knowing then I would do my part even more readily. Now I have three days of hard work to repeat: retouch until she becomes like an expressionless doll, sweat in dark-room, mount, ship and wait her next move. This is sob stuff I suppose. Well! that's out of my system!

The sittings of Hans and Perry most successful. Perry has one of the most flexible faces ever before my camera. A fine, human being, lovable person.

I went on with peppers, my wonder and vision increasing. Twenty negatives made, from which ten at least will be finished: but this proportion does not indicate my surety, for many viewpoints were repeated two or three times on account of the shifting light.

And now I have two new peppers of quite as amazing contours,—unintentionally discovered while shopping. But my mind is no longer carefree.

July 22—early. I wanted to sleep, needed to, after a week of confusion,—especially the last two days, but Sonya kept me awake,—just her presence, asleep beside me, the warmth of her body, her breathing. We must sleep apart most of the time when she comes to live here. I have never before slept so often all night with anyone, and at first slept well. But I must not spoil our beautiful contact.

I shipped again the Eastern order,—and wait. Tourists are arriving for vaca-tion: many come in. I grow weary of my work, showing it so often. No praise moves me, I know all of it is part of my past. The new pepper negatives are exciting, as are several recent portraits: printing them will be an event. Sybil and Vasia used my studio last week for a party: their guests of honor, Mr. and Mrs. Balaban,—he of the American Opera Co. A fine party,—everyone happy. Ramiel danced,—impromtu. Many years had passed since I first saw him, and his dramatic power and artistry was revived for me. Then—Saturday last a party was planned at the Flavins'—Ramiel to dance, Vasia to sing. In compari-son the affair was flat. The setting was perfect, the drinks real, the service per-fect,—food such as only the wealthy can find time to prepare: but it was planned, —certain ones to perform at a given time, and the spontaneity of the other party was lacking. The Flavins I like,—and their home on the coast, with a miniature Point Lobos, is a place of wonder.

A sitting yesterday and one today. Yesterday's of the daughter of Louis Ed-brooke my boyhood friend, who found me again in Carmel.

I lost my eyebrows the other day! Well, that's an exaggeration,—a barber trimmed them! I always feel denuded coming from the barber shop,—quite immodest: and seated in the chair I feel helpless,—anything may happen. But I never had this experience before: I was not prepared to protest. Suddenly—snip, snip, and one was neatly trimmed. Of course I had to have the other match. I was chagrined, angry, but said nothing: he was trying his best to beautify me. And when I left he remarked—"You look like yourself again."

Dr. H. Gurlitt of the König Albert Museum, Zwickau, seeing the exhibit in Stuttgart has ordered three of my prints: the head—Galván, the knees—Bertha, and a shell.

Two sittings yesterday. I'm always saved at the last moment. I'm thinking there will be no more personal "expression" for awhile. I gaze longingly at several fine crooknecked squashes Ramiel brought home to tempt me. I should not take time now. But will I?

July 26. I have had nine sittings within the last ten days, and two more dated ahead, besides selling four prints. My personal work more than pays expenses now. The stars must be right for my bank account!

imre weisshauss here to supper. I am growing to like him personally. He has reached an impasse in his work which has mellowed his outlook, and manner. He said: "If you ask me what I know, I would tell you,—nothing!" Well, this condition will pass, and he will be all the stronger. I recall my dissatisfaction before going to New York, 1922. I was changing, and going in the right direction too: Stieglitz—my two hours with him focussed me. Yet "Steel" and several other things made in Ohio, before seeing Stieglitz, were a forecast of my present work. In fact I still show them as part of my present.

Despite being busy with sittings I have found time, or stolen it, to work with more peppers, and the exquisite squash. I find myself seeing well despite all distraction.

Sunday, July 28. A $210 order in from first proofs shown—A Mr. Joseph Quinn and three children. I enjoyed the whole family. Then I sold another of my favorite rocks from Mojave Desert group: Lula Boyd having purchased the other last year.

If I could only get hold of a decent amount of ready cash to pay off a few bills and send for the boys.

Saturday, August 3. Another order from second set of proofs—Theodora Willard —amounts to $105, and she bought three prints besides. I have had one more sitting and have three more sets of proofs to hear from. And yet I am nearly broke! Fact is the Eastern order I had to reprint has never paid: each day I expectantly wait. I feel bitter toward this person, who could easily respond, whether she is pleased, or not.

Now I must leave to wither several eggplants, the finest I have ever noted that Ramiel discovered, and start on one of the orders, to get ready cash. I tried to work with them yesterday—and failed. I admit they are difficult, not easy to do justice to, but my failure was partly due to working under pressure, knowing it was my last chance, that money was low.

When I last printed orders, I took time to include two of my pepper negatives.

They are like sculpture, carved obsidian, and can be placed with my finest expression.

Mary Bulkley—a person I want to know better—brought a Mr. Swope, who was very much interested in my work, and very intelligent. Yesterday came Earl V. Ovington, an aviator, and old friend of my father in his archery days.

August 10. I write while a half hour exposure is being staged: a pepper the sole actor. Ramiel persists in bringing new peppers nearly every day, despite my warning that we will soon live on wind and water if I am not allowed to work on orders,—and how can I when ten or more of the most amazing forms intrigue me! I have almost thirty new negatives already, peppers and two or three squash, and at last, one excellent eggplant.

We have been living on deposits from sittings, more than I have ever had in a given period of time. I have over a thousand dollars, either outstanding, or due when orders are delivered. This will put me out of debt, give me enough to send Flora $100, and still something to live on! But most satisfying is the sale of personal work, amounting to $90 the last month.

The sittings have been mostly tourists here for a short time, so I must make them on a moment's notice,—or lose out. I have had no time for finishing due to this "run," and of course due to the peppers.

One sitting I did make for myself,—Frederick O'Brien. I had not seen him in years, did not recognize him at first. Ramiel talked with him, leaving me to watch and capture the right moment,—which I did,—to my satisfaction.

August 21 — 5:00 a.m. My hour: alone with my coffee, and a pen to put down my thoughts,—which are rather scattered in many directions, or divided between many subjects. But this hour of mine, this aloneness, I have not had in many weeks or months, and only have today because I fell into bed—literally—at 8:30 last night, after an exhausting day of printing, actually eight hours in the darkroom.

The children are here,—Brett, Neil, Cole,—a worse time to have them could not be! I have no time, except the supper hour and a brief visit or walk before bedtime to give them. All I can do these days is to keep up with work: or better, try not to get too far behind. Sittings, and very good ones, still pour in. Quite amazing! I no longer accept a sitting unless unlimited time is granted for finishing.

Brett walks a mile or more without a cane, and with only a slight limp.

Ramiel is worn out with the extra confusion. He is high-strung and takes matters too seriously. Last night an episode took place which I deeply regret, for it may have lasting consequences. I was in bed, trying to direct the dish-washing, general cleaning up before bedtime. The boys were arguing among themselves over respective duties, which led to teasing and half-playful blows. Ramiel in

131

his excitement slapped Neil,—something I have not done for years, and always regretted, had terrific reactions when I did. The boys are not going to forget this,—punishment by one, in their eyes, without authority.

If Flora gets wind of this, I will not hear the end of it. One of my big quarrels with her was over the slapping of Neil by Ruth Shaw. And I have always protested when she—Flora—resorts to blows. Children must, and can be, handled without beating. But it takes infinite patience.

August 27. A letter from Flora with the astonishing news of Chandler's marriage!—and at the age of nineteen!!! and to Maxine who is seventeen!! How futile all my warnings against tying himself too young. Sister warned me, tried her best to dissuade me. Despite the unfortunate, inevitable separation, I see the four boys, and am glad I married when I married. Each one of us must learn our own lesson.

I am showing at Courvoisier's, San Francisco—twenty prints. A fine column, intelligently written by Aline Kistler, *S.F. Chronicle,* about my exhibit. Her comment at length on the print, "Cypress, Point Lobos" is what I expected from a good critic: "But Weston has not done the cypress that others have seen." That is the key note from which she elaborated.

I must not go out evenings again until this rush is over. Last night it was Buhlig's last of three concerts here. I slept through most of his very interesting talk,—I know it was, for I heard snatches. I slept through a program I wanted to hear, only coming to for the last number, a Bach, which was superb! I do not pretend to know music, my response can only be emotional,—or better, intuitive.

Ramiel danced, but not with the abandon and fire he expressed at the O'Sheas'. Oh that was a party! If I had been or were now in a writing mood, several pages would be devoted to that memorable night.

Richard comes in an hour for a sitting. I must prepare.

Sunday, September 14—in studio—morning coffee. I have moved my bed over here, —which makes more room, less confusion at the house. Sonya is still asleep in the corner. She moved here several weeks ago, after a nervous breakdown from over-tension at "Tilly Polak's." It seems as though I have at last found someone to go through life with. What to do with K., I don't know: she writes me burning love letters, and having once told her to come here, it is not so easy to tell her of my change—without hurting her. C. may come for her vacation this month. But she knows of Sonya,—I told her.

The children have gone. Flora has promised to send Neil back with me, when I make a visit—the Xmas holidays. I am glad this could happen without a quarrel for I want Neil, and should have him during his adolescence.

After a brief lull, sittings have picked up again,—three last week. Several good orders in, one for $320. Also I have made several fine portraits for myself: one of Rudhyar, and one of Neil, especially noteworthy. The average quality of my professional sittings has been excellent.

September 20. Up at 4:00 and in my darkroom straightening prints from work of yesterday and the day before: work which was strenuous enough to put me to bed at 8:30. At last I have been printing the peppers.

I had to have an excuse to do them for my conscience' sake, for orders are still behind: the excuse was Pauline's request for several prints for *Vogue*. But I notice that instead of just printing one, I found it necessary to print five,—for selection! Well they are gorgeous,—the strongest things I have done, outside of some portraits.

Frederick O'Brien here for a time,—hunting a place to write. "I have been all over the world trying to find a place to write." Does this fruitless search indicate he is through,—nothing more to say? He and —— over to supper recently. A jolly evening he can make with his charming wit.

Sonya is such a lovable and altogether charming companion.

What shall I do about K.? And C. will be here soon for a holiday! But she has more poise. And B. wants to come here to dance in my studio!

A big mask party planned for tomorrow night, which Ramiel is engineering. Over fifty invited from all walks of life: Pebble Beach and Highlands Society to Carmel Bohemians!

I am in the excitement only as a spectator: until the night!

September 26. The Carmelite's society reporter (if it had one) writes about the grand mask ball: "It started out to be a farewell gathering for Ramiel McGehee; before it was over it had become the social event of the season." Also, every one seemed to be having a good time,—and without alcohol! The morning after, viewing the room carpeted with confetti and serpentines, fragments of costumes, discarded masks, floors stained with spilled punch, a great log gone to embers in the fire place, I felt like writing: of the grand march which Myrto and I led, as King & Queen, down Ocean Avenue, astonishing the natives, of the many amusing, bizarre or exquisite costumes, of the overflow of amorous couples found in our nearby house, of Ramiel's directing, and of Sonya as a modiste,—but most of the details will live as a memory only, for I have no time!

Peter and Rose are here, a grand surprise,—C. came and went, and Ramiel returns with Peter next Monday. With all due love hereby expressed, I shall be glad to be alone!

October 1. Peter, Rose and Ramiel embraced us three who are permanent residents and waved farewell: so ends another epoch. Last night the supper table gathering was by contrast very quiet: almost awkwardly so. I found myself trying to make conversation. Neither Brett, Sonya nor myself are much on talk. After Ramiel's tenseness and excitement of these last weeks, to which has been added the constant flow of Rose's strained and raucous voice, the evening had a stillness of pine trees in heavy fog.

The change from confusion to peace, the sudden break in existing rhythms, had effect upon me. I could not eat, and went to sleep sitting by the fire before eight o'clock. But today I must brace up: work!

October 2. Supper with Myrto Childe (how well I recall her as Dorothea Childs, a tall awkward girl, whom I met at the studio of Robo and Tina nine years ago. She was tight, and dancing together, top-heavily reeled and crashed to the floor pulling me along)—but to return, the talk returned to the masked revel. Myrto, my queen of five feet eleven, made an adorable consort for me of five feet five or so. Enthroned in state as rulers of the vegetable kingdom, all who entered were made to kneel and kiss our hands. If they refused, or hesitated, "Off with their heads." There were innumerable executions by way of the saw!

My crown was a hollowed-out cabbage with jewels of onions and radishes. I wore a vermin-trimmed robe and a necklace of green peppers, onions and a cucumber pendant.

Notable costumes were Henry Dickinson as a Zulu chieftan, Mary Bulkley as a "pity the blind" Negress, Molly O'Shea, a Portuguese peasant, Jimmie Hopper, pirate, Frederick O'Brien, Chinese potentate: but I could easily give a page to the notables.

Speaking of O'Brien,—Brett photographed him and got better things than I did, in fact, as Frederick said, the best portraits he has ever had, and he has been done by many important photographers.

I photographed Ramiel the day before he left. Out of two dozen negatives I will finish—eventually—fourteen, which indicates I am pleased, and he is. One negative of his hands alone is a big thing, and the portraits are a sensitive recording of one I know so well, and technically fine. The hands were entirely unposed, uncalculated: I was about to make a head, saw the gesture, and had it in a flash. So do I wish to work.

How beautiful, how grateful was Ramiel in his parting words!

October 8. Yesterday,—Monday, we closed the studio, hanging out a sign "Closed Mondays," and went to Point Lobos. A holiday of work, but work which was play. I became physically exhausted any number of times, carrying and manipulating my 8 × 10 camera, but always revived, came back. If I had worked as hard with a sitting which might bring me a hundred dollars, I'd think myself half killed! And I developed after supper, couldn't see a night's rest ahead without knowing results. I made seven negatives: seven negatives will be printed,

—all well-seen, all well-timed. My exposures ranged from 3 seconds in bright sun at noon, to 16 minutes in fog at 5:30, just before leaving. All were of cypress trunks or roots. All were made with the smallest aperture.

Brett worked very well: that is putting it mildly. Several negatives are brilliant both in technique and vision.

Sunday, October 13. B. is here: the third of my old loves for Sonya to meet, and help entertain. All three have gotten along very well with Sonya,—but who could not!

B. will dance here next Saturday night. With orders promised, and dance preparations, and trying to get away next Monday for San Francisco, — I am scheduled to talk at the Berkeley Museum—there will be a hectic week ahead.

Sunday, October 27. Returned from S. F. with Merle Armitage and—his bride! They stayed here two days and left, taking B. Now, I thought, for a week of hard work before going north again to make sittings: but no such luck,—Dr. and Mrs. Lovell arrived wanting to take Brett or me to a football game. Another afternoon lost, at least for work. Friends arrive here on their vacations, and in vacation moods. One cannot always deny them.

But yesterday I made good with my work, printing a $320 order, 24 prints from 12 negatives, in 5 hours. When I returned from the north, Brett had an exhibit of his work,—all new, and some I had not seen, hung in the studio. I can say without hesitation that he is now one of the finest photographers in this country —which means the world.

B. danced to a small but sympathetic and enthusiastic audience: danced as I have never seen her before!

I have raised my price for portraits: now the first two prints $40, duplicates $15. Also my personal work, most of the prints now $15. I'm getting back to where I was seven years ago!

A little rat, ——— ——— to whom I was kind enough, and foolish enough to make rates, is trying to beat me out of the small balance of $15 due on his prints, claiming they are not up to my standard. They are! He is a thief, and a cheap one. He has the prints, and I have $10 for $40 worth of work.

5. "So that the buckeye isn't one—"

November 16. I should not spend five minutes writing for myself: but I will! The second trip to S. F., for sittings, not a success,—two sittings only from which I pay commission,—actually not worthwhile. Then the work for *The California Monthly*, doing the Berkeley campus: I was to make six photographs for $120,—I made not a one: except a great eucalyptus—close up—its two white trunks filling the whole plate,—of course this was done for E. W. I could see nothing else! Fifteen years ago or so I would have found plenty to do,—even though not for myself I could have seen with the popular eye. But my mind was a blank that Sunday, and with money at stake.

But the tragedy is that I find they were depending on me for the next issue, so I must go way back, 140 miles, and do the job over!

S. F. was impossible, any city would be to me now: the dirt, noise, cramped quarters, the drabness of humanity struggling for money enough for food, then hunting excitement. One must grub for money, no matter where, but here at least are trees to look out upon, the ocean nearby, clean sparkling air, and few people, elbow room, breathing space, and for excitement, I don't want the passive kind,—entertainment—I want the thrill of work.

I had that yesterday—at Point Lobos. We went with Willard Van Dyke, who came to study photography with me for a week, who knows enough to make me feel I have little to give him, who will go a long ways from present indications.

I worked well.

Chandler "beat" his way here to take a ten day course with me, having been offered a position in a studio to make sittings! Poor Ted!—he must be desperate. And he has nerve, and guts,—or perhaps steps in "where angels fear to tread!"

The outstanding event of our trip north and one reason I went at the time was to see *The Passion of Joan of Arc*—a French film: a silent drama in which, great as was the acting and directing, the camera played even a greater part in making it one of the three or four outstanding films ever produced. This importance of the camera was stressed in a long article by Arthur Millier in the *Times*. He also mentioned me in the article having "discovered and developed to its highest pitch, right under the noses of the movie magnates" the principles upon which this film was based. And he wonders why they did not "smell him out and tempt him from the still to the moving camera." They are blind, Arthur.

Monday, November 19. — no, today is Tuesday, but I had Monday in mind because it was an important day in my work. Willard, Brett, and I went out on the 17 Mile Drive: between the hours of 10:00 and 4:00 I made nine negatives of cypress roots and rocks, eight of which will be finished without question as among the best seen and most brilliant technically I have yet done. The one not to be finished was a very fine negative, badly fogged. I have had trouble recently with fog, and spent an hour before going out hunting the source: finding two small bellows leaks I thought I was out of danger. My long exposures out-of-doors, never less than three or four seconds to as many minutes necessitate extraordinary precautions. I could easily have made two or three more negatives of equal value, for I was working on a magnificent root when the shutter to my $5 rectilinear lens closed, and stayed closed despite all coaxing. This lens I use most of the time in preference to my anastigmat.

I also made a portrait of Willard. Turning to speak, I saw him in a fine, easy, lounging position, sprawled on the rocks, beautifully lighted. I captured the moment.

To encourage the promoters of an "International" Salon at Portland, because of a new system of judging, and also because I was over-persuaded, I sent five prints. One feature of the plan was to return the judge's ballots to each entrant: each ballot slip supposed to have comments for or against and why. One old boy certainly did not like my work! His name H. Doty. His comments: "Head not pleasingly placed," (Johan Hagemeyer), "Interesting but fails as work of art," (back of Cristal, my best), "Interesting as Natural Subject, but where is picture? Feel that camera cannot deal with pattern such as this, and produce aesthetic appeal," (my first cypress root, and still one of best), "Pepper or gnarled piece of wood—which? My interest is aroused—but not my aesthetic interest." Evidently the old boy *was* interested, but rebelled at having his complacency upset. The only one he voted "yes" on was my first single shell, which is sure fire with all types, because it is lovely, aside from any other quality it may have.

One, H. Berger, Jr., voted yes on all my prints, commenting, "A pleasure to pass on these five outstanding prints of the exhibition."

Prints from this show and Berkeley came back in deplorable condition. If for no other reason I am through except for one-man shows, under glass.

Friday, November 29. — and up at 5:00, because we leave for S. F. early: that campus work to do over! The one of the eucalyptus is surely beautiful! Its two white trunks brilliantly white, against an overcorrected sky,—no, this is a misstatement, the original negative is correct in value, but I printed on a very contrasty paper, so the sky is apparently overcorrected, but so is the tree out of value: the sky very dark, the tree very white. Anyway, it is aesthetically thrilling. The question is, will Mr. Zobel respond?

Monday the 25th, also Sonya's birthday, we went to Point Lobos again. This time I worked with rocks,—mostly quite close, details, exquisite patterns from erosion, some quite geometric, others flaming rhythms. Fourteen negatives made, thirteen to be finished: the only discard was one fogged. I spent an hour hunting for that leak before we went: a mystery.

December 4. We arrived on the Berkeley Campus in a dense fog, the first in weeks, only rain could have been worse. I waited a day, then went ahead, despite the weather. This time I made ten negatives, "picturesque" views, buildings framed by trees, etc. Why do they hire me for work to be done with the viewpoint of the average commercial photographer? But I made at least one which I like quite well, and think they will: the base of the campanile, seen behind one of the leafless plane trees, cut at the top where the myriad branches hung with a few last leaves reach upward. This sounds too picturesque, but actually it is a simple, strong viewpoint.

The important event of our trip was the purchase, on the 30th of Nov. about 5:30, of Brett's first camera, a 4 × 5 Graflex, second hand, $50. My first was a $3\frac{1}{2}$ × $3\frac{1}{2}$ Bulls Eye, cost $5 new.

December 20. I have been up an hour—it is now 6:00—and still dark, with a brilliant moon and glittering stars. I have been in a "Xmas rush"—not in volume like my summer tourist work—but more tiring, nerve-wracking, because orders must be finished by a certain day. Yesterday I made four sittings—my last—to be finished within four days! How, I don't know, but somehow. Then we go south for the holidays, to be with my boys. After a week's visit, we plan a trip; to Arizona, to New Mexico, to Death Valley, depending on information about rains.

This year has been a success, financially. I have paid off a doctor's bill of large dimensions, kept up all current expenses, helped Flora all that I could,—considerably for me,—purchased a new phonograph, $125, Brett's Graflex, supported a family of from three to four, and have $800 in the bank, with at least $300, yet coming in, up to a possible $500. Not so bad for an "artist!"

And I have not neglected personal work, with fifty new negatives to print. This year's sales from my personal negatives amounts to over $400,—more than on a basis of paying expenses.

December 23. We do not leave for Xmas day with the boys in Southland. I could not make it. I am up at 4:30 to print four orders for delivery tomorrow. So now I plan to stay over most of next week, print my own late work, and leave for New Year's day.

Data from Dr. Lillian Whiting—

Chandler	born	4 — 26 — 1910	12:30 p.m.
Brett	„	12 — 16 — 1911	2:30 p.m.

| Neil | born | 12 — 6 — 1916 | 6:00 a.m. |
| Cole | „ | 1 — 30 — 1919 | 4:20 p.m. |

December 27. — To record that yesterday I actually printed for myself!—making eighteen prints from seventeen negatives in six hours and a half. This speed, rather indicative of the fine quality of my negatives, rather than undue haste. They were simple to print: and, not working for "effects," knowing exactly what I wished in the prints, time and correct contrast were the only concern.

We leave for the south next Monday, before New Year's.

December 29, 1929. My last entry this year,—after hunting for my ink for half an hour, and finding it in Brett's room. That is the boy's great problem in life. How to overcome carelessness, to create order, without which no one can reach great heights as an artist, or anything else. Brett loses everything he touches, breaks things right and left, is forever hurting himself. All symptoms of a disorderly mind. And art is based on order! The world is full of sloppy "Bohemians," and their work betrays them.

My press is heating in preparation for mounting forty-five new prints all done in the last two days. This is a record, and I felt the strain yesterday, piling into bed at 8:30; but up this a.m. at 3:45, and feeling quite fit. I am blessed with great recuperative power, though I abuse myself, knowing this, by working on my nerve force.

That I was able to print forty-five different negatives in two days does not indicate lack of proper consideration. Rather, that I had near to perfect negatives, and that I know in a flash exactly what I want, which is always that feeling for the thing which I had,—and have carried over in my mind, at the time of exposure. A letter from Walt Kuhn, with this thought—"To paint a thing which looks like a buckeye and isn't is not so easy. You know what it is, you have done it."

This is a thought for all photographers, who work with an apparently mechanical device. To make an exact record of the thing before one's lens, sharp, decisive, with no subterfuge: but so seen and presented that "the buckeye isn't one." Aline Kistler wrote down a similar thought, re my little desk lamp, shown at East West Gallery. "It expresses the interesting paradox of being an emotional abstraction produced by direct representation."

These words of Walt Kuhn's and Aline Kistler's are a fine ending for the Chapter 1929, and a good start for the new one of 1930.

6. *"High praise...I work all the harder—"*

January 31, 1930. Some day I may find time to write about our vacation adventures: how a monumental rock lured us off the highway in Arizona, with dire result: digging out of river bottom silt for eight hours. How we made our way by inches through a snow storm in the California mountains,—three feet of snow on the level—while other cars were abandoned on every side. I did no work, but I have no regrets. It was a memorable experience.

At a concert by imre weisshaus I met, through Howard Putzell,—Walter Arensberg. Later to his home, where I saw the most concentrated collection of fine art that has ever been my privilege. Four Brancusis, four Rousseaus, four Cézannes,—Picasso, Matisse, Derain, Renoir, African sculpture, early American paintings—my surprise and admiration—well, I could cover a page with names. The work was carefully chosen too,—not just for a name.

Brancusi's bird, and princess,—these two I remember with most amazement. The princess was curiously like one of my peppers. I took my work. It was accepted with such thrilling understanding. "The most important photography being done." And Arensberg knows personally all the outstanding workers. He asked me to come again, bought two prints, my very first cypress root, and one of the last, a root flowing like lava through rocks. And—"I will acquire more from time to time."

Howard acquired three prints, chosen well. He bought one, and asked to trade a Boris Deutch drawing for two more: which I did, because of his great appreciation and desire. But I do like the drawing.

Howard then took me to Henry Braxton, Hollywood, who has a gallery showing only "modern" art. He dated me for an exhibit at once, opening Feb. 3.

Returning here "Denny-Watrous" were waiting for me, another show for the 8th! And St. Louis Public Library exhibit starts in March!

Yesterday I started working again. My patiently waiting bones. As so often happens, I was sidetracked from bones,—seeing an old bedpan, I took one look, and fell hard. I have an exquisite negative. It might easily be called "The Princess" or "The Bird!" It has a stately, aloof dignity—stood on end — — "form follows function" again.

Neil returned to live with me. Another chapter started for both of us. And I want a fine one.

Sunday, February 2. Point Lobos again,—after nearly two months away: no, over two months have passed since working there on Sonya's birthday, and

140

very well I worked that day, with fifteen good negatives. Yesterday I started late, and working over old ground I found several things I had in mind, and a couple more, making seven, all good but for fog on two. I have exhausted my resources and patience to discover the light which enters in some mysterious way and causes such havoc. And I paid the repair shop well for going over all my cameras.

I have from yesterday, a negative of dried, taut kelp, wrapped around rock: another snake-like kelp, salt white, dried, hanging over rocks where a tide had carried it: three more eroded rocks, details like flower forms: a great shadow, from a rock above onto rocks below: and an allover pattern of slender pines in evening, sun—a poetic thing, which I might have done years ago,—but not so well.

Friday,—my bones at last: one like two iris with a jar,—then a single iris with jar: an egg with bone base: two of the jaw bone combined with another,—this jaw bone is thrilling like the prow of a ship: and finally two eggs in a shell. I only indicate the likeness of bones or kelp, or anything else, to other forms in nature, to show the relativity of everything. Certainly I did not do them because of their similarity.

February 17. Entries about every two weeks seem to be my limit. Correspondence comes from all over the states and Europe too: requests for prints for exhibits and publication, questions to answer, would-be apprentices.

The exhibit at Braxton has brought me two fine notices, from Arthur Millier,— "we believe that the work and influence of this photographer will be written large in the history of art in the West and in America," and from Merle Armitage,—"The rather small group who have been aware of E. W. for some years, know that in him, America is making one of its strongest bids toward an art consciousness."

Whether true or not, and of course I believe they are right, such high praise has a salutory effect upon me. Instead of sitting back and thinking, well I've arrived, I work all the harder, as though I must not fail those who believe in me, that I must go on and on!

Yesterday I started work with an electric iron, which caused me to further explore the kitchen, hunting for backgrounds, accessories. I wound up by doing an egg beater in front of a washboard, and after, two views of a newly found bone,—a fine one.

Sonya I must mention re her first work, almost her very first: a negative of Neil's hands, the back of a chair, and a halved red cabbage. Any one of these I would sign as my own. And I could not give higher praise. She is a surprise!

Besides the Braxton showing, I have twenty-five here at the Denny-Watrous Gallery, one ahead for St. Louis Public Library, and another for the Fine Arts

141

Museum of Houston, Texas. A request came, the second from New York, but I feel like playing for time: I am ready, but Kuhn advises me to wait until I can come personally, which seems out of the question. Anyway there's no rush.

These days are golden, the nights silver. Point Lobos in moonlight is enchanted! Robinson and Una Jeffers gave me presentation copy "C" of the limited edition of *Dear Judas*. A cordial and fine gesture.

February 18. After four perfect days of warm, even hot sun, and nights balmy, and brilliant as Mexico, Carmel is again shrouded in fog. Knowing such weather could not last we closed yesterday and went to the Point.

I worked with a newly discovered group of eroded rocks,—some in quite different forms than any I have done before: making twelve negatives from 9:00 to 5:00, with no rest but a ten minute plunge in the ocean, naked, of course,—then ten more drying in the hot sun.

Well, I might as well quit writing, or anything else. I am never alone anymore unless I arise at 4:00, not so easy for me these days being more or less exhausted and sleeping late. My family, Brett, Neil or Sonya congregate around my desk the moment they arise. I should have a room with locked doors.

How much I want, and need to be alone! Even an hour a day—

February 19. Nine, out of twelve exposed, to finish,—the other three in the waste barrel, fogged! Since I have not been able to find any leak, after hours of searching, my trouble must come when inserting the dark slides: naturally I take the greatest care at the time, but my camera is old, the back does not fit as tight as it once did, warped perhaps, going from Mexican sun to Carmel fog, and the slightest move is enough to part the holder from back,— a sixteenth of an inch, and,—enters light!

What can I do? I wish for a new and light 8 × 10.

February 22. Thursday I went to photograph Molly and John O'Shea, at their Highlands home: real persons both of them! Evidently well-to-do which hasn't hurt them, indeed they are amongst the few, one might say, whom money has enriched,—added to their inherent charm. I did Molly first, in John's (or Shawn's—is that the Irish spelling?—I think not, but like the sound better)—studio. She is difficult to work with, camera shy to a degree,—why I cannot see, being a beautiful woman of fine carriage. While working I noted Leda, their police-dog, asleep in a most beautiful posture, and made three negatives, which I look forward to with great interest.

After lunch, and cocktails, too many for me not used to drink, Sean (I think this correct) took me to see their rocks. I was amazed at the concentrated drama and strength of that point. A heavy sea (Neil has certainly made this page illegible, putting down a book on the wet ink).

142

Sunday, February 23. No use going on with yesterday's thoughts,—the family gathering broke the thread as usual. But I will mention this, that after the rocks and sea, Sean and I went back to warm up, being soaked with the spray, and added a little internal heat with numerous glasses of *real* bourbon taken over a period of two hours' conversation. When Brett and Sonya arrived they were given every opportunity to add to the merriment. So we drove home very gay, relaxed, forgot our supper, slept well, and awakened fresh and no head. All of which I put down because drinking to this extent is an unusual event for me.

I have my horoscope at last. Mrs. Severy, after making many charts, decided on Gemini as my rising sign: and, I have a bad year ahead! Which does not worry me for time passes. Too, the human element enters in. She may be wrong, not having my hour. Eight charts were made before Gemini was decided upon. I am not a skeptic, I am always inclined toward unorthodox viewpoints, I see no reason to doubt that the stars have a definite effect upon the human race, but I wonder whether anyone can interpret them. An orthodox belief is merely a prevailing one, popular at the moment: astrology was no doubt once quite orthodox, just as vaccination is now. And someday vaccination will be generally regarded as a superstition comparable to witchcraft.

February 24. Tina, according to newspaper reports has been deported from Mexico, because of her communistic activities,—"an undesirable citizen!" She expected this move, and so wrote me, long ago sending me her books to care for. Dear, lovely Tina! You seem much more remote in Germany—so the paper stated her destination—for now I cannot picture your surroundings.

One of the best chapters in Anita's book [Anita Brenner—see Vol. I] on Mexico is "Francisco Goitia." Quoting his ideas she writes, "He takes for granted the mastery which permits him to do so,"—that is break rules. And, "line and color both are exact when the spirit is comprehended, or the inverse." And, "that man who for the sake of a pure work of art tenders his people the sacrifice of an unworldly life."

February 25.—And it is still raining: has been off and on for five days. These days would be fine for reading, writing, forgetting the economic pressure. But I cannot forget, not entirely, with no cash coming in, and a new worry, Johan sick with pneumonia.

At the O'Sheas' Monday late, we met Mable Dodge Luhan and her Indian husband. One might expect a young, handsome, dashing sort of buck,—instead of the rather stolid, heavy old Indian we met. With them was Ella Young, who impressed me more than any of the party. They will come here today.

Sean showed a number of paintings I had not seen. He has a dazzling color sense, and often achieves fine form.

February 28, 1930. A letter from John Schaffer—a young man met at Merle's—who wrote me in a burst of enthusiasm after viewing my exhibit at Braxton's:

"Splendid! You are a better grocer than Matisse or Picasso.... Those peppers were at once Rembrandtesque and Chaplin—the titanic strength of Rembrandt and the wistfulness of our inimitable Charles. .... I could only think of Van Gogh when I saw your trees. You have seen fragments which I had never suspected to exist, bits of life and matter that have found expression due to your omnipresent eye. Thanks a dozen times for the experience your exhibition afforded me."

Now I consider my exhibit a success, though I sell not a print.

Also came a letter from Walter Arensberg to whom I sent my bedpan, or "form follows function," as I half facetiously named the print.

"I can't express how bowled over I was by the vision of "f. f. f." It is certainly one of your most profound, and shall hang in my study."

Two more letters to spur me on, if I needed them for a spurring—

Well, I have new material! Sonya went mushroom hunting and returned with several of the most exquisite and powerful bones. I have seen, just studying them, that is the two important ones, seven different views or combinations to do, seven new and strong negatives.

And yet this work of mine which creates such response from individuals, I have removed, for economic reasons, part of it from my Denny-Watrous exhibit, and substituted very conventional portraits. One painter, a nice lady-like painter who makes pastel color canvases and decorations suitable for boudoirs, a Mr. Johnnet, when asked how he liked my showing, stammered and said that I had extraordinary subject matter. Well—of course I have, and why should I be even bothered by an ordinary person. But I am displeased with his nerve in hanging one of his "pretty" embroideries over my bedpan during his lecture on art. I shall change it to a place he cannot cover it. A most unethical discourteous gesture, his,—covering fine art with applied art!

Sunday, March 2. A jolly evening at Drew Chidester's home. He and his wife are both very real vital people and excellent hosts. Good cocktails, wine, and a bountiful supper cooked by Madame Mika Mikoun—"Sculpteur Ceramiste," who knows her garlic, no matter how she sculps.

I've been working with bones: the first day, not a single exposure, the extension bed came loose from my fast-disintegrating camera, the muslin curtain on the porch where I work, rotten when I came, finally ripped off, visitors interrupted, until evening finished my attempts, and I who work so easily, smoothly, felt finished. The next day was better, I made six well-seen negatives, but one was moved, bone slipped, another was slightly undertimed, rare for me to do, and another, my favorite, the two bones were not separated enough in value: so I had only a 50 % success, a very poor average for me. But my viewing, my feeling on the ground glass, was strong, and the three perfect negatives will be worthy additions.

Later Bob Howard called to see my new work, but purchased an old print, vintage of 1922. A nude Diego has, Margrethe, fragment on sand with parasol. I certainly would have chosen, and preferred that he would have, a later work. Thinking over Anita's paragraph about Goitia,—breaking rules: during my exhibit for the Japanese, 1927, a Japanese critic wrote, "There is growing a Weston style of composition from Mr. Weston who disregards composition." Actually, one does not, or I do not, *consciously* disregard composition, or *try* to break rules. I see things in my own way, thus establishing precedents, making rules,—for others!

7. "How little subject matter counts in the ultimate reaction!"

Saturday, March 8. Yesterday I made photographic history: for I have every reason and belief that two negatives of kelp done in the morning will someday be sought as examples of my finest expression and understanding. Another is almost as good, and yet another might be considered a very strong example of a more usual viewpoint: this latter several steps beyond the salon type of photograph. But my two best,—they are years beyond.

I had found the kelp the evening before, almost at the foot of Ocean Avenue, washed there by the recent storm, the heavy sea. I knew it would not stay put, perhaps not even the night, so early next morning I walked down to see what the tides had done: and there it lay unchanged, twisted, tangled, interwoven, a chaos of convulsed rhythms, from which I selected a square foot, organized the apparently complex maze, and presented it, a powerful integration. This was done of course with no manual arrangement,—the selection was entirely my viewpoint as seen through the camera. I get a greater joy from finding things in Nature, already composed, than I do from my finest personal arrangements. After all, selection is another way of arranging: to move the camera an eighth of an inch is quite as subtle as moving likewise a pepper.

These kelp negatives are as strong as any of my rocks: indeed I think they are stronger. A few of my rock details have lace-like delicacy. How little subject matter counts in the ultimate reaction!

March 11. On Monday, my day off, we drove early to the beach—the Carmel front. I wishing to work with kelp, noted on a Sunday evening walk. But alas, kelp does not stay put, like rocks and trees, so the several noted arrangements had disappeared, or were disarranged, maybe by the tide, or Sunday revelers. So I found and worked with dried kelp, three negatives. They were far different from the powerful kelp of the previous week: exquisite curves, almost dainty lines. Then we drove to a remembered beach ten miles down the coast where there were rock forms of amazing texture. But the extension bed of my camera pulled out, the screw loose, so I found working close to impossible, and there was not much I could do: one negative only made. While working the tide came in and my camera case was turned over in the salt water and holders pretty well saturated. A poor day for me!

8. "The stark beauty a lens can so exactly render—"

March 15. Long ago I thought of printing my own work,—work not done for the public—on high gloss paper. This was some years back in Mexico: but habit is so strong that not until this last month did I actually start mounting glossy prints for my collection.

I had to make some twenty such prints for an article in *Touring Topics*—they purchased thirteen. When I compared the returned balance with the same copies in my portfolio I made my decision at once. It will take a long time to print even my favorite negatives again: I imagine two thirds of my older work will never be reprinted, and too, the expense would be prohibitive. But I have already made a showing, and hope my next exhibit will be on glossy paper. What a storm it will arouse!—from the "Salon Pictorialists." It is but a logical step, this printing on glossy paper, in my desire for photographic beauty. Such prints retain most of the original negative quality. Subterfuge becomes impossible, every defect is exposed, all weakness equally with strength. I want the stark beauty that a lens can so exactly render, presented without interference of "artistic effect." Now all reactions on every plane must come directly from the original seeing of the thing, no secondhand emotion from exquisite paper surfaces or color: only rhythm, form and perfect detail to consider. Honesty unembellished—first conceptions coming straight through unadulterated—no suggestion, no allegiance to any other medium. While on the subject of printing: I recall an article, about Stieglitz if my memory serves. It spoke of his making a hundred prints or so to get one just right. At the time, though I admired the effort and patience, it seemed to indicate a woeful lack of surety, or lack of skill, or a pretty poor negative, or maybe just good publicity. But now more than ever, I want to be able—and am most of the time—to make one or two tests, and then the final print, as I would have it. This way is my ideal. It indicates decisive thinking in making the negative, and carrying that already formed image conception, without wavering, on through into the print. It necessitates fine negatives and printing ability.

Sunday, March 16. For two Saturdays now, I have "received" at my exhibit,—Denny-Watrous Gallery. The last time most interesting, and most profitable. A tourist purchased a print of cypress branches,—not one of my important things: and John O'Shea bought the first print sold of my kelp, and the first print sold, done in my new way, on glossy paper. He said, "I am going to have a whole portfolio of your prints." The kelp, shown for the first time, created quite a stir: and I will say they are photographs to be proud of.

Late in the evening came half a dozen press photographers, here from all over the country. They were all most enthusiastic and wish to call at my studio. I forgot to tell why they are here: because of Lindbergh, and his glider experiments nearby. They showed a fine spirit in begging me to go with them and try to get Lindbergh. But though I should very much like to do him, in my way, which must mean some personal contact, I cannot be enthusiastic about working as they do, "snooping" around, waiting their chance, not wholly against his will, but with no cooperation nor desire,—for which I do not blame him. My arrival on the scene would mean just another press photographer to bother him.

March 18.—And writing the date recalls that it is Sister's birthday— — I must send her a print for greeting.

Looking over old letters to find stamps for Neil, I came across this one of historical value!

"Dear Papa,
Received camera in good shape. It's a dandy. I think I can work it all right. Took a snap at the chickens."

—and so on — — dated Aug. 20, 1902. I wrote this, and father saved it, twenty-eight years ago.

Photographed William Ritschel at his home. A rugged old man, with a beautiful young wife, or mistress, one never can know these days, who assured me he disliked a "posed"-appearing photograph,—and then posed all over the place. His work showed little sense of form, but he understands, and paints well in an academic way, the emotional, dramatic side of the sea: in other words paints good sea pictures,—and sells them.

One whole magazine was fogged: which proves my trouble must come from the magazine. These troubles I have with fog are absolutely distressing and depressing.

Sunday, March 23. Sonya, Brett, and I, to hear Buhlig play Beethoven's Hammerklavier Sonata. I had not heard it before, and I did not hear it all last night. I slept through part of the tremendous piano forte! And we sat in the front row, near to touching Richard! I certainly feel that I must give up going out evenings. What is the use! Maybe I'll try an afternoon nap before important evenings. Is it that Richard's playing could not hold me absolutely? But I wanted to hear, and I have slept through other programmes that conscious mind desired to hear, or see,—for instance a Chaplin film!

Beethoven cannot move me as does Bach: nor do any of the moderns—that I have heard—move me as does Bach: none have the transcending grandeur, the irresistible force, and surety which sweeps me along with neither intellectual questioning nor emotional excitement. Bach is,—Bach — — —

148

I worked with a new load of manzanita roots, brought for the fireplace,—and with one negative, have a good result. Two out of three fogged. Oh, God!

March 25. A chicken dinner for me last night with all the trimmings of a usual American dinner, mashed potatoes, gravy, etc., in honor of my 44th birthday. Chicken to honor a vegetarian! It looked good I must say, this festive table, but the eating of it was a disillusionment,—I would have prefered, and many times over, a fine avocado, a crisp salad, and for desert, Ramiel's ambrosia,—oranges, fresh coconut, and honey—instead of pudding.

Mable Dodge Luhan in, and bought two more heads of Lawrence and one of Jeffers: a nice birthday present. Ella Young with her, and I asked for a sitting, because I admire her and because her portraits may sell. Ella Young believes in fairies,—and of course that would appeal to me, anything unorthodox does. I told her that I had slept during most of her talk, but felt that my subconscious self had listened very attentively. She was not surprised, in fact she was pleased, and said this often happened when the subconscious mind wished to especially listen in. This partial understanding of my desire to sleep through important evenings, came to me as I told her of my nap during her talk. I knew she would not mind, or rather would understand and be complimented.

Now I shall not be tortured by the effort to keep awake, but go expecting and prepared for a good nap,—choosing a back seat. Hope I don't snore all through a Bach fugue! some might not understand.

March 26. I am a grandfather!!
Edward Frank Weston—the fifth Edward in succession—arrived on my 44th birthday — — Strange coincidence—if it is coincidence. Almost, it seems, there must be a deep significance in this sharing of birthdates.

Monday, March 31. I have been printing,—new negatives, and reprinting some old ones. The reprinting of old negatives has been a revelation,—using glossy paper. Because the prints do not "dry down," losing shadow detail and flattening highlights I am able to print much deeper and use a more contrasty grade of paper, with a resulting brilliance and richness which puts an entirely new value on my old work,—like unto new negatives in the pleasure they give me. I am shipping today my first exhibit on glossy paper: to Munich, Germany.

I worked one morning with a boxer, who is also an artist, Stanley Quackenbush. I had to work much faster with his movements, even when arrested, than with B. dancing, for instance: I made 1/10 sec. exposures, at f/4.5 in brilliant reflected sunlight, indoors. But I did not always get a fine definition. So in order to stop down and focus with more sureness, I must find a brighter room, or work out doors.

Then I did that fairy-like person, Ella Young, with good results,—worked with David Alberto's hands—not so good—too posed, artificial, and had another day

149

at Point Lobos,—not as good as usual, making but two negatives: did not find material in spot where Brett left us.

Willard Van Dyke here, and brought the new book on Steichen with foreword by Sandburg. I was disappointed, had hoped to find his personal work far ahead of his reproductions in *Vanity Fair*, always too clever, artificial, which I was willing to blame on [the] magazine's policy. Willard left sooner than expected so I did not look through the book at leisure, nevertheless we went once over the plates together and my memory recalls but little of outstanding value: a sunflower, a head of sunburned girl, the flower pots he considers, or likes as his best,—better did Brett see in a similar way, the sewer pipe, done when he was fifteen. Willard also brought *Camera Work* of seventeen years ago, and how much stronger and finer are the plates of Paul Strand. The blind woman, the white fence,—these and others dim the work of Steichen. The foreword by Sandburg, he, Steichen, does not live up to. Sandburg in making excuses for Steichen, contradicts himself. When he decries art for art's sake, he then writes, "or by revolutionists who stood clear and clean outside that of commerce and fought it tooth and nail and worked for its destruction." What is this but art for art's sake. And then he rings in Michelangelo, claiming he sold his life work to the church and then writing,—Angelo revolted when he had to please! Same old story—anyone working for *Vanity Fair* has to be clever to hold his place. Steichen's work is just that,—clever. Again he writes of Steichen, and contradicts his underlying thought that all great art has been for a price: "A fellow can't stay on Broadway a long time and give the customers what they want without becoming something like the north end of a horse going south." With this the whole defense collapses.

The best sentence in the foreword: "Creative art gives an object or experience a new existence and essence of its own."

I have five new negatives, and of new subject matter from Monday last, my holiday: they are of succulents in the garden of Sally Flavin. All well-seen and to be printed, pointing a new series which will be important as the peppers, roots and rocks. Kelp, worthwhile, I have not seen of late, excepting last eve, but too far to carry my heavy camera.

150

9. *"The flame of recognition—"*

April 7. Galka Scheyer and Michael Schindler have been here and we have seen much of them these two days past. A stimulating contact it has been. Galka repelled me at the very start of our acquaintance but now I find myself wishing she would drop in once more before leaving. She is a dynamo of energy. She would wear me out in a few days,—but insight of unusual clarity, and an ability to express herself in words, brilliantly, forcefully, to hit the nail cleanly, buoys me up for the time. She is an ideal "go-between" for the artist and his public. She and Michael had a two day controversy over one of my prints,— whether or no it could legitimately be hung upside down, both of them agreeing that it was stronger upside down but Michael insisting that the objectivity of photography required the print to be shown as originally seen: she protesting the imposed limitation, insisting that no rule should bind one's freedom of expression. I inclined to Michael's side, at least in the case of the print in question, fish and kelp, for one cannot get away from objective rendering of perspective and the fish turned upside down gave me a disagreeable feeling of falling out of the print, maybe only because I made the negative. Granted the lines, pattern, etc., became more dynamic reversed, art must be more than pattern, form, for otherwise anyone could learn to compose by rule and be an artist,—which could never be.

The flame started first by amazement over subject matter, that flame which only a great artist can have—not the emotional pleasure of the layman—but the intuitive understanding and recognition relating obvious reality to the esoteric, must then be confined to a *form* within which it can burn with a focussed intensity: otherwise it flares, smokes and is lost like in an open bonfire.

So writing, I do not place the artist on a pedestal, as a little god. He is only the interpreter of the inexpressable, for the layman, the link between the known and the unknown, the beyond.

This is mysticism,—of course! How else can one explain why a combination of lines by Kandinsky, or a form by Brancusi, not obviously related to the cognized world, does bring such intense response. Science might explain—try to—by saying that a Kandinsky excites certain reflex action upon the optic center. No doubt my words are most unscientific, but my thought is correct, and in line with most of the naive explanations of science. These scientists, so many of them see not beyond their noses! Granted, the eye becomes excited. Why does it? Another example of narrow outlook, in an article on the newly-discovered

151

planet, conjecturing on the possibility of life there,—and as always from the standpoint of earthly temperature, etc. Is this earth the last word! Why not life on the sun?—A superior life maybe.

I said Galka could express herself forcefully in words: actually she stumbles over words, being new to English,—but the effect is forceful, and she is not an orator. Which calls to mind that Paul Rosenfeld—in his writing—weakens his critical analyses by words, words, straining for unusual combinations, tossing the glass balls. Yet his feeling for Stieglitz—it was the *Port of New York* I reread after some years—the chapter on Stieglitz which I gave Sonya to read—is well rendered, if only it were not so cluttered with flowery phrases.

A summer sea and sky these past days—and lazy breakers with the tide at ebb: more like the Southland. The valley is carpeted with spring wild flowers, yellow one week, the next purple: and wild iris on Point Lobos.

I am going to start numbering my best work, editions up to fifty. It is time to protect those who have confidence in me. And too, I will be able to raise prices.

April 9. We went to hear Claire Dux sing. I do not care for professional soloists bellowing for a price, but the Chidesters were giving a party after the concert and Claire Dux was invited, so were we,—for politeness' sake I had to hear her sing. The singing neither offended nor thrilled me—nor did I sleep! I passively listened,—no more.

The party though was right jolly, a well-chosen gathering, good food and plenty of superlative Scotch. I was plied with liquor, dragged into a bedroom, dressed in a white silk evening gown and made to dance. It went over well enough, if the roars of laughter were indicative. A brilliant climax to the concert!

Yesterday, lunch with the Luhans. And after, Don Antonio—"Tony"—was persuaded to go out on the rocks with me and my Graflex. I made three dozen negatives, and some brilliant ones. Most of one magazine were fogged. I am going to the city and have my Graflex operated on.

April 12. I printed a head of Tony Luhan to have ready when they came after proofs. The print was extraordinary,—about the limit in brilliance of chemical quality, and powerful in presentation of the person. I was more than happy.

Now Tony is a rather flabby Indian, settled down into a life of ease, well-fed, middle-aged inactivity. In my print, I gave him a heroic strength he does not possess.

So when he lumbered in, I got out the enlargement, anticipating at least a grunt of approval.

Silence—

Well, I thought, Indians are never ecstatic.

Mable Luhan was in the car. We took the print and proofs to her. She responded, exclaiming, "like a head of bronze." "How do you like it Tony?"

"I don't like."

"Why?" I ventured at last.

"I look too old,—a hundred years maybe."

!!!!!—Collapse of the photographer — — —

April 13. —this moment returned from the dance program of Ronny Johansson. I left at the intermission—blood boiling—fighting mad. I only stutter—trying to tell how I feel—which is as though I had been insulted—my intelligence affronted—really I am in a fury—I don't often get this way. And when I think of B.—dancing here to a handful—then this, this — — —

It is a chagrin—disappointment — — this dance—"act"—I might have seen as a movie prologue, and been quite "entertained"—but somehow here in Carmel—at the "Golden Bough," sponsored by Kuster, I, at least, expected something—God knows what—but *something!* Not surely the same old gags of 20 years back—child's play—no, a child would play better—and to think that I dragged Neil away from his swimming hole to educate him!

This—after Claire Dux—who bellowed sweetly last week, is just too much. But I had no hopes when I went to hear her: so I was mildly amused while my supper digested. At this moment I could not digest a lettuce leaf.

Usually I can laugh—I can't even smile just now — — shades of "Frisco"— and that buck nigger—Bertha and I saw together—how they danced — — or to watch the rabble in Solomon's penny dance hall—or the Camioneros in Salon Azteca—that was dancing! honest dancing.

And all the time I realized she (maybe) was dancing well—what she did—but *what* she did—that's the sickening, infuriating part. Maybe this explosion has been good for me—getting complacent?—make my work grow—push it to the limit in my reaction—realize one cannot conform—or emphasize that realization —this rebellion will force me ahead—I would not weep if I had spent $50 on tickets—I will go on ahead—see more than I ever saw before—be hard to please —desperate over mediocrity—all thanks to Ronny Johansson.

April 17. After the above explosion I felt cleansed, purged, I sat down and drafted a "manifesto," announcing that I would no longer retouch my professional portraits. This is a drastic move! Dare I put it into effect? Will I gain or lose—I mean my bank account?

I don't care—but my family — —

April 21. Brilliant, warm days again: fine weather for the Easter week-enders. I usually have some acquaintance, or old friend call, or stay here. Last week Aline Kistler and Warren, this week Alfred Honigbaum, also Mr. and Mrs. Henry Swift, Berkeley, came, she whom I showed the sights to her first day in Mexico. He bought two prints, a cypress detail, and a rock, choosing with excellent judgment, and preferring the glossy paper.

153

Myrto Childe, now living here, spent the day. We called up the past, and the days of 1920—I, at Tina's and Robo's,—when Robelo lived, and I was first enamoured of Tina: Robelo was too, and God knows, many others. The parade of suitors marched in and out, until my last day in Mexico, keeping me in hot water. Tina was to be my great test and lesson,—my last possessive love.

April 24. I sent the following statement to Houston, Texas, where I am showing forty prints during May:

Clouds, torsos, shells, peppers, trees, rocks, smoke stacks, are but interdependent, interrelated parts of a whole, which is Life.

Life rhythms felt in no matter what, become symbols of the whole.

The creative force in man, recognizes and records these rhythms with the medium most suitable to him, to the object, or the moment, feeling the cause, the life within the outer form. Recording unfelt facts by acquired rule, results in sterile inventory. To see the *Thing Itself* is essential: the quintessence revealed direct without the fog of impressionism,—the casual noting of a superficial phase, or transitory mood.

This then: to photograph a rock, have it look like a rock, but be *more* than a rock.

Significant presentation,—not interpretation.

—and I sent these Technical Notes:

These photographs—excepting portraits—are contact prints from direct 8 × 10 negatives, made with a rectilinear lens costing $5, —this mentioned because of previous remarks and questions. The portraits are enlarged from $3\frac{1}{4}$ × $4\frac{1}{4}$ Graflex negatives, the camera usually held in hands.

My way of working—

I start with no preconceived idea — —

discovery excites me to focus — —

then rediscovery through the lens — —

final form of presentation seen on ground glass, the finished print previsioned complete in every detail of texture, movement, proportion, *before exposure* — — the shutter's release automatically and finally fixes my conception, allowing no after manipulation — —

the ultimate end, the print, is but a duplication of all that I saw and felt through my camera.

April 26. Someone reading over my statement questioned my use of the word "impressionism." To me it has always meant for example, a tree momentarily shimmering in a brilliant sun or the same tree rain drenched, half hidden by a passing storm: painted, etched or photographed under such conditions,—the transitory instead of the eternal.

154

But I do not want the play of sunlight to excite the fancy, nor the mystery of gloom to invoke the imagination—wearing colored glasses — —

I want the *greater mystery* of *things revealed more clearly than the eyes see*, at least more than the layman,—the casual observer notes. I would have a microscope, shall have one some day.

On the other hand what a valuable way of recording just such passing moments is the camera! And I certainly would be the first to grasp the opportunity, if I were ready at the time! I cannot, never have been bound by any theory or doctrine, not even my own. Anything that excites me, for any reason, I will photograph: not searching for unusual subject matter, but making the commonplace unusual, nor indulging in extraordinary technique to attract attention. Work only when desire to the point of necessity impels,—then do it honestly. Then so called "composition" becomes a personal thing to be developed along with technique as a personal way of seeing. So composition cannot be taught. Rules of composition are theories deducted by the disciples of some master who without thought of how or why, recorded his own intense observations in his own way. Others then copy and set to formulae.

April 28. I have finished, since starting to print on glossy paper, eighty-five prints. All new negatives,—that is, those made last year but not printed, and a number of old favorites which have become new favorites, so incomparably finer do they register on glossy paper. It is a joy like unto making a first print, to reprint negatives I was tired of. No other surface is now to be thought of. I can print much deeper than heretofore, with no fear of losing shadows, or muddying half tones by drying down: or I can use a more contrasty grade of paper, resulting in amazingly rich blacks yet retaining brilliant whites.

I actually look forward to the great labor of reprinting all my best work. Then I shall have a bargain sale of the old!

Besides giving me all possible quality from a given negative, glossy paper deprives me of any chance to spot—repair—a print from a damaged or carelessly seen negative. Everything is revealed—retouching on the negative or spotting on the print. And too, there can be no relying upon beautiful paper textures,—one is faced with the real issue, significant presentation of the Thing Itself with photographic quality.

April 29. The widely used arguments against photography ever being considered a fine art are: the element of chance which enters in,—finding things ready-made for a machine to record, and of course the mechanics of the medium. Besides disproving chance with my own work amongst others, finding everywhere ready-made "arrangements," I say that chance enters into all branches of art: a chance word or phrase starts a trend of thought in a writer, a chance sound may bring new melody to a musician, a chance combination of lines,

155

new composition to a painter. I take advantage of chance—which in reality is not chance—but being ready, attuned to one's surroundings—and grasp my opportunity in a way which no other medium can equal in spontaneity, while the impulse is fresh, the excitement strong. The nearest to photography is a quick line sketch, done usually as a note for further elaboration. And how much finer, stronger, more vivid these sketches usually are than the finished painting.

So in photography,—the first fresh emotion, feeling for the thing, is captured complete and for all time at the very moment it is seen and felt. Feeling and recording are simultaneous,—hence the great vitality in *pure* photography and its loss in manipulated photography,—by the devitalizing influence of the hand.

As to photography's mechanicalness,—art is a way of seeing, not a matter of technique. A moron can be a superb technician. And besides the spontaneity of the machine,—camera, time, and energy can be saved for creative thought, inner development.

This is not a defense of photography to bolster up my own misgivings. I would not change to any other way of working. This is a dissertation with morning coffee, the trend of thought started by Myrto, who said she wrote better, her thoughts registered more directly through her typewriter: the machine again—

May 7. Until yesterday, I had not been away on an outing for over five weeks. Brett has been in the south with car and camera. He returned last week bringing Cole! Almost at once, the peace we had ended, the clash of personalities began, the quiet evenings turned noisy. Neil changed the moment Cole appeared. Cole the restless, excitable, exciting others, mischievous,—but a dear, fine boy, with a certain sadness beneath his roguishness.

So we started for Point Lobos. I made but four negatives all day. I should find a new place to work: the excitement over new subject matter is no longer there. Not that I have done everything, or even done as well as could be, many things already worked with,—but that necessary thrill of discovery, amazement over new material, I no longer have.

However I have three new negatives to print, (one discarded, moved, camera wind-shaken).

This from foreword to exhibit, *Das Lichtbild*, München,—

"There will scarcely be anyone who now and then, has not been deeply impressed by a photo... for the mere fact that its subject modified and improved his own imagination of the universe, granting him an outlook far beyond his visible surroundings."

Monday, May 12. Jack Black, ex-convict, five timer, sat to me yesterday. I read his book, *You Can't Win*, and I heard much about him from Lincoln Steffens, so I decided he would be an interesting addition to my rogue's gallery!

156

He has a lot of humour. When he greeted me he said, "I've never been invited to have a portrait made except for a rogue's gallery! They keep you several days before the 'sitting,' till you look sufficiently rough and dirty,—like they think you should be. Stupid!—When you get out, clean up, no one can recognize you from the photo."

A slender, almost delicate figure,—grey, slightly bowed, deeply lined—some of the furrows are scars from the strait jacket,—a devil to manage in prison, hated by the police, said Lincoln Steffens. He gave forth warmth, friendliness, even his cold blue eyes, but one could sense how quickly he could change to steel in emergency. He showed but flashes of bitterness, whenever he mentioned police,—said he never passed one, not now, without cursing him under his breath. He stayed the afternoon. I asked would he have wine or tea,—he said tea. A fascinating afternoon, with Jack Black reminiscing,—a background, he has, to draw from.

When we walked down the street to Steffens', I noted how far down over his eyes he pulled his hat. A habit from old maybe!

In the evening he talked at the Denny-Watrous Gallery,—and held his audience for two hours.—Subjects: prison reform, how criminals get that way,—and stay so, and his own return to society: no dry statistics, but facts from an under-world expert, told without bitterness. Nor did he once become sentimental, maudlin,—rather he put over his case against the good people with a mellow sarcasm, a subtle humour which brought laughter,—used wisely the most powerful weapon of propaganda—at least to move a sophisticated audience—ridicule. His classification of gangs,—other than underworld—real estate gangs, bank gangs, Hoover's gang,—who have greater success because they hire better lawyers—put one at once in sympathy with the underdog.

But—the sad fact is, that an audience who would go to hear Jack Black is already composed 99–100 percent of those understanding and in sympathy with his cause. Others,—right-minded pillars of society, would not be seen in such a crowd. They would spend their money for jails,—bigger and better, police,—more efficient, or rather "hard-boiled." But these "pillars" are getting a first hand contact with uniformed bandits,—police, in these days of traffic violations. Maybe they will see the light!

I have several fine negatives of Jack Black: Graflex in hand, rapid, spontaneous shots.

May 14. Point Lobos yesterday.

How many times the last year or so have I written this line! I never tire of that wonder spot, nor could I ever forget it, no matter where I go from here.

It was a perfect day, of brilliant sun, and the laziest sea I have yet seen in the north: scarce a ripple laved the shore.

I decided to work with cypress for the first time in months: the sun on their weather-polished trunks,—torsos nude of bark,—reveals every tiny line, etched black on a surface glistening as ivory.

Harder work to isolate details of a cypress than to work with rocks. And I have done so many, that to find new forms was not easy. I worked with but two trees all day: but these two were so difficult, my hazard so great that I returned home exhausted.

The first one on a precipitous earth bank was bad enough—I strained every tendon trying to focus—but I could have saved myself, supposing a slip, by digging into the soft earth on the way down. The second was a marvellous old root. I had found it long ago, and it was difficult to reach without a camera: but added to handling myself, the 8 × 10, its weight, and worse, unwieldiness, made my task as dangerous, no, more dangerous than any I have faced in photography.

The tree hung over a cliff, a sheer drop to the ocean, with only a couple of possible ledges to hold the camera. I planned carefully every step down, removed all loose rocks and branches, before making the descent. One misstep as I stood there focussing, and I never would have focussed again. I was never so limited in viewpoint, so fixed in position, but from that one available spot, which did not allow me to move six inches in any direction, I found a very fine combination of roots. The light was perfect,—for a few moments: before I had finished focussing it was not, for a cast shadow started to move across my arrangement, quite ruining it. I waited over an hour, resting in the hot sun, dozing, then forcing myself up for fear of rolling off into the ocean. Then just about time for my little eclipse to pass, another, uncalculated, was on! I saw that it would last until sunset: reluctantly picked up my camera, noting where tripod legs were placed and how long, then worked for an hour on the other side of the tree.

Just before the shadow passed, fleecy clouds veiled the sun, and helped kill the shadow without dulling too much the brilliance. I have a hard-earned negative.

Sunday morning, May 18, 1930. Another chapter of my life ended, our lives,— Brett and mine. This morning he left for the south to start a life on his own.

It all happened so suddenly, the actual parting, yet conditions leading up to it date back many months. In the last analysis, I would say, the question of money was the great factor in our separation: other causes seem more immediate, obvious, such as incompatibility with Sonya, irritation over the children,—but money, or in other words the satisfaction of his ego, was the basis of his going. He must sweat and suffer before he even begins to have the meagre, simple comfort I have given him.

We are much alike in many ways, yet so very different in others. Maybe the differences are only in the matter of years.

Brett needs money, I think always will, or for many years. He is a thoughtless spender,—and he wants the best. His thoughtlessness is not a mean selfishness, for he has always been the most generous boy. I wonder how much he will change, earning by his own sweat the money he spends.

He will make money, for he will have to have it!—Good clothes, good food, a new car, the best in cameras. Well, I was extravagant in the matter of cameras —anything photographic—I had to have the best. But that was to further my work. In most things I have gone along with the plainest,—or without.

When Brett returned from the South last month, I had hoped for a change in him. He had a taste there of rushing and worrying, being on his own,—I thought he would realize and be more thoughtful.

But Brett has grown his wings,—no longer a child, yet so much a child in many ways that my heart aches when I think of what he faces now alone. But it had to be for his own growth. He no longer fitted into this nest, yet while he used it he had to be part of the routine, which no longer interested him. If he had no little brothers needing just what I have tried to do for him, if Sonya had not been there, we might have gone on for years together. Our mutual love, compatibility, would have held us together,—and maybe—no, I'm sure,—to his detriment. It had to come, our separation. Neil, Cole, Sonya, are actually only incidents—he had to spread his wings and fly!

Yesterday I was sick at heart, the same awful feeling that always has come over me, when, whether deserved or not, I have cuffed or scolded the children: knowing that if I had been big enough, I could have handled the situation differently. I thrashed Chandler and Brett once in a great while, when we were all young together! I vividly remember cuffing Neil the last time,—one of the few times. I do not recall ever striking Cole. I have grown at least!

It happened this way,—the break between Brett and me. Friday night at the supper table, he pushed Cole's face into his food, for leaning over onto the table. A few moments later Cole saw his chance and knocked Brett's own hand, holding buttered bread, into his face. Brett turned, made ridiculous, face grease-smeared, and in his fury, slapped Cole, rather too hard. The least slap would have been too hard. I have warned him, and the little boys, that I am to mete out all punishment. I became furious, ordered Brett to his room, told him the next offense he could leave, would have to. The next morning he was packing to go. I talked with him, told him not to be hasty, let him know I did not expect him, nor want him to leave. But I knew all the time the moment had come,— Brett was no longer a child,—he would have to be while here. The episode was only a symbol.

Brett never held a grudge. He always laughed while in tears. Fine quality that! We made mutual confessions of fault, but he made up his mind to go,—"there

159

were other reasons." I knew them all, have known them, couldn't change them. This parting had to be.

But we parted in deep love. We know that neither of us will ever forget the other. So today I am both happy and sad.

May 19. A sculptor—Jo Davidson—of whom I have heard—from the Steffenses—whose good friend he is—and of course through magazines I long ago became acquainted with his work—has been house guest at the Steffenses—and while there doing a bust of Robinson Jeffers. I went over, asked by Ella Winter to photograph the "maestro," his subject and his sculpture together.

What happened, the many reactions evoked by the afternoon, would involve me in a chapter I may not find time to finish in this short morning hour.

For instance—am I too politic with friends or acquaintances? Yes, I am! I know it and it hurts me. But if I spoke out frankly my thoughts, what a storm I would arouse! And what about my pocketbook? My policy is either silence, avoiding the issue, or finding all possible good—and there is always some good in most work—discreetly confining myself to that. Is this weak? It all comes down to economics with me.

Take yesterday as an example: what if I had exploded at the Steffenses as I was sorely tempted to—and before the assembled guests paying homage to Davidson? Should I have hurt them and started a free-for-all by proclaiming the lion of the moment a clown, a boor, a cheap, fresh personality: and his work, that he was doing third-rate photographs in sculpture, that I could see him being a very successful bulb-squeezer in a photographic studio catering to middle class minds?

At first meeting I was amused, he had a disarming way, his exhibitionism, his pose, the antics of this droll, pot-bellied, bewhiskered little monkey were really funny. But later when I got a taste of his crude arrogance, not the dignified sureness of one who really knows they are great,—the quiet poise of Jeffers—what a contrast between those two men! The real—the artificial! If I had wished to cartoon Davidson, I would have photographed the two heads together,—no intentional caricature could have been more revealing: perhaps I have caught this contrast in the group.

He did not like my portraits, the several he had seen,—of course this accounts for the above tirade! I'm sore!? No,—one gets weary of continual praise—it might easily harm a weak person—even the strong might momentarily become complacent. A constructive thought, a good stiff jolt from a fine mind to start one thinking—that is to be welcomed. It was his manner that infuriated me! If there is one thing that makes me boil, it is the familiarity, the boorishness that allows another to put his hand on my shoulder, stick his face within six inches of mine and try to put over with loud talk a boring idea. He was patronizing—

160

the great Jo Davidson—condescending to impart his profound wisdom,—so others could hear him: harping on "intention," all art must have "intention." How very brilliant!

This explosion on paper is the result of being decent yesterday. Keeping my temper—well, one should do that with inferiors—for the sake of the Steffenses, fine persons both.

Davidson was jealous of my work, his aggressiveness was a defense. My portraits of Jeffers made his bust of Jeffers look weak. That's the whole story. He had to keep his exalted position on a shaky pedestal. Now I know my portraits, and I realize they seldom reach the importance that my other work has, not even when I make them for myself—with intention. In the first place my professional routine worries me, so I throw my best creative effort into trees, rocks, peppers, to escape the other: I admit too, that twenty years of pleasing others,—probably I have made near to five thousand portraits, always trying to please the sitter, for a price, this must often tinge my conception when I work for myself,—habit! This is my "out." But I do know when I rise above habit, often enough to place me far ahead of Davidson, often enough to have me considered by some very fine minds, the best portrait photographer in America which means the world so far as I know from reproductions.

"Well," I would ask Lincoln Steffens, "now where is my 'humility' you felt I should have?" What would he feel from this noise from my tin trumpet?

But there is a *man* to talk with. Lincoln Steffens is *real*, he is a gentleman,—courteous, lovable, intelligent. He speaks—says something, doesn't puff and blow to put over a thought, doesn't have to. When he puts his hand on my arm, —my heart warms: when Davidson puts his hand on my shoulder, and leers, I could slap him for impertinence. His instructions to me to dominate my subject were amusing. I wonder if he got the sarcasm when I asked him if he dominated Jeffers! One glance of Jeffers could wither him—the eagle noticing the chipmunk. He saw Robinson Jeffers exactly as Jeffers wanted him to see, only he failed in the execution.

How vulgar he was when he almost shouted, "I would dominate Mussolini, I'd grab his nose if necessary"—then he tweaked mine to show me and at that moment I nearly failed and spit in his face. If Davidson had been a gentleman or intelligent, I might have given him a word on photography. I must dominate in a very subtle way, I must depend upon "chance"—if there is such a thing. To present to me at the moment when my camera is ready, the person revealed, and capture that moment in a fraction of a second or a few seconds, with no opportunity to alter my result. A painter or sculptor may see as quickly as I do, but they can carry their conception on mentally, change it, or if the model changes in mood or position, keep on with their original idea in mind.

161

Photography's great difficulty lies in the necessary coincidence of the sitter's revealment, the photographer's realization, the camera's readiness. But when these elements do coincide, portraits in any other medium, sculpture or painting, are cold dead things in comparison. In the very overcoming of the mechanical difficulties which would seem to restrict the camera, and does if one is not aware, and turns these apparent barriers to advantage, lies its tremendous strength. For when the perfect spontaneous union is consummated, a human document, the very bones of life are bared.

Later, it was suggested I show my portfolio (no portraits, though now I wish I had included some) to Davidson. I did not take my work for him to criticize or praise, but for his education.

He changed his tune, couldn't have done otherwise: but *now* I was no longer in competition with his portraits!

Enough time wasted letting off steam—too much, considering my subject matter — — —

May 21. Awake at 4:00, up at 5:00,—old habits again, all but lying in bed for an hour before arising.

I was sick yesterday. The strain of Brett's leaving, then the episode with Davidson, was too much for the back of my neck. I came to in the afternoon, had to, for I had an appointment with Una Jeffers to photograph the twins, Garth and Don, going soon with the Luhans to Taos. I did them with their father, and alone together.

From several sources,—one, the Jeffers, I find that I came out victorious in the Davidson episode: victorious in defeat!—defeat because I kept my mouth shut, and he had the last word. The climax to my nonresistant victory happened at the Jeffers'. Robin told me this: a crowd gathered to say goodbye,—the Steffenses, Jo Davidson, Jimmie Hopper and so on: my portraits of Robin were brought out to show Davidson: he couldn't put down the head against the rocks, even examined it through a reading glass, said, "Why, I could make a bust from this." So if I needed revenge I have it. But such episodes have their value: after, one feels cleansed, purged,—and stronger, as Jack Black did after his flogging in the Canadian prison. His arms were tied so he couldn't fight back, my tongue was tied so I couldn't: partly tied by courtesy, partly—I must admit—because my words come slowly in a verbal duel, I answer better in writing.

May 22. Helen Forbes and a friend—can't think of her name—never know names until heard ten times—then forget a month later—viewed my work last eve. The friend gave me a rare and spontaneous compliment,—genuine because unpremeditated. I was showing the print of egg balanced on bone: she started to pick up the print, then hesitated, then laughed, exclaiming, "I reached for

162

that print, then drew back for fear of unbalancing the egg!" I certainly have achieved something very real to cause such a gesture.

A recent, very enthusiastic visitor was Dr. Becking, scientist. In fact I have rarely had such understanding response,—and he reacted *as a scientist.* "You see things from the scientists' viewpoint. I wish we could afford to have you around our laboratory," he said. We are going to walk together all over Point Lobos someday: use each other's eyes!

If Davidson publicly admitted he could use my head of Jeffers to work from, I should retract several remarks from my explosion, privately acknowledging that I misjudged him, or was a bit hard on him. Another item—he had been drinking much wine that day, thus revealing his true self,—to his disadvantage.

Yesterday I enlarged a head of Jack Black which is very strong, hard, though the other one which started the duel at Steffenses, the very human, tender expression was Jack Black quite as much and maybe more so at this time of his life.

A letter from him reveals his warmth,—for that, I think his book does too. The letter in part: "The proofs came, and I want to say that they are not the photographs I have known...best of all No. 4—I look so much like a judge staring at a defendant in the dock and trying to decide whether to give him 5, 10 or 20 years. I'm going to have some of them before I go back to N. Y. if only to let them know what can be done with the camera when the man behind it hasn't the undertaker's technique. Hope to see you and thank you with fewer words and more feeling before I go East.

Love to you and yours
John Black."

The reference to the undertaker's technique: he said, after I had made a few negatives, "I went to a photographer once in N. Y. for a newspaper photo. First he started to fix my tie, said it wouldn't do, then brushed my hair—I told him he was an undertaker, that I wasn't a stiff in a morgue,—grabbed my hat and got out quick."

Saturday, May 24. Helen Forbes took us to Point Lobos yesterday: she went to paint, so I took advantage of an invitation to join her. I wanted to get away from here, to lie in the grass, forget, relax: my head still bothered me. But I couldn't resist taking along my camera,—just for possibilities. Toward evening I did recuperate and made one negative, a cypress, a fine one. Not till I focussed, did I realize, recognize, that I was using one of Brett's details, an insignificant bit—at first glance—which he had glorified, used in one of his best-seen negatives. Brett and I were always seeing the same things to do—we have the same kind of vision. He didn't like this: naturally enough he felt that even when he had done the thing first, the public would not know and he would be blamed for imitating me.

Reading over my chapter on Davidson it seems childish! I couldn't stand being publicly "chastised." Now I find the "public" all with me!

So I will say this in J. D.'s favor, seeing the first print in my portfolio he said: "Well—this has 'intention'—this is art—I wouldn't have spoken so if I had seen these first." And I will also say that I might have quite liked him, at least as a jolly, lively human being if we had not clashed on "art."

I was called over to photograph him, with Fremont Older and his bust—while he worked. I took along two new prints of Jack Black to show Older who was most enthusiastic, and so was Davidson! *After* seeing my photographs, or rather while looking at them he got a sudden inspiration to also do him. I can't resist this little "dig." He excitedly inquired how long Jack was to be south—he would wire him, etc. Enough!

Finally, Steffens presented one of my peppers to Davidson, "he liked it so much." Curtain!

Sunday, May 25. I had long promised to do Jeffers and the twins together. The right time came to keep my word, before the boys left with Mabel Luhan and Tony for a month in Taos. When I arrived the plans had changed to include the whole family; so—there was a large crock of wine in the making which would spoil without attention. Robin put it in the old Ford and drove us home. Now the crock stands by our fireplace.

I have promised to dance tomorrow night in a comedia for the members of the music society. I tried to say no—it was not accepted. This will be a new experience for me: heretofore I have played the fool for friends. This doing a planned stunt, before a mixed crowd—takes on a different flavor. Hope I do not have stage fright!

May 27. No stage fright—but I could feel that I was not doing my best—despite laughter and applause—and after congratulations. It was not spontaneous enough. I went cold waiting near an hour for my delayed cue. I danced Rachmaninoff's *Prelude in C Sharp Minor,*—great to satirize: for an encore Mendelssohn's *Spring Song,* also an opportunity. Sonya made me a classic Greek tunic—with variations—which I am sure shared with my dancing—the honors. I wore—as several times in Mexican parties—little pointed breasts. After my overwhelming success, Kuster asked me to take part in his coming production *The Three Penny Opera,*—and Bert Heron put in his bid for me to be a Roman citizen in *Julius Caesar.* Maybe I will finish my career on the stage! I refused both: what time?—my own work—and tourist season starting.

The last number of the evening was Henry Cowell in *Grand Opera*: very well-done,—subtle, screamingly funny. Henry has keen humour. And so has Dr. Becking who was one of the hits of the evening, and kept up the fun at Peter Steffens' afterward where we went to dance.

Altogether I put in a full day, for in the afternoon I talked to the school children of the 6th and 7th grades,—Cole's and Neil's classes, took my prints from Mexico and Point Lobos,—also vegetables, bones, shells. I felt quite complimented in that I held the children's attention every moment. I had not been in a school-room for twenty five years! More fun to talk to children than to grown-ups.

This from Lincoln Steffens: "Think, the intellectuals advise. The artists don't think, the mechanics and scientists don't. A group of researchers, comparing notes, agreed one evening that they proceeded by hunches."

And this I wrote to Seymour Stern in reaction to some remarks in *Experimental Cinema*,—the first issue of a magazine destined to live through maybe five issues! "Intuition, despite Einstein, is the basis of all great art. A 'hunch,'—that is, intuition is back of all forms of creation: engineering, that is, construction, or composition follows to put into a form the primal flame."

We put down the same thought with the same word "hunch" as an axis.

May 29. 4:30—unusual for me to be up so early these recent days: I thought I was losing my old habits. I don't want to! This still, alone hour I would miss, have missed.

I have had another explosion!—of a different kind,—but following that out-burst over the dancer, then Jo Davidson, a revolution in my life may be in-dicated: perhaps only change of life!

Yesterday's flare-up was over economics,—started by hours in the darkroom printing copies of a drawing for which I am to receive less than a carpenter would ask for his time. I did not need to take this job: but I needed money — — I have no one to blame but myself. I made my own bed. I could have been well-to-do—if not rich—by this time, if I had taken advantage of all the publicity I have had these years past,—if I had thought in terms of money instead of my work. I really have just what I deserve, or wanted: a bare living and plenty of time for my work. But I should be getting more than a bare living, and yet have time for myself. When I work for others I should be paid more. How to achieve this I know: go to a big city, get a manager, open a studio,—well-located, do the society stunt, become fashionable — — I could make good, I have the personality, and know how to deliver the goods. I could have been a good businessman: making money is thinking in terms of money. Maybe if I would put all else from mind but money for a few years I could gather together a modest sum, and quit. But those precious years! If I was only clever enough to figure out an easy way to extract the public's nickels, dimes, dollars—a patent medicine, a catchy song,—which reminds me of one I started, and Johan was to set to music, called—"I'm never so homesick as when I'm at home." Just so, do some become rich!

Sunday, June 1. A recent evening Sonya and I, walking as usual, met Orrick Johns and Caroline. He had known Jo Davidson in Europe. Also he had been present during our one-sided controversy. He told me of a conversation once with Davidson, a sort of confession, in which J. D. revealed himself as a very sad figure: said that he had definitely cultivated a grand manner for his "business," but actually considered himself a failure as an artist.

Now I better understand the reason for our clash, though I already put it down to jealousy. And I do feel guilty that I exploded, even to myself. The outburst was likely good for me: J. D. only incidental. It was an episode which brought me face to face with myself, to ask a question or two. Do I overrate my work? Am I becoming self-satisfied? Am I repeating successes?

The several recent outbursts are more significant than surface causes might indicate. One effect,—I have dared to hang my manifesto on the wall, stating emphatically that I will no longer sign retouched portraits.

10. *"Unretouched portraits"*

June 13. Back from San Francisco where I went to shop, buy clothes to replace the rags I was using, and to make contacts hoping for sale of prints. My shopping was aplenty, my sales, one lone print to Bob Howard, artist. How glad I was to return! To return from noise, dirt, stench, hurry, to the sea and cypress. The machine it seems to me should give man a life of leisure, time for inner expansion, instead of the terrible maelstrom engendered. I believe it will. Cities will be depopulated except for a few to press buttons a few hours a week: no—my imagination is not wide enough—the wheels can be started just as well from a distance. Anyhow I detested the week of walking Market St., miles to save a nickel, or more often, to find ready-made, fine combinations.

I landed in Carmel, nearly broke, finding a letter from Johan asking for $180 advance rent to pay on the mortgage of this place. I might have paid $1.80! The thought came—if Johan should lose—what next for me?

Sometimes being broke, facing an uncertain tomorrow, has a stiffening effect on my spine. It makes me hard, and even reckless in spending, as though I said to myself—I have nothing anyhow—I might as well go the limit. I bought a new Bach album for $10, I decided to put a sign in my showcase, a manifesto to the public similar to the one on my wall,—"no retouching," and I had printed a contract form to be signed *before* sittings, courteously telling those who want my work, *how* they can get it: by paying a deposit, and by sending a check in advance for finished work, unless they wished it sent C.O.D. Also mentioning the work will be finished according to *my* wishes, and unretouched or I will not sign my name. Now I will change my sign on Ocean Ave., to read "E. W. Photographer—unretouched portraits." In fact, go the limit in every way.

A good omen came, the same day I put out my manifesto, when a none too beautiful girl came in, who wanted my unretouched work. Of men I have plenty—it is the women I will lose—some—the question how many? The girl could not afford my work at present—but the omen brightened me. There are those who will come, if they can find me!

Another way to stiffen my spine is to hear music. There is nothing like a Bach fugue to remove me from a discordant moment. I have learned something in buying records: or in having them: only Bach holds up fresh and strong after repeated playing. I can always return to Bach when the other records, even some moderns, weary me.

June 18. After several days of a bad head, a tight, sore spot at the base of my skull, I decided to try for a cure, a few negatives for myself. Irving and Ruby had a fascinating cutter for slicing hard-boiled eggs which they gave me to work with. The taut wire strings for slicing give it the appearance of a musical instrument, a miniature harp. I put the hard-boiled egg, stripped for cutting into it, a couple more eggs were commandeered to balance, and two aluminum baking dishes, the halved kind, made to fit together in a round steamer were used in back. Result,—excellent, I made two more negatives of these halved pots,—both important, except that in each I allowed a necessary line to be almost lost in the background. I shall work more, for these are fine material. I cured my head!

June 19. The above recorded work was only a beginning,—yesterday I made eleven perfect negatives, ten of them of the egg cutter. In contrast to the day before of fog, I had brilliant sun. Feeling my way as I do so often, allowing things to happen, be presented to me, waiting like a hawk to pounce upon an idea, I placed the little egg cutter on a white blotter—fascinating form—almost any angle held interest: then suddenly the sun burst through the fog and my day's work was presented. The black shadow of the cutter upon the blotter was my hunch. The form doubled, but the excitement of opposing lines, interplay of forms, far more than doubled the interest.

Now I have not used shadows of an object as part of the composition for years: not for ten or fifteen years. At that time I began making portraits casting a strong shadow of the head on the background. It was often too grotesque, and I began to have imitators, so I quit. I had done it,—I was through. Popular magazines such as *Vanity Fair* still publish such abominations!

But yesterday's shadows of the egg cutter were strong—never detached—never competing. Looking straight down—or nearly so—upon the cutter—the shadows added to the construction, building up the delicate little form until it assumed the strength of a powerful machine. With every turn came something new. I did not take over two hours to do the ten negatives. The speed with which I worked recalls a conversation with Consuela in San Francisco at a party Jean Roy gave. She, slightly inebriated, took me to task for being prolific, —mentioning a well-known N. Y. photographer who made maybe one negative a year—but it was so perfect.

Well I can make—given time—one thousand negatives a year not only perfect technically, but fresh and strong in seeing. Then I am just one thousand times as important as Consuela's shining example! A slight exaggeration to make my point. Which is this: photography suits the tempo of this age—of active bodies and minds. It is a perfect medium for one whose mind is teeming with ideas, imagery, for a prolific worker who would be slowed down by painting or sculpting, for one who sees quickly and acts decisively, accurately.

168

It is an abominable medium for the slow-witted, or the sloppy worker: he, the slow one, cannot use the speed to advantage, or cannot grasp the passing moment quickly enough to record it in an instant,—or, if sloppy, the ease of execution tends to exaggerate his weakness. Now one does not think *during* creative work: any more than one thinks when driving a car. One has a background of years —learning—unlearning—success—failure—dreaming—thinking—experience— back it goes—farther back than one's ancestors: all this,—then the moment of creation, the focussing of all into the moment. So I can make—"without thought" —fifteen carefully-considered negatives one every fifteen minutes,—given material with as many possibilities.

I had a rare opportunity yesterday—to work alone—everyone away — — but an equally rare phenomenon found me unable to take advantage of my opportunity: I found nothing to work with. I went through my chest full of bones, shells, stones, finding nothing new enough to excite me. The kitchen yielded nothing as fine as my egg cutter or the egg beater. I considered the grocery store: a halved red cabbage, yes, but out of season—peppers, squash, eggplant, eggs,—the latter, and the eggplant too, I am not through with, but as yet it has not come to me how to use them again. So I played a Caesar Franck Symphony, a Bach Concerto,—read, sunned myself, dreamed. A rare day after all.

In the evening to the store for supper groceries, where I found material which will start me and keep me going for days to come: bananas,—not new to my work; I had done two negatives in 1927, and then was sidetracked. But how much better I can do them now! And what exciting curves, forms, this bunch had. I know from my thrill upon seeing them that something important is coming. One group awaits me now: put together last night,—strong, dynamic —it should go with my kelp.

11. *"Composition is a way of seeing—"*

June 22. Ten negatives of the bananas! I knew what to expect from my excited condition of yesterday. I had five bananas to work with, all of them unusually curved. They had endless possibilities, combined. I worked without effort.

One group slipped during exposure, one I had to repeat, being slightly under-timed, the rest are all fine negatives. Three of them are obviously arranged: the rest, and really the strongest, appear as though they might have been thrown together,—only analysis would reveal a very careful building up. Careful—yes—but not laborious: for I worked with the rapidity and ease which indicates I am working well. In the evening I quit for a walk on the beach with Sonya, on the way stopping at the P.O. A letter from Peter Steffens, who took several of my prints to N. Y. to find a publisher, which indicated success. If this could happen—a beautifully printed book of my work—it would "make" me. And the wider distribution of my work,—knowing that it was being seen by hundreds or thousands, instead of the handful who come in here, would have a fine, strengthening effect upon me. As it is now, I have hundreds of prints that no one ever sees,—wrapped and stored away, for I rarely show more than fifty prints to visitors. Even that number takes too much of my time, and more would be confusing to see,—each one so vital and shown so rapidly.

The letter in part: "Well, I think it's all fixed—anyway Mitchell Kennerly is crazy about your work and is sending someone to Calif. next week to see more of it and you. He's a millionaire and cares only about putting out rare beautiful things beautifully. He had not seen your things before and they hit him hard."

I think a combination of banana negatives, this letter, Bach's *Passacaglia*, run-ning through my mind, plus chattering blue birds, cooing doves, horses kicking at stable stalls, awakened me at 4:00, when I got up.

June 25. A walk on the beach Saturday night discovered me great piles of fresh kelp. Sunday I dared not leave for fear of losing business. Monday early I walked down again to see if there was aught of value left. I found aplenty and also a dead seafowl spread out so exquisitely that I could hardly wait to return with my camera for fear someone might give it a kick and spoil its flight of death. I missed the car, for it was a long walk, but Neil and Cole helped me down. The seafowl—I guess it was a cormorant—though lying there the neck seemed too short—had not been moved. I photographed it first—then went kelp hunting until mid-afternoon, making three negatives, none so powerful as my first kelp, but fine in rhythm and texture.

170

By the way, Herbert Klein purchased my favorite of the first kelp group, and three other prints.

The same evening after my beach adventuring I found more bananas, a perfectly straight bunch. So yesterday morn I started with a view of them which I have had in mind three years, and carried it out better than I visioned it. Made six new negatives,—then a sitting of Fred Bechdoldt in the afternoon to add to my Carmel Rogue's Gallery.

June 26. In rare hours when the sun breaks through the summer fog which blankets Carmel at this time of year, I dash for the roof of Neil's cottage, around which we stretched muslin, strip to the sun and wind, bake and burn until I sweat, then dash back for a cold tub. What a glorious sensation!—the sun penetrates right through me to the board beneath and then back again, until every pore is open and every nerve tingles with joy. My body is tanned to a rich brown, and I am better able to stand the devitalizing darkroom hours.

Training for art!

The new banana negative is great! A bunch of five standing on end, still joined at the top,—and how beautiful the fruit is at the point of radiation from the main stalk,—the concave side to the camera. The three centre bananas are perfectly straight, the two outer ones swell out from the top, then almost straighten to cut diagonally across all but the centre fruit. It is a classic conception and I am proud to have made it.

I should have said the *front* row of the bunch of five, for in the back several more are hidden, all but a slight curve from the outer two which join and complete at the top the front line sweep.

One more negative of the bananas from Tuesday is important, a closeup, lines radiating from the main stalk, the axis. And two I must confess were under-timed and discarded. One I did over again and better-seen yesterday: the other will have to wait for a new purchase, for I changed the group by trimming.

A sitting yesterday, but not much immediate help, for I will be paid by the month at $10 per. Against my rules,—but better break them—and eat!

Friday. Yestereve with Jeanne D'Orge and Carl Cherry, to hear the latter's new phonograph amplifier. He played records I well knew—a Bach fugue—Ravel's *Bolero*. The volume was overpowering—actually—like sitting in the midst of, right in front of, a tremendous orchestra. The tone was excellent too. He had a new invention destined to make them rich: a savings bank for home use which cannot be opened except by a magnetic key which is held at the main Bank. The inventor seems to have financial distress equal to the artist, and needs more capital to swing his project. But he has one advantage, his product can be patented, for his gain. The artist no sooner exposes his work to the public than a coast-to-coast flock of imitators spring up like toadstools in the night.

June 28. I have often noted Sonya sitting in the little Mexican chair, knees crossed, and one leg twined around the other in a seemingly impossible way,—impossible to me at least—suggesting one vine twisting around another. Anyhow it had a dynamic flow which at once suggested new subject matter. With time, and a new idea, I get into action at once. So this morning I have a new negative before me. No doubt as to its value. It may start a whole series in a new vein. Maybe I'll travel legwise up to other fragments. I have not done nudes for several years and methinks I am ready, and better able than ever before.

There is something out of place in my back. This morning I could hardly move in bed with pain. Each day I have thought it would pass. I so dislike doctors—unknown ones—but I must find one to snap me together.

June 30. I have already spoken of art as a way of seeing. The following, written for *The Carmelite* about Brett's work is in the same vein.

"He learned in the only way one can learn anything—by working.... No one can teach another how to *see.* If composition could be taught, anyone might become an artist. Composition is a way of seeing—strong or weak according to the individual. Rules of composition are deduced from the work of strong masters and used by weak imitators to produce—nothing!" E. W.

July 3. Within 5 hours I printed from 11 negs.—2 prints each — — each one was a fine negative easy to print—all were new, that is, never before printed from, which took more time, having no data for reference—which also I always keep:—once made, I can remember and duplicate, given the same paper, any print, even ten years back. I mention, or record these details, to fix in my mind about the limit of speed with which I can print, with all possible care and consideration, without attempting to hurry, making the best possible print from each negative.

To the casual observer this may seem far too many "exhibition" prints to pull in so short a time. But remember my prints are all visually "printed" when I focus on the ground glass, my negatives are so fine and my mind so clear that I do not have to make dozens,—or a hundred prints, to get one!

Becking and I took an early Sunday morning walk on and near Point Lobos: the scientist and the artist coming together for the avowed purpose of getting each other's viewpoint, on mutually exciting ground.

It was not difficult—in our case—to get together. Becking has much of the artist in him, which the scientist of the future must have,—that is imagination: and I must have much of the scientist in me. Becking is not the narrow, one-track-mind scientist I have exploded over: his mind is fluid, he "erects card castles to knock them down,"—as he puts it. With malice in mind—well, no—not quite malice—for I felt Becking broad,—I casually brought up the subject of evolution—in which I cannot believe—though I have no data nor study to

172

enable me to start an argument with a scientist,—neither defense nor offense could I offer, to back my doubt, my heretical stand against the modern religion of science,—except science's inability, after years of effort, to prove evolution and my own intuitive non-acceptance. A very weak case, mine!

To my astonishment, Becking said, "I do not believe in evolution." And then to my question, "If the study of physics is carried far enough does it not lead to metaphysics?" he answered "Yes."

Back from our walk we stopped for "brunch" in Becking's patio. He showed me a book of primitive drawings, reproduced from a cave in Spain,—50,000 years old. At once I knew that here was a case against evolution, and that now I was on ground that was common to me. I could speak with authority. "Becking," I said, "these drawings are from a highly-cultured race, they were done by extremely sensitive artists, certainly as fine as anything contemporary."

The fact that some primitive drawings are crude, ugly, childish, proves nothing: for is not most of the art of our time equally crude and ugly? Then as now, and as it ever will be, a few great artists stood out from the rest. There never was a race of artists. Take the Greek vase which every museum must present—some very fine, others weak copies or downright ugly. Take Mexican contemporary popular art: some artist creates a fine form in pottery or beautiful pattern in weaving, and follows a whole school of imitators,—the original flame finally dies out, until another artist starts a new masterpiece to be copied and in turn die. One can buy in la Via de Guadalupe a thousand of the strange horned lion I have and prize, all alike, from the same mold: but some one person made the original—and what a prize that original would be!

July 4. 4:30—with rain-like fog: not so pleasant for weekenders. I arose early, to be alone, to see my new work now mounted, to write and think quietly. Always someone sociably inclined to drop in for morning coffee,—Sonya, Cole, an early riser, Everett Ruess, camping in our garage,—a boy who has potentialities in painting and writing, and though I agree morning coffee can be a delightful ceremony, it is the one time I wish to be alone. Every day I must write with chattering all around me,—no wonder I feel like destroying as poorly-said my entries of the day before. This sounds like a poor excuse for poor writing,— maybe is. I should not attempt to write then?—but I must write—Well, what luck! Here comes Sonya at this ungodly hour—couldn't sleep with a bad cold— and Everett rushes from the garage with paper in his hand bound for the woods on a hurry call—I am finished again — — just this one thought—if my technique in writing was as strong as my technique in photography could I not write despite confusion?—for I am usually surrounded by near or distant confusion while photographing. I lack technique in writing, hence weak or incomplete expression. I have to *think*—and one must not think—have no need to while creating. Yet I go stumbling along, and someday may arrive.

July 10 — 4:30 a.m. A form of insomnia for me to rise so early, having gone to bed late: but I sleep sound while it lasts, and drop off immediately [after] I hit the pillow. I have been under tension in many ways. No sittings, bad check returned, money due for months, day after day of fog. I printed long hours yesterday, and that keyed me up: concentrated, exhausting work,—so many hours on one's feet in the dark.

One negative printed was made the same morning. Myrto brought me a Passion Flower. I put it in a glass bowl, with a white floor ground—I pointed straight down upon it—and without much hesitation made the negative. The hesitation —because I have used so often a centered bowl or basket: but for the moment I saw no other way—and the flower would soon wilt. What a truly marvelous flower, and in water, with shimmer of glass, all delicate, keyed high, I could not resist, and am glad I did not, so different it is from anything I have done, —recently.

Some admirers will say, "Can this be Weston?" Some old admirers will say, "Weston is finding his old beauty!" To both I will say, "Don't try to pigeonhole me!" I might photograph a sweet pea one hour,—the next hour a coil of guts.

I wrote an article, published this July with examples of my work in *Camera Craft*, a photo magazine which offers its readers just what they want. I need not explain—the average want is obvious. Why did I contribute then?—over-persuasion, partly, and the hope of reaching a few ready for change. I tempered my words, fearing the editor might not stand up under full blast. But seeing some unusually awful reproductions in the same issue by one Boris, with a laudatory article by the editor, I spent an hour writing him my mind. These cheap abortions which need no description other than their titles, "Prayer," "Greek Slave," "Orphans," "Unlucky Day," have nothing to do with Art, nor Life, nor Photography. So I not very gently explained. But why did I waste my time? I know the Editor's policy, his outlook from his writing and magazine in general: backing my work and opinions, his publication would fail!

I am in a mood to stir things up! My "Bed Pan" was published in *U. S. A.* That was a worthwhile move on my part,—and they deserve all praise for nerve. They also published "Cypress and Rocks," and printed it horizontal instead of vertical: I should be complimented that my composition can be seen in any way!

Stanley Wood is showing at Denny-Watrous: his water colors very fine,—and I can't often respond to painting with my greater interest in photography—the most important medium of our day. Now I am speaking more honestly my mind. Too often I have tried to explain photography,—why it is important. Old stuff!—necessary twenty years ago,—not now! Photographers who still try to paint with the camera should be dismissed with this advice: "Go buy a brush and paint box—you are not worthy nor strong enough to be a photographer."

174

I like Stanley, and regret his wife blocks our contact. She belongs to the wives' union, and publicly disapproves of me.

"Art is not imitation nor an ethnological curiosity staged for tourists. Only when an artist realizes perfectly which is his right and proper function in the social body, and sees with his own eyes, feels with his own heart and thinks with his own mind, will appear a new art on the American continent, the creation of a new race."

José Clemente Orozco

Fine! Also I read in these words a "dig" at Diego—

Orozco is in S. F. Wish I might meet him again. I had almost no contact in Mexico.

Herb Klein who bought my favorite kelp, wrote,—"interweaving like a Bach fugue, yet keeping its dynamic tension through the complexity."

Whenever I can feel a Bach fugue in my work I know I have arrived.

July 19. A week after making the above wish, I had a phone call from Alfred Honigbaum. I was in the darkroom when long distance rang, giving Alfred's name. I knew at once, intuitively that he was bringing Orozco down, though I did not know they had even met. And I was right: Orozco, Alma Reed, and Alfred will arrive tonight!

Since my last entry, much has happened. I have worked with summer squash, —one afternoon, making some very beautiful and strong negatives: the squash nearly white in the sun, a grey ground, and intense black shadow,—the simple massing of the three values, most satisfying.

And I have worked with peppers again, surprising myself! Sonya brought several home, and I could not resist, though I thought to have finished with peppers. But peppers never repeat themselves: shells, bananas, melons, so many forms, are not inclined to experiment,—not so the pepper, always exciting-ly individual. So I have three new negatives, and two more under way. One of these, and they are already printed along with the squash, is extraordinarily fine and different. It is the most exquisite one I have done; the former negatives [were] usually powerful. This slender, delicate pepper, I placed on a green-glazed oval dish,—it might be a strange tropical plant in itself, spiraling up from the roots, partly unfolded at the top like a fern. It has a mystic significance.

Other recent and important notes: I am to have a frame at Hotel Del Monte, which should bring sittings unfortunately from the class of unhealthy parasites I detest: I lost a sitting (this came to me after) because I only charge $40— instead of $500—! this is tragedy.

Chan and Max and baby will probably come here, replacing Cole,—a trial ahead for me, but I owe Ted a chance to study photography since he wants to

175

— — Cole I shall be sad to lose, but he can return when older and less likely to clash with Neil. Flora may drive up for a few days—what confusion ahead— if I can only keep my head!

The *Carmelite* reprinted an article of mine making a typographical error which will enrage certain of the "Carmel Art Association": My sentence read— "Photography will eventually negate *much* painting" — — the "much" was omitted!

Ford Sterling and Henry Cowell—recent visitors of whom I made negatives. The above a kaleidoscope of recent happenings.

12. *José Clemente Orozco*

July 21. The coming of Clemente Orozco and Alma Reed will go down as an important day in my personal history. I am to open the season with a one-man exhibit in Alma Reed's New York Gallery: but more important she is to keep my work, feature it along with Orozco's, to the exclusion of all other artists'.

My years of effort, seemingly to no end but my personal growth, my "labor of love" one might say, and the response of a few friends and admirers, seem now to be justified,—that I will reap a reward, enough maybe to enable me to carry on as I wish. The several explosions of past months all lead to this climax.

Around the grate fire Saturday night I showed my work. Orozco had not seen it since Mexico. I showed my kelp first, the one which caused me to write down in this book, "I have today (or yesterday) made photographic history." Clemente started forward in his chair, —he had not expected this. He is not the explosive type of Mexican, but his response and few words meant all the more. Then followed an hour of deep interest, enthusiasm. Alma Reed, trying to decide where I *must* exhibit:—"These prints will cause a sensation in New York," —and so on.

Morning: Hazel and Dene to breakfast and then they drove us to Point Lobos. Walking over the Point with Alma Reed, she explained a remark from the back seat of the old Ford. "When could you be ready to exhibit in New York?" "Tomorrow," I answered.

So she told me: "I had decided to discontinue the work of handling, showing, all other artists except Clemente,—the gallery was really started to 'put him over,'—because of my belief in his greatness. Now I have seen your work. It complements his—there is no conflict—you both are striving toward the same end. Clemente and I have discussed it,—we want you to be the only other artist the gallery will show and promote. And you will open the season in October."

The future unfolded in a flash, all justified by the past.

Orozco brought a number of his new lithographs. Stark beauty, stripped of all frosting. The very bones, the quintessence revealed,—structural and emotional. No compromise in Clemente Orozco.

Now for October—with all my strength—mind—heart!

Sunday, July 27.—awaiting three sittings, really four,—a mother and two children, separately and then in group. At last my season begins.

This last week I have lived several weeks in one. No sooner had Orozco left than Ford Sterling phoned from L. A.,—he was driving up again Tuesday,—could he bring me anything?

When he arrived I was on the beach working with kelp, just finishing the tenth negative from endless material freshly washed up. I made some very exciting new negatives. Ford explained his return this way: "I could not get your work out of mind, the greatest photographs of their kind I have seen. I need a mental cathartic. I want to be with you a few days, watch you work, get a new slant. I will pay my way."

Later in the day he told me this. "I am in a little jam financially, but later I am going to send you the finest 8 × 10 camera and tripod on the market. I made up my mind when I saw you working with that old box that I would throw in a junk pile." I gave to him my best for four days. When he left he bought ten prints for $100.

One day I went with Ford to Point Lobos. We worked around the cannery: entirely new material, old boats, fences, shacks, great heaps of abalone shells. Again I worked well,—making thirteen negatives.

Another day I printed for him, contacts and amplifications: kelp, bananas, eggplant, Orozco,—the latter is one of my finest portraits, his piercing eyes I accentuated by using to great advantage the reflections from unscreened light upon the thick lenses he wears. Orozco sent word that "It is the first time he has known himself in a photograph, in spite of all that he has had made." The sitting was made in the failing light of evening after a day crowded with events. Holding the Graflex,—there was no time for working with tripod, I could not stop down beyond 6.3, so the definition is not perfect, but practically satisfactory.

The bananas finished were done as a "lesson" for Ford: fortunately I already had in mind exactly the way I would do them, so his presence did not prevent me from seeing well. A sitting, unheralded, came while we worked. I told Ford to return in an hour. I was through in half the time. I picked an eggplant Sonya had brought me, thinking to use it for another lesson. At once it came to me how to use it: balanced on an inverted wooden bowl. The eggplant curved definitely one way, unsymmetrical,—the two curves had the slightest point of contact. The eggplant almost soars away from the sweeping curve below. I could not wait for Ford with light failing: twenty minutes' exposure, holding my breath for fear a passing car would disturb the breathless balance. Ford was thrilled with the result, Sonya was too, and so am I.

I have met a man whom I liked at once, Henry Ohloff,—a minister, but what a minister!—radical, sensitive, virile. I was showing my new pepper to Hazel

178

and Dene: tears came to his eyes. Later he purchased it, though he could ill afford to, I happen to know.

July 26. Last eve came Hazel and Dene bringing Mr. and Mrs. Folger, Maroni Olsen, Henry Ohloff: later Roi and Imogen arrived. I had an audience for my work whose response thrilled me. Maroni Olsen bought a print,—the classic banana group. Sittings, sales, fresh contacts, future possibilities, everything points to success in more than one way. My stars must have changed!

July 29. —another sitting ahead for this morning! My personal work will have to be curtailed for the summer. It cannot be stopped, for last night Sonya brought me a glorious pepper!

Well, I have a formula for portraits which enables me to make a sitting in not more than half an hour, and do it well.

At Denny-Watrous Gallery is a most awful exhibit of paintings by the "Carmel Art Association." A compromise on the part of Dene and Hazel, for business. They told me this story which must be preserved. One of the exhibitors said to Hazel, "if anyone shows an interest in my painting you can give them permission to take it home, try it on their walls, and if they desire any change I will be glad to repaint it to suit them."

This is certainly applying the modern slogan of "Service,"—for the sake of gain as is usually the case—to art! Art!

August 1. The half hour sitting done while Ford waited brought me an order for $175!

The glorious new pepper Sonya brought me has kept me keyed up all week and caused me to expose eight negatives:—I'm not satisfied yet! These eight were all from the same viewpoint: rare for me to go through this. I started out with an underexposure—by the time I had developed the light had failed, and though I tripled my time again I undertimed! Again I tried, desperately determined to get it because I could ill afford the time. Giving an exposure of 50 minutes at 5:00 I timed correctly, but during exposure the fire siren shrieked, and promptly the fire truck roared by followed by every car in town: the old porch trembled, my wobbly old camera wobbled, the pepper shimmied, and I developed a moved negative. Next morning I went at it again: interruptions came, afternoon came, light weak, prolonged exposures necessary,—result, one negative possible, but possible also to improve upon it.

I tried the light from the opposite side in the next morning light,—brilliant sun through muslin. Better! A reason for my failures. Three negatives made, on a new angle so different as to be another pepper. And more failures, this time sheer thoughtlessness: a background of picture backing was placed too close and came into focus when stopped down which I could not see but should have realized, the corrugations plainly show and spoil the feeling. The one exposure from a new angle was perfect. So I have made eight negatives from the same angle and yet must go on. Today it is foggy and I am faced with an entirely new approach.

All this work has been done between moments of greeting tourists, printing, mounting, etc. Small wonder I have failed.

But the pepper is well worth all time, money, effort. If peppers would not wither, I certainly would not have attempted this one when so preoccupied. I must get this one today: it is beginning to show the strain and tonight should grace a salad. It has been suggested that I am a cannibal to eat my models after a masterpiece. But I rather like the idea that they become a part of me, enrich my blood as well as my vision. Last night we finished my now famous squash, and had several of my bananas in a salad.

transition, Paris, a new magazine to me, and the last one to be printed, going the way of so many experiments—transitions—published my "Knees" and two peppers: but not well-reproduced.

August 3. Sonya, as Ramiel did last year, keeps tempting me with new peppers! Two more have been added to my collection. While experimenting with one of these, which was so small that I used my 21 cm. Zeiss to fill the 8 × 10 size, I tried putting it in a tin funnel for background. It was a bright idea, a perfect relief for the pepper and adding reflected light to important contours. I still had the pepper which caused me a week's work, I had decided I could go no further with it, yet something kept me from taking it to the kitchen, the end of all good peppers. I placed it in the funnel, focussed with the Zeiss, and, knowing just the viewpoint, recognizing a perfect light, made an exposure of six minutes, with but a few moments' preliminary work,—the real preliminary was done in hours passed. I have a great negative,—by far the best!

August 4. Sold a print yesterday and one the day before, bringing my total within a week, which Ford started, to nearly $170. But I also lost $144, with the news of Alexander Lefturich's failure and inability to pay any bills.

A letter from Lincoln Steffens from Paris, telling me that Kennerly procrastinates, but was genuinely excited over my prints, even discussed the make-up of proposed book. So I revived my waning hope.

In the late afternoon I made three more peppers in funnel, all with the Zeiss [lens], all very close, filling entire plate. The one great objection to the Zeiss is that I cannot stop down as far as I am used to.

August 7. Many visitors these days. I have to use my intuition plus a little subtle detective work to find out whether they have either of two attributes, money, or real understanding. With the latter, lacking the former,—with such individuals I am willing to spend my time freely and willingly: with the former, lacking the latter,—with these too I spend time,—while there seems hope of their spending

180

money in return. But those with neither money nor good taste, I get rid of quickly,—unless they seem to have possibilities of growth: youth groping.

Two rather satisfied artists from Boston came in,—they evidently had no money, but I was all prepared to bring out my portfolio, when they praised the pastels of a female artist here, which gave me my cue, and the portfolio was not forthcoming, saving me an hour's time.

One very appreciative visitor was Rodriguez—a Guatemalan—a writer, friend of many friends of mine. I had known of him many years, but our paths never crossed before. With him I spent the whole evening willingly, for he gained in the seeing,—took something away, and I gained in the giving,—he left something behind.

Those last new peppers!

They are powerful! I actually have added to my former work with them, and am all set to go on!

August 8. I could wait no longer to print them,—my new peppers, so I put aside several orders, and yesterday afternoon had an exciting time with seven new negatives.

First I printed my favorite, the one made last Saturday, Aug. 2, just as the light was failing,—quickly made, but with a week's previous effort back of my immediate, unhesitating decision. A week?—Yes, on this certain pepper,—but twenty-eight years of effort, starting with a youth on a farm in Michigan, armed with a No. 2 Bull's Eye, $3\frac{1}{2} \times 3\frac{1}{2}$, have gone into the making of this pepper, which I consider a peak of achievement.

It is a classic, completely satisfying,—a pepper—but more than a pepper: abstract, in that it is completely outside subject matter. It has no psychological attributes, no human emotions are aroused: this new pepper takes one beyond the world we know in the conscious mind.

To be sure, much of my work has this quality,—many of my last year's peppers, but this one, and in fact all the new ones, take one into an inner reality,—the absolute,—with a clear understanding, a mystic revealment. This is the "significant presentation" that I mean, the presentation through one's intuitive self, seeing "through one's eyes, not with them": the visionary.

My recent work more than ever indicates my future.

José Rodriguez came upstairs to my darkroom—to say adiós. He was deeply moved when I showed the new print just made. So was Sonya, so will be many others.

Monday, August 11. J. Nilsen Laurvik, with Lillian Hodghead, both have been house guests for three days, coming last Friday afternoon and ending last night. Friday night was the reunion party for which Laurvik procured a gallon of red wine. Much gayety, until I thought of the morrow's sittings, Lillian H., director

181

of S. F. Conservatory of Music, who came for the express purpose, and Laurvik whom I had long wanted to do.

I was sick the next morning, I am not used to and don't stand drinking. But by noon, braced up, and worked quite well.

Yesterday we picnicked at Point Lobos—quite a joyous day. Laurvik is grand fun on a party, and so were the rest. I took the Graflex, and watching hawk-like every opportunity, made 24 negatives as Laurvik and Lillian sat, sprawled, or stood on the rocks. If I got technically what I saw, I will have many unusual photographs. A tall Viking, Laurvik, he felt the Point deeply, belonged there on the rocks, by the sea. Laurvik wishes to write the foreword to my exhibit catalogue for New York.

He could do it well.

August 14. Cole has gone — — life is so marked with partings: Chandler, Maxine, and baby "Ted," arrive tomorrow — — and so is life balanced with meetings.

Cole,—the baby, yet I would guess the oldest soul of them all: a little rogue, but a dear rogue, with mischievous ways and dancing eyes,—yet he does at times evoke in me much sadness: I have seen his face in repose filled with indescribable pathos, as though he'd known, knew, or would know a world's affliction.

How different the two young girls of the day before, deeply moved, all questions because it was an experience in their lives. Hazel had told them I had a few prints at $5. I showed them these, from discarded negatives, not prints I am ashamed of, but not comparable to my best. Evidently not girls of means, and expecting to spend but $5,—after much hesitating they counted out ten $1 bills for a very fine pepper, chosen with excellent judgment, or better, intuition: then thanked me, apologizing for taking my time.

August 17. Sales continue. This stimulates me tremendously,—this recognition which allows me to go on, knowing I cannot lose. I would anyway—always have: but now I have the satisfaction of monetary reward, slowly, surely growing, and without compromise, pleasing only myself. My one great desire is that eventually I will feel secure enough to take the stand of no compromise in portraiture.

Yesterday I sold my old "Circus Tent,"—then later my favorite new pepper,—its first sale, to Miss Cornish, who has a school—I think of music—in Seattle.

But is this pepper my favorite?—for I have another which is just as great in another way, a pepper so dynamic it becomes terrific with implied esoteric force: while the first one has an elegant classic movement, a stately aloofness.

I worked hard all week on orders, to earn the right to go on with—more peppers! I found four or five of extraordinary beauty which will fit well my present way of seeing.

182

If today, Sunday, will bring me any leisure,—tourists are thick as ants,—I will work. I want them—but I want to do these peppers too. So many called yesterday, at least twelve or fifteen, winding up with Ford Sterling again.

An amusing story: a letter came from the secretary at "Asilomar," a kind of resort, convention grounds, Y.W.C.A., asking me to talk at a photographic banquet, the subject, "Photography as a Hobby for Women!"

I answered that I was hardly fitted to speak with authority from that angle: photography being my lifework, and for me a high explosive.

Much fun could be had with a satirical treatment of the subject, for instance, built around the multi-colored Kodaks now manufactured to fit into women's vanity cases! But who cares to waste time.

Monday. If I got anything from yesterday's work it will either be a miracle or indicative of super concentration on my part. To be sure I knew just about what I wished to do with each pepper, and the background was selected,—the tin funnel: but the niceties of absolutely correct exposure, advantageous illumination, critical definition, all had to be considered with an audience which included at one time—Richard Buhlig, just arrived for his concert, Ruhdyar and wife, Ford and Aloyse, Fritz Wurzman, Winifred Howe with mother and friend, to say nothing of Sonya and several curiosity seekers who wandered in and out.

I really have no place to work except this studio porch, and I cannot close this room which is really public, to receive visitors; one never knows when might arrive a "prospect." Fortunately I am not bothered so much on week days.

Richard was thrilled with my "classic" bananas and Ruhdyar with a pepper— new—which is one of my favorites too: a single pepper of amazing convolutions, a most mystic form, low in key, but sunlit in the center: it fills the entire negative, horizontally.

Saturday, August 23. My grandchild is here, and incidentally his parents. He is a "grand" child! A strong, hearty boy with a fine head. Ruhdyar was here when he arrived, took a look at his palms and said, "What a head line!" "Ted," —he is Ted the third, for so my father called me, and I in turn called Chandler, and now the baby succeeds to the title,—Ted and I made friends at once and already have had long conversations, both humorous and serious: nobody understands our talk, but we do!

Chandler is thin, worn: Max is sobered down for one so young. They have been through a severe test. I want to see them surmount their trial, come out the stronger for it.

I have been working fast, furious, and very well.

Cows! Cabbages! Auto headlights and curtains! Hands! And another pepper! The cows I found at Point Lobos. I had my Graflex with me thinking to do

Ford in action: but there they were, these spotted Holsteins, with swelling bellies, lying all over the landscape. I made nearly three dozen negatives, camera in hand, mostly rear ends to get the ample volume as they lay, lazily cud-chewing. I have chosen four, representative ones to print as a start: and am all excited to finish. We had a picnic lunch, after which I turned the 8 × 10 on Ford's Lincoln. Auto fragments have been done quite often, but I had to have my say.

The hands I mentioned are Ruhdyar's—and what I saw on the ground glass thrilled me: what I got saddened me. I will never know why I drew eight blanks! Maybe I did not wind my curtain up, or maybe left my slide in,—but Oh, what might have been! Well, I have several, but the big fish got away—

Then yesterday was another important event—the start with halved and quartered red cabbage: for months in mind to do. I put on the Zeiss, stretched out the bellows, entirely filled the plate with the center, not showing the outer form,—curve of cabbage, and in brilliant sun, made five negatives, changing the pattern by slicing off a thin layer each time, which also gave me a fresh surface.

Whether I do more or not, these will go at once into my printing file for N. Y. show. They are extraordinary, significant,—more than a cabbage.

Sunday, August 24. An awful day, Saturday, of visitors, in and out, until I was in a whirl, and still feel the strain. Results,—one sitting ahead and a print sold. Also waiting to hear from M. J. B., coffee advertising manager, who drove down yesterday to interview me re photographs for a campaign in the newspapers. No printing done, and I have my doubts about today: and my desire is overwelming!—to print new work.

Last night to Henry Cowell's new Operetta, *The Building of Bamba,* given at Forest Theatre: So poorly produced that one could hardly say whether it had possibilities or not. Many of the cast were from Halcyon, colony of mystics. I have my doubts about the esoteric when it does not include the aesthetic! I certainly would not have gone to an opera, disliking staged bellowing,—worse combined with acting, even when the bellowers are good: these were awful,— most of them, but I had hopes this might be a new note, or new music from Henry. But no, much of it sounded like old church hymns poorly sung.

Monday. My price of $35 a negative to M. J. B.—which was very low, in fact cannot compete with my portrait profits, was accepted without question. I quoted low, in order to get a start: advertising interests me. But they request the first print by Wednesday or within three days: ridiculous! I wrote that I must have three weeks or a month, otherwise we could end negotiations at once. The trouble with these large business concerns is that they are used to dictating terms: dozens of commercial photographers competing for the work, put them in the position of dictator.

Well, I am not anxious to add another "hurry" to my life. I do the dictating if they want me, want carefully planned work, want craftsmanship.

August 28, 1930. M. J. B. phoned me long-distance, very much modified in their demands: if I could get out the first negative by Friday they would pay me $50, and afterward try to plan further in advance. I accepted, they seem to want me especially, and their money is not tight. But here it is Thursday—and I have not made a single negative! The first of the week I had to get other work finished, then I was delayed in getting lettering done on a package which goes into the ad. Today starts with a heavy fog and I intended to use sunlight, as I can do so well.

After printing orders, I printed several cow negatives. They were certainly well-seen, but enlargements from Graflex negatives, camera in hand, $1/_{10}$ sec., f/18, can hardly compare with contacts from 8 × 10 on tripod stopped down beyond f/256! All I can say is, that they are surprisingly good, considering. One day, I'll try the cows with 8 × 10.

September 11. In selecting prints for my N. Y. exhibit, I chose, for the sake of variety from the many subjects I have used—peppers, kelp, bananas, shells, rocks, and what not, to show what can be done with anything, how each is related to all. This relativity is indicated in the course of selection: for I often place a kelp along with a pepper, or a shell with a melon, choosing on the basis of finest print quality or clearest expression in feeling, regardless of subject, for they are the same, varying only in degree.

José Rodriguez in an article for *California Arts & Architecture*, has started from a basis seldom touched upon—and it is the real base of my work, the very inner core:

"Weston is crazy about photography in the same sense that Hokusai was crazy about drawing. There is, in fact, a strong affinity between these two artists—born in different centuries of different races. To both, the physical thing is immensely significant. Superficially, this would make them both stark realists, but the second thought follows irresistibly that this very preoccupation with shape as a fundamental definition makes them both out-and-out mystics."

Then he goes on to make a valuable explanation to the public who are always finding symbolic meanings, literal association of forms, ideas, comparing a pepper to a madonna and child, or finding the face of Lincoln in a tree! He kills that idea. I never see these associated forms when I work, only parts of life as symbols of all life. After, when someone with literal mind points them out, the print is sullied thereby!

I am very weary these days. Rushing to clean up orders, that I may print more new work, with N. Y. in view.

M. J. B. quite pleased, and a check by return mail. Orders are printed to date. Now I am printing Orozco's frescos,—52 negatives and difficult ones, I do them so carefully there is no profit,—but I must please him and Alma Reed: they will work for me I know. They have faith in me.

Yesterday I printed only 21 negatives in six hours,—one print each. But after these first prints the next should be more simple, for I keep all data on time, paper, etc.

Sunday morn, September 14. — 4:30—wide awake with thoughts on my yesterday's negatives: squash—winter squash—marvellous cream white forms—one like a starfish—one a pointed comet sweeping through space—another, fluted like a Greek column: solid, smooth, absolute,—abstract? I am fishing for words to give my feeling for their detached quality—their gesture of complete beauty.

So! I am in the same class I rebel against? Comparing a rock to Lincoln's face! No—I am trying to give a *feeling* for these forms in *words*. With the prints before one, they should stand alone in their own significance, any associated thought should come as a matter of course,—of course one can see, must see the startling similarity of forms, the repetitions all through nature. I suppose the layman is amazed and has to exclaim, because he, a non-observer, sees for the first time through the artist. The artist then becomes an interpreter, a go-between.

And my negatives,—I have several as detached, silent, complete as were my reactions to the squash. What an awful word—"squash!" They deserve a better name.

Just after writing the above, I made ready to repeat one of the squash negatives of yesterday which had a defect in background. For this ground, I have been using a white cardboard funnel. It gives me a gradation from white to grey to nearly black around the squash, depending on how far forward or back I place the object.

Well—I miscalculated my time,—because I went contrary to my intuition—it looked so bright, yet I said to myself,—this is early morning, 7:00 a.m.—don't be deceived, give it thirteen minutes. Exactly five minutes had passed when squash, funnel, and all toppled to the floor. Stunned for a moment, I came to and capped the lens. I looked on my ground glass at the void left by the accident and found no bright objects which could have been recorded in the few elapsed seconds nor did I think the quick fall of my "set" would show, so I went into the darkroom and developed: easier to develop, take a chance, than to do over,—that would take maybe an hour, even if the light stayed put,—which it wouldn't! Result—a perfectly timed negative. The fall was timely! Thirteen minutes would have been far too much. Maybe some unseen hand knocked down that squash,—and saved me!

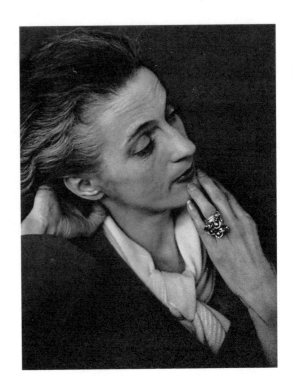

17. Robinson Jeffers, Tor House, 1929

18. Alice Rohrer, 1933

19. José Clemente Orozco, 1930

20. La Teresina, 1933

21. COLE WESTON, 1929

22. SONYA NOSKOWIAK, 1929

23. ZOHMA & JEAN CHARLOT, 1933

24. ALBERT BENDER, 1928

25. IVANOS & BUGATTI, 1931

26. BED PAN, 1930

27. EGGSLICER, 1930

28. ERODED PLANK FROM BARLEY SIFTER, 1931

September 17. I am dull this morning. I can't drink without paying,—I mean drink even moderately. Two or three cocktails, and a glass of wine,—this was enough to make me weary, flat, today. But I can't blame drinking alone: maybe the dinner last eve, even more than the drinks, causes my weariness. I, who am satisfied with a big salad, or a bowl of spinach, or a few bananas and grapes, cannot put down a baked ham dinner,—with all the trimmings, and not know it. But there is another reason, which combined with the other two, has let me down,—a psychic reason: I was at variance with my host,—John O'Shea. The difference started ten days ago when Schindler talked here. His treatment by some of the pillars of society in the audience was contemptible. One can allow for a difference of opinion on modern architecture, or any other art, but one cannot excuse insulting conduct: talking in undertones which were anything but whispers, walking around,—yes clumping around during the after-discussion, asking trivial questions—actually poking fun. Schindler bore himself with dignity, he was a gentleman, the others were not. I admit John O'Shea had been drinking: good,—one's character is revealed with a few drinks. After the lecture he made disparaging remarks, even indulging in personalities in a loud voice standing near Schindler, head turned toward him, face a leering mask. Disgusting!

I sat down and wrote for the *Carmelite* an article giving full vent to my feelings, not using names, but the several offenders were plainly enough indicated.

So when John phoned me to come to a stag party, I hesitated: but I went. I had not entered the door before he started the whole thing over, he and Dickinson. I tried to turn the conversation—what was there to argue about? I live today—they live back in the middle ages — — I spent my evening trying to keep them off "art" and keep my temper. Dickinson said, "Weston is too serious!" But they were the serious ones—that article had a sting! I was sober enough to sit back and watch the others, especially John: and his face revealed much. I saw a man, soured, cynical, negative. Perhaps he knows that he can not, never can, reach the heights he tried for. A fine painter, but nowhere near a great artist. I felt sorry for him, but that does not excuse his childish nonsense.

Frederick O'Brien was the artist of the evening,—in word and action he had the fine approach to life and art. He was fluid,—the others congealed in negation.

September 18. Getting closer—using a 5 inch Cooke lens on the 8 × 10—making the heart of an artichoke to fill the entire plate—a celery heart becomes heroic— a new field is opening to me—on the horizon I see a microscope! Celery is great material: the stalk done close—a twisted tree trunk—white as a palm—fluted like great pillars. I see celery as a staple, even as peppers have been!

But I must stop photographing and print: over forty new negatives awaiting in the darkroom.

September 29. Two weeks have passed which seem two months. A letter from Alma Reed with the news that my exhibit would open October 15th,—two weeks sooner than expected. When the letter arrived I had several sittings dated, Brett had just arrived with Elinore, his new love—and I certainly don't blame him!—a lovely person, beautiful in face and form, a fine frank attitude, and considerate. I had orders to print, and new negatives too, for consideration as additions to my exhibit.

Working under pressure has advantages. I quickly eliminated for printing those negatives which seemed to repeat in form or feeling those already on hand, if I thought they had not gone beyond the old ones. I lived the exhibit for ten days, and now fifty prints are ready to ship.

What a task to choose! I could give another equally representative, almost as important, exhibit of one hundred prints from those left in my portfolio. This fact surprised even me: thirty-three out of the fifty prints chosen were from negatives made this year,—all but three shells done in 1927, and the head of Galván from Mexico, were from last year's work. In other words these last two years, especially the last eight months, have been my most significant. I have worked well and prolifically.

I have yet to get off the catalogue. Laurvik offered to write the foreword, but not a word from my "special delivery" note. Last night Becking came over to see the prints before shipping. Several remarks he made gave me the idea, why not a scientist for the foreword! I suggested his thoughts would be an excellent introduction. He promptly and enthusiastically offered to write them for me. It was so good to see dear Brett Boy again!

18. "Reality makes him dream—"

September 30. Becking was prompt—which is more than I can say of Laurvik—and I can easily guess that Becking is the busier man. What makes me a bit peeved is the fact that Laurvik offered to write the foreword—his own initiative—then failed me. But I don't know his circumstances, and I gave him short notice.

However, I am happy. Becking's concise statement could hardly be improved upon: and I like the idea of a scientist introducing me to the art-hunting public: "Natural science, as an impartial student of form, cannot but marvel at the rediscovery of fundamental shapes and structures by an artist. Weston has described the 'skeleton' materials of our earth; rock, bone, and wood, in a way both naive and appealing: in other words like an inspiring scientific treatise. He shows living matter, contorted like wrestlers' limbs, fighting the unseen forces of environment. He has seen the serene display of the spirals in the shell, the soft but stubborn curves of the kelps. . . . Reality makes him dream."

October 2. My exhibit goes forward today. I had fought it out with myself,—which prints to send—for so long, that when Henrietta Shore arrived I was glad to get her critical estimate of my selections. We agreed amazingly well: She suggested but four changes out of the fifty, all of them I had to admit she had good reason for. The bedpan,—because I might be labelled "Brancusi," the dead cormorant,—which she violently protested was unworthy of me, and though I felt she somewhat exaggerated its unworthiness, I had to admit to myself that I was carried away by the unusual subject matter, the summer squash,—which I had improved on in the recent winter squash, and the portrait of Perry Newberry,—which I had long hesitated over and finally included because it has always been extremely popular,—not a good reason to include it in my most important exhibit.

When it came to choosing substitutes, she had the same trouble I had,—picking out a dozen or more which "simply had to go." Last night I began looking over old catalogues for some idea of the usual form for the cover. I could have used my own idea, but I felt that for Alma Reed, I should follow traditional form of announcement, that is, be on the safe side since we could not confer. The first one I picked up was Paul Strand's. I found that his exhibit was largely made up of rocks, trees, uprooted trees, even one seaweed! Some of my titles were the same!—naturally they would be since neither of us indulge in poetic titles.

I suppose my exhibit coming a year and a half later, there will be hints of plagiarism tacked on me! I look forward with interest to the press notices. But as curiosity only, for I know these prints are all my own. I arose at 3:30 this morning: the exhibit on my mind, last details to attend to, the several changes to make.

October 3. With the exhibit off I decided to take a rest, which meant work for myself. I had seen some very fine piles of kelp, washed in by the recent storm, —an early rain which at least laid the dust. The day was brilliant, warm, with no wind. I found it difficult to work without repeating myself,—those very first kelp set a standard hard to surpass. So I made but one negative, until, in search for starfish, I found a perfect specimen of the short, stocky seaweed which stands upright on wave-washed rocks, and sways with the waves like miniature palms. The roots of this were as grand as those of a cypress, the struggle for existence, the battle with the elements, had twisted and gnarled them until, seen close on the ground glass, one felt a giant century-old tree. I kept it wet with sea water,—the surface and rock background: it sparkled in the sun, a most exciting subject. If development shows what I saw—and of course it will, barring accidents—then I will regret not having it ready for exhibit.

October 13. I have written dozens of personal letters, and sent out 200 announcements of my exhibit: now I am ready to relax and await returns. Well no, not exactly relax!—For there are some seventy negatives to be printed, many new ones, besides those to be reprinted.

I have six recent invitations to show,—in Chicago, Berkeley, Seattle, Denver, and two in San Francisco. It has come to the point where I must have on hand several sets of fifty prints each, ready to exhibit, and, if my New York exhibit sells well, indicating steady demand, I will have to make at least several prints each from the most popular negatives, to have on hand: it is far too much work to make only one print at a time as heretofore.

Last week we took Henry to Point Lobos. I gave her a personally conducted tour of the Point. She was so excited that every turn discovered something she wished to paint. Well I knew her feeling! I left my camera home: I made up my mind to rest,—and saw new places to work that brought regrets — —

We go again today. Sharp took me to a deep rock-bound pool full of the most amazing sea life. Starfish! Marvellous form!—today I will hunt them.

October 16. My New York exhibit opened yesterday: for a few hours the day before, it seemed as though it might not. A telegram from Alma Reed, "—prints not here," hit me like news of death — — — — I had sent them with a week's allowance of time before the opening. I kept wires hot until they were located, undelivered in New York: someone's stupidity nearly brought tragedy.

This trouble combined with having a lunatic on our hands for the night, left me rather low for two sittings yesterday,—the first in some time.

Dene didn't realize this man was mad: thought he was overwrought from trouble and exhaustion,—he had walked from San José with bleeding feet. She wished him on me for the night. I knew at once he was mildly mad at least, a religious fanatic,—a Messiah with a persecution complex. Such a person might wax violent with anyone. I got him to bed in the studio, and the next day— with money wired from the south—Myrto and John almost shoved him on board a train.

Hazel asked me to duplicate my N. Y. show in her gallery, to hang next Wednesday: which means reprinting twenty-eight negatives by then! And I have had seven more requests for exhibits, four from the Bay region, besides Seattle, Denver, and Chicago.

If I could give up commercial portraiture, I could be kept busy every moment with furthering the sale of my personal work.

This is my hope.

October 17. A wire from Alma Reed: "Opening real success—all your old friends and sister present—many new admirers—sold long slender shell—everything most promising—Felicidades."

This brought me great joy. Especially "sister present!" It seems, and is, a reunion with her — —

4 a.m., Saturday, October 25. —and my exhibit ready to hang at Denny-Watrous: awaiting dawn so that I can have it up before the opening at 10:00. It was really quite a task, more rushing, to get this show done in time: especially since I made three prints, each negative, to have on hand for other exhibits,—the latest request for a one-man exhibit at the "Palace of the Legion of Honor," S. F. What bad taste in the use of "Palace!" Sacking Royalty—we democratic Americans must ring in some suggestion of "class."

Clemente Orozco hung my N. Y. exhibit: this news pleased me.—The prints were not in their hands until 4:30 the afternoon before opening day!

Sister wrote: "Your exhibit is a knockout." She *would* be prejudiced,—to a degree!

Ever faithful friend, Jean Charlot wrote: "I hope critics will recognize fully what a great artist you are." His comments, upon various avenues of approach in my work, were so interesting, intelligent, keen, that some morning I wish to devote to discussing them with myself,—if time for writing ever comes again!

The first notice in the *N. Y. Times* was favorable enough to me, but I felt (though H. Shore did not agree) that it was insinuated photography could not be an "art." At least the writer suggests that, and contradicts herself. "And his artist's power of selection realizes light, color, and form more handsome than many of the forms discovered by those working in a more direct medium." (What medium could be more *direct* than photography?) "But photography always remains an art of selection and taste, making greater demands on the object beautifully composed in light and shadow than on the creative mind of the artist."

Well, let's see!—let me look at my work, comparing it with work being done in the graphic arts,—the best. Imagination and varied selection in subject matter, power and originality in presentation, a realization of form, and the importance of light in which to reveal that form, and a feeling for the life force within the form: and besides, the technical ability to use my medium to record exactly what I felt. What more then! All hinges on the fact that I use a machine —which has been proved to be flexible—according to the user, while the "creative mind of the artist" must use the hand—and to what purpose? Often to bungle with!

I recall reading years ago, Leonardo da Vinci, complaining because the musicians had placed painting among the mechanical arts: it was not abstract enough —being done with the hand!

But after I have proved—to my satisfaction—my point, I am constrained to add, what difference does it make? Why bother to answer? Let me be labeled scientist, or just photographer!—quite sufficient—

This much is sure. I am releasing a powerful creative force which has profound effect upon many persons,—individuals from many walks of life. And I am doing this without hope of sufficient monetary compensation, because the urge will not be denied.

This last sentence sums up everything. What I am doing must have value— call it what you will.

October 29. A very fine letter came from Charles Sheeler with congratulations and good wishes: he writes—"I am among the many who will thank you for having shown your photographs in New York. . . . It must always be encouraging to those who insist that photography should stay within the bounds of the medium to witness such an outstanding demonstration as you have given that the medium is adequate."

This pleases me about as well as anything that could have been said, especially since written by Sheeler, whose work both as a photographer and painter is so important.

Two more prints have sold,—my eggslicer and portrait of Clemente. Alma Reed writes: "Steadily growing interest—scores of admirers—some of the artists, Walt Kuhn for instance, are boosting [you] all over town. Steiner (a very fine photographer from the few things I have seen) was in, and told Ione Robinson it was a 'magnificent show.' It really does look superb."

All this is most gratifying to me. I put my best into the N. Y. exhibit. Success means more than glory to me: it means maybe a sort of release. Surely now (for I have wavered this bad year) I can insist—"no retouched portraits."

Now I have work for an all Mexican show, at Alma Reed's Gallery, immediately following my exhibit. The only preparation will be in cleaning the mounts of my old platinum prints. I cannot take time to reprint. Having made my stand with the glossy prints, I feel the older work should be shown as it was first presented. In fact I rather welcome the opportunity to show this period—the clouds—juguetes—landscapes—pottery—and maybe some portraits.

We have been going to Point Lobos twice a week to give Henry a chance to work: which excuse to go I take advantage of, without much urging! And I have worked exceptionally well, making more than a few things I would have sent to N. Y. if they had been ready: rocks and trees of course, but done with fresh enthusiasm and all advantage of past experience,—also starfish, over which I am now quite excited.

A recent day we sat in the Gallery at Denny-Watrous, my exhibit being on the walls. Henry made known rather nervously, hesitatingly, that sometime she had something to tell me—maybe she would—perhaps it would hurt me. Well, I usually "handle" Henry to make her talk, so after much preliminary explaining to assure me of how highly she valued my work, out it came.

"You will be a much greater artist if you can approach your subject—go to nature, with no preconceived idea. You will lose many admirers, but gain others." And so on, elaborating none too clearly. But I understood,—agreed and disagreed. I always have had that faculty of seeing both sides—being able to say—"yes and no"—in the same breath. This quality I believe has given me a breadth and balance in my work,—has accounted for variety, in subjects and approach. It also gives an impression of indecision to those who do not know me well, this ability to see all around a premise and argue against my-self.

In this age of communication, through books, reproductions, exhibits brought from all over the world, who can be free from influence,—preconception? But —it all depends upon what one does with this cross-fertilization:—is it digested, or does it bring indigestion?

When I start out in the field, for instance at "the Point," it seems to me no one could be more free from intention, preconceptions than I am: allowing whatever crosses my path to incite me to work—and working I do not think: of course there is one's subconscious memory to draw upon,—all the events, all the eyes have seen in this life and how many more lives? to influence one. But no one starts alone, apart,—we only add to that which has gone before, we are only parts of the whole. The "individual" adds more or combines more than the mass does, he stands out more clearly, a prophet, with a background, a future,

193

and the strength, clarity to speak,—in his chosen way,—music—paint—words: a Bach or Blake.

Henry admits she is fighting the same thing in herself: she adds that she means by "preconceived," a personal idea of what nature *should be* like—instead of an effort to find out what nature *is* like. The photographer—the purist—like myself, going directly to record nature exactly, without the human interference of the hand, must be singularly free from personal interpretation of nature. I have used the phrase "significant presentation" to indicate my way of seeing "the thing itself." My personal viewpoint, my individualism comes forth, in the parts I select to present the fundamental structure I feel and extract from nature, isolate in my negative. I have been related in articles to Brancusi in my use of "abstract form." Yet they are all forms abstracted from nature: my seeing of life, recognition of cause, intuitive understanding. Or whatever you will! Maybe I have tried too hard to speak. Maybe a wire from N. Y. asking for personal data for a special story in the Sunday *Times*, which has broken my trend of thought, is just as well to have come.

But I will go on...and go into Jean's letter! "The pepper series look more like photography of sculpture than they exist as photographs alone." And also: "Others are perhaps too heavy with implications coming from the subject-matter like the red cabbage and artichoke (with the idea of growth, etc.) to know which of its beauty is in the print—which in the mental correlation."

As to this last thought—why not both beauty of print and mental correlation with idea of growth?

But this must end for today!

Sunday morn, November 1. Chandler and I met at 3:30 a.m. He just going to bed after printing all night,—I just arising! So we had coffee together. The night was as balmy as in Mexico: very hot weather for Carmel.

Yesterday, following a wire from Alma Reed, I shipped air mail an exhibit of ten prints to the Harvard Society of Contemporary Arts, Cambridge.

Then she writes: "Day by day the show gains in interest. All the photographers are most excited. Arnold Genthe called yesterday and stated that your work 'opened up entirely new paths for photographers.' Mitchell Kennerly bought pepper No. 35 P. He was thrilled with the exhibition. (Nothing from him about publication!) *The New York Times* Sunday magazine have just accepted an article and six photos." All most encouraging news. And I am certainly kept busy answering telegrams, rushing out prints.

I photographed Ratan Devi recently. She sang and played at Denny-Watrous. Exquisite artistry. So I tried to record facial expression and her hands in movement while actually singing. A difficult problem,—to keep in focus her ever swaying body, to release the shutter at the most significant moment. Usually I would have developed at once, unable to wait: these days I have to wait!

November 13. Rain!—it started in the night. The first rain is an event worth recording. Lucky we chose yesterday to work at Point Lobos. I saw one of Henry's nearly completed trees: superb! She has surpassed herself, and that is saying much. I have too!—these late rocks and trees are a definite advance.

Exhibit news: "The 'great Steichen' was in this evening and seemed quite thrilled. He purchased No. 18, (Rock 37). He said that it was a magnificent exhibition and that N. Y. should be truly ashamed for not buying out the entire collection. He has the reputation of being a hermit, but the noise about the exhibition forced him out. At first he sent his assistant to 'see if it were worth while'."

But the prints have not sold any too well,—five to date. The financial depression we must blame. Well—the foundation is being laid for a future which I believe sure to come.

Tuesday eve was a great event, maybe *the* event for me, in music: *Walter Gieseking*, pianist, played at the "Golden Bough." No use my making musical comments. I only know I was listening to a master whose playing was an achievement. How different from the virtuosity of Horowitz of wide acclaim: the latter left me cold. But Gieseking!—His Bach, *Partita B flat major, No. 1,* — — I felt that he and his piano were one,—an inseparable whole. But why Bach at the start of the program? It should be the climax! After Bach, one must let down for the others. Beethoven followed, and I found my thoughts wandering. Then came the moderns—not so "modern" any more—Debussy—Ravel—exquisite, delicately romantic—but not Bach.

November 14. —thinking of Jean's letter: I too felt that my peppers resemble sculpture: but not while doing them,—afterwards, maybe helped by others who have even thought I copied "modern" sculpture.

Well, a sculptor might have exactly copied a pepper, and been accused of realistic (photographic) viewpoint, or of taking liberties with Nature! I have only discovered unusually important forms in nature and presented them to an unseeing public. I have had time and again persons tell me, "I never go to a market now, without looking at the peppers, or cabbage, or bananas!" And even they bring me vegetables to work with, as the Mexicans used to bring me toys. So I have actually made others *see* more than they did. Is not that important?

When I work in the field with rocks, trees, what not, I think that this is my important way: then comes a period of "still-life" which excites me equally. So the best way is not to theorize, but do whatever I am impelled to do at the moment. I have always had the faculty of seeing two sides, positive and negative, to a question. No sooner do I say "no," than out pops "yes." Of this I am sure: the intimate "close-up" study of single objects has helped my work outside.

As to Jean's remark re implications of growth—If I get into my work that very feeling of growth—livingness—I am deeply satisfied.

195

November 20. The days, past and present, are full of work: sittings come in regularly enough, twice weekly excursions to Point Lobos, preparations for coming exhibit at Vickery, Atkins and Torrey. I have in mind now a new Ford. The old Packard—Flora's—is about shot—a car of some kind is a necessity if I am to continue working in the field—a Ford is the only sensible buy. But I dread spending $800,—it comes too hard!—though writing this I catch myself, for actually my portrait sittings are "easy money": an hour, or less for the sitting, a few hours, often only an hour for the finishing, and I have from $40 to several hundred. I figure on earning from a fair size order $1 a minute, with small overhead and small stock bills. I have a formula for portraits, and it works!

If the sittings would come in large enough quantities to keep me busy every working day, I would soon be rich: but right here comes the rub—I refuse to spend the time earning a living—I will more and more give time to *my* work. Even—I think now of several large portrait commissions a year, then all thought, energy, time to personal growth. This cannot be realized until the boys are on their own.

Back to thought of the Ford. If it were not for the business need of a car, home portraits even now awaiting me—north and south, I might decide on a microscope for the year to come, and retire from the field. But that would mean more confining work, and work out of doors is what I need most of all.

Takane Nambu, Japanese opera singer, in recital here. Tickets free for my family, otherwise nothing could have tempted me. She sang Japanese folk songs with Italian Opera voice, then *Madame Butterfly*. It was just too bad for comment. Personally she had much charm.

A letter and catalogue from Harvard Society of Contemporary Arts. It is an important group exhibit, with such names as Atget, Sheeler, Strand, Stieglitz, Steiner,—and Tina too!—seventeen exhibitors. The secretary wrote that mine have been among the most admired. This should lead to something quite important,—for me. I am on the way to more than local recognition. My biographical data read, "born in the late 90's." Making me a grandfather at about thirty-five!

November 22. The *N. Y. Times Magazine* for last Sunday—the 16th, published an article, nearly two pages with four illustrations about my work. The writer, Frances McMullen, did well. She used many of my thoughts, or press notices, paraphrased them or quoted exactly. The article has dignity, the reproductions for a newspaper excellent. Also, *California Arts & Architecture* out with José Rodriguez' article and seven reproductions: a very fine display.

Too bad all this publicity during hard times! But maybe it has saved me from failure, from hunger, or what not!

I have printed six new negatives,—trees and rocks. Any one of them I would have included in my N. Y. exhibit if ready. Next year will be a definite advance. Today we go to *the* Point.

Sunday. —I have on my desk before me, a halved red onion which is so absolutely marvellous as to bring desire to start still-life again: indeed I would, but where the time? Xmas only a month away, and orders must be kept moving to make ready for last moment rush. Then I may go to the city: several sittings await me, and I could be there for the opening of my exhibit. But I dread "home portraits,"—I can't use my formula! I waste too much time for the money.

Work at the Point yesterday was most satisfactory. The tide was higher than I have ever seen it, and then correspondingly lower. The gravel washed out, revealing eight inches of base I had never seen before, offering new forms to work with, or variations of old forms. I made seven negatives,—eight, but I don't count the last one of an abalone which moved during a prolonged exposure at 5:00. Arriving upon my scene of action, a number of sea gulls took off, rather reluctantly I noted. Descending to the beach, I found eight or more enormous abalones washed ashore. Why, I cannot guess, for there had been no storm, and it seems to me a terrific force must be necessary to loosen the grip of an abalone. Several were very much alive, and I was spellbound with the beauty of their form and rhythm of movement, not to mention color. One, who had given up and lay half slid off his shell, was too fine to resist, but during exposure slid some more.

All afternoon the gulls sat upon the rocks above me or sailed overhead, angrily squawking at me for spoiling their feast.

December 3. Henry returned from S. F. last eve: tells me my exhibit is superbly hung, that a print sold the first day,—the egg slicer—which also sold in N. Y. I suppose it is purchased because it's "modern." I am so sick of the word! My squash is just as "modern." One's spirit of approach may be contemporary, but subject matter is immaterial, and fine art of any period is "modern," and much that is labeled "modern" is very academic, decked out with a few frills.

The N. Y. *Theatre Arts Monthly* published four full page reproductions: a pepper, one of my finest, and egg slicer, one of my worst, the cypress and rocks of Arensberg's purchase, and two bones,—the latter I would not include again in an exhibit. But the egg slicer I am distressed over. I have learned a lesson! I printed it to study. When Alma Reed wrote me for "newspaper" prints, for advance publication, I went through my extra box and sent anything that might reproduce well, thinking—it will look like hell when reproduced anyway! Well, I am paid for my uncraftsmanlike attitude, for I am shamed by this page. This carelessness on my part has decided me to have a great bonfire after Xmas, destroying all work not absolutely my best. I can at least do this for posterity, for I know that even though I am recognized now—the *Theatre Arts Monthly* as an example, wrote in the caption, "No painter of modern times is more cognizant of dramatic form"—I will be more widely acclaimed and my work sought for after I am gone. I *must* realize that every print I send out (God forgive the portraits) with my signature is going to be severely criticized by those who know—if it is bad—for a crown is jealously eyed: and worse, the tyro, the public, will consider all my prints as praiseworthy. If I am indiscriminate, the public will be.

Henry is drawing my portrait. The drawing fine—the likeness I do not see!—and she keeps asking me if I see myself, and I keep answering "yes": for what can I say? Anatomically it may be correct—even that I doubt—and she is trying for an exact likeness—but she misses me—as I see me. On the other hand if she sees me so it must be right—through her eyes!

One of my recent finds on the beach at the Point is a sea-bleached seal bone, —an "abstraction" in ivory. Now, no more excursions to the beach, to Point Lobos until I have a new car,—the old one has passed out. If I can only enter into the purchase of a new Ford in a carefree spirit,—knowing it *should be* for business, but far more important, for my work. And my sale of prints will actually pay for it.

December 14. Just returned from a week in S. F., mostly spent waiting around at my exhibit, for sittings which did not come,—and losing sittings in Carmel—which I found out to my sorrow when I came back.

The exhibit is beautifully hung, the most stunning presentation I have had, or rather that I have seen, for reports from N. Y. tell me the prints were superbly presented.

I cannot say my trip north was fruitless. The first day I found most extraordinary curly-leaved cabbage; took it back to Henry's where we stayed, and made my first sitting in S. F. Also it was the last sitting I made, for I halved it while waiting for Hans to arrive for the return, making three more negatives.

Then there were other contacts besides the cabbage! Margrethe Mather,—a fine renewal of an old friendship: but she seems as lost, or more so, than ever, —in her work. I have promised to help her if she will come to Carmel,—but it really seems futile.

I met Diego! I stood behind a stone block, stepped out as he lumbered down stairs into Ralph's courtyard on Jessop Place,—and he took me clear off my feet in an embrace. I photographed Diego again, his new wife—Frieda—too: she is in sharp contrast to Lupe, petite,—a little doll alongside Diego, but a doll in size only, for she is strong and quite beautiful, shows very little of her father's German blood.

Dressed in native costume even to huaraches, she causes much excitement on the streets of San Francisco. People stop in their tracks to look in wonder. We ate at a little Italian restaurant where many of the artists gather, recalled old days in Mexico, with promises of meeting soon again in Carmel.

Pflueger—architect—was another contact worthwhile. He sat to me—on the roof at Ralph's.

December 18. I have real news this morning. I arose very early, awakened with thoughts of yesterday, and unable to sleep again because of my excitement.

I printed for myself for the first time since the New York exhibit two months ago. I do not count reprinting a negative: once the first print is made the thrill is over. Yesterday's work was all from new negatives, some made months ago, thirteen all told. Without question, any one of them could go into a one-man show of my best. I printed thirteen in five hours, living up to my manifesto that the first print from a negative should be as fine as one could make.

Briefly, these are the prints before me: little succulents around the top and sides, with a cypress root of exquisite texture, flowing from them like a cascade of water: a cypress—which Henry did not like because of its exaggerated perspective, but which in reality was but slightly exaggerated,—being one of those strange cypress forms which narrow quite violently from a wide base: then my halved red onion, just the center, enlarged about four diameters, not perfectly sharp all over, but solid, and easily one of my amazing photographs: the new halved cabbage too, or kale I think the variety is called, Henry likes better than my other earlier cabbage—I think it is a "knock out" but no more so than the first: cypress branches forming absolute rectangles against the sky, one of them making two sharp angles,—this startling technique: and the next one I come to equally startling, but that is hardly the word—for these white beach rocks, brilliant but not contrasty, have the most amazing chemical or photographic quality, plus simple statement of form so directly seen and untheatrical that it becomes stronger than many of my obviously powerful constructions: the next, in contrast to the rectangular branches, swirl upwards like fire,—a dozen of them with the same movement: cypress trees, like peppers, do not repeat a family pattern, each one facing a different problem in battling wind and finding foothold, so another rises for a ways as straight as a pine from rocky base with great dignity: and now I come to a cypress, which, if a painter had done it, he would be accused of fantasy, of creating a fairyland,—it is one of the most "imaginative" things I've ever done, if one can so call a literal record!—From all this one might think I had departed from my usual uncompromising way of seeing, and it is different, but I am as proud of my vision as when I made good with an overly picturesque scene in Mexico, or discovered more than the exterior of a beautiful girl — — in an evening sun which tips the branches, a cypress, fragile, formed to a letter S, clings to a steep grassy bank, with clusters of star-like sea flowers studding the slope — — a lichen-covered rock, nearly a circle in form fits into one of the cypress curves — —

199

it breaths mystery and I know there must be fairies in the deep dark recesses!—and yet there is not a grain of impressionism in this print—it is sharp, clear, definite—but—those who *affect* modernism will not like it: they will see more in the next I come to of another "abstract" rock, a fine thing, but no finer than my "dainty" tree and flower-covered slope: a rocky grotto almost with the qualities of the cypress fairyland—and I am through—having indulged in superlatives—without regret!

December 23. All Xmas work finished several days ago,—which means there has been very little. I am backing down on buying the Ford. I would gamble if I were alone,—but not with so many dependents. Neil leaves within an hour for Los Angeles: a visit only, he wishes to return. His mother will be amazed over his growth and change. He has grown a full head this last year,—now towers over me.

I would like to go south,—to see Cole,—Ramiel, Johan?—I hesitate, writing that I would *like* to see Johan, for he depresses me terribly now, or did the last several times we met.

I have kept on with my printing and have everything ready for my trip south, —my proposed trip! Everyone (I always mean everyone who counts) is enthused over these new prints. Henry thinks them the finest things I have done.

Xmas morn. —Rain threatens, after a brilliant cloudless week: a grand Xmas gift to the parched land, to our health and happiness, if it comes. The air has been so electrical, one's nerves are kept on the jump. We had a little Xmas tree for Teddy—his first—and opened presents around the fire—mostly gifts for the baby. I had two packages,—a corduroy shirt from Ramiel, and a book of reproductions,—the work of Atget—Paris photographer—from Jean Charlot. Then I bought a record for the family—which really means myself—a Bach fugue played by Segovia—guitarist. Come to think—I made myself another present which I might call a Xmas gift, though it came Dec. 19th,—I quit smoking. And really stopped this time, for the attempt in 1928 failed. This time it was so easy—so unexpectedly easy—that I surprised myself. To make the first step—that *was* difficult. I tried the plan of cutting down gradually, kidding myself along: it did not work! Then I said to myself—just a cigarette with morning coffee—but once starting the day I kept on. I decided that far more than overcoming the physical craving—I had to fight against habit—I had to establish a mental condition definite enough to place me beyond desire. I had often fought with myself, thrown away cigarettes, hid them, resorted to such childlike ways, until last week, when I created a state of mind in which smoking already seemed a part of my far distant past. I simply put them out of my existence. I do not say I had absolutely no desire—but it was so slight that it almost seems I deserve little credit for my victory! Up to the day I quit, I had not missed cigarettes with morning coffee and followed with at least a package a day, for fifteen years.

200

To be honest, the first several days I puffed once or twice a day from Sonya's cigarette, but I really mean *only one* or *two* inhalations. I did this partly from desire, partly curiosity. But it was not that desire got the better of me,—I *knew* that at last I had control, that I would not slip again,—so the puff was partly curiosity to note the effect. I became, with just the one inhaling, as dizzy as though I had taken several cocktails. How quickly then does Nature begin her house cleaning!

Already my nerves are much calmer. Smoking is a vicious circle—I smoked when I was nervous to calm my nerves, thereby adding to my nervousness!

December 26. Clear, and a cloudless horizon today. A few scattered drops of rain fell yesterday of not so much value as a good fog. Xmas day was my test— and a good one—to see if I had really quit smoking. I have!—not even one puff—with all the heavy food, meat and sweets, and wine, which calls for smoking after, to say nothing of loafing and smoking by the roaring fireplace. But I am rejoicing in my new freedom — — —

December 27. Zigrosser wrote me last year that they were to have an exhibit of photographs by Atget, whom he considered one of the greatest photographers of all time. I was curious and excited over this new name to me,—and I knew Zigrosser to have good taste,—since he chose my work as the most important art of the West!

So when Jean sent the book of Atget—I prepared to be thrilled—or that's a cheap word, let's say deeply moved! Instead I was interested,—held to attention all through the book—but nothing profound — —

Atget establishes at once with his audience a sympathetic bond: for he has a tender approach to all that he does,—a simple, very understanding way of seeing, with kindly humor, with direct honesty, with a reporter's instinct for items of human interest.

But I feel no great flame: almost, in plate 94 of tree roots,—if I had seen it before doing my own I would have thought it great. How much it resembles my viewpoint.

Unless the plates were poorly reproduced Atget was not a fine technician,— not always: halation destroyed much, and color correction not good. The poor man being dead he had no "say" in this book and perhaps would have omitted many plates. I can see no excuse for publishing 32,—for example. Too often he uses such poor judgment in lighting, getting messy, spotty results like plate 24. Certainly it has value as a record, but not as important photography. Again a plate like 48, his instinct for subject matter was keen, but his recording weak,— his construction inexcusable. Cut off the sky and present the wagon—and what he felt but did not get is there. So often one feels he just missed the real thing: for example 55 of the agave,—or the flowers 53,—or the wagon, above-mentioned.

But on the other hand his intimate interiors,—the bedrooms,—are as fine as a Van Gogh: and his store windows a riot,—superb. In these I find him at his best, and in such plates as his merry-go-round and circus or side show front.

Atget's importance is unquestioned. If I started out to criticize, it was from disappointment. I had expected a flame, and found but a warm glow. What I admire most of all is the man's simple honesty. He has no bag of tricks. He makes me feel ashamed in recalling certain prints—most all destroyed now—in which I found myself trying to call attention with cleverness, or shall I say by a forced viewpoint—for I hope I have never been cheaply clever!

And recalling the usual "Photo Salon" of pretty trees, romantic nudes, sentimental postures, Atget stands out, so very far apart, in extraordinary dignity.

One day I worked with bananas, a bunch I could not resist, and I have a white cabbage laid aside to do with first opportunity. Twice we went to Point Lobos and I did not make a negative! I might blame the tide the first day which was too high for certain work, but the next time out I went among the cypress with no results. I have lost my amazement, for awhile, with that subject matter, and should stay away, go elsewhere. My camera is in such a rickety condition that I have no pleasure using it, and the car is done for: last time out we returned on a rim, so I must either buy tires, or a new car, or stay home. So, for the time, I seem to be in a period of transition. Maybe going south will bring me new light as to the next step. I am certainly not depressed,—much—or most of this momentary hesitation is due to economics. I feel very fortunate considering general depression, my big family all well and eating. I do not owe a cent. I have $500 cash, all bills paid for this month and about $300 due me, and a good sitting yesterday besides selling a print of my halved onion. And yet I do not have the nerve to plunge and buy a car. I am not enough businessman to see or guess ahead. Is anyone? Should I save for a worse day?

January 9, 1931 — — 4 a.m. I leave for L. A. at 8:00 with Brett. Being all packed there is no reason but the usual one for this early hour rising: the reason before given,—my desire for escape,—to be alone. Sleep is also escape of a kind, but mine is not a passive desire to give up, find oblivion, for I am one of intense action. And I am one who must have order,—so these recent days have been trying. Sonya is the only orderly individual in this house besides myself; the little boys might be if they had rooms of their own, but Chan, Brett, and the two girls are not.—Everywhere they leave everything they happen to be using and never know where anything is.

I am not of the same type of order Ramiel is. His housekeeping is a marvel of perfection,—so perfect that he must spend much time in the attainment. I do not like dust and cobwebs, but I can overlook them, I have to, or spend hours or minutes I cannot spare. My claim to order is in keeping things in their place, and knowing the place.

Also I am one who does not stand quarreling, bickering,—not even between the children with whom it is half playful. So Cole and Neil must be separate until they are older.

Since the first of the year I have done several negatives for myself: of a cabbage, of an orchid! The cabbage excited me most, with finer results. This time it was a single leaf I used, achieving the strongest, most abstract results. The orchid, which was given me by Marion Simpson, was not so easy to do: too perfect—like trying to photograph a cathedral. And yet if I were not leaving today, I could spend a whole day or several days with it, could do something—in fact I have several negatives of much interest, but know there is so much more I could do, for it has possibilities far beyond a literal recording. I made several negatives in the tin funnel, direct sunlight, giving all the orchid's exotic quality, and a couple close up, more direct, powerful, abstract as it were: these latter are in the spirit I would go on with, given time. I don't know where I will attain to another orchid!—cabbages and peppers are easier to possess. But I am quite as happy without orchids,—the power in that cabbage leaf is in mind as I write this.

Instead of a new Ford, I am buying tires for the old Packard, and with a few other parts and much work by mechanic Chandler it will do for the time and give him a car when he leaves me.

February 21, 1931. Peace again!—the exquisite hour before dawn, here at my old desk — — — seldom have I realized so keenly, appreciated so fully, these still, dark hours.

I have escaped—but a day ago—from a madhouse! A week spent near Flora when she is nursing, is nothing less — — They sent for me to come,—Cole very sick with Diphtheria. I refused, knowing Flora's fear complex, and my reaction, which always caused me to leave,—and then get blamed for shirking, deserting. I said to Chan—"If the doctor sends for me I'll go to you at once." A week passed, another call to come. In an hour I was on the stage for Los Angeles.

Poor little Cole — — terrible disease — — I am glad that I went to him. He might have pulled through without me, but I'm sure I gave him confidence, calmed his own fears. He has inherited or acquired—probably the latter—Flora's appalling terror. I could see that he was thoroughly frightened, that the idea of death was strangling him. The house was in quarantine: Chan, Brett, Elinore, Flora, and myself, a mad mixture, imprisoned together in that little shack! Flora right in her element,—for if ever she "feels her oats," asserts her ego, rises to supernal heights, it is when nursing: and she is the world's worst nurse. Efficient,—yes—so damned efficient that the patient, nor anyone near, is allowed no moment of calm. We all went around like jumping jacks with Flora pulling the wires,—issuing the orders, commanding, nagging, countermanding, —anything that popped into her poor old rattlebrained pate. When anyone relaxed—high treason—she would find another job—to be done at once!—a spot wiped off the sink —a can taken to the garbage: and when the order was ignored—children become deaf, inert, impervious under continued nagging—then would come over her that look of self-pity, and indignation—toward me —that I would not back up her hysteria. I admit being too easy with the boys, —a reaction to Flora's neverceasing wrangle. But I can get more out of them, promptly and willingly and with respect, than she can. Flora's great cry has been that I would never back up her orders. Of course not,—never!

I called Flora efficient, and that is misleading: I meant to indicate that she is a hard worker, a slave, one who would die for the children, extravagantly generous, but with qualities which lead to utter confusion. The order she so much desires, and could have with half the effort, is dissipated through her most disorderly mind.

I return with memories, of Chan and Flora roaring at each other, of Brett telling her to "shut up," or paying no attention at all while she chattered or screamed on. In another room Cole calling for help, going into spasms, half brought on by fear, and intensified the moment Flora entered.

All my past has been revived by this experience, and I am satisfied that I did the only possible thing,—leave forever.

As I entered Glendale there stood my old studio and home, *my* home, painted a bright blue, topped by a huge sign, "Auto Loans." It was stripped, stark naked, every vine,—which used to shield me from the prying pillars of Glendale society,—cut down: the flesh had sloughed off, the spirit escaped, only dry bleached bones left.

I had only been back a week or so when Chandler phoned me to come to Cole. The first trip south had a few days worth recalling: hours mostly spent in the dentist's chair or going back and forth,—it took me over an hour on the bus from Pauline's, who lived in a Frank Lloyd Wright house in the foothills. Brett has his studio there, so I stayed with him rather than Flora. Paul, I got to know and appreciate better than ever, to really love her.

Two outstanding evenings were those at Arensbergs and Grants.

Walter Arensberg bought two more prints—not to say this was the important item of the evening—but the purchase was a symbol of his very deep appreciation. I can say that there are few persons I show my work to who respond so fully, that I myself feel a great inner joy, and I must include Mrs. Arensberg too. They asked me to come again, that Mr. and Mrs. George Middleton,—she the daughter of Robert La Follette—wished to see my work: again fine understanding, and a purchase.

Grant is a protegé of Ramiel, one of several aspiring writers under his guidance, —another is Lee. Grant is in charge of a beach club bathhouse at Palos Verdes, now closed for the winter. The two boys and Ramiel pulled a party for me there,

to be recorded as memorable. Arriving late, I stepped into an enormous room,
—one long table, feast-laden, extended the full lenth. In front of the fireplace
in which great eucalyptus logs blazed, a regiment of lobsters, in uniforms red,
awaited the attack. Old friends greeted me,—Merle, Arthur, José, Fay, Jake,
and a new one, Ione Robinson. I had but entered the room when someone
slipped me a glass of scotch (real) and so the fun began. Ramiel, the perfect
host, bustled vigilantly everywhere, hawk-eyed to further every want, to provoke
all means to joy.

For contrast I was in the dentist's chair at 9:00 the next day, and from there
to make a sitting!

Carmel was a refuge for one weary person.

14. *"I am the adventurer on a voyage of discovery—"*

February 23. Before my call to Cole's bedside, I had started working with new subject matter,—fungus growths,—mushrooms, toadstools: extraordinary forms which added several negatives with new direction, to my ever growing portfolio,—no—that was a misstatement,—not "new direction," they belong with the rest of my recent vegetable forms.

Since returning I have done—in mind only, but safely recorded there until time permits a photograph—a new and much finer version of the egg and bone. I placed an egg upon my sea-bleached seal bone, in the course of experimenting one rainy afternoon: but this was not at all what I started out to do,—I have quite forgotten my primal impulse. I had gathered together shells, bones, eggs, wood, dried kelp, whatnot, as I often do, to see what these things, or one of the, or combinations, *will do to me*: I am the adventurer on a voyage of discovery, ready to receive fresh impressions, eager for fresh horizons, not in the spirit of a militant conqueror to impose myself or my ideas, but to identify myself in, and unify with, whatever I am able to recognize as significantly part of me: the "me" of universal rhythms. Nature must not be recorded with a viewpoint colored by psychological headaches or heartaches: petty personal reactions from everyday situations are not to be exploited, such can be recorded in daybooks,—a good place to evacuate, cleanse the heart and head, preparatory to an honest, direct, and reverent approach when granted the flash of revealment.

March 6. Quiet, balmy days have passed, for work, the time and conditions could not have been better: but instead of doing new things for myself, I have been destroying some of my past,—so far fifteen negatives, and house-cleaning, generally ordering up books, papers, and my mind. I tried to work, had desire, —always have that, but no still-life excited me, not after doing the egg and bone successfully. I started several times with pine cones, shells, leaves, etc., but nothing excited me. I always realized I was repeating myself. If I had a nude body to work with — — a Negress, a black fat Negress, then I could have worked! This desire keeps popping into my mind. Or B. if she had been here, I know that something fine would have happened: to go on from where I left off with her in 1927. Or, with a car, I would have gone adventuring: but still-life I could not see — — —

March 10. —late morning—after ten hours sleep! Rather a record for me, and with no exhaustion to have caused it. Truth is, I feel quite balmy these last days,—there seems no incentive to spring out of bed at 4:00, so I lazily stretch at 8:00! This condition will not last, so I am taking advantage of it,—actually enjoying it. Henry has bought a car, and when she returns from the north, we will be going to the Point again: then I will begin to function normally.

My mind has been active, very much so,—rather trimming off loose ends, patching up holes. Reading too,—and what a book! Waldo Frank's *Rediscovery of America*. Everything that I have been feeling about life, all that I have put into recent work,—gradually for the last few years, Frank has presented so clearly, forcefully, conclusively, that his words became my own. For me, he brought together my random thoughts into words, sentences,—a book, which were I a writer, I would have tried to write, and as photographer, if I have approached his understanding, then I have fulfilled my intention.

To one who believes in America, despite the chaos, despite the ridicule of superficial thinkers, the refusal of weaklings, even to the acceptance of Hollywood, and all the cults of Los Angeles,—this book must give fresh hope, new impetus, desire to carry on, to see through.

Before going to Mexico—the war just over—(and I am proud of my war record of non-support, of absolute refusal) I was embittered: this condition intensified by certain associations, by discord at home. I was never fooled into thinking that Mexico was an escape, but it was necessary to go there—or somewhere— for readjustment, to gain perspective. Fortunate that I chose Mexico, or that my instinct told me to go when the opportunity was presented. Mexico was a great battlefield,—I lost forever in the jealous fury of three years, all concrete love,—personal and grasping, and won a new abstract, all embracing love, which has placed me safely beyond any danger of becoming a neurotic misfit. Is this sojourn in Carmel an attempt to escape, a refusal? Not at all! I am not a reformer, a missionary, a propagandist,—not in a militant concrete way. I have one clear way to give, to justify myself as part of this whole,—through my work. Here I can work, and from here I send out the best of my life, focussed onto a few sheets of silvered paper.

March 11. Returning home from the concert last night, a south wind bellied out my cape—the sky was murky—I smelled and said "rain"—and this morning there is rain. God knows we need it. Which makes me question the faith of people who pray for rain or sun or whatnot. With implicit faith why pray for any change? Is it not questioning God's judgment, His business? This is too deep for me—

Piatigorsky played the 'cello. Widely heralded like Horowitz, he was no disappointment, though he did not move me as did Gieseking—I meant not so profoundly: but he was not the virtuoso like Horowitz. His pianissimo was extraordinary, but at times I wished for more power. The event of the evening

207

was Suite in C Major—for 'cello alone—Bach. Then a Debussy Sonata, which was most exciting — — and I had thought that I was weary of Debussy.

I dreamed strangely last night: I went to the studio, found the big French doors had been unhinged, taken off, the place wide open and stripped of everything: cameras, furniture, books, all gone! What now?

March 15. Willard and Preston came down for the weekend. I like them very much,—very! Intelligent—clean—positive—they are of the youth who will "rediscover America." Jerome Melquist comes to mind,—he is another?—and Brett and Elinore: Chandler?—if he is strong enough to rise above his early marriage,—a man's job on a boy's shoulders. He, Max, Teddy, and Cole will be here soon! And I will have a severe test again. I cannot go on with all of them on my hands indefinitely,—I must concentrate on Neil and Cole. Chan and Max alone would have to battle their own way as Brett and Elinore are doing,—or trying to! But the baby? I feel so close to "Teddy." Soon we will have our birthday together,—his first.

March 17. This last month has been most non-productive: it may be more than lack of exciting new material, weariness with still-life, and yet I think I could have worked at the Point, given a way to get there. But come to think of it, I did not do much the last few times we went out. Perhaps an entirely new scene will be necessary. Ironically,—there has been no business to interfere, and perfect weather: I could have had a period of peace and quiet rarely granted me. And no "family!" on my hands, on my mind!—Quite too sad the opportunity lost: a month of perfect conditions for work.

I was cheered this week by an order for six prints from my portfolio. David S. Spector, San Francisco, asked me to send fifteen to select from: which means a much-needed $90, and more of my work out in the world to be seen by a wider circle,—or a different one than might come here.

I came across a choice bit of writing, which is my own! I had saved it from the bonfire of my daybooks kept three years prior to Mexico, and destroyed when I returned in 1925: destroyed for the very reason indicated in this one saved page. I am proud of having saved it,—evidently as a warning to myself, and I am proud to have written it.

To quote from my "awakening": "...perhaps hating to admit that my depressions were at least partially due to my own realized shortcomings,—and turning back over the pages of this daybook, I find recorded continual proof of my weaknesses. Ever and anon I am putting down remarks which such and such a person had said about my work, and then clinching my faith in it by setting forth that person's own greatness. Further—I like to pretend my friends are great—this gives me added ego—that my loves have been marvelous and my conquests unusual—my experiences different—while really I am quite naive and unsophisticated. I have put down much rubbish fearing some detail might be missed. Also I have tried to philosophize, *tried* to write, when I should have been content in the recording of daily events, indeed, such records are the best things I have written. "Well I know you Edward Weston, and I say you have spent a year of writing in trying to build up a fine defense around yourself and your work,—excusing your weakness! And yet knowing all this, you are not strong enough to destroy most of your work, nor these notebooks! I, who have preached against backscratching, have not withstood it." This I call good self-analysis. The question now comes, was I strong or weak in destroying? One might easily say weak!—For I certainly realized that I had made myself ridiculous, really exposed myself, that I feared to have this record stand!

The above quotation was written in 1920,—I was over thirty. Seen in perspective, I was shaking off a veneer acquired late in life. I had been a quite naive, simple youth,—much alone, especially after my first camera. I would play hookey from school to wander over the south parks photographing snow and landscape, until my father put me to work. So I had little schooling beyond eighth grade, read only photographic literature, and my contacts were those of the business world. Then came California, early marriage, starting a home, children, and the opening of my studio in Tropico.

With this background I was suddenly thrown into contact with a sophisticated group,—actually they were drawn to me through my photography which had gone steadily ahead,—was my development. They were well-read, worldly wise, clever in conversation,—could garnish with a smattering of French: they were parlor radicals, could sing I. W. W. songs, quote Emma Goldman on freelove: they drank, smoked, had affairs,—I had practically no experience with drinking and smoking, never a mistress before marriage, only adventures with two or three whores.

I was dazzled—this was a new world—these people had something I wanted: actually they *did* open up new channels, started me thinking from many fresh angles, looking toward hitherto unconsidered horizons. But there had to be a personal house-cleaning afterwards,—for, not to expose my real self to these clever new friends, I had to pretend much, to become one of them, parrot their thoughts, ape their mannerisms. Then came the day of reckoning when I saw through my own pretence. In the reaction I must have written the above quoted page.

March 20. When in Los Angeles, Seymour [Stern] showed me a copy of *American Annual of Photography* which he had promised to review for a new magazine of "radical & experimental art" called *The Left*. I offered to do the job for he was very busy: but I was not altogether altruistic,—I saw a chance to make a stand for real photography as against the salon type "pictorialism,"—the bastard bromoils, etc., done by would-be painters. *The Left* just came (first issue). It is

209

certainly "red!"—politically red—almost entirely politics. And in the back is an ad for next issue of *Experimental Cinema*, (Seymour's magazine) in which I am announced a feature, and titled "*Left-wing American Photographer.*" I simply roared with laughter! I had been adopted — — Seymour, so intensely earnest, would have been hurt by my mirth. But I was not laughing at his cause,—a cause so many would die for. He gave me the greatest compliment, from his viewpoint, possible to confer. There was no derision in my laughter, I was laughing at myself, as though out of a clear sky I had suddenly been knighted! —with a title I knew not how to wear. A radical I have always been considered, but only in my work. Politically, my convictions are unformed, excepting to realize, to know, that a change must come, that the world, and these States are in a mess: what form the change should take—evolution or revolution—I leave to those who have given it a life study. For me evolution offers a stronger base for a unified future. Prohibition failed here because it was forced upon a people not ready, not evoluted: they needed the escape drink offers. I cannot see the possibility of success in proletarian revolution here: too many workers hope to become bosses, or even President,—too many individuals out for themselves, to get all they can at any cost.

One thing is certain, unless the machine is turned into a public utility for universal benefit, it will devour all of us—capital and labor alike.

My deepest concern is for the youth now growing up in this land: so many of them will be utterly wasted, when they might become of tremendous importance to the state,—talent, genius all directed in our system into an effort to make a bare living, or to get rich. Misfits, suicides, neurotics, gunmen, convicts, who might have become the flower of the nation,—the finest, most sensitive ones, are those who refuse to fit in, cannot be moulded.

To really blossom, one must feel wanted, loved: must feel a place is open for one's especial capacity—not just any job. One's work must have social significance, be needed,—to be vital. Art for art's sake is a failure: the musician cannot play forever to an empty house. There must be balance—giving and receiving —of equal import whether in sex or art. The creative mind demands an audience, must have one for fulfillment, to give reason for existence. I am not trying to turn the artist into a propagandist, a social reformer, but I say that art must have a living quality which relates it to present needs, or to future hopes, opens new roads for those ready to travel, those who were ripe but needed an awakening shock,—impregnation. Nor am I in any way suggesting that the artist consciously tries to put a message into his work—he may, as Orozco does—who, whipped into a flame by injustice, releases himself with scathing satire: but his work will live, one might say, despite the social theme, as done by a creative mind, a visionary functioning positively, giving direction and meaning to life, which had been suffocating in sunless middle-class parlors, or falsified in "Bohe-

210

mian" attics. The same theme put down by a lesser artist, be he ever so fiery a radical, would no more live than a skyscraper erected by a schoolboy.

March 21. What started me on yesterday's subject was a desire to find the reason why my work has meaning to many people in many walks of life: not only artists and intellectuals respond, but businessmen, the butcher, the baker, etc., —children too. And now I have been adopted by the left wing!—though my work has no trace of political propaganda. But it is none the less radical,—it predicates a changing order: and that is why it is so disturbing to the bourgeoisie—I have watched them—who fear change.

My work has vitality because I have helped, done my part, in revealing to others the living world about them, showing to them what their own unseeing eyes had missed: I have thus cleared away the haze of a futile romanticism, allowing identification with all things by those who had been drifting apart.

Most certainly I have not done this consciously,—tried to put a message into my work. But my own desire for identification and its realization has placed me in the van as a pioneer, focussing a universal need.

Universal need?—Yes, but not universal acceptance! I am misunderstood because in the van,—have violent opposition, especially from bourgeois painters and their satellites in photography.

But have I not wasted several pages in putting down the obvious!

April 5. —And not yet have I worked! Even Point Lobos did not start me, possibly because I tried a spot already too well-known and worked. Late in the day I did become excited over several rocks, but the light had failed.

Maybe the great effort of last autumn, preparing for the New York exhibit, the impetus of which lasted until just before leaving for the south, has brought reaction: but this sterile period is unique for me. My only regret is that the peace and quiet of these weeks has also been unique. And now it is over, for Max and Teddy are here and Chan will soon arrive. Max returned with— Brett and Elinore—Cole *and* Flora! We had two mad days — — Cole, to his sorrow, went back south with his mother to continue treatments for nose and throat,—aftereffects of his sickness. Another effect is a psychic growth: suffering has matured him as it did Brett.

Brett may drive to New York. Why not?—he has nothing to lose—and will gain adventuring.

Henry took us to the Point in her new Ford, the result of a few sales. For a beginner she drove well, even though we near to ran down a Packard limousine!

April 7. I agreed to write an article for the *Carmelite* on the John O'Shea exhibit at Denny-Watrous Gallery: I sweat in doing it,—because, to a degree I had to resort to evasion, and I don't like to, it's not my way. I was overpersuaded,—

Hazel—Dene (so I speak of the two girls, always collectively)—wanted me to, so did John and Molly O'Shea: each one of these friends has not only been very kind to me, but has helped materially to raise my economic status. Of course I am trying to excuse a guilty conscience.

Fortunately I could respond to his banana canvases. I could see them much greater,—yet they have value, so I wrote around and about them.

Now I face an ironical situation: I wrote in a way which gives an impression that I accept John's work as a whole, that I value it higher than I actually do, —and John, from his remarks, I gather, feels that I should have said much more. To be sure, he jested in his cynical way, praised my "style," but I felt behind his mask an ego which would have had me use superlatives, placing John O'Shea as the foremost painter in the West. I couldn't do that, John! You are a brilliant painter, clever as can be, but most of your work I see as very fine illustrations, with the bananas on the way to something beyond.

April 11. I have just had an order from Jerome Hill—portraits of himself— amounting to $265—printed from 15 negatives. This is the largest single order I have had in Carmel: it would not have been so unusual in the old Glendale days, almost 10 years ago! Best of all I really approve of most of the prints ordered, and I like Jerome very much,—a quite unspoiled rich boy, sensitive and intelligent. He will also buy from my personal collection: his brother has already taken two.

Well, I will certainly need every cent I can amass. Chandler will have to have a large amount to start him in business, and if indications come true, I will have Johan, dead broke and very sick, on my hands this summer. To even think about this prospect makes me ill. In the first place he is mentally sick, embittered, neurasthenic,—a morbid unhealthy person to have around: a well person on top of my already too large family would be unthinkable. The extra expense is the least consideration, it is the confusion of personalities which will be maddening. And so far as helping Johan I feel utterly helpless. The old Johan, always difficult but with redeeming graces, is dead; a shell full of poison remains. But when Elsa phoned me from S. F. his wish, what could I say but "yes"—and then have violent reactions. I am living in his house, albeit no more than a good tenant, and I am full of memories of our past friendship.

April 14. Yesterday April 13, 1931, was the record so far as I can recall for sale of my prints. Jerome Hill purchased 10, excellent selections, his brother ordered 2, his mother one: a total of $195. And this month is a record one with sales amounting to nearly $300. If Spector orders, which is quite sure, this will be a memorable period. Jerome Hill's portrait order amounted to $280, his cousin's $40 so far, and his mother will sit to me soon. I like Jerome, a sensitive, and very intelligent boy, who thinks for himself.

Sunday was an intense day. I wrote Johan to send me a lease by return mail which would assure me this place until next January, or I would move out. And I laid down a few rules for him to observe if he came to live with me. I had to do this,—better a break now than after he arrives.

Also on Sunday I was called upon to make important decisions for two persons, Henry and Willard. Henry phoned, asking to see me. I was printing and could see no one! So then she asked me to decide:—through a mistake in numbering a $600 painting had been marked for $400, the dealer could sell it for the latter price, it was one of her finest, should she let it go?

I said—you painted this canvas six years ago—you agree that now you are a finer artist in every way — — that you could paint as well or better any day in the week — — that times are bad — — that you need money to go on with your work — — that selling it means a larger circle seeing it — — my answer is to sell! She agreed.

Willard drove down from San Francisco to ask me his question. He had been offered a position which in 25 years—when he would be 49—assured him $50,000 cash, and a respectable salary the while. An opportunity most young men would jump at. But Willard is not among the "most." The very fact that he hesitated, that he drove way down here to question, to ask for help in deciding was significant: he wanted me to back up a decision he had already made. I said no—do not sell yourself to an oil company for 25 years, to earn money to die on! You would ruin a life that holds promise, become one of the many misfits, maybe a hopeless neurotic. Willard beamed all over! He wanted no more backing. His conscience was hurting because he felt it almost a duty to accept.

There may come days when Willard will have doubts,—wish that he could look forward to retiring with $50,000 or more, and colorless comfort. But I am glad that I said no, emphatically, without hesitation. At least one brilliant young American saved from becoming a cow!

April 23. Rain sweeping over the shingled roof awakened me at 4:30. It lasted but twenty minutes, a most thrilling twenty minutes, and a heavy sky promises more. Drought must be a ghastly, frightening condition! I say "must be," for though we have had one this winter, and some parts of the state are in a pathetic condition, here on this peninsula, with cool weather, and blankets of fog, we do not suffer physically.

For the first time in months, I am excited to work, and by "still-life,"—though I do not like the designation still-life, a misnomer for my most living artichokes, peppers, onions, cabbage! Cabbage has renewed my interest, marvellous hearts, like carved ivory, leaves with veins like flame, with forms curved like the most exquisite shell. These forms—which Sonya discovered—came to me, coincident with a letter from Alma Reed in which my *next N. Y.* exhibit is discussed! I

213

knew it was coming, but to see the words "I am already thinking of your next exhibition here," made me sit up and take notice.

I have "some" reputation to live up to! I cannot fail to give even more than last year,—must not fail my friends! Not glory, nor money—these come as results of working and doing one's best—but the feeling of functioning, being needed by others,—fulfillment.

I began to go over work already completed, better than or different from my last exhibit, worthy of me,—and found at least thirty! I could even give an entirely new fifty print exhibit today, and not fall below last year's, indeed many prints are definitely beyond anything heretofore shown, especially the rocks. And I have at least eight months ahead before I show again.

My last year's exhibit is being circulated: Brooklyn Museum, Grace Horne Gallery, Boston, Walden Gallery, Chicago,—and I am sending to San Diego Museum in May.

April 28. We surprised Chandler on his 21st birthday,—last Sunday the 26th, with a party which was really a surprise. And he gave me one of his latest prints,—a strongly-seen, finely-constructed arrangement of rope and lever which gives promise of an important future.

Yesterday's express brought me a present from Lincoln Steffens,—his autobiography. I practically knew he would do this. But I wanted the books so much that they came almost as a thrilling surprise. One of my portraits was used for a frontispiece: well-reproduced but unfortunately not up to my usual technical excellence, and I have done better ones from viewpoint of likeness. But he should know!

I worked again with the cabbage fragment, bettering my first efforts. I enlarged this bit, of an inch high, to almost 8 × 10. It will go in my next exhibit.

Another book received which I have wanted, Oh, very much, ever since it was announced in preparation. A monograph of over 400 reproductions of the work of that great Mexican artist, Posada. Frances Toor sent it to me,—always generous and thoughtful Frances.

A day of great import yesterday,—I searched for a new place! Johan came to see me Sunday. He would give me a lease but with an increase of $15, bringing the rent to $75. If I must pay that amount I might as well improve my location. But aside from this consideration, I must break all dealings with Johan. I am afraid our friendship has broken forever. I wrote him a very plain letter telling him exactly what I would expect, even demand of him if he came to live with me this summer. I received a bitterly sarcastic answer.

I have found a beautiful room in the centre of town,—a very important location, and a small house nearby: the total rent will come to only $10 more than Johan now asks.

214

I don't like the idea of working for the landlord,—but I realize that one additional sitting from transients, which now I seldom get, will cover my extra expenses: why, even the sale of a print could do that. Transients too, are going to be very much of a nuisance: I mean the many who will come unheralded,—just sightseeing curiosity seekers, rubbernecks! But I will find some way to handle them, even as I do now in a lesser way.

All considered, change is fresh adventure, should bring new impetus to work and life. Already I feel changed in spirit. Ready for whatever comes.

Johan has hinted that if I do move he may have to return. I took it as a threat. The idea of competition does not bother me as does the nightmare of meeting Johan even casually on the streets, or even knowing he is here. A ghost of my past, our past which cannot be recalled.

May 30. Today Ramiel, Merle and Grant arrive for a week's visit! Great excitement ahead—

Tuesday Henry drove Sonya and me to the Point. My work proved that I am not through with trees and rocks, not if I can find new ones of enough difference to stimulate me. I worked with three trees, all within a short radius, but very difficult to get with my 8 × 10: and on a sheer, smooth, rocky slope, on which working was a real hazard. I am still sore from the strain of bracing myself while focussing, to keep from sliding off into the ocean far below.

Yesterday I printed from the negatives made but the day before, adding seven new prints to my portfolio: and besides, two very important cabbage fragments from last week's work. One of these especially is most amazing.

May 9. After eleven hours sleep,—the consequence of a week's visit from Ramiel, Merle and Grant. The whole affair was just too much!—friends whom I really love, but coming at this time, prescient with change, and all the detail in connection, the visit was almost catastrophe. Ramiel had said they would bring money for expenses and would help in the work. We had practically no money, nor help: and the latter deficiency hurt the most. One can understand being broke! After all the extra expense was not so great, though I need every cent for Chandler, whose venture into business will cost me well over a thousand,—but not to have assisted in the work seems all too thoughtless. To be sure they were on a holiday, coming here worn out and troubled, but so are we here. It was not fair! To cap the climax, Brett, Elinore, and Cole arrived, after I had warned Brett not to come at this time. I give Brett credit for planning to camp out, bringing his own food,—but I could not let him eat in his car, or on the roof where they slept, while the rest of us were gay (or trying to be) inside around the fire. So I had them eat with us. But then Brett should have offered to help, Elinore too,—which they did in a halfhearted way, not in the spirit which would have made me grateful. Few there are who understand or fulfill social amenities.

May 14. —and a misty rain is falling, most likely the last this season. Reading over my last entry: I was rather cross with my friends and children, but with reason. I am inclined to excuse faults, try to understand, and put down much as thoughtlessness. I do know that these very persons would do anything for me, have already proven. But I also know that neither Sonya nor I would have rested on our bums in another's home under like conditions. If each of these visitors had given one half-hour of their time a day to helping, no one would have been overworked and the gesture would have brought a feeling of gratefulness and goodwill all around.

Ramiel has spent many hours in the kitchen here before,—far more than I wanted him to. And I know that he was a tired and halfsick person. All I can say is that we were just as weary. I regret especially the visit with Brett. The morning of his departure I had risen to find a mountain of dishes left from the day before. I was thoroughly angry, and to shame the rest I started to wash them. Of course protests followed but I would not accept them. Instead of the talk and last breakfast together which I wanted, he wanted, I communed with the dishpan.

And now Brett is in S. F. trying to ship to Alaska!

I am with him in this venture. He has tried to make this goal since he ran away when 15, and was ignominiously captured and returned to me!

But I wish so much that we might have a real farewell!

May 24. I note my last entry was made on a rainy day: and so is today's. But this is a real rain, drenching the bone-dry soil, while the last did not lay the dust.

I also note my last entry was written in rebellion, like so many of my entries,—letting off steam to avoid explosion.

Poor Brett!—he returned to Carmel, unable to ship. But he has not given up! We had a quiet, happy contact for several days.

A week from today we will be away from this place,—moved, and starting a new experience. I leave with no regrets. I have had a very important period of my life here,—a memorable two years and a half. Is it possible! But I have had to destroy a depressing "something," which enveloped this spot like a noxious vapour: something more than the physical gloominess of dead trees and underbrush, of tin cans and empty gin bottles, of collected rubbish, to say nothing of leaky roofs, overflowing cesspool and the dank, cheerless air of the home hidden from the sun by too many towering pines: only in the evenings was the spell broken by a roaring grate fire. Johan left behind him some emanation which pervaded every nook: a ghost of his own unhealthy attitude, his bitterness, his sick mind and body.

One thing I look forward to, which the change will bring, is a chance to be really alone for a few hours a day or even a week: for the house and studio are

216

separate. I may have some time to sit alone, be with myself, renew an old acquaintance.

May 28, 1931. —before 5:00—the last day in this studio. I feel somewhat depressed. Of course I should not, useless to worry!—But I do,—some.

It all comes down to my personal work,—in this way: Johan is definitely coming back—this means that he will make every effort to re-establish himself,—he is broke, he is bitter toward me because of my frank letter telling him how to conduct himself if he came to convalesce here. He makes portraits of women more flattering than mine, so out-of-focus that they reveal nothing. Of course I *can* do this too, but only by reviving my past. Then, his work will be cheaper than mine, a point in his favor these hard times. But his advantage will be in being the underdog!—Which will make him fight for recognition. And here is where my personal work enters in. He cares little or nothing for his personal expression, he will spend all of his effort and time in getting "business." *I will not! I begrudge every moment so spent.* Also my rent and other expenses will be about $35 more a month than heretofore.

Well—let me figure my advantages. I will have a much better location, a sign which can be seen down Ocean Ave., two showcases in the center of activity, more publicity than ever before, locally and internationally, and the goodwill of the community, which Johan lost by his actions, bitter denunciations when he left, thinking never to return.

But all I ask is that my personal work will not be even temporarily sidetracked. It has been already too much this spring. It must go on, and on!

The last few days I have been before the public, and much discussed, even acclaimed!—But not through my work. The annual frolic of the Carmel Music Society took place Monday,—a burlesque on opera. I danced Carmen, and made a hit. Later in the evening, I danced impromtu, an improvisation barefoot, interpreting a "spring song." This especially brought down the house. Never had I appeared on a stage before, and I found it quite exciting to feel the audience responding, to *make* them laugh.

Henry Cowell was a scream as Madame Butterfly.

The evening is the talk of Carmel.

June 9. In my new studio—rather early—and feeling rather dull — — who wouldn't with neither coffee in my belly, nor cigarette smoke in my lungs. But do I feel any worse than sometimes,—in fact usually, *just after* starting to dope myself in the morning? No, I am not saying I will quit,—I'm too disgusted with myself after so many failures. I don't seem to care. I really don't fight. I should think that I would. With health and money at stake, with my personal work affected by the dulling of my nervous system. I wonder were life more simple— if one were not continually under a pressure—economic pressure—whether then the dope factories would not fail?

Today is a reaction from yesterday. I smoked much, because I was bored: but I was bored because I was trapped,—caught here in my new cage! Is it of my own making, or am I victim of circumstances? Is this condition a penalty I am to pay, or is it just blind fate? I wonder now whether I chose this location too hurriedly? After all it is but a glorified office building, and I a businessman waiting for business. In the old place I waited too, but I could wait,—and work, out in the sun and air, on the soil. Now my sun is filtered through glass, and I can only step out into a court, stone paved,—to meet other shopkeepers!—Or loafing, gossiping clerks. Now I have friends, socially inclined, who wander in and break the continuity of thought and work. And I fear to put out a warning sign which might drive away a real sitting or buyer.

But there are advantages here, to make the most of. I am alone in the early hours,—more so than when home was within talking distance. I have a splendid light for stills or portraits,—not continually shifting and changing through the pines. I am away from the family,—from domestic scenes. And if business is as much better here as it should be, I can easier buy myself freedom, a few holidays.

It rains this morning,—gently. Has for the last three days—on and off. And this is almost the halfway of June!

July 6. —a month, nearly, since making an entry in this daybook. Some one has said that only those suffering some unfulfillment keep diaries. But who isn't! All but bovine ruminators must have some void to fill. In Mexico, I registered pages of unfulfillment,—all physical,—jealousy, disappointment. Since returning, my tears have been mostly economic. Often a chapter has been just an explosion, an outlet for outraged feelings, when I momentarily forget to laugh. But I am more inclined to write when in a period of exciting work. I have not had such a period for months, hardly this year. I have had flashes. Several fine things from the Point, and last week hunting eroded soil, mostly in cuts made for new roads, I recorded half a dozen negatives which add a new note to the erosion series. And I must mention the wing of a dead pelican in which I foresee a moving print.

Ramiel and Merle have come and gone. The latter to show his print collection and to talk on "The Impresario Racket." I was in no condition to enjoy them, hardly knew they were here, except for added confusion.

Sunday the 4th who should appear but Gjura Stojana and Ara! I had not seen him since a tiny monetary disagreement of 1927. We had a happy renewal and parted with the old embrace. It is well. He showed new drawings, far ahead in technique, and fighting for a greater vision: but at times the fight showed too plainly,—he had tried too hard.

Also came Lloyd LaPage Rollins with his sister. We had a jolly evening at Henry's. He invited me to show at the de Young Museum in October.

218

July 16. Merle gave me Keyserling's *Travel Diary.* Like many philosophers he fails with art as a subject: doesn't know what it's all about! I suppose philosophers imagine they are omniscient on all subjects. He betrays his weakness, the way I do when philosophizing,—say upon economic conditions.

He writes: "Artists owe the enormous esteem in which they are held to a circumstance...." (of accidental nature): "...our body, thanks to its having been clothed throughout many centuries, has lost the power of manifesting its innate expressive values, for which reason we regard it as a revelation when an artist realizes it in his creations."

The above is in a discussion of the naked Negroes in Africa, their magnificence. "Sculpture in all seriousness would be meaningless here." "There are only very few sculptors who have done better work than Nature..." Well, I would go him one better, and say that *no* sculptor has *ever* done better than Nature,—when copying Nature! One would have to start with the A B C's of art, explain that artists (fine ones) don't copy Nature, and when they do record quite literally, the presentation is such as to arouse connotations quite apart from the subject matter. The camera recording Nature exactly can yet be used to convey an abstract idea. Peppers are reproduced in seed catalogues, but they have no relation to my peppers. The former were photographed to appeal to the belly, mine to arouse an impersonal creative understanding. How often do I hear exclamations, "I will see vegetables with different eyes from now on," or "I don't think I can eat a pepper again without feeling like a cannibal!"

No—Nature cannot be improved upon, considered physically. No use to exactly copy a butterfly,—better to see it crowning a blossom or floating in summer sky: but to find a dead pelican, photograph a few inches of its wing, so that white quills dart from black barbs like rays of light cutting a night sky,—this is not copying Nature, but using her with imaginative intent to a definite end.

Keyserling is weak on art: but he is one of my best-loved contemporary writers.

August 9. My entries used to be daily,—now once a month. My mind is concerned with business. Also, I have been disturbed over family relations. I can be more quickly wrecked over bickerings, hostile tensions, than in any other way. Max and Sonya seem forever at dagger's point. And I see both sides, and no remedy. What a relief when Chan and family leave. I could get along with them in peace, but I can't adjust others' difficulties. Chandler and I could work together in perfect harmony. He is more than willing to do his share, and do it efficiently. I am deeply thankful to have had this renewed contact. It has brought us together, and I have seen his admirable traits.

I came upon another example of Keyserling's mistaken approach to art,—on the same page. "It is impossible to conceive a higher degree of harmonious and general perfection of the human body than that which Greek art has revealed to us: this is why we call its creations absolutely beautiful." Obviously he writes of a period—the popular—of Greek art which was absolutely bad—when it was concerned more with eugenics than fine art.

Further on he writes: "Anyone who presents perfectly the appearance of things, which is what the great painter and poet does, in fact expresses its spiritual significance—but his soul may be ignorant of it."

I have always said,—an abstract idea can be expressed by literal or exact representation, but I do not think it can be done unless the "soul" be very much aware of it. If a soul be unaware, and a camera be used to copy an apple, the result can be no more than a record of an apple: but give the same camera and apple to one who sees more than said apple's surface and edible qualities, who understands the apple's significance,—then, the result will be—more than an apple!

15. "Things seen into things known"

August 14. My work is always a few jumps ahead of what I say about it! I am simply a means to an end: I cannot, at the time, say why I record a thing in a certain way, nor why I record it at all! Why indeed does one give up material comfort for the sake of an idea,—for "art?" Certainly public applause no longer spurs me on, though I want it, need it for my belly's sake:—I mean applause in the sense of wide fame. An audience is needed, if only a handful, or maybe one person. The artist must function, must fulfill his place as a giver—but maybe I am not an "artist," nor my product "art!"

This question, an old and hackneyed one was brought up again by a group of "real artists," painters of course, while viewing my recent retrospective exhibit, 1914–31, at Denny-Watrous'. I set about at once to prove by logical deduction that photography could be an art,—or at least an art in the very terms these painters think in, and I proved it very easily to my own satisfaction, though I am sure my logic would not even dent their defense mechanism. Then I suddenly realized I did not care what photography was labeled, that what I was doing had so much more importance, more vitality than their painting, that a great gulf separated their intent and mine. Of course this I have known for years, but have not clearly stated my case in words. These painters, most painters, and the photographers who imitate them, are "expressing themselves": "Art" is considered as a "self-expression." I am no longer trying to "express myself," to impose my own personality on nature, but without prejudice, without falsification, to become identified with nature, to see or *know* things as they are, their very essence, so that what I record is not an *interpretation—my idea* of what nature *should be*—but a *revelation*, a piercing of the smoke screen artificially cast over life by neurosis, into an absolute, impersonal recognition. Art is weakened in degree, according to the amount of personality expressed: to be explicit, according to the warping and twisting of knowledge by inhibitions. Granting we all have inhibitions, economic, sexual,—these must not color our work. The artist is not a petty individual God on a throne, free to exploit and expose his heartaches and bellyaches,—he is an instrument through which inarticulate mankind speaks: he may be a prophet who at a needed moment points the way, forming the future, or he may be born at a time when his work is a culmination, a flowering in soil already prepared.

So, when a few years ago I wrote that I was no longer interested in interpretation, but in presentation, I was only stating a half-truth, for after all the commercial

221

photographer, the illustrator of catalogues, also "presents." Then what is the difference between the "presentation" I would make of a cabbage and that made by the commercial man? The latter with matter-of-fact approach sees a cabbage as an unrelated fact, devoid of interest except as a means to sauerkraut. I feel in the same cabbage, all the mystery of life force, I am amazed, emotionally stirred, and by my way of presentation my recognition of the reason for the cabbage form, its significance in relation to all forms, I am able to communicate my experience to others.

This "emotional stirring" is not to be understood as melodrama, nor the vague rhapsodies of a mooning poet counting daisy petals for an answer to his doubts, —but as a great flame of recognition—the significance of facts—wisdom controlling the means (brush, chisel, camera)—and presenting this knowledge in a communicable form.

August 21. These thoughts are continually broken. Last week I feel that I was on the way toward the most clarified statement I have made. Well—to try again — —

In discussing "self-expression" with a visitor, she said—"but these prints of yours are different from other workers',—you are expressing your personality."

I will answer by quoting Dora Hagemeyer who wrote in a very clear, understanding way about my exhibit. "But in Carmel, we find him moving beyond the artist. It is here that he has transcended art and become the seer. Seen through his eyes, the concealed flight in the wing of a bird, the sculpture of a bud, are transformed from things *seen* to things *known*."

A "seer" is one who sees with the inner eye and is able to give concrete expression to his knowledge of facts, things,—conveying this intelligent perception, without personal bias, in a direct, clarified form, so that the spectator can participate in the revelation.

The form,—composition, construction—must not be considered as a formula to be learned by rule. It is far more important. It is the most clarified, forceful way the seer (see-er) can command for the presentation and communication of his experience. It will vary according to the special qualities, the significance of the thing to be presented.

August 30. Maybe I can pick up the threads of thought on the above subject, with which I was not through.

I have had the most miserable week I can remember of in years. Awakened with a very lame back, last Monday, fell down trying to dress: went to a chiropractor, who found "something" out of place, one leg half an inch too short, etc. I felt relief at once, when he snapped my back, but I am by no means right, suffer considerable pain — — I suppose I should not have been working, but Sonya brought me a most marvellous chard from the Big Sur,—powerful white stalks and veins running into dark green leaves with a variety of movement absolutely amazing. I worked despite great handicap, for it would not last for long. I saw well,—but had tragic failures. The leaves would wilt imperceptibly during a 20 minute or more exposure, so that I only got two negatives out of ten, and these two not perfect. I could not work out of doors in the wind, and I had to stop down to the limit, hence my failures. The chard is still fresh, but I do not feel equal to going on with it. And besides, we await the arrival of Brett, Elinore, Neil, Cole, Ramiel! Well, this will be a last grand climax of visitors, for Brett comes to talk over the pros and cons of going into business with Chan. Ramiel comes to enter the discussion. I feel all discussion futile. All the objections which might be raised, I have considered and agree to. But the fact remains, and I explained all this in detail, that I have not enough money to start Chan, to buy his equipment and also provide him a living until he gets under way. Brett has the equipment, and he is out of work,—in other words he has not enough to live on, to wait on, while times are so bad.

No matter what the decision, Chan must go now. He has worked with me a year. I could go on with him as a partner. He is willing, intelligent and responsive. But I cannot go on living with the confusion and conflicting interests of the two families. The baby is a fine one, I love him, but I have had my share of babies. Mine are just now at the point where I can have some peace. So the little family must go, for their own good as well as mine.

I thought I could go on writing today, but my back twitches, and shooting pains go down my right thigh. I must remain quiet if possible.

A painter from Seattle, a very intelligent one, Mark Tobey, has been here for several days. He bought my work several years ago from an exhibit, and four more while here. I had a very stimulating contact, and one which may lead to something important, for Tobey is on his way to teach in the south of England in a settlement founded by the Harry Payne Whitney fortune. He took well over 100 numbers of my prints and will recommend the purchase of a large collection for a permanent exhibit.

It has just started raining! A very early first rain. Another dry winter would about finish this country—

October 1. It does not seem possible a month has passed since my last entry! I have been very busy, working continually under pressure, but more than physical frustration, I have been psychically distressed. More?—well maybe it's a 50-50 interference with my desire to write,—mind and body both so well-occupied that my pen has kept out of mischief. But no—thinking of a letter I wrote to a Dr. Thorek—Chicago "Pictorialist," I must admit my pen was very naughty.

I had some fun out of the correspondence, but the doctor, lacking, I am sure, any sense of humor, didn't realize I was making him ridiculous. I knew before

I answered his article on my work—shown at Fort Dearborn Camera Club—
that I was entering a futile argument, but I wrote for my own amusement,
answering all those,—and there have been many, who find phallic symbolism
in my photographs. The doctor found nothing else,—but the desire to see
"reproductive organs" in kelp, vegetables, rocks, peppers,—natural forms. It
was too good a chance,—I had to come back, and blamed his own "psycho-
pathological" condition, turned his own words back upon himself, hinted that
he belonged with the sexually unemployed, with the hordes of neurasthenic
disciples of Freud, who find sex in one's every word or gesture. I admitted he
had a far greater imagination than mine, or else he "knew his organs" better
than a layman, because only with effort could I find more than faint resemblance
to "reproductive organs" in any of my prints: besides, there could not be phallic
symbolism where none was intended or felt,—in fact no symbolism of any kind
was premeditated. I do not feel that direct symbolism ever goes into the work
of a really important artist, certainly not in the sense of preaching or making
sly allusions. If there is symbolism in my work, it can only be in a very broad
consideration of life, the seeing of parts, fragments as universal symbols, the
understanding of relativity everywhere, the resemblance of all natural forms to
each other.

Of course the doctor came back just as I knew he would: said my defense
mechanism was working, that if I had not consciously intended phallic symbols,
that something in my subconscious prompted my creations!

If this were so, if my subconscious had "gone phallic," it would indicate, according to theory, sex repressions of some sort, and so far as I know I have none,
—am about as free from inhibitions as one can possibly be.

But maybe I have the solution,—why others find sex in my work and I do not:
it came from an artist (painter) who called on me recently, Edward Biberman,
from New York. I told him the story, and he gave me a possible solution,—at
least to me it was logical.

He said, in effect, that I had seen vegetables and other natural forms, *fundamental*
forms, with such intensity, such direct honesty that a tremendous force like sex,
which enters into, permeates all nature, could not but be revealed. All basic
forms are so closely related as to be visually equivalent. Seeing parts of life always in relation to the whole, recording their essence with a simplification which
can be called an "abstraction," I have had a back (before close inspection)
taken for a pear, knees for shell forms, a squash for a flower, and rocks for
almost everything imaginable!

Here it might be well to mention a few instances where phallic symbolism has
been seen by others and my own reaction, when I could see suggestions of
phallic and other forms, with *effort*,—for let me state that it is only the literal
minded who at once start to find what a thing resembles,—faces in clouds,

elephants in rocks—etc., etc. The creative artist is of course aware of universal spiritual connotations in his work, but is never concerned with literary allusions. I have had pointed out faces and forms in prints which I had lived with for years, and never seen,—though unfortunately they were plain enough afterwards! Am I so blind, so unseeing? No—when I look at a print, I see only that form or force which was my original stimulus, most assuredly never a literary impulse. So when someone saw a vulva in a certain rock, I recalled that when first discovered I had thought it must be the imprint of a prehistoric camel: but I photographed it because of its own intrinsic beauty. Another vulva found in my halved artichoke—and very farfetched the likeness—I had often thought would make a fine modern stage set. A rock made on the Mojave—often likened to a great penis—(I might coin a word and say it has penistic insinuations), actually does look like a mighty erection. Nevertheless I can honestly state that when I focussed my camera on it that broiling desert morning, all I felt was the great diagonal cutting the plate, its relation to other forms in background, with tiny grasses giving scale at the base: someone likened this grass to pubic hair! Either I must be very naive, or the others neurotic! The peppers which are more libeled than anything I have done,—in them has been found vulvas, penises or combinations, sexual intercourse, madonna with child, wrestlers, modern sculpture, African carving, ad nauseam, according to the state of mind of the spectator: and I have a lot of fun sizing people up from their findings! I have done perhaps fifty negatives of peppers: because of the endless variety in form manifestations, because of their extraordinary surface texture, because of the power, the force suggested in their amazing convolutions. A box of peppers at the corner grocery holds implications to stir me emotionally more than almost any other edible form, for they run the gamut of natural forms, in experimental surprises. If any of them more than remotely resemble "reproductive organs," it must be an organ the likes of which I've never seen, and a mighty queer one.

Now call the above explanation my defense mechanism become active, I say that it is disgust and weariness over having my work labeled and pigeonholed by those who bring to it their own obviously abnormal, frustrated condition: the sexually unemployed belching gaseous irrelevancies from an undigested Freudian ferment.

16. Transition—"a way I have been seeing lately—"

October 14. A damp, cold, grey day. I would welcome it, if rain was indicated, —but this is only Carmel fog. Yesterday at the "Point," it stopped my work,— a wet blanket which swept in from the ocean like fine rain, saturating my camera, shivering my bones. But I had already made four negatives, one open landscape, or rather a viewpoint which combines my close-up period with distance, a way I have been seeing lately,—sometimes a suggestion of sea in the corner, or rocks reaching back to a distant horizon. The other exposures were of bones—a skull and jawbone of a cow, which I took with me, to find suitable backgrounds among the rocks. Artificial,—to place them? Not if they do not look placed, or if they are frankly placed. Since I ask this question, I must be having doubts. I have such violent reactions over faking, dishonesty in others, —half-nude flappers, holding water jars, obviously studio lighted and posed, called "The Greek Slave," that I have become more questioning about my own "arrangements." However I am by no means ready, or even expect to give up arrangements, thereby discrediting some of my most important work,—all the peppers, vegetables, etc. Selection in the field is only another form of arrange-ment,—the camera being moved instead of the subject.

Yesterday, I made a very obvious arrangement, placing the skull in a hollowed out rock; it stands on horn end, exactly in the center of a rocky landscape. I have done this too boldly, honestly, to be accused of pretence,—that I had found it so placed. I did this after I had used the same setting for a shell, perhaps in reaction, because Cole said—and I always listen to children's honest remarks —"Dad, that's artificial, isn't it?" This remark made me pause to consider, for I had never intended it should be considered as anything but placed. My own response in making it was one of emotion from contrasting scale,—the tiny shell in a vast expanse, yet the shell dominating.

Maybe I am on the defensive! But I must go on doing anything I feel impelled to do without theorizing,—at least not till afterwards.

I am returning to old habits, early rising, from 4:00 to 5:00. I hope this means renewed creative energy. But after all, the few things done this summer are significantly good, indicating that only lack of time based on uncontrollable conditions and distractions has prevented me from doing work perhaps finer than ever. I cannot hope to always have such an explosion of unthwarted crea-tive energy as I had last year — —

The last few weeks has brought several stimulating contacts: a renewal with Howard Putzell (now Parker) who stopped to see me on his way to Mexico, presenting me with his usual response and enthusiasm concretely expressed in the purchase of four prints. I have already mentioned Edward Biberman. I liked him the moment we met,—asked him to dine with us. We had several evenings together. He had seen and liked my N. Y. show. Without seeing his work, I know it must have value. He had just returned from painting in Arizona, and so fired me with enthusiasm that my one great urge (not a new one) is to go there. Then recently came with Vasia,—Dobrowen—conductor of S. F. orchestra. Though he spoke Russian I did not need to understand to get his response. I felt it deeply....

Sonya is away, visiting her parents. Do I miss her? Yes and no. I miss her as much as I would anyone: but, though my friends mean very much to me, I have grown away from any need of their presence,—indeed to be alone is a condition I welcome, greatly desire. To know that my friends love me and I them, to see them at rare intervals, is enough. More and more I am absorbed in my life's work. I have set a goal: when the boys are finally started in life, I retire. This means that I will find me an isolated spot as far away from the general public as possible, a place where only those who have a great desire can reach me, and there I will work undisturbed, sending my prints to city markets. I can live on the sale of four prints a month. I will do portraits only when I want to, of those I want to, the way I want to,—and charge well for the privilege. I will have my revenge for all the prettified, retouched females I have had to do, for all the portraits I have sent out which *were not my work*: portraits so nauseating that I have covered them over when signing my name. Some are horrified at physical prostitution, and I agree it must be inconvenient and often disgusting. But I am prostituting my spiritual self every week in the year. A few might feel and share the shame of my degradation.

Returning to Sonya: She is industrious, thoughtful, sensitive, and loves me, I'm sure. She has indications of going far in a creative way.... Since the other family left, Chan, Max, and Teddy, the house is more at peace,—the tension I felt has gone, except when the boys nag or fight. But we four get along quite well together. Praises be that Sonya is a quiet little mouse.

Two Days was really too bad! Cheap sentimentality, too obvious propaganda, tiresome repetition, dragging tempo. The "radicals" who managed the show were utterly unorganized,—an 8th grade schoolboy could have done better. I left with mixed feelings of pity and contempt. As Hazel said, one felt the need of a good hot bath afterwards.

October 16, 1931. A balmy star-lit morning. I downed my coffee hurriedly before 4:00. I am considering these early mornings as "omenous": maybe there is such a word?—if not there should be.

To return to the discussion which raged at my exhibit: "Photography versus Art." I will try to prove with logic that, unfortunately, photography can be art, that is in the sense these "critics" approach art, as a means of personal—very personal—expression.

The controversy reminds me of one which took place in the 16th century: painting was on the defensive—the intelligentsia of the day had placed it among the mechanical arts because it was done with the hand, not the mind. Ironically, a similar attitude is now held by the painters toward photography,—the hand, finally accepted as a means to an end, after a fight in which Leonardo da Vinci rose to defend painting,—the painters now assume the hand omnipotent, and label photography mechanical because it is done with a machine. (Wouldn't it be funny, if one could pierce the future, and find that photography was accepted as the great art form, because the mind,—"intelligence" is more comprehensive, —could be directed through a machine in a purer form, without the bungling interference of the hand!)

To quote Leonardo: "If thou, O musician, sayest that painting is mechanical because it is wrought by the work of the hands, music is wrought by the mouth, but not by the tasting faculties of the mouth; just as the hand indeed is employed in the case of painting, but not for its faculties of touch, . . . I will answer that painting is mental."

Before I write more, let it be understood, *of course*, that I am discussing "straight photography," not the bastard half-painted gum or bromoil prints,—photography devitalized by the use of the hand.

First of all, the weighty discussion might have been ended by the very obvious, visual proof in my own exhibition,—for, standing at one point where my oldest work, 1914, met my latest, 1931, there was exposed work so different in technique, and conception, that it was as though two radically different persons were exhibiting together: but the same camera was used by "both" individuals. So the camera is only a means to an end, it can see only, or whatever the user sees. Carry on this thought: give the same camera and subject matter, say an apple on dish, to ten photographers, tell them to do what they will with it, and I will promise ten results as widely varying, not only in arrangement and lighting, but in quality in feeling for the thing, as any ten painters might produce.

But, someone objects, the camera, used in the field, where one can't "arrange," takes in everything,—a painter can eliminate. So can the photographer, by change of viewpoint, or change to a different focal length lens: and if this does not solve the difficulty he can find another subject "around the corner." Ever see a painter search for the right viewpoint! Each medium has its own limitations. Photography has proved that nature offers an endless number of perfect "compositions,"—order everywhere. The painter has always (most of them) tried to improve nature by self-imposition, with a usual understatement resulting in travesty. Instead of going to nature in a spirit of inquiry, to learn from her, to take what she has to give, they go with arrogance, to tell her how she ought to look, to be.

To return to the painter's hands, his one claim to superiority: supposing an armless person had great creative ability—which is something *within us*, not at our finger tips—and learned to paint with brush in foot or mouth!—Would his work be of less importance *because* he had not used his hands? Or is the perfect draughtsmanship of some commercial artist, "art," because hand made?

The whole controversy seems to be concerned with the painter's hand as a means to self-expression, his ability to add to, leave out, or change nature at will (this includes the most abstract art done in a room with blinds down: for we cannot conceive of a form not already known in nature) while the photographer uses a machine which reproduces exactly, everything toward which it is pointed.

But does it! I will even go so far as to say that the camera is not mechanical unless the photographer's attitude be mechanical. Lenses of a dozen different focal lengths can be used, completely altering the viewpoint of perspective, changing, even distorting nature at will, or revealing so much more than the average eye sees that photography has opened the blinds to a new world vision.

Then carry on the possibilities of personal choice into the selection of films and printing papers, dozens of manufacturers each making dozens of varieties of films of different color or speed, sensitivity to be used with or without filters which can actually cut out certain colors entirely, and as many papers of infinite surface textures, and grades of contrast, to shorten, lengthen or render exactly the scale of gradation in the original view: add to these, chemicals of widest possible choice, and one has far greater opportunity for self-expression through material opportunity than is granted the painter. The trouble has been with photographers, not photography!

And the trouble with the "critics," under examination in this inquiry, is that they are afraid,—this new and vital way of seeing has made their soft, gutless painting look ridiculous. It will be noted that if they do condescend to notice photography, it is always the kind which looks like their painting,—there is no competition to fear in imitation!

I understand that one photographer—a musician or composer—from Santa Barbara, entered this controversy, on the side of the painters!—using their arguments. His work has been described to me: the usual camera painting. His music must be just as bad, couldn't be otherwise, for to produce work of any value in any line of creative endeavor, one must bore into the spirit of today. Old ideals are crashing on all sides, and the precise uncompromising camera vision is, and will be more so, a world force in the revaluation of life.

229

The above-mentioned composer could not go beyond my work of about 1920, —this had "artistic" qualities. The present work, though it "intrigued" him, was not "art!" And so they wrangled on!

I notice that the average layman is not concerned over "artistic qualities" (though they often say "these mean more to me than painting"),—he accepts photography for what it is without question.

One of the arguments used centered on my nudes: that photography always failed with nudes, they had no life. Now my dancing figures of B. seem quite alive to me, though the "abstract" backs might be questioned: but the latter were made with a different intent. However, compare any of my nudes with one by an A. N. A.—one of this group—shown after my exhibit,—well it looks like a partially fried or decayed fish, with about as much life!

This could go on for many more reams. One might ask if singing is a greater art than piano or violin playing, because the latter are mechanical aids to producing sound? The answer is of course anticipated, that the musician bends these mechanical aids to his will: but I have already shown that the camera can "see" in as many ways as there are individuals back of it. So I will finish—and it's about time—by declaring that *fortunately* it is difficult to be dishonest toward nature, to become too personal with the very impersonal lens—eye. Only with effort can the camera be forced to lie: basically it is an honest medium: so the photographer is much more likely to approach nature in a spirit of inquiry, of communion, instead of with the saucy swagger of self-dubbed "artists." And contemporary vision, the new life, is based on honest approach to all problems, be they morals or art. False fronts to buildings, false standards in morals, subterfuge and mummery of all kinds, must be, will be scrapped. And the crafty, senile old men who head the cumbersome outdated governmental failure called democracy must be, will be figuratively chloroformed. Youth will no longer stand for their stupid nonsense.

I want to be a spiritual force in this new world vision, and feel that I am so functioning.

October 19. I have a new record which I have played to the exclusion of all others for a month: Bach's *Brandenburg Concerto No. 3, in G Major*, Philharmonic Orchestra, Berlin, Fürtwangler conducting. It is such a complete work, so absolute, holding everything that music, or any art means to me, that I can hear it daily, ten times daily, and never tire.

If astrology has any significance—and from even a "common sense" viewpoint I cannot see why not—though some, or most, astrologers can be doubted— then my feeling for Bach can be understood, for I noted recently we were born under the same sign.

With all the response to contemporary art and music, no composer of the day moves me as does this master!

Henry showed me the new mural she is painting. It is most obviously phallic! Now she would protest just as vigorously as I have in my recent explosion, against this label, or libel! Or would she? For I have heard her remark that sex enters into her work, as a part of life: which indicates she consciously does think of phallic symbols, while my work, if it has such tendencies, could only have them by virtue of my subconscious,—naughty—naughty subconscious!— what am I depriving you of?

Of course knowing Henry, the very inhibited life she must lead, I may be constrained to at once look for phallic symbols, and especially since she is spoken of as a pathological painter! I hope Henry never hears this remark! But I must admit that sex is very obvious in a great deal of her work, and I'm not the kind who is on the hunt for an artist's sexual aberrations—or a layman's either.

I made a negative recently—I started to say nude—which I can never show unless I wish to prove to (the satisfaction of) my traducers that they are right, and that I am phallic-minded!

Molly O'Shea brought me a horse-radish which was so ridiculously like a woman's torso that I could not resist doing it,—in that spirit. The print looks for all the world like a reclining nude. I could never live it down, explain that I had in this case, laughed up my sleeve, frankly done it for its connotations, but with a sense of humor. Well, I'm labeled anyway so I might as well show my naked horse-radish hussy!

More echoes from my exhibit: objections because I had made peppers into some-thing they were not,—whether in this case phallic symbols entered in I don't know, but I hope some new note was struck—one wearies — — Because I chose unusually strong and beautiful peppers to photograph—and why not—because I glorified them in dramatic isolation, because I saw their finest points, because I see more than a housewife who picks commonplace peppers for stuffing,—so I have in some way violated these poor peppers!

My only answer is that I have not the eyes of a Hausfrau.

Countess Lavatelli (or something like that) showed her weaving at the same time my exhibit was on. It was awful!—all except one piece in an old traditional pattern.

Her own work,—that in which she expressed herself, was just cheap. A theoso-phist, she weaves into her patterns propaganda for theosophy, pretty little stories, which have to be explained with poetical quotations pinned onto the weaving. This is worth mentioning, because she, and some Italian doctor (of philosophy I guess) who sponsored her, missed no chance to ridicule Americans, their bad taste, crude manners: while she, the "countess," exposed the worst possible taste, and the pair showed very crude manners, by criticizing their hosts in front of them,—in French.

231

October 26. Contrasting reactions to my work: the British editor of a book just published in England on *International Photography*, refused to admit my work and Stieglitz'. I feel greatly honored!

While Dobrowen told Vasia that seeing my prints gave him emotional reactions comparable to when he first viewed the Sistine Chapel: I could not understand his Russian, but I did catch the word Michelangelo.

I am preparing the largest exhibit I have ever given—150 prints—to open Nov. 17, at the de Young Museum, S. F. For a change, I am going to include about 50 portraits. I know they have value despite my reaction against portraiture, so strong that I can scarcely grant them any consideration.

One new work which pleases me, is of a board taken from a grainsifter. The sifting grain has eroded the board, following the lines of the wood's grain, into an amazing sculptured relief.

October 29. In reading over a book which listed various deficiencies which lead to complexes and consequent psychic derangements, I could not but feel how fortunate I have been. My shortcomings have never been serious enough to cause any profound disturbance. Never rich, I was raised in comparative comfort, and even now when I am economically distressed, I actually do not suffer, nor want wealth, only the necessities for the children's education. I could increase my income today if I would compromise, that is to a greater extent.

Rather frail as a child, I built myself up to become by far the fastest runner in our neighborhood and a Junior record holder at the Central Y.M.C.A., Chicago. A bit short—5 ft.5½ in.—I can never remember this bothered me, for the average was less in my youth—I was, on the other hand, possessed of a finely-knit frame, and good looks, so that I never had to compensate for physical deficiencies.

I have always attracted women, had more than I needed, though at times—twice in my life—I have been upset over certain ones. Jealousy is, I suppose, an inferiority complex. But these were passing phases, more than compensated for.

In school I was well up in my classes, and when I failed, I at least knew it was my own fault from lack of interest and application.

I can recall being extremely bashful in my youth. I do not account for it, unless all sensitive children are so. But once in business, meeting the public, this condition was more or less overcome.

From the very start of my photographic career, I have been successful, had recognition.

So it seems I have had a very well-balanced basis to start from, in every way, —to create without inhibitions which might warp my viewpoint.

One more thing: though I once wanted to be an artist,—that is to paint; photography was not taken up as a substitute, a compensation, for I always was one

232

of the best painters in my school classes. But once I became interested in photography, I lost all desire to paint, and have never seriously considered it since.

Danger, in my case, might have come from overpraise, too much recognition, some no doubt, premature and undeserved. But I have never been satisfied, —praise always spurred me on to greater effort. I have been my own severest critic. I believe my greatest pleasure, at least in recent years, has been the feeling of having given to others, rather than a personal satisfaction in receiving acclaim.

One thing I must note: from youth I have taken for granted, accepted the fact, that some day I was to be a leader. This state of mind I held even before I knew what direction my life and work would take.

No doubt such self-realization has been of value, given impetus to the attaining of my goal.

November 14. The first *real* rain today, ushered in this early morning by a gale of wind. A day I would wish to be alone,—a day for self-consideration. But it is Saturday, the boys will be home, and Cole especially never cares to be alone, while Neil doesn't like company. Neil is quite self-sufficient,—Cole quite the extrovert. Speaking of Cole,—he said "Just think Dad, Octopi have eight testicles."

Today under Ramiel's direction I open in the Japanese quarter, Los Angeles. He sent me an S.O.S. for nudes. In disgust, I picked out thirteen old negatives, as far back as 1920, and printed fifty prints in two hours.... It's too sad—they want my name but incidentally,—they really want naked women, occidentals. It disgusted me to puking — — why could they not buy obscene postcards? The Mexican men were the same: I've watched them at my exhibits in Mexico, snickering over nudes that I certainly made with a clean mind. I can laugh too, at sex, its humorous side, a good story: but discrimination, good taste are indicated when one laughs at the right time or place.

American men may be just as bad, but they never go to exhibits, so one can't judge! Even so, I can stand a crude horselaugh better than the babble of club-women about composition or values,—"art." I will probably be hearing a lot of it soon, if I go to S. F. for the opening of my exhibit Tuesday. Fifty of the one hundred and fifty prints are portraits. I am rather proud of them, having selected a group of *individuals*,—excluding all pretty people,—not one adenoidal movie queen type among them. Jack Black, Sean O'Malley, Tony Luhan, will glower down, or looking beyond, will not even notice the chattering, tricked-out lies,—"society" women, who pass below them,—or Ann Davies Thomas, Elizabeth Hale Severy, will smile indulgently at them, while six-months-old Betty Ann McCarthy, lost in baby dreams, will be as indifferent as Tony is to their shallow patter, their varnished faces, tinsel, and fripperies.

I had a visit from three women, real salt of the earth, who came to see my exhibit, a private view before it left: Mrs. Beatty, Miss Husted, Miss Smith.

Afterwards Miss Husted phoned me. She and Mrs. Beatty had been playing a game,—the point was to see how many of my prints they could recall. They had definitely placed 125, out of the 150 hurriedly shown prints. I consider this an extraordinary tribute worth recording.

December 10. While in S. F. I had an evening with Consuela. She told me of a conversation with Stieglitz in N. Y. in which I was concerned. Stieglitz felt hurt that in my several recent "writeups," I had not mentioned him as an influence in my life. Strange, that Consuela was the cause of my not mentioning him. After showing him some of my new work, she wrote me that he thought they lacked vitality, had no connection with contemporary life, etc. (I went into this in detail at the time, 1927 or '28). So why should I mention Stieglitz when he expressed disapproval,—might not wish to be connected with my name?

But I wrote him at once, explaining my stand as above, and await with some curiosity his answer. If he *is* hurt, wants to be known as an influence in my work, (I told him I would mention him the next chance I had), it will show an approval he denied.

This talk with C. started me thinking: what have been the outstanding influences, "inspirations" in my life,—upon my work?

I feel that I have been more deeply-moved by music, literature, sculpture, painting than I have by photography,—that is by the other workers in my own medium. This needs explanation. I am not moved to emulate,—neither to compete with or imitate, these other creative expressions, but seeing, hearing, reading something fine excites me to greater effort,—("inspires" is just the word, but how it has been abused!). Reading about Stieglitz, for instance, means more to me than seeing his work. Kandinsky, Brancusi, Van Gogh, El Greco, have given me fresh impetus: and of late Keyserling, Spengler, Melville, (catholic taste!) in literature. I never hear Bach without deep enrichment,—I almost feel he has been my greatest "influence." It is as though, in taking to me these great conceptions of other workers, the fallow soil in my depths, emotionally stirred, receptive, has been fertilized.

Even my own work has excited me, spurred me to greater effort,—knowing I have almost reached a peak,—though there are always higher, more distant ones. And praise of my work, response, even favorable press notices, has always had a positive effect upon me: for I have accepted it as a trust which I must be worthy of and carry on with. Besides I have never been much of a hero worshipper, so opinions I have accepted or rejected, according to my own understanding, no matter from what source, mighty or humble. My children's opinions, always fresh, unbiased, I listen to as readily as those of an important critic. Early in life I learned a lesson. Showing my work to various artists, critics, in whom I had great faith, I would receive such widely divergent opinions that I soon realized there could be no universal standard of criticism, no absolute opinion. So, listening to my superiors, I accepted and rejected, went my own way: if the wrong way, the realization had to come through me, when I was ready. This acceptance and rejection has entered in to my approach to the work of others. From Brancusi to Bach, I have gratefully taken what was mine by right of understanding,—more cannot be taken without merely copying. Diego once wrote, "Each artist carries the seed of another." No one man invents something, say the airplane. But the efforts of many may come to the sharpest focus in one man. I have always felt the great importance of my closest friends as influence: names unsung to the wider public. And further back in time parents,—father, sister, uncle, aunts,—and so on, an endless chain, each link of importance to an impressionable child, and man. But,—I cannot recall, give credit to a single school teacher!

Schools, I only remember as dreary wastelands. I cannot believe that I learned anything of value in school, unless it be the will to rebel, to "play hookey," which I have done on numerous occasions since those first days with my camera in the snow-covered Chicago parks: "played hookey" from my first job, from my own "business," from my family life,—not without some sense of responsibility, but never with after-regrets.

I started writing on Stieglitz, and have covered much territory. To return: —from reading about him, what he stood for and had done, I went to meet him in as near a state of hero worship as I had ever been in. Yet I can recall saying to Margrethe as I packed my prints, "I hope Stieglitz will like my work, but it will make no difference to me if he does not." Undoubtedly I was building up a defense, for I was in a period of change, dissatisfaction. Bravado of a sort caused that remark, clinging to my old but falling ideals. *On the way* to meet Stieglitz I made a photograph ("Steel") which I still show—it's hanging now in S. F.—as belonging to my present period. So Stieglitz did not change me, I went to him because *I was changing.*

But meeting him was no disillusionment, on the contrary I was profoundly impressed, not so much by his work (I recall quite as well the work of Sheeler and Strand) as by his personality. I was ready for what he had to say, to give. His photographs did not overawe me. Acknowledging his superior technique, I felt some of my portraits held their own by comparison. Technically I gained from that Eastern trip, not in formulae for developers, but in precision of expression, in the use of the formulae and tools I had. And today if I go to a photographic exhibit it is to see what is being done technically, that I might use. The other man's viewpoint seldom gives me anything.

I have written down the influence, inspiration of other workers upon myself, but now I will finish by saying that I have learned, and am learning more from a direct communion with nature, which is the final step in growth.

January 27, 1932. Entries are becoming rare. But I still have desire. I have been extremely active. Before Xmas, the usual rush of finishing orders intended for gifts. Since the holidays, getting off three exhibits: Hotchkiss School, Conn., Scripps College, Claremont, Stanford University. Now I am preparing my New York show, to open Feb. 29th. I could ship it tomorrow if necessary,— selections practically all made, excepting the possibility of new negatives better than the chosen ones. And this is possible, for I have had a spell of work, thanks to no business!

I have also completed a tremendous task, approached with the greatest enthusiasm: that of reprinting my entire New York exhibit on a new paper. A demonstrator for "Velour Black" sent me a trial package:—it is so much superior to the paper I had been using, that I changed without hesitation. The blacks are richer, the whites clearer, and despite the fact that it has more contrast, the shadows actually have more detail. In other words this paper has a longer scale or range from black to white. Also the surface quality is more beautiful. The prints I have been making are a joy,—almost as though I were printing from new negatives,—over 75 new ones!

The actually new negatives I have done since the 1st have been most satisfactory. A cypress on Pebble Beach, than which I have done nothing finer in a tree, indeed it will go with my best of all time past. This week I have worked with sand,—patterns of sand,—patterns of sand and earth mixed, after the rain had washed the latter down the beach: and miniature sand erosions on the banks at edge of beach which without scale might be the cliff dwellings, but actually are but a foot or so high. Now I am considering a squash,—a remarkable one of the "turkish turban"—so called—variety which Shore loaned me.

What storms we have had! A veritable deluge of rain—with unusual variations —hail—a thunder storm which lasted an hour—and in Los Angeles—two inches of snow. All this takes me back to the California I knew twenty-five years ago—when rain *was* rain. Essentially a lover of sun, I hope it will pour all winter, it has been so much needed for years.

I have deeply felt the death of Frederick O'Brien,—a friend to be really missed. Fred came to see me only a short time before he was stricken. He was very gay and kept us hilarious with the tales he so loved to tell. He was a raconteur rather than writer: and he well knew this,—told me he would never write again if he did not have to. But I think he loved his *Carmelite* column. Joe Coughlin never blue-pencilled! Fred made the most of this unusual opportunity. It was his chance to use that most subtle of weapons—ridicule—to attack on his "Paper Wings" all shams,—hypocrisy, pretence, fraud: to expose the smug, the mediocre, the vulgar. His fight was against intolerance, whether it came from King, Demagogue, or the "Sovereign People,"—the great herd level: against the manipulating, regulating, exploiting of our fellowmen. He saw clearly the

236

sinister encroachment taking place upon our traditional guarantees of individual liberty.

Fred was a rare human being. The Gods do not often mould his kind.

January 28. I have heard twice from Stieglitz: neither letter quite satisfactory, not quite frank and open,—at least so I feel. He wrote: "I feel Kanaga failed to convey to you the spirit of our meeting.... I could not fully agree with her 100% enthusiasm for those prints.... that same morning I ran across an article you had written about yourself. (*Creative Art*, 1928.) ... I could not grasp why photographers invariably mentioned famous painters and writers as forces in their lives and avoided mentioning photographers ... Photography has its tradition. Why will photographers be ashamed to recognize it when putting themselves in print? ... Don't worry about the future reference to me. Your photography needs all your attention.... I am glad you are making a name for yourself and have now a host of admirers."

Deliberate or not, there is in the above a distorting of my intention in the article mentioned, which was *obviously* anecdotal and started with my Mexican period, after meeting Stieglitz. It was composed of notes from my daybook, and the painter mentioned, Rivera, entered the picture as a brief incident, in no way as an influence.

It struck me as particularly ironical that Stieglitz insinuated I was ashamed of the tradition of photography. There are many out here who could testify to the contrary,—and of course this diary is proof enough though hidden from public view. So Stieglitz' assumption from this article was quite unwarranted, —and I vaguely feel ulterior motives. Is he sore because I have gone ahead without his sanction, dared to enter New York unattached to his group, and meet success? His sentence—"Don't worry about the future reference to me. Your photography needs all your attention"—is an example of his veiled way of answering my frank letter to him. I can only read it as a verbal whack.

A few days after Stieglitz' letter came one from Alma Reed, which would, if not distorted in the interpretation, the retelling of the story, make Stieglitz out as two-faced: one face to me,—not wanting credit as an "influence," the other face to others,—"claiming the credit for your creations," to quote from Alma's letter.

Alma wrote: "Stieglitz has been showing a letter you wrote him, claiming credit for your creations. The person who told me was enraged. He said if there ever was a pure 'original' it was yourself and that you derived from no one and owed nothing to any other photographer. Well that proves what I say, you are beginning to be feared by the mighty."

I wonder who my unknown champion is?

I wrote Stieglitz again, answering his insinuation, that I was ashamed of the traditions of photography: a charge too ridiculous to become angry over! He wrote again—and in quite a different tone—more conciliatory—and a bit of rather condescending praise over a group of prints of mine he had seen "ten days ago." I don't know whose collection they could have been—I have no Eastern "collector." The balance of the letter was a long apology for not having gone to my exhibit last year, or I might say an explanation. . . .

This last remark sounds like a rather nasty "dig,"—but actually Stieglitz can do a lot of boresome whining over his hard luck—lack of public appreciation—failure of friends—never having a darkroom—years of hard work—etc., when apparently he has had marvellous "breaks,"—appreciation everywhere, to the point of making him a superman.

Well, let this be enough of the Stieglitz episode. I give him all due credit for an important contact at a moment in my life when I knew what I wanted, and got it. That time has long since passed.

17. "Nature, the great stimulus—"

January 29. —And more Stieglitz, which confirms my own reactions. Samuel Kootz writes me: "I have had a great deal of trouble with Alfred Stieglitz. We have, of late, become so estranged because of my published opinions of O'Keeffe that he is selecting that reason for refusing to allow me to reproduce his photographs. It is a silly, and rather senile attitude to assume, but I have come to know that Mr. Stieglitz requires fawning over, and that is an obeisance I will not accord him or anyone."

I think the above, added to my own experience, needs no further comment!

This correspondence with Stieglitz has caused me to ponder over "influence," "inspiration," or better yet *stimulus*. I have thought back to my beginnings— 1902—which I recently noted was the year Stieglitz founded the "Photo Secession" and *Camera Work*—a great year for photography!

Though city-bred I always preferred the country, all that hills and valleys, lakes and skies symbolize. But I think my first great realization came through my camera: at least it brought me into closer contact with nature, taught me to observe more carefully, awakened me to something more than casual noting and romantically enjoying. Even then I was trying to understand, getting closer, becoming identified with nature. She was then as now, the great stimulus. These periods when I have been influenced by sophisticated friends or looks, I consider a real loss.

February 1. I have a splendid negative of the "turkish-turban" squash: it will go with my New York exhibit. My interest continues in the sand and soil patterns, but rain keeps me from work. These patterns are elusive: formed by soil washed over sand they change continually,—no use going out to search for them unless I take my camera,—they are changed by the time I could return. Ansel Adams wrote an article on my S. F. show: it contains debatable parts, though on the whole intelligently considered.

I will quote several paragraphs from my letter to him. I have covered some of these thoughts before but they can bear repeating.

Ansel did not care for my vegetables,—least of all the halved ones. This is nothing new! I seem to be continually defending them! I can see the resemblance of some of them, especially the oft-maligned peppers, to modern sculpture, —or Negro carving—but I certainly did not make them for this reason.

"No sculptor can be wholly abstract. We cannot imagine forms not already existing in nature,—we know nothing else. Take the extreme abstractions of

Brancusi: they are all based upon natural forms, I have been accused of imitating his work,—and I do admire, and may have been 'inspired' by it,—which means I have the same kind of (inner) eye, otherwise Rodin might have influenced me. Actually, I have proved through photography, that nature has all the abstract (simplified) forms, that Brancusi or any other artist could imagine. With my camera I go direct to Brancusi's *source*. I find *ready to use*,—select and isolate, what he has to 'create.' One might as well say that Brancusi imitates nature, as to accuse me of imitating Brancusi;—just because I found these forms firsthand in nature.

"I have on occasion used the expression, 'to make a pepper more than a pepper.' I now realize it is a misleading phrase. I did not mean 'different' from a pepper, but a pepper *plus*,—an intensification of its own important form and texture, —a revelation.

"Photography as a creative expression—or what you will—must be seeing *plus*. Seeing alone means factual recording. Photography is not at all seeing in the sense that the eyes see. Our vision is binocular, it is in a continuous state of flux, while the camera captures but a single isolated condition of the moment. Besides, we use lenses of various focal lengths to purposely exaggerate actual seeing, we 'overcorrect' color for the same reason. In printing we carry on our willful distortion of fact—'seeing'—by using papers to intensify the contrast of the original scene or object. This is all legitimate procedure: but it is not seeing literally, it is seeing with intention, with reason.

"An idea, just as abstract as could be conceived by sculptor or painter, can be expressed through 'objective' recording with the camera, because nature has everything that can possibly be imagined by the artist: and the camera, controlled by wisdom, goes beyond statistics.

"But after all, I am not limiting myself by theories, so I never question the rightness of my approach. If I am interested, amazed, stimulated to work, that is sufficient reason to thank the Gods, and go ahead! Dare to be irrational!— keep free from formulae, open to any fresh impulse, fluid. Our time is becoming more and more bound by logic, by absolute rationalism, by the mediocrity of mass thinking, a dangerous strait jacket! The really great scientist dares to differ from accepted 'facts,'—to think irrationally, and so discover, grow. Theories lead directly to the academic if they are allowed to crystallize.

"Let the photographers who are taking new or different paths beware of the very theories through which they advance, lest they accept them as final. Let the eyes work from inside out,—do not imitate 'photographic painting' by limiting yourself to statistics in a worthy desire to be 'photographic!' ('photographic painting' is being used by Rexroth in an article about me, showing the expression to be a misnomer).

"I have at times done some dangerous reasoning, but fortunately something beyond reason always steps in to save me."

I wrote a statement for the de Young Museum at the time of my recent exhibit. It sums up thoughts scattered over many of these pages: so I will copy.

"Photography is not for the escapist, the 'mooning poet,' the revivalist crying for dead cultures, nor the cynic,—a sophisticated weakling: it is for the man of action, who as a cognizant part of contemporary life, uses the means most suitable for a clear statement of his recognition. This recognition is not limited to the physical means or manifestations of our day,—such as machinery, sky-scrapers, street scenes, but anything—flower, cloud or engine—is subject matter, if seen with an understanding of the rationale of a new medium, which has its own technique and approach, and has no concern with outworn forms of ex-pression,—means nor ends.

"*Fortunately* it is difficult to be dishonest, to become *too personal* with the very impersonal lens-eye. So the photographer is forced to approach nature in a spirit of inquiry, of communion, with desire to learn. Any expression is weakened in degree, by the injection of personality:—the warping of knowledge by petty inhibitions, life's exigencies.

"I do not wish to impose my personality upon nature, (any of life's manifesta-tions) but without prejudice or falsification to become *identified* with nature, to know things in their very essence, so that what I record is not an interpretation —*my* idea of what nature *should* be—but a *revelation*,—a piercing of the smoke screen artificially cast over life by irrelevant, humanly limited exigencies, into an absolute, impersonal recognition.

"'Self expression,' so called, is usually biased opinion, willful distortion, under-statement. Discounting statistical recording, any divergence from nature must be toward a clearer understanding, an intentional emphasis of the essential qualities in things.

"Through photography I would present the *significance of facts*, so they are transformed from things *seen* to things *known*. Wisdom controlling the means —the camera—makes manifest this knowledge, this revelation, in form commu-nicable to the spectator."

February 2. Instead of "transformed," as used in the above, would not "subli-mated" better indicate my meaning?

The point I made yesterday about not limiting subject matter to physical mani-festations of our day concerns quite a group of young intellectuals, radicals, who imagine that to be "modern" one must "shoot" a skyscraper at a dizzy angle. It is not certain subject matter that makes one contemporary, it is how you see *any* subject matter. Once exciting, the repeated photographing of dis-torted perspectives is becoming boresome. I recall with pleasure Sheeler's dignified, austere photographs of New York buildings seen ten years ago. I remember no attempt to force attention by clever viewpoint. He didn't *try* to be different,—he *was*.

When making a portrait, my approach is quite the same as when I am portraying a rock. I do not wish to impose my personality upon the sitter, but, keeping myself open to receive reactions from his own special ego, record this with nothing added: except of course when I am working professionally, when money enters in,—then for a price, I become a liar,—and a good one I can be whether with pencil or subtle lighting or viewpoint. I hate it all, but so do I support not only my family, but *my own* work. The latter I will never, not if I starve, make to please others for their price.

A coincidence: yesterday I wrote,—"Nature has all the abstract forms that Brancusi or any artist could imagine. With my camera I go direct to Brancusi's *source*. I find *ready to use* what he has to 'create.'"

Today in Keyserling's *Travel Diary*,—chapter on Hong Kong, I find this,— "And the nature of the Far East induces a process like no other: in it the lines are of a purity, and the transitions of a neatness, *such as are created among us only by the artist's capacity for abstraction: this nature has already been stylized by God.*"

February 4. Great excitement for me yesterday: the sale of eight prints, and to one person. Who purchased, I don't know, for Jake Zeitlin made the sale in Los Angeles. All the money I have received this year has been from my print sales,—not a single sitting since Xmas. San Jose State College, Hotchkiss School, Connecticut, Scripps College, Claremont, each acquired one or more prints from my exhibits,—and I almost forgot the de Young Museum. I have yet to hear from Stanford. Exhibits are beginning to pay direct dividends.

This is all most encouraging. I see a future with independence from portrait sittings. I must be patient, and bide my time. Also I feel more free to spend time and money on my real work. I have been waiting all this week for the weather to clear so that I can work with the soil-washed sand on the beach: the difference in va ues between soil and sand is not sufficient,—sun is needed, a low sun to outline the slight ridge of deposit.

February 5. I am "old-fashioned" enough to believe that beauty—whether in art or nature, exists as an end in itself: at least it does for me. This in no way interferes with Sullivan's "Form follows Function," for form that is beautiful is so because its function is the ultimate expression of potentiality,—and so is beauty in nature which cannot always be explained by logic, by ascribing it to efficiency,—to practical or remunerative values. If the Indian decorating a jar adds nothing to its utility, I cannot see why nature must be considered strictly utilitarian when she bedecks herself in gorgeous color, assumes magnificent forms, or bursts into song. Has man the sole prerogative to use beauty as an end?—which he most certainly does!

Of course I am on dangerous ground: rational minds, "right thinkers," will attack this credo with scholastic common sense,—very common, blind sense.

Especially will some social workers howl: communists who consider art subservient to morals, who would have it function as a missionary to improve sanitary conditions or bank balances.

I suppose my stand is that of the now universally condemned "art for art's sake," for I make no apologies, though admitting it calls to mind a kind of loafing "Bohemian" dabbler,—misplaced barbers, "counter jumpers," or parasitic females, frittering away on daubs and baubles to decorate the homes of our great democracy, using art as an excuse to loaf, to be supported, and petted like poodles by sexually unemployed dowagers,—art patrons!

But this is no fault of the idea of beauty or art as an end: it means that good taste in a democracy, or in any form of popular government in which competitive commerce rules, in which money-changers rise to power from the scum of the earth, and plumbers, garbage collectors, realtors, ride in limousines, is dictated by the vulgarity of the commonplace. We have, in this golden era of democracy, "artistic" barbers, bootblacks,—anything,—in Los Angeles—and where else could this happen!—I saw a billboard announcing, "artistic lots for sale cheap."

Art is the work of individuals,—it is aristocratic: which is not to be confused with the Americans' idea of aristocracy,—wealth of money. Of course there have been horrible examples of rulers influencing the taste of a period, say Louis XV: but better chance the taste of a temporary figurehead than that of the "sovereign people" which is always bad en masse. Today the artist is forced into an isolated, unappreciated existence, unless he caters to popular vulgarity.

I am not wailing,—this is not sour grapes. I would not change my place for limousines, fripperies, mode and etiquette conformity,—all excess baggage, breeding physical and mental constipation.

February 6. Rain, and more rain ahead. It is quite warm. I sit here at 6:00 a.m. with window open and no fire. This is unusual. California rains are not warm like April showers in the East. Almost 20 inches of rain has fallen this season in Carmel, with two months more to go. This is about four times the total for all last year.

Yesterday's entry leads me directly to the pros and cons of a mooted question: Can the masses be educated, really acquire good taste, appreciation of fine expressions in painting, literature, music, theatre, so that these things become more than a veneer, a false front?

I certainly doubt it, yet there might be room for debate. Take for example the demand for really beautiful automobiles, smart, clean lines, free from excess ornamentation: manufacturers are not altruistic, they would make Louis XV coaches if they would sell better, they would trick them out like Xmas trees for

243

an extra dollar. I can only believe that "the people" are aping those who, with good taste, fortunately set the pace. Take for example, a popular expression, the motion picture palace—and what is shown thereabout is the last word in vulgarity. There is a credulous idea among certain liberal persons that the public could be led to demand better things, that they have never been given a chance. Nonsense,—they have had every chance, and the few good things shown always fail. The movie magnates watch the way of the wind and cater to box office, not to intelligence. Russia is held up as an example of fine expression coming from a people. Again nonsense,—what we get from Russia is the result of dictatorship,—has nothing to do with the proletariats' taste. They might discriminate politically due to efficient propaganda, but I wager that the cheap melodramas, the treacle which the American public eats up, would be equally popular in Russia: they were in Mexico, with audiences largely Indian, who loved the lurid Italian films, more crude than ours.

I have been amazed at one good omen, a recent phenomenon in America: the tremendous success of the magazine *Ballyhoo*, which has swept the country over night. There must be hope for this nation if we have a sense of humor so indicated,—*can laugh at ourselves,* the absurd antics of our business men, the preposterous bombast of our ad writers. It would seem that we are not so gullible if we can enjoy poking fun at Blisterine, Wiggley's Gum, and Schools for Scientific Slaughter. I will take credit for anticipating *Ballyhoo's* game by about ten years. I used to write ads for Tina's and Brett's amusement in Mexico, quite along the same line: more recently (before *Ballyhoo*) I wrote a burlesque on advertising for Fred O'Brien, published in *The Carmelite*. Too bad I did not think of commercializing my fun.

February 8. —Steady rain.

I have, ready to ship, my N.Y. exhibition: selected, listed, and after much deliberation, approved. Now questions come:—shall I write my own "foreword," a statement or credo, perhaps to regret my words later,—or shall I select several choice press notices,—or shall I merely announce the exhibition, catalogue the prints, and call it enough. I must decide today.

I have recently read Stuart Chase and Carleton Beals on Mexico. Why not get busy on my own daybook,—turn it into a little cash? The time is ripe—I am in the limelight as a photographer—and Mexico is on everyone's lips,—Mexico and her artists.

If I could become even slightly successful as a writer, my problem would be solved. With a living from sale of prints and writing, I could give up professional portraiture, and a lot of overhead with it.

I will make a start, find out if I can stand the reactions from past thoughts, see if I have enough left for a book after I have done severe cutting.

I said to Henry: "I have decided not to include my 'W. C.' in N.Y. show."
Cole said: "It's too personal, isn't it Dad."

Recent writing would seem to indicate that I am not overly fond of humanity at large, with grave doubts over popular rule. Yet I am not a misanthropist, I can sympathize, feel friendly with almost anyone as an individual: but I do not stand mass actions nor contacts.

I recall as a boy, walking miles in bitter winter weather rather than ride on a crowded Cottage Grove Ave. cable car. It was not because I would be physically uncomfortable, jostled or stepped on, but because I became psychically distressed,—though I didn't reason this way in my teens. The same reaction used to come from Xmas shopping crowds, the solid, suffocating mass on State Street. And today I have similar reactions when living in a city. Something quite poisonous exudes from people "canned" in dreary rows of ugly houses. God knows the houses in Carmel are the ugliest in the world with their crooked roofs, —affected quaintness: but the effect is silly rather than sordid, and pines and gay gardens, clean air and space, all take the curse off.

I especially dislike most radicals: as types they are the least imaginative of mortals, and the most arrogant: combined with evangelistic qualities they are quite impossible. So my mixed feelings toward Russia are understandable. In their present stage of collectivism, sharing homes, kitchens, baths, herding together, I would commit suicide, or freeze in the gutter. This is all very personal, petty,—one should sacrifice for the big idea!

If it is true that Lenin said that communism is but a step toward anarchism, then I might be more enthusiastic. But Lenin is dead. In the end will Russia, communism, foster personal liberty of action and thought, or become more and more meddlesome in the individual's own problems, negating growth which can only come through personal decisions, at least in questions which do not basically effect the community? We have lost enough individual liberty in these United States; a *more* paternalistic government would be unthinkable!

February 22. —Up before 5:00. I never sleep well with another,—which is unfortunate if the other does enjoy company. I can go to sleep easily, but after actual exhaustion is slept off and I awaken to find myself against the heat of another's body I become really distressed,— to the point of revulsion. So, nights in which I should sleep more, I usually sleep less.

My N. Y. exhibit has at last gone forward: the announcements too. I wrote my own statement, credo, what you will. I hope the reaction will not come too soon. One changes, but the published word does not, and ten years hence, or even tomorrow!—Those who read will accept it as my present. I used material already written, pruning, condensing, clarifying, so I feel it is the best I have done to date.

Of course my exhibition is the best I have ever given. Whether it will please as many people as last year, I doubt. But as one improves, fewer will follow. I gave a preview to a few Carmelites,—Lincoln Steffens and "Peter," Mary Bulkley, Mr. and Mrs. Frederick Burt, (Helen Ware), Dora and Hurd Comstock, Mr. and Mrs. Frank Sheridan. I could tell that my audience was moved.

In checking over the dates of my prints, I was amazed to find I had chosen 19 made in 1930: which means that with one or two exceptions this group was done in the last three months of 1930, after my first N. Y. show. That was a big year, 1930! I went back to 1929 for two selections,—1931 gave me 24, and 1932, 6. This year starts out well! One print of a toadstool I added to the catalogue after it went to press. So, given material, I seem to be working well. But I have a desire to work with people this year, portraits of figures, do a series to suit myself and show nothing else in New York next year. It might prove a sensational change. There are not many who can work equally well in portraiture, or landscape, or still-life, or however my details can be classified,—they are not still in the sense of "nature morte."

I append the statement from my catalogue. Too long to write out longhand.

I have no unalterable theories to proclaim, no personal cause to champion, no symbolism to connote. Too often theories crystallize into academic dullness,— bind one in a strait jacket of logic,—of common, very common sense. To be directed or restrained by unyielding reason is to put doubt as a check on amazement, to question fresh horizons, and so hinder growth. It is essential to keep fluid by thinking irrationally, by challenging apparent evidence and accepted ideas,—especially one's own.

In a civilization severed from its roots in the soil—cluttered with nonessentials, blinded by abortive desires, the camera can be a way of self-development, a means to rediscover and identify oneself with all manifestation of basic form,— with nature, the source.

Fortunately, it is difficult to see too personally with the very impersonal lens-eye: through it one is prone to approach nature with desire to learn from, rather than impose upon, so that a photograph, done in this spirit, is not an interpretation, a biased opinion of what nature should be, but a revelation,— an absolute, impersonal recognition of the significance of facts.

The camera controlled by wisdom goes beyond obvious, statistical recording,— sublimating things seen into things known.

"Self expression" is usually an egotistical approach, a willful distortion, resulting in over or understatement. The direction should be toward a clearer understanding through intentional emphasis of the fundamental reality of things, so that the presentation becomes a synthesis of their essence.

Edward Weston

Carmel, California: February 1932

March 2. Lorenzo in Taos,—Mabel Luhan's book on D. H. Lawrence just out, with most of illustrations by myself,—Lawrence, Tony, Jeffers. I was angry and disgusted to find they had changed the shape of my portraits to fit the page of the book. They would not have done this with paintings!—but just photographs. — The quality of the reproductions is quite good. I am not at all proud of the Lawrence portrait. I certainly did a poor technical job that day.

My portrait of Lincoln Steffens used as frontispiece in the autobiography, though very popular, did not please me. It was soft, moved. I can only blame myself for letting it go out, giving them a chance to choose it, in my desire to please others.

The Lawrence book was interesting and amusing, quite as revealing of Mabel Luhan as of Lawrence.

Cristal is here for a week or so: a very dear person, she. C. brought the latest issue of *Experimental Cinema* from Seymour. The illustrations are stills from Eisenstein's *Que Viva Mexico*. Of course one cannot judge the film from a few stills, nor even the stills as a whole from several selections, but I was disappointed. The full page reproductions are very bad technically, with no excuse for bad focus when they could have been stopped down. I can forgive much when movement must be stopped, but these figures were obviously placed and static. Also they were picturesque to a degree,—a fault which permeated my first work there. I admit my failure in Mexico,—not complete, I have some strong records, —but as a whole I now realize how much more profoundly I could have seen. Of course I am a different person now! I can blame three things, conditions, for my failure in Mexico: immaturity, psychic distress, and economic pressure. The latter condition kept me waiting in the studio for work which seldom came. It turned me to photographing toys,—juguetes, which have their place, still live: but I should have had more chance to go out.

March 5. First news from N. Y. from "Sis." Ira Martin, Pres. of P. P. A. made the first purchase, "Shell and Rock—Arrangement," said it was the high point of photography. I cannot agree. I call it an interesting experiment. Ira Martin it seems went to my exhibit, reserved his opinion until he had seen Stieglitz' retrospective exhibit, and that of a group of outstanding European photographers at Julien Levy Gallery, both exhibits, fortunately for me, on at the same time mine is. He then hailed me as . . . .

Of course this is all very flattering,—if I needed flattery. I think it is futile to use the word "greatest." Each one of us must recognize that we are part of a whole, and develop our part to the limit of our individual capabilities, stimulated and strengthened by the fine work of others.

From the angle of publicity, having these two other exhibits on, is extraordinary good fortune. Photography will be much discussed, many the arguments.

March 7. Marvellous days these,—warm, even hot, sun from dawn to dusk. I laze around on the beach in trunks only. We are slowly advancing to an acceptance of nudity. Those with ugly bodies and dirty minds will make the last protest. Women are becoming quite "daring,"—their latest suits barely cover breasts and mound of Venus.

Two more prints sold in N. Y. This about covers expenses. I am hoping for, needing, print sales to make up for almost three months without a sitting! This condition cannot go on without dire consequences. Yet I cannot consider that my business is worse than last year. I have really done better. If I had not spent so much on the boys, I would have well over a thousand dollars in the bank. And now I must give up my camera, 8 x 10,—send it to Chandler. It means cash returns to him: to me a means of creative expression. I am not so altruistic, so ready to sacrifice, as this gesture seems. In the first place it has to be done, willingly or not, and the fact that I do it more or less willingly can be considered from several angles: I am about through with the trees and rocks of Point Lobos for the time, nor do the vegetables or still-life indoors excite me: then the camera is so old and wobbly that I have no pleasure in its use nor confidence in results. I feel like turning to portraits for awhile, which would include any human parts, clothed or unclothed, or any gestures, head, hands, hips or feet. I would like a new Graflex, larger, 4 x 5. This size I would not enlarge from, contacts would be large enough. My technique in portraiture would improve, I could send an exhibit of portraits to N. Y. next year. I have this desire. I feel this will be my next step.

A letter from Seymour. Like most "radicals," he is impertinently arrogant. Instead of a love for humanity, I feel his motivating impulse to be a form of the will to power. In fact I wonder if this does not account for many radicals, as well as businessmen. Persecution has made them desire power. Seymour uses words, words, to build up his defense, or offense, as you will. He writes that I have "enveloped my art in mystico-sentimental wrappings,"—that is through my statements about it, but admits that it "contains the *germs* (!) of a mature scientific approach." He calls himself "a materialist, a realist, a utilitarian formalist," but belies this self-portrait by choosing for publication, Eisenstein's very picturesque, rather sentimental approach to the Indian!

March 11, 1932. I have often mentioned the importance of Bach in my life; recently, Dec. 10, I called him my greatest influence. Today reading Keyserling's *Travel Diary,* I came to this: "No musician has ever . . . as deep as Bach; to the metaphysician he is therefore more congenial than any other." So a philosopher more congenial to me than any I have read, finds Bach more congenial to him. Maybe it is significant that Bach was born under the same sign that I was.

Sister has written to me almost every day. She has been a sort of assistant curator for my show. Seven prints sold the first week. Considering the economic distress, this is a good record. So far, in the press, I have had favorable comparison with the European group showing at Julien Levy's. One critic, Carlyle Burrows, after commenting upon the European group, writes, "Most extraordinary however, are the studies shown by Edward Weston...." This is as it should be,—logical that America should lead in photography.

March 15. —Seymour's letter again: he writes, "As to the 'nonrelationship' of art and the social-economic structure,—Comrade Eisenstein himself is just now finding out, ...how seriously the social order—the *particular* social order, with whatever ruling class it has, proletariat or capitalist—can interfere with, and impede, even the greatest art in the world."

This is quite an admission from Seymour!

I find in a large majority of radicals, two very strong motivating forces,—forces they profess to abhor: the will to power, and sentimentality. And proletariats are but the bourgeoisie in the making.

In Mabel Luhan's book I liked very much her thoughts on the artist as the transformer, or, "Man is the transforming animal,"—to quote her correctly: and "unless he gives back to life as much as he takes from it, his acute reception faculty fails him."

Yes, unless one gives forth, and regardless of the $, one is finished. I have said, when my work is over, when I stop, then with no reason for existence, I die.

Another thought: unless one is merely a copyist,—in which case, no matter how faithful the copy, it is valueless, the work of an opportunist,—one cannot be influenced except by that which, by right of understanding, is already one's own.

18. *East Coast vs. West Coast—"Theatrical?"*

March 19. Another echo from the N. Y. exhibit: this time from sister who has been on a brother debauch for the last two weeks! Quite sister-like she arose in wrath when some man viewing my show said it "lacked the dignity of Stieglitz," that I was "theatrical." This astonished me. I could not have had a more unwelcome criticism! Not that I agree!

Well—adverse comments can be more stimulating than praise, at least can bring forth a fighting quality, and turn one inward too, for a little self consideration. This is all to the good. How much value *my* opinion has of *my* work can be questioned. It must be a biased valuation. I have worked hard and long, with much sweat and love,—how could I be otherwise than biased? So I must deny any "theatrical" quality in my work without hesitation. But I can try to find reason for the "critic's" viewpoint, taking for granted that he, as a friend of Stieglitz, is not also biased.

I have several times noted that Eastern people do not at once see Western values: to them our values are not "correct." I have observed painters first coming to this coast and painting here with Eastern eyes: and I have watched them change. I have had my work criticized as having false values. At times I do exaggerate, print with more contrast, with reason, but usually I feel my values are true.

This leads to further consideration of the difference between East and West: a difference which could easily lead an unacquainted Easterner to think my work "theatrical," though I think a more just observation would be to call it "dramatic." Everything is relative. To the New Yorker of fifty years ago the present startling architecture—now accepted as a matter of course—would be dramatic, maybe called "theatrical." So to one not used to the West, to the scale of things out here,—nature must seem very dramatic. But can nature ever be labeled "theatrical?" Of course not, or only by those not used to, or not big enough to feel a part of nature on a grand dimension. Only an inability to commune with, be on a close terms with a given nature, can account for the label "theatrical." It is fear of a thing which makes it strange.

Everything in the West is on a grander scale, more intense, vital, dramatic. Forms are here which never occur in the East,—in fruits, flowers, vegetables, in mountains, rocks, trees. Go to Mexico, and there one finds an even greater drama, values more intense,—black and white, cutting contrasts, am I theatrical because I see important forms importantly?

250

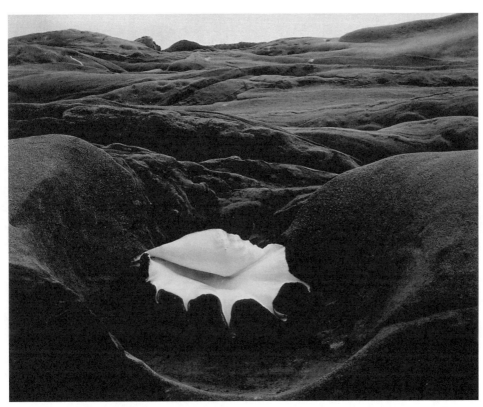

29. SHELL & ROCK – ARRANGEMENT, 1931

30. CHURCH, NEW MEXICO, 1934

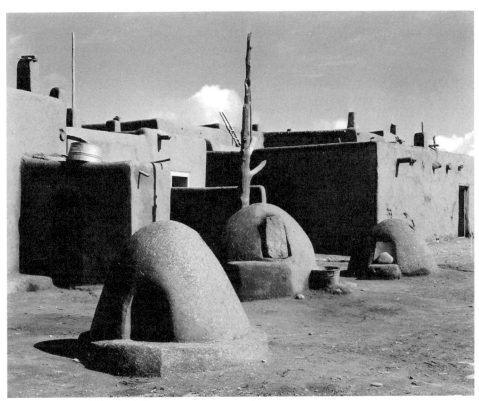

31. Ovens, Taos Pueblo, New Mexico, 1934

32. DUNES, OCEANO, 1934

33. & 34. UNTITLED, 1934

35. & 36. UNTITLED, 1934

37. & 38. UNTITLED, 1934

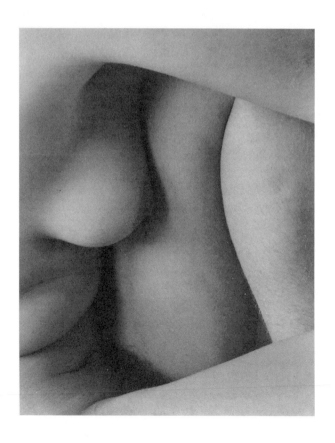

39. & 40. Untitled, 1934

All these forms,—trees, rocks, natural manifestations of Western vitality are my neighbors, my friends,—I understand and love them. I do not lie about them. After living here for ten years, I made a trip back East. Nature seemed soft there, poetic, tenderly lyrical, almost too sweet. Someone pointing out the sights to me from the train window said, "See the mountains." I looked and saw not! —then I realized they meant what, to me, were low rolling hills! But I must have had some apprehension that several of my prints would be misunderstood, probably because last year many did not know our Western kelp. I recall now laying aside one cypress, saying to myself, "I will not include this, no one would believe it true!"

Now then—what about E. W. himself, who has done this work called "theatrical?" That I am emotional to a degree I well know: that I feel intensely the drama of this life around me, and feel a part of it, I acknowledge: that I have been theatrical in my seeing I do not believe. If, with a clear vision, I have seen more than the average person sees,—well that's my job!—to reveal, to sublimate. To say my exhibit lacked dignity is to mark at once the observer as prejudiced, and perhaps indicate some of his own deficiencies. "Dignity" can be misused: can actually mean a sort of repressed tightness, anaemic viewpoint. I don't intend to so class Stieglitz,—I am thinking of my "critic." Dignity in his case might indicate pathology.

But all this controversy over who is the greatest this or that, is futile, leads nowhere. There will always be opinions and more opinions. Better to realize each worker as part of a great pattern, complementing each other, each seeing and doing his share. Why competition in arts?—Too much like bawling hucksters. Civilization accounts for much intolerance—the right to live is contested, fought for like wolves. No one is to blame, it's the damned system. Enough to compete with oneself, to forget the others, and try to carry to the limit the possibilities one was born with.

March 26. I wrote to sister, thoughts similar to those above. She thought me too concerned with the "unimportant critic" just discussed. No. This person's importance has no import for me. The value of an unfavorable criticism is in the self-questioning which should follow. If a criticism is decided to be undeserved, then one is strengthened in conviction: if it contains a hint of truth, a whole new line of thought may be aroused. Either way one is enriched.

But why not a more catholic viewpoint, admitting the value,—the necessity, of many ways of seeing? We do not expect everyone to prefer red cabbage to white: the fragrance of a magnolia to sage. There is place for both tastes and both odors, and there are different stages of development to be accounted for. Even such banal painting as Howard Chandler Christie's or the photographs of Dr. Max Thorek must be granted a rung on the ladder if only the lowest. At the top of the ladder will be found various viewpoints, tendencies carried to ultimate conclusions, as many as there are artists with differing psyches. The opinions as to their values will again be legion.

I wonder if Blake, the visionary, could be called theatrical because he saw things out of the ordinary! And if the answer be that photography is documentary,—well, why not document the extraordinary! I see no reason for recording the obvious. For example, by selecting an unusual pepper,—called "grotesque" by some who object to my seeing, I have brought attention to the dual force in this hybrid, the outer covering and inner lining, of different contractile forces inherited from diverse ancestral sources, which pull against each other like warring elements in a mestizo,—causing the strangely beautiful forms,—these I have felt and recorded. Have they not more interest than the commonplace pepper which a cook might prefer to stuff?

To close the above discussion before my long defense might be considered admission of defeat, I will quote a quite different viewpoint of my work. In a review of the various photographic exhibits held simultaneously in N. Y., Lincoln Kirstein in the *Arts Weekly* writes of mine: "Edward Weston has a really impressive show ... recorded with intense penetration and simplicity .... Weston is a serious and exhaustive artist, perhaps more genuinely creative in his various aspects than anyone else mentioned in this hasty review."

Of Stieglitz he comments: "The prints of faces and human figures have a quality, which when disassociated from his explanations are still attractive." I think Stieglitz deserves this "slam" on his explanations, his farfetched titles, relating clouds to people, etc. They are certainly undignified and theatrical!

March 27. Una Jeffers brought me a beautiful author's copy of Robin's new book, *Thurso's Landing.* Last night I read aloud to the boys and Sonya. I think the boys got a surprise, that great poetry could at the same time be exciting. Cole said, "Dad, that's as exciting as a wild West movie!"—and later—"It sounds like a song—I didn't know poetry was like that." They didn't want me to stop reading.

In a short poem "The Bed by the Window,"—his chosen deathbed—is a thought I have always held, that we live on until our reason for existence ends, until we have finished our work. I grant that many deaths seem hard to justify, but I hold this conviction nevertheless. Jeffers writes: "We are safe to finish what we have to finish."

Yesterday came a Mr. Kendall. I liked him immediately. He is making an exhaustive study of genius. He asked me if Jeffers was interested in the occult. I could not answer, except from his writing, which would indicate that he is. Then he said, "I have not yet found an authentic genius, neither in history nor contemporary life, who was not a student of the occult." He is making a special study of the eyes of genius, which seem to have certain unique qualities.

252

April 6. Within the last few days I have been disappointed twice, in what are heralded as important achievements in their respective fields: *China Express*, a Soviet film, and Harold Kreutzberg, German dancer, called "modern."

Since the former is communist propaganda and the latter "capitalistic" entertainment, I cannot be accused of being socially biased in my reactions. Nor were my reactions the result of expecting too much with a subsequent letdown. Kreutzberg of course has had much acclaim in the press, and from my friends too, excepting Henry, and I believe Bertha, both fine critical minds: but I went in a very open frame of mind.

Probably I did hope for something new—a beginning—instead I saw the last word in sophisticated entertainment, a theatrical peak. The last number, a group dance, in which the dancing was secondary to a vaudevillish act such as are given for women's clubs by dancing school classes, had a cheap popular appeal. In fact the whole evening smacked of program music. It was descriptive dancing. Perhaps all art can be called descriptive, even the most abstract, but in great expressions the descriptive elements become so sublimated as to be secondary to the form. I did not feel that Kreutzberg achieved this sublimation. What he attempted was done with amazing skill and good taste, but I was not once emotionally moved, rather held by this brilliant virtuosity, as in the case of Horowitz. His end left me cold; I did not feel the creative force that was within Isadora, whom I saw in her decadence, nor the power of Nijinsky (spelling?) whom I saw in his prime. It was all too artificial,—posturing, not dancing as I felt it in the two just-mentioned artists. Kreutzberg was also too effeminate for me. In the Mozart group dance in which they were all costumed alike, he might easily have been one of the girls, quite as lyrically lovely, no contrast of masculinity as a foil to the feminine charm.

Maybe I *am* too severe,—expecting a new horizon and finding an exquisite flowering of old forms obstructing the way.

I was quite as let down by *China Express* from a different angle. As propaganda I can find excuses for the boresome repetition of ideas through the much-acclaimed montage, for after all the film was made to convert a mass of illiterate peasants who need an insistent emphasis of the obvious. The tempo was painfully slow: quick consecutive flashes do not necessarily speed action. Not that speed is always desirable, but if slow, there must be material of sufficient interest to hold one, to compensate.

The plot had great possibilities: a background more human and honestly dramatic than 99 44/100 % of Hollywood abominations made for the box office to titillate yokels, money grubbers, and offering false ideals and an absurd society.

But the characters in *China Express* were quite as overdrawn, melodramatic, sentimental in their ways as those of a Hollywood film. The subtitles often ridiculous. Does not "I have a little sister too," sound like Hollywood? And the American or Anglo-Saxon overseers, the old maid with corkscrew curls, the violated Chinese girl—obviously placed in a glorifying light to play the better on one's heartstrings—all these were maudlin portrayals, maybe good propaganda for mob minds, but why label a film a great expression! No doubt these characters *could* be true, but they were not at all convincing. It brought to mind the old stage melodramas of my youth.

The photography was uneven—some of it poor.| The crosslightings so often used in the night scenes belong to the portrait studio effects of the 90's. And the low key of the first part was no excuse for losing much in a smudge of obscurity. This latter criticism I may have no right to make since I saw it projected by a portable outfit. But I made due allowance for that by comparing the loss in the daylight scenes with those of the night.

I am quite in accord with the *idea* of montage as expressed in the Russian films, but I have yet to see one that wholly convinced me that they had reached any degree of absolute expression.

I eagerly wait Eisenstein's new film on Mexico.

April 12. Kreutzberg came to my exhibit at Denny-Watrous. I asked him to sit to me. He was really happy as could be. We went at once to the hills nearby where I did his head against the sky. He "posed" all over the place, could not get away from the theatre even in the open, and clad in conventional clothes. Finally for the last few negatives I got his shirt off, and stripped, I did a couple of extraordinary heads.

He is really a charming and unassuming person: even his posing seemed but an expression of naiveté.

Next day a letter was mailed from Brett. He had also done Kreutzberg! The proofs were fine,—and done indoors, more flattering than mine. But again the forced gestures, which were incongruous in a tweed coat. Brett, too, realized this. He should have been done in costume.

Brett's opening exhibit in Santa Barbara was a great success. Five sittings arranged the first day! I knew he would do it—

April 14. These days are so inexpressibly beautiful, no fog, but yesterday a quickly clearing April shower, which gathered unheralded, washed air and refreshed earth. The sun is almost hot, it penetrates luxuriously, one feels to be actually growing, expanding along with the wild flowers, so profuse this year. I have never seen the oaks such a tender green, glistening with life, nor the pines so festooned with candelabra. The wild lilacs are a mass of lavender bloom, wild iris line the roadside, the fungi are extraordinary in size, color, variety. Recently at Point Lobos I saw what must be a rare bird, an albino among its kind, a white jay. In the twenty-eight years I have lived in California I have never seen one before. At first I could not believe my eyes,—that saucy, raucous call, the swaggering, jaunty airs, and that glistening white bird. So I sat me down and watched him quietly for half an hour. He came quite close, there was no mistake, here was a snow white jay,—only the side of his tail feathers seemed a shade darker, a light grey or grey-blue. It was a thrilling sight.

My 8 × 10 camera has gone on to Chandler; it served me well for ten years, all through Mexico, my finest period here in Carmel,—a friend, through which I have seen and recorded many a fine negative. But I did not feel sentimental over the parting,—like saying farewell to an old love, one knows that a new one will come to compensate. And I have already ordered a new camera, the finest made, a Century Universal, Folmer-Schwing. I think I have earned it.

A real shock has come to me in the news from Sybil that Vasia, long ailing, has been diagnosed as having a cancerous growth in his throat. How ironical for a singer! He cannot be operated on. This latter fact might be his salvation, if he could be convinced of the only possible way to cure or at least stop the progress of the growth,—through natural methods, fasting, inner house-cleaning, and a positive mental attitude. I have done all I can to bring some light to Sybil, but I doubt if she will listen, until all else fails, and it may be too late. People must have the witchcraft of drugs, injections, the ballyhoo of new "cures," —to give nature a chance, even half a chance, is too simple a procedure!

And Vasia—the kindest, dearest of humans—condemned!

April 21. At noon hour we walk,—to the beach or toward the valley—the latter straight down Monte Verde to Santa Lucia, from village pines into the open country. There we lie in a secluded bower of wild growth, wind-protected, hot, and watch the river empty into the ocean. Often the tides wash up a natural dam until the river spreads over the low lands. Before us is a meadow of yellow mustard, sprinkled with purple, a home for meadowlarks. The background of rounded hills, Point Lobos, foam-washed in the distance, eastward a barn, protected by lone black cypress, sea gulls soaring inland, wisps of swift-sailing fog, or banks of April shower clouds,—all rich in fulfillment, Life. And not so many miles away "bread lines," hunger, mobs, murder, Death.

19. *The Mass and the Individual*

April 22. What is to be the solution, what cure for the hunger, murder, Death? Will our system—Capitalism—fall? Will it slowly die,—evolution, or suddenly end,—revolution? Is Communism the solution? Despite the splendid arguments in its favor, many of which I can agree to, indeed have always held to,—equal opportunity for all, not admitting that all are born free and equal,—the destruction of money value, doing away with the *need* for making money,—the shortening of necessary working hours by collectively owned machines, leaving time for the individual to develop himself: despite these undeniably fine ideals, which would benefit the capitalist even more than the proletarian, turning his exceptional capacities into finer channels than those of grubbing or grafting for money,—yet I draw back instinctively from communism, at least as I have seen it in the making, not admitting that I have been fooled for a moment by propaganda against it. I know too well how propaganda works, having lived through the disgusting "ballyhoo" of the World War. My record during that period I am proud of; I was against it from the start and remained so, I contributed not one penny in "Liberty Bonds" nor "Red Cross," I was with the aristocratic minority.

But what has been my background, what has conditioned me to draw back from communism? It might be easier if I had been born under a czar, but living in a democracy, watching the antics of popular rule, people fooled by demagogues, bullied by their own paid hirelings, police, soldier, politicians: the destruction of personal liberty by mass minds, the perpetuation of the weakling, the vulgarization in every walk of life, the cheapening by popular approval. A sensitive person is either swallowed and lost in the grey dead level, or becomes militantly an individual, or retires to an ivory tower. The latter is not as the radicals would have it, a bourgeois artist,—he is a rebel against bourgeois surroundings.

I realize that I have been so conditioned by my fight as an individual in a back-slapping, mob-spirited, intolerant, self-righteous, familiar, evangelistic, regulating, levelling "democracy,"—that the very thought of collectivism, community ownership, of *one another* actually sickens me, literally.

I know the communist's answer—their way will work out to a different end—it's too early to judge them yet — — and to be fair one must agree. But they have made a bad beginning—blaming necessity—with all the evils of capitalism under another name.

256

I can, do, love individuals; I dislike and mistrust the sovereign mass. I have sympathy for the underdog, but so have I for real dogs, stray, lost, abused, just as much if not more—

I believe, I know, that the mass, the proletariat, hates the artist, the intelligentsia, —would gladly tear him to pieces. It is envy, fear, his own will to power. Only a few great souls are really humanitarian.

Who, as an individual, has not experienced the hatred of a group of laborers, say telephone linemen, or a group of corner loafers in a small town,—the muttering insolence, the sneering faces, or outright jibes? Why? Because one dresses differently, walks with assurance, *is* different, belongs in a world they could never reach.

The ordinary bourgeois type they do not notice, they understand him, for they are bourgeois in the making: with energy, good luck, back scratching they can rise to foremen, and lord it over their fellow Joneses.

Can communism change human nature? Or am I wrong, has human nature been perverted? Is there a basic fineness that I will not admit?

I look into faces that pass in the street, or gather in crowds,—and feel hopeless.

April 23. The foregoing sounds like an all too personal bellyache: as though I were not strong enough to stand, see beyond, the disagreeable episodes of a few crude yokels. Maybe so. Freedom has to be forced upon the mass. Minorities always have to lead, or even force them to accept freedom as well as slavery, and what seems unsolvable to me is that what means freedom to one spells slavery to another, and conversely. Minorities in turn are led by one great individual, unique, whose mould is destroyed at birth. Even the disciples of a leader, the second lieutenants, are impossible, —arrogant, bigoted, proselyting parrots, who, with no creative understanding, stabilize the master's living thought. This is true whether the disciples follow religion, art, philosophy: Christ, El Greco, or Nietzsche. Always formulae instead of fluid Life.

A "John Reed Club" has been started in Carmel. Many of my friends have joined, or organized it. They want me. I went to a meeting. It was dull, humorless, vague. "Comrade" Weston tickles me: it's so much like "Brother" Weston of the Methodist Church. Both groups are honest, sincere, no doubt, though one must admit the comrades are more intelligent and contemporary. By joining the club one automatically accepts communism, admits it rightness, countenances revolution, collectivization, and so on into the night!

How can I join,—honestly, without reservation agree? "Dialectic materialism" —words and more words, leading where? But maybe this world needs just this materialistic "logical conclusion" (their very words connote a restraint they deny, a crystalization into unyielding reason) before man can "take off" again for fresh heights.

April 26. Recently Harriet Dean, whom I first met with Margrethe, fifteen years ago, called: with her came Xavier Martinez, wife and daughter, and a Virginia Hale, who bought one of my prints. They spent hours with my work, deeply responsive. Later they came again with a dancer—Lester Horton. I saw him give superb interpretations of American Indian dances, so fine they seemed far removed from "interpretations," as though he were a reincarnation of an Indian brave. He was equally responsive to my work.

The same week I met Martinez' family, he wrote me, having seen and approved of Jeffers' head used on cover of *Time.* I visited "Marty" years ago, in Piedmont, our only contact. Thinking he would make a grand head for my next N. Y. show (I have decided to hang only portraits) and desiring to know him better, I invited him to sit to me. I enclosed my N. Y. catalogue statement. "Marty" answered, accepting, "sometime next May." He liked my statement, "a sane philosophy," but disagreed with my ideas on "self-expression" which "is egotistical just as genius is egotistical." "It is self-expression or point of view that differentiates Rembrandt from Greco,...that makes your photographs so wonderful and unlike the artificial ones of Steichen."

I fear that many misread my statement. I said "Self-expression is *usually* an egotistical approach." I had no intention of denying individual viewpoint. I had in mind the vast horde of modern artists, hell-bent on being different, exposing their own uninteresting (except maybe to a psychologist) inhibitions at the expense of things in themselves,—"interpreting" nature, life, through their own inflated egos,—unwarranted egotism.

I would go further in saying that the real artist,—genius in any line of creative endeavor,—does not interpret anything: he creates a new world in opposition to the thought of his own age. Always ahead and alone, he is the leader who clears the way for revolution. And revolution is but one surface manifestation of evolution; like a boil on the neck it hastens the cure. Whether individual or racial, boils should not be suppressed, driven back into the blood: fresh boils, worse ones, result, or death.

April 28. In the last issue of *The Left,* an article by Leon Dennen on "Plechanov and the Marxian approach to Art," is about the only mature writing in the magazine. *Left* is supposed to be published by and for the revolutionary intelligentsia. Peevish indulgences, "slamming Amurken" writers, etc.

Dennen's article should be read by the rest of the contributors, the class who think art must be political, evangelistic, who say, "What has kelp got to do with the revolution?"

To quote: "The Marxian approach to art has suffered most from misinterpretation by exponents as well as opponents of historical materialism. The majority of American Marxist critics have gone no further than analyzing art and the development of ideologies in general, in terms of economic evolution," and goes on to explain other elements that condition the development of ideologies and art, the whole social psychology of a given epoch, and further, since when is universal literature revolutionary? Plechanov frees the Marxian method of criticism from the narrowness of duty. "Revolutionary aesthetics does not prescribe (cannot, I would say) what the artist is to do." Sociology does not close the doors against aesthetics...the analysis of the sociological equivalent would remain unaccomplished if the critic refused to give an evaluation of its aesthetic qualities. The Marxian critic welds the utilitarian and aesthetic aspect into one life."

The Mexican Syndicate of Painters and Sculptors who were avowedly allied to the U.S.S.R. published this statement, I think written by Siqueiros: "Art for art's sake is an aesthetic fallacy,"—(I have said that such an attitude is the result of the artist rebelling against his condition, his time)—art for the people is a phrase of inconsistent and hypocritical sentimentalism. Art is necessarily a thing of the people, not an abstract concept, nor a vehicle for exploiting whims. The search for true expression of mass feeling is not to be confused with the doctrine that plastic art to be reconstructive or revolutionary, must be subservient to the propagation of prescribed ideas. A panel ('fresco' was being discussed) sincerely and forcefully conceived from pure emotion, and portrayed according to the aesthetic laws of the craft, will generate its own morale."

May 16. After ten days visiting Chan—Max—Teddie and Brett—Eleanor—L. The latter contact, unexpected, at least in the direction it took, and very beautiful. Our meeting on the 8th took a rapid course which left nothing to desire on the next day but a complete fulfillment.... L. will be here soon. Not so easy, an affair in Carmel. Nor would I hurt Sonya for worlds: she has been too fine and square with me. I must conclude that I cannot remain a faithful husband to anyone. Yet I never go out hunting affairs, they seem presented to me, —inevitable.

Teddie is a glorious child. I think he remembered me. Anyway we became fast friends.

I left Santa Maria depressed. I think there is no future there for Chan, not even a present living. And what solution? I spent so much. But Santa Barbara buoyed me up: Brett will succeed there I'm sure.

May 17. I have done no work for myself, comparatively none, since January! Partially due to having no camera. This does not distress me—a rest is simply getting up steam—but I do regret that this period of inaction came at a time when, with no business, I had leisure to create without interruption.

Now my camera has arrived but the back does not fit when reversed to vertical. The idea of sending out an expensive camera that does not function disgusts me.

259

I will return to Wilton Co. tomorrow. Sonya and I drive to S. F. with Drew Chidester to see Willard's exhibit at de Young Museum.

Today I photograph a bride!—the first in years. I must do her at Del Monte Lodge. I tried to find every excuse to myself not to accept the job. I detest the idea, the artificial surroundings, but my conscience would not permit a refusal, not with Chan in distress, a new camera to pay for, children's clothes to renew, not when millions are glad to be even eating. The job will pay a month's rent! There's really no way out of it. I can't be so damn particular.

June 23. —over a month since an entry—and what a month! The consummation of love between L. and Edward. I say "love," meaning no less. I feel that few humans are granted such good fortune in finding, and knowing each other. L. wrote me she was coming north. I found pressing "business" in S. F. We met on the train at Salinas. That night, it was May 25th, we came to know each other.

June 26. A gentle rain is falling — — as it was when we last parted. But this time there is no definite future. A farewell note came yesterday, just a month, to the day, from our first night together: "A temporary au revoir," she writes. And: "Bless you, my love, I take you to me and I love you with my whole being—Your L."

What can be the meaning of all this!—this cutting short of a stalk just starting to bloom? Is this love to but live in our memories,—or is the cutting with reason, a test?—or to force our roots down into richer, firmer soil, a preparation for future blooming?

I ask myself, if I had been free, would I have allowed L. to go to another without protest? I am sure not! And she, being loyal, having some real or imagined obligation, would have been torn asunder. And if I had "overpersuaded" her, successfully — — what then but sore hearts, scandal, to who knows what end.

Sonya is my problem. I love her now as a *best* friend, a true one, never was there truer. But would she accept this change? She has given me the most peaceful "married" life I have ever had, three years of it. She has stood by me, worked for me, saved for me. We are companionable, physically and mentally. Why then this desire to change, to go from a comfortable arrangement, a reasonable adjustment, into the unknown! Or should I say unknown? Do not L. and I know each other, even though our days have been few together? Yes!

I have been "untrue" to Sonya once before: the first year. But I knew the adventure for what it was, a passing excitement. W. and I met at a party. Wine and familiarity, her evident willingness, my curiosity, led to a week's "romance." A difficult one to achieve. Climbing out the window after I had retired for the night. Creeping up the creaking studio stairs. Getting safely back to bed. I was a welcome rebound from her first affair. She was a charming child, who had been well taught. There was no basis to continue on.

But recently, before meeting L., on the way to a party at the Highlands, I sat in the back seat of a car with P. She snuggled close, dropped her head on my shoulder, and I, almost too astonished, caressed her hair. I had known P. for three years, with never the slightest hint of this. But I was willing—no great desire—more curiosity. I photographed her soon after. Kisses followed. We went to a cottage in the Highlands. Once there, she said "No, it's not the right time." I was but slightly impassioned, so shrugged my shoulders,—to myself: could she come to my studio at night? I hesitated,—there was no hesitation with L., for her I would take any chance. Finally I gave her a key, which has not been used. Never the "right time." A psychically different person, P. Admitting she likes to make the conquest — — wanting my assurance that I would do anything without being shocked — — explaining that she loved to sleep with a man without doing anything — — that she liked women too — — In fact I don't think she was sure what she wanted. And I was not interested enough to press "my" suit. Lately she has shown renewed desire. It's too late. I am too filled with L. I will be true to her "in my fashion."

July 6. Fog, thick, wet, has shrouded Carmel for almost two weeks. It has brought to me most definitely that this is no permanent place for me. Will any one place give me lasting interest, a home? Or any one woman? Strange question, the latter, following my recent love affair. But now is just the time to question. I do doubt my ability to remain for long in one place. The very nature of my work, requiring fresh fields to conquer. Or am I making excuses for a desire to change that has come over me?

I know that I have home-making instincts, yes, and marital ones. I should have a permanent home to return to — — and a wife — — to return to?

The R.O.T.C. "Summer School for scientific slaughter"—credit "Ballyhoo"— is noisily shooting away the taxpayer's money in preparation for the next war to preserve the sovereign people,—to protect them from the shock of having to think in new terms,—to keep them comfortably static.

July 11. I went to L. A., night train, returning the following night,—to photograph Richard Day, for a frontispiece to his book which Merle is planning. He is also to do one on me,—my work. There seem to be a few "ifs": if the money can be raised,—for it will be privately printed, and if the preliminary work can be done before Merle's vacation ends.

Sheldon Cheney talked on "Revolution in Art" at Denny-Watrous. An intelligent, prophetic, and very human individual, but not so dynamic in speaking as in writing. A group of "reds" were in the audience, waiting for the discussion. They started the old discussion,—the relation of art to society, trying to prove that art must serve some "cause," of course the only cause, theirs,—communism. One man

261

with Peter Steffens, Levy by name, made me boil. Why don't "reds" stick to politics and leave art alone, a subject they cannot grasp. This man was narrow, bigoted, crude, with the voice and eyes of a religious fanatic. If such persons are to rule this country when their end is achieved, I hope I am dead. Conditions would be as bad as if the Ku Klux Klan were in power. Every time a "red" opens his mouth, I become more conservative!

What I am now, where I stand, in this epochal time, fast-changing world, I frankly don't know. I certainly am not for the capitalist, nor the sovereign mass. The communists I know are "mouthing Puritans." I do know where I stand re my work, though the "radicals" (political) don't think so. Funny, I have always been considered a radical by academic artists, but the communists probably would damn me as "bourgeois liberal,"—because I do not portray the worker's cause.

Despite all criticism my work is functioning. I receive continued and growing response from sensitive persons from all walks of life—yes, I do know my work has revolutionary significance, despite its lack of literary connotations. Peter Steffens said that Trotsky believes that new and revolutionary art forms may be of more value in awakening a people, or disturbing their complacency, or challenging old ideals with constructive prophecy of a coming change. I am not quoting him, rather using my own ideas to explain his thought as given to me. Now I must locate his own reference.

We also discussed the reason for the unhappy, disturbed condition of so many American artists. It cannot be economic distress alone: artists have always been willing to suffer privation for their work. And besides, the most flagrant examples of a tortured psyche I know of belong to artists with economic security. Their condition in every case seems to me to be because they are not functioning in terms of their racial psyche, the collective subconscious. They have hangovers from European or other native ties, they are not assimilated, adapted to this soil. That they were American-born, even for several generations makes no difference, if they are still in the process of becoming adapted. The way of seeing and the means must grow from our own needs. All of the artists I have in mind are easel painters. They have stacks of paintings stored away. The fact that these are not purchased with money means nothing to these artists. But the fact that they are unsought means everything. The artist must have an audience, must give. I am happy in my work because I am giving, changing the lives, the viewpoint of hundreds. So does any fine photographer. Photography, as Walter Arensberg said, has brought a new world vision. People want my work, buy it, would buy more if times were better. So my work is functioning, is needed.

Photography is peculiarly adapted to the American psyche. No argument as to whether it is art or not can destroy its value. The fact is, it is not a medium which has reached the end of its value as an expression: it is vital in that it belongs to an epoch, a race in the making, the becoming.

20. *"A book on my work—"*

October 24. Since July 11th, over three months ago, I have made no entry in this book. On that date, I casually noted that Merle had in mind a book on my work. It has now gone to press! For these last three months I have "lived" this book, literally. Weeks passed, with prints under consideration strewn all over my room. The first dozen or so were easy to select, work that *had* to be included, prints that were epochal in my life. But after these, came the struggle to eliminate from amongst a hundred or more possibilities. To confine myself to the limit of thirty reproductions, lay aside dozens that I wanted to use, was a task which made me question my own decisive ability. Merle raised the number to thirty-six; but even then I wavered between my desires. Probably I will always regret certain omissions.

I have learned much from this struggle. For one thing, my critical faculty toward my work has sharpened. I have always thought that I was severe enough in judging my photographs, but faced with presenting them in a book, from which I could never escape, I discovered the word "but"; "this print is fine *but—*" And I have learned something about writing! That it is one thing to jot down thoughts in a daybook; another to present them to an audience,— again, one from which I could not escape! Continually, I would face myself, and say, "Do I really mean this?—Could it be misunderstood?—Have I clearly expressed my meaning?—And how about my technique, my choice of words, their exact relation to my thoughts?—Have I been pedantic?"

I wrote, and I destroyed, until I had corns on my bum, bleary eyes, writer's cramp, and a befogged brain. Finally I achieved a clarified, concise statement, —at least I think so today, and mailed it yesterday.

I am weeks behind in my finishing of orders, have done no work for myself for months,—hardly any this year. But I know that I have grown. I am now ready to go ahead with fresh desire and added strength.

The book will be out in November. The story of its growth from an idea, from Merle's imagination, to its publication, should be told. But it is a long story, for another day.

21. *Group f/64*

November 8. I only thought that I was through writing my statement! Soon after mailing it, Merle advised me it was eight lines too long. This meant rewriting much of the article, but in doing so I achieved a greater clarification, caught myself in a couple of equivocal statements.

A letter from Walter Arensberg in which he can't agree with all of my selections, and thinks Steff's appreciation rhetorical and irrelevant. As to the latter criticism, I fear he is right. I feel that my fondness for Steff made me blind to the reactions of those who do not know him personally. Considering my selections, Walter's reactions really bother me. Maybe—as I wrote him—I should have had a jury (of my own selection) sit on the job. Perhaps I tried too hard, had stage fright; certain it is I took the matter seriously, considered every angle in my attempt to assemble a well-balanced group of my finest work. I know how futile it is to try pleasing everyone in a "jury" of the best critics in the world. I would like to have had Walter's approval, but in pleasing him, others of equal discrimination would have disagreed. Some of the portraits might be questioned from the technical side. Merle overpersuaded me to include several because of their wide appeal as outstanding figures of the age, D. H. Lawrence for instance. Well, I must stop worrying; it's done, the book has gone to press.

These are the most glorious days I have ever seen in Carmel; brilliant sun, warm. I went in the ocean yesterday, and dozed on the beach for an hour. But this past summer has been dreary; fog added to fog for weeks.

My desk is cleared of unanswered letters, orders to date all printed. So a few days ago Henry drove Xenia, Sonya, and myself to Oliver's cacti garden in Monterey. There was amazing material and I worked hard and well. Yesterday I worked with an extraordinary squash—it would have to be, for me to return to old subject matter—and today I have started on another, with real interest. While we were in S. F. several weeks ago, a party was given exclusively for photographers, at Willard's. Those who gathered and partook of wine and photo-technique, were Imogen, John Paul, Ansel, Sonya, Willard, and E. W. Others were present, but the six above formed a group with the primary purpose of stimulating interest in real photography and encouraging new talent. Henry Swift was added to the above-mentioned. The original plan was to rent a room in S. F. and give a succession of exhibits. This idea was abandoned out of consideration for Lloyd Rollins who has done so much for photography during his directorship at the museum. Lloyd felt we would be directly in competition with him, and offered an alternative; to give us a group show, several galleries at the museum. This offer was accepted and "Group f/64" will open Nov. 15th. Invited to show with the group are: Preston Holder, who has added photography to poetry, Consuela Kanaga, Alma Lavenson, who fought my criticism (self-invited) of her work a few years ago, but now has seen the light, and Brett. Some have expressed astonishment that I should join a group, having gone my own way for years. But I see it as purely educational. We are all friends, free from politics; and I have no desire to be the founder of a cult!

December 8. Just a month since my last entry; and what a month, equal to a whole season of months. My book is out!—and it *is* a fine work throughout of which I am proud. Merle and Lynton spared no effort in making it an outstanding contribution; to it was given understanding, love, and fine craftmanship. The reproductions as a whole are superb; though several could have been better, but even these only suffer by comparison with the others.

I went to Los Angeles for the signing of my name. Returned with Merle, Brett, and Hugh King to Carmel, thence to San Francisco. So much has been crowded into this month that I despair of going into more than a bare outline; and why do that? I am faced with enough problems, work ahead, without recalling the past. For instance: Chandler must leave his studio in Santa Maria, with no money to start elsewhere — L. has been in a serious mental state, and I seem to be, and gladly am, one of the few points of contact which may lead her to a rebirth — Sybil is faced with earning a living for a very sick Vasia and her child; so I am, with Sonya's help, teaching her photography —

Merle is to publish a book on Shore, which means I do all the copying of her work, for Henry is penniless, and would have none other anyway; besides I have been asked to write the foreword, an even greater task, though a labor of love; I can only hope that this is to be my swan song as an art critic! Besides these several problems, Cole is leaving to live with his mother, which is sad for me, for he has gained health and improved his morale while here, and I fear he may slump back in "Toonerville." But it may be best to have him away from Neil for awhile; they bicker continually. All these vital considerations come to me during a flurry of Xmas work, arranging two exhibits, and most important of all a time when I am revolutionizing my way of working in portraiture. I have purchased a 4 × 5 Graflex and will start making contact prints, *unretouched*. From now on I will not sign retouched portraits! This is a daring step to make during a major economic crisis, but it *had to be done*! I have been psychically ill at times from signing my name to work which was not *my* work. I have done enough aesthetic whoring. I paid for the camera by the biggest and worst job of whoring I have done in years. At times during the work, I came near to throwing it in the fire and telling the poor unsuspecting subjects that I did not want their lousy money. I kept going by repeating to myself: "$380,

265

$380!—you must not give in, this means a new camera, a new life." And so I went through with it.

The 4 × 5 size is large enough, I hope, so that I will not be asked to enlarge; which means greater technical perfection; for no matter how well done, an enlargement does lose quality, cannot compare with a contact from the same negative. I do not dare to say "no enlargements," not yet; that will be the next step. But I will not sign, except duplicate prints from old negatives, any retouched order. This still leaves another step, which will follow logically, that I will accept no order that I am ashamed to sign, that I will never retouch again. But I must go carefully, I cannot let others suffer from my rashness.

December 11. A week ago I was taking my daily sun bath on the beach, clad in trunks only; so warm it was that I sweat a bit, and even ventured into the surf, finding the water more endurable than some summer days. Yesterday it snowed in Carmel at sea level! This morning the gutters are icy, the roofs white with snow!

My book is going to be the sensation we expected. Already I have been receiving congratulations,—verbal, written, and yesterday a wire from Mrs. Maitland. How thankful I am that previous negotiations for the publishing of my work fell through. No one but Merle could have designed a book to so perfectly present my photographs; and Lynton's craftsmanship and knowledge carried on the plans to a notable achievement.

December 16. Brett is 21 today; bless that grand boy always. How blessed I am to have him as a son, and friend!

The weather remained cold for days; the north slopes of roofs held snow in the gutters for two days. But this morning it is cloudy, a south wind, blowing, and the sunrise red. Rain perhaps.

A different kind of storm broke yesterday; one of wrath over a print included in my book,—"Shell and Rock—Arrangement." I am a good weather-prophet in matters of art, for I predicted this storm when I made my decision at the last moment to include it.

From Bob Sanborn and Ramiel came the first protest. Ramiel did his best to prevent or dissuade me from using it; but to no avail. I *would* publish and I'm *glad* that I did! The issue taken seems to be that it is a "stunt," theatrical, not true to nature; as Bob wrote: "—the greatness of your work, Edward, is that you allow nature to talk her own language." Of course I went all through this controversy long ago,—*with myself*; despite all the logic I could bring to bear against the print, it held out, and won. Are not these friends pedantic, wasn't I, in reasoning it out of existence? And are their reasons consistent? Why did they not flay me for including the "Shells" on p. 117—three shells each from different parts of the world, arbitrarily arranged. The only difference I can see, is that the latter is a still-life indoors, the "Shell and Rock" a still-life outdoors. And Bob has an early shell "composite" which he values highly! Ramiel writes: "Even adding the word 'arrangement' does not save it for me." But I did not add that word as an apology, rather to forestall criticism from *naturalists* that I was "nature-faking."

After all arguments, pro and con, the justification of this questionable print is in that it has deeply moved an intelligent audience, as I was moved when I saw its first presentation on my ground glass. For instance, Walter Arensberg bought it "on sight." And I have amusedly seen how it fascinated several who are most positive in their theories as to the logic which conditions the direction photography *must* take.

One thing is certain; I had no intention of doing a stunt. I am not a "showman" wanting to attract attention. I can honestly say,—claim for my work, that it is done with no regard for public opinion, not reactions; that I do a thing because I want to, I feel it. I don't *have to* please the public, not anyone, for thank the Gods, my portraits earn my salt! Obviously then, I am not interested in making the public gasp, titillating it by "stunts"; that's a juvenile approach. I may or may not do another "Shell & Rock—Arrangement,"—something in that vein, but I'm glad I did it, and I'm glad it's in the book!

Enough—

January 18, 1933. Pouring today; much needed,—this rain. The south is pathetically dry. I returned from there Friday. Now Sonya has gone,—returned with Merle for a week's stay. Just Neil and I left. It is well. I like to be alone; it has connotations of adventure! And this rain augments the feeling I have of something pending. Maybe Sonya is having the adventure. I hope so; then my conscience might be eased. But am I not expressing that thing one is *supposed* to have,—a conscience? Actually, I have never felt guilt over my philandering; only a desire not to be discovered for *her* sake; not yet at least. And I could feel quite as guilty toward L., from whose arms I went to H. in L. A. To be sure it was unpremeditated, and we had both reached a delightful intoxication but that does not absolve me from the guilt I should feel,—and don't! Yes, and before going south I made love to both S. and X.! Am I then so weak that I fall for every petticoat? Am I so oversexed that I cannot restrain myself? Neither question can be dismissed with a "yes." First, I can go long periods with no desire, no need; then I see the light in a woman's eyes which calls me, and can find no good reason—if I like her—not to respond. I have never deliberately gone out of my way to make a conquest, to merely satisfy sex needs. It amounts to this; that I was meant to fill a need in many a woman's life, as in turn each one stimulates me, fertilizes my work. And I love them all in turn, at least it's more than lust I feel, for the months, weeks, or days we are together. Maybe I flatter myself, but so I feel. So what will you answer to this, Sonya?—and L.?

267

L. is my most difficult problem; for I am in a position which amounts to saving her sanity, if not her life. I am not conceited in this; it is all too true. She lives for the day when we can be together. And if it can become possible and I cannot remain true to her—from past records it would seem improbable—what then? I love her, yes, but so have I loved others; and they all pass, not the love, but the emotion, the flame. I love Sonya, but only with tenderness, the calm affection of a friend. And that is not enough for most women, not even the emancipated; they are basically conservative no matter how intellectually radical.

22. *"End of a period—"*

January 19. —and still raining; has for the last twelve hours.

Cole in L. A. seemed a bit pathetic. His new school with 2500 pupils confused him. And he is too high-strung to be near Flora. I hated to leave him behind. He will be happy to know that a plaque was awarded him as the outstanding boy in his graduating class at the Sunset School.

Neil has been in a mix-up with the "authorities," along with seven other boys, all sons of "leading citizens" in Carmel. From the front lawn of a local drayman, one dark night, the boys removed a ridiculous marble atrocity, a nude in Italian marble, placing it in the road some blocks away, plastered with a "for sale" sign. Then the boys made the classic mistake of all "criminals,"—curiosity took them back to the seat of their crime. Hidden in shrubbery "the law" awaited, and arrested them with a flourish of guns. The drayman, Wermuth, a vicious, vindictive type brought charge of grand theft!—a ridiculous charge which the district attorney refused to consider. So criminal proceedings have been dropped, but I understand a civil suit is in order for $500 damages. The atrocity isn't worth 50 cents as a work of art. But the drayman has been made ridiculous, and is full of rage.

I feel as though I had contributed to the boys' delinquency, for I have often said it would be a pleasure to blow up this nude vulgarity.

My visit to L. A. was a hectic one. Merle drove me from one visit to another,—everywhere to receive congratulations on my book. It has been a veritable sensation. If I could not detach myself, hear the applause as one of the audience, I might be sunk by homage. But even when I think the praise deserved something always answers within me, "Well, what of it?" Maybe even this is vanity! However, I think not. This book, like an exhibit, marks the end of a period. I turn the pages, each plate an old friend, each recalling red-letter days,—and know that I must go on from these, leave them as I leave my love affairs, still loving them, but with no regrets.

On my way to L. A., driving with Brett, Elinore, Chester, Chan, I worked; my subject an imposing grain elevator; result, an excellent negative. I worked again in Santa Barbara, with cacti; result, at least three good things. I am wild to be working again!

January 26. Printed recent negatives; adding to my collection the grain elevator and two cacti, all worthy additions. I destroyed two of the cacti negatives; one which would have been excellent in a different light; sunset came on while I worked with it, so that what I saw at the start faded before my eyes. I should have been strong enough not to waste a film—not because of the few cents involved—but because I knew at the time that my labor was in vain. The other was destroyed as not quite meaningful. Again I knew it at the time of making, but that desire to be working overpowered my judgment. I made but one negative, and felt that I had to have more to show for the afternoon. Foolish reason! The one I made—and it was done a few moments after I started to work—can go with my best; it was seen and made with *no hesitation*, and that is the way to work!

The time I went to L. A. for the signing of my books, Merle and I had supper with Madeleine Ruthven. Later came Elise Seeds. Merle fell hard! And I must say that Elise is an unique person. The last visit to L. A. we dined with Elise. My appreciation of her very personal qualities increased. Elise is a comedian— and she must be a rare one—but she is also an artist with pencil and brush who has a slant on things quite her own. Merle has a goat's head, really striking, and I came away with a drawing of a hand—I almost said hands—but it is one hand drawn in different movements superimposed, which is finely seen.

I asked Elise to sit to me. She answered: "I will not! You would discover things inside of me to record which are none of your damn business!" Finally we compromised on an ear. I might sneak in a little more than the ear—

February 2, 1933. The first of February opened to a new page in my book of loves: S. came to me! We had hours of exceeding beauty. I could easily wax emotional! How we can continue I can't foresee; the danger in her coming here at night is too great,—would be fatal to both of us if she were seen. And her striking carriage, her Junoesque figure could be recognized from a block away.

I have worked with my new 4 × 5 Graflex: made sittings on successive days of Sybil, Sonya and Xenia. The Meyer Plasmat, 10 5/8, f/5.5—which I have on trial, has fine quality, but unless the day is fairly brilliant, I doubt if the speed I use of 1/5 sec. will give sufficient exposure, even using the extra fast Pans [Panchromatic films]. Of course I can usually select my hour and day for sitting, but sometimes a "last day here" client comes in, and I should be prepared for bad light conditions. I will not consider artificial light: a sitter always feels artificial, and besides it's just another thing to bother with. So I have written to find out if the f/4 lens of 10 5/8 in. focus will fit my front board, and the extra cost.

The claim of extra depth for the Plasmat seems justified. A head nearly filling the ground glass has good definition from nose to ear, with lens wide open; and this of course is the same as extra speed.

270

February 7. I have definitely decided on the 10 5/8, f/5.5 double Plasmat. The sitting, which settled my choice, was of Alice Rohrer, who came here with Kathryn Hulme. Besides the lens quality which I proved, I made a number of very fine portraits. The year starts auspiciously for my work. Alice is as lovely as ever. Last evening we had tea with Mable Luhan and Lady Brett; a really good time. I had not seen Brett (one can hardly think or speak of her otherwise) since our meeting in Mexico with Lawrence and Frieda. That meeting was no more than a greeting. I feel that I will like her; in fact I do. When Mable Luhan asked Brett to show her paintings, I had mixed feelings of curiosity and dread. It's not easy, as a guest, to be honest! But I found to my relief, imagination, a very individual viewpoint, and a feeling for form.

Brett does not know my work, other than a few portraits. She has promised to come here soon.

February 22. This great, high-roofed room has been, in winter, rather bleak and cold,—cold in aspect, not temperature: the gas stove heated well enough, but that isn't enough: a *feeling* of coziness is necessary, and the ugly gas stove, made to look like a phonograph—an aesthetic insult—gave out no cheer; on the contrary it was a dreary, smelly thing of no character. I finally couldn't stand it, so Bert installed a jolly coal, or wood stove. It has "made" the room! It glows and crackles, the kettle sings; it is really human. I actually enjoy the extra work in caring for it.

Henry brought me a most amazing white radish. I made seven negatives with great enthusiasm, immediate response. One day Henry drove Sonya, Xenia, and me to Monterey, I made two important negatives: a cactus cristata in Oliver's garden, and a group of silvered gas tanks. The latter I have had my eyes on ever since coming here; a great spheroid backed by two upright tanks. Driving home from the cacti,—there they were all glittering in a setting sun. It was the time. They were not easy to do; a neatly trimmed hedge in the foreground, which the gas company must have put there to take the curse off of industrialism, while it actually nearly ruins the ensemble, made the problem difficult. But as usual, a difficulty surmounted results in something even finer, or at least differently important, than one's first conception.

By using my longest focus element I was able to achieve a fine construction: the spheroid cut just above the hedge—if it had been an inch higher I would have been thwarted—and the two upright forms almost filling the background.

Excellent result with my new lens: Max, Brett, Imogen, Kees Van Niel all sat to me, and I worked well.

February 26. I slept at home last night—or should I call home the place where I become domestic, where I eat and sleep by the fire afterwards?—But I slept none too well and arose at 5:00. My life has been crowded every moment these last weeks with work and adventure. A new love seems always to bring with it new work! And so it seems to be working out. How I am going to take proper care of three women remains to be seen. I place my difficulties in the hands of the good Pagan Gods. The coming into my life of — was dramatically sudden. I had always felt that it would happen sometime; I have been drawn to her for three years,—since she was a child—albeit a mature one—of sixteen. And she was attracted to me, that was evident. I sensed her virginal desire for experience, and wanted to initiate her, but at the time there were—or I thought so—too many difficulties. Then she went away, returning after a year or so,—with experience. Seeing the light in her eyes, I soon found a way to be with her alone. There was no resistance to the first kiss. But still there were difficulties,—or again I thought so; Carmel is so small a place! Matters drifted along, with only an occasional surreptitious embrace,—until Saturday night (2:25) when — slightly tight—"bingy" she called her condition—took the initiative and came to me.

I had just returned to the studio, tired from a sitting of Robin, had turned back my bedcovers, when a tap-tap came on my door. I turned on the lights and quickly turned them off, seeing who stood there, and sensing at once, why. She was delightfully the child, though a very poised one, in explaining her call. She was delicately apologetic for coming to me, yet direct and frank;—not the least brazen. She knew what she wanted, and what I wanted—but she knew my difficulties and so cleared the way.

I assured — that having acquired knowledge through experience it was obviously a duty—and a pleasant one to hand on to her all that I knew! So we wasted no more time in talk. I am not exaggerating when I say, that she had the most beautiful breasts I have ever seen or touched; breasts such as Renoir painted, swelling without the slightest sag,—high, ample, firm.

— stayed the night. We slept but little. She moved me profoundly. A dear child, with a desire to learn, no inhibitions and much passion.

But now for the work I have been doing: sittings for portraits of Dorothy Brett, a charming girl called Sally Lasher, who wanted to exchange an old ivory carved cross for a sitting (when I saw her I didn't care whether I got the cross or not!), Robin, and nudes of both Sonya and Sybil. These nudes—all 4 × 5 Graflex negatives—go beyond any I have done. The sitting of "Brett" (we have discovered that we are related) with her ear trumpet was a great success. Robin's new portraits are finer than his old ones. And Sally Lasher's portraits are excellent. I am quite excited and happy. To climax a big week Kees took us to his laboratory where I worked with some amazing forms in glass;—and consider the day a forerunner of many more there.

March 25. Yesterday my birthday, with festivities which started with my morning coffee. I went over early, as usual before Neil or Sonya were up; and there found my table laden with gifts, greetings and flowers,—the latter an enormous bowl filled with sweet alyssum. Neil had made a poster greetings, Sonya gave me Lawrence's *Apocalypse*, and the Heron's silk pyjamas which Stella made. Later came Sybil with short stories by Dostoevsky and a lovely rose. A supper "surprise" followed at Sybil's, with Kees and Mimi also there. And who should arrive later but Lloyd Rollins with another book, Charles Morgan's *Portrait in a Mirror*. Bert Heron added to my collection with Peter Arno's *Circus*, over which I have had liver-stirring laughs all day mixed with admiration for Arno as artist. The table last night, covered with spring blossoms, was so very beautiful; and Sybil radiant as hostess.

April 18. Sunday night we held a party to be remembered, a rare gathering which brought together congenial persons who like to play, be gay; not one of them was a false note, each contributing to the fun, and spontaneously. Came: Fernando Felix, who plays the guitar and sings—Mexican songs of course—Nacho Bravo, who dances the rumba,—these two here with the newly-established Mexican consulate; Wilna Hervey and Nan Mason, who played and sang in their delightful way; and then the group who have been gathering recently for dancing and vino,—Xenia, Francis, Elaine, Nan and Ed; finally, there was Michael Schindler here for a few days. We had plenty of good vino, white and red, Ferando's singing was memorable, Xenia sang in Russian, Sonya in Spanish and Polish, I improvised, danced a Kreutzberg and a "Spring" number, also I danced with Wilna who is almost a foot taller than I am, and must weigh 350! It was a party without one dull moment, ending dramatically when, with a knock at the front door about 1:00, the night watchman complained of too much noise! His nearest "beat" is a block away.

Saturday the boys of the "Venus case" and their parents had to appear before the Juvenile Court, Salinas,—Judge Jorgenson presiding. After much wrangling between the lawyers, cross examination of witnesses, in which Chief Gus got quite confused and lost some of his august presence, the prosecuting attorney was granted a continuance. Our lawyer asked for a recess, during which we decided to put the boys on the stand to tell their story, confess, and let the judge use his common sense. First we put on the stand Mr. Bardarson, principal of Sunset grammar school, and Mr. Morehead, principal of Monterey high school who testified that the eight boys in question had spotless records and amongst the highest scholastic standing; then each boy in turn told his story, all coinciding. The judge, in questioning the boys, was most sympathetic, asked questions which went to show that the boys had no intention of damaging the statue, had nothing "against" Wermuth personally, that the whole affair was a prank. He denied the prosecution a continuance and dismissed the case after being assured by each boy that he had learned a lesson. The judge saw no reason to put the boys on probation. But now Wermuth threatens a civil suit for damages.

April 25. After days of fog, a surprise rain fell last night. We walked over to Steff's; he was alone, fortunately I took my new 4 × 5 portraits and nudes. He "got them," was really moved by them. Steff may not know art lingo, but he *knows*, instinctively. Followed a long talk on diverse topics; why he is no longer a liberal, his unaccepted challenge to ministers of the gospel to debate on Christ —he claiming to be a better Christian than they—and his recent lecture tours, —how he loves to sway an audience, to talk, but finds writing difficult, a job. He told of a recent visit with Jeffers. Robin spoke of their long friendship, of how they complemented each other; Steff seeing the humor in the kaleidoscope of life, Robin the tragedy. "It is because you see, are interested in masses, 'the crowd' which is always humorous, while I see and write of the individual who is always a tragedy."

We discussed the lack of humor in most communists, those "in" the movement; noting that even those who had humor fast lose it when "converted." "But you have not lost yours, Steff." "No, but I'm not a communist."

Henry has been making some of the finest drawings of her life; and gave me one, a magnolia, superbly felt and executed. I have been drawing too!—for the first time since grammar school days. The *Beaux Arts Gallery*, S. F., is to hang a non-artist exhibit.

Nell Chidester invited me. Should I be insulted! I sent three drawings, all to do with myself, my subject matter and camera. I am quite fond of them!

We—Willard, Mary J., Sonya and I may go to New Mexico, probably in June. Mabel has offered us a cottage while there. To go to Arizona and now New Mexico has been a dream of years. But first I go to L. A. to make sittings—Jack is to campaign for them—and to see the children, and L.

23. *Landcapes—"the heavens and earth become one—"*

July 7. We, Willard, Sonya and I, have returned from N. Mexico. Gone but two weeks, counting traveling time, I feel the time and expense well-spent. Besides the visual memories brought back of a magnificent country—Arizona, New Mexico and my own California—I have some fine new work; landscapes with gorgeous heavens—I was continuously reminded of old Mexico—details of various pueblos,—the old church at Laguna, the perfectly formed and functional ovens against equally perfect walls of adobe, some few rock details and one of a juniper; but mostly open landscape,—for in N. Mexico the heavens and earth become one, while here in California the sky is usually monotonous, unimportant. But this statement may well be arbitrary, or ill-considered; for the last stretch of our return trip, from San Miguel to Salinas was one of the most visually thrilling of the entire expedition. The aged hills, eroded until they had become smoothly swelling mounds on the near horizon, perfectly outlined, revealed in a low summer sun, were literally breath-taking. The point I wish to make, which contradicts my remark re California sky, is that the sky was cloudless; but, one single cloud would have been superfluous,—actually would have spoiled the perfect serenity of that moment.

I wanted to work! I couldn't ask Willard to stop, though he offered to. I knew how weary he must have been, how much he wanted to be home. And I knew I could go back,—it is but a day's journey. But when? It must be soon, for only this time of year is the light at its best. Five years ago, with Brett and Henry, we passed these hills at the same hour, the same month. Then as now we were "on our way,"—the destination S. Francisco. I wanted to work. I thought to return. But when? It must be soon!

September 14. The last two months—it seems a year since my last entry—have been so filled with events, tourists, visitors, work, that now with tourists leaving town, visitors gone—guests of the Weston Hotel, Merle would say—and work more or less finished, I feel a bit letdown, stale; the natural reaction.

The most important event of the summer was a visit from Jean Charlot who spent several weeks with us, bringing with him Zohmah Day, a strange little sprite of whom we became quite fond. As to Jean, I found that we were as close together, in friendship and in work, as before, though seven years had separated us since Mexican days.

Jean is an artist who functions in work as easily as he breathes. He has none of the "artistic temperament" for he *is* an artist. He has clear, direct knowledge;

275

intuition rather than reason. He has a subtle humor which comes through in his work and in most original and unexpected remarks. He has a quiet, strong reserve which made it possible for me to have him around at a time when almost any other person would have been quite impossible. Much as I wanted to see him, see more of him, most of the time I was too busy; we each had to go our way. There was never a demand, obvious or implied on his part.

Jean's arrival came just as I was about to select my Chicago exhibit of 100 prints to be held at the Increase Robinson Gallery on Michigan Ave. With curiosity and desire to see which prints another would select for this show— such another as Jean—I handed him some 400 prints to choose from, holding a mental reservation that if he did not please me I would make my own changes. After several days the selecting was finished; several of my favorite prints had been left out, and many added which I would not have considered. Then I started in to make my corrections. Result, I left Jean's selections intact. I decided that it was as good an exhibition as one that I would have chosen and probably better balanced; my tendency being to overlook older work that I have wearied of. Jean gave me renewed interest in certain works I have neglected. But what a job his selections made me face; I had to reprint at least two-thirds of the total. In doing this I made the best set of prints of my life; so fine that many are like new work to me.

I owe this exhibit to my sister. She made the contact and arrangements with Mrs. Robinson, whom, by the way, I like very much through our correspondence. I open the coming Saturday, Sept. 16. I have taken a great interest in this, to me, important event. It will be the first showing in my "old home-town," unless I wish to count the prints Alma sent to the Fort Dearborn Camera Club a couple of years ago. I don't!

Neil, Sonya and I are alone. It is unnaturally quiet! Cole spent most of the summer here. I hardly had a real contact with the dear boy. Chandler has gone to S. F. to try for a job,—taking Teddie with him. What a child Teddie is! A definite, strong personality, even at three. And with a disposition too good to believe possible.

September 15. Besides my Chicago exhibition I got together 50 prints—old extras —for Lita Coughlin to take with her and show in Shanghai; I sent five of my new nudes to the opening of Ansel Adams' new gallery in S. F.—a showing by "Group f/64." And I assembled for 683 Brockhurst, Willard's and Mary's gallery, the most important retrospective show I have given; "Thirty Years of Photography," starting in 1903, with work done at 17. Seeing the work on the wall I realized that my photographs of thirty years ago are closer in approach and technique—though immature of course—to my latest work, than are several of the photographs dating 1913–20; a period in which I was trying to be "artistic." I recall that in those days I used to affect a flowing tie and feel myself very much the "artist." I also recall that I was very conscious of myself as a spectacle, felt uncomfortable, but stubbornly went through with it. There seemed to be two forces warring for supremacy, for even as I made the soft "artistic" work with poetic titles, I would secretly admire sharp, clean, technically perfect photographs in showcases of very mediocre photographers. I was dangerously near to becoming a "Bohemian" artist in a garret;—but always a stronger side has saved me in the end.

At the very height of all my recent work, when I was near to physical and mental exhaustion, I received a letter from L. asking me to come to a definite decision, write her my intentions. It was the last straw! But it brought much to a focus. I wrote in a more definite way—albeit a bit hysterical—than I would have at a calmer moment. I gave her to understand that the possibility of our actually living together was more remote than ever; that if we ever did, she must realize that I have never been noted for my constancy; that now my greatest desire and need was to be absolutely alone for awhile,—that I had been too long pushed and pulled in every direction,—that I could not stand another responsibility, another complication. And then I asked her for once to be the strong one, to help me, as I had tried to help her. I knew she would either rise or fall on this latter request. And she rose! Told me that my letter was the best thing that could have happened to her. It must have given L. a hard jolt, such as she needed,—we all need at critical times.

I suppose my enthusiasm of the moment, plus desire to help her, even save her, led me to give L. false hopes. Will I ever learn to be careful!

October 21. A difficult month,—the past. Chandler got a "job"—nothing more— in S. F., and I have full responsibility for Teddie. How completely can the demands of a child of his age command one's time! Friends were very kind in relieving me for a few hours at a time; but those hours were not much more than a physical relief. I found it almost impossible to "get going" before my free moments were over. I must confess that I felt rebellious,—even felt a bit of the martyr which I really detest. It was the old story; anything which stands in the way of my work causes psychic distress.

Yet I consider—in retrospect—that I learned much. What self-control, subtlety, wisdom is needed to understand and direct a child, especially such a child! Extremely sensitive, strong willed and responding to affection, with a sense of humor subtle beyond his years, combined with remarkable understanding, Teddie presents a problem to solve in the way of correct approach. He is so plastic that one needs to be ever alert to set an example. To keep that balance which would not destroy initiative, yet maintain the control which a child demands, needs, is a task requiring great patience and wisdom. And he is so basically good, so really adorable, that one could easily harm him with misguided affection. He matches his wits against yours, in the spirit of a game, at every moment, and he knows that you know this!

There is a very close bond between that child and me,—at least as great as that which I felt for my own children. Because he has my birthdate? Possibly. Being older, learning from experience, I realize mistakes which I made with my own boys and would rectify them in Teddie. We seem destined to play an important part in each other's lives. How can this be without taking too much from my work? In no case must this relation resolve into mere duty on my part.

My Chicago exhibition can be considered a success; large attendance, excellent publicity, even that of Bulliet, who used several columns to defend his opinion that photography cannot be considered art!—And eight sales so far. Mrs. Robinson has proved to be an excellent "dealer." Prompt in all matters, she mailed checks from sales with no delay. She has asked to retain 50 prints, to act as my Chicago representative. One unexpected result from the Chicago exhibition was a wire from Alma Reed wanting to know if the Increase Robinson prints were available for a N. Y. showing. Also, that she had found a number of my missing prints and was clearing balance by mail!

I will show with her this winter if we can agree on different terms; but I cannot give her the Chicago prints. Half of them remain there, the rest I need for Ansel Adams Gallery, where I open Nov. 10, and for a National Tree contest which closes this month.

Bulliet's article amused me. He admits that I may be "within shooting distance," —he writes, "You get excited, wonder why it is the 'cubists' can't think up things as good," and then "realizes their art emptiness." The paragraph which starts with, "A score of etchings by Picasso and Braque after the Weston patterns would send you to a sleepless bed," he finishes with, "but eventually you walk calmly if not a bit wearily away." Rather amusing contrasts! Bulliet calls me "of the Man Ray School!" This is ironical for I have never—except in a few examples—cared for Man Ray,—too clever. He says I am "a little more poetical—a bit sentimental and less flinty than Man Ray" who "belonged to the age of iron!" I can't see anything hard as iron in Man Ray, and have thought his portraits—some—very sentimental!

I am not particularly proud of being placed in the Man Ray "School,"— whatever that is. As far back as my daybook of Mexico, I put down unfavorable reactions to Man Ray's work. Perhaps if I had selected Chicago show, more of the hard, stronger items would have been included. Jean's tendency was to select the more subtle work. Did I mention that Jean selected this show? But just because a thing is subtle, or delicate, or "poetical," it need not be sentimental. Is one to avoid nature when she elects to be unusual or even fantastic, —consider her sentimental? I am thinking now of my "Cypress and Succulents,"

"42 T." If I had placed a nude figure under the tree and called it "Fairyland" then I might be labeled sentimental. Yet a critic friend of Blanche Matthias thought my work showed no trace of sentimentality except in this print. If I were to choose a print from my show which might be so labeled, I would say the lone shack by the sea, one of the "Deserted Landings." This might arouse definite connotations in those prone to sentimentalize.

October 24. Farewells today. Sybil, Chan, and Teddie drove to Los Angeles. At these crossroads many friends stop for a day, a month or a year, with consequent farewells. Teddie will remain with his mother indefinitely. The house will be quiet, I will be able to work better; but I shall miss him very much. They drove away in a drift of fog. Well, all the better a day for darkroom work.

December 31, 1933. The old year is being ushered out in a pouring rain. So far the winter has been unusually mild. For two months before Xmas, Carmel had extraordinary weather,—warm sun, no fog. I bathed in the ocean almost daily, —the last time Dec. 24th; then Xmas day fog!

It does not seem possible that I have made no entry since Chan left for Los Angeles with Teddie, to once more try to make a living by photography. I regretted their going, but Chan had to leave for his own good. I miss Teddie, when I have time to think of him; the same could be said of Cole, in fact all those who are close to me. I have a faculty of going for days or weeks without thinking of my dearest friends and relatives; then suddenly I become conscious of them.

January 6, 1934. At this point, almost a week ago, I was interrupted by a phone call which brought two sittings,—to Sonya. I did not have a single sitting during Dec. This has been the worst year of the Depression for me. Nevertheless I have held to my determination not to lower my prices for portraits; which stand the same as in 1929. If I had lowered them I would have lost more than gained; of this I feel sure.

There might be a question as to whether my stand on retouching, and new small size, has not hurt "business"; but again I feel sure that it has not. Before making a definite stand, retouching was the exception; and the 4 × 5 contact prints have been almost always chosen in preference to the 8 × 10 enlargements. The personal result of my new way of working in portraiture has been that I have done the finest portraits of my life. For the first time in years, portraiture has meant more to me than just a job, has been a creative expression. So I am justified, no matter what the economic result. Also, this year's nudes—4 × 5 contacts—have reached a place barely indicated before. Portraits, nudes, and open landscapes have been my expression this last year; only two or three "close-ups" have been added to my portfolio. The landscapes which I did in New Mexico please me, and have moved others,—even to the point of buying! I

279

think they mark a definite step in advance, and indicate the next phase of my work.

Recent sittings include: Jean and Zohmah, James Cagney, Muriel Draper, John Evans and Claire Spencer, Teresina and Teddie. Each one a success, I would say. Perhaps in retrospect I will write of the various and interesting persons who have passed before my lens; but if this idea ever materializes, it probably will not until the day comes when my vision is dimmed and I cannot function as a photographer.

Alma wired me for an exhibition to open Jan. 29th. I answered that I could not "afford the luxury of a New York show this year." A lot of truth in my reply; but I was also "calling her bluff," or better, I was bluffing. She has owed me money for prints sold months ago; has promised it "return mail," time and again. I need the money, and I'm tired of her unbusinesslike approach.

Marvellous warm days again. I have been in the ocean daily this week.

Tonight we hear Roland Hayes sing; I, for the first time. I hope that I am not expecting too much.

February 13, 1934. I was not disappointed in Roland Hayes; indeed he gave me a deep emotional experience, a real fulfillment. An artist faced his audience and gave to them from his innermost spiritual achievement. There may be greater voices,—louder, with more amazing virtuosity, but Hayes ranged beyond all technical barriers. Back of a small, dark Negro facing his white audience, one felt the race which he almost defiantly represented, and because of which he surmounted all obstacles to triumph.

Brett had photographed Hayes, and pleased him, so he told me after the concert when I introduced myself as "Brett Weston's father." A charming, sincere, vital man whom I wish to know better.

April 20. The busier I am, the more vital and interesting my life, the less time I find to write down my experiences, naturally. Since Jan.| so much has happened.

Perhaps most important, from the effect it will have upon my future, is the step I took to regain my personal freedom and its achievement. First L. wrote me,—a sadly beautiful note, telling me that she realized that we could not go on, that we must start on another basis. She must have sensed this from our last contact. When I have nothing more to give, I do not easily simulate. My reply must have been too unemotional, showing all too ready acceptance (I had made up my own mind months past), because her answer showed that I had caused her a great hurt. Oh, these difficult relations which involve the tragic—because misunderstood—differences between man and woman.

This step toward my freedom, though I did not literally take it, I actually did. She sensed that I held out no hope; this plus my lack of ability to act a part unfelt, caused her to take the initiative.

But I did take the first step with Sonya. On our fifth anniversary, April 17, just passed, I wrote her frankly that I must have my freedom, that I could no longer live a lie; of course granting her the same. She rose to the occasion in fine spirit, better by far than I had expected, considering her jealous nature. Perhaps she too had already realized, and become partially reconciled to the fact that she would always have to share me. I told Sonya, and mean it, that I had no desire to live with any other woman, that she was an ideal companion; but that others in my life were as inevitable as the tides, that I rebelled against being tied, that if her jealousy stood in my way, we would have to part.

Since January, and until a few weeks ago, I have been working on the Public Works of Art Project, So. Calif. region, with Merle, the director, as my boss. For the first time since my early twenties I have been on a salary. The weekly check, starting at $42.50 and finally because of shortage of funds reduced to $38.50, saved me during a very dull period. So far as I know, I am the only photographer in America who worked on the project as a creative artist; this due entirely to Merle. No provision had been made for photographers as artists. Dr. Heil, northern director, could see no way to use me, excepting later to copy the work of painters and sculptors for government records. Even if Heil was not politically tied, even though he had not lacked imagination, or initiative, I doubt if he at all sympathizes with contemporary photography as an expression. Lloyd Rollins would have tried to use me, I'm sure. But Merle having initiative, imagination and sympathy, wired Heil asking him to put me on the S. Calif. project. This agreed, I went to work here in Carmel; for the first time in my life getting paid in advance for doing anything I wanted to do; for Merle allowed me just that freedom. Such halcyon days could not last. Merle was actually overstepping his privilege in putting me on as an artist; so to keep me on I had to go south to copy frescoes, paintings, etc. I went down twice; exciting at first, though hard, exacting work, long hours; but finally I resigned, for it seemed senseless to be down there, the while I was supporting my overhead here, and chancing the loss of sittings, one of which might more than equal a month's work on the P.W.A.P. So it proved. I had no sooner returned than I had one equal to over two month's work on the project,—the largest single order I have had in Carmel,—$370. More recently in rapid succession I have had six more sittings, and sold a book. Have I mentioned this? The E. W. Book received the 50 Best Books of the Year award from the Am. Inst. of Graphic Arts. So much for those who criticized it in an unwarranted manner!

When I resigned from the P.W.A.P., I was successful, through Merle, in having Chan take my place. I understand he is doing good work. Then Brett was put on as a sculptor; for the first time in his life receiving a real salary. Merle selected his carving as one of the three best things done on his entire project. Willard was selected from some 50 applicants to be official photographer for the northern region.

I had two delightful adventures in Los Angeles; one a renewal with X., a memorable night; another with a most passionate, and pathetically repressed virgin. This adventure started just before I left never reached fulfillment. I feel that if the time had been propitious, and with more time, the story would be different. X. on the other hand is most delightfully unmoral, pagan,—a grand person to love.

I have been doing good work; open landscapes on the P.W.A.P. and excellent nudes. One weekend Willard came down after just quitting his job with the Shell Oil Co.: we took his car, I paying the expenses, and drove to Oceano. There, I made several dune negatives that mark a new epoch in my work. I must go back there,—the material made for me!

Cole is now living with me. Begged his mother until she consented to let him come up. He is developing finely, has gained physically and grown mentally. I am blessed with four grand boys. And Teddie! We had our first birthday celebration together. I bought him a "two wheel" bicycle. What excitement! At four he sits in Chan's lap at the wheel of his Chevrolet and drives it; he can turn corners, puts on the hand brake, shuts off the ignition.

Fog hangs heavy over Carmel now, but we have had a warm winter with brilliant sun. *The* musical event of the year was Gieseking's concert. The next day I photographed him with fine results. He liked them immensely. It came back to me that he considered my sitting the best he had ever had done.

A great tragedy came to Sybil with the suicide in Shanghai of Bubbles, her sister who jumped eight stories, carrying her two children with her. As a result Sybil's parents committed suicide! What suffering Sybil has gone through these last two years. But she has come through!

24. *"Peace to enjoy, fulfill, this beauty—"*

December 9, 1934. I have not opened this book for almost 8 months,—and with good reason; I have been too busy, busy living. I notice the last entry was 4–20. On 4–22 a new love came into my life, a most beautiful one, one which will, I believe, stand the test of time.

I met C. [Charis Wilson]—a short time before going South on the P.W.A.P. work, saw her at a concert, was immediately attracted, and asked to be introduced. I certainly had no conscious designs in mind at the time, but I am not in the habit of asking for introductions to anyone which means that the attraction was stronger then than I realized. I saw this tall, beautiful girl, with finely proportioned body, intelligent face well-freckled, blue eyes, golden brown hair to shoulders,—and had to meet. Fortunately this was easy. Her brother was already one of my good friends, which I, of course, did not know.

I left for the south before our paths crossed again. While there a letter from S. said she had a new model for me, one with a beautiful body. It was C.——Poor S.——How ironical. But what happened was inevitable.

The first nudes of C. were easily amongst the finest I had done, perhaps the finest. I was definitely interested now, and knew that she knew I was. I felt a response. But I am slow, even when I feel sure, especially if I am deeply moved.

I did not wait long before making the second series which was made on April 22, a day to always remember. I knew now what was coming; eyes don't lie and she wore no mask. Even so I opened a bottle of wine to help build up my ego. You see I really wanted C. hence my hesitation.

And I worked with hesitation; photography had a bad second place. I made some eighteen negatives, delaying always delaying, until at last she lay there below me waiting, holding my eyes with hers. And I was lost and have been ever since. A new and important chapter in my life opened on Sunday afternoon, April 22, 1934.

After eight months we are closer together than ever. Perhaps C. will be remembered as the great love of my life. Already I have achieved certain heights reached with no other love.

Domestic relations have been severely strained, quite to the breaking point, casting a shadow over my association with C. A change must take place and soon. I must have peace to enjoy, fulfill, this beauty.

PART IV

Carmel, April 22, 1944

"Ten years—"

April 22, 1944. —Carmel—Ten years ago today on a Sunday afternoon was the beginning; now Charis and I are married, have been for five years. This is the first entry in my once-well-kept daybook since 1934. I laughingly blame Ch. for cramping my style as a writer—and there may be some truth in this charge—but the fact is that I have not had much time, nor necessary aloneness for keeping an intimate journal.

In no period of my life has there been a comparable series of important events, coming one upon another as if to crowd into ten years all that might happen to some in a lifetime. I doubt if I can take time to recall more than the highlights of these years, or scratch the surface of all the changes which in turn have changed me, colored my thoughts, directed my actions. Without comment—not until in some later entry explanation is necessary—

I will write down some of the outstanding events and experiences of these missing ten years; incidents, of course, especially concerning me. It will be obvious soon enough—if I go on writing—what such a cataclysm as the war has done to me. So this list, without too much pride and with shameless prejudice.

1935: I left my Carmel, once-happy-home, and moved to S. Monica where Brett and I with Cole and Neil set up housekeeping with an eye open for sittings. 1936: Charis came to live with me. 1937: I received a Guggenheim Fellowship, the first ever granted a photographer; renewal in 1938. We traveled 35,000 miles mostly through California as told in that exciting book *California and the West* by Charis Wilson Weston—so well-told that I need not recount any of the Guggenheim period. 1938: Moved to Carmel Highlands because of H. L's [Harry Leon Wilson, writer, father of Charis] sickness. Neil built us a one-big-room house which Walter Arensberg calls the palatial shack. 1938: divorced Flora after 16 years separation. 1939: married Charis after 5 years of sin. 1941: Contract with Limited Editions Club Inc., N. Y. to illustrate *Leaves of Grass*; we travel cross-country for 10 months covering 20,000 miles, 24 states, from the old South to Maine. This story will also be told, God and Charis willing. Travel was done during a national emergency. When war broke out we scurried home. Charis did not want to scurry. I did.

Many deaths have saddened these last 10 years, but two were especially poignant to me—Tina and Ramiel. Tina returned to Mexico to die. Ramiel went to sleep in his little Redondo home, after a long painful struggle. Tina and Ramiel, always linked in my mind, always clasped to my heart.

"Oh, there will pass with your great passing
Little of beauty not your own,—"

Edna St. Vincent Millay

One birth has gladdened; Erica, born to Brett and Cicely, my first granddaughter, and the first girl in the family.

Something almost worse than death came to my only sister Mary—a stroke which crippled her right side. She has come through in heroic fashion, learning to write with left hand, learning to walk, to talk.

Glossary of Mexican Words and Phrases

aguacate – avocado, alligator pear
atole – non-alcoholic cornflour drink
azotea – flat roof
bastón – walking cane
batea – painted tray
bizcocho – biscuit
bomba – pump
borrachito – slightly drunk, exhilarated
camión – bus
cargador – porter
chango – monkey
charro – cowboy with special skills, as against *vaquero* – a cowhand
chirimoya – cherimoya, a tropical fruit
criada – servant girl
crudo – hangover
diana – fanfare
encargado – agent, attorney
enchilada – pancake of maize with chile
equipal – Weston's mishearing of *episcapodo* or *episcopal?* – a bishop's chair
faja – sash
frijoles – small kidney beans
habanero – a rum drink
huarache – Mexican sandal woven of strips of leather
jefe – chief, head man, mayor of a village
jicara – small jug
juguetes – toys
loza – pottery
mariposa – butterfly
mole de guajalote – turkey with a chile and chocolate sauce
naranja – orange

negro – black
olla – pot
petate – straw mat
piñatas – papier maché figures made to be filled with gifts or candies and then broken in a blindfold attack
pollo – chicken
pozole – hominy, usually cooked with a hog's head, sometimes with chicken
puestos – booths, stalls at a market or fair
pulque – fermented juice of the maguey cactus
pulque curado – pulque prepared with pineapple or orange and sugar
pulquería – bar where pulque is served
rebozo – shawl or scarf, worn by women
serape – blanket, worn by men
tamale – crushed maize, minced meat and chile, dipped in oil and then steamed or boiled
tequila – distilled liquor made from the roasted stems of the century plant, *tequila*
tierra caliente – hot country
tortilla – pancake
tostada – toasted bread
trastero – whatnot
vaquero – cowhand; see *charro*
viejitos – little old ones; Los Viejitos is a famous folkdance caricaturing elderly white men
vino rioja – red wine from La Rioya, Spain
zaguán – entrance hall, foyer

289

Edward Weston's Technique

Edward Weston brought to Mexico an 8 × 10 view camera and a 3¼ × 4¼ Graflex. His battery of lenses included an "expensive anastigmat" of unspecified make and several soft focus, or diffused focus, lenses, among them a Wollensak Verito and a Graf Variable. These lenses had the characteristic that the degree of diffusion (i.e., spherical aberration) could be altered at will.

The Variable was basically an anastigmat, fully corrected for its maximum aperture, f/3.8. By changing the distance between the front and the rear elements of this double lens, varying amounts of spherical aberration could be induced. Theoretically it thus produced either a needle-sharp image or one so diffused that it hardly seemed to be produced by a lens.

The f/4 Verito was described by its manufacturer as "a specially designed double lens . . . which, while it gives the desired diffused or soft optical effect, shows no distortion, double lines, or other optical imperfections, and being rectilinear gives an even diffusion over the whole plate. . . . Will not make sharp negatives with wiry definition unless stopped down to f:8."

When Weston wrote, on Easter, 1924, "Sharper and sharper I stopped down my lens; the limit of my diaphragm, f/32, was not enough, so I cut a smaller hole from black paper," he was referring to this characteristic of the Verito as well as to the fact that great depth of field is given with small lens openings.

Weston had trouble with the Variable. Although he stopped it down to the smallest aperture, he found troublesome flares. An optometrist deduced that this was caused by the large glass surface of the f/3.8 lens. On June 24, 1924, Weston purchased for 25 pesos a second-hand Rapid Rectilinear lens. This type of lens had long been considered obsolete, if not archaic. Years later he gave this lens to his son Brett, who generously presented it to the George Eastman House. It bears no maker's name. On the barrel is inscribed: "8 × 10 THREE FOCUS," and the scratched dedication, "To Brett—Dad, 1937." Examination on an optical bench proves it to be an unsymmetrical form of Rapid Rectilinear of 11¼-inch focal length, well made and well centered. It has no shutter—Weston used a behind-the-lens Packard shutter—but an iris diaphram marked "R.O.C.

and C.CO." (Rochester Optical and Camera Co."). The smallest opening is marked "256." Measurement proves this to be the long-obsolete "Uniform System," the equivalent of f/64.

Weston used panchromatic sheet film. This material, capable of recording all visible wavelengths—in contrast to orthochromatic emulsion, which is relatively insensitive to red and overly sensitive to blue—was an innovation in film form: it was first marketed in America by the Eastman Kodak Company only two years before Weston sailed to Mexico. Notations of exposures in the Mexican Daybook indicate that the speed of this "pan-chro" film would be rated today at 16 by the American Standards Association system. A portrait in full sunlight required ⅒ sec. at f/11; an open landscape was stopped down to f/32 for an exposure of ⅒ sec. with a K-1 filter. He had no meter to calculate the exposure. Experience guided him: "I dislike to figure out time, and find my exposures more accurate when only *felt*."

On August 24, 1924, Weston noted: "I have returned, after several years' use of Metol-Hydroquinone open-tank developer, to a three-solution Pyro developer, and I develop one at a time in a tray, instead of a dozen in a tank!" This technique he used for the rest of his life. It is classic; he undoubtedly learned of it at the "photographic college" he briefly attended. The 1908 instruction manual of a similar institution—the American School of Art and Photography—recommends it as the standard developer. Weston used it with less than the usual amount of sodium carbonate. (Interestingly, the Wollensak Optical Co. advised: "Negatives made with the Verito should be fully timed, and slightly underdeveloped, using any standard developer with a minimum amount of carbonate of soda. . . .")

Weston printed on several kinds of paper. In his early years in Mexico he was especially fond of the platinum and palladium paper made by Willis & Clement, which he imported from England. This paper, which became obsolete in the 1930s, was sensitized with the salts of iron and platinum (or palladium), rather than silver. It gave soft, rich effects quite unlike any other kind of paper, and was cherished by pictorial photographers. Prints were exposed in sunlight for minutes, developed in potassium oxalate, and fixed in hydrochloric acid. The addition of potassium bichromate to the developer gave an increased brilliance in the whites; this technique Weston used in his struggle to get prints of the dramatic white clouds that so moved him. The paper had a tendency, especially if damp, to solarize, that is, partially to reverse in the highlights, giving a dark edge instead of a light one. Printing was slow work. To make fourteen prints from

292

as many negatives in one day, as he did on September 30, 1924, was unusual.

On this day Weston noted with surprise that proof prints, made on Azo paper, gave him as much satisfaction as platinotypes. This material was a typical gelatino-chloride developing-out paper exposed to artificial light. Weston always referred to it as "gaslight paper," a name given to it in the 1890s, but which was retained decades after electricity became universal.

Although Weston preferred an 8 × 10 camera (he rejoiced in "the precision of a view box planted firmly on a sturdy tripod"), he made increasing use while in Mexico of his 3¼ × 4¼ Graflex—hand held even at exposures as long as ⅒ second. To enlarge these negatives on platinum or palladium paper was tedious. An enlarged negative had to be made. First an 8 × 10-inch glass positive was made from the small negative. From this, in turn, he made a new negative, which he then printed by contact. On his return to California, he abandoned platinum and palladio papers, and settled on glossy chloro-bromide papers—which he invariably printed by contact.

This simple technique Weston used throughout his life. It was a direct outgrowth of his formative Mexican days.

BEAUMONT NEWHALL

Acknowledgments

The photographs for this book were
loaned by the following:

Cole Weston: Daybook I, plates 2, 5,
6, 8, 9, 10, 11, 13, 15, 21, 22, 24,
27, 28; Daybook II, plates 1, 2, 4, 5,
6, 7, 8, 9, 11, 12, 14, 16, 19, 26, 31,
35, 36

Philadelphia Museum of Art: Daybook
I, plates 1, 4, 12, 17, 18, 20, 23, 29,
31; Daybook II, plates 10, 13, 29,
30, 37, 40

The Center for Creative Photography:
Daybook I, plates 3, 7, 14, 16, 19,
25, 26, 30, 32; Daybook II, plates 3,
15, 18, 20, 21, 22, 23, 25, 28, 32,
33, 34, 38, 39

Aperture Foundation, Inc.: Daybook
II, plates 17, 24

Sheldon Memorial Art Gallery, University of Nebraska: Daybook II, plate
27

Selected Bibliography

Armitage, Merle, ed. *50 Photographs by Edward Weston*. New York: Duell, Sloan & Pearce, 1947.

Bunnell, Peter C. *Edward Weston on Photography*. Salt Lake City: Gibbs M. Smith, Inc., 1983.

Bunnell, Peter C., and David Featherstone, eds. *EW 100: Centennial Essays in Honor of Edward Weston*. Carmel, California: Friends of Photography, 1986.

Conger, Amy. *Edward Weston in Mexico, 1923–1926*. Albuquerque: University of New Mexico Press, 1983.

Davis, Keith. *Edward Weston: One Hundred Photographs from the Nelson Atkins Museum of Art and the Hallmark Photographic Collection*. Kansas City: William Rockhill Nelson Trust, 1982.

Maddow, Ben. *Edward Weston: His Life*. New York: Aperture, 1989.

Newhall, Beaumont. *Supreme Instants: The Photography of Edward Weston*. Boston: Little, Brown and Company, 1986.

Newhall, Beaumont, and Amy Conger, eds. *Edward Weston Omnibus: An Anthology*. Salt Lake City: Gibbs M. Smith Books, 1984.

Newhall, Nancy. *The Photographs of Edward Weston*. New York: The Museum of Modern Art, 1946.

Newhall, Nancy, ed. *Edward Weston: The Flame of Recognition*. Millerton, New York: Aperture, 1975.

Edward Weston: Masters of Photography, No. 7. Essay by R. H. Cravens. New York: Aperture, 1989.

Edward Weston: Nudes. Remembrance by Charis Wilson. Millerton, New York: Aperture, 1977.

Whitman, Walt. *Leaves of Grass*. With photographs by Edward Weston. New York: Limited Editions Club, 1942.

Wilson, Charis, and Edward Weston. *California and the West*. New York: Aperture, 1978.

Wilson, Charis, and Edward Weston, *The Cats of Wildcat Hill*. New York: Duell, Sloan & Pearce, 1947.

Index

I. MEXICO

Moore, George, 120
Morley, Dr. Sylvanus, 158, 160
Movies, 56, 121, 127, 131, 142

Nacional Museum, 54, 55, 59
Negatives, enlarged, 95, 96
Neil, *see* Weston, Laurence Neil
New York, City of, 4–8, 34, 139
Niven, William, *Scottish archaeologist*, 59
Nude of A., pl. 21, 136, 138, 145, 147
Nudes, 26, 27, 30, 55, 57, 83, 90, 93, 97, 99, 101, 110, 118–19, 129, 136, 138, 143, 146, 194–95

Oaxaca, 156, 157, 159, 162–71, 183, 191, 200
Oaxaca, SS, 25
Obregón, Alvaro, *Mexican soldier and president*, 36, 42, 101
O'Keeffe, Georgia, *painter*, 5, 6, 140
Olín, Nahui (Carmen Mondragon), *writer and painter, pl. 9*, 26, 30, 52, 55, 97, 100, 104, 114
Organ cactus, 64, 66
Orozco, Carlos, 127
Orozco, José Clemente, *painter and muralist*, 138, 146, 158

Pacheco, Máximo, *painter*, 141
Palladiotype, 22, 60, 62, 91, 92, 93, 129, 142, 143, 146, 199, 202
Palma Cuernavaca, I., 90, 91, 93, 99, 100, 101, 139
Palma Cuernavaca, II., pl. 23, 139, 201
Palma Santa, pl. 24, 155
Partridge, Roi, *etcher*, 7, 80, 100
Passion Play of Oberammergau, The, 155
Pátzcuaro, 171–75
Pelota, 104
Pepe, *see* Quintanilla, Pepe
Peter, Dr., 99, 155, 156
Photographic beauty, 129
Photography, 46, 55, 80, 91, 92, 93, 94, 99, 105, 129, 135, 136, 139,

147, 156, 185, 188. *See also* Charlot, D'Harnoncourt, Mayorga, Pintao, Stieglitz, Siqueiros
Picasso, Pablo, 17, 29, 31, 57, 73, 147
Picturesqueness, 66, 81, 90
Pintao—*see* Martínez Pintao, Manuel
Pipes and Stacks, Armco, pl. 5, 41, 66
Pirámide del Sol, pl. 10, 33, 40, 66, 98
Platinum, 31, 41, 59, 66, 94
Portraits, 5, 30, 33, 42, 46, 47, 49, 51, 55, 95, 97, 103, 104, 105, 106, 129
Portraiture, professional, 36, 39, 45, 49, 74, 87, 89, 91, 92, 102, 137, 141, 158, 159
Printing, 3, 59, 64, 89, 91, 93, 94, 129, 143, 146, 147
Prints, 4, 61, 65, 66, 67, 92, 107
Puebla, 159, 162–71, 191
Puerta Vallarta, 126
Pulquerías, *pls. 17, 25*, 16, 32, 48, 56, 71, 73–74, 97, 106, 108, 110, 154, 161, 165, 188, 193, 194
Pyramids, 34, 72

Querétaro, 171, 194
Quintanilla, Luis, *Spanish painter and etcher*, 98, 100
Quintanilla, Pepe, 102, 104, 129, 154, 202

Ramiel, *see* McGehee, Ramiel
R. R. (Rapid Rectilinear) lens, 66, 76, 79, 80, 90, 91, 98, 99, 134, 135
Ray, Man, *painter, photographer*, 69, 190
Realism, 55, 90, 150
Retablos, 165
Retouching, 36, 39, 90, 135
Revolution, 21, 36, 37, 41, 42, 51, 66, 81, 82, 86, 150
Rivera, Diego, *painter and muralist, pl. 16*, 17, 19, 26, 31, 32, 33, 34, 35, 41, 42, 43, 45, 51, 55, 57, 77, 98, 99, 100, 103, 104–05, 106, 127, 128, 129, 130, 133, 137, 138, 139,

Index

II. CALIFORNIA